PENGUIN CLASSICS

THE FIGHT AND OTHER WRITINGS

William Hazlitt was born in 1778 at Maidstone. His parents were revolutionaries and intellectual deists familiar with the works of Priestley, Price and Godwin. In 1783 the family emigrated to America, but they found life there disappointing and returned to England in 1788, settling at Wem in Shropshire. Hazlitt rejected his father's wish that he should become a Unitarian Minister, but in 1798 he heard Coleridge's last sermon, which proved a turning-point in his career. Coleridge encouraged him to pursue his interest in philosophy and Hazlitt later wrote several such works, including *An Essay on the Principles of Human Action* (1805), *An Abridgement of 'The Light of Nature pursued by Abraham Tucker'* (1807) and his great attack on Malthus, *A Reply to the Essay on Population* (1807). Art was one of his greatest passions and his training in Paris left its mark on his writing. Unlike his literary contemporaries, such as Wordsworth and Coleridge, Hazlitt remained a radical all his life, and this commitment made him many enemies. Much of his writing is ephemeral, but there is a body of literary and social criticism which holds an important place in English literature. A great essayist, he handled a wide range of styles, from the abstract and formal ideas in 'On Reason and Imagination' to the colloquialism of 'The Fight'. In 1812 he became Parliamentary Reporter for the *Morning Chronicle* and was soon filling its columns with essays on diverse subjects and brilliant accounts of the London stage. His collected essays from the *Examiner*, published under the title of *The Round Table*, are a notable contribution to the literature of radical protest. In 1820 he began submitting essays to the *London Magazine*, which were to become the first volume of *Table Talk* (2 vols., 1821–2). In the same year he fell in love with a young girl, and this disastrous period in his life is recounted in *Liber Amoris*. Hazlitt recovered and began writing again, and in 1825 *The Spirit of the Age* was published. His last great task was *The Life of Napoleon Buonaparte* (4 vols., 1828–30). William Hazlitt died in 1830.

Tom Paulin was born in Leeds in 1949 and grew up in Belfast. He was educated at the universities of Hull and Oxford, and is G. M. Young Lecturer in English at Hertford College, Oxford. He is a regular critic on BBC2's *Late Review*. His most recent volume of poems is *The Wind Dog*,

T0315590

and his most recent critical study is *The Day-Star of Liberty: William Hazlitt's Radical Style*.

David Chandler received a BA in English and History of Art at University College London, an M.Phil and D.Phil at Corpus Christi College, Oxford, and is now Lecturer in English at Kyoto University. He has published many articles, mostly on aspects of Romantic Period writing or Shakespeare, in such journals as *Notes and Queries*, *English Language Notes*, *Studies in Bibliography*, *The Wordsworth Circle* and *Romanticism on the Net*.

INTRODUCTION

Poets ... are ambitious, vain, and indolent – more busy in preparing idle ornaments, which take their chance of bringing in somehow or other, than intent on eliciting truths by fair and honest inquiry. It should seem as if they considered prose as a sort of waiting-maid to poetry, that could only be expected to wear her mistress's cast-off finery.

William Hazlitt, 'On the Prose-Style of Poets'

In an exciting and famous passage in his autobiography, Benvenuto Cellini describes how he had a problem melting down the lumps of copper and bronze which were to form his statue of Perseus. Noticing that the metal was not running as easily as it should, and realizing the alloy would be consumed in the terrific heat, he sends for all his 'pewter plates, bowls and salvers' – about two hundred of them – and puts these household objects into the channels which directed the flowing metal into the mould. When the cast has cooled, he removes the mould and finds that he has cast a perfect statue – until he reaches the right foot, which is slightly imperfect.

Hazlitt was fascinated by Cellini's account of the casting of Perseus, and in his travel book, *Notes of a Journey Through France and Italy*, from which I've included some extracts, he gives a typically vigorous version of the episode:

He found that the copper which he had at first thrown in did not work kindly. After one or two visits to the furnace, he grew impatient, and seizing on all the lead, iron, and brass he could lay his hands on in the house, threw it *pell-mell*, and in a fit of desperation, into the melting mass, and retired to wait the result. After passing an hour in the greatest agitation, he returned; and inspecting the cast, to his extreme joy discovered it to be smooth and perfect, without a flaw in any part, except a dint in the heel. He then sat down to enjoy his triumph over his enemies, and to devour a cold chicken (which he had provided for his supper) with vast composure and relish.

That detail of the cold chicken is characteristic of Hazlitt – it's reminiscent of the Cheshire cheese which Wordsworth demolishes in 'My First Acquaintance with Poets', and is just one among many examples of Hazlitt's sensuous style of introducing food images into his essays. This preference for the physically tangible – for touch and taste – is explained in the seminal essay 'On Reason and Imagination', where he argues against writers who adopt 'dry and husky' abstractions and ignore individual facts and experiences. As he explains in this essay, the imagination is an associating principle, and has an 'intuitive perception' when a thing belongs to a system, or is 'only an exception to it'.

This principle of association – it is the grammar of perception – is illustrated in an extraordinary passage in 'On Genius and Common Sense' that's like a moment from a political thriller, where Hazlitt describes how the radical writer and poet John Thelwall had a strangely discomfiting experience after being acquitted at the Treason Trials which were held in London in 1794. He then argues that genius and taste are not strictly reducible to rules, that in art, taste, life, speech we decide from feeling, not from reason, and he suggests that common sense is 'tacit reason', and that conscience is the same unspoken sense of right and wrong. This is the abstract idea he makes sensuous, exact and particular in the Thelwall anecdote.

The source of the idea in 'On Genius and Common Sense' is a very interesting passage in *Leviathan* where Hobbes analyses unguided thoughts which wander and 'seem impertinent to one another as in a dream'. And yet, he says, in this wild ranging of the mind,

a man may oft-times perceive the way of it, and the dependence of one thought upon another. For in a discourse of our present civil war, what could seem more impertinent, than to ask (as one did) what was the value of a Roman Penny? Yet the coherence to me was manifest enough. For the thought of war, introduced the thought of the delivering up of the king to his enemies; the thought of that, brought in the thought of the delivering up of Christ; and that again the thought of the 30 pence, which was the price of that treason: and thence easily followed that malicious question; and all this in a moment of time; for thought is quick.

Hazlitt greatly admired Hobbes, and he draws on this passage to argue that any impression in a series can recall any other impression in that series without running through the whole in sequence. The mind 'drops the intermediate links' and passes on with rapid stealth to the 'more striking' effects of pleasure or pain which have 'naturally taken the strongest hold of it'. And he deduces this type of instantaneous, subconscious, mnemonic shortcutting from the account he gives of John Thelwall, whom he knew and whose portrait he painted. Thelwall began a wandering journey through Wales after he had been imprisoned in the Tower of London for five months in 1794, then was kept in the 'dead-hole' in Newgate with the corpses of those who had died of jail fever. Thelwall, as I've noted, was acquitted at the Treason Trials in December 1794, one of the great public events which shaped the young Hazlitt (he was a pupil at a Unitarian academy in Hackney at the time).

Thelwall left London to recover from the government's attempt on his life, and Hazlitt describes how one morning he arrived at an inn (always a favourite location for an epiphany in the essays), ordered breakfast:

and was sitting at the window in all the dalliance of expectation when a face passed of which he took no notice at the instant − but when his breakfast was brought in presently after, he found his appetite for it gone, the day had lost its freshness in his eye, he was uneasy and spiritless; and without any cause that he could discover, a total change had taken place in his feelings. While he was trying to account for this odd circumstance, the same face passed again − it was the face of Taylor the spy; and he was no longer at a loss to explain the difficulty. He had before caught only a transient glimpse, a passing side-view of the face; but though this was not sufficient to awaken a distinct idea in his memory, his feelings, quicker and surer, had taken the alarm; a string had been touched that gave a jar to his whole frame, and would not let him rest, though he could not at all tell what was the matter with him. To the flitting, shadowy, half-distinguished profile that had glided by his window was linked unconsciously and mysteriously, but inseparably, the impression of the trains that had been laid for him by this person; – in this brief moment, in this dim, illegible short-hand of the mind he had just escaped the speeches of the Attorney and Solicitor-General over again; the gaunt figure of Mr Pitt glared by him; the walls of a prison enclosed him; and he felt the hands of the executioner near him, without knowing it till the tremor and disorder of his nerves gave information to his reasoning faculties that all was not well within.

From this exceptionally succinct example, which he cites in his essay on genius and common sense, Hazlitt deduces that the same state of mind – a deep nervous horror – was recalled by one circumstance in the series of associations that had been produced by the whole set of circumstances at the time of Thelwall's trial. In explaining a philosophical point, he also lodges a highly significant time-spot in the historical memory and makes a political statement. The result is a sensible image – concrete, not abstract – which functions as a type of poem in prose as well as an illustration of his theme. It's like a cinematic moment – Godwin's *Caleb Williams* on film – which combines Hazlitt's practice as a painter with his philosophical interests. That passing face is one of the many motion pictures which Hazlitt designs in his prose, a technique which combines his enormous knowledge of the visual arts (he is the first great art critic in English) with a fascination he had for early popular forms of visual entertainment – the magic lantern shows, phantasmagorias, dioramas, fantascopes, which were first brought to London in the early 1800s.

Often Hazlitt uses the term 'transparency' to praise a work of art, and here he's both thinking of the illuminated transparencies in magic lantern shows and offering the term as a figure for his own, often highly visual, journalism. Coleridge, he says in 'My First Acquaintance with Poets', can make the entire universe become 'a transparency of fine words', and Hazlitt nourishes a wish to make his own prose acquire the glossy glow of an illuminated slide. What we begin to notice here is the way certain images in Hazlitt's writing have a self-reflexive quality which obliquely insists that we appreciate them as symbols of the art of critical prose. The account of Cellini casting Perseus is one such self-referring symbol, and if we look at Hazlitt's work the image of a furnace appears significantly often: it is one of his symbols for a particular type of creative imagination shared by certain writers – Milton and Burke primarily. Thus, in his essay on Shakespeare and Milton, he remarks:

Milton has borrowed more than any other writer, and exhausted every source of imitation, sacred or profane; yet he is perfectly distinct from every other writer. He is a writer of centos, and yet in originality scarcely inferior to Homer. The power of his mind is stamped on every line. The fervour of his imagination melts down and renders malleable, as in a furnace, the most contradictory materials.

And he repeats this image of scrap metal melting in a furnace in an essay on personal identity where he again alludes to Cellini's Perseus: 'I have run myself out of my materials for this essay, and want a well-turned sentence or two to conclude with.' Here, he's being deliberately curt and unpolished, and then he produces a simile which gives a lovely, paradoxical lift to his admission of failure, saying that in this he resembles Benvenuto Cellini, who complained that 'with all the brass, tin, iron, and lead he could muster in the house, his statue of Perseus was left imperfect, with a dent in the heel of it'. The implication is that an essayist, like a sculptor in metal, melts down not raw, but already processed material into a new and beautiful shape. This is a symbol of the essay as cento, as a patchwork of quotations, and it's part of the deep structure of Hazlitt's imagination, one of the means by which he seeks to transform criticism into an art form. Deep down he wants his readers to recognize that criticism isn't a second-order, subservient form of writing, where the critic is simply the humble handmaiden of great art, the deferential servant of genius – rather the essayist is creating a form of art, a type of what is now termed *bricolage*. Yeats, too, was fascinated by the way in which art can be thrown together from scraps, from the bits and pieces that litter the floor of the heart's rag-and-bone shop, or from objects which are recycled into dissonant form:

I, the poet William Yeats,
With old mill boards and sea-green slates,
And smithy work from the Gort forge,
Restored this tower for my wife George;
And may these characters remain
When all is ruin once again.

The lasting monument of Hazlitt's prose is made up of phrases and fragments from Edmund Burke, as well as images, phrases, or whole lines and passages from Shakespeare, Milton and an immense number of other writers. But where Yeats can assert his art in the symbol of an actual tower, Hazlitt might have been drawn to Elizabeth Bishop's more equivalent, more ephemeral symbol of a paper house:

a gray wasp's nest
of chewed-up paper
glued with spit.

In Bishop, as in Hazlitt, there is a theme of temporariness and deracination, going on journeys, vulnerablity to the big power structures.

If the critic is an epic compiler of centos, a Cellini melting down prefabricated materials, he is also an actor, someone who imaginatively participates in the works he evaluates. The crucial moment in Hazlitt's early career was the night of 26 January 1814, when Edmund Kean opened as Shylock in *The Merchant of Venice*. Sitting in the small audience that freezing night in the Drury Lane Theatre, Hazlitt was overwhelmed by Kean's performance. His review of it appeared the next day in the *Morning Chronicle*. Kean became sensationally famous and Hazlitt's reputation was also made.

Though he praised Kean's acting of Shylock, he predicted that the actor would become 'a greater favourite' in other parts:

There was a lightness and vigour in his tread, a buoyancy and elasticity of spirit, a fire and animation, which would accord better with almost any other character than with the morose, sullen, inward, inveterate, inflexible malignity of Shylock.

If we consider this sentence in relation to other moments in Hazlitt's writing, we can see that that noun 'elasticity' is crucial:

Hickman might be compared to Diomed, light, vigorous, elastic, and his back glistened in the sun, as he moved about, like a panther's hide. ('The Fight')

If the rope-dancer had performed his task in this manner, leaving so many gaps and botches in his work, he would have broke his neck long ago; I should never have seen that vigorous elasticity of nerve and precision of movement! ('The Indian Jugglers')

Like any critic, Hazlitt is discussing an object external to him, but his critical vocabulary has also that self-referential quality I've spoken of. He is offering the lithe, muscular, elastic human body as a symbol for his own active and engaged prose style.

In a footnote to *Notes of a Journey Through France and Italy*, he says that in the Elgin Marbles there is:

a flexibility and sway of the limbs and of the whole body. The flesh has the softness and texture of flesh, not the smoothness or stiffness of stone. There is an undulation and a liquid flow on the surface, as the breath of genius moved the mighty mass: they are the finest forms in the most striking attitudes, and with every thing in its place, proportion, and degree, uniting the ease, truth, force, and delicacy of Nature. They shew nothing but the artist's thorough comprehension of, and entire docility to that great teacher. There is no *petit-maîtreship*, no pedantry, no attempt at a display of science, or at forcing the parts into an artificial symmetry, but it is like cutting a human body out of a block of marble, and leaving it to act for itself with all the same springs, levers, and internal machinery.

In other sculptures the limbs appear to be cased in marble, and to answer to one another, like rhymes in verse, but the Elgin Marbles are 'harmonious, flowing, varied prose'. This is a central, sudden, critical epiphany, because here a petrified substance – marble – has been made to flow by the sculptor's art. His chisel, a tool analogous to Hazlitt's pen, challenges the view that prose is a petrific, plodding, boring medium which is inferior to poetry. By identifying other classical sculptures with rhyming verse, and then comparing harmoniously varied prose to the aesthetic illusion in the Elgin Marbles of flowing stone, liquid stone, Hazlitt has let his own prose run free and united classical form with nature. Melting into and out of the Parthenon frieze, he has asserted the unique dignity of his chosen art, prose.

His essential theme, throughout his career, is the nature of prose style, a subject that reaches its summation in 'On the Prose-Style of Poets', the essay that opened his last collection of essays, *The Plain Speaker*. In this seminal account, he praises Burke's prose style and offers a symbolic figure which is a version of the image of the rope dancer he employs in 'The Indian Jugglers':

Burke's style is airy, flighty, adventurous, but it never loses sight of the subject; nay, is always in contact with, and derives its increased or varying impulse from it. It may be said to pass yawning gulfs 'on the unstedfast footing of a spear'; still it has an actual resting-place and tangible support under it – it is not suspended on nothing.

The unsteady spear, like the stretched rope, is an image of the sinewy elasticity of impassioned prose. Prose deals with the actual, the tangible; it aims to 'impart conviction', and nothing can be admitted by way of 'ornament or relief' that doesn't add 'new force or clearness' to the original idea.

Deep in Hazlitt's aesthetic of prose is an idea of energetic motion which finds its most sustained treatment in 'On Gusto', where he argues that in Titian's paintings: 'The blood circulates here and there, the blue veins just appear, the rest is distinguished throughout only by that sort of tingling sensation to the eye, which the body feels within itself. This is gusto.' As so often in Hazlitt, the physical body and the visible are identified, so that sight and touch are merged, not separate, senses. And though the subject here is Titian's painting, it is also a symbolic figure for journalistic prose. Thus Jeffrey, the formidable Whig editor of the *Edinburgh Review*, has a 'glancing brilliancy and rapidity of style . . . His pen is never at a loss, never stands still; and would dazzle for this reason alone, like an eye that is ever in motion.' Again and again, Hazlitt returns to the moving eye as a figure for active, engaged prose. Writing in an age of popular visual entertainment, he anticipates cinema and television, partly because he notices the way people walk, and so gives the effect of a flickering series of images when he describes Bentham's rapid walk up and down his garden, or Southey walking stiffly through the streets of London, his umbrella tucked under one arm. The face of Taylor the spy passing the window of Thelwall's inn is, as I've suggested, another example of this technique of brushing his texts with visual motion. The vigilant eyes of Titian's subjects which, Hazlitt suggests, seem to follow the observer around the room, are another example of the optical tingling effect he wants to give to his prose.

In 'The Fight' he offers the rapid, sloggering, muscular action of boxers as his supreme image for prose: 'There was little cautious sparring – no half-hits – no tapping and trifling, none of the *petit-maîtreship* of the art – they were almost all knock-down blows: – the fight was a good stand-up fight.' That phrase '*petit-maîtreship*' is one which he uses of the Georgian polemicist Junius in an essay on Burke where he says that Burke's style 'has the stalk of a giant' – again the walking image – while Junius's has 'the strut of a *petit-maître*'. The phrase for a pedantic, uptight, schoolmasterly style occurs again in the footnote on the Elgin Marbles where Hazlitt says of the sculptures: 'There is no *petit-maîtreship*, no pedantry, no attempt at a display of science.' And, as we've seen, he clinches his account by asserting that the Marbles are 'harmonious, flowing, varied prose' – they symbolize the qualities he wants his own prose to possess.

Noticing this, we realize that we need to bring to our reading of his essays an active and subtle poetics of prose style which allows us to relish the way in which his prose works formally. Even when he is turning out a piece of jobbing journalism, he can suddenly texture his language with a unique sensuousness that is subtle and arresting. For example, a year before he died, he wrote two pieces for *The Atlas* which were entitled 'Trifles Light as Air'. They are entirely and candidly ephemeral, but at one moment the prose flexes wittily into life:

It is a curious speculation to take a modern *belle*, or some accomplished female acquaintance, and conceive what her great-great-grandmother was like, some centuries ago. Who was the Mrs —— of the year 200? We have some standard of grace and elegance among eastern nations 3000 years ago, because we read accounts of them in history; but we have no more notion of, or faith in, our own ancestors than if we had never had any. We *cut the connexion* with the Druids and the Heptarchy; and cannot fancy ourselves (by any transformation) inmates of caves and woods, or feeders on acorns and sloes. We seem *engrafted* on that low stem – a bright, airy, and insolent excrescence.

There is nothing especially remarkable about this passage, until Hazlitt introduces some concrete detail and sets up a playful assonance between *acorns, sloes, low, insolent*, that culminates in the ugly word *excrescence*, which completes the sentence like a bubble bursting, or like a sloe or a pustule being squeezed. The passage works towards this final, tiny, bravura performance, and we enjoy it for that almost physically affective moment. It's casual and spontaneous, but perfectly timed. From the phrase 'caves and woods' to the penultimate word in the sentence, the prose has a subtle keeping until its unity is deliberately blown and dispersed by the final ugly polysyllable which is catapulted forward by the flick of the *t* in 'insolent' and the tiny pause that follows.

We are so used to reading critical prose as being simply about something else – a work of art – that it's hard to appreciate it as performance, as a medium that in Hazlitt's case aspires to the condition of human bodies moving on stage or in a ring in front of an audience that has paid to view the performance and will jeer or walk out if it isn't kept continuously interested. Except in his first book, the philosophical essay on the natural disinterestedness of the human mind, Hazlitt never loses sight of his audience. His moments of autobiography – telling us he's unhappy in love, describing the road from Wem to Shrewsbury – are ways of relaxing his readers by making him appear vulnerable, but they are also pointers to the prose *Prelude* he wants to write.

Take another French phrase he sometimes uses – *un beau jour*. It occurs in the passage from 'On the Pleasure of Painting: The Same Subject Continued' where he describes his first visit to the Louvre:

The first day I got there, I was kept for some time in the French Exhibition-room, and thought I should not be able to get a sight of the old masters. I just caught a peep at them through the door (vile hindrance!) like looking out of purgatory into paradise – from Poussin's noble mellow-looking landscapes to where Rubens hung out his gaudy banner, and down the glimmering vista to the rich jewels of Titian and the Italian school. At last, by much importunity, I was admitted, and lost not an instant in making use of my new privilege. – It was *un beau jour* to me.

The phrase appears again in 'The Fight' where the moon 'gave promise *d'un beau jour* for the morrow, and shewed the ring undrenched by envious showers, arrayed in sunny smiles'. In both passages, Hazlitt is alluding to a passage in Burke's *Reflections on the Revolution in France* where Burke angrily attacks those who supported the French National Assembly's removal of Louis XVI and Marie-Antoinette from Versailles to Paris:

Miserable king! miserable Assembly! How must that assembly be silently scandalized with those of their members, who could call a day which seemed to blot the sun out of Heaven 'un beau jour'!

For Hazlitt, the phrase '*un beau jour*' is both an allusion to this passage and a mnemonic device triggering his discovery of what he terms Burke's 'powerful inimitable prose-style'. As a young man of twenty he bought a copy of Burke's *Reflections* and a copy of *Paradise Lost* in Shrewsbury, then walked home to his parents in Wem, dipping into the books, giddy with excitement at his 'double prize'. That day in 1798 is the *beau jour* of his discovery of Burke's polemic against the Revolution. Where Wordsworth responds to natural objects – mountains, celandines, daffodils – Hazlitt returns to certain texts – Shakespeare's plays, *Paradise Lost, Reflections on the Revolution in France* – and reworks quotations from them into his essays. Though he disagreed with Burke's monarchism, the late counter-revolutionary prose is central to the formation of his style. Also the fact that he can admire Burke, while rejecting his politics, is the backbone of Hazlitt's critical position – this is the disinterested ability to appreciate the arguments of an enemy, and it is one of the fundamental values he acquired from his Unitarian upbringing.

That culture – high-minded, rational, politically engaged – is honoured in 'My First Acquaintance with Poets', where he celebrates

Coleridge's genius. Looking out at the Welsh mountains 'that skirt the horizon with their tempestuous confusion', he remarks:

As we passed along between W—m and Shrewsbury, and I eyed their blue tops seen through the wintry branches, or the red rustling leaves of the sturdy oak-trees by the roadside, a sound was in my ears as of a Siren's song; I was stunned, startled with it, as from deep sleep; but I had no notion then that I should ever be able to express my admiration to others in motley imagery or quaint allusion, till the light of his genius shone into my soul, like the sun's rays glittering in the puddles of the road.

This moment of plenary inspiration is recalled in an essay Hazlitt wrote as he lay dying in a Soho rooming-house:

the long line of blue hills near the place where I was brought up waves in the horizon, a golden sunset hovers over them, the dwarf-oaks rustle their red leaves in the evening-breeze, and the road from [Wem] to [Shrewsbury] by which I first set out on my journey through life, stares me in the face as plain, but from time and change not less visionary and mysterious, than the pictures in the *Pilgrim's Progress*.

The same moment is more obliquely recalled in an important essay he wrote eight years earlier, 'On a Landscape of Nicolas Poussin', which is an elegy for his hero Napoleon and his friend Keats, both of whom died in 1822, the year he saw Poussin's masterpiece.

In this essay, Hazlitt discusses the figure of Orion:

He stalks along, a giant upon earth, and reels and falters in his gait, as if just awaked out of sleep, or uncertain of his way; – you see his blindness, though his back is turned. Mists rise around him, and veil the sides of the green forests; earth is dank and fresh with dews, the 'grey dawn and the Pleiades before him dance', and in the distance are seen the blue hills and sullen ocean.

This is a version of Hazlitt beginning his journey through life on the road between Wem and Shrewsbury, but Burke is also a subtle presence here – his style has the 'stalk of a giant', so the stalking figure of Orion is on one level a symbol for Hazlitt's and Burke's prose styles. And when Orion, in the opening sentence, is called 'the classical Nimrod', there is an allusion to a famous passage in Burke's

Letter to a Noble Lord, where he attacks the French revolutionary ideologists as 'a misallied and disparaged branch of the house of Nimrod'.

Hazlitt, then, layers his prose in a complicated and allusive manner. Like Cellini, he recycles all sorts of bits and pieces, like Milton he works innumerable quotations into the fabric of his essays. Above all, he refuses to allow prose to play second fiddle to poetry — to be a mere servant of a greater art — and he affirms constantly the strict, subtle, joyous, elastic laws of prose-writing. One of the very greatest masters of English prose style, this neglected genius needs to be celebrated and studied. If anyone makes criticism into an art form, it is William Hazlitt.

A NOTE ON THE TEXT

The text of the essays included in this edition is, wherever applicable, that of the first edition of the first collected volume of his works in which Hazlitt included them (*Characters of Shakspeare's Plays* (1817), *The Round Table* (1817), *A View of the English Stage* (1818), *Lectures on the English Poets* (1818), *Political Essays, With Sketches of Public Characters* (1819), *Lectures on the Dramatic Literature of the Age of Elizabeth* (1820), *Table-Talk* (1821–2), *The Spirit of the Age* (1825), *The Plain Speaker* (1826), and *Notes of a Journey Through France and Italy* (1826)). Details of previous newspaper or periodical publications are included in the brief bibliographical notes incorporated with the annotation at the end of this edition. For uncollected essays the text used is that of earliest publication. The text of *A Letter to William Gifford, Esq.* (1819) is similarly taken from the first published edition of that work.

The editors would like to acknowledge their gratitude to Duncan Wu for all his help in locating Hazlitt's texts. They would also like to acknowledge a Small Research Grant from the British Academy.

Because the essays selected for this edition have been taken from a variety of different sources, certain changes have been made in order to standardize style across the volume: words with 'ise' endings have been made consistently 'ize'; single quotation marks have been used, and punctuation at the end of a quotation has been standardized; long em dashes have been changed to spaced en dashes for parentheses in the text; full points have been removed after titles such as 'Mr', 'Dr', and 'Mrs'; book, play, long poem and journal titles have been italicized as have titles of works of art.

Certain typographical features, such as a line of asterisks, have been removed, but where an extract from an essay has been included, a single asterisk before the first line or after the last line indicates that a preceding or final portion of the essay has been omitted for this edition.

In addition, spelling mistakes or typographical errors from the original editions have been silently corrected, as have some period or archaic spellings that were used inconsistently. Hazlitt spelled certain names, like Shakespeare, in a number of ways; for this edition we have standardized spelling as 'Shakespeare' and corrected certain other spellings of names where they appeared inconsistently.

THE FIGHT AND OTHER WRITINGS

'The Customs and the Grande Chartreuse'

*

At Pont Beau-Voisin, the frontier town of the King of Sardinia's dominions, we stopped to breakfast, and to have our passports and luggage examined at the Barrier and Custom-house. I breakfasted with the Spaniard, who invited himself to our tea-party, and complimented Madame (in broken English) on the excellence of her performance. We agreed between ourselves that the Spaniards and English were very much superior to the French. I found he had a taste for the Fine Arts, and I spoke of Murillo and Velázquez as two excellent Spanish painters. 'Here was sympathy.'[1] I also spoke of *Don Quixote* – 'Here was more sympathy.' What a thing it is to have produced a work that makes friends of all the world that have read it, and that all the world have read! Mention but Don Quixote, and who is there that does not own him for a friend, countryman, and brother? There is no French work, at the name of which (as at a talisman) the scales of national prejudice so completely fall off; nay more, I must confess there is no English one. We were summoned from our tea and patriotic effusions to attend the *Douane*.[2] It was striking to have to pass and repass the piquets of soldiers stationed as a guard on bridges across narrow mountain-streams that a child might leap over. After some slight dalliance with our great-coat pockets, and significant gestures as if we might or might not have things of value about us that we should not, we proceeded to the Custom-house. I had two trunks. One contained books. When it was unlocked, it was as if the lid of Pandora's box flew open. There could not have been a more sudden start or expression of surprise, had it been filled with cartridge-paper or gunpowder. Books were the corrosive sublimate that eat out despotism and priestcraft – the artillery that battered down castle and dungeon-

3

walls – the ferrets that ferreted out abuses – the lynx-eyed guardians that tore off disguises – the scales that weighed right and wrong – the thumping make-weight thrown into the balance that made force and fraud, the sword and the cowl, kick the beam – the dread of knaves, the scoff of fools – the balm and the consolation of the human mind – the salt of the earth – the future rulers of the world! A box full of them was a contempt of the constituted Authorities; and the names of mine were taken down with great care and secrecy – Lord Bacon's *Advancement of Learning*, Milton's *Paradise Lost*, De Stutt-Tracey's *Ideologie*, (which Buonaparte said³ ruined his Russian expedition), Mignet's *French Revolution*, (which wants a chapter on the English Government), *Sayings and Doings*,⁴ with pencil notes in the margin, *Irving's Orations*,⁵ the same, an *Edinburgh Review*, some *Morning Chronicles*, *The Literary Examiner*, a collection of Poetry, a Volume bound in crimson velvet, and the Paris edition of *Table-Talk*.⁶ Here was some questionable matter enough – but no notice was taken. My box was afterwards corded and *leaded* with equal gravity and politeness, and it was not till I arrived at Turin that I found it was a prisoner of state, and would be forwarded to me anywhere I chose to mention, out of his Sardinian Majesty's dominions. I was startled to find myself within the smooth polished grasp of legitimate power, without suspecting it; and was glad to recover my trunk at Florence, with no other inconvenience than the expense of its carriage across the country.*

* At Milan, a short time ago, a gentleman had a Homer, in Greek and Latin, among his books. He was surlily asked to explain what it meant. Upon doing so, the Inspector shook his head doubtingly, and said, 'It might pass this time,' but advised him to beware of a second. 'Here, now, is a work,' he continued, pointing to —'s *Lives of the Popes*,⁷ containing all the abominations (public and private) of their history, 'You should bring such books as this with you!' This is one specimen of that learned conspiracy for the suppression of light and letters, of which we are sleeping partners and honorary associates. The Allies complain at present of Mr Canning's 'faithlessness'. Oh! that he would indeed play them false and earn his title of 'slippery George'! Faithful to anything he cannot be – faithless to them would be something. The Austrians, it is said, have lately attempted to strike the name of Italy out of the maps, that that country may neither have a name, a body, or a soul left to it, and even to suppress the publication of its finest historians, that it may forget it ever had one. Go on, obliging creatures! Blot the light out of heaven, tarnish the blue sky with the blight and fog of despotism, deface and trample on the green earth; for while one trace of what is fair or lovely is left in the earth under our feet, or the sky over

It was noon as we returned to the inn, and we first caught a full view of the Alps over a plashy meadow, some feathery trees, and the tops of the houses of the village in which we were. It was a magnificent sight, and in truth a new sensation. Their summits were bright with snow and with the mid-day sun; they did not seem to stand upon the earth, but to prop the sky; they were at a considerable distance from us, and yet appeared just over our heads. The surprise seemed to take away our breath, and to lift us from our feet. It was drinking the empyrean. As we could not long retain possession of our two places in the interior, I proposed to our guide to exchange them for the cabriolet; and, after some little chaffering and candid representations of the outside passengers of the cold we should have to encounter, we were installed there to our great satisfaction, and the no less contentment of those whom we succeeded. Indeed I had no idea that we should be steeped in these icy valleys at three o'clock in the morning, or I might have hesitated. The view was cheering, the clear air refreshing, and I thought we should set off each morning about seven or eight. But it is part of the *sçavoir vivre*[9] in France, and one of the methods of adding to the *agrémens*[10] of travelling, to set out three hours before daybreak in the depth of winter, and stop two

---

our heads, or in the mind of man that is within us, it will remain to mock your impotence and deformity, and to reflect back lasting hatred and contempt upon you. Why does not our Eton scholar, our classic Statesman, suggest to the Allies an intelligible hint of the propriety of inscribing the name of Italy once more on the map,

'Like that ensanguined flower inscribed with woe' –[8]

of taking off the prohibition on the Histories of Guicciardini and Davila? Or why do not the English people – the English House of Commons, suggest it to him? Is there such a thing as the English people – as an English House of Commons? Their influence is not felt at present in Europe, as erst it was, to its short-lived hope, bought with flat despair. The reason is, the cause of the people of Europe has no echo in the breasts of the British public. The cause of Kings had an echo in the breast of a British Monarch – that of Foreign Governments in the breasts of British Ministers! There are at present no fewer than fifteen hundred of the Italian nobility of the first families proscribed from their country, or pining in dungeons. For what? For trying to give to their country independence and a Constitutional Government, like England! What says the English House of Lords to that? What if the Russians were to come and apply to us and to them the benefits and the principles of the Holy Alliance – the bayonet and the thumbscrew? Lord Bathurst says, 'let them come'; – and they will come when we have a servile people, dead to liberty, and an arbitrary government, hating and ready to betray it!

hours about noon, in order to arrive early in the evening. With all the disadvantages of preposterous hours and of intense cold pouring into the cabriolet like water the two first mornings, I cannot say I repented of my bargain. We had come a thousand miles to see the Alps for one thing, and we *did* see them in perfection, which we could not have done inside. The ascent for some way was striking and full of novelty; but on turning a corner of the road we entered upon a narrow defile or rocky ledge, overlooking a steep valley under our feet, with a headlong turbid stream dashing down it, and spreading itself out into a more tranquil river below, a dark wood of innumerable pine-trees covering the side of the valley opposite, with broken crags, morasses, and green plots of cultivated ground, orchards, and quiet homesteads, on which the sun glanced its farewell rays through the openings of the mountains. On our left, a precipice of dark brown rocks of various shapes rose abruptly at our side, or hung threatening over the road, into which some of their huge fragments, loosened by the winter's flaw,[11] had fallen, and which men and mules were employed in removing − (the thundering crash had hardly yet subsided, as you looked up and saw the fleecy clouds sailing among the shattered cliffs, while another giant-mass seemed ready to quit its station in the sky) − and as the road wound along to the other extremity of this noble pass, between the beetling rocks and dark sloping pine-forests, frowning defiance at each other, you caught the azure sky, the snowy ridges of the mountains, and the peaked tops of the Grande Chartreuse, waving to the right in solitary state and air-clad brightness. − It was a scene dazzling, enchanting, and that stamped the long-cherished dreams of the imagination upon the senses. Between those four crystal peaks stood the ancient monastery of that name, hid from the sight, revealed to thought, halfway between earth and heaven, enshrined in its cerulean atmosphere, lifting the soul to its native home, and purifying it from mortal grossness. I cannot wonder at the pilgrimages that are made to it, its calm repose, its vows monastic. Life must there seem a noiseless dream; − Death a near translation to the skies! Winter was even an advantage to this scene. The black forests, the dark sides of the rocks gave additional and inconceivable brightness to the glittering summits of the lofty mountains, and received a deeper tone and a more solemn gloom from them; while in the open spaces the unvaried sheets of snow fatigue the eye, which requires the contrast of the green tints or luxuriant foliage of summer or of spring. This was more particularly perceptible as the day closed, when the golden sunset streamed in vain over frozen valleys that imbibed no richness from it, and repelled its smile from their polished marble surface. But in the more gloomy and desert regions, the difference is less remarkable between summer and winter, except in the beginning of spring, when the summits of the hoary rocks are covered with snow, and the clefts in their sides are filled with fragrant shrubs and flowers. I hope to see this miracle when I return.

We came to Echelles, where we changed horses with great formality and preparation, as if setting out on some formidable expedition. Six large strong-boned horses with high haunches (used to ascend and descend mountains) were put to, the rope-tackle was examined and repaired, and our two postilions mounted and dismounted more than once, before they seemed willing to set off, which they did at last at a hand-gallop, that was continued for some miles. It is nothing to see English blood-horses get over the ground with such prodigious fleetness and spirit, but it is really curious to see the huge cart-horses, that they use for Diligences abroad, lumbering along and making the miles disappear behind them with their ponderous strength and persevering activity. The road for some way rattled under their heavy hoofs, and the heavy wheels that they dragged or whirled along at a thundering pace; the postilions cracked their whips, and the one in front (a dark, swarthy, short-set fellow) flourished his, shouted and hallooed, and turned back to vociferate his instructions to his companion with the robust energy and wildness of expression of a smuggler or a leader of banditti, carrying off a rich booty from a troop of soldiers. There was something in the scenery to favour this idea. Night was falling as we entered the superb tunnel cut through the mountain at La Grotte (a work attributed to Victor-Emanuel, with the same truth that Falstaff took to himself[12] the merit of the death of Hotspur), and its iron floor rang, the whips cracked, and the roof echoed to the clear voice of our intrepid postilion as we dashed through it. Our path then wound among romantic defiles, where huge masses of snow and the gathering gloom threatened continually to bar our way; but it seemed cleared by the lively shout of our guide, and the carriage-wheels, clogged with ice, rolled after the heavy tramp of the horses. In this manner we rode on through a country full of wild grandeur and shadowy fears, till we had nearly reached the end of our day's journey, when we dismissed our two fore-horses and their rider, to whom I presented a trifling *douceur*[13] 'for the sake of his good voice and cheerful countenance'. The descent into Chambéry was the most dangerous part of the road, and our horses were nearly thrown on their haunches several times. The road was narrow and slippery; there were a number of market-carts returning from the town, and there was a declivity on one side, which, though not a precipice, was quite sufficient to have dashed us to pieces in a common-place way. We arrived at Chambéry in the dusk of the evening; and there is surely a charm in the name, and in that of the Charmettes near it (where he who relished all more sharply than his fellows, and made them feel for him as for themselves, alone felt peace or hope), which even the Magdalen Muse of Mr Moore[14] has not been able to *unsing*![15] We alighted at the inn fatigued enough, and were delighted on being shown to a room to find the floor of wood, and English teacups and saucers. We were in Savoy.

We set out early the next morning, and it was the most trying part of our whole journey. The wind cut like a scythe through the valleys, and a cold, icy feeling struck from the sides of the snowy precipices that surrounded us, so that we seemed enclosed in a huge well of mountains. We got to St Jean de Maurienne to breakfast about noon, where the only point agreed upon appeared to be to have nothing ready to receive us. This was the most tedious day of all; nor did we meet with any thing to repay us for our uncomfortable setting out. We travelled through a scene of desolation, were chilled in sunless valleys or dazzled by sunny mountain-tops, passed frozen streams or gloomy cavities, that might be transformed into the scene of some Gothic wizard's spell, or reminded one of some German novel. Let no one imagine that the crossing the Alps is the work of a moment, or done by a single heroic effort – that they are a huge but detached chain of hills, or like the dotted line we find in the map. They are a sea or an entire kingdom of mountains. It took us three days to traverse them in this, which is the most practicable direction, and travelling at a good round pace. We passed on as far as eye could see, and still we appeared to have made little way. Still we were in the shadow of the same enormous mass of rock and snow, by the side of the same creeping stream. Lofty mountains reared themselves in front of us – horrid abysses were scooped out under our feet. Sometimes the road wound along the side of a steep hill, overlooking some village-spire or hamlet, and as we ascended it, it only gave us a view of remoter scenes, 'where Alps o'er Alps arise',[16] tossing about their billowy tops, and tumbling their unwieldy shapes in all directions – a world of wonders! – Any one, who is much of an egotist, ought not to travel through these districts; his vanity will not find its account in them; it will be chilled, mortified, shrunk up: but they are a noble treat to those who feel themselves raised in their own thoughts and in the scale of being by the immensity of other things, and who can aggrandize and piece out their personal insignificance by the grandeur and eternal forms of nature! It gives one a vast idea of Buonaparte to think of him in these situations. He alone (the Rob Roy of the scene) seemed a match for the elements, and able to master 'this fortress, built by nature for herself'.[17] Neither impeded nor turned aside by immoveable barriers, he smote the mountains with his iron glaive, and made them malleable; cut roads through them; transported armies over their ridgy steeps; and the rocks 'nodded to him, and did him courtesies'![18]

We arrived at St Michelle at night-fall (after passing through beds of ice and the infernal regions of cold), where we met with a truly hospitable reception, with wood-floors in the English fashion, and where they told us the King of England had stopped. This made no sort of difference to me.

We breakfasted the next day (being Sunday) at Lans-le-Bourg, where I observed my friend the Spaniard busy with his tables, taking down the name of the place. The landlady was a little, round, fat, good-humoured, black-eyed Italian or Savoyard, *saying* a number of good things to all her guests, but sparing of them otherwise. We were now at the foot of Mount Cénis, and after breakfast we set off on foot before the Diligence, which was to follow us in half an hour. We passed a melancholy-looking inn at the end of the town, professing to be kept by an Englishwoman; but there appeared to be nobody about the house, English, French, or Italian. The mistress of it (a young woman who had married an Italian) had, in fact, died a short time before of pure chagrin and disappointment in this solitary place, after having told her tale of distress to every one, till it fairly wore her out. We had leisure to look back to the town as we proceeded, and which, with its church, stone-cottages, and slated roofs, shrunk into a miniature-model of itself as we continued to advance farther and higher above it. Some straggling cottages, some vineyards planted at a great height, and another compact and well-built village, that seemed to defy the extremity of the seasons, were seen in the direction of the valley that we were pursuing. Else all around were shapeless, sightless piles of hills covered with snow, with crags or pine-trees or a foot-path peeping out, and in the appearance of which no alteration whatever was made by our advancing or receding. We gained on the mountain by a broad, winding road that continually doubles, and looks down upon the point from whence you started half an hour before. Some snow had fallen in the morning, but it was now fine, though cloudy. We found two of our fellow-travellers following our example, and they soon after overtook us. They were both French. We noticed some of the features of the scenery; and a lofty hill opposite to us being scooped out into a bed of snow, with two ridges or promontories projecting (something like an arm-chair) on each side. '*Voilà!*' said the younger and more volatile of our companions, '*c'est un trône, et le nuage est la gloire!*'[19] — A white cloud indeed encircled its misty top. I complimented him on the happiness of his allusion, and said that Madame was pleased with the exactness of the resemblance. He then turned to the valley, and said, '*C'est un berceau.*'[20] This is the height to which the imagination of a Frenchman always soars, and it can soar no higher. Any thing that is not cast in this obvious, common-place mould, that had been used a thousand times before with applause, they think barbarous, and as they phrase it, *originaire*. No farther notice was taken of the scenery, any more than if we had been walking on the Boulevards at Paris, and my young Frenchman talked of other things, laughed, sung, and smoked a cigar with a gaiety and lightness of heart that I envied. 'What has become', said the elder of the Frenchmen, 'of Monsieur l'Espagnol? He does not easily quit his seat; he sits in one corner, never looks out, or if you point to any object, takes no notice of it; and when you come to the end of the stage, says — "What is the name of that place we passed by last?" — takes out his pocket-book, and makes a note of it. "That is droll."' And what made it more so, it turned out that our Spanish friend was a painter, travelling to Rome to study the Fine Arts! All the way as we ascended, there were red posts placed at the edge of the road, ten or twelve feet in height, to point out the direction of the road in case of a heavy fall of snow, and with notches cut to shew the depth of the drifts. There were also scattered stone-hovels, erected as stations for the *Gens d'armes*, who were sometimes left here for several days together after a severe snow-storm, without being approached by a single human being. One of these stood near the top of the mountain, and as we were tired of the walk (which had occupied two hours) and of the uniformity of the view, we agreed to wait here for the Diligence to overtake us. We were cordially welcomed in by a young peasant (a soldier's wife) with a complexion as fresh as the winds, and an expression as pure as the mountain-snows. The floor of this rude tenement consisted of the solid rock; and a three-legged table stood on it, on which were placed three earthen bowls filled with sparkling wine, heated on a stove with sugar. The woman stood by, and did the honours of this cheerful repast with a rustic simplicity and a pastoral grace that might have called forth the powers of Hemskirk and Raphael. I shall not soon forget the rich ruby colour of the wine, as the sun shone upon it through a low glazed window that looked out on the boundless wastes around, nor its grateful spicy smell as we sat round it. I was complaining of the trick that had been played by the waiter at Lyons in the taking of our places, when I was told by the young Frenchman, that, in case I returned to Lyons, I ought to go to the Hôtel de l'Europe, or to the Hôtel du Nord, 'in which latter case he should have the honour of serving me'. I thanked him for his information, and we set out to finish the ascent of Mount Cénis, which we did in another half-hour's march. The *traiteur*[21] of the Hôtel du Nord and I had got into a brisk theatrical discussion on the comparative merits of Kean and Talma, he asserting that there was something in French acting which an English understanding could not appreciate; and I insisting loudly on bursts of passion as the *forte* of Talma, which was a language common to human nature; that in his *Œdipus*, for instance, it was not a Frenchman or an Englishman he had to represent – *'Mais c'est un homme, c'est Œdipe'* – when our cautious Spaniard brushed by us, determined to shew he could descend the mountain, if he would not ascend it on foot. His figure was characteristic enough, his motions smart and lively, and his dress composed of all the colours of the rainbow. He strutted on before us in the snow, like a flamingo or some tropical bird of variegated plumage; his dark purple cloak fluttered in the air, his Montero cap, set a little on one side, was of fawn colour; his waistcoat a bright scarlet, his coat a reddish brown, his trousers a pea-green, and his boots a perfect yellow. He saluted us with a national politeness as he passed, and seemed bent on redeeming the sedentary sluggishness of his character by one bold and desperate effort of locomotion.

The coach shortly after overtook us. We descended a long and steep declivity, with the highest point of Mount Cénis on our left, and a lake to the right, like a landing-place for geese. Between the two was a low, white monastery, and the barrier where we had our passports inspected, and then went forward with only two stout horses and one rider. The snow on this side of the mountain was nearly gone. I supposed myself for some time nearly on level ground, till we came in view of several black chasms or steep ravines in the side of the mountain facing us, with water oozing from it, and saw through some *galleries*, that is, massy stone-pillars knit together by thick rails of strong timber, guarding the road-side, a perpendicular precipice below, and other galleries beyond, diminished in a fairy perspective, and descending 'with cautious haste and giddy cunning',[22] and with innumerable windings and re-duplications to an interminable depth and distance from the height where we were. The men and horses with carts, that were labouring up the path in the hollow below, shewed like crows or flies. The road we had to pass was often immediately under that we were passing, and cut from the side of what was all but a precipice out of the solid rock by the broad, firm master-hand that traced and executed this mighty work. The share that art has in the scene is as appalling as the scene itself – the strong security against danger as sublime as the danger itself. Near the turning of one of the first galleries is a beautiful waterfall, which at this time was frozen into a sheet of green pendent ice – a magical transformation. Long after we continued to descend, now faster and now slower, and came at length to a small village at the bottom of a sweeping line of road, where the houses seemed like dove-cotes with the mountain's back reared like a wall behind them, and which I thought the termination of our journey. But here the wonder and the greatness began: for, advancing through a grove of slender trees to another point of the road, we caught a new view of the lofty mountain to our left. It stood in front of us, with its head in the skies, covered with snow, and its bare sides stretching far away into a valley that yawned at its feet, and over which we seemed suspended in mid air. The height, the magnitude, the immoveableness of the objects, the wild contrast, the deep tones, the dance and play of the landscape from the change of our direction and the interposition of other striking objects, the continued recurrence of the same huge masses, like giants following us with unseen strides, stunned the sense like a blow, and yet gave the imagination strength to contend with a force that mocked it. Here immeasurable columns of reddish granite shelved from the mountain's sides; here they were covered and stained with furze and other shrubs; here a chalky cliff shewed a fir-grove climbing its tall sides, and that itself looked at a distance like a huge, branching pine-tree; beyond was a dark, projecting knoll, or hilly promontory, that threatened to bound the perspective – but, on drawing nearer to it, the cloudy vapour that shrouded it (as it were) retired, and opened another vista beyond, that, in its own unfathomed depth, and in the gradual obscurity of twilight, resembled the uncertain gloom of the back-ground of some fine picture. At the bottom of this valley crept a sluggish stream, and a monastery or low castle stood upon its banks. The effect was altogether grander than I had any conception of. It was not the idea of height or elevation that was obtruded upon the mind and staggered it, but we seemed to be descending into the bowels of the earth – its foundations seemed to be laid bare to the centre; and abyss after abyss, a vast, shadowy, interminable space, opened to receive us. We saw the building up and frame-work of the world – its limbs, its ponderous masses, and mighty proportions, raised stage upon stage, and we might be said to have passed into an unknown sphere, and beyond mortal limits. As we rode down our winding, circuitous path, our baggage (which had been taken off) moved on before us; a grey horse that had got loose from the stable followed it, and as we whirled round the different turnings in this rapid, mechanical flight, at the same rate and the same distance from each other, there seemed something like witchcraft in the scene and in our progress through it. The moon had risen, and threw its gleams across the fading twilight; the snowy tops of the mountains were blended with the clouds and stars; their sides were shrouded in mysterious gloom, and it was not till we entered Susa, with its fine old drawbridge and castellated walls, that we found ourselves on *terra firma*, or breathed common air again. At the inn at Susa, we first perceived the difference of Italian manners; and the next day arrived at Turin, after passing over thirty miles of the straightest, flattest, and dullest road in the world. Here we stopped two days to recruit our strength and look about us.

On the Pleasure of Painting

'There is a pleasure in painting which none but painters know.'[1] In writing, you have to contend with the world; in painting, you have only to carry on a friendly strife with Nature. You sit down to your task, and are happy. From the moment that you take up the pencil, and look Nature in the face, you are at peace with your own heart. No angry passions rise to disturb the silent progress of the work, to shake the hand, or dim the brow: no irritable humours are set afloat: you have no absurd opinions to combat, no point to strain, no adversary to crush, no fool to annoy – you are actuated by fear or favour to no man. There is 'no juggling here',[2] no sophistry, no intrigue, no tampering with the evidence, no attempt to make black white, or white black: but you resign yourself into the hands of a greater power, that of Nature, with the simplicity of a child, and the devotion of an enthusiast – 'study with joy her manner, and with rapture taste her style'.[3] The mind is calm, and full at the same time. The hand and eye are equally employed. In tracing the commonest object, a plant or the stump of a tree, you learn something every moment. You perceive unexpected differences, and discover likenesses where you looked for no such thing. You try to set down what you see – find out your error, and correct it. You need not play tricks, or purposely mistake: with all your pains, you are still far short of the mark. Patience grows out of the endless pursuit, and turns it into a luxury. A streak in a flower, a wrinkle in a leaf, a tinge in a cloud, a stain in an old wall or ruin grey, are seized with avidity as the *spolia opima*[4] of this sort of mental warfare, and furnish out labour for another half-day. The hours pass away untold, without chagrin, and without weariness; nor would you ever wish to pass them otherwise. Innocence is joined with industry, pleasure with business; and the mind is satisfied, though it is not engaged in thinking or in doing any mischief.*

I have not much pleasure in writing these Essays, or in reading them afterwards; though I own I now and then meet with a phrase that I like, or a thought that strikes me as a true one. But after I begin them, I am only anxious to get to the end of them, which I am not sure I shall do, for I seldom see my way a page or even a sentence beforehand; and when I have as by a miracle escaped, I trouble myself little more about them. I sometimes have to write them twice over: then it is necessary to read the *proof*, to prevent mistakes by the printer; so that by the time they appear in a tangible shape, and one can con them over with a conscious, sidelong glance to the public approbation, they have lost their gloss and relish, and become 'more tedious than a twice-told tale'.[6] For a person to read his own works over with any great delight, he ought first to forget that he ever wrote them. Familiarity naturally breeds contempt. It is, in fact, like poring fondly over a piece of blank paper: from repetition, the words convey no distinct meaning to the mind, are

* There is a passage in Werter[5] which contains a very pleasing illustration of this doctrine, and is as follows.

'About a league from the town is a place called Walheim. It is very agreeably situated on the side of a hill: from one of the paths which leads out of the village, you have a view of the whole country; and there is a good old woman who sells wine, coffee, and tea there: but better than all this are two lime-trees before the church, which spread their branches over a little green, surrounded by barns and cottages. I have seen few places more retired and peaceful. I send for a chair and table from the old woman's, and there I drink my coffee and read Homer. It was by accident that I discovered this place one fine afternoon: all was perfect stillness; every body was in the fields, except a little boy about four years old, who was sitting on the ground, and holding between his knees a child of about six months; he pressed it to his bosom with his little arms, which made a sort of great chair for it; and notwithstanding the vivacity which sparkled in his eyes, he sat perfectly still. Quite delighted with the scene, I sat down on a plough opposite, and had great pleasure in drawing this little picture of brotherly tenderness. I added a bit of the hedge, the barn-door, and some broken cart-wheels, without any order, just as they happened to lie; and in about an hour I found I had made a drawing of great expression and very correct design, without having put in any thing of my own. This confirmed me in the resolution I had made before, only to copy nature for the future. Nature is inexhaustible, and alone forms the greatest masters. Say what you will of rules, they alter the true features, and the natural expression.'

mere idle sounds, except that our vanity claims an interest and property in them. I have more satisfaction in my own thoughts than in dictating them to others: words are necessary to explain the impression of certain things upon me to the reader, but they rather weaken and draw a veil over than strengthen it to myself. However I might say with the poet, 'My mind to me a kingdom is,'[7] yet I have little ambition 'to set a throne or chair of state in the understandings of other men'.[8] The ideas we cherish most, exist best in a kind of shadowy abstraction,

'Pure in the last recesses of the mind';[9]

and derive neither force nor interest from being exposed to public view. They are old familiar acquaintance, and any change in them, arising from the adventitious ornaments of style or dress, is little to their advantage. After I have once written on a subject, it goes out of my mind: my feelings about it have been melted down into words, and *them* I forget. I have, as it were, discharged my memory of its old habitual reckoning, and rubbed out the score of real sentiment. For the future, it exists only for the sake of others. – But I cannot say, from my own experience, that the same process takes place in transferring our ideas to canvas; they gain more than they lose in the mechanical transformation. One is never tired of painting, because you have to set down not what you knew already, but what you have just discovered. In the former case, you translate feelings into words; in the latter, names into things. There is a continual creation out of nothing going on. With every stroke of the brush, a new field of inquiry is laid open; new difficulties arise, and new triumphs are prepared over them. By comparing the imitation with the original, you see what you have done, and how much you have still to do. The test of the senses is severer than that of fancy, and an over-match even for the delusions of our self-love. One part of a picture shames another, and you determine to paint up to yourself, if you cannot come up to nature. Every object becomes lustrous from the light thrown back upon it by the mirror of art: and by the aid of the pencil we may be said to touch and handle the objects of sight. The air-drawn visions that hover on the verge of existence have a bodily presence given them on the canvas: the form of beauty is changed into a substance: the dream and the glory of the universe is made 'palpable to feeling as to sight'.[10] – And see! a rainbow starts from the canvas, with all its humid train of glory, as if it were drawn from its cloudy arch in heaven. The spangled landscape glitters with drops of dew after the shower. The 'fleecy fools'[11] show their coats in the gleams of the setting sun. The shepherds pipe their farewell notes in the fresh evening air. And is this bright vision made from a dead dull blank, like a bubble reflecting the mighty fabric of the universe? Who would think this miracle of Rubens's pencil possible to be performed? Who, having seen it, would not spend his life to do the like? See how the rich fallows, the bare stubble-field, the scanty harvest-home, drag in Rembrandt's landscapes! How often have I looked at them and nature, and tried to do the same, till the very 'light thickened',[12] and there was an earthiness in the feeling of the air! There is no end of the refinements of art and nature in this respect. One may look at the misty glimmering horizon till the eye dazzles and the imagination is lost, in hopes to transfer the whole interminable expanse at one blow upon the canvas. Wilson said,[13] he used to try to paint the effect of the motes dancing in the setting sun. At another time, a friend coming into his painting-room when he was sitting on the ground in a melancholy posture, observed that his picture looked like a landscape after a shower: he started up with the greatest delight, and said, 'That is the effect I intended to produce, but thought I had failed.' Wilson was neglected; and, by degrees, neglected his art to apply himself to brandy. His hand became unsteady, so that it was only by repeated attempts that he could reach the place, or produce the effect he aimed at; and when he had done a little to a picture, he would say to any acquaintance who chanced to drop in, 'I have painted enough for one day: come, let us go somewhere.' It was not so Claude left his pictures, or his studies on the banks of the Tiber, to go in search of other enjoyments, or ceased to gaze upon the glittering sunny vales and distant hills; and while his eye drank in the clear sparkling hues and lovely forms of nature, his hand stamped them on the lucid canvas to last there for ever! – One of the most delightful parts of my life was one fine summer, when I used to walk out of an evening to catch the last light of the sun, gemming the green slopes or russet lawns, and gilding tower or tree, while the blue sky gradually turning to purple and gold, or skirted with dusky grey, hung its broad marble pavement over all, as we see it in the great master of Italian landscape. But to come to a more particular explanation of the subject.

The first head I ever tried to paint was an old woman[14] with the upper part of the face shaded by her bonnet, and I certainly laboured it with great perseverance. It took me numberless sittings to do it. I have it by me still, and sometimes look at it with surprise, to think how much pains were thrown away to little purpose, – yet not altogether in vain if it taught me to see good in every thing,[15] and to know that there is nothing vulgar in nature seen with the eye of science or of true art. Refinement creates beauty everywhere: it is the grossness of the spectator that discovers nothing but grossness in the object. Be this as it may, I spared no pains to do my best. If art was long,[16] I thought that life was so too at that moment. I got in the general effect the first day; and pleased and surprised enough I was at my success. The rest was a work of time – of weeks and months (if need were) of patient toil and careful finishing. I had seen an old head by Rembrandt at Burleigh-House, and if I could produce a head at all like Rembrandt in a year, in my life-time, it would be glory and felicity and wealth and fame enough for me! The head I had seen at Burleigh was an exact and wonderful facsimile of nature, and I resolved to make mine (as nearly as I could) an exact facsimile of nature. I did not then, nor do I now believe, with Sir Joshua,[17] that the perfection of art consists in giving general appearances without individual details, but in giving general appearances with individual details. Otherwise, I had done my work the first day. But I saw something more in nature than general effect, and I thought it worth my while to give it in the picture. There was a gorgeous effect of light and shade: but there was a delicacy as well as depth in the *chiaro scuro*, which I was bound to follow into all its dim and scarce perceptible variety of tone and shadow. Then I had to make the transition from a strong light to as dark a shade, preserving the masses, but gradually softening off the intermediate parts. It was so in nature: the difficulty was to make it so in the copy. I tried, and failed again and again; I strove harder, and succeeded as I thought. The wrinkles in Rembrandt were not hard lines; but broken and irregular. I saw the same appearance in nature, and strained every nerve to give it. If I could hit off this edgy appearance, and insert the reflected light in the furrows of old age in half a morning, I did not think I had lost a day. Beneath the shrivelled yellow parchment look of the skin, there was here and there a streak of the blood colour tinging the face; this I made a point of conveying, and did not cease to compare what I saw with what I did (with jealous lynx-eyed watchfulness) till I succeeded to the best of my ability and judgment. How many revisions were there! How many attempts to catch an expression which I had seen the day before! How often did we try to get the old position, and wait for the return of the same light! There was a puckering up of the lips, a cautious introversion of the eye under the shadow of the bonnet, indicative of the feebleness and suspicion of old age, which at last we managed, after many trials and some quarrels, to a tolerable nicety. The picture was never finished, and I might have gone on with it to the present hour.* I used to set it on the ground when my day's work was done, and saw revealed to me with swimming eyes the birth of new hopes, and of a new world of objects. The painter thus learns to look at nature with different eyes. He before saw her 'as in a glass darkly, but now face to face'.[18] He understands the texture and meaning of the visible universe, and 'sees into the life of things',[19] not by the help of mechanical instruments, but of the improved exercise of his faculties, and an intimate sympathy with nature. The meanest thing is not lost upon him, for he looks at it with an eye to itself, not merely to his own vanity or interest, or the opinion of the world. Even where there is neither beauty nor use – if that ever were – still there is truth, and a sufficient source of gratification in the indulgence of curiosity and activity of mind. The humblest painter is a true scholar; and the best of scholars – the scholar of nature. For myself, and for the real comfort and satisfaction of the thing, I had rather have been Jan Steen, or Gerard Dow, than the greatest casuist or philologer that ever lived. The painter does not view things in clouds or 'mist, the common gloss of theologians',[20] but applies the same standard of truth and

---

* It is at present covered with a thick slough of oil and varnish (the perishable vehicle of the English school) like an envelope of gold-beaters' skin, so as to be hardly visible.

disinterested spirit of inquiry, that influence his daily practice, to other subjects. He perceives form, he distinguishes character. He reads men and books with an intuitive eye. He is a critic as well as a connoisseur. The conclusions he draws are clear and convincing, because they are taken from the things themselves. He is not a fanatic, a dupe, or a slave: for the habit of seeing for himself also disposes him to judge for himself. The most sensible men I know (taken as a class) are painters; that is, they are the most lively observers of what passes in the world about them, and the closest observers of what passes in their own minds. From their profession they in general mix more with the world than authors; and if they have not the same fund of acquired knowledge, are obliged to rely more on individual sagacity. I might mention the names of Opie, Fuseli, Northcote, as persons distinguished for striking description and acquaintance with the subtle traits of character.* Painters in ordinary society, or in obscure situations where their value is not known, and they are treated with neglect and indifference, have sometimes a forward self-sufficiency of manner: but this is not so much their fault as that of others. Perhaps their want of regular education may also be in fault in such cases. Richardson, who is very tenacious of the respect in which the profession ought to be held, tells a story of Michael Angelo,[21] that after a quarrel between him and Pope Julius II, 'upon account of a slight the artist conceived the pontiff had put upon him, Michael Angelo was introduced by a bishop, who, thinking to serve the artist by it, made it an argument that the Pope should be reconciled to him, because men of his profession were commonly ignorant, and of no consequence otherwise: his holiness, enraged at the bishop, struck him with his staff, and told him, it was he that was the blockhead, and affronted the man himself would not offend; the prelate was driven out of the chamber, and Michael Angelo had the Pope's benediction accompanied with presents. This bishop had fallen into the vulgar error, and was rebuked accordingly.'

* Men in business, who are answerable with their fortunes for the consequences of their opinions, and are therefore accustomed to ascertain pretty accurately the grounds on which they act, before they commit themselves on the event, are often men of remarkably quick and sound judgments. Artists in like manner must know tolerably well what they are about, before they can bring the result of their observations to the test of ocular demonstration.

Besides the exercise of the mind, painting exercises the body. It is a mechanical as well as a liberal art. To do any thing, to dig a hole in the ground, to plant a cabbage, to hit a mark, to move a shuttle, to work a pattern, – in a word, to attempt to produce any effect, and to *succeed*, has something in it that gratifies the love of power, and carries off the restless activity of the mind of man. Indolence is a delightful but distressing state. We must be doing something to be happy. Action is no less necessary than thought to the instinctive tendencies of the human frame; and painting combines them both incessantly.* The hand furnishes a practical test of the correctness of the eye; and the eye thus admonished, imposes fresh tasks of skill and industry upon the hand. Every stroke tells, as the verifying of a new truth; and every new observation, the instant it is made, passes into an act and emanation of the will. Every step is nearer what we wish, and yet there is always more to do. In spite of the facility, the fluttering grace, the evanescent hues, that play round the pencil of Rubens and Vandyke, however I may admire, I do not envy them this power so much as I do the slow, patient, laborious execution of Correggio, Leonardo da Vinci, and Andrea del Sarto, where every touch appears conscious of its charge, emulous of truth, and where the painful artist has so distinctly wrought,

'That you might almost say his picture thought!'[23]

In the one case, the colours seem breathed on the canvas as by magic, the work and the wonder of a moment: in the other, they seem inlaid in the body of the work, and as if it took the artist years of unremitting labour, and of delightful never-ending progress to perfection.† Who would wish ever to come to the close of such works, – not to dwell on them, to return to them, to be wedded to them to the last? Rubens, with his florid, rapid style, complained that when he had just learned his art, he should be forced to die. Leonardo, in the slow advances of his, had lived long enough!

---

* The famous Schiller used to say,[22] that he found the great happiness of life, after all, to consist in the discharge of some mechanical duty.

† The rich *impasting*[24] of Titian and Giorgione combines something of the advantages of both these styles, the felicity of the one with the carefulness of the other, and is perhaps to be preferred to either.

Painting is not, like writing, what is properly understood by a sedentary employment. It requires not indeed a strong, but a continued and steady exertion of muscular power. The precision and delicacy of the manual operation makes up for the want of vehemence, – as to balance himself for any time in the same position the rope-dancer must strain every nerve. Painting for a whole morning gives one as excellent an appetite for one's dinner, as old Abraham Tucker acquired for his by riding over Banstead Downs. It is related of Sir Joshua Reynolds,[25] that 'he took no other exercise than what he used in his painting-room', – the writer means, in walking backwards and forwards to look at his picture; but the act of painting itself, of laying on the colours in the proper place, and proper quantity, was a much harder exercise than this alternate receding from and returning to the picture. This last would be rather a relaxation and relief than an effort. It is not to be wondered at, that an artist like Sir Joshua, who delighted so much in the sensual and practical part of his art, should have found himself at a considerable loss when the decay of his sight precluded him, for the last year or two of his life, from the following up of his profession, – 'the source', according to his own remark, 'of thirty years' uninterrupted enjoyment and prosperity to him'.[26] It is only those who never think at all, or else who have accustomed themselves to brood incessantly on abstract ideas, that never feel *ennui*.

To give one instance more, and then I will have done with this rambling discourse. One of my first attempts was a picture of my father,[27] who was then in a green old age, with strong-marked features, and scarred with the small-pox. I drew it with a broad light crossing the face, looking down, with spectacles on, reading. The book was Shaftesbury's *Characteristics*, in a fine old binding, with Gribelin's etchings. My father would as lieve it had been any other book; but for him to read was to be content, was 'riches fineless'.[28] The sketch promised well; and I set to work to finish it, determined to spare no time nor pains. My father was willing to sit as long as I pleased; for there is a natural desire in the mind of man to sit for one's picture, to be the object of continued attention, to have one's likeness multiplied; and besides his satisfaction in the picture, he had some pride in the artist, though he would rather I should have written a sermon than painted like Rembrandt or like Raphael. Those winter days, with the gleams of sunshine coming through the chapel-windows, and cheered by the notes of the robin-redbreast in our garden (that 'ever in the haunch of winter sings'[29]) – as my afternoon's work drew to a close, – were among the happiest of my life. When I gave the effect I intended to any part of the picture for which I had prepared my colours, when I imitated the roughness of the skin by a lucky stroke of the pencil, when I hit the clear pearly tone of a vein, when I gave the ruddy complexion of health, the blood circulating under the broad shadows of one side of the face, I thought my fortune made; or rather it was already more than made, in my fancying that I might one day be able to say with Correggio, '*I also am a painter!*'[30] It was an idle thought,[31] a boy's conceit; but it did not make me less happy at the time. I used regularly to set my work in the chair to look at it through the long evenings; and many a time did I return to take leave of it before I could go to bed at night. I remember sending it with a throbbing heart to the Exhibition, and seeing it hung up there by the side of one of the Honourable Mr Skeffington (now Sir George). There was nothing in common between them, but that they were the portraits of two very good-natured men. I think, but am not sure, that I finished this portrait (or another afterwards) on the same day that the news of the battle of Austerlitz[32] came; I walked out in the afternoon, and, as I returned, saw the evening star set over a poor man's cottage with other thoughts and feelings than I shall ever have again. Oh, for the revolution of the great Platonic year,[33] that those times might come over again! I could sleep out the three hundred and sixty-five thousand intervening years very contentedly! – The picture is left: the table, the chair, the window where I learned to construe Livy, the chapel where my father preached, remain where they were; but he himself is gone to rest, full of years,[34] of faith, of hope, and charity!

The Same Subject Continued

The painter not only takes a delight in nature, he has a new and exquisite source of pleasure opened to him in the study and contemplation of works of art —

> 'Whate'er Lorraine light touch'd with soft'ning hue,
> Or savage Rosa dash'd, or learned Poussin drew'.[1]

He turns aside to view a country-gentleman's seat with eager looks, thinking it may contain some of the rich products of art. There is an air round Lord Radnor's park,[2] for there hang the two Claudes, the *Morning and Evening of the Roman Empire* — round Wilton-house, for there is Vandyke's picture of the Pembroke family — round Blenheim, for there is his picture of the Duke of Buckingham's children, and the most magnificent collection of Rubenses in the world — at Knowsley, for there is Rembrandt's Hand-writing on the Wall — and at Burleigh, for there are some of Guido's angelic heads. The young artist makes a pilgrimage to each of these places, eyes them wistfully at a distance, 'bosomed high in tufted trees',[3] and feels an interest in them of which the owner is scarce conscious: he enters the well-swept walks and echoing arch-ways, passes the threshold, is led through wainscoted rooms, is shown the furniture, the rich hangings, the tapestry, the massy services of plate — and, at last, is ushered into the room where his treasure is, the idol of his vows — some speaking face or bright landscape! It is stamped on his brain, and lives there thenceforward, a tally for nature, and a test of art. He furnishes out the chambers of the mind from the spoils of time, picks and chooses which shall have the best places — nearest his heart. He goes away richer than he came, richer than the possessor; and thinks that he may one day return, when he perhaps shall have done something like them, or even from failure shall have learned to admire truth and genius more.

My first initiation in the mysteries of the art was at the Orleans Gallery:[4] it was there I formed my taste, such as it is; so that I am irreclaimably of the old school in painting. I was staggered when I saw the works there collected, and looked at them with wondering and with longing eyes. A mist passed away from my sight: the scales fell off. A new sense came upon me, a new heaven and a new earth stood before me. I saw the soul speaking in the face – 'hands that the rod of empire had swayed'[5] in mighty ages past – 'a forked mountain or blue promontory',

> —'with trees upon't
> That nod unto the world, and mock our eyes with air'.[6]

Old Time had unlocked his treasures, and Fame stood portress at the door. We had all heard of the names of Titian, Raphael, Guido, Domenichino, the Caracci – but to see them face to face, to be in the same room with their deathless productions, was like breaking some mighty spell – was almost an effect of necromancy! From that time I lived in a world of pictures. Battles, sieges, speeches in parliament seemed mere idle noise and fury, 'signifying nothing',[7] compared with those mighty works and dreaded names that spoke to me in the eternal silence of thought. This was the more remarkable, as it was but a short time before that I was not only totally ignorant of, but insensible to the beauties of art. As an instance, I remember that one afternoon I was reading the *Provoked Husband*[8] with the highest relish, with a green woody landscape of Ruysdael or Hobbema just before me, at which I looked off the book now and then, and wondered what there could be in that sort of work to satisfy or delight the mind – at the same time asking myself, as a speculative question, whether I should ever feel an interest in it like what I took in reading Vanbrugh and Cibber?

I had made some progress in painting when I went to the Louvre[9] to study, and I never did any thing afterwards. I never shall forget conning over the Catalogue which a friend lent me just before I set out. The pictures, the names of the painters, seemed to relish in the mouth. There was one of Titian's Mistress at her toilette. Even the colours with which the painter had adorned her hair were not more golden, more amiable to sight, than those which played round and tantalized my fancy ere I saw the picture. There were two portraits by the same hand – 'A young Nobleman with a glove' – Another, 'a companion to it' – I read the description over and over with fond expectancy, and filled up the imaginary outline with whatever I could conceive of grace, and dignity, and an antique *gusto* – all but equal to the original. There was the Transfiguration too. With what awe I saw it in my mind's eye, and was overshadowed with the spirit of the artist! Not to have been disappointed with these works afterwards, was the highest compliment I can pay to their transcendent merits. Indeed, it was from seeing other works of the same great masters that I had formed a vague, but not disparaging idea of these. – The first day I got there, I was kept for some time in the French Exhibition-room, and thought I should not be able to get a sight of the old masters. I just caught a peep at them through the door (vile hindrance!) like looking out of purgatory into paradise – from Poussin's noble mellow-looking landscapes to where Rubens hung out his gaudy banner, and down the glimmering vista to the rich jewels of Titian and the Italian school. At last, by much importunity, I was admitted, and lost not an instant in making use of my new privilege. – It was *un beau jour* [10] to me. I marched delighted through a quarter of a mile of the proudest efforts of the mind of man, a whole creation of genius, a universe of art! I ran the gauntlet of all the schools from the bottom to the top; and in the end got admitted into the inner room, where they had been repairing some of their greatest works. . Here the *Transfiguration*, the *St Peter Martyr*, and the *St Jerome of Domenichino* stood on the floor, as if they had bent their knees, like camels stooping, to unlade their riches to the spectator. On one side, on an easel, stood *Hippolito de Medici* (a portrait by Titian) with a boar-spear in his hand, looking through those he saw, till you turned away from the keen glance: and thrown together in heaps were landscapes of the same hand, green pastoral hills and vales, and shepherds piping to their mild mistresses underneath the flowering shade. Reader, 'if thou hast not seen the Louvre, thou art damned!' [11] – for thou hast not seen the choicest remains of the works of art; or thou hast not seen all these together, with their mutually reflected glories. I say nothing of the statues; for I know but little of sculpture, and never liked any till I saw the Elgin Marbles ... Here, for four months together, I strolled and studied, and daily heard the warning sound – '*Quatres heures passées, il faut fermer, Citoyens*' – (Ah! why did they ever change their style?) muttered in coarse provincial French; and brought away with me some loose draughts and fragments, which I have been forced to part with, like drops of life-blood, for 'hard money'. How often, thou tenantless mansion of godlike magnificence – how often has my heart since gone a pilgrimage to thee!

It has been made a question, whether the artist, or the mere man of taste and natural sensibility, receives most pleasure from the contemplation of works of art? and I think this question might be answered by another as a sort of *experimentum crucis*,[12] namely, whether any one out of that 'number numberless'[13] of mere gentlemen and amateurs, who visited Paris at the period here spoken of, felt as much interest, as much pride or pleasure in this display of the most striking monuments of art as the humblest student would? The first entrance into the Louvre would be only one of the events of his journey, not an event in his life, remembered ever after with thankfulness and regret. He would explore it with the same unmeaning curiosity and idle wonder as he would the Regalia in the Tower, or the Botanic Garden in the Tuileries, but not with the fond enthusiasm of an artist. How should he? His is 'casual fruition, joyless, unendeared'.[14] But the painter is wedded to his art, the mistress, queen, and idol of his soul. He has embarked his all in it, fame, time, fortune, peace of mind, his hopes in youth, his consolation in age: and shall he not feel a more intense interest in whatever relates to it than the mere indolent trifler? Natural sensibility alone, without the entire application of the mind to that one object, will not enable the possessor to sympathize with all the degrees of beauty and power in the conceptions of a Titian or a Correggio; but it is he only who does this, who follows them into all their force and matchless grace, that does or can feel their full value. Knowledge is pleasure as well as power. No one but the artist who has studied nature and contended with the difficulties of art, can be aware of the beauties, or intoxicated with a passion for painting. No one who has not devoted his life and soul to the pursuit of art, can feel the same exultation in its brightest ornaments and loftiest triumphs which an artist does. Where the treasure is, there the heart is also. It is now seventeen years since I was studying in the Louvre (and I have long since given up all thoughts of the art as a profession), but long after I returned, and even still, I sometimes dream of being there again – of asking for the old pictures – and not finding them, or finding them changed or faded from what they were, I cry myself awake! What gentleman-amateur ever does this at such a distance of time – that is, ever received pleasure or took interest enough in them to produce so lasting an impression?

But it is said that if a person had the same natural taste, and the same acquired knowledge as an artist, without the petty interests and technical notions, he would derive a purer pleasure from seeing a fine portrait, a fine landscape, and so on. This however is not so much begging the question as asking an impossibility: he cannot have the same insight into the end without having studied the means; nor the same love of art without the same habitual and exclusive attachment to it. Painters are, no doubt, often actuated by jealousy, partiality, and a sordid attention to that only which they find useful to themselves in painting. W——[15] has been seen poring over the texture of a Dutch cabinet-picture, so that he could not see the picture itself. But this is the perversion and pedantry of the profession, not its true or genuine spirit. If W—— had never looked at any thing but megilps and handling, he never would have put the soul of life and manners into his pictures, as he has done. Another objection is, that the instrumental parts of the art, the means, the first rudiments, paints, oils, and brushes, are painful and disgusting; and that the consciousness of the difficulty and anxiety with which perfection has been attained, must take away from the pleasure of the finest performance. This, however, is only an additional proof of the greater pleasure derived by the artist from his profession; for these things which are said to interfere with and destroy the common interest in works of art, do not disturb him; he never once thinks of them, he is absorbed in the pursuit of a higher object; he is intent, not on the means but the end; he is taken up, not with the difficulties, but with the triumph over them. As in the case of the anatomist, who overlooks many things in the eagerness of his search after abstract truth; or the alchemist who, while he is raking

into his soot and furnaces, lives in a golden dream; a lesser gives way
to a greater object. But it is pretended that the painter may be supposed
to submit to the unpleasant part of the process only for the sake of the
fame or profit in view. So far is this from being a true state of the case,
that I will venture to say, in the instance of a friend of mine[16] who has
lately succeeded in an important undertaking in his art, that not all the
fame he has acquired, not all the money he has received from thousands
of admiring spectators, not all the newspaper puffs, – nor even the praise
of the *Edinburgh Review*, – not all these, put together, ever gave him at
any time the same genuine, undoubted satisfaction as any one half-hour
employed in the ardent and propitious pursuit of his art – in finishing
to his heart's content a foot, a hand, or even a piece of drapery. What is
the state of mind of an artist while he is at work? He is then in the act
of realizing the highest idea he can form of beauty or grandeur: he
conceives, he embodies that which he understands and loves best: that
is, he is in full and perfect possession of that which is to him the
source of the highest happiness and intellectual excitement which he
can enjoy.

In short, as a conclusion to this argument, I will mention a
circumstance which fell under my knowledge the other day. A friend
had bought a print of Titian's *Mistress*, the same to which I have
alluded above. He was anxious to shew it me on this account. I told
him it was a spirited engraving, but it had not the look of the original.
I believe he thought this fastidious, till I offered to show him a rough
sketch of it, which I had by me. Having seen this, he said he perceived
exactly what I meant, and could not bear to look at the print afterwards.
He had good sense enough to see the difference in the individual
instance; but a person better acquainted with Titian's manner and
with art in general, that is, of a more cultivated and refined taste,
would know that it was a bad print, without having any immediate
model to compare it with. He would perceive with a glance of the
eye, with a sort of instinctive feeling, that it was hard, and without that
bland, expansive, and nameless expression which always distinguished
Titian's most famous works. Any one who is accustomed to a head
in a picture can never reconcile himself to a print from it: but to the
ignorant they are both the same. To a vulgar eye there is no difference
between a Guido and a daub, between a penny-print or the vilest

scrawl, and the most finished performance. In other words, all that excellence which lies between these two extremes, – all, at least, that marks the excess above mediocrity, – all that constitutes true beauty, harmony, refinement, grandeur, is lost upon the common observer. But it is from this point that the delight, the glowing raptures of the true adept commence. An uninformed spectator may like an ordinary drawing better than the ablest connoisseur; but for that very reason he cannot like the highest specimens of art so well. The refinements not only of execution but of truth and nature are inaccessible to unpractised eyes. The exquisite gradations in a sky of Claude's are not perceived by such persons, and consequently the harmony cannot be felt. Where there is no conscious apprehension, there can be no conscious pleasure. Wonder at the first sight of works of art may be the effect of ignorance and novelty; but real admiration and permanent delight in them are the growth of taste and knowledge. 'I would not wish to have your eyes,' said a good-natured man to a critic, who was finding fault with a picture, in which the other saw no blemish. Why so? The idea which prevented him from admiring this inferior production was a higher idea of truth and beauty which was ever present with him, and a continual source of pleasing and lofty contemplations. It may be different in a taste for outward luxuries and the privations of mere sense; but the idea of perfection, which acts as an intellectual foil, is always an addition, a support, and a proud consolation!

Richardson, in his *Essays* which ought to be better known, has left some striking examples of the felicity and infelicity of artists, both as it relates to their external fortune, and to the practice of their art. In speaking of *the knowledge of hands*, he exclaims –[17] 'When one is considering a picture or a drawing, one at the same time thinks this was done by him* who had many extraordinary endowments of body and mind, but was withal very capricious; who was honoured in life and death, expiring in the arms of one of the greatest princes of that age, Francis I, King of France, who loved him as a friend. Another is of him† who lived a long and happy life, beloved of Charles V, emperor; and many others of the first princes of Europe. When one

* Leonardo da Vinci.
† Titian.

has another in hand, we think this was done by one* who so excelled in three arts, as that any of them in that degree had rendered him worthy of immortality; and one moreover that durst contend with his sovereign (one of the haughtiest Popes that ever was) upon a slight offered to him, and extricated himself with honour. Another is the work of him† who, without any one exterior advantage but mere strength of genius, had the most sublime imaginations, and executed them accordingly, yet lived and died obscurely. Another we shall consider as the work of him‡ who restored Painting when it had almost sunk; of him whom art made honourable, but who neglecting and despising greatness with a sort of cynical pride, was treated suitably to the figure he gave himself, not his intrinsic worth; which, not having philosophy enough to bear it, broke his heart. Another is done by one§ who (on the contrary) was a fine gentleman and lived in great magnificence, and was much honoured by his own and foreign princes; who was a courtier, a statesman, and a painter; and so much all these, that when he acted in either character, *that* seemed to be his business, and the others his diversion. I say when one thus reflects, besides the pleasure arising from the beauties and excellences of the work, the fine ideas it gives us of natural things, the noble way of thinking it may suggest to us, an additional pleasure results from the above considerations. But, oh! the pleasure, when a connoisseur and lover of art has before him a picture or drawing, of which he can say this is the hand, these are the thoughts of him¶ who was one of the politest, best-natured gentlemen that ever was; and beloved and assisted by the greatest wits and the greatest men then in Rome: of him who lived in great fame, honour, and magnificence, and died extremely lamented; and missed a Cardinal's hat only by dying a few months too soon; but was particularly esteemed and favoured by two Popes, the only ones who filled the chair of St Peter in his time, and as great men as ever sat there since that apostle, if at least he ever did: one, in short, who could have been a Leonardo,

* Michael Angelo.
† Correggio.
‡ Annibale Caracci.
§ Rubens.
¶ Raphael.

a Michael Angelo, a Titian, a Correggio, a Parmegiano, an Annibal, a Rubens, or any other whom he pleased, but none of them could ever have been a Raphael.'

The same writer speaks feelingly of the change in the style of different artists from their change of fortune, and as the circumstances are little known, I will quote the passage relating to two of them.

'Guido Reni from a prince-like affluence of fortune (the just reward of his angelic works) fell to a condition like that of a hired servant to one who supplied him with money for what he did at a fixed rate; and that by his being bewitched with a passion for gaming, whereby he lost vast sums of money; and even what he got in this his state of servitude by day, he commonly lost at night: nor could he ever be cured of this cursed madness. Those of his works, therefore, which he did in this unhappy part of his life, may easily be conceived to be in a different style to what he did before, which in some things, that is, in the airs of his heads (in the gracious kind) had a delicacy in them peculiar to himself, and almost more than human. But I must not multiply instances. Parmegiano is one that alone takes in all the several kinds of variation, and all the degrees of goodness, from the lowest of the indifferent up to the sublime. I can produce evident proofs of this in so easy a gradation, that one cannot deny but that he did this, might do that, and very probably did so; and thus one may ascend and descend, like the angels on Jacob's ladder, whose foot was upon the earth, but its top reached to Heaven.

'And this great man had his unlucky circumstance: he became mad after the philosopher's stone, and did but very little in painting or drawing afterwards. Judge what that was, and whether there was not an alteration of style from what he had done, before this devil possessed him. His creditors endeavoured to exorcize him, and did him some good, for he set himself to work again in his own way: but if a drawing I have of a Lucretia be that he made for his last picture, as it probably is (Vasari says that was the subject of it) it is an evident proof of his decay: it is good indeed, but it wants much of the delicacy which is commonly seen in his works; and so I always thought before I knew or imagined it to be done in this his ebb of genius.'

We have had two artists of our own country, whose fate has been as singular as it was hard. Gandy was a portrait-painter in the beginning of the last century, whose heads were said to have come near to Rembrandt's, and he was the undoubted prototype of Sir Joshua Reynolds's style. Yet his name has scarcely been heard of; and his reputation, like his works, never extended beyond his own country. What did he think of himself and of a fame so bounded! Did he ever dream he was indeed an artist? Or how did this feeling in him differ from the vulgar conceit of the lowest pretender? The best known of his works is a portrait of an alderman of Exeter, in some public building in that city.

Poor Dan Stringer! Forty years ago he had the finest hand and the clearest eye of any artist of his time, and produced heads and drawings that would not have disgraced a brighter period in the art. But he fell a martyr (like Burns) to the society of country-gentlemen, and then of those whom they would consider as more his equals. I saw him many years ago when he treated the masterly sketches he had by him (one in particular of the group of citizens in Shakespeare 'swallowing the tailor's news'[18]) as 'bastards of his genius, not his children'[19]; and seemed to have given up all thoughts of his art. Whether he is since dead, I cannot say: the world do not so much as know that he ever lived!

On a Landscape of Nicolas Poussin

'And blind Orion hungry for the morn.'[1]

Orion, the subject of this landscape,[2] was the classical Nimrod; and is called by Homer, 'a hunter of shadows, himself a shade'.[3] He was the son of Neptune; and having lost an eye in some affray between the Gods and men, was told that if he would go to meet the rising sun, he would recover his sight. He is represented setting out on his journey, with men on his shoulders to guide him, a bow in his hand, and Diana in the clouds greeting him. He stalks along, a giant upon earth, and reels and falters in his gait, as if just awaked out of sleep, or uncertain of his way; — you see his blindness, though his back is turned. Mists rise around him, and veil the sides of the green forests; earth is dank and fresh with dews, the 'grey dawn and the Pleiades before him dance',[4] and in the distance are seen the blue hills and sullen ocean. Nothing was ever more finely conceived or done. It breathes the spirit of the morning; its moisture, its repose, its obscurity, waiting the miracle of light to kindle it into smiles: the whole is, like the principal figure in it, 'a forerunner of the dawn'.[5] The same atmosphere tinges and imbues every object, the same dull light 'shadowy sets off'[6] the face of nature: one feeling of vastness, of strangeness, and of primeval forms pervades the painter's canvas, and we are thrown back upon the first integrity of things. This great and learned man might be said to see nature through the glass of time: he alone has a right to be considered as the painter of classical antiquity. Sir Joshua has done him justice in this respect.[7] He could give to the scenery of his heroic fables that unimpaired look of original nature, full, solid, large, luxuriant, teeming with life and power; or deck it with all the pomp of art, with temples and towers, and mythologic groves. His pictures 'denote a foregone conclusion'.[8] He applies nature to his purposes, works out her images according to the standard of his thoughts, embodies high fictions; and the first conception being given, all the rest seems to grow out of, and be assimilated to it, by the unfailing process of a studious imagination. Like his own Orion, he overlooks the surrounding scene, appears to 'take up the isles as a very little thing, and to lay the earth in a balance'.[9] With a laborious and mighty grasp, he put nature into the mould of the ideal and antique; and was among painters (more than any one else) what Milton was among poets. There is in both something of the same pedantry, the same stiffness, the same elevation, the same grandeur, the same mixture of art and nature, the same richness of borrowed materials, the same unity of character. Neither the poet nor the painter lowered the subjects they treated, but filled up the outline in the fancy, and added strength and reality to it; and thus not only satisfied, but surpassed the expectations of the spectator and the reader. This is held for the triumph and the perfection of works of art. To give us nature, such as we see it, is well and deserving of praise; to give us nature, such as we have never seen, but have often wished to see it, is better, and deserving of higher praise. He who can show the world in its first naked glory, with the hues of fancy spread over it, or in its high and palmy state,[10] with the gravity of history stamped on the proud monuments of vanished empire, – who, by his 'so potent art',[11] can recall time past, transport us to distant places, and join the regions of imagination (a new conquest) to those of reality, – who shows us not only what nature is, but what she has been, and is capable of, – he who does this, and does it with simplicity, with truth, and grandeur, is lord of nature and her powers; and his mind is universal, and his art the master-art!

There is nothing in this 'more than natural',[12] if criticism could be persuaded to think so. The historic painter does not neglect or contravene nature, but follows her more closely up into her fantastic heights, or hidden recesses. He demonstrates what she would be in conceivable circumstances, and under implied conditions. He 'gives to airy nothing a local habitation',[13] not 'a name'. At his touch, words start up into images, thoughts become things. He clothes a dream, a phantom with form and colour and the wholesome attributes of reality. *His* art is a second nature; not a different one. There are those, indeed, who think that not to copy nature, is the rule for attaining perfection. Because they cannot paint the objects which they have seen, they fancy themselves qualified to paint the ideas which they have not seen. But it is possible to fail in this latter and more difficult style of imitation, as well as in the former humbler one. The detection, it is true, is not so easy, because the objects are not so nigh at hand to compare, and therefore there is more room both for false pretension and for self-deceit. They take an epic motto or subject, and conclude that the spirit is implied as a thing of course. They paint inferior portraits, maudlin lifeless faces, without ordinary expression, or one look, feature, or particle of nature in them, and think that this is to rise to the truth of history. They vulgarize and degrade whatever is interesting or sacred to the mind, and suppose that they thus add to the dignity of their profession. They represent a face that seems as if no thought or feeling of any kind had ever passed through it, and would have you believe that this is the very sublime of expression, such as it would appear in heroes, or demi-gods of old, when rapture or agony was raised to its height. They show you a landscape that looks as if the sun never shone upon it, and tell you that it is not modern – that so earth looked when Titan first kissed it with his rays. This is not the true *ideal*. It is not to fill the moulds of the imagination, but to deface and injure them: it is not to come up to, but to fall short of the poorest conception in the public mind. Such pictures should not be hung in the same room with that of Orion.*

Poussin was, of all painters, the most poetical. He was the painter of ideas. No one ever told a story half so well, nor so well knew what

---

* Every thing tends to show the manner in which a great artist is formed. If any person could claim an exemption from the careful imitation of individual objects, it was Nicolas Poussin. He studied the antique, but he also studied nature. 'I have often admired', says Vignuel de Marville,[14] who knew him at a late period of his life, 'the love he had for his art. Old as he was, I frequently saw him among the ruins of ancient Rome, out in the Campagna, or along the banks of the Tyber, sketching a scene that had pleased him; and I often met him with his handkerchief full of stones, moss, or flowers, which he carried home, that he might copy them exactly from nature. One day I asked him how he had attained to such a degree of perfection, as to have gained so high a rank among the great painters of Italy? He answered, I HAVE NEGLECTED NOTHING.' – *See his* Life *lately*

was capable of being told by the pencil. He seized on, and struck off with grace and precision, just that point of view which would be likely to catch the reader's fancy. There is a significance, a consciousness in whatever he does (sometimes a vice, but oftener a virtue) beyond any other painter. His Giants sitting on the tops of craggy mountains, as huge themselves, and playing idly on their Pan's-pipes, seem to have been seated there these three thousand years, and to know the beginning and the end of their own story. An infant Bacchus or Jupiter is big with his future destiny. Even inanimate and dumb things speak a language of their own. His snakes, the messengers of fate, are inspired with human intellect. His trees grow and expand their leaves in the air, glad of the rain, proud of the sun, awake to the winds of heaven. In his *Plague of Athens*, the very buildings seem stiff with horror. His picture of the *Deluge* is, perhaps, the finest historical landscape in the world. You see a waste of waters, wide, interminable: the sun is labouring, wan and weary, up the sky; the clouds, dull and leaden, lie like a load upon the eye, and heaven and earth seem commingling into one confused mass! His human figures are sometimes 'o'er-informed'[15] with this kind of feeling. Their actions have too much gesticulation, and the set expression of the features borders too much on the mechanical and caricatured style. In this respect, they form a contrast to Raphael's, whose figures never appear to be sitting for their pictures, or to be conscious of a spectator, or to have come from the painter's hand. In Nicolas Poussin, on the contrary, every thing seems to have a distinct understanding with the artist: 'the very stones prate of their whereabouts':[16] each object has its part and place assigned, and is in a sort of compact with the rest of the picture. It is this conscious keeping, and, as it were, *internal* design, that gives their peculiar character to the works of this artist. There

published. It appears from this account that he had not fallen into a recent error, that nature puts the man of genius out. As a contrast to the foregoing description, I might mention, that I remember an old gentleman once asking Mr West in the British Gallery, if he had ever been at Athens? To which the President made answer, No; nor did he feel any great desire to go; for that he thought he had as good an idea of the place from the Catalogue, as he could get by living there for any number of years. What would he have said, if any one had told him, he could get as good an idea of the subject of one of his great works from reading the Catalogue of it, as from seeing the picture itself! Yet the answer was characteristic of the genius of the painter.

was a picture of Aurora in the British Gallery a year or two ago. It was a suffusion of golden light. The Goddess wore her saffron-coloured robes, and appeared just risen from the gloomy bed of old Tithonus. Her very steeds, milk-white, were tinged with the yellow dawn. It was a personification of the morning. – Poussin succeeded better in classic than in sacred subjects. The latter are comparatively heavy, forced, full of violent contrasts of colour, of red, blue, and black, and without the true prophetic inspiration of the characters. But in his Pagan allegories and fables he was quite at home. The native gravity and native levity of the Frenchman were combined with Italian scenery and an antique gusto, and gave even to his colouring an air of learned indifference. He wants, in one respect, grace, form, expression; but he has every where sense and meaning, perfect costume and propriety. His personages always belong to the class and time represented, and are strictly versed in the business in hand. His grotesque compositions in particular, his Nymphs and Fauns, are superior (at least, as far as style is concerned) even to those of Rubens. They are taken more immediately out of fabulous history. Rubens's Satyrs and Bacchantes have a more jovial and voluptuous aspect, are more drunk with pleasure, more full of animal spirits and riotous impulses; they laugh and bound along –

'Leaping like wanton kids in pleasant spring:'[17]

but those of Poussin have more of the intellectual part of the character, and seem vicious on reflection, and of set purpose. Rubens's are noble specimens of a class; Poussin's are allegorical abstractions of the same class, with bodies less pampered, but with minds more secretly depraved. The Bacchanalian groups of the Flemish painter were, however, his masterpieces in composition. Witness those prodigies of colour, character, and expression, at Blenheim. In the more chaste and refined delineation of classic fable, Poussin was without a rival. Rubens, who was a match for him in the wild and picturesque, could not pretend to vie with the elegance and purity of thought in his picture of Apollo giving a poet a cup of water to drink, nor with the gracefulness of design in the figure of a nymph squeezing the juice of a bunch of grapes from her fingers (a rosy wine-press) which falls into the mouth of a chubby infant below. But, above all, who shall celebrate, in terms of fit praise, his picture of the shepherds in the Vale of Tempe going out in a fine morning of the spring, and coming to a tomb with this inscription: – ET EGO IN ARCADIA VIXI![18] The eager curiosity of some, the expression of others who start back with fear and surprise, the clear breeze playing with the branches of the shadowing trees, 'the valleys low, where the mild zephyrs use',[19] the distant, uninterrupted, sunny prospect speak (and for ever will speak on) of ages past to ages yet to come!*

Pictures are a set of chosen images, a stream of pleasant thoughts passing through the mind. It is a luxury to have the walls of our rooms hung round with them, and no less so to have such a gallery in the mind, to con over the relics of ancient art bound up 'within the book and volume of the brain, unmixed (if it were possible) with baser matter'![20] A life passed among pictures, in the study and the love of art, is a happy noiseless dream: or rather, it is to dream and to be awake at the same time; for it has all 'the sober certainty of waking bliss',[21] with the romantic voluptuousness of a visionary and abstracted being. They are the bright consummate essences of things, and 'he who knows of these delights to taste and interpose them oft, is not unwise'![22] – The *Orion*, which I have here taken occasion to descant upon, is one of a collection of excellent pictures, as this collection is itself one of a series from the old masters, which have for some years back embrowned the walls of the British Gallery, and enriched the public eye. What hues (those of nature mellowed by time) breathe around, as we enter! What forms are there, woven into the memory! What looks, which only the answering looks of the spectator can express! What intellectual stores have been yearly poured forth from the shrine of ancient art! The works are various, but the names the same – heaps of Rembrandts frowning from the darkened walls, Rubens's glad gorgeous groups, Titians more rich and rare, Claudes always exquisite, sometimes beyond compare, Guido's endless cloying sweetness, the learning of Poussin and the Caracci, and Raphael's princely magnificence, crowning all. We read certain

---

* Poussin has repeated this subject more than once, and appears to have revelled in its witcheries. I have before alluded to it, and may again. It is hard that we should not be allowed to dwell as often as we please on what delights us, when things that are disagreeable recur so often against our will.

letters and syllables in the Catalogue, and at the well-known magic
sound, a miracle of skill and beauty starts to view. One might think
that one year's prodigal display of such perfection would exhaust the
labours of one man's life; but the next year, and the next to that, we
find another harvest reaped and gathered in to the great garner of
art, by the same immortal hands –

> 'Old GENIUS the porter of them was;
> He letteth in, he letteth out to wend. – '[25]

Their works seem endless as their reputation – to be many as they
are complete – to multiply with the desire of the mind to see more
and more of them; as if there were a living power in the breath of
Fame, and in the very names of the great heirs of glory 'there were
propagation too'![24] It is something to have a collection of this sort to
count upon once a year; to have one last, lingering look yet to come.
Pictures are scattered like stray gifts through the world; and while
they remain, earth has yet a little gilding left, not quite rubbed off,
dishonoured, and defaced. There are plenty of standard works still to
be found in this country, in the collections at Blenheim, at Burleigh,
and in those belonging to Mr Angerstein, Lord Grosvenor, the Marquis
of Stafford, and others, to keep up this treat to the lovers of art for
many years: and it is the more desirable to reserve a privileged
sanctuary of this sort, where the eye may dote, and the heart take its
fill of such pictures as Poussin's *Orion*, since the Louvre is stripped
of its triumphant spoils, and since he, who collected it,[25] and wore it
as a rich jewel in his Iron Crown, the hunter of greatness and of
glory, is himself a shade! –

Mr Kean's Shylock

January 27, 1814.

Mr KEAN (of whom report had spoken highly) last night made his appearance at Drury-Lane Theatre in the character of Shylock. For voice, eye, action, and expression, no actor has come out for many years at all equal to him. The applause, from the first scene to the last, was general, loud, and uninterrupted. Indeed, the very first scene in which he comes on with Bassanio and Antonio, showed the master in his art, and at once decided the opinion of the audience. Perhaps it was the most perfect of any. Notwithstanding the complete success of Mr KEAN in the part of Shylock, we question whether he will not become a greater favourite in other parts. There was a lightness and vigour in his tread, a buoyancy and elasticity of spirit, a fire and animation, which would accord better with almost any other character than with the morose, sullen, inward, inveterate, inflexible malignity of Shylock. The character of Shylock is that of a man brooding over one idea, that of its wrongs, and bent on one unalterable purpose, that of revenge. In conveying a profound impression of this feeling, or in embodying the general conception of rigid and uncontrollable self-will, equally proof against every sentiment of humanity or prejudice of opinion, we have seen actors more successful than Mr KEAN; but in giving effect to the conflict of passions arising out of the contrasts of situation, in varied vehemence of declamation, in keenness of sarcasm, in the rapidity of his transitions from one tone and feeling to another, in propriety and novelty of action, presenting a succession of striking pictures, and giving perpetually fresh shocks of delight and surprise, it would be difficult to single out a competitor. The fault of his acting was (if we may hazard the objection), an over-display of the resources of the art, which gave too much relief to the hard, impenetrable, dark ground-work of the character of Shylock. It would be endless to point out individual beauties, where almost every passage was received with equal and deserved applause. We thought, in one or two instances, the pauses in the voice were too long, and too great a reliance placed on the expression of the countenance, which is a language intelligible only to a part of the house.

The rest of the play was, upon the whole, very respectably cast. It would be an equivocal compliment to say of Miss SMITH, that her acting often reminds us of Mrs SIDDONS. RAE played Bassanio; but the abrupt and harsh tones of his voice are not well adapted to the mellifluous cadences of SHAKESPEARE's verse.

*

February 2.

Mr KEAN appeared again in Shylock, and by his admirable and expressive manner of giving the part, fully sustained the reputation he had acquired by his former representation of it, though he laboured under the disadvantage of a considerable hoarseness. He assumed a greater appearance of age and feebleness than on the first night, but the general merit of his playing was the same. His style of acting is, if we may use the expression, more significant, more pregnant with meaning, more varied and alive in every part, than any we have almost ever witnessed. The character never stands still; there is no vacant pause in the action; the eye is never silent. For depth and force of conception, we have seen actors whom we should prefer to Mr KEAN in Shylock; for brilliant and masterly execution, none. It is not saying too much of him, though it is saying a great deal, that he has all that Mr KEMBLE *wants* of perfection. He reminds us of the descriptions of the 'far-darting eye'[1] of GARRICK. We are anxious to see him in Norval and Richard,[2] and anticipate more complete satisfaction from his performance of the latter part, than from the one in which he has already stamped his reputation with the public.

Miss SMITH played Portia with much more animation than the last time we saw her, and in delivering the fine apostrophe on Mercy, in the trial-scene, was highly impressive.

Mr Macready's Othello

Oct. 12, 1816.

We have to speak this week of Mr MACREADY's Othello, at Covent-Garden Theatre, and though it must be in favourable terms, it cannot be in very favourable ones. We have been rather spoiled for seeing any one else in this character, by Mr KEAN's performance of it, and also by having read the play itself lately. Mr MACREADY was more than respectable in the part; and he only failed because he attempted to excel. He did not, however, express the individual bursts of feeling, nor the deep and accumulating tide of passion which ought to be given in Othello. It may perhaps seem an extravagant illustration, but the idea which we think any actor ought to have of this character, to play it to the height of the poetical conception, is that of a majestic serpent wounded,[1] writhing under its pain, stung to madness, and attempting by sudden darts, or coiling up its whole force, to wreak its vengeance on those about it, and falling at last a mighty victim under the redoubled strokes of its assailants. No one can admire more than we do the force of genius and passion which Mr KEAN shows in this part, but he is not stately enough for it. He plays it like a gipsy, and not like a Moor. We miss in Mr KEAN not the physiognomy, or the costume, so much as the *architectural* building up of the part. This character always puts us in mind of the line –

'Let Afric on its hundred thrones rejoice.'[2]

It not only appears to hold commerce with meridian suns, and that its blood is made drunk with the heat of scorching skies; but it indistinctly presents to us all the symbols of eastern magnificence. It wears a crown and turban, and stands before us like a tower. All this, it may be answered, is only saying that Mr KEAN is not so tall as a tower: but any one, to play Othello properly, ought to look taller and grander than any tower. We shall see how Mr YOUNG will play it. But this is from our present purpose. Mr MACREADY is tall enough for the part, and the looseness of his figure was rather in character with the flexibility of the South: but there were no sweeping outlines, no massy movements in his action.

The movements of passion in Othello (and the motions of the body should answer to those of the mind) resemble the heaving of the sea in a storm; there are no sharp, slight, angular transitions, or if there are any, they are subject to this general swell and commotion. Mr KEAN is sometimes too wedgy and determined; but Mr MACREADY goes off like a shot, and startles our sense of hearing. One of these sudden explosions was when he is in such haste to answer the demands of the Senate on his services: 'I do agnize a natural hardness,'[3] &c. as if he was impatient to exculpate himself from some charge, or wanted to take them at their word lest they should retract. There is nothing of this in Othello. He is calm and collected; and the reason why he is carried along with such vehemence by his passions when they are roused, is, that he is moved by their collected force. Another fault in Mr MACREADY's conception was, that he whined and whimpered once or twice, and tried to affect the audience by affecting a pitiful sensibility, not consistent with the dignity and masculine imagination of the character: as where he repeated, 'No, not much moved,'[4] and again, 'Othello's occupation's gone,'[5] in a childish treble. The only part which should approach to this effeminate tenderness of complaint is his reflection, 'Yet, oh the pity of it, Iago, the pity of it!'[6] What we liked best was his ejaculation, 'Swell, bosom, with thy fraught, *for 'tis of aspick's tongues.*'[7] This was forcibly given, and as if his expression were choked with the bitterness of passion. We do not know how he would have spoken the speech, 'Like to the Pontic sea that knows no ebb,'[8] &c. which occurs just before, for it was left out. There was also something fine in his uneasiness and inward starting at the name of Cassio, but it was too often repeated, with a view to effect. Mr MACREADY got most applause in such speeches as that addressed to Iago, 'Horror on horror's head accumulate!'[9] This should be a lesson to him. He very injudiciously, we think, threw himself on a chair at the back of the stage, to deliver the farewell apostrophe to Content, and to the 'pride, pomp, and circumstance of glorious war'.[10] This might be a relief to him, but it distressed the audience. — On the whole, we think Mr MACREADY's powers are more adapted to the declamation than to the acting of passion: that is, that he is a better orator than actor. As to Mr YOUNG's Iago, 'we never saw a gentleman acted finer'.[11] Mrs FAUCIT's Desdemona was very pretty. Mr C. KEMBLE's Cassio was excellent.

Mrs Siddons

June 15, 1816.

Players should be immortal, if their own wishes or ours could make them so; but they are not. They not only die like other people, but like other people they cease to be young, and are no longer themselves, even while living. Their health, strength, beauty, voice, fails them; nor can they, without these advantages, perform the same feats, or command the same applause that they did when possessed of them. It is the common lot: players are only *not* exempt from it. Mrs SIDDONS retired once from the stage: why should she return to it again? She cannot retire from it twice with dignity; and yet it is to be wished that she should do all things with dignity. Any loss of reputation to her, is a loss to the world. Has she not had enough of glory? The homage she has received is greater than that which is paid to Queens. The enthusiasm she excited had something idolatrous about it; she was regarded less with admiration than with wonder, as if a being of a superior order had dropped from another sphere to awe the world with the majesty of her appearance. She raised Tragedy to the skies, or brought it down from thence. It was something above nature. We can conceive of nothing grander. She embodied to our imagination the fables of mythology, of the heroic and deified mortals of elder time. She was not less than a goddess, or than a prophetess inspired by the gods. Power was seated on her brow, passion emanated from her breast as from a shrine. She was Tragedy personified. She was the stateliest ornament of the public mind. She was not only the idol of the people, she not only hushed the tumultuous shouts of the pit in breathless expectation, and quenched the blaze of surrounding beauty in silent tears, but to the retired and lonely student, through long years of solitude, her face has shone as if an eye had appeared from heaven; her name has been as if a voice had opened the chambers of the human heart, or as if a trumpet had awakened the sleeping and the dead. To have seen Mrs SIDDONS, was an event in every one's life; and does she think we have forgot her? Or would she remind us of herself by showing us what *she· was not*? Or is she to continue on the stage to the very last, till all her grace and all her grandeur gone, shall leave behind them only a melancholy blank? Or is she merely to be played off as 'the baby of a girl'[1] for a few nights? – 'Rather than so,'[2] come, Genius of Gil Blas,[3] thou that didst inspire him in an evil hour to perform his promise to the Archbishop of Grenada, 'and champion us to the utterance' of what we think on this occasion.

It is said that the Princess CHARLOTTE has expressed a desire to see Mrs SIDDONS in her best parts, and this, it is said, is a thing highly desirable. We do not know that the Princess has expressed any such wish, and we shall suppose that she has not, because we do not think it altogether a reasonable one. If the Princess CHARLOTTE had expressed a wish to see Mr GARRICK, this would have been a thing highly desirable, but it would have been impossible; or if she had desired to see Mrs SIDDONS *in her best days*, it would have been equally so; and yet without this, we do not think it desirable that she should see her at all. It is said to be desirable that a Princess should have a taste for the Fine Arts, and that this is best promoted by seeing the highest models of perfection. But it is of the first importance for Princes to acquire a taste for what is reasonable: and the second thing which it is desirable they should acquire, is a deference to public opinion: and we think neither of these objects likely to be promoted in the way proposed. If it was reasonable that Mrs SIDDONS should retire from the stage three years ago, certainly those reasons have not diminished since, nor do we think Mrs SIDDONS would consult what is due to her powers or her fame, in commencing a new career. If it is only intended that she should act a few nights in the presence of a particular person, this might be done as well in private. To all other applications she should answer – 'Leave me to my repose.'[4]

Mrs SIDDONS always spoke as slow as she ought: she now speaks slower than she did. 'The line too labours, and the words move slow.'[5] The machinery of the voice seems too ponderous for the power that wields it. There is too long a pause between each sentence, and between each word in each sentence. There is too much preparation. The stage waits for her. In the sleeping scene, she produced a different impression from what we expected. It was more laboured, and less natural. In coming on formerly, her eyes were open, but the sense was shut. She was like a person bewildered, and unconscious of what she did. She moved her lips involuntarily; all her gestures were involuntary and mechanical. At present she acts the part more with a view to effect. She repeats the action when she says, 'I tell you he cannot rise from his grave,'[6] with both hands sawing the air, in the style of parliamentary oratory, the worst of all others. There was none of this weight or energy in the way she did the scene the first time we saw her, twenty years ago. She glided on and off the stage almost like an apparition. In the close of the banquet scene, Mrs SIDDONS condescended to an imitation which we were sorry for. She said, 'Go, go,'[7] in the hurried familiar tone of common life, in the manner of Mr KEAN, and without any of that sustained and graceful spirit of conciliation towards her guests, which used to characterize her mode of doing it. Lastly, if Mrs SIDDONS has to leave the stage again, Mr HORACE TWISS will write another farewell address[8] for her: if she continues on it, we shall have to criticize her performances. We know which of these two evils we shall think the greatest.

Too much praise cannot be given to Mr KEMBLE's performance of Macbeth. He was 'himself again',[9] and more than himself. His action was decided, his voice audible. His tones had occasionally indeed a learned quaintness, like the colouring of POUSSIN; but the effect of the whole was fine. His action in delivering the speech, 'To-morrow and to-morrow',[10] was particularly striking and expressive, as if he had stumbled by an accident on fate, and was baffled by the impenetrable obscurity of the future. – In that prodigious prosing paper, *The Times*, which seems to be written as well as printed by a steam-engine,[11] Mr KEMBLE is compared to the ruin of a magnificent temple, in which the divinity still resides. This is not the case. The temple is unimpaired; but the divinity is sometimes from home.

Coriolanus

Shakespeare has in this play shown himself well versed in history and state-affairs. *Coriolanus* is a store-house of political commonplaces. Any one who studies it may save himself the trouble of reading Burke's *Reflections*, or Paine's *Rights of Man*, or the Debates in both Houses of Parliament since the French Revolution or our own. The arguments for and against aristocracy or democracy, on the privileges of the few and the claims of the many, on liberty and slavery, power and the abuse of it, peace and war, are here very ably handled, with the spirit of a poet and the acuteness of a philosopher. Shakespeare himself seems to have had a leaning to the arbitrary side of the question, perhaps from some feeling of contempt for his own origin; and to have spared no occasion of bating the rabble. What he says of them is very true: what he says of their betters is also very true, though he dwells less upon it. – The cause of the people is indeed but little calculated as a subject for poetry: it admits of rhetoric, which goes into argument and explanation, but it presents no immediate or distinct images to the mind, 'no jutting frieze, buttress, or coigne of vantage' for poetry 'to make its pendent bed and procreant cradle in'.[1] The language of poetry naturally falls in with the language of power. The imagination is an exaggerating and exclusive faculty: it takes from one thing to add to another: it accumulates circumstances together to give the greatest possible effect to a favourite object. The understanding is a dividing and measuring faculty: it judges of things not according to their immediate impression on the mind, but according to their relations to one another. The one is a monopolizing faculty, which seeks the greatest quantity of present excitement by inequality and disproportion; the other is a distributive faculty, which seeks the greatest quantity of ultimate good, by justice and proportion. The one is an aristocratical, the other a republican faculty. The principle of poetry is a very anti-levelling principle. It aims at effect, it exists by contrast. It admits of no medium. It is every thing by excess. It rises above the ordinary standard of sufferings and crimes. It presents a dazzling appearance. It shews its head turretted, crowned, and crested. Its front is gilt and blood-stained. Before it 'it carries noise, and behind it leaves tears'.[2] It has its altars and its victims, sacrifices, human sacrifices. Kings, priests, nobles, are its train-bearers, tyrants and slaves its executioners. — 'Carnage is its daughter.'[3] — Poetry is right-royal. It puts the individual for the species, the one above the infinite many, might before right. A lion hunting a flock of sheep or a herd of wild asses is a more poetical object than they; and we even take part with the lordly beast, because our vanity or some other feeling makes us disposed to place ourselves in the situation of the strongest party. So we feel some concern for the poor citizens of Rome when they meet together to compare their wants and grievances, till Coriolanus comes in and with blows and big words drives this set of 'poor rats',[4] this rascal scum, to their homes and beggary before him. There is nothing heroical in a multitude of miserable rogues not wishing to be starved, or complaining that they are like to be so: but when a single man comes forward to brave their cries and to make them submit to the last indignities, from mere pride and self-will, our admiration of his prowess is immediately converted into contempt for their pusillanimity. The insolence of power is stronger than the plea of necessity. The tame submission to usurped authority or even the natural resistance to it has nothing to excite or flatter the imagination: it is the assumption of a right to insult or oppress others that carries an imposing air of superiority with it. We had rather be the oppressor than the oppressed. The love of power in ourselves and the admiration of it in others are both natural to man: the one makes him a tyrant, the other a slave. Wrong dressed out in pride, pomp, and circumstance, has more attraction than abstract right. — Coriolanus complains of the fickleness of the people: yet, the instant he cannot gratify his pride and obstinacy at their expense, he turns his arms against his country. If his country was not worth defending, why did he build his pride on its defence?

He is a conquerer and a hero; he conquers other countries, and makes this a plea for enslaving his own; and when he is prevented from doing so, he leagues with its enemies to destroy his country. He rates the people 'as if he were a God to punish, and not a man of their infirmity'.[5] He scoffs at one of their tribunes for maintaining their rights and franchises: 'Mark you his absolute *shall*?'[6] not marking his own absolute *will* to take every thing from them, his impatience of the slightest opposition to his own pretensions being in proportion to their arrogance and absurdity. If the great and powerful had the beneficence and wisdom of Gods, then all this would have been well: if with a greater knowledge of what is good for the people, they had as great a care for their interest as they have themselves, if they were seated above the world, sympathizing with the welfare, but not feeling the passions of men, receiving neither good nor hurt from them, but bestowing their benefits as free gifts on them, they might then rule over them like another Providence. But this is not the case. Coriolanus is unwilling that the senate should shew their 'cares' for the people, lest their 'cares' should be construed into 'fears',[7] to the subversion of all due authority; and he is no sooner disappointed in his schemes to deprive the people not only of the cares of the state, but of all power to redress themselves, than Volumnia is made madly to exclaim,

'Now the red pestilence strike all trades in Rome,
And occupations perish.'[8]

This is but natural: it is but natural for a mother to have more regard for her son than for a whole city; but then the city should be left to take some care of itself. The care of the state cannot, we here see, be safely entrusted to maternal affection, or to the domestic charities of high life. The great have private feelings of their own, to which the interests of humanity and justice must curtsy. Their interests are so far from being the same as those of the community, that they are in direct and necessary opposition to them; their power is at the expense of *our* weakness; their riches of *our* poverty; their pride of *our* degradation; their splendour of *our* wretchedness; their tyranny of *our* servitude. If they had the superior knowledge ascribed to them (which they have not) it would only render them so much more formidable; and from Gods would convert them into Devils.

The whole dramatic moral of *Coriolanus* is that those who have little shall have less,[9] and that those who have much shall take all that others have left. The people are poor; therefore they ought to be starved. They are slaves; therefore they ought to be beaten. They work hard; therefore they ought to be treated like beasts of burden. They are ignorant; therefore they ought not to be allowed to feel that they want food, or clothing, or rest, that they are enslaved, oppressed, and miserable. This is the logic of the imagination and the passions; which seek to aggrandize what excites admiration and to heap contempt on misery, to raise power into tyranny, and to make tyranny absolute; to thrust down that which is low still lower, and to make wretches desperate: to exalt magistrates into kings, kings into gods; to degrade subjects to the rank of slaves, and slaves to the condition of brutes. The history of mankind is a romance, a mask, a tragedy, constructed upon the principles of *poetical justice*;[10] it is a noble or royal hunt, in which what is sport to the few is death to the many, and in which the spectators halloo and encourage the strong to set upon the weak, and cry havoc in the chase though they do not share in the spoil. We may depend upon it that what men delight to read in books, they will put in practice in reality.

One of the most natural traits in this play is the difference of the interest taken in the success of Coriolanus by his wife and mother. The one is only anxious for his honour; the other is fearful for his life.

> '*Volumnia.* Methinks I hither hear your husband's drum:
> I see him pluck Aufidius down by th' hair:
> Methinks I see him stamp thus – and call thus –
> Come on, ye cowards; ye were got in fear
> Though you were born in Rome; his bloody brow
> With his mail'd hand then wiping, forth he goes
> Like to a harvest man, that's task'd to mow
> Or all, or lose his hire.
>
>   *Virgilia.* His bloody brow! Oh Jupiter, no blood.
>
>   *Volumnia.* Away, you fool; it more becomes a man
> Than gilt his trophy. The breast of Hecuba,
> When she did suckle Hector, look'd not lovelier

Than Hector's forehead, when it spit forth blood
At Grecian swords contending.'[11]

When she hears the trumpets that proclaim her son's return, she says in the true spirit of a Roman matron,

'These are the ushers of Martius: before him
He carries noise, and behind him he leaves tears.
Death, that dark spirit, in's nervy arm doth lie,
Which being advanc'd, declines, and then men die.'[12]

Coriolanus himself is a complete character: his love of reputation, his contempt of popular opinion, his pride and modesty, are consequences of each other. His pride consists in the inflexible sternness of his will; his love of glory is a determined desire to bear down all opposition, and to extort the admiration both of friends and foes. His contempt for popular favour, his unwillingness to hear his own praises, spring from the same source. He cannot contradict the praises that are bestowed upon him; therefore he is impatient at hearing them. He would enforce the good opinion of others by his actions, but does not want their acknowledgments in words.

'Pray now, no more: my mother,
Who has a charter to extol her blood,
When she does praise me, grieves me.'[13]

His magnanimity is of the same kind. He admires in an enemy that courage which he honours in himself; he places himself on the hearth of Aufidius with the same confidence that he would have met him in the field, and feels that by putting himself in his power, he takes from him all temptation for using it against him.

*

'Introduction to Elizabethan Literature'

The age of Elizabeth was distinguished, beyond, perhaps, any other in our history, by a number of great men, famous in different ways, and whose names have come down to us with unblemished honours; statesmen, warriors, divines, scholars, poets, and philosophers, Raleigh, Drake, Coke, Hooker, and higher and more sounding still, and still more frequent in our mouths, Shakespeare, Spenser, Sidney, Bacon, Jonson, Beaumont and Fletcher, men whom fame has eternized in her long and lasting scroll, and who, by their words and acts, were benefactors of their country, and ornaments of human nature. Their attainments of different kinds bore the same general stamp, and it was sterling: what they did, had the mark of their age and country upon it. Perhaps the genius of Great Britain (if I may so speak without offence or flattery), never shone out fuller or brighter, or looked more like itself, than at this period. Our writers and great men had something in them that savoured of the soil from which they grew: they were not French, they were not Dutch, or German, or Greek, or Latin; they were truly English. They did not look out of themselves to see what they should be; they sought for truth and nature, and found it in themselves. There was no tinsel, and but little art; they were not the spoiled children of affectation and refinement, but a bold, vigorous, independent race of thinkers, with prodigious strength and energy, with none but natural grace, and heartfelt unobtrusive delicacy. They were not at all sophisticated. The mind of their country was great in them, and it prevailed. With their learning and unexampled acquirement, they did not forget that they were men: with all their endeavours after excellence, they did not lay aside the strong original bent and character of their minds. What they performed was chiefly nature's handy-work; and time has claimed it for his own. – To these, however, might be added others not less learned, nor with a scarce less happy vein, but less fortunate in the event, who, though as renowned in their day, have sunk into 'mere oblivion',[1] and of whom the only record (but that the noblest) is to be found in their works. Their works and their names, 'poor, poor dumb names',[2] are all that remains of such men as Webster, Dekker, Marston, Marlowe, Chapman, Heywood, Middleton, and Rowley! 'How lov'd, how honour'd once, avails them not':[3] though they were the friends and fellow-labourers of Shakespeare, sharing his fame and fortunes with him, the rivals of Jonson, and the masters of Beaumont and Fletcher's well-sung woes! They went out one by one unnoticed, like evening lights; or were swallowed up in the headlong torrent of puritanic zeal which succeeded, and swept away every thing in its unsparing course, throwing up the wrecks of taste and genius at random, and at long fitful intervals, amidst the painted gew-gaws and foreign frippery of the reign of Charles II and from which we are only now recovering the scattered fragments and broken images to erect a temple to true Fame! How long, before it will be completed?

If I can do any thing to rescue some of these writers from hopeless obscurity, and to do them right, without prejudice to well-deserved reputation, I shall have succeeded in what I chiefly propose. I shall not attempt, indeed, to adjust the spelling, or restore the pointing, as if the genius of poetry lay hid in errors of the press, but leaving these weightier matters of criticism to those who are more able and willing to bear the burden, try to bring out their real beauties to the eager sight, 'draw the curtain of Time, and shew the picture of Genius',[4] restraining my own admiration within reasonable bounds!

There is not a lower ambition, a poorer way of thought, than that which would confine all excellence, or arrogate its final accomplishment to the present, or modern times. We ordinarily speak and think of those who had the misfortune to write or live before us, as labouring under very singular privations and disadvantages in not having the benefit of those improvements which we have made, as buried in the grossest ignorance, or the slaves 'of poring pedantry';[5] and we make a cheap

and infallible estimate of their progress in civilization upon a graduated scale of perfectibility, calculated from the meridian of our own
times. If we have pretty well got rid of the narrow bigotry that would
limit all sense or virtue to our own country, and have fraternized,
like true cosmopolites, with our neighbours and contemporaries, we
have made our self-love amends by letting the generation we live in
engross nearly all our admiration and by pronouncing a sweeping
sentence of barbarism and ignorance on our ancestry backwards, from
the commencement (as near as can be) of the nineteenth, or the latter
end of the eighteenth century. From thence we date a new era, the
dawn of our own intellect and that of the world, like 'the sacred
influence of light'[6] glimmering on the confines of Chaos and old
night; new manners rise, and all the cumbrous 'pomp of elder days'[7]
vanishes, and is lost in worse than Gothic darkness. Pavilioned in
the glittering pride of our superficial accomplishments and upstart
pretensions, we fancy that every thing beyond that magic circle is
prejudice and error; and all, before the present enlightened period,
but a dull and useless blank in the great map of time. We are so
dazzled with the gloss and novelty of modern discoveries, that we
cannot take into our mind's eye the vast expanse, the lengthened
perspective of human intellect, and a cloud hangs over and conceals
its loftiest monuments, if they are removed to a little distance from
us – the cloud of our own vanity and short-sightedness. The modern
sciolist *stultifies* all understanding but his own, and that which he
conceives like his own. We think, in this age of reason and consummation of philosophy, because we knew nothing twenty or thirty
years ago, and began to think then for the first time in our lives, that
the rest of mankind were in the same predicament, and never knew
any thing till we did; that the world had grown old in sloth and
ignorance, had dreamt out its long minority of five thousand years
in a dozing state, and that it first began to wake out of sleep, to rouse
itself, and look about it, startled by the light of our unexpected
discoveries, and the noise we made about them. Strange error of our
infatuated self-love! Because the clothes we remember to have seen
worn when we were children, are now out of fashion, and our
grandmothers were then old women, we conceive with magnanimous
continuity of reasoning, that it must have been much worse three

hundred years before, and that grace, youth, and beauty are things of modern date – as if nature had ever been old, or the sun had first shone on our folly and presumption. Because, in a word, the last generation, when tottering off the stage, were not so active, so sprightly, and so promising as we were, we begin to imagine, that people formerly must have crawled about in a feeble, torpid state, like flies in winter, in a sort of dim twilight of the understanding; 'nor can we think what thoughts they could conceive',[8] in the absence of all those topics that so agreeably enliven and diversify our conversation and literature, mistaking the imperfection of our knowledge for the defect of their organs, as if it was necessary for us to have a register and certificate of their thoughts, or as if, because they did not see with our eyes, hear with our ears, and understand with our understandings, they could hear, see, and understand nothing. A falser inference could not be drawn, nor one more contrary to the maxims and cautions of a wise humanity. 'Think', says Shakespeare, the prompter of good and true feelings, 'there's livers out of Britain.'[9] So there have been thinkers, and great and sound ones, before our time. They had the same capacities that we have, sometimes greater motives for their exertion, and, for the most part, the same subject-matter to work upon. What we learn from nature, we may hope to do as well as they; what we learn from them, we may in general expect to do worse. – What is, I think, as likely as any thing to cure us of this overweening admiration of the present, and unmingled contempt for past times, is the looking at the finest old pictures; at Raphael's heads, at Titian's faces, at Claude's landscapes. We have there the evidence of the senses, without the alterations of opinion or disguise of language. We there see the blood circulate through the veins (long before it was known that it did so),[10] the same red and white 'by nature's own sweet and cunning hand laid on',[11] the same thoughts passing through the mind and seated on the lips, the same blue sky, and glittering sunny vales, 'where Pan, knit with the Graces and the Hours in dance, leads on the eternal spring'.[12] And we begin to feel, that nature and the mind of man are not a thing of yesterday, as we had been led to suppose; and that 'there are more things between heaven and earth, than were ever dreamt of in our philosophy'.[13] – Or grant that we improve, in some respects, in a uniformly progressive ratio, and build,

Babel-high, on the foundation of other men's knowledge, as in matters of science and speculative inquiry, where by going often over the same general ground, certain general conclusions have been arrived at, and in the number of persons reasoning on a given subject, truth has at last been hit upon, and long-established error exploded; yet this does not apply to cases of individual power and knowledge, to a million of things beside, in which we are still to seek as much as ever, and in which we can only hope to find, by going to the fountain-head of thought and experience. We are quite wrong in supposing (as we are apt to do), that we can plead an exclusive title to wit and wisdom, to taste and genius, as the net produce and clear reversion of the age we live in, and that all we have to do to be great, is to despise those who have gone before us as nothing.

Or even if we admit a saving clause in this sweeping proscription, and do not make the rule absolute, the very nature of the exceptions shows the spirit in which they are made. We single out one or two striking instances, say Shakespeare or Lord Bacon, which we would fain treat as prodigies, and as a marked contrast to the rudeness and barbarism that surrounded them. These we delight to dwell upon and magnify; the praise and wonder we heap upon their shrines, are at the expense of the time in which they lived, and would leave it poor indeed. We make them out something more than human, 'matchless, divine, what we will',[14] so to make them no rule for their age, and no infringement of the abstract claim to superiority which we set up. Instead of letting them reflect any lustre, or add any credit to the period of history to which they rightfully belong, we only make use of their example to insult and degrade it still more beneath our own level.

It is the present fashion to speak with veneration of old English literature; but the homage we pay to it is more akin to the rites of superstition, than the worship of true religion. Our faith is doubtful; our love cold; our knowledge little or none. We now and then repeat the names of some of the old writers by rote; but we are shy of looking into their works. Though we seem disposed to think highly of them, and to give them every credit for a masculine and original vein of thought, as a matter of literary courtesy and enlargement of taste, we are afraid of coming to the proof, as too great a trial of our candour and patience. We regard the enthusiastic admiration of these obsolete authors, or a desire to make proselytes to a belief in their extraordinary merits, as an amiable weakness, a pleasing delusion; and prepare to listen to some favourite passage, that may be referred to in support of this singular taste, with an incredulous smile; and are in no small pain for the result of the hazardous experiment; feeling much the same awkward condescending disposition to patronize these first crude attempts at poetry and lispings of the Muse, as when a fond parent brings forward a bashful child to make a display of its wit or learning. We hope the best, put a good face on the matter, but are sadly afraid the thing cannot answer. – Dr Johnson said of these writers generally,[15] that 'they were sought after because they were scarce, and would not have been scarce, had they been much esteemed'. His decision is neither true history nor sound criticism. They were esteemed, and they deserved to be so.

One cause that might be pointed out here, as having contributed to the long-continued neglect of our earlier writers, lies in the very nature of our academic institutions, which unavoidably neutralizes a taste for the productions of native genius, estranges the mind from the history of our own literature, and makes it in each successive age like a book sealed. The Greek and Roman classics are a sort of privileged text-books, the standing order of the day, in a University education, and leave little leisure for a competent acquaintance with, or due admiration of, a whole host of able writers of our own, who are suffered to moulder in obscurity on the shelves of our libraries, with a decent reservation of one or two top-names, that are cried up for form's sake, and to save the national character. Thus we keep a few of these always ready in capitals, and strike off the rest, to prevent the tendency to a superfluous population in the republic of letters; in other words, to prevent the writers from becoming more numerous than the readers. The ancients are become effete in this respect, they no longer increase and multiply; or if they have imitators among us, no one is expected to read, and still less to admire them. It is not possible that the learned professors and the reading public should clash in this way, or necessary for them to use any precautions against each other. But it is not the same with the living languages, where there is danger of being overwhelmed by the crowd of competitors; and pedantry has combined with ignorance to cancel their unsatisfied claims.

We affect to wonder at Shakespeare, and one or two more of that period, as solitary instances upon record; whereas it is our own dearth of information that makes the waste; for there is no time more populous of intellect, or more prolific of intellectual wealth, than the one we are speaking of. Shakespeare did not look upon himself in this light, as a sort of monster of poetical genius, or on his contemporaries as 'less than smallest dwarfs',[16] when he speaks with true, not false modesty, of himself and them, and of his wayward thoughts, 'desiring this man's art, and that man's scope'.[17] We fancy that there were no such men, that could either add to or take any thing away from him, but such there were. He indeed overlooks and commands the admiration of posterity, but he does it from the *table-land* of the age in which he lived. He towered above his fellows, 'in shape and gesture proudly eminent';[18] but he was one of a race of giants, the tallest, the strongest, the most graceful, and beautiful of them; but it was a common and a noble brood. He was not something sacred and aloof from the vulgar herd of men, but shook hands with nature and the circumstances of the time, and is distinguished from his immediate contemporaries, not in kind, but in degree and greater variety of excellence. He did not form a class or species by himself, but belonged to a class or species. His age was necessary to him; nor could he have been wrenched from his place in the edifice of which he was so conspicuous a part, without equal injury to himself and it. Mr Wordsworth says of Milton, that 'his soul was like a star, and dwelt apart'.[19] This cannot be said with any propriety of Shakespeare, who certainly moved in a constellation of bright luminaries, and 'drew after him a third part of the heavens'.[20] If we allow, for argument's sake (or for truth's, which is better), that he was in himself equal to all his competitors put together; yet there was more dramatic excellence in that age than in the whole of the period that has elapsed since. If his contemporaries, with their united strength, would hardly make one Shakespeare, certain it is that all his successors would not make half a one. With the exception of a single writer, Otway, and of a single play of his (*Venice Preserv'd*), there is nobody in tragedy and dramatic poetry (I do not here speak of comedy) to be compared to the great men of the age of Shakespeare, and immediately after. They are a mighty phalanx of kindred spirits closing him round, moving in the same orbit, and impelled by the same causes in their whirling and eccentric career. They had the same faults and the same excellences; the same strength and depth and richness, the same truth of character, passion, imagination, thought and language, thrown, heaped, massed together without careful polishing or exact method, but poured out in unconcerned profusion from the lap of nature and genius in boundless and unrivalled magnificence. The sweetness of Dekker, the thought of Marston, the gravity of Chapman, the grace of Fletcher and his young-eyed wit, Jonson's learned sock,[21] the flowing vein of Middleton, Heywood's ease, the pathos of Webster, and Marlowe's deep designs, add a double lustre to the sweetness, thought, gravity, grace, wit, artless nature, copiousness, ease, pathos, and sublime conceptions of Shakespeare's Muse. They are indeed the scale by which we can best ascend to the true knowledge and love of him. Our admiration of them does not lessen our relish for him: but, on the contrary, increases and confirms it. – For such an extraordinary combination and development of fancy and genius many causes may be assigned; and we may seek for the chief of them in religion, in politics, in the circumstances of the time, the recent diffusion of letters, in local situation, and in the character of the men who adorned that period, and availed themselves so nobly of the advantages placed within their reach.

I shall here attempt to give a general sketch of these causes, and of the manner in which they operated to mould and stamp the poetry of the country at the period of which I have to treat; independently of incidental and fortuitous causes, for which there is no accounting, but which, after all, have often the greatest share in determining the most important results.

The first cause I shall mention, as contributing to this general effect, was the Reformation, which had just then taken place. This event gave a mighty impulse and increased activity to thought and inquiry, and agitated the inert mass of accumulated prejudices throughout Europe. The effect of the concussion was general; but the shock was greatest in this country. It toppled down the full-grown, intolerable abuses of centuries at a blow; heaved the ground from under the feet of bigoted faith and slavish obedience; and the roar and dashing of opinions, loosened from their accustomed hold, might be heard like the noise of an angry sea, and has never yet subsided. Germany first broke the spell of misbegotten fear, and gave the watchword; but England joined the shout, and echoed it back with her island voice, from her thousand cliffs and craggy shores, in a longer and a louder strain. With that cry, the genius of Great Britain rose, and threw down the gauntlet to the nations. There was a mighty fermentation: the waters were out; public opinion was in a state of projection. Liberty was held out to all to think and speak the truth. Men's brains were busy; their spirits stirring; their hearts full; and their hands not idle. Their eyes were opened to expect the greatest things, and their ears burned with curiosity and zeal to know the truth,[22] that the truth might make them free. The death-blow which had been struck at scarlet vice and bloated hypocrisy, loosened their tongues, and made the talismans and love-tokens of Popish superstition, with which she had beguiled her followers and committed abominations with the people, fall harmless from their necks.

The translation of the Bible was the chief engine in the great work. It threw open, by a secret spring, the rich treasures of religion and morality, which had been there locked up as in a shrine. It revealed the visions of the prophets, and conveyed the lessons of inspired teachers (such they were thought) to the meanest of the people. It gave them a common interest in the common cause. Their hearts burnt within them as they read. It gave a *mind* to the people, by giving them common subjects of thought and feeling. It cemented their union of character and sentiment: it created endless diversity and collision of opinion. They found objects to employ their faculties, and a motive in the magnitude of the consequences attached to them, to exert the utmost eagerness in the pursuit of truth, and the most daring intrepidity in maintaining it. Religious controversy sharpens the understanding by the subtlety and remoteness of the topics it discusses, and braces the will by their infinite importance. We perceive in the history of this period a nervous masculine intellect. No levity, no feebleness, no indifference; or if there were, it is a relaxation from the intense activity which gives a tone to its general character. But there is a gravity approaching to piety; a seriousness of impression, a conscientious severity of argument, an habitual fervour and enthusiasm in their mode of handling almost every subject. The debates of the schoolmen were sharp and subtle enough; but they wanted interest and grandeur, and were besides confined to a few: they did not affect the general mass of the community. But the Bible was thrown open to all ranks and conditions 'to run and read',[23] with its wonderful table of contents from Genesis to the Revelations. Every village in England would present the scene so well described in Burns's 'Cotter's Saturday Night'. I cannot think that all this variety and weight of knowledge could be thrown in all at once upon the mind of a people, and not make some impression upon it, the traces of which might be discerned in the manners and literature of the age. For to leave more disputable points, and take only the historical parts of the Old Testament, or the moral sentiments of the New, there is nothing like them in the power of exciting awe and admiration, or of rivetting sympathy. We see what Milton has made of the account of the Creation, from the manner in which he has treated it, imbued and impregnated with the spirit of the time of which we speak. Or what is there equal (in that romantic interest and patriarchal simplicity which goes to the heart of a country, and rouses it, as it were, from its lair in wastes and wildnesses) to the story of Joseph and his Brethren, of Rachael and Laban, of Jacob's Dream, of Ruth and Boaz, the descriptions in the book of Job, the deliverance of the Jews out of Egypt, or the account of their captivity and return from Babylon? There is in all these parts of the Scripture, and numberless more of the same kind, to pass over the Orphic hymns of David, the prophetic denunciations of Isaiah, or the gorgeous visions of Ezekiel, an originality, a vastness of conception, a depth and tenderness of feeling, and a touching simplicity in the mode of narration, which he who does not feel, need be made of no 'penetrable stuff'.[24] There is something in the character of Christ too (leaving religious faith quite out of the question) of more sweetness and majesty, and more likely to work a change in the mind of man, by the contemplation of its idea alone, than any to be found in history, whether actual or feigned. This character is that of a sublime humanity, such as was never seen on earth before, nor since. This shone manifestly both in his words and actions. We see it in his washing the Disciples' feet the night before his death, that unspeakable instance of humility and love, above all art, all meanness, and all pride, and in the leave he took of them on that occasion, 'My peace I give unto you, that peace which the world cannot give, give I unto you';[25] and in his last commandment, that 'they should love one another'.[26] Who can read the account of his behaviour on the cross, when turning to his mother he said, 'Woman, behold thy son',[27] and to the Disciple John, 'Behold thy mother',[28] and 'from that hour that Disciple took her to his own home', without having his heart smote within him! We see it in his treatment of the woman taken in adultery, and in his excuse for the woman who poured precious ointment on his garment as an offering of devotion and love, which is here all in all. His religion was the religion of the heart. We see it in his discourse with the Disciples as they walked together towards Emmaus, when their hearts burned within them;[29] in his sermon from the Mount, in his parable of the Good Samaritan, and in that of the Prodigal Son – in every act and word of his life, a grace, a mildness, a dignity and love, a patience and wisdom worthy of the Son of God. His whole life and being were imbued, steeped in this word, *charity*; it was the spring, the well-head from which every thought and feeling gushed into act; and it was this that breathed a mild glory from his face in that last agony upon the cross, 'when the meek Saviour bowed his head and died',[30] praying for his enemies. He was the first true teacher of morality; for he alone conceived the idea of a pure humanity. He redeemed man from the worship of that idol, self, and instructed him by precept and example to love his neighbour as himself, to forgive our enemies, to do good to those that curse us and despitefully use us. He taught the love of good for the sake of good, without regard to personal or sinister views, and made the affections of the heart the sole seat of morality, instead of the pride of the understanding or the sternness of the will. In answering the question, 'who is our neighbour?'[31] as one who stands in need of our assistance, and whose wounds we can bind up, he has done more to humanize the thoughts and tame the unruly passions, than all who have tried to reform and benefit mankind. The very idea of abstract benevolence, of the desire to do good because another wants our services, and of regarding the human race as one family, the offspring of one common parent, is hardly to be found in any other code or system. It was 'to the Jews a stumbling block, and to the Greeks foolishness'.[32] The Greeks and Romans never thought of considering others, but as they were Greeks or Romans, as they were bound to them by certain positive ties, or, on the other hand, as separated from them by fiercer antipathies. Their virtues were the virtues of political machines, their vices were the vices of demons, ready to inflict or to endure pain with obdurate and remorseless inflexibility of purpose. But in the Christian religion, 'we perceive a softness coming over the heart of a nation, and the iron scales that fence and harden it, melt and drop off'.[33] It becomes malleable, capable of pity, of forgiveness, of relaxing in its claims, and remitting its power. We strike it, and it does not hurt us: it is not steel or marble, but flesh and blood, clay tempered with tears, and 'soft as sinews of the new-born babe'.[34] The gospel was first preached to the poor, for it consulted their wants and interests, not its own pride and arrogance. It first promulgated the equality of mankind in the community of duties and benefits. It denounced the iniquities of the chief Priests and Pharisees, and declared itself at variance with principalities and powers,[35] for it sympathizes not with the oppressor, but the oppressed. It first abolished slavery, for it did not consider the power of the will to inflict injury, as clothing it with a right to do so. Its law is good, not power. It at the same time tended to wean the mind from the grossness of sense, and a particle of its divine flame was lent to brighten and purify the lamp of love!

There have been persons who, being sceptics as to the divine mission of Christ, have taken an unaccountable prejudice to his doctrines, and have been disposed to deny the merit of his character; but this was not the feeling of the great men in the age of Elizabeth (whatever might be their belief) one of whom says of him, with a boldness equal to its piety:

'The best of men
That e'er wore earth about him, was a sufferer;
A soft, meek, patient, humble, tranquil spirit;
The first true gentleman that ever breathed.'[56]

This was old honest Dekker, and the lines ought to embalm his memory to every one who has a sense either of religion, or philosophy, or humanity, or true genius. Nor can I help thinking, that we may discern the traces of the influence exerted by religious faith in the spirit of the poetry of the age of Elizabeth, in the means of exciting terror and pity, in the delineation of the passions of grief, remorse, love, sympathy, the sense of shame, in the fond desires, the longings after immortality, in the heaven of hope, and the abyss of despair it lays open to us.*

The literature of this age then, I would say, was strongly influenced (among other causes), first by the spirit of Christianity, and secondly by the spirit of Protestantism.

The effects of the Reformation on politics and philosophy may be seen in the writings and history of the next and of the following ages. They are still at work, and will continue to be so. The effects on the poetry of the time were chiefly confined to the moulding of the character, and giving a powerful impulse to the intellect of the country. The immediate use or application that was made of religion to subjects of imagination and fiction was not (from an obvious ground of separation) so direct or frequent, as that which was made of the classical and romantic literature.

For much about the same time, the rich and fascinating stores of the Greek and Roman mythology, and those of the romantic poetry of Spain and Italy, were eagerly explored by the curious, and thrown open in translations to the admiring gaze of the vulgar. This last circumstance could hardly have afforded so much advantage to the poets of that day, who were themselves, in fact, the translators, as it shows the general curiosity and increasing interest in such subjects,

* In some Roman Catholic countries, pictures in part supplied the place of the translation of the Bible: and this dumb art arose in the silence of the written oracles.

as a prevailing feature of the times. There were translations of Tasso by Fairfax, and of Ariosto by Harington, of Homer and Hesiod by Chapman, and of Virgil long before, and Ovid soon after; there was Sir Thomas North's translation of Plutarch, of which Shakespeare has made such admirable use in his *Coriolanus* and *Julius Caesar*; and Ben Jonson's tragedies of Catiline and Sejanus may themselves be considered as almost literal translations into verse, of Tacitus, Sallust, and Cicero's *Orations* in his consulship. Boccaccio, the divine Boccaccio, Petrarch, Dante, the satirist Aretine, Machiavelli, Castiglione, and others, were familiar to our writers, and they make occasional mention of some few French authors, as Ronsard and Du Bartas; for the French literature had not at this stage arrived at its Augustan period, and it was the imitation of their literature a century afterwards, when it had arrived at its greatest height (itself copied from the Greek and Latin), that enfeebled and impoverished our own. But of the time that we are considering, it might be said, without much extravagance, that every breath that blew, that every wave that rolled to our shores, brought with it some accession to our knowledge, which was engrafted on the national genius. In fact, all the disposable materials that had been accumulating for a long period of time, either in our own, or in foreign countries, were now brought together, and required nothing more than to be wrought up, polished, or arranged in striking forms, for ornament and use. To this every inducement prompted, the novelty of the acquisition of knowledge in many cases, the emulation of foreign wits, and of immortal works, the want and the expectation of such works among ourselves, the opportunity and encouragement afforded for their production by leisure and affluence; and, above all, the insatiable desire of the mind to beget its own image, and to construct out of itself, and for the delight and admiration of the world and posterity, that excellence of which the idea exists hitherto only in its own breast, and the impression of which it would make as universal as the eye of heaven, the benefit as common as the air we breathe. The first impulse of genius is to create what never existed before: the contemplation of that, which is so created, is sufficient to satisfy the demands of taste; and it is the habitual study and imitation of the original models that takes away the power, and even wish to do the like. Taste limps after genius, and from copying the artificial models, we lose sight of the living principle of nature. It is the effort we make, and the impulse we acquire, in overcoming the first obstacles, that projects us forward; it is the necessity for exertion that makes us conscious of our strength; but this necessity and this impulse once removed, the tide of fancy and enthusiasm, which is at first a running stream, soon settles and crusts into the standing pool of dulness, criticism, and *virtù*.[37]

What also gave an unusual *impetus* to the mind of man at this period, was the discovery of the New World, and the reading of voyages and travels. Green islands and golden sands seemed to arise, as by enchantment, out of the bosom of the watery waste, and invite the cupidity, or wing the imagination of the dreaming speculator. Fairy land was realized in new and unknown worlds. 'Fortunate fields and groves and flowery vales, thrice happy isles',[38] were found floating 'like those Hesperian gardens famed of old',[39] beyond Atlantic seas, as dropt from the zenith. The people, the soil, the clime, every thing gave unlimited scope to the curiosity of the traveller and reader. Other manners might be said to enlarge the bounds of knowledge, and new mines of wealth were tumbled at our feet. It is from a voyage to the Straits of Magellan that Shakespeare has taken the hint of Prospero's Enchanted Island, and of the savage Caliban with his god Setebos.* Spenser seems to have had the same feeling in his mind in the production of his *Faerie Queene*, and vindicates his poetic fiction on this very ground of analogy.

> 'Right well I wote, most mighty sovereign,
> That all this famous antique history
> Of some the abundance of an idle brain
> Will judged be, and painted forgery,
> Rather than matter of just memory:
> Since none that breatheth living air, doth know
> Where is that happy land of faery
> Which I so much do vaunt, but no where show,
> But vouch antiquities, which nobody can know.

* See *A Voyage to the Straits of Magellan*, 1594.

> But let that man with better sense avise,
> That of the world least part to us is read:
> And daily how through hardy enterprize
> Many great regions are discovered,
> Which to late age were never mentioned.
> Who ever heard of th' Indian Peru?
> Or who in venturous vessel measured
> The Amazons' huge river, now found true?
> Or fruitfullest Virginia who did ever view?
>
> Yet all these were when no man did them know,
> Yet have from wisest ages hidden been:
> And later times things more unknown shall show.
> Why then should witless man so much misween
> That nothing is but that which he hath seen?
> What if within the moon's fair shining sphere,
> What if in every other star unseen,
> Of other worlds he happily should hear,
> He wonder would much more; yet such to some appear.'[40]

Fancy's air-drawn pictures after history's waking dream showed like clouds over mountains; and from the romance of real life to the idlest fiction, the transition seemed easy. — Shakespeare, as well as others of his time, availed himself of the old *Chronicles*, and of the traditions or fabulous inventions contained in them in such ample measure, and which had not yet been appropriated to the purposes of poetry or the drama. The stage was a new thing; and those who had to supply its demands laid their hands upon whatever came within their reach: they were not particular as to the means, so that they gained the end. *Lear* is founded upon an old ballad; *Othello* on an Italian novel; *Hamlet* on a Danish, and *Macbeth* on a Scotch tradition: one of which is to be found in Saxo-Grammaticus, and the last in Holinshed. The Ghost-scenes and the Witches in each, are authenticated in the old Gothic history. There was also this connecting link between the poetry of this age and the supernatural traditions of a former one, that the belief in them was still extant, and in full force and visible operation among the vulgar (to say no more) in the time of our authors. The appalling and wild chimeras of superstition and ignorance, 'those bodiless creations that ecstasy is very cunning in',[41] were inwoven with existing manners and opinions, and all their effects on the passions of terror or pity might be gathered from common and actual observation – might be discerned in the workings of the face, the expressions of the tongue, the writhings of a troubled conscience. 'Your face, my Thane, is as a book where men may read strange matters.'[42] Midnight and secret murders too, from the imperfect state of the police, were more common; and the ferocious and brutal manners that would stamp the brow of the hardened ruffian or hired assassin, more incorrigible and undisguised. The portraits of Tyrrel and Forrest were, no doubt, done from the life. We find that the ravages of the plague, the destructive rage of fire, the poisoned chalice, lean famine, the serpent's mortal sting, and the fury of wild beasts, were the common topics of their poetry, as they were common occurrences in more remote periods of history. They were the strong ingredients thrown into the cauldron of tragedy, to make it 'thick and slab'.[43] Man's life was (as it appears to me) more full of traps and pit-falls; of hair-breadth accidents by flood and field;[44] more way-laid by sudden and startling evils; it trod on the brink of hope and fear; stumbled upon fate unawares; while the imagination, close behind it, caught at and clung to the shape of danger, or 'snatched a wild and fearful joy'[45] from its escape. The accidents of nature were less provided against; the excesses of the passions and of lawless power were less regulated, and produced more strange and desperate catastrophes. The tales of Boccaccio are founded on the great pestilence of Florence, Fletcher the poet died of the plague, and Marlowe was stabbed in a tavern quarrel. The strict authority of parents, the inequality of ranks, or the hereditary feuds between different families, made more unhappy loves or matches.

'The course of true love never did run even.'[46]

Again, the heroic and martial spirit which breathes in our elder writers, was yet in considerable activity in the reign of Elizabeth. 'The age of chivalry was not then quite gone, nor the glory of Europe extinguished for ever.'[47] Jousts and tournaments were still common with the nobility in England and in foreign countries: Sir Philip Sidney was particularly distinguished for his proficiency in these exercises (and indeed fell a martyr to his ambition as a soldier) – and the gentle Surrey was still more famous, on the same account, just before him. It is true, the general use of firearms gradually superseded the necessity of skill in the sword, or bravery in the person: and as a symptom of the rapid degeneracy in this respect, we find Sir John Suckling soon after boasting of himself as one –

> 'Who prized black eyes, and a lucky hit
> At bowls, above all the trophies of wit'.[48]

It was comparatively an age of peace,

> 'Like strength reposing on his own right arm';[49]

but the sound of civil combat might still be heard in the distance, the spear glittered to the eye of memory, or the clashing of armour struck on the imagination of the ardent and the young. They were borderers on the savage state, on the times of war and bigotry, though in the lap of arts, of luxury, and knowledge. They stood on the shore and saw the billows rolling after the storm: 'they heard the tumult, and were still'.[50] The manners and out-of-door amusements were more tinctured with a spirit of adventure and romance. The war with wild beasts, &c. was more strenuously kept up in country sports. I do not think we could get from sedentary poets, who had never mingled in the vicissitudes, the dangers, or excitements of the chase, such descriptions of hunting and other athletic games, as are to be found in Shakespeare's *Midsummer Night's Dream*, or Fletcher's *Noble Kinsmen*.

With respect to the good cheer and hospitable living of those times, I cannot agree with an ingenious and agreeable writer[51] of the present day, that it was general or frequent. The very stress laid upon certain holidays and festivals, shows that they did not keep up the same Saturnalian licence and open house all the year round. They reserved themselves for great occasions, and made the best amends they could, for a year of abstinence and toil by a week of merriment and convivial indulgence. Persons in middle life at this day, who can afford a good dinner every day, do not look forward to it as any particular subject of exultation: the poor peasant, who can only contrive to treat himself to a joint of meat on a Sunday, considers it as an event in the week.

So, in the old Cambridge comedy of *The Returne from Parnassus*, we find this indignant description of the progress of luxury in those days, put into the mouth of one of the speakers.

> 'Why is't not strange to see a ragged clerke,
> Some stammell weaver, or some butcher's sonne,
> That scrubb'd a late within a sleeveless gowne,
> When the commencement, like a morrice dance,
> Hath put a bell or two about his legges,
> Created him a sweet cleane gentleman:
> How then he 'gins to follow fashions.
> He whose thin sire dwelt in a smokye roofe,
> Must take tobacco, and must wear a locke.
> His thirsty dad drinkes in a wooden bowle,
> But his sweet self is served in silver plate.
> His hungry sire will scrape you twenty legges
> For one good Christmas meal on new year's day,
> But his mawe must be capon cramm'd each day.'
>
> *Act III. Scene 2.*

This does not look as if in those days 'it snowed of meat and drink',[52] as a matter of course throughout the year! – The distinctions of dress, the badges of different professions, the very signs of the shops, which we have set aside for written inscriptions over the doors, were, as Mr Lamb observes,[53] a sort of visible language to the imagination, and hints for thought. Like the costume of different foreign nations, they had an immediate striking and picturesque effect, giving scope to the fancy. The surface of society was embossed with hieroglyphics, and poetry existed 'in act and complement extern'.[54] The poetry of former times might be directly taken from real life, as our poetry is taken from the poetry of former times. Finally, the face of nature, which was the same glorious object then that it is now, was open to them; and coming first, they gathered her fairest flowers to live for ever in their verse: – the movements of the human heart were not hid from them, for they had the same passions as we, only less disguised, and less subject to control. Dekker has given an admirable description of a mad-house in one of his plays.[55] But it might be perhaps objected, that it was only a literal account taken from Bedlam at that time: and it might be answered, that the old poets took the same method of describing the passions and fancies of men whom they met at large, which forms the point of communion between us: for the title of the old play, *A Mad World, my Masters*,[56] is hardly yet obsolete; and we are pretty much the same Bedlam still, perhaps a little better managed, like the real one, and with more care and humanity shewn to the patients!

Lastly, to conclude this account; what gave a unity and common direction to all these causes, was the natural genius of the country, which was strong in these writers in proportion to their strength. We are a nation of islanders, and we cannot help it; nor mend ourselves if we would. We are something in ourselves, nothing when we try to ape others. Music and painting are not our *forte*: for what we have done in that way has been little, and that borrowed from others with great difficulty. But we may boast of our poets and philosophers. That's something. We have had strong heads and sound hearts among us. Thrown on one side of the world, and left to bustle for ourselves, we have fought out many a battle for truth and freedom. That is our natural style; and it were to be wished we had in no instance departed from it. Our situation has given us a certain cast of thought and character; and our liberty has enabled us to make the most of it. We are of a stiff clay, not moulded into every fashion, with stubborn joints not easily bent. We are slow to think, and therefore impressions do not work upon us till they act in masses. We are not forward to express our feelings, and therefore they do not come from us till they force their way in the most impetuous eloquence. Our language is, as it were, to begin anew, and we make use of the most singular and boldest combinations to explain ourselves. Our wit comes from us, 'like birdlime, brains and all'.[57] We pay too little attention to form and method, leave our works in an unfinished state, but still the materials we work in are solid and of nature's mint; we do not deal in counterfeits. We both under- and over-do, but we keep an eye to the prominent features, the main chance. We are more for weight than show; care only about what interests ourselves, instead of trying to impose upon others by plausible appearances, and are obstinate and intractable in not conforming to common rules, by which many arrive at their ends with half the real waste of thought and trouble. We neglect all but the principal object, gather our force to make a great blow, bring it down, and relapse into sluggishness and indifference again. *Materiam superabat opus*,[58] cannot be said of us. We may be accused of grossness, but not of flimsiness; of extravagance, but not of affectation; of want of art and refinement, but not of a want of truth and nature. Our literature, in a word, is Gothic and grotesque; unequal and irregular; not cast in a previous mould, nor of one uniform texture, but of great weight in the whole, and of incomparable value in the best parts. It aims at an excess of beauty or power, hits or misses, and is either very good indeed, or absolutely good for nothing. This character applies in particular to our literature in the age of Elizabeth, which is its best period, before the introduction of a rage for French rules and French models; for whatever may be the value of our own original style of composition, there can be neither offence nor presumption in saying, that it is at least better than our second-hand imitations of others. Our understanding (such as it is, and must remain to be good for any thing) is not a thoroughfare for commonplaces, smooth as the palm of one's hand, but full of knotty points and jutting excrescences, rough, uneven, overgrown with brambles; and I like this aspect of the mind (as some one said of the country), where nature keeps a good deal of the soil in her own hands. Perhaps the genius of our poetry has more of Pan than of Apollo; 'but Pan is a God, Apollo is no more!'[59]

On Gusto

Gusto in art is power or passion defining any object. – It is not so difficult to explain this term in what relates to expression (of which it may be said to be the highest degree) as in what relates to things without expression, to the natural appearances of objects, as mere colour or form. In one sense, however, there is hardly any object entirely devoid of expression, without some character of power belonging to it, some precise association with pleasure or pain: and it is in giving this truth of character from the truth of feeling, whether in the highest or the lowest degree, but always in the highest degree of which the subject is capable, that gusto consists.

There is a gusto in the colouring of Titian. Not only do his heads seem to think – his bodies seem to feel. This is what the Italians mean by the *morbidezza*[1] of his flesh-colour. It seems sensitive and alive all over; not merely to have the look and texture of flesh, but the feeling in itself. For example, the limbs of his female figures have a luxurious softness and delicacy, which appears conscious of the pleasure of the beholder. As the objects themselves in nature would produce an impression on the sense, distinct from every other object, and having something divine in it, which the heart owns and the imagination consecrates, the objects in the picture preserve the same impression, absolute, unimpaired, stamped with all the truth of passion, the pride of the eye, and the charm of beauty. Rubens makes his flesh-colour like flowers; Albano's is like ivory; Titian's is like flesh, and like nothing else. It is as different from that of other painters, as the skin is from a piece of white or red drapery thrown over it. The blood circulates here and there, the blue veins just appear, the rest is distinguished throughout only by that sort of tingling sensation to the eye, which the body feels within itself. This is gusto. – Vandyke's flesh-colour, though it has great truth and purity, wants gusto. It has not the internal character, the living principle in it. It is a smooth surface, not a warm, moving mass. It is painted without passion, with indifference. The hand only has been concerned. The impression slides off from the eye, and does not, like the tones of Titian's pencil, leave a sting behind it in the mind of the spectator. The eye does not acquire a taste or appetite for what it sees. In a word, gusto in painting is where the impression made on one sense excites by affinity those of another.

Michael Angelo's forms are full of gusto. They every where obtrude the sense of power upon the eye. His limbs convey an idea of muscular strength, of moral grandeur, and even of intellectual dignity: they are firm, commanding, broad, and massy, capable of executing with ease the determined purposes of the will. His faces have no other expression than his figures, conscious power and capacity. They appear only to think what they shall do, and to know that they can do it. This is what is meant by saying that his style is hard and masculine. It is the reverse of Correggio's, which is effeminate. That is, the gusto of Michael Angelo consists in expressing energy of will without proportionable sensibility, Correggio's in expressing exquisite sensibility without energy of will. In Correggio's faces as well as figures we see neither bones nor muscles, but then what a soul is there, full of sweetness and of grace – pure, playful, soft, angelical! There is sentiment enough in a hand painted by Correggio to set up a school of history painters. Whenever we look at the hands of Correggio's women or of Raphael's, we always wish to touch them.

Again, Titian's landscapes have a prodigious gusto, both in the colouring and forms. We shall never forget one that we saw many years ago in the Orleans Gallery[2] of Actæon hunting. It had a brown, mellow, autumnal look. The sky was of the colour of stone. The winds seemed to sing through the rustling branches of the trees, and already you might hear the twanging of bows resound through the tangled mazes of the wood. Mr West, we understand, has this landscape. He will know if this description of it is just. The landscape back-ground of the St Peter Martyr is another well known instance of the power of this great painter to give a romantic interest and an appropriate character to the objects of his pencil, where every circumstance adds to the effect of the scene, – the bold trunks of the tall forest trees, the trailing ground plants, with that cold convent spire rising in the distance, amidst the blue sapphire mountains and the golden sky.

Rubens has a great deal of gusto in his Fauns and Satyrs, and in all that expresses motion, but in nothing else. Rembrandt has it in every thing; every thing in his pictures has a tangible character. If he puts a diamond in the ear of a Burgomaster's wife, it is of the first water; and his furs and stuffs are proof against a Russian winter. Raphael's gusto was only in expression; he had no idea of the character of any thing but the human form. The dryness and poverty of his style in other respects is a phenomenon in the art. His trees are like sprigs of grass stuck in a book of botanical specimens. Was it that Raphael never had time to go beyond the walls of Rome? That he was always in the streets, at church, or in the bath? He was not one of the Society of Arcadians.*

Claude's landscapes, perfect as they are, want gusto. This is not easy to explain. They are perfect abstractions of the visible images of things; they speak the visible language of nature truly. They resemble a mirror or a microscope. To the eye only they are more perfect than any other landscapes that ever were or will be painted; they give more of nature, as cognizable by one sense alone; but they lay an equal stress on all visible impressions; they do not interpret one sense by another; they do not distinguish the character of different objects as we are taught, and can only be taught, to distinguish them by their effect on the different senses. That is, his eye wanted imagination: it did not strongly sympathize with his other faculties. He saw the atmosphere, but he did not feel it. He painted the trunk of a tree or a rock in the foreground as smooth – with as complete an abstraction of the gross, tangible impression, as any other part of the picture; his trees are perfectly beautiful, but quite immoveable;

---

* Raphael not only could not paint a landscape; he could not paint people in a landscape. He could not have painted the heads or the figures, or even the dresses of the St Peter Martyr. His figures have always an *indoor* look, that is, a set, determined, voluntary, dramatic character, arising from their own passions, or a watchfulness of those of others, and want that wild uncertainty of expression, which is connected with the accidents of nature and the changes of the elements. He has nothing *romantic* about him.

they have a look of enchantment. In short, his landscapes are unequalled imitations of nature, released from its subjection to the elements, – as if all objects were become a delightful fairy vision, and the eye had rarefied and refined away the other senses.

The gusto in the Greek statues is of a very singular kind. The sense of perfect form nearly occupies the whole mind, and hardly suffers it to dwell on any other feeling. It seems enough for them *to be*, without acting or suffering. Their forms are ideal, spiritual. Their beauty is power. By their beauty they are raised above the frailties of pain or passion; by their beauty they are deified.

The infinite quantity of dramatic invention in Shakspeare takes from his gusto. The power he delights to show is not intense, but discursive. He never insists on any thing as much as he might, except a quibble. Milton has great gusto. He repeats his blow twice; grapples with and exhausts his subject. His imagination has a double relish of its objects, an inveterate attachment to the things he describes, and to the words describing them.

> —— 'Or where Chinese drive
> With sails and wind their *cany* waggons *light*.'[3]

> 'Wild above rule or art, *enormous* bliss.'[4]

There is a gusto in Pope's compliments, in Dryden's satires, and Prior's tales; and among prose-writers, Boccaccio and Rabelais had the most of it. We will only mention one other work which appears to us to be full of gusto, and that is *The Beggar's Opera*. If it is not, we are altogether mistaken in our notions on this delicate subject.

On Shakespeare and Milton

In looking back to the great works of genius in former times, we are sometimes disposed to wonder at the little progress which has since been made in poetry, and in the arts of imitation in general. But this is perhaps a foolish wonder. Nothing can be more contrary to the fact, than the supposition that in what we understand by the *fine arts*, as painting, and poetry, relative perfection is only the result of repeated efforts in successive periods, and that what has been once well done, constantly leads to something better. What is mechanical, reducible to rule, or capable of demonstration, is progressive, and admits of gradual improvement: what is not mechanical, or definite, but depends on feeling, taste, and genius, very soon becomes stationary, or retrograde, and loses more than it gains by transfusion. The contrary opinion is a vulgar error, which has grown up, like many others, from transferring an analogy of one kind to something quite distinct, without taking into the account the difference in the nature of the things, or attending to the difference of the results. For most persons, finding what wonderful advances have been made ·in biblical criticism, in chemistry, in mechanics, in geometry, astronomy, &c. *i. e.* in things depending on mere inquiry and experiment, or on absolute demonstration, have been led hastily to conclude, that there was a general tendency in the efforts of the human intellect to improve by repetition, and, in all other arts and institutions, to grow perfect and mature by time. We look back upon the theological creed of our ancestors, and their discoveries in natural philosophy, with a smile of pity: science, and the arts connected with it, have all had their infancy, their youth, and manhood, and seem to contain in them no principle of limitation or decay: and, inquiring no farther about the matter, we infer, in the intoxication of our pride, and the height of our self-congratulation, that the same progress has been made, and will continue to be made, in all other things which are the work of man. The fact, however, stares us so plainly in the face, that one would think the smallest reflection must suggest the truth, and overturn our sanguine theories. The greatest poets, the ablest orators, the best painters, and the finest sculptors that the world ever saw, appeared soon after the birth of these arts, and lived in a state of society which was, in other respects, comparatively barbarous. Those arts, which depend on individual genius and incommunicable power, have always leaped at once from infancy to manhood, from the first rude dawn of invention to their meridian height and dazzling lustre, and have in general declined ever after. This is the peculiar distinction and privilege of each, of science and of art: − of the one, never to attain its utmost limit of perfection; and of the other, to arrive at it almost at once. Homer, Chaucer, Spenser, Shakespeare, Dante, and Ariosto, (Milton alone was of a later age, and not the worse for it) − Raphael, Titian, Michael Angelo, Correggio, Cervantes, and Boccaccio, the Greek sculptors and tragedians, − all lived near the beginning of their arts − perfected, and all but created them. These giant-sons of genius stand indeed upon the earth, but they tower above their fellows; and the long line of their successors, in different ages, does not interpose any object to obstruct their view, or lessen their brightness. In strength and stature they are unrivalled; in grace and beauty they have not been surpassed. In after-ages, and more refined periods, (as they are called) great men have arisen, one by one, as it were by throes and at intervals; though in general the best of these cultivated and artificial minds were of an inferior order; as Tasso and Pope, among poets; Guido and Vandyke, among painters. But in the earlier stages of the arts, as soon as the first mechanical difficulties had been got over, and the language was sufficiently acquired, they rose by clusters, and in constellations, never so to rise again!

The arts of painting and poetry are conversant with the world of thought within us, and with the world of sense around us − with what we know, and see, and feel intimately. They flow from the sacred shrine of our own breasts, and are kindled at the living lamp of nature. But the pulse of the passions assuredly beat as high, the depths and soundings of the human heart were as well understood three thousand, or three hundred years ago, as they are at present: the face of nature, and 'the human face divine'[1] shone as bright then as they have ever done. But it is *their* light, reflected by true genius on art, that marks out its path before it, and sheds a glory round the Muses' feet, like that which

> 'Circled Una's angel face,
> And made a sunshine in the shady place'.[2]

The four greatest names in English poetry, are almost the four first we come to – Chaucer, Spenser, Shakespeare, and Milton. There are no others that can really be put in competition with these. The two last have had justice done them by the voice of common fame. Their names are blazoned in the very firmament of reputation; while the two first, (though 'the fault has been more in their stars than in themselves that they are underlings'[3]) either never emerged far above the horizon, or were too soon involved in the obscurity of time. The three first of these are excluded from Dr Johnson's *Lives of the Poets*[4] (Shakespeare indeed is so from the dramatic form of his compositions): and the fourth, Milton, is admitted with a reluctant and churlish welcome.

In comparing these four writers together, it might be said that Chaucer excels as the poet of manners, or of real life; Spenser, as the poet of romance; Shakespeare as the poet of nature (in the largest use of the term); and Milton, as the poet of morality. Chaucer most frequently describes things as they are; Spenser, as we wish them to be; Shakespeare, as they would be; and Milton as they ought to be. As poets, and as great poets, imagination, that is, the power of feigning things according to nature, was common to them all: but the principle or moving power, to which this faculty was most subservient in Chaucer, was habit, or inveterate prejudice; in Spenser, novelty, and the love of the marvellous; in Shakespeare, it was the force of passion, combined with every variety of possible circumstances; and in Milton, only with the highest. The characteristic of Chaucer is intensity; of Spenser, remoteness; of Milton, elevation; of Shakespeare, every thing. – It has been said by some critic,[5] that Shakespeare was distinguished from the other dramatic writers of his day only by his wit; that they had all his other qualities but that; that one writer had as much sense, another as much fancy, another as much knowledge of character, another the same depth of passion, and another as great a power of language. This statement is not true; nor is the inference from it well-founded, even if it were. This person does not seem to have been aware that, upon his own showing, the great distinction of Shakespeare's genius was its virtually including the genius of all the great men of his age, and not his differing from them in one accidental particular. But to have done with such minute and literal trifling.

The striking peculiarity of Shakespeare's mind was its generic quality, its power of communication with all other minds – so that it contained a universe of thought and feeling within itself, and had no one peculiar bias, or exclusive excellence more than another. He was just like any other man, but that he was like all other men. He was the least of an egotist that it was possible to be. He was nothing in himself; but he was all that others were, or that they could become. He not only had in himself the germs of every faculty and feeling, but he could follow them by anticipation, intuitively, into all their conceivable ramifications, through every change of fortune or conflict of passion, or turn of thought. He had 'a mind reflecting ages past',[6] and present: – all the people that ever lived are there. There was no respect of persons with him. His genius shone equally on the evil and on the good, on the wise and the foolish, the monarch and the beggar: 'All corners of the earth, kings, queens, and states, maids, matrons, nay, the secrets of the grave',[7] are hardly hid from his searching glance. He was like the genius of humanity, changing places with all of us at pleasure, and playing with our purposes as with his own. He turned the globe round for his amusement, and surveyed the generations of men, and the individuals as they passed, with their different concerns, passions, follies, vices, virtues, actions, and motives – as well those that they knew, as those which they did not know, or acknowledge to themselves. The dreams of childhood, the ravings of despair, were the toys of his fancy. Airy beings waited at his call, and came at his bidding. Harmless fairies 'nodded to him, and did him courtesies':[8] and the night-hag bestrode the blast[9] at the command of 'his so potent art'.[10] The world of spirits lay open to him, like the world of real men and women: and there is the same truth in his delineations of the one as of the other; for if the preternatural characters he describes could be supposed to exist, they would speak, and feel, and act, as he makes them. He had only to think of any thing in order to become that thing, with all the circumstances belonging to it. When he conceived of a character, whether real or imaginary, he not only entered into all its thoughts and feelings, but seemed instantly, and as if by touching a secret spring, to be surrounded with all the same objects, 'subject to the same skyey influences',[11] the same local, outward, and unforeseen accidents which would occur in reality. Thus the character of Caliban not only stands before us with a language and manners of its own, but the scenery and situation of the enchanted island he inhabits, the traditions of the place, its strange noises, its hidden recesses, 'his frequent haunts and ancient neighbourhood',[12] are given with a miraculous truth of nature, and with all the familiarity of an old recollection. The whole 'coheres semblably together'[13] in time, place, and circumstance. In reading this author, you do not merely learn what his characters say, – you see their persons. By something expressed or understood, you are at no loss to decypher their peculiar physiognomy, the meaning of a look, the grouping, the bye-play, as we might see it on the stage. A word, an epithet paints a whole scene, or throws us back whole years in the history of the person represented. So (as it has been ingeniously remarked)[14] when Prospero describes himself as left alone in the boat with his daughter, the epithet which he applies to her, 'Me and thy *crying* self',[15] flings the imagination instantly back from the grown woman to the helpless condition of infancy, and places the first and most trying scene of his misfortunes before us, with all that he must have suffered in the interval. How well the silent anguish of Macduff is conveyed to the reader, by the friendly expostulation of Malcolm – 'What! man, ne'er pull your hat upon your brows!'[16] Again, Hamlet, in the scene with Rosencrantz and Guildenstern, somewhat abruptly concludes his fine soliloquy on life by saying, 'Man delights not me, nor woman neither, though by your smiling you seem to say so.'[17] Which is explained by their answer – 'My lord, we had no such stuff in our thoughts. But we smiled to think, if you delight not in man, what lenten entertainment the players shall receive from you, whom we met on the way': − as if while Hamlet was making this speech, his two old schoolfellows from Wittenberg had been really standing by, and he had seen them smiling by stealth, at the idea of the players crossing their minds. It is not 'a combination and a form'[18] of words, a set speech or two, a preconcerted theory of a character, that will do this: but all the persons concerned must have been present in the poet's imagination, as at a kind of rehearsal; and whatever would have passed through their minds on the occasion, and have been observed by others, passed through his, and is made known to the reader. − I may add in passing, that Shakespeare always gives the best directions for the costume and carriage of his heroes. Thus to take one example, Ophelia gives the following account of Hamlet; and as Ophelia had seen Hamlet, I should think her word ought to be taken against that of any modern authority.

> '*Ophelia.* My lord, as I was reading in my closet,
> Prince Hamlet, with his doublet all unbrac'd,
> No hat upon his head, his stockings loose,
> Ungartred, and down-gyved to his ancle,
> Pale as his shirt, his knees knocking each other,
> And with a look so piteous,
> As if he had been sent from hell
> To speak of horrors, thus he comes before me.
>   *Polonius.* Mad for thy love!
>   *Oph.* My lord, I do not know,
> But truly I do fear it.
>   *Pol.* What said he?
>   *Oph.* He took me by the wrist, and held me hard,
> Then goes he to the length of all his arm;
> And with his other hand thus o'er his brow,
> He falls to such perusal of my face,
> As he would draw it: long staid he so;
> At last, a little shaking of my arm,
> And thrice his head thus waving up and down,
> He rais'd a sigh so piteous and profound,

As it did seem to shatter all his bulk,
And end his being. That done, he lets me go,
And with his head over his shoulder turn'd,
He seem'd to find his way without his eyes;
For out of doors he went without their help,
And to the last bended their light on me.'

Act. II. Scene 1.

How after this airy, fantastic idea of irregular grace and bewildered melancholy any one can play Hamlet, as we have seen it played, with strut, and stare, and antic right-angled sharp-pointed gestures, it is difficult to say, unless it be that Hamlet is not bound, by the prompter's cue, to study the part of Ophelia. The account of Ophelia's death begins thus:

'There is a willow hanging o'er a brook,
That shows its hoary leaves in the glassy stream' —[19]

Now this is an instance of the same unconscious power of mind which is as true to nature as itself. The leaves of the willow are, in fact, white underneath, and it is this part of them which would appear 'hoary' in the reflection in the brook. The same sort of intuitive power, the same faculty of bringing every object in nature, whether present or absent, before the mind's eye, is observable in the speech of Cleopatra, when conjecturing what were the employments of Antony in his absence: — 'He's speaking now, or murmuring, where's my serpent of old Nile?'[20] How fine to make Cleopatra have this consciousness of her own character, and to make her feel that it is this for which Antony is in love with her! She says, after the battle of Actium, when Antony has resolved to risk another fight, 'It is my birth-day; I had thought to have held it poor: but since my lord is Antony again, I will be Cleopatra.'[21] What other poet would have thought of such a casual resource of the imagination, or would have dared to avail himself of it? The thing happens in the play as it might have happened in fact. — That which, perhaps, more than any thing else distinguishes the dramatic productions of Shakespeare from all others, is this wonderful truth and individuality of conception. Each of his characters is as much itself, and as absolutely independent of the rest, as well as of the author, as if they were living persons, not fictions of the mind. The poet may be said, for the time, to identify himself with the character he wishes to represent, and to pass from one to another, like the same soul successively animating different bodies. By an art like that of the ventriloquist, he throws his imagination out of himself, and makes every word appear to proceed from the mouth of the person in whose name it is given. His plays alone are properly expressions of the passions, not descriptions of them. His characters are real beings of flesh and blood; they speak like men, not like authors. One might suppose that he had stood by at the time, and overheard what passed. As in our dreams we hold conversations with ourselves, make remarks, or communicate intelligence, and have no idea of the answer which we shall receive, and which we ourselves make, till we hear it: so the dialogues in Shakespeare are carried on without any consciousness of what is to follow, without any appearance of preparation or premeditation. The gusts of passion come and go like sounds of music borne on the wind. Nothing is made out by formal inference and analogy, by climax and antithesis: all comes, or seems to come, immediately from nature. Each object and circumstance exists in his mind, as it would have existed in reality: each several train of thought and feeling goes on of itself, without confusion or effort. In the world of his imagination, every thing has a life, a place, and being of its own!

Chaucer's characters are sufficiently distinct from one another, but they are too little varied in themselves, too much like identical propositions. They are consistent, but uniform; we get no new idea of them from first to last; they are not placed in different lights, nor are their subordinate *traits* brought out in new situations; they are like portraits or physiognomical studies, with the distinguishing features marked with inconceivable truth and precision, but that preserve the same unaltered air and attitude. Shakespeare's are historical figures, equally true and correct, but put into action, where every nerve and muscle is displayed in the struggle with others, with all the effect of collision and contrast, with every variety of light and shade. Chaucer's characters are narrative, Shakespeare's dramatic, Milton's epic. That is, Chaucer told only as much of his story as he pleased, as was required for a particular purpose. He answered for his characters himself. In Shakespeare they are introduced upon the stage, are liable to be asked all sorts of questions, and are forced to answer for themselves. In Chaucer we perceive a fixed essence of character. In Shakespeare there is a continual composition and decomposition of its elements, a fermentation of every particle in the whole mass, by its alternate affinity or antipathy to other principles which are brought in contact with it. Till the experiment is tried, we do not know the result, the turn which the character will take in its new circumstances. Milton took only a few simple principles of character, and raised them to the utmost conceivable grandeur, and refined them from every base alloy. His imagination, 'nigh sphered in Heaven',[22] claimed kindred only with what he saw from that height, and could raise to the same elevation with itself. He sat retired and kept his state alone, 'playing with wisdom';[23] while Shakespeare mingled with the crowd, and played the host, 'to make society the sweeter welcome'.[24]

The passion in Shakespeare is of the same nature as his delineation of character. It is not some one habitual feeling or sentiment preying upon itself, growing out of itself, and moulding every thing to itself; it is passion modified by passion, by all the other feelings to which the individual is liable, and to which others are liable with him; subject to all the fluctuations of caprice and accident; calling into play all the resources of the understanding and all the energies of the will; irritated by obstacles or yielding to them; rising from small beginnings to its utmost height; now drunk with hope, now stung to madness, now sunk in despair, now blown to air with a breath, now raging like a torrent. The human soul is made the sport of fortune, the prey of adversity: it is stretched on the wheel of destiny, in restless ecstasy. The passions are in a state of projection. Years are melted down to moments, and every instant teems with fate. We know the results, we see the process. Thus after Iago has been boasting to himself of the effect of his poisonous suggestions on the mind of Othello, 'which, with a little act upon the blood, will work like mines of sulphur',[25] he adds –

'Look where he comes! not poppy, nor mandragora,
Nor all the drowsy syrups of the East,
Shall ever medicine thee to that sweet sleep
Which thou ow'dst yesterday.' –

And he enters at this moment, like the crested serpent, crowned with his wrongs and raging for revenge! The whole depends upon the turn of a thought. A word, a look, blows the spark of jealousy into a flame; and the explosion is immediate and terrible as a volcano. The dialogues in *Lear*, in *Macbeth*, that between Brutus and Cassius, and nearly all those in Shakespeare, where the interest is wrought up to its highest pitch, afford examples of this dramatic fluctuation of passion. The interest in Chaucer is quite different; it is like the course of a river, strong, and full, and increasing. In Shakespeare, on the contrary, it is like the sea, agitated this way and that, and loud-lashed by furious storms; while in the still pauses of the blast, we distinguish only the cries of despair, or the silence of death! Milton, on the other hand, takes the imaginative part of passion – that which remains after the event, which the mind reposes on when all is over, which looks upon circumstances from the remotest elevation of thought and fancy, and abstracts them from the world of action to that of contemplation. The objects of dramatic poetry affect us by sympathy, by their nearness to ourselves, as they take us by surprise, or force us upon action, 'while rage with rage doth sympathize':[26] the objects of epic poetry affect us through the medium of the imagination, by magnitude and distance, by their permanence and universality. The one fill us with terror and pity, the other with admiration and delight. There are certain objects that strike the imagination, and inspire awe in the very idea of them, independently of any dramatic interest, that is, of any connexion with the vicissitudes of human life. For instance, we cannot think of the pyramids of Egypt, of a Gothic ruin, or an old Roman encampment, without a certain emotion, a sense of power and sublimity coming over the mind. The heavenly bodies that hang over our heads wherever we go, and 'in their untroubled element shall shine when we are laid in dust, and all our cares forgotten',[27] affect us in the same way. Thus Satan's address[28] to the Sun has an epic, not a dramatic interest; for though the second person in the dialogue makes no answer and feels no concern, yet the eye of that vast luminary is upon him, like the eye of heaven, and seems conscious of what he says, like an universal presence. Dramatic poetry and epic, in their perfection, indeed, approximate to and strengthen one another. Dramatic poetry borrows aid from the dignity of persons and things, as the heroic does from human passion, but in theory they are distinct. – When Richard II calls for the looking-glass to contemplate his faded majesty in it, and bursts into that affecting exclamation: 'Oh, that I were a mockery-king of snow, to melt away before the sun of Bolingbroke',[29] we have here the utmost force of human passion, combined with the ideas of regal splendour and fallen power. When Milton says of Satan:

> '—— His form had not yet lost
> All her original brightness, nor appear'd
> Less than archangel ruin'd, and th' excess
> Of glory obscur'd;' —[30]

the mixture of beauty, of grandeur, and pathos, from the sense of irreparable loss, of never-ending, unavailing regret, is perfect.

The great fault of a modern school of poetry is, that it is an experiment to reduce poetry to a mere effusion[31] of natural sensibility; or what is worse, to divest it both of imaginary splendour and human passion, to surround the meanest objects with the morbid feelings and devouring egotism of the writers' own minds. Milton and Shakespeare did not so understand poetry. They gave a more liberal interpretation both to nature and art. They did not do all they could to get rid of the one and the other, to fill up the dreary void with the Moods of their own Minds.[32] They owe their power over the human mind to their having had a deeper sense than others of what was grand in the objects of nature, or affecting in the events of human life. But to the men I speak of there is nothing interesting, nothing heroical, but themselves. To them the fall of gods or of great men is the same. They do not enter into the feeling. They cannot understand the terms. They are even debarred from the last poor, paltry consolation of an unmanly triumph over fallen greatness; for their minds reject, with a convulsive effort and intolerable loathing, the very idea that there ever was, or was thought to be, any thing superior to themselves. All that has ever excited the attention or admiration of the world, they look upon with the most perfect indifference; and they are surprised to find that the world repays their indifference with scorn. 'With what measure they mete, it has been meted to them again.'[33]

Shakespeare's imagination is of the same plastic kind as his conception of character or passion. 'It glances from heaven to earth, from earth to heaven.'[34] Its movement is rapid and devious. It unites the most opposite extremes; or, as Puck says, in boasting of his own feats, 'puts a girdle round about the earth in forty minutes'.[35] He seems always hurrying from his subject, even while describing it; but the stroke, like the lightning's, is sure as it is sudden. He takes the widest possible range, but from that very range he has his choice of the greatest variety and aptitude of materials. He brings together images the most alike, but placed at the greatest distance from each other; that is, found in circumstances of the greatest dissimilitude. From the remoteness of his combinations, and the celerity with which they are effected, they coalesce the more indissolubly together. The more the thoughts are strangers to each other, and the longer they have been kept asunder, the more intimate does their union seem to become. Their felicity is equal to their force. Their likeness is made more dazzling by their novelty. They startle, and take the fancy prisoner in the same instant. I will mention one or two which are very striking, and not much known, out of *Troilus and Cressida*. Æneas says to Agamemnon,

> 'I ask that I may waken reverence,
> And on the cheek be ready with a blush
> Modest as morning, when she coldly eyes
> The youthful Phœbus.'[36]

Ulysses urging Achilles to show himself in the field, says –

> 'No man is the lord of any thing,
> Till he communicate his parts to others:
> Nor doth he of himself know them for aught,
> Till he behold them formed in the applause,

> Where they're extended! which like an arch reverberates
> The voice again, or like a gate of steel,
> Fronting the sun, receives and renders back
> Its figure and its heat.'[37]

Patroclus gives the indolent warrior the same advice.

> 'Rouse yourself; and the weak wanton Cupid
> Shall from your neck unloose his amorous fold,
> And like a dew-drop from the lion's mane
> Be shook to air.'[38]

Shakespeare's language and versification are like the rest of him. He has a magic power over words: they come winged at his bidding; and seem to know their places. They are struck out at a heat, on the spur of the occasion, and have all the truth and vividness which arise from an actual impression of the objects. His epithets and single phrases are like sparkles, thrown off from an imagination, fired by the whirling rapidity of its own motion. His language is hieroglyphical. It translates thoughts into visible images. It abounds in sudden transitions and elliptical expressions. This is the source of his mixed metaphors, which are only abbreviated forms of speech. These, however, give no pain from long custom. They have, in fact, become idioms in the language. They are the building, and not the scaffolding to thought. We take the meaning and effect of a well-known passage entire, and no more stop to scan and spell out the particular words and phrases, than the syllables of which they are composed. In trying to recollect any other author, one sometimes stumbles, in case of failure, on a word as good. In Shakespeare, any other word but the true one, is sure to be wrong.[39] If any body, for instance, could not recollect the words of the following description,

> '———— Light thickens,
> And the crow makes wing to the rooky wood,'[40]

he would be greatly at a loss to substitute others for them equally expressive of the feeling. These remarks, however, are strictly applicable only to the impassioned parts of Shakespeare's language, which flowed from the warmth and originality of his imagination, and were his own. The language used for prose conversation and ordinary business is sometimes technical, and involved in the affectation of the time. Compare, for example, Othello's apology to the senate, relating 'his whole course of love',[41] with some of the preceding parts relating to his appointment, and the official dispatches from Cyprus. In this respect, 'the business of the state does him offence'. —[42] His versification is no less powerful, sweet, and varied. It has every occasional excellence, of sullen intricacy, crabbed and perplexed, or of the smoothest and loftiest expansion — from the ease and familiarity of measured conversation to the lyrical sounds

> '—— Of ditties highly penned,
> Sung by a fair queen in a summer's bower,
> With ravishing division to her lute.'[43]

It is the only blank verse in the language, except Milton's, that for itself is readable. It is not stately and uniformly swelling like his, but varied and broken by the inequalities of the ground it has to pass over in its uncertain course,

> 'And so by many winding nooks it strays,
> With willing sport to the wild ocean.'[44]

It remains to speak of the faults of Shakespeare. They are not so many or so great as they have been represented; what there are, are chiefly owing to the following causes: — The universality of his genius was, perhaps, a disadvantage to his single works; the variety of his resources, sometimes diverting him from applying them to the most effectual purposes. He might be said to combine the powers of Æschylus and Aristophanes, of Dante and Rabelais, in his own mind. If he had been only half what he was, he would perhaps have appeared greater. The natural ease and indifference of his temper made him sometimes less scrupulous than he might have been. He is relaxed and careless in critical places; he is in earnest throughout only in *Timon, Macbeth,* and *Lear.* Again, he had no models of acknowledged excellence constantly in view to stimulate his efforts, and by all that appears, no love of fame. He wrote for the 'great vulgar and the small',[45] in his time, not for posterity. If Queen Elizabeth and the maids of honour laughed heartily at his worst jokes, and the catcalls in the gallery were silent at his best passages, he went home satisfied, and slept the next night well. He did not trouble himself about Voltaire's criticisms.[46] He was willing to take advantage of the ignorance of the age in many things; and if his plays pleased others, not to quarrel with them himself. His very facility of production would make him set less value on his own excellences, and not care to distinguish nicely between what he did well or ill. His blunders in chronology and geography do not amount to above half a dozen, and they are offences against chronology and geography, not against poetry. As to the unities, he was right in setting them at defiance. He was fonder of puns than became so great a man. His barbarisms were those of his age. His genius was his own. He had no objection to float down with the stream of common taste and opinion: he rose above it by his own buoyancy, and an impulse which he could not keep under, in spite of himself or others, and 'his delights did show most dolphin-like'.[47]

He had an equal genius for comedy and tragedy; and his tragedies are better than his comedies, because tragedy is better than comedy. His female characters, which have been found fault with as insipid, are the finest in the world. Lastly, Shakespeare was the least of a coxcomb of any one that ever lived, and much of a gentleman.

Shakespeare discovers in his writings little religious enthusiasm, and an indifference to personal reputation; he had none of the bigotry of his age, and his political prejudices were not very strong. In these respects, as well as in every other, he formed a direct contrast to Milton. Milton's works are a perpetual invocation to the Muses; a hymn to Fame. He had his thoughts constantly fixed on the contemplation of the Hebrew theocracy, and of a perfect commonwealth; and he seized the pen with a hand just warm from the touch of the ark of faith.[48] His religious zeal infused its character into his imagination; so that he devotes himself with the same sense of duty to the cultivation of his genius, as he did to the exercise of virtue, or the good of his country. The spirit of the poet, the patriot, and the prophet, vied with each other in his breast. His mind appears to have held equal communion with the inspired writers, and with the bards and sages of ancient Greece and Rome; –

> 'Blind Thamyris, and blind Mæonides,
> And Tiresias, and Phineus, prophets old.'[49]

He had a high standard, with which he was always comparing himself, nothing short of which could satisfy his jealous ambition. He thought of nobler forms and nobler things than those he found about him. He lived apart, in the solitude of his own thoughts, carefully excluding from his mind whatever might distract its purposes or alloy its purity, or damp its zeal. 'With darkness and with dangers compassed round',[50] he had the mighty models of antiquity always present to his thoughts, and determined to raise a monument of equal height and glory, 'piling up every stone of lustre from the brook',[51] for the delight and wonder of posterity. He had girded himself up, and as it were, sanctified his genius to this service from his youth. 'For after', he says, 'I had from my first years, by the ceaseless diligence and care of my father, been exercised to the tongues, and some sciences as my age could suffer, by sundry masters and teachers, it was found that whether aught was imposed upon me by them, or betaken to of my own choice, the style by certain vital signs it had, was likely to live; but much latelier, in the private academies of Italy, perceiving that some trifles which I had in memory, composed at under twenty or thereabout, met with acceptance above what was looked for; I began thus far to assent both to them and divers of my friends here at home, and not less to an inward prompting which now grew daily upon me, that by labour and intense study (which I take to be my portion in this life), joined with the strong propensity of nature, I might perhaps leave something so written to after-times as they should not willingly let it die. The accomplishment of these intentions, which have lived within me ever since I could conceive myself any thing worth to my country, lies not but in a power above man's to promise; but that none hath by more studious ways endeavoured, and with more unwearied spirit that none shall, that I dare almost aver of myself, as far as life and free leisure will extend. Neither do I think it shame to covenant with any knowing reader, that for some few years yet, I may go on trust with him toward the payment of what I am now indebted, as being a work not to be raised from the heat of youth or the vapours of wine; like that which flows at waste from the pen of some vulgar amourist, or the trencher fury of a rhyming parasite, nor to be obtained by the invocation of Dame Memory and her Siren daughters, but by devout prayer to that eternal spirit who can enrich with all utterance and knowledge, and sends out his Seraphim with the hallowed fire of his altar, to touch and purify the lips of whom he pleases: to this must be added industrious and select reading, steady observation, and insight into all seemly and generous arts and affairs. Although it nothing content me to have disclosed thus much before-hand; but that I trust hereby to make it manifest with what small willingness I endure to interrupt the pursuit of no less hopes than these, and leave a calm and pleasing solitariness, fed with cheerful and confident thoughts, to embark in a troubled sea of noises and hoarse disputes, from beholding the bright countenance of truth in the quiet and still air of delightful studies.'[52]

So that of Spenser:

> 'The noble heart that harbours virtuous thought,
>   And is with child of glorious great intent,
> Can never rest until it forth have brought
>   The eternal brood of glory excellent.'[53]

Milton, therefore, did not write from casual impulse, but after a severe examination of his own strength, and with a resolution to leave nothing undone which it was in his power to do. He always labours, and almost always succeeds. He strives hard to say the finest things in the world, and he does say them. He adorns and dignifies his subject to the utmost: he surrounds it with every possible association of beauty or grandeur, whether moral, intellectual, or physical. He refines on his descriptions of beauty; loading sweets on sweets, till the sense aches at them; and raises his images of terror to a gigantic elevation, that 'makes Ossa like a wart'.[54] In Milton, there is always an appearance of effort: in Shakespeare, scarcely any.

Milton has borrowed more than any other writer, and exhausted every source of imitation, sacred or profane; yet he is perfectly distinct from every other writer. He is a writer of centos, and yet in originality scarcely inferior to Homer. The power of his mind is stamped on every line. The fervour of his imagination melts down and renders malleable, as in a furnace, the most contradictory materials. In reading his works, we feel ourselves under the influence of a mighty intellect, that the nearer it approaches to others, becomes more distinct from them. The quantity of art in him shows the strength of his genius: the weight of his intellectual obligations would have oppressed any other writer. Milton's learning has the effect of intuition. He describes objects, of which he could only have read in books, with the vividness of actual observation. His imagination has the force of nature. He makes words tell as pictures.

> 'Him followed Rimmon, whose delightful seat
> Was fair Damascus, on the fertile banks
> Of Abbana and Pharphar, lucid streams.'[55]

The word *lucid* here gives to the idea all the sparkling effect of the most perfect landscape.

And again:

> 'As when a vulture on Imaus bred,
> Whose snowy ridge the roving Tartar bounds,
> Dislodging from a region scarce of prey,
> To gorge the flesh of lambs and yeanling kids
> On hills where flocks are fed, flies towards the springs
> Of Ganges or Hydaspes, Indian streams;
> But in his way lights on the barren plains
> Of Sericana, where Chineses drive
> With sails and wind their cany waggons light.'[56]

If Milton had taken a journey for the express purpose, he could not have described this scenery and mode of life better. Such passages are like demonstrations of natural history. Instances might be multiplied without end.

We might be tempted to suppose that the vividness with which he describes visible objects, was owing to their having acquired an unusual degree of strength in his mind, after the privation of his sight; but we find the same palpableness and truth in the descriptions which occur in his early poems. In 'Lycidas' he speaks of 'the great vision of the guarded mount',[57] with that preternatural weight of impression with which it would present itself suddenly to 'the pilot of some small night-foundered skiff':[58] and the lines in the 'Penseroso', describing 'the wandering moon,

> 'Riding near her highest noon,
> Like one that had been led astray
> Through the heaven's wide pathless way',[59]

are as if he had gazed himself blind in looking at her. There is also the same depth of impression in his descriptions of the objects of all the different senses, whether colours, or sounds, or smells – the same absorption of his mind in whatever engaged his attention at the time. It has been indeed objected to Milton, by a common perversity of criticism, that his ideas were musical rather than picturesque, as if because they were in the highest degree musical, they must be (to keep the sage critical balance even, and to allow no one man to possess two qualities at the same time) proportionably deficient in other respects. But Milton's poetry is not cast in any such narrow, commonplace mould; it is not so barren of resources. His worship of the Muse was not so simple or confined. A sound arises 'like a steam of rich distilled perfumes';[60] we hear the pealing organ, but the incense on the altars is also there, and the statues of the gods are ranged around! The ear indeed predominates over the eye, because it is more immediately affected, and because the language of music blends more immediately with, and forms a more natural accompaniment to, the variable and indefinite associations of ideas conveyed by words. But where the associations of the imagination are not the principal thing, the individual object is given by Milton with equal force and beauty. The strongest and best proof of this, as a characteristic power of his mind, is, that the persons of Adam and Eve, of Satan, &c. are always accompanied, in our imagination, with the grandeur of the naked figure; they convey to us the ideas of sculpture. As an instance, take the following:

'—— He soon
Saw within ken a glorious Angel stand,
The same whom John saw also in the sun:
His back was turned, but not his brightness hid;
Of beaming sunny rays a golden tiar
Circled his head, nor less his locks behind
Illustrious on his shoulders fledge with wings
Lay waving round; on some great charge employ'd
He seem'd, or fix'd in cogitation deep.
Glad was the spirit impure, as now in hope
To find who might direct his wand'ring flight
To Paradise, the happy seat of man,
His journey's end, and our beginning woe.
But first he casts to change his proper shape,
Which else might work him danger or delay:
And now a stripling cherub he appears,
Not of the prime, yet such as in his face
Youth smiled celestial, and to every limb
Suitable grace diffus'd, so well he feign'd:
Under a coronet his flowing hair
In curls on either cheek play'd; wings he wore
Of many a colour'd plume sprinkled with gold,
His habit fit for speed succinct, and held
Before his decent steps a silver wand.'[61]

The figures introduced here have all the elegance and precision of a Greek statue; glossy and impurpled, tinged with golden light, and musical as the strings of Memnon's harp!

Again, nothing can be more magnificent than the portrait of Beelzebub:

'With Atlantean shoulders fit to bear
The weight of mightiest monarchies':[62]

Or the comparison of Satan, as he 'lay floating many a rood', to 'that sea beast,

'Leviathan, which God of all his works
Created hugest that swim the ocean-stream!'[65]

What a force of imagination is there in this last expression! What an idea it conveys of the size of that hugest of created beings, as if it shrunk up the ocean to a stream, and took up the sea in its nostrils as a very little thing! Force of style is one of Milton's greatest excellences. Hence, perhaps, he stimulates us more in the reading, and less afterwards. The way to defend Milton against all impugners, is to take down the book and read it.

Milton's blank verse is the only blank verse in the language (except Shakespeare's) that deserves the name of verse. Dr Johnson, who had modelled his ideas of versification on the regular sing-song of Pope, condemns the *Paradise Lost* as harsh and unequal.[64] I shall not pretend to say that this is not sometimes the case; for where a degree of excellence beyond the mechanical rules of art is attempted, the poet must sometimes fail. But I imagine that there are more perfect examples in Milton of musical expression, or of an adaptation of the sound and movement of the verse to the meaning of the passage, than in all our other writers, whether of rhyme or blank verse, put together, (with the exception already mentioned). Spenser is the most harmonious of our stanza writers, as Dryden is the most sounding and varied of our rhymists. But in neither is there any thing like the same ear for music, the same power of approximating the varieties of poetical to those of musical rhythm, as there is in our great epic poet. The sound of his lines is moulded into the expression of the sentiment, almost of the very image. They rise or fall, pause or hurry rapidly on, with exquisite art, but without the least trick or affectation, as the occasion seems to require.

The following are some of the finest instances:

'—— His hand was known
In Heaven by many a tower'd structure high; —
Nor was his name unheard or unador'd
In ancient Greece: and in the Ausonian land

Men called him Mulciber: and how he fell
From Heaven, they fabled, thrown by angry Jove
Sheer o'er the chrystal battlements; from morn
To noon he fell, from noon to dewy eve,
A summer's day; and with the setting sun
Dropt from the zenith like a falling star
On Lemnos, the Ægean isle: thus they relate,
Erring.' —[65]

*

'—— But chief the spacious hall
Thick swarm'd, both on the ground and in the air,
Brush'd with the hiss of rustling wings. As bees
In spring time, when the sun with Taurus rides,
Pour forth their populous youth about the hive
In clusters; they among fresh dews and flow'rs
Fly to and fro: or on the smoothed plank,
The suburb of their straw-built citadel,
New rubb'd with balm, expatiate and confer
Their state affairs. So thick the airy crowd
Swarm'd and were straiten'd; till the signal giv'n,
Behold a wonder! They but now who seem'd
In bigness to surpass earth's giant sons,
Now less than smallest dwarfs, in narrow room
Throng numberless, like that Pygmean race
Beyond the Indian mount, or fairy elves,
Whose midnight revels by a forest side
Or fountain, some belated peasant sees,
Or dreams he sees, while over-head the moon
Sits arbitress, and nearer to the earth
Wheels her pale course: they on their mirth and dance
Intent, with jocund music charm his ear;
At once with joy and fear his heart rebounds.'[66]

I can only give another instance, though I have some difficulty in leaving off.

'Round he surveys (and well might, where he stood
So high above the circling canopy
Of night's extended shade) from th' eastern point
Of Libra to the fleecy star that bears
Andromeda far off Atlantic seas
Beyond the horizon: then from pole to pole
He views in breadth, and without longer pause
Down right into the world's first region throws
His flight precipitant, and winds with ease
Through the pure marble air his oblique way
Amongst innumerable stars that shone
Stars distant, but nigh hand seem'd other worlds;
Or other worlds they seem'd or happy isles,' &c.[67]

The verse, in this exquisitely modulated passage, floats up and down as if it had itself wings. Milton has himself given us the theory of his versification –

'Such as the meeting soul may pierce
In notes with many a winding bout
Of linked sweetness long drawn out.'[68]

Dr Johnson and Pope would have converted his vaulting Pegasus into a rocking-horse. Read any other blank verse but Milton's, – Thomson's, Young's, Cowper's, Wordsworth's, – and it will be found, from the want of the same insight into 'the hidden soul of harmony',[69] to be mere lumbering prose.

To proceed to a consideration of the merits of *Paradise Lost*, in the most essential point of view, I mean as to the poetry of character and passion. I shall say nothing of the fable, or of other technical objections or excellences; but I shall try to explain at once the foundation of the interest belonging to the poem. I am ready to give up the dialogues in Heaven, where, as Pope justly observes, 'God the Father turns a school-divine';[70] nor do I consider the battle of the angels as the climax of sublimity, or the most successful effort of Milton's pen. In a word, the interest of the poem arises from the daring ambition and fierce passions of Satan, and from the account of the paradisaical happiness, and the loss of it by our first parents. Three-fourths of the work are taken up with these characters, and nearly all that relates to them is unmixed sublimity and beauty. The two first books alone are like two massy pillars of solid gold.

Satan is the most heroic subject that ever was chosen for a poem; and the execution is as perfect as the design is lofty. He was the first of created beings, who, for endeavouring to be equal with the highest, and to divide the empire of heaven with the Almighty, was hurled down to hell. His aim was no less than the throne of the universe; his means, myriads of angelic armies bright, the third part of the heavens, whom he lured after him with his countenance, and who durst defy the Omnipotent in arms. His ambition was the greatest, and his punishment was the greatest; but not so his despair, for his fortitude was as great as his sufferings. His strength of mind was matchless as his strength of body; the vastness of his designs did not surpass the firm, inflexible determination with which he submitted to his irreversible doom, and final loss of all good. His power of action and of suffering was equal. He was the greatest power that was ever overthrown, with the strongest will left to resist or to endure. He was baffled, not confounded. He stood like a tower; or

> '—— As when Heaven's fire
> Hath scathed the forest oaks or mountain pines.'[71]

He was still surrounded with hosts of rebel angels, armed warriors, who own him as their sovereign leader, and with whose fate he sympathizes as he views them round, far as the eye can reach; though he keeps aloof from them in his own mind, and holds supreme counsel only with his own breast. An outcast from Heaven, Hell trembles beneath his feet, Sin and Death are at his heels, and mankind are his easy prey.

> 'All is not lost; th' unconquerable will,
> And study of revenge, immortal hate,
> And courage never to submit or yield,
> And what else is not to be overcome',[72]

are still his. The sense of his punishment seems lost in the magnitude of it; the fierceness of tormenting flames is qualified and made innoxious by the greater fierceness of his pride; the loss of infinite happiness to himself is compensated in thought, by the power of inflicting infinite misery on others. Yet Satan is not the principle of malignity, or of the abstract love of evil – but of the abstract love of power, of pride, of self-will personified, to which last principle all other good and evil, and even his own, are subordinate. From this principle he never once flinches. His love of power and contempt for suffering are never once relaxed from the highest pitch of intensity. His thoughts burn like a hell within him;[73] but the power of thought holds dominion in his mind over every other consideration. The consciousness of a determined purpose, of 'that intellectual being, those thoughts that wander through eternity',[74] though accompanied with endless pain, he prefers to nonentity, to 'being swallowed up and lost in the wide womb of uncreated night'.[75] He expresses the sum and substance of all ambition in one line. 'Fallen cherub, to be weak is miserable, doing or suffering!'[76] After such a conflict as his, and such a defeat, to retreat in order, to rally, to make terms, to exist at all, is something; but he does more than this – he founds a new empire in hell, and from it conquers this new world, whither he bends his undaunted flight, forcing his way through nether and surrounding fires. The poet has not in all this given us a mere shadowy outline; the strength is equal to the magnitude of the conception. The Achilles of Homer is not more distinct; the Titans were not more vast; Prometheus chained to his rock was not a more terrific example of suffering and of crime. Wherever the figure of Satan is introduced, whether he walks or flies, 'rising aloft incumbent on the dusky air',[77] it is illustrated with the most striking and appropriate images: so that we see it always before us, gigantic, irregular, portentous, uneasy, and disturbed – but dazzling in its faded splendour, the clouded ruins of a god. The deformity of Satan is only in the depravity of his will; he has no bodily deformity to excite our loathing or disgust. The horns and tail are not there, poor emblems of the unbending, uncon-quered spirit, of the writhing agonies within. Milton was too magnani-mous and open an antagonist to support his argument by the bye-tricks of a hump and cloven foot; to bring into the fair field of controversy the good old catholic prejudices of which Tasso and Dante have availed themselves, and which the mystic German critics would restore. He relied on the justice of his cause, and did not scruple to give the devil his due. Some persons may think that he has carried his liberality too far, and injured the cause he professed to espouse by making him the chief person in his poem. Considering the nature of his subject, he would be equally in danger of running into this fault, from his faith in religion, and his love of rebellion; and perhaps each of these motives had its full share in determining the choice of his subject.

Not only the figure of Satan, but his speeches in council, his soliloquies, his address to Eve, his share in the war in heaven, or in the fall of man, shew the same decided superiority of character. To give only one instance, almost the first speech he makes:

> 'Is this the region, this the soil, the clime,
> Said then the lost archangel, this the seat
> That we must change for Heaven; this mournful gloom
> For that celestial light? Be it so, since he
> Who now is sov'rain can dispose and bid
> What shall be right: farthest from him is best,
> Whom reason hath equal'd, force hath made supreme
> Above his equals. Farewel happy fields,
> Where joy for ever dwells: Hail horrors, hail
> Infernal world, and thou profoundest Hell,
> Receive thy new possessor; one who brings
> A mind not to be chang'd by place or time.
> The mind is its own place, and in itself
> Can make a Heav'n of Hell, a Hell of Heav'n.
> What matter where, if I be still the same,
> And what I should be, all but less than he
> Whom thunder hath made greater? Here at least
> We shall be free; th' Almighty hath not built
> Here for his envy, will not drive us hence:
> Here we may reign secure, and in my choice
> To reign is worth ambition, though in Hell:
> Better to reign in Hell, than serve in Heaven.'[78]

The whole of the speeches and debates in Pandemonium are well worthy of the place and the occasion – with Gods for speakers, and angels and archangels for hearers. There is a decided manly tone in the arguments and sentiments, an eloquent dogmatism, as if each person spoke from thorough conviction; an excellence which Milton probably borrowed from his spirit of partisanship, or else his spirit of partisanship from the natural firmness and vigour of his mind. In this respect Milton resembles Dante, (the only modern writer with whom he has any thing in common) and it is remarkable that Dante, as well as Milton, was a political partisan. That approximation to the severity of impassioned prose which has been made an objection to Milton's poetry, and which is chiefly to be met with in these bitter invectives, is one of its great excellences. The author might here turn his philippics against Salmasius[79] to good account. The rout in heaven is like the fall of some mighty structure, nodding to its base, 'with hideous ruin and combustion down'.[80] But, perhaps, of all the passages in *Paradise Lost*, the description of the employments of the angels during the absence of Satan, some of whom 'retreated in a silent valley, sing with notes angelical to many a harp their own heroic deeds and hapless fall by doom of battle',[81] is the most perfect example of mingled pathos and sublimity. – What proves the truth of this noble picture in every part, and that the frequent complaint of want of interest in it is the fault of the reader, not of the poet, is that when any interest of a practical kind take a shape that can be at all turned into this, (and there is little doubt that Milton had some such in his eye in writing it,) each party converts it to its own purposes, feels the absolute identity of these abstracted and high speculations; and that, in fact, a noted political writer of the present day[82] has exhausted nearly the whole account of Satan in the *Paradise Lost*, by applying it to a character whom he considered as after the devil, (though I do not know whether he would make even that exception) the greatest enemy of the human race. This may serve to show that Milton's Satan is not a very insipid personage.

Of Adam and Eve it has been said, that the ordinary reader can feel little interest in them, because they have none of the passions, pursuits, or even relations of human life, except that of man and wife, the least interesting of all others, if not to the parties concerned, at least to the by-standers. The preference has on this account been given to Homer, who, it is said, has left very vivid and infinitely diversified pictures of all the passions and affections, public and private, incident to human nature – the relations of son, of brother, parent, friend, citizen, and many others. Longinus preferred the *Iliad* to the *Odyssey*,[85] on account of the greater number of battles it contains; but I can neither agree to his criticism, nor assent to the present objection. It is true, there is little action in this part of Milton's poem; but there is much repose, and more enjoyment. There are none of the every-day occurrences, contentions, disputes, wars, fightings, feuds, jealousies, trades, professions, liveries, and common handicrafts of life; 'no kind of traffic; letters are not known; no use of service, of riches, poverty, contract, succession, bourne, bound of land, tilth, vineyard none; no occupation, no treason, felony, sword, pike, knife, gun, nor need of any engine'.[84] So much the better; thank heaven, all these were yet to come. But still the die was cast, and in them our doom was sealed. In them

> 'The generations were prepared; the pangs,
> The internal pangs, were ready, the dread strife
> Of poor humanity's afflicted will,
> Struggling in vain with ruthless destiny.'[85]

In their first false step we trace all our future woe,[86] with loss of Eden. But there was a short and precious interval between, like the first blush of morning before the day is overcast with tempest, the dawn of the world, the birth of nature from 'the unapparent deep',[87] with its first dews and freshness on its cheek, breathing odours. Theirs was the first delicious taste of life, and on them depended all that was to come of it. In them hung trembling all our hopes and fears. They were as yet alone in the world, in the eye of nature, wondering at their new being, full of enjoyment and enraptured with one another, with the voice of their Maker walking in the garden, and ministering angels attendant on their steps, winged messengers from heaven like rosy clouds descending in their sight. Nature played around them her virgin fancies wild; and spread for them a repast where no crude surfeit reigned. Was there nothing in this scene, which God and nature alone witnessed, to interest a modern critic? What need was there of action, where the heart was full of bliss and innocence without it! They had nothing to do but feel their own happiness, and 'know to know no more'.[88] 'They toiled not, neither did they spin; yet Solomon in all his glory was not arrayed like one of these.'[89] All things seem to acquire fresh sweetness, and to be clothed with fresh beauty in their sight. They tasted as it were for themselves and us, of all that there ever was pure in human bliss. 'In them the burthen of the mystery, the heavy and the weary weight of all this unintelligible world, is lightened.'[90] They stood awhile perfect, but they afterwards fell and were driven out of Paradise, tasting the first fruits of bitterness as they had done of bliss. But their pangs were such as a pure spirit might feel at the sight – their tears 'such as angels weep'.[91] The pathos is of that mild contemplative kind which arises from regret for the loss of unspeakable happiness, and resignation to inevitable fate. There is none of the fierceness of intemperate passion, none of the agony of mind and turbulence of action, which is the result of the habitual struggles of the will with circumstances, irritated by repeated disappointment, and constantly setting its desires most eagerly on that which there is an impossibility of attaining. This would have destroyed the beauty of the whole picture. They had received their unlooked-for happiness as a free gift from their Creator's hands, and they submitted to its loss, not without sorrow, but without impious and stubborn repining.

> 'In either hand the hast'ning angel caught
> Our ling'ring parents, and to th' eastern gate
> Led them direct, and down the cliff as fast
> To the subjected plain; then disappear'd.
> They looking back, all th' eastern side beheld
> Of Paradise, so late their happy seat,
> Wav'd over by that flaming brand, the gate
> With dreadful faces throng'd, and fiery arms:
> Some natural tears they dropt, but wip'd them soon;
> The world was all before them, where to choose
> Their place of rest, and Providence their guide.'[92]

'The Manager'

*

It is no insignificant epoch in one's life the first time that odd-looking thing, a play-bill, is left at our door in a little market-town in the country (say W—m in S—shire).[1] The Manager, somewhat fatter and more erect, 'as Manager beseems', than the rest of his company, with more of the man of business, and not less of the coxcomb, in his strut and manner, knocks at the door with the end of a walking cane (a badge of office!) and a bundle of papers under his arm; presents one of them printed in large capitals, with a respectful bow and a familiar shrug; hopes to give satisfaction in the town; hints at the liberal encouragement they received at W—ch,[2] the last place they stopped at; had every possible facility afforded by the Magistrates; supped one evening with the Rev. Mr J—s,[3] a dissenting clergyman, and really a very well-informed, agreeable, sensible man, full of anecdote – no illiberal prejudices against the profession: – then talks of the strength of his company, with a careless mention of his own favourite line – his benefit fixed for an early day, but would do himself the honour to leave farther particulars at a future opportunity – speaks of the stage as an elegant amusement, that most agreeably enlivened a spare evening or two in the week, and, under proper management (to which he himself paid the most assiduous attention), might be made of the greatest assistance to the cause of virtue and humanity – had seen Mr Garrick act the last night but one before his retiring from the stage – had himself had offers from the London boards, and indeed could not say he had given up all thoughts of one day surprising them – as it was, had no reason to repine – Mrs F— tolerably advanced in life – his eldest son a prodigious turn for the higher walks of tragedy – had said perhaps too much of himself –

had given universal satisfaction – hoped that the young gentleman
and lady, at least, would attend on the following evening, when the
West-Indian[4] would be performed at the market-hall, with the farce
of *No Song No Supper*[5] – and so having played his part, withdraws
in the full persuasion of having made a favourable impression, and
of meeting with every encouragement the place affords! Thus he
passes from house to house, and goes through the routine of topic
after topic, with that sort of modest assurance, which is indispensable
in the manager of a country theatre. This fellow, who floats over the
troubles of life as the froth above the idle wave, with all his little
expedients and disappointments, with pawned paste-buckles, mort-
gaged scenery, empty exchequer, and rebellious orchestra, is not of
all men the most miserable: – he is little less happy than a king,
though not much better off than a beggar. He has little to think of,
much to do, more to say; and is accompanied, in his incessant daily
round of trifling occupations, with a never-failing sense of authority
and self-importance, the one thing needful (above all others) to the
heart of man. This however is their man of business in the company;
he is a sort of fixture in their little state; like Nebuchadnezzar's image,[6]
but half of earth and half of finer metal: he is not 'of imagination all
compact':[7] he is not, like the rest of his aspiring crew, a feeder upon
air, a drinker of applause, tricked out in vanity and in nothing else;
he is not quite mad, nor quite happy. The whining Romeo, who goes
supperless to bed, and on his pallet of straw dreams of a crown of
laurel, of waving handkerchiefs, of bright eyes, and billets-doux
breathing boundless love: the ranting Richard, whose infuriate
execrations are drowned in the shouts of the all-ruling pit; he who,
without a coat to his back, or a groat in his purse, snatches at Cato's
robe, and binds the diadem of Cæsar on his brow; – these are the
men that Fancy has chosen for herself, and placed above the reach
of fortune, and almost of fate. They take no thought for the morrow.
What is it to them what they shall eat, or what they shall drink, or
how they shall be clothed?[8] 'Their mind to them a kingdom is.'[9] – It
is not a poor ten shillings a week, their share in the profits of the
theatre, with which they have to pay for bed, board, and lodging,
that bounds their wealth. They share (and not unequally) in all the
wealth, the pomp, and pleasures of the world. They wield sceptres,

conquer kingdoms, court princesses, are clothed in purple, and fare sumptuously every night. They taste, in imagination, 'of all earth's bliss, both living and loving':[10] whatever has been most the admiration or most the envy of mankind, they, for a moment, in their own eyes, and in the eyes of others, become. The poet fancies others to be this or that; the player fancies himself to be all that the poet but describes. A little rouge makes him a lover, a plume of feathers a hero, a brazen crown an emperor. Where will you buy rank, office, supreme delights, so cheap as at his shop of fancy? Is it nothing to dream whenever we please, and *seem* whatever we desire? Is real greatness, is real prosperity, more than what it seems? Where shall we find, or where shall the votary of the stage find, Fortunatus's Wishing Cap,[11] but in the wardrobe which we laugh at: or borrow the philosopher's stone[12] but from the *property-man* of the theatre? He has discovered the true Elixir of Life, which is freedom from care: he quaffs the pure *aurum potabile*,[13] which is popular applause. He who is smit with the love of this *ideal* existence, cannot be weaned from it. Hoot him from the stage, and he will stay to sweep the lobbies or shift the scenes. Offer him twice the salary to go into a counting-house, or stand behind a counter, and he will return to poverty, steeped in contempt, but eked out with fancy, at the end of a week. Make a laughing-stock of an actress, lower her salary, tell her she is too tall, awkward, stupid, and ugly; try to get rid of her all you can – she will remain, only to hear herself courted, to listen to the echo of her borrowed name, to live but one short minute in the lap of vanity and tinsel show. Will you give a man an additional ten shillings a week, and ask him to resign the fancied wealth of the world, which he 'by his so potent art'[14] can conjure up, and glad his eyes, and fill his heart with it? When a little change of dress, and the muttering a few talismanic words, make all the difference between the vagabond and the hero, what signifies the interval so easily passed? Would you not yourself consent to be alternately a beggar and a king, but that you have not the secret skill to be so? The player has that 'happy alchemy of mind;'[15] – why then would you reduce him to an equality with yourself? – The moral of this reasoning is known and felt, though it may be gainsaid. Wherever the players come, they send a welcome before them, and leave an air in the place behind them.* They shed a light upon the day, that does not very soon pass off. See how they glitter along the street, wandering, not where business but the bent of pleasure takes them, like mealy-coated butterflies, or insects flitting in the sun. They seem another, happier, idler race of mortals, prolonging the carelessness of childhood to old age, floating down the stream of life, or wafted by the wanton breeze to their final place of rest. We remember one (we must make the reader acquainted with him) who once overtook us loitering by 'Severn's sedgy side',[16] on a fine May morning, with a score of play-bills streaming from his pockets, for the use of the neighbouring villages, and a music-score in his hand, which he sang blithe and clear, advancing with light step and a loud voice! With a sprightly *bon jour*, he passed on, carolling to the echo of the babbling stream, brisk as a bird, gay as a mote, swift as an arrow from a twanging bow, heart-whole, and with shining face that shot back the sun's broad rays! — What is become of this favourite of mirth and song? Has care touched him? Has death tripped up his heels? Has an indigestion imprisoned him, and all his gaiety, in a living dungeon? Or is he himself lost and buried amidst the rubbish of one of our larger, or else of one of our Minor Theatres?

> —'Alas! how changed from him,
> That life of pleasure, and that soul of whim!'[17]

But as this was no doubt the height of his ambition, why should we wish to debar him of it?

* So the old song joyously celebrates their arrival: —

> 'The beggars are coming to town,
> Some in rags, and some in jags, and some in velvet gowns.'

*

The Indian Jugglers

Coming forward and seating himself on the ground in his white dress and tightened turban, the chief of the Indian Jugglers begins with tossing up two brass balls, which is what any of us could do, and concludes with keeping up four at the same time, which is what none of us could do to save our lives, nor if we were to take our whole lives to do it in. Is it then a trifling power we see at work, or is it not something next to miraculous? It is the utmost stretch of human ingenuity, which nothing but the bending the faculties of body and mind to it from the tenderest infancy with incessant, ever-anxious application up to manhood can accomplish or make even a slight approach to. Man, thou art a wonderful animal, and thy ways past finding out![1] Thou canst do strange things, but thou turnest them to little account! – To conceive of this effort of extraordinary dexterity distracts the imagination and makes admiration breathless. Yet it costs nothing to the performer, any more than if it were a mere mechanical deception with which he had nothing to do but to watch and laugh at the astonishment of the spectators. A single error of a hair's-breadth, of the smallest conceivable portion of time, would be fatal: the precision of the movements must be like a mathematical truth, their rapidity is like lightning. To catch four balls in succession in less than a second of time, and deliver them back so as to return with seeming consciousness to the hand again, to make them revolve round him at certain intervals, like the planets in their spheres, to make them chase one another like sparkles of fire, or shoot up like flowers or meteors, to throw them behind his back and twine them round his neck like ribbons or like serpents, to do what appears an impossibility, and to do it with all the ease, the grace, the carelessness imaginable, to laugh at, to play with the glittering mockeries, to follow them with his eye as if he could fascinate them with its lambent fire or as if he had only to see that they kept time with the music on the stage — there is something in all this which he who does not admire may be quite sure he never really admired any thing in the whole course of his life. It is skill surmounting difficulty, and beauty triumphing over skill. It seems as if the difficulty once mastered naturally resolved itself into ease and grace, and as if to be overcome at all, it must be overcome without an effort. The smallest awkwardness or want of pliancy or self-possession would stop the whole process. It is the work of witchcraft, and yet sport for children. Some of the other feats are quite as curious and wonderful, such as the balancing the artificial tree and shooting a bird from each branch through a quill; though none of them have the elegance or facility of the keeping up of the brass balls. You are in pain for the result and glad when the experiment is over; they are not accompanied with the same unmixed, unchecked delight as the former; and I would not give much to be merely astonished without being pleased at the same time. As to the swallowing of the sword, the police ought to interfere to prevent it. When I saw the Indian Juggler do the same things before, his feet were bare, and he had large rings on the toes, which kept turning round all the time of the performance, as if they moved of themselves. The hearing a speech in Parliament, drawled or stammered out by the Honourable Member or the Noble Lord, the ringing the changes on their common-places, which any one could repeat after them as well as they, stirs me not a jot, shakes not my good opinion of myself: but the seeing the Indian Jugglers does. It makes me ashamed of myself. I ask what there is that I can do as well as this? Nothing. What have I been doing all my life? Have I been idle, or have I nothing to show for all my labour and pains? Or have I passed my time in pouring words like water into empty sieves, rolling a stone up a hill and then down again,[2] trying to prove an argument in the teeth of facts, and looking for causes in the dark, and not finding them? Is there no one thing in which I can challenge competition, that I can bring as an instance of exact perfection, in which others cannot find a flaw? The utmost I can pretend to is to write a description of what this fellow can do. I can write a book: so can many others who have not even learned to spell. What abortions are these Essays! What errors, what ill-pieced transitions, what crooked reasons, what lame conclusions! How little is made out, and that little how ill! Yet they are the best I can do. I endeavour to recollect all I have ever observed or thought upon a subject, and to express it as nearly as I can. Instead of writing on four subjects at a time, it is as much as I can manage to keep the thread of one discourse clear and unentangled. I have also time on my hands to correct my opinions, and polish my periods: but the one I cannot, and the other I will not do. I am fond of arguing: yet with a good deal of pains and practice it is often as much as I can do to beat my man; though he may be a very indifferent hand. A common fencer would disarm his adversary in the twinkling of an eye, unless he were a professor like himself. A stroke of wit will sometimes produce this effect, but there is no such power or superiority in sense or reasoning. There is no complete mastery of execution to be shown there: and you hardly know the professor from the impudent pretender or the mere clown*.

I have always had this feeling of the inefficacy and slow progress of intellectual compared to mechanical excellence, and it has always made me somewhat dissatisfied. It is a great many years since I saw Richer, the famous rope-dancer, perform at Sadler's Wells. He was matchless in his art, and added to his extraordinary skill exquisite ease, and unaffected, natural grace. I was at that time employed in copying a half-length picture of Sir Joshua Reynolds's; and it put me out of conceit with it. How ill this part was made out in the drawing! How heavy, how slovenly this other was painted! I could not help saying to myself, 'If the rope-dancer had performed his task in this manner, leaving so many gaps and botches in his work, he would have broke his neck long ago; I should never have seen that vigorous

---

* The celebrated Peter Pindar (Dr Wolcot)⁵ first discovered and brought out the talents of the late Mr Opie, the painter. He was a poor Cornish boy, and was out at work in the fields, when the poet went in search of him. 'Well, my lad, can you go and bring me your very best picture?' The other flew like lightning, and soon came back with what he considered as his master-piece. The stranger looked at it, and the young artist, after waiting for some time without his giving any opinion, at length exclaimed eagerly, 'Well, what do you think of it?' — 'Think of it?' said Wolcot, 'why, I think you ought to be ashamed of it — that you who might do so well, do no better!' The same answer would have applied to this artist's latest performances, that had been suggested by one of his earliest efforts.

elasticity of nerve and precision of movement!' – Is it then so easy an undertaking (comparatively) to dance on a tight-rope? Let any one, who thinks so, get up and try. There is the thing. It is that which at first we cannot do at all, which in the end is done to such perfection. To account for this in some degree, I might observe that mechanical dexterity is confined to doing some one particular thing, which you can repeat as often as you please, in which you know whether you succeed or fail, and where the point of perfection consists in succeeding in a given undertaking. – In mechanical efforts, you improve by perpetual practice, and you do so infallibly, because the object to be attained is not a matter of taste or fancy or opinion, but of actual experiment, in which you must either do the thing or not do it. If a man is put to aim at a mark with a bow and arrow, he must hit it or miss it, that's certain. He cannot deceive himself, and go on shooting wide or falling short, and still fancy that he is making progress. The distinction between right and wrong, between true and false, is here palpable; and he must either correct his aim or persevere in his error with his eyes open, for which there is neither excuse nor temptation. If a man is learning to dance on a rope, if he does not mind what he is about, he will break his neck. After that, it will be in vain for him to argue that he did not make a false step. His situation is not like that of Goldsmith's pedagogue. –

> 'In argument they own'd his wondrous skill,
> And e'en though vanquish'd, he could argue still.'[4]

Danger is a good teacher, and makes apt scholars. So are disgrace, defeat, exposure to immediate scorn and laughter. There is no opportunity in such cases for self-delusion, no idling time away, no being off your guard (or you must take the consequences) – neither is there any room for humour or caprice or prejudice. If the Indian Juggler were to play tricks in throwing up the three case-knives, which keep their positions like the leaves of a crocus in the air, he would cut his fingers. I can make a very bad antithesis without cutting my fingers. The tact of style is more ambiguous than that of double-edged instruments. If the Juggler were told that by flinging himself under the wheels of the Jaggernaut,[5] when the idol issues forth on a gaudy day, he would immediately be transported into Paradise, he might believe it, and nobody could disprove it. So the Brahmins may say what they please on that subject, may build up dogmas and mysteries without end, and not be detected: but their ingenious countryman cannot persuade the frequenters of the Olympic Theatre that he performs a number of astonishing feats without actually giving proofs of what he says. — There is then in this sort of manual dexterity, first a gradual aptitude acquired to a given exertion of muscular power, from constant repetition, and in the next place, an exact knowledge how much is still wanting and necessary to be supplied. The obvious test is to increase the effort or nicety of the operation, and still to find it come true. The muscles ply instinctively to the dictates of habit. Certain movements and impressions of the hand and eye, having been repeated together an infinite number of times, are unconsciously but unavoidably cemented into closer and closer union; the limbs require little more than to be put in motion for them to follow a regular track with ease and certainty; so that the mere intention of the will acts mathematically like touching the spring of a machine, and you come with Locksley in *Ivanhoe*, in shooting at a mark, 'to allow for the wind'.⁶

Farther, what is meant by perfection in mechanical exercises is the performing certain feats to a uniform nicety, that is, in fact, undertaking no more than you can perform. You task yourself, the limit you fix is optional, and no more than human industry and skill can attain to: but you have no abstract, independent standard of difficulty or excellence (other than the extent of your own powers). Thus he who can keep up four brass balls does this *to perfection*; but he cannot keep up five at the same instant, and would fail every time he attempted it. That is, the mechanical performer undertakes to emulate himself, not to equal another.* But the artist undertakes to imitate another, or to do what nature has done, and this it appears is more difficult, *viz.* to copy what she has set before us in the face of nature or 'human face divine',⁷ entire and without a blemish, than to keep up four brass balls at the same instant, for the one is done by the power of human skill and industry, and the other never was nor will be. Upon the whole, therefore, I have more respect for

---

* If two persons play against each other at any game, one of them necessarily fails.

Reynolds, than I have for Richer; for, happen how it will, there have been more people in the world who could dance on a rope like the one than who could paint like Sir Joshua. The latter was but a bungler in his profession to the other, it is true; but then he had a harder task-master to obey, whose will was more wayward and obscure, and whose instructions it was more difficult to practise. You can put a child apprentice to a tumbler or rope-dancer with a comfortable prospect of success, if they are but sound of wind and limb: but you cannot do the same thing in painting. The odds are a million to one. You may make indeed as many H—s and H—s,[8] as you put into that sort of machine, but not one Reynolds amongst them all, with his grace, his grandeur, his blandness of *gusto*, 'in tones and gestures hit',[9] unless you could make the man over again. To snatch this grace beyond the reach of art is then the height of art[10] – where fine art begins, and where mechanical skill ends. The soft suffusion of the soul, the speechless breathing eloquence, the looks 'commercing with the skies',[11] the ever-shifting forms of an eternal principle, that which is seen but for a moment, but dwells in the heart always, and is only seized as it passes by strong and secret sympathy, must be taught by nature and genius, not by rules or study. It is suggested by feeling, not by laborious microscopic inspection: in seeking for it without, we lose the harmonious clue to it within: and in aiming to grasp the substance, we let the very spirit of art evaporate. In a word, the objects of fine art are not the objects of sight but as these last are the objects of taste and imagination, that is, as they appeal of the sense of beauty, of pleasure, and of power in the human breast, and are explained by that finer sense, and revealed in their inner structure to the eye in return. Nature is also a language. Objects, like words, have a meaning; and the true artist is the interpreter of this language, which he can only do by knowing its application to a thousand other objects in a thousand other situations. Thus the eye is too blind a guide of itself to distinguish between the warm or cold tone of a deep blue sky, but another sense acts as a monitor to it, and does not err. The colour of the leaves in autumn would be nothing without the feeling that accompanies it; but it is that feeling that stamps them on the canvas, faded, seared, blighted, shrinking from the winter's flaw,[12] and makes the sight as true as touch –

'And visions, as poetic eyes avow,
Cling to each leaf and hang on every bough.'[13]

The more ethereal, evanescent, more refined and sublime part of art is the seeing nature through the medium of sentiment and passion, as each object is a symbol of the affections and a link in the chain of our endless being. But the unravelling this mysterious web of thought and feeling is alone in the Muse's gift, namely, in the power of that trembling sensibility which is awake to every change and every modification of its ever-varying impressions, that

'Thrills in each nerve, and lives along the line.'[14]

This power is indifferently called genius, imagination, feeling, taste; but the manner in which it acts upon the mind can neither be defined by abstract rules, as is the case in science, nor verified by continual unvarying experiments, as is the case in mechanical performances. The mechanical excellence of the Dutch painters in colouring and handling is that which comes the nearest in fine art to the perfection of certain manual exhibitions of skill. The truth of the effect and the facility with which it is produced are equally admirable. Up to a certain point, every thing is faultless. The hand and eye have done their part. There is only a want of taste and genius. It is after we enter upon that enchanted ground that the human mind begins to droop and flag as in a strange road, or in a thick mist, benighted and making little way with many attempts and many failures, and that the best of us only escape with half a triumph. The undefined and the imaginary are the regions that we must pass like Satan, difficult and doubtful, 'half flying, half on foot'.[15] The object in sense is a positive thing, and execution comes with practice.

Cleverness is a certain *knack* or aptitude at doing certain things, which depend more on a particular adroitness and off-hand readiness than on force or perseverance, such as making puns, making epigrams, making extempore verses, mimicking the company, mimicking a style, &c. Cleverness is either liveliness and smartness, or something answering to *sleight of hand*, like letting a glass fall sideways off a table, or else a trick, like knowing the secret spring of a watch.

Accomplishments are certain external graces, which are to be learnt from others, and which are easily displayed to the admiration of the beholder, *viz.* dancing, riding, fencing, music, and so on. These ornamental acquirements are only proper to those who are at ease in mind and fortune. I know an individual[16] who if he had been born to an estate of five thousand a year, would have been the most accomplished gentleman of the age. He would have been the delight and envy of the circle in which he moved – would have graced by his manners the liberality flowing from the openness of his heart, would have laughed with the women, have argued with the men, have said good things and written agreeable ones, have taken a hand at piquet or the lead at the harpsichord, and have set and sung his own verses – *nugæ canoræ* [17] – with tenderness and spirit; a Rochester without the vice, a modern Surrey! As it is, all these capabilities of excellence stand in his way. He is too versatile for a professional man, not dull enough for a political drudge, too gay to be happy, too thoughtless to be rich. He wants the enthusiasm of the poet, the severity of the prose-writer, and the application of the man of business. – Talent is the capacity of doing any thing that depends on application and industry, such as writing a criticism, making a speech, studying the law. Talent differs from genius, as voluntary differs from involuntary power. Ingenuity is genius in trifles, greatness is genius in undertakings of much pith and moment. A clever or ingenious man is one who can do any thing well, whether it is worth doing or not: a great man is one who can do that which when done is of the highest importance. Themistocles said he could not play on the flute,[18] but that he could make of a small city a great one. This gives one a pretty good idea of the distinction in question.

Greatness is great power, producing great effects. It is not enough that a man has great power in himself, he must show it to all the world in a way that cannot be hid or gainsaid. He must fill up a certain idea in the public mind. I have no other notion of greatness than this two-fold definition, great results springing from great inherent energy. The great in visible objects has relation to that which extends over space: the great in mental ones has to do with space and time. No man is truly great, who is great only in his life-time. The test of greatness is the page of history. Nothing can be said to be great that has a distinct limit, or that borders on something evidently greater than itself. Besides, what is short-lived and pampered into mere notoriety, is of a gross and vulgar quality in itself. A Lord Mayor is hardly a great man. A city orator or patriot of the day only show, by reaching the height of their wishes, the distance they are at from any true ambition. Popularity is neither fame nor greatness. A king (as such) is not a great man. He has great power, but it is not his own. He merely wields the lever of the state, which a child, an idiot, or a madman can do. It is the office, not the man we gaze at. Any one else in the same situation would be just as much an object of abject curiosity. We laugh at the country girl who having seen a king expressed her disappointment by saying, 'Why, he is only a man!' Yet, knowing this, we run to see a king as if he was something more than a man. – To display the greatest powers, unless they are applied to great purposes, makes nothing for the character of greatness. To throw a barley-corn through the eye of a needle, to multiply nine figures by nine in the memory, argues infinite dexterity of body and capacity of mind, but nothing comes of either. There is a surprising power at work, but the effects are not proportionate, or such as take hold of the imagination. To impress the idea of power on others, they must be made in some way to feel it. It must be communicated to their understandings in the shape of an increase of knowledge, or it must subdue and overawe them by subjecting their wills. Admiration to be solid and lasting must be founded on proofs from which we have no means of escaping; it is neither a slight nor a voluntary gift. A mathematician who solves a profound problem, a poet who creates an image of beauty in the mind that was not there before, imparts knowledge and power to others, in which his greatness and his fame consists, and on which it reposes. Jedediah Buxton will be forgotten; but Napier's bones will live.[19] Lawgivers, philosophers, founders of religion, conquerors and heroes, inventors and great geniuses in arts and sciences, are great men, for they are great public benefactors, or formidable scourges to mankind. Among ourselves, Shakespeare, Newton, Bacon, Milton, Cromwell, were great men, for they showed great power by acts and thoughts, which have not yet been consigned to oblivion. They must needs be men of lofty stature, whose shadows lengthen out to remote posterity. A great farce-writer may be a great man; for Molière was but a great farce-writer. In my mind, the author of *Don Quixote* was a great man. So have there been many others. A great chess-player is not a great man, for he leaves the world as he found it. No act terminating in itself constitutes greatness. This will apply to all displays of power or trials of skill, which are confined to the momentary, individual effort, and construct no permanent image or trophy of themselves without them. Is not an actor then a great man, because 'he dies and leaves the world no copy'?[20] I must make an exception for Mrs Siddons, or else give up my definition of greatness for her sake. A man at the top of his profession is not therefore a great man. He is great in his way, but that is all, unless he shows the marks of a great moving intellect, so that we trace the master-mind, and can sympathize with the springs that urge him on. The rest is but a craft or *mystery*. John Hunter was a great man – *that* any one might see without the smallest skill in surgery. His style and manner showed the man. He would set about cutting up the carcase of a whale with the same greatness of *gusto* that Michael Angelo would have hewn a block of marble. Lord Nelson was a great naval commander; but for myself, I have not much opinion of a sea-faring life. Sir Humphry Davy is a great chemist, but I am not sure that he is a great man. I am not a bit the wiser for any of his discoveries, nor I never met with any one that was. But it is in the nature of greatness to propagate an idea of itself, as wave impels wave, circle without circle. It is a contradiction in terms for a coxcomb to be a great man. A really great man has always an idea of something greater than himself. I have observed that certain sectaries and polemical writers have no higher compliment to pay their most shining lights than to say that 'Such a one was a considerable man in his day.' Some new elucidation of a text sets aside the authority of the old interpretation, and a 'great scholar's memory outlives him half a century',[21] at the utmost. A rich man is not a great man, except to his dependants and his steward. A lord is a great man in the idea we have of his ancestry, and probably of himself, if we know nothing of him but his title. I have heard a story of two bishops, one of whom said (speaking of St Peter's at Rome) that when he first entered it, he was rather awestruck, but that as he walked up it, his mind seemed to swell and dilate with it, and at last to fill the whole building – the other said that as he saw more of it, he appeared to himself to grow less and less every step he took, and in the end to dwindle into nothing. This was in some respects a striking picture of a great and little mind – for greatness sympathizes with greatness, and littleness shrinks into itself. The one might have become a Wolsey; the other was only fit to become a Mendicant Friar – or there might have been court-reasons for making him a bishop. The French have to me a character of littleness in all about them; but they have produced three great men that belong to every country, Molière, Rabelais, and Montaigne.

To return from this digression, and conclude the Essay. A singular instance of manual dexterity was shown in the person of the late John Cavanagh, whom I have several times seen. His death was celebrated at the time in an article in the *Examiner* newspaper, (Feb. 7, 1819) written apparently between jest and earnest: but as it is *pat* to our purpose, and falls in with my own way of considering such subjects, I shall here take leave to quote it.

'Died at his house in Burbage-street, St Giles's, John Cavanagh, the famous hand fives-player. When a person dies, who does any one thing better than any one else in the world, which so many others are trying to do well, it leaves a gap in society. It is not likely that any one will now see the game of fives[22] played in its perfection for many years to come – for Cavanagh is dead, and has not left his peer behind him. It may be said that there are things of more importance than striking a ball against a wall – there are things indeed that make more noise and do as little good, such as making war and peace, making speeches and answering them, making verses and blotting them; making money and throwing it away. But the game of fives is what no one despises who has ever played at it. It is the finest exercise for the body, and the best relaxation for the mind. The Roman poet said that "Care mounted behind the horseman and stuck to his skirts." But this remark would not have applied to the fives-player. He who takes to playing at fives is twice young. He feels neither the past nor future "in the instant". Debts, taxes, "domestic treason, foreign levy, nothing can touch him further". He has no other wish, no other thought, from the moment the game begins, but that of striking the ball, of placing it, of *making* it! This Cavanagh was sure to do. Whenever he touched the ball, there was an end of the chase. His eye was certain, his hand fatal, his presence of mind complete. He could do what he pleased, and he always knew exactly what to do. He saw the whole game, and played it; took instant advantage of his adversary's weakness, and recovered balls, as if by a miracle and from sudden thought, that every one gave for lost. He had equal power and skill, quickness, and judgment. He could either outwit his antagonist by finesse, or beat him by main strength. Sometimes, when he seemed preparing to send the ball with the full swing of his arm, he would by a slight turn of his wrist drop it within an inch of the line. In general, the ball came from his hand, as if from a racket, in a straight horizontal line; so that it was in vain to attempt to overtake or stop it. As it was said of a great orator that he never was at a loss for a word, and for the properest word, so Cavanagh always could tell the degree of force necessary to be given to a ball, and the precise direction in which it should be sent. He did his work with the greatest ease; never took more pains than was necessary; and while others were fagging themselves to death, was as cool and collected as if he had just entered the court. His style of play was as remarkable as his power of execution. He had no affectation, no trifling. He did not throw away the game to show off an attitude, or try an experiment. He was a fine, sensible, manly player, who did what he could, but that was more than any one else could even affect to do. His blows were not undecided and ineffectual—lumbering like Mr Wordsworth's epic poetry, nor wavering like Mr Coleridge's lyric prose, nor short of the mark like Mr Brougham's speeches, nor wide of it like Mr Canning's wit, nor foul like the *Quarterly*, nor *let* balls like the *Edinburgh Review*. Cobbett and Junius together would have made a Cavanagh. He was the best *up-hill* player in the world; even when his adversary was fourteen, he would play on the same or better, and as he never flung away the game through carelessness and conceit, he never gave it up through laziness or want of heart. The only peculiarity of his play was that he never *volleyed*, but let the balls hop; but if they rose an inch from the ground, he never missed having them. There was not only nobody equal, but nobody second to him. It is supposed that he could give any other player half the game, or beat them with his left hand. His service was tremendous. He once played Woodward and Meredith together (two of the best players in

England) in the Fives-court, St Martin's-street, and made seven and twenty aces following by services alone − a thing unheard of. He another time played Peru, who was considered a first-rate fives-player, a match of the best out of five games, and in the three first games, which of course decided the match, Peru got only one ace. Cavanagh was an Irishman by birth, and a house-painter by profession. He had once laid aside his working-dress and walked up, in his smartest clothes, to the Rosemary Branch to have an afternoon's pleasure. A person accosted him, and asked him if he would have a game. So they agreed to play for half a crown a game, and a bottle of cider. The first game began − it was seven, eight, ten, thirteen, fourteen, all. Cavanagh won it. The next was the same. They played on, and each game was hardly contested. "There," said the unconscious fives-player, "there was a stroke that Cavanagh could not take: I never played better in my life, and yet I can't win a game. I don't know how it is." However, they played on, Cavanagh winning every game, and the by-standers drinking the cider and laughing all the time. In the twelfth game, when Cavanagh was only four, and the stranger thirteen, a person came in, and said, "What! are you here, Cavanagh?" The words were no sooner pronounced than the astonished player let the ball drop from his hand, and saying, "What! have I been breaking my heart all this time to beat Cavanagh?" refused to make another effort. "And yet, I give you my word," said Cavanagh, telling the story with some triumph, "I played all the while with my clenched fist." − He used frequently to play matches at Copenhagen-house for wagers and dinners. The wall against which they play is the same that supports the kitchen-chimney, and when the wall resounded louder than usual, the cooks exclaimed, "Those are the Irishman's balls," and the joints trembled on the spit! − Goldsmith consoled himself that there were places where he too was admired: and Cavanagh was the admiration of all the fives-courts, where he ever played. Mr Powell, when he played matches in the Court in St Martin's-street, used to fill his gallery at half-a-crown a head, with amateurs and admirers of talent in whatever department it is shown. He could not have shown himself in any ground in England, but he would have been immediately surrounded with inquisitive gazers, trying to find out in what part of his frame his unrivalled skill lay, as politicians wonder to see the balance of Europe suspended in Lord Castlereagh's face, and admire the trophies of the British Navy lurking under Mr Croker's hanging brow. Now Cavanagh was as good-looking a man as the Noble Lord, and much better looking than the Right Hon. Secretary. He had a clear, open countenance, and did not look sideways or down, like Mr Murray the bookseller. He was a young fellow of sense, humour, and courage. He once had a quarrel with a waterman at Hungerford-stairs, and they say, served him out in great style. In a word, there are hundreds at this day, who cannot mention his name without admiration, as the best fives-player that perhaps ever lived (the greatest excellence of which they have any notion) – and the noisy shout of the ring happily stood him in stead of the unheard voice of posterity! – The only person who seems to have excelled as much in another way as Cavanagh did in his, was the late John Davies, the racket-player. It was remarked of him that he did not seem to follow the ball, but the ball seemed to follow him. Give him a foot of wall, and he was sure to make the ball. The four best racket-players of that day were Jack Spines, Jem. Harding, Armitage, and Church. Davies could give any one of these two hands a time, that is, half the game, and each of these, at their best, could give the best player now in London the same odds. Such are the gradations in all exertions of human skill and art. He once played four capital players together, and beat them. He was also a first-rate tennis-player, and an excellent fives-player. In the Fleet or King's Bench, he would have stood against Powell, who was reckoned the best open-ground player of his time. This last-mentioned player is at present the keeper of the Fives-court, and we might recommend to him for a motto over his door – "Who enters here, forgets himself, his country, and his friends." And the best of it is, that by the calculation of the odds, none of the three are worth remembering! – Cavanagh died from the bursting of a blood-vessel, which prevented him from playing for the last two or three years. This, he was often heard to say, he thought hard upon him. He was fast recovering, however, when he was suddenly carried off, to the regret of all who knew him. As Mr Peel made it a qualification of the present Speaker, Mr Manners Sutton, that he was an excellent moral character, so Jack Cavanagh was a zealous Catholic, and could not be persuaded to eat meat on a Friday, the day on which he died. We have paid this willing tribute to his memory.

> "Let no rude hand deface it,
> And his forlorn *'Hic Jacet.'*"

Character of Cobbett

People have about as substantial an idea of Cobbett as they have of Cribb. His blows are as hard, and he himself is as impenetrable. One has no notion of him as making use of a fine pen, but a great mutton-fist; his style stuns his readers, and he 'fillips the ear of the public with a three-man beetle'.[1] He is too much for any single newspaper antagonist; 'lays waste'[2] a city orator or Member of Parliament, and bears hard upon the government itself. He is a kind of *fourth estate*[3] in the politics of the country. He is not only unquestionably the most powerful political writer of the present day, but one of the best writers in the language. He speaks and thinks plain, broad, downright English. He might be said to have the clearness of Swift, the naturalness of Defoe, and the picturesque satirical description of Mandeville; if all such comparisons were not impertinent. A really great and original writer is like nobody but himself. In one sense, Sterne was not a wit, nor Shakespeare a poet. It is easy to describe second-rate talents, because they fall into a class and enlist under a standard: but first-rate powers defy calculation or comparison, and can be defined only by themselves. They are *sui generis*, and make the class to which they belong. I have tried half a dozen times to describe Burke's style without ever succeeding; – its severe extravagance; its literal boldness; its matter-of-fact hyperboles; its running away with a subject, and from it at the same time – but there is no making it out, for there is no example of the same thing any where else. We have no common measure to refer to; and his qualities contradict even themselves.

Cobbett is not so difficult. He has been compared to Paine; and so far it is true there are no two writers who come more into juxta-position from the nature of their subjects, from the internal resources on which they draw, and from the popular effect of their writings and their adaptation (though that is a bad word in the present case) to the capacity of every reader. But still if we turn to a volume of Paine's (his *Common Sense* or *Rights of Man*) we are struck (not to say somewhat refreshed) by the difference. Paine is a much more sententious writer than Cobbett. You cannot open a page in any of his best and earlier works without meeting with some maxim, some antithetical and memorable saying, which is a sort of starting-place for the argument, and the goal to which it returns. There is not a single *bon-mot*, a single sentence in Cobbett that has ever been quoted again. If any thing is ever quoted from him, it is an epithet of abuse or a nickname. He is an excellent hand at invention in that way, and has 'damnable iteration in him'.[4] What could be better than his pestering Erskine year after year with his second title of Baron Clackmannan? He is rather too fond of *The Sons and Daughters of Corruption*. Paine affected to reduce things to first principles, to announce self-evident truths. Cobbett troubles himself about little but the details and local circumstances. The first appeared to have made up his mind beforehand to certain opinions, and to try to find the most compendious and pointed expressions for them: his successor appears to have no clue, no fixed or leading principles, nor ever to have thought on a question till he sits down to write about it; but then there seems no end of his matters of fact and raw materials, which are brought out in all their strength and sharpness from not having been squared or frittered down or vamped up to suit a theory – he goes on with his descriptions and illustrations as if he would never come to a stop; they have all the force of novelty with all the familiarity of old acquaintance; his knowledge grows out of the subject, and his style is that of a man who has an absolute intuition of what he is talking about, and never thinks of any thing else. He deals in premises and speaks to evidence – the coming to a conclusion and summing up (which was Paine's *forte*) lies in a smaller compass. The one could not compose an elementary treatise on politics to become a manual for the popular reader; nor could the other in all probability have kept up a weekly journal for the same number of years with the same spirit, interest, and untired perseverance. Paine's writings are a sort of introduction to political arithmetic on a new

plan: Cobbett keeps a day-book and makes an entry at full of all the
occurrences and troublesome questions that start up throughout the
year. Cobbett with vast industry, vast information, and the utmost
power of making what he says intelligible, never seems to get at the
beginning or come to the end of any question: Paine in a few short
sentences seems by his peremptory manner 'to clear it from all
controversy, past, present, and to come'.[5] Paine takes a bird's-eye view
of things. Cobbett sticks close to them, inspects the component parts,
and keeps fast hold of the smallest advantages they afford him. Or if
I might here be indulged in a pastoral allusion, Paine tries to enclose
his ideas in a fold for security and repose; Cobbett lets *his* pour out
upon the plain like a flock of sheep to feed and batten. Cobbett is a
pleasanter writer for those to read who do not agree with him; for
he is less dogmatical, goes more into the common grounds of fact
and argument to which all appeal, is more desultory and various, and
appears less to be driving at a previous conclusion than urged on by
the force of present conviction. He is therefore tolerated by all parties,
though he has made himself by turns obnoxious to all; and even those
he abuses read him. The Reformers read him when he was a Tory,
and the Tories read him now that he is a Reformer. He must, I think,
however, be *caviare* to the Whigs.*

If he is less metaphysical and poetical than his celebrated prototype,
he is more picturesque and dramatic. His episodes, which are numerous
as they are pertinent, are striking, interesting, full of life and *naïveté*,
minute, double measure running over, but never tedious – *nunquam
sufflaminandus erat.*[6] He is one of those writers who can never tire
us, not even of himself; and the reason is, he is always 'full of matter'.[7]
He never runs to lees, never gives us the vapid leavings of himself,
is never 'weary, stale, and unprofitable',[8] but always setting out afresh
on his journey, clearing away some old nuisance, and turning up new
mould. His egotism is delightful, for there is no affectation in it. He
does not talk of himself for lack of something to write about, but
because some circumstance that has happened to himself is the best
possible illustration of the subject, and he is not the man to shrink from

---

* The late Lord Thurlow used to say that Cobbett was the only writer that deserved the
name of a political reasoner.

giving the best possible illustration of the subject from a squeamish delicacy. He likes both himself and his subject too well. He does not put himself before it, and say – 'admire me first' – but places us in the same situation with himself, and makes us see all that he does. There is no blindman's-buff, no conscious hints, no awkward ventrilo-quism, no testimonies of applause, no abstract, senseless self-complacency, no smuggled admiration of his own person by proxy: it is all plain and above-board. He writes himself plain William Cobbett, strips himself quite as naked as any body would wish – in a word, his egotism is full of individuality, and has room for very little vanity in it. We feel delighted, rub our hands, and draw our chair to the fire, when we come to a passage of this sort: we know it will be something new and good, manly and simple, not the same insipid story of self over again. We sit down at table with the writer,[9] but it is to a course of rich viands, flesh, fish, and wild-fowl, and not to a nominal entertainment, like that given by the Barmecide in the *Arabian Nights*,[10] who put off his visitors with calling for a number of exquisite things that never appeared, and with the honour of his company. Mr Cobbett is not a *make-believe* writer. His worst enemy cannot say that of him. Still less is he a vulgar one. He must be a puny, common-place critic indeed, who thinks him so. How fine were the graphical descriptions he sent us from America:[11] what a transatlantic flavour, what a native *gusto*, what a fine *sauce piquante* of contempt they were seasoned with! If he had sat down to look at himself in the glass, instead of looking about him like Adam in Paradise, he would not have got up these articles in so capital a style. What a noble account of his first breakfast after his arrival in America! It might serve for a month. There is no scene on the stage more amusing. How well he paints the gold and scarlet plumage of the American birds, only to lament more pathetically the want of the wild wood-notes of his native land! The groves of the Ohio that had just fallen beneath the axe's stroke 'live in his description',[12] and the turnips that he transplanted from Botley 'look green'[13] in prose! How well at another time he describes the poor sheep that had got the tick and had tumbled down in the agonies of death! It is a portrait in the manner of Bewick, with the strength, the simplicity, and feeling of that great naturalist. What havoc he makes,[14] when he pleases, of the curls of Dr Parr's wig and of the Whig consistency of Mr —![15] His *Grammar*[16] too is as entertaining as a story-book. He is too hard upon the style of others, and not enough (sometimes) on his own.

As a political partisan, no one can stand against him. With his brandished club, like Giant Despair in the *Pilgrim's Progress*, he knocks out their brains; and not only no individual, but no corrupt system could hold out against his powerful and repeated attacks, but with the same weapon, swung round like a flail, that he levels his antagonists, he lays his friends low, and puts his own party *hors de combat*. This is a bad propensity, and a worse principle in political tactics, though a common one. If his blows were straightforward and steadily directed to the same object, no unpopular Minister could live before him; instead of which he lays about right and left, impartially and remorselessly, makes a clear stage, has all the ring to himself, and then runs out of it, just when he should stand his ground. He throws his head into his adversary's stomach, and takes away from him all inclination for the fight, hits fair or foul, strikes at every thing, and as you come up to his aid or stand ready to pursue his advantage, trips up your heels or lays you sprawling, and pummels you when down as much to his heart's content as ever the Yanguesian carriers[17] belaboured Rosinante with their pack-staves. '*He has the back-trick simply the best of any man in Illyria.*'[18] He pays off both scores of old friendship and new-acquired enmity in a breath, in one perpetual volley, one raking fire of 'arrowy sleet'[19] shot from his pen. However his own reputation or the cause may suffer in consequence, he cares not one pin about that, so that he disables all who oppose, or who pretend to help him. In fact, he cannot bear success of any kind, not even of his own views or party; and if any principle were likely to become popular, would turn round against it to show his power in shouldering it on one side. In short, wherever power is, there is he against it: he naturally butts at all obstacles, as unicorns are attracted to oak-trees, and feels his own strength only by resistance to the opinions and wishes of the rest of the world. To sail with the stream, to agree with the company, is not his humour. If he could bring about a Reform in Parliament, the odds are that he would instantly fall foul of and try to mar his own handy-work; and he quarrels with his own creatures as soon as he has written them into a little vogue — and a prison. I do not think this is vanity or fickleness so much as a pugnacious disposition, that must have an antagonist power to contend with, and only finds itself at ease in systematic opposition. If it were not for this, the high towers and rotten places of the world would fall before the battering-ram of his hard-headed reasoning: but if he once found them tottering, he would apply his strength to prop them up, and disappoint the expectations of his followers. He cannot agree to any thing established, nor to set up any thing else in its stead. While it is established, he presses hard against it, because it presses upon him, at least in imagination. Let it crumble under his grasp, and the motive to resistance is gone. He then requires some other grievance to set his face against. His principle is repulsion, his nature contradiction: he is made up of mere antipathies, an Ishmaelite[20] indeed without a fellow. He is always playing at *hunt-the-slipper* in politics. He turns round upon whoever is next him. The way to wean him from any opinion, and make him conceive an intolerable hatred against it, would be to place somebody near him who was perpetually dinning it in his ears. When he is in England, he does nothing but abuse the Boroughmongers,[21] and laugh at the whole system: when he is in America, he grows impatient of freedom and a republic. If he had stayed there a little longer, he would have become a loyal and a loving subject of his Majesty King George IV. He lampooned the French Revolution when it was hailed as the dawn of liberty by millions: by the time it was brought into almost universal ill-odour by some means or other (partly no doubt by himself) he had turned, with one or two or three others, staunch Buonapartist. He is always of the militant, not of the triumphant party: so far he bears a gallant show of magnanimity; but his gallantry is hardly of the right stamp. It wants principle: for though he is not servile or mercenary, he is the victim of self-will. He must pull down and pull in pieces: it is not in his disposition to do otherwise. It is a pity; for with his great talents he might do great things, if he would go right forward to any useful object, make thorough-stitch work of any question, or join hand and heart with any principle. He changes his opinions as he does his friends, and much on the same account. He has no comfort in fixed principles: as soon as any thing is settled in his own mind, he quarrels with it. He has no satisfaction but in the chase after truth, runs a question down, worries and kills it, then quits it like vermin, and starts some new game, to lead him a new dance, and give him a fresh breathing through bog and brake, with the rabble yelping at his heels and the leaders perpetually at fault. This he calls sport-royal. He thinks it as good as cudgel-playing or single-stick, or any thing else that has life in it. He likes the cut and thrust, the falls, bruises, and dry blows of an argument: as to any good or useful results that may come of the amicable settling of it, any one is welcome to them for him. The amusement is over, when the matter is once fairly decided.

There is another point of view in which this may be put. I might say that Mr Cobbett is a very honest man with a total want of principle, and I might explain this paradox thus. I mean that he is, I think, in downright earnest in what he says, in the part he takes at the time; but in taking that part, he is led entirely by headstrong obstinacy, caprice, novelty, pique or personal motive of some sort, and not by a steadfast regard for truth or habitual anxiety for what is right uppermost in his mind. He is not a feed, time-serving, shuffling advocate (no man could write as he does who did not believe himself sincere) – but his understanding is the dupe and slave of his momentary, violent, and irritable humours. He does not adopt an opinion 'deliberately or for money';[22] yet his conscience is at the mercy of the first provocation he receives, of the first whim he takes in his head; he sees things through the medium of heat and passion, not with reference to any general principles, and his whole system of thinking is deranged by the first object that strikes his fancy or sours his temper. – One cause of this phenomenon is perhaps his want of a regular education. He is a self-taught man, and has the faults as well as excellences of that class of persons in their most striking and glaring excess. It must be acknowledged that the Editor of the *Political Register* (the *two-penny trash*, as it was called, till a bill passed the House to raise the price to sixpence[23]) is not 'the gentleman and scholar':[24] though he has qualities that, with a little better management, would be worth (to the public) both those titles. For want of knowing what has been discovered before him, he has not certain general landmarks to refer to, or a general standard of thought to apply to individual cases. He relies on his own acuteness and the immediate evidence, without being acquainted with the comparative anatomy or philosophical structure of opinion. He does not view things on a large scale or at the horizon (dim and airy enough perhaps) – but as they affect himself, close, palpable, tangible. Whatever he finds out, is his own, and he only knows what he finds out. He is in the constant hurry and fever of gestation: his brain teems incessantly with some fresh project. Every new light is the birth of a new system, the dawn of a new world to him. He is continually outstripping and overreaching himself. The last opinion is the only true one. He is wiser to-day than he was yesterday. Why should he not be wiser to-morrow than he was to-day? – Men of a learned education are not so sharp-witted as clever men without it: but they know the balance of the human intellect better; if they are more stupid, they are more steady; and are less liable to be led astray by their own sagacity and the over-weening petulance of hard-earned and late-acquired wisdom. They do not fall in love with every meretricious extravagance at first sight, or mistake an old battered hypothesis for a vestal, because they are new to the ways of this old world. They do not seize upon it as a prize, but are safe from gross imposition by being as wise and no wiser than those who went before them.

Paine said on some occasion – 'What I have written, I have written'[25] – as rendering any farther declaration of his principles unnecessary. Not so Mr Cobbett. What he has written is no rule to him what he is to write. He learns something every day, and every week he takes the field to maintain the opinions of the last six days against friend or foe. I doubt whether this outrageous inconsistency, this headstrong fickleness, this understood want of all rule and method, does not enable him to go on with the spirit, vigour, and variety that he does. He is not pledged to repeat himself. Every new *Register* is a kind of new Prospectus. He blesses himself from all ties and shackles on his understanding; he has no mortgages on his brain; his notions are free and unincumbered. If he was put in trammels, he might become a vile hack like so many more. But he gives himself 'ample scope and verge enough'.[26] He takes both sides of a question, and maintains one as sturdily as the other. If nobody else can argue against him, he is a very good match for himself. He writes better in favour of Reform than any body else; he used to write better against it. Wherever he is, there is the tug of war, the weight of the argument, the strength of abuse. He is not like a man in danger of being *bed-rid* in his faculties – he tosses and tumbles about his unwieldy bulk, and when he is tired of lying on one side, relieves himself by turning on the other. His shifting his point of view from time to time not merely adds variety and greater compass to his topics (so that the *Political Register* is an armoury and magazine for all the materials and weapons of political warfare) but it gives a greater zest and liveliness to his manner of treating them. Mr Cobbett takes nothing for granted as what he has proved before; he does not write a book of reference. We see his ideas in their first concoction, fermenting and overflowing with the ebullitions of a lively conception. We look on at the actual process, and are put in immediate possession of the grounds and materials on which he forms his sanguine, unsettled conclusions. He does not give us samples of reasoning, but the whole solid mass, refuse and all.

> —'He pours out all as plain
> As downright Shippen or as old Montaigne.'[27]

This is one cause of the clearness and force of his writings. An argument does not stop to stagnate and muddle in his brain, but passes at once to his paper. His ideas are served up, like pancakes, hot and hot. Fresh theories give him fresh courage. He is like a young and lusty bridegroom that divorces a favourite speculation every morning, and marries a new one every night. He is not wedded to his notions, not he. He has not one Mrs Cobbett among all his opinions. He makes the most of the last thought that has come in his way, seizes fast hold of it, rumples it about in all directions with rough strong hands, has his wicked will of it, takes a surfeit, and throws it away. – Our author's changing his opinions for new ones is not so wonderful: what is more remarkable is his facility in forgetting his old ones. He does not pretend to consistency (like Mr Coleridge); he frankly disavows all connexion with himself. He feels no personal responsibility in this way, and cuts a friend or principle with the same decided indifference that Antipholis of Ephesus cuts Ægeon of Syracuse.[28] It is a hollow thing. The only time he ever grew romantic was in bringing over the relics of Mr Thomas Paine with him from America[29] to go a progress with them through the disaffected districts. Scarce had he landed in Liverpool when he left the bones of a great man to shift for themselves; and no sooner did he arrive in London than he made a speech to disclaim all participation in the political and theological sentiments of his late idol, and to place the whole stock of his admiration and enthusiasm towards him to the account of his financial speculations, and of his having predicted the fate of paper-money. If he had erected a little gold statue to him, it might have proved the sincerity of this assertion: but to make a martyr and a patron-saint of a man, and to dig up 'his canonized bones'[30] in order to expose them as objects of devotion to the rabble's gaze, asks something that has more life and spirit in it, more mind and vivifying soul, than has to do with any calculation of pounds, shillings, and pence! The fact is, he *ratted* from his own project. He found the thing not so ripe as he had expected. His heart failed him: his enthusiasm fled, and he made his retractation. His admiration is short-lived: his contempt only is rooted, and his resentment lasting. – The above was only one instance of his building too much on practical *data*. He has an ill habit of prophesying, and goes on, though still deceived. The art of prophesying does not suit Mr Cobbett's style. He has a knack of fixing names and times and places. According to him, the Reformed Parliament was to meet in March, 1818 – it did not, and we heard no more of the matter. When his predictions fail, he takes no farther notice of them, but applies himself to new ones – like the country-people who turn to see what weather there is in the almanac for the next week, though it has been out in its reckoning every day of the last.

Mr Cobbett is great in attack, not in defence: he cannot fight an up-hill battle. He will not bear the least punishing. If any one turns upon him (which few people like to do) he immediately turns tail. Like an overgrown school-boy, he is so used to have it all his own way, that he cannot submit to any thing like competition or a struggle for the mastery; he must lay on all the blows, and take none. He is bullying and cowardly; a Big Ben[31] in politics, who will fall upon others and crush them by his weight, but is not prepared for resistance, and is soon staggered by a few smart blows. Whenever he has been set upon, he has slunk out of the controversy. The *Edinburgh Review* made[32] (what is called) a dead set at him some years ago, to which he only retorted by an eulogy on the superior neatness of an English kitchen-garden to a Scotch one. I remember going one day into a bookseller's shop in Fleet-street to ask for the *Review*; and on my expressing my opinion to a young Scotchman, who stood behind the counter, that Mr Cobbett might hit as hard in his reply, the North Briton said with some alarm — 'But you don't think, Sir, Mr Cobbett will be able to injure the Scottish nation?' I said I could not speak to that point, but I thought he was very well able to defend himself. He however did not, but has borne a grudge to the *Edinburgh Review* ever since, which he hates worse than the *Quarterly*. I cannot say I do.*

---

* Mr Cobbett speaks almost as well as he writes. The only time I ever saw him he seemed to me a very pleasant man — easy of access, affable, clear-headed, simple and meek in his manner, deliberate and unruffled in his speech, though some of his expressions were not very qualified. His figure is tall and portly. He has a good sensible face — rather full, with little grey eyes, a hard, square forehead, a ruddy complexion, with hair grey or powdered; and had on a scarlet broad-cloth waistcoat with the flaps of the pockets hanging down, as was the custom for gentlemen-farmers in the last century, or as we see it in the pictures of Members of Parliament in the reign of George I. I certainly did not think less favourably of him for seeing him.

The Fight

—'The *fight*, the *fight's* the thing,
Wherein I'll catch the conscience of the king.'[1]

Where there's a will, there's a way, – I said so to myself, as I walked
down Chancery-lane, about half-past six o'clock on Monday the 10th
of December, to inquire at Jack Randall's where the fight the next
day was to be; and I found 'the proverb' nothing[2] 'musty' in the
present instance. I was determined to see this fight, come what would,
and see it I did, in great style. It was my *first fight*, yet it more
than answered my expectations. Ladies! it is to you I dedicate this
description; nor let it seem out of character for the fair to notice the
exploits of the brave. Courage and modesty are the old English virtues;
and may they never look cold and askance on one another! Think,
ye fairest of the fair, loveliest of the lovely kind, ye practisers of soft
enchantment, how many more ye kill with poisoned baits than ever
fell in the ring; and listen with subdued air and without shuddering,
to a tale tragic only in appearance, and sacred to the FANCY!

I was going down Chancery-lane, thinking to ask at Jack Randall's
where the fight was to be, when looking through the glass-door of
the *Hole in the Wall*, I heard a gentleman asking the same question
at Mrs Randall, as the author of *Waverley* would express it.[3] Now
Mrs Randall stood answering the gentleman's question, with the
authenticity of the lady of the Champion of the Light Weights.
Thinks I, I'll wait till this person comes out, and learn from him how
it is. For to say a truth, I was not fond of going into this house of call
for heroes and philosophers, ever since the owner of it (for Jack is no
gentleman) threatened once upon a time to kick me out of doors for

wanting a mutton-chop at his hospitable board, when the conqueror in thirteen battles was more full of *blue ruin*[4] than of good manners. I was the more mortified at this repulse, inasmuch as I had heard Mr James Simpkins, hosier in the Strand, one day when the character of the *Hole in the Wall* was brought in question, observe – 'The house is a very good house, and the company quite genteel: I have been there myself!' Remembering this unkind treatment of mine host, to which mine hostess was also a party, and not wishing to put her in unquiet thoughts at a time jubilant like the present, I waited at the door, when, who should issue forth but my friend Joe Toms, and turning suddenly up Chancery-lane with that quick jerk and impatient stride which distinguishes a lover of the FANCY, I said, 'I'll be hanged if that fellow is not going to the fight, and is on his way to get me to go with him.' So it proved in effect, and we agreed to adjourn to my lodgings to discuss measures with that cordiality which makes old friends like new, and new friends like old, on great occasions. We are cold to others only when we are dull in ourselves, and have neither thoughts nor feelings to impart to them. Give a man a topic in his head, a throb of pleasure in his heart, and he will be glad to share it with the first person he meets. Toms and I, though we seldom meet, were an *alter idem*[5] on this memorable occasion, and had not an idea that we did not candidly impart; and 'so carelessly did we fleet the time',[6] that I wish no better, when there is another fight, than to have him for a companion on my journey down, and to return with my friend Jack Pigott, talking of what was to happen or of what did happen, with a noble subject always at hand, and liberty to digress to others whenever they offered. Indeed, on my repeating the lines from Spenser in an involuntary fit of enthusiasm,

> 'What more felicity can fall to creature,
> Than to enjoy delight with liberty?'[7]

my last-named ingenious friend stopped me by saying that this, translated into the vulgate, meant '*Going to see a fight*'.

Joe Toms and I could not settle about the method of going down. He said there was a caravan, he understood, to start from Tom Belcher's at two, which would go there *right out* and back again the next day. Now I never travel all night, and said I should get a cast to Newbury by one of the mails. Joe swore the thing was impossible, and I could only answer that I had made up my mind to it. In short, he seemed to me to waver, said he only came to see if I was going, had letters to write, a cause coming on the day after, and faintly said at parting (for I was bent on setting out that moment) – 'Well, we meet at Philippi!'[8] I made the best of my way to Piccadilly. The mail coach stand was bare. 'They are all gone,' said I – 'this is always the way with me – in the instant I lose the future – if I had not stayed to pour out that last cup of tea, I should have been just in time' – and cursing my folly and ill-luck together, without inquiring at the coach-office whether the mails were gone or not, I walked on in despite, and to punish my own dilatoriness and want of determination. At any rate, I would not turn back: I might get to Hounslow, or perhaps farther, to be on my road the next morning. I passed Hyde Park Corner (my Rubicon),[9] and trusted to fortune. Suddenly I heard the clattering of a Brentford stage, and the fight rushed full upon my fancy. I argued (not unwisely) that even a Brentford coachman was better company than my own thoughts (such as they were just then), and at his invitation mounted the box with him. I immediately stated my case to him – namely, my quarrel with myself for missing the Bath or Bristol mail, and my determination to get on in consequence as well as I could, without any disparagement or insulting comparison between longer or shorter stages. It is a maxim with me that stage-coaches, and consequently stage-coachmen, are respectable in proportion to the distance they have to travel: so I said nothing on that subject to my Brentford friend. Any incipient tendency to an abstract proposition, or (as he might have construed it) to a personal reflection of this kind, was however nipped in the bud; for I had no sooner declared indignantly that I had missed the mails, than he flatly denied that they were gone along, and lo! at the instant three of them drove by in rapid, provoking, orderly succession, as if they would devour the ground before them. Here again I seemed in the contradictory situation of the man in Dryden who exclaims,

'I follow Fate, which does too hard pursue!'[10]

If I had stopped to inquire at the White Horse Cellar, which would not have taken me a minute, I should now have been driving down the road in all the dignified unconcern and *ideal* perfection of mechanical conveyance. The Bath mail I had set my mind upon, and I had missed it, as I missed every thing else, by my own absurdity, in putting the will for the deed, and aiming at ends without employing means. 'Sir,' said he of the Brentford, 'the Bath mail will be up presently, my brother-in-law drives it, and I will engage to stop him if there is a place empty.' I almost doubted my good genius; but, sure enough, up it drove like lightning, and stopped directly at the call of the Brentford Jehu.[11] I would not have believed this possible, but the brother-in-law of a mail-coach driver is himself no mean man. I was transferred without loss of time from the top of one coach to that of the other, desired the guard to pay my fare to the Brentford coachman for me as I had no change, was accommodated with a great coat, put up my umbrella to keep off a drizzling mist, and we began to cut through the air like an arrow. The mile-stones disappeared one after another, the rain kept off; Tom Turtle, the trainer, sat before me on the coach-box, with whom I exchanged civilities as a gentleman going to the fight; the passion that had transported me an hour before was subdued to pensive regret and conjectural musing on the next day's battle; I was promised a place inside at Reading, and upon the whole, I thought myself a lucky fellow. Such is the force of imagination! On the outside of any other coach on the 10th of December with a Scotch mist drizzling through the cloudy moonlight air, I should have been cold, comfortless, impatient, and, no doubt, wet through; but seated on the Royal mail, I felt warm and comfortable, the air did me good, the ride did me good, I was pleased with the progress we had made, and confident that all would go well through the journey. When I got inside at Reading, I found Turtle and a stout valetudinarian, whose costume bespoke him one of the FANCY, and who had risen from a three months' sick bed to get into the mail to see the fight. They were intimate, and we fell into a lively discourse. My friend the trainer was confined in his topics to fighting dogs and men, to bears and badgers; beyond this he was 'quite chap-fallen',[12] had not a word to throw at a dog,[13] or indeed very wisely fell asleep, when any other game was started. The whole art of training (I, however, learnt from him), consists in two things, exercise and abstinence, abstinence and exercise, repeated alternately and without end. A yolk of an egg with a spoonful of rum in it is the first thing in a morning, and then a walk of six miles till breakfast. This meal consists of a plentiful supply of tea and toast and beef-steaks. Then another six or seven miles till dinner-time, and another supply of solid beef or mutton with a pint of porter, and perhaps, at the utmost, a couple of glasses of sherry. Martin trains on water, but this increases his infirmity on another very dangerous side. The Gas-man takes now and then a chirping glass (under the rose) to console him, during a six weeks' probation, for the absence of Mrs Hickman – an agreeable woman, with (I understand) a pretty fortune of two hundred pounds. How matter presses on me! What stubborn things are facts! How inexhaustible is nature and art! 'It is well', as I once heard Mr Richmond observe, 'to see a variety.' He was speaking of cock-fighting as an edifying spectacle. I cannot deny but that one learns more of what *is* (I do not say of what *ought to be*) in this desultory mode of practical study, than from reading the same book twice over, even though it should be a moral treatise. Where was I? I was sitting at dinner with the candidate for the honours of the ring, 'where good digestion waits on appetite, and health on both'.[14] Then follows an hour of social chat and native glee; and afterwards, to another breathing over heathy hill or dale. Back to supper, and then to bed, and up by six again – Our hero

'Follows so the ever-running sun,
With profitable *ardour* – '[15]

to the day that brings him victory or defeat in the green fairy circle. Is not this life more sweet than mine?[16] I was going to say; but I will not libel any life by comparing it to mine, which is (at the date of these presents) bitter as coloquintida and the dregs of aconitum!

The invalid in the Bath mail soared a pitch above the trainer, and did not sleep so sound, because he had 'more figures and more fantasies'.[17] We talked the hours away merrily. He had faith in surgery, for he had had three ribs set right, that had been broken in a *turn-up* at Belcher's, but thought physicians old women, for they had no antidote in their catalogue for brandy. An indigestion is an excellent common-place for two people that never met before. By way of ingratiating myself, I told him the story of my doctor, who, on my earnestly representing to him that I thought his regimen had done me harm, assured me that the whole pharmacopeia contained nothing comparable to the prescription he had given me; and, as a proof of its undoubted efficacy, said, that 'he had had one gentleman with my complaint under his hands for the last fifteen years'. This anecdote made my companion shake the rough sides of his three great coats with boisterous laughter; and Turtle, starting out of his sleep, swore he knew how the fight would go, for he had had a dream about it. Sure enough the rascal told us how the three first rounds went off, but 'his dream', like others, 'denoted a foregone conclusion'.[18] He knew his men. The moon now rose in silver state, and I ventured, with some hesitation, to point out this object of placid beauty, with the blue serene beyond, to the man of science, to which his ear he 'seriously inclined',[19] the more as it gave promise *d'un beau jour* for the morrow, and showed the ring undrenched by envious showers,[20] arrayed in sunny smiles. Just then, all going on well, I thought on my friend Toms, whom I had left behind, and said innocently, 'There was a blockhead of a fellow I left in town, who said there was no possibility of getting down by the mail, and talked of going by a caravan from Belcher's at two in the morning, after he had written some letters.' 'Why,' said he of the lapels, 'I should not wonder if that was the very person we saw running about like mad from one coach-door to another, and asking if any one had seen a friend of his, a gentleman going to the fight, whom he had missed stupidly enough by staying to write a note.' 'Pray Sir,' said my fellow-traveller, 'had he a plaid-cloak on?' – 'Why, no,' said I, 'not at the time I left him, but he very well might afterwards, for he offered to lend me one.' The plaid-cloak and the letter decided the thing. Joe, sure enough, was in the Bristol mail, which preceded us by about fifty yards. This was droll enough. We had now but a few miles to our place of destination, and the first thing I did on alighting at Newbury, both coaches stopping at the same time, was to call out, 'Pray, is there a gentleman in that mail of the name of Toms?' 'No,' said Joe, borrowing something of the vein of Gilpin,[21] 'for I have just got out.' 'Well!' says he, 'this is lucky; but you don't know how vexed I was to miss you; for,' added he, lowering his voice, 'do you know when I left you I went to Belcher's to ask about the caravan, and Mrs Belcher said very obligingly, she couldn't tell about that, but there were two gentlemen who had taken places by the mail and were gone on in a landau, and she could frank us. It's a pity I didn't meet with you; we could then have got down for nothing. But *mum's the word*.' It's the devil for any one to tell me a secret, for it is sure to come out in print. I do not care so much to gratify a friend, but the public ear is too great a temptation to me.

Our present business was to get beds and a supper at an inn; but this was no easy task. The public-houses were full, and where you saw a light at a private house, and people poking their heads out of the casement to see what was going on, they instantly put them in and shut the window, the moment you seemed advancing with a suspicious overture for accommodation. Our guard and coachman thundered away at the outer gate of the Crown for some time without effect — such was the greater noise within: — and when the doors were unbarred, and we got admittance, we found a party assembled in the kitchen round a good hospitable fire, some sleeping, others drinking, others talking on politics and on the fight. A tall English yeoman (something like Matthews in the face, and quite as great a wag) —

'A lusty man to ben an abbot able, — '[22]

was making such a prodigious noise about rent and taxes, and the price of corn now and formerly, that he had prevented us from being heard at the gate. The first thing I heard him say was to a shuffling fellow who wanted to be off a bet for a shilling glass of brandy and water — 'Confound it, man, don't be *insipid*!' Thinks I, that is a good phrase. It was a good omen. He kept it up so all night, nor flinched with the approach of morning. He was a fine fellow, with sense, wit, and spirit, a hearty body and a joyous mind, free-spoken, frank, convivial — one of that home English breed that went with Harry the Fifth to the siege of Harfleur — 'standing like greyhounds on the slips',[23] &c. We ordered tea and eggs (beds were soon found to be out of the question) and this fellow's conversation was *sauce piquante*. It did one's heart good to see him brandish his oaken towel and to hear him talk. He made mince-meat of a drunken, stupid, red-faced, quarrelsome, *frowzy* farmer, whose nose 'he moralized into a thousand similes',[24] making it out a firebrand like Bardolph's.[25] 'I'll tell you what, my friend,' says he, 'the landlady has only to keep you here to save fire and candle. If one was to touch your nose, it would go off like a piece of charcoal.' At this the other only grinned like an idiot, the sole variety in his purple face being his little peering grey eyes and yellow teeth; called for another glass, swore he would not stand it; and after many attempts to provoke his humorous antagonist to single combat, which the other turned off (after working him up to a ludicrous pitch of choler) with great adroitness, he fell quietly asleep with a glass of liquor in his hand, which he could not lift to his head. His laughing persecutor made a speech over him, and turning to the opposite side of the room, where they were all sleeping in the midst of this 'loud and furious fun', said, 'There's a scene, by G — d, for Hogarth to paint. I think he and Shakespeare were our two best men at copying life!' This confirmed me in my good opinion of him. Hogarth, Shakespeare, and Nature, were just enough for him (indeed for any man) to know. I said, 'You read Cobbett, don't you? At least,' says I, 'you talk just as well as he writes.' He seemed to doubt this. But I said, 'We have an hour to spare: if you'll get pen, ink and paper, and keep on talking, I'll write down what you say; and if it doesn't make a capital *Political Register*, I'll forfeit my head. You have kept me alive to-night, however. I don't know what I should have done without you.' He did not dislike this view of the thing, nor my asking if he was not about the size of Jem Belcher; and told me soon afterwards, in the confidence of friendship, that 'the circumstance which had given him nearly the greatest concern in his life, was Cribb's beating Jem after he had lost his eye by racket playing'. — The morning dawns; that dim but yet clear light appears, which weighs like solid bars of metal on the sleepless eyelids; the guests drop down from their chambers one by one — but it was too late to think of going to bed now (the clock was on the stroke of seven), we had nothing for it but to find a barber's (the pole that glittered in the morning sun lighted us to his shop), and then a nine miles' march to Hungerford. The day was fine, the sky was blue, the mists were retiring from the marshy ground, the path was tolerably dry, the sitting-up all night had not done us much harm — at least the cause was good; we talked of this and that with amicable difference, roving

and sipping of many subjects, but still invariably we returned to the
fight. At length, a mile to the left of Hungerford, on a gentle eminence,
we saw the ring surrounded by covered carts, gigs, and carriages, of
which hundreds had passed us on the road; Toms gave a youthful
shout, and we hastened down a narrow lane to the scene of action.

Reader! have you ever seen a fight? If not, you have a pleasure to
come, at least if it is a fight like that between the Gas-man and Bill
Neate. The crowd was very great when we arrived on the spot; open
carriages were coming up, with streamers flying and music playing,
and the country-people were pouring in over hedge and ditch in all
directions, to see their hero beat or be beaten. The odds were still on
Gas, but only about five to four. Gully had been down to try Neate,
and had backed him considerably, which was a damper to the sanguine
confidence of the adverse party. About two hundred thousand pounds
were pending. The Gas says, he has lost 3,000*l.* which were promised
him by different gentlemen if he had won. He had presumed too
much on himself, which had made others presume on him. This
spirited and formidable young fellow seems to have taken for his
motto the old maxim, that 'there are three things necessary to success
in life – *Impudence*! *Impudence*! *Impudence*!'[26] It is so in matters of
opinion, but not in the *Fancy*, which is the most practical of all
things, though even here confidence is half the battle, but only half.
Our friend had vapoured and swaggered too much, as if he wanted
to grin and bully his adversary out of the fight. 'Alas! the Bristol man
was not so tamed!'[27] – 'This is *the grave-digger*' (would Tom Hickman
exclaim in the moments of intoxication from gin and success, showing
his tremendous right hand), 'this will send many of them to their
long homes; I haven't done with them yet!' – Why should he –
though he had licked four of the best men within the hour, yet why
should he threaten to inflict dishonourable chastisement on my old
master Richmond, a veteran going off the stage, and who has borne
his sable honours meekly? Magnanimity, my dear Tom, and bravery,
should be inseparable. Or why should he go up to his antagonist, the
first time he ever saw him at the Fives Court, and measuring him
from head to foot with a glance of contempt, as Achilles surveyed
Hector, say to him – 'What, are you Bill Neate? I'll knock more blood
out of that great carcase of thine, this day fortnight, than you ever

knock'd out of a bullock's!' It was not manly, 'twas not fighter-like. If he was sure of the victory (as he was not), the less said about it the better. Modesty should accompany the *Fancy* as its shadow. The best men were always the best behaved. Jem Belcher, the Game Chicken (before whom the Gas-man could not have lived) were civil, silent men. So is Cribb, so is Tom Belcher, the most elegant of sparrers, and not a man for every one to take by the nose. I enlarged on this topic in the mail (while Turtle was asleep), and said very wisely (as I thought) that impertinence was a part of no profession. A boxer was bound to beat his man, but not to thrust his fist, either actually or by implication, in every one's face. Even a highwayman, in the way of trade, may blow out your brains, but if he uses foul language at the same time, I should say he was no gentleman. A boxer, I would infer, need not be a blackguard or a coxcomb, more than another. Perhaps I press this point too much on a fallen man – Mr Thomas Hickman has by this time learnt that first of all lessons, 'That man was made to mourn'.[28] He has lost nothing by the late fight but his presumption; and that every man may do as well without! By an over-display of this quality, however, the public had been prejudiced against him, and the *knowing-ones* were taken in. Few but those who had bet on him wished Gas to win. With my own prepossessions on the subject, the result of the 11th of December appeared to me as fine a piece of poetical justice as I had ever witnessed. The difference of weight between the two combatants (14 stone to 19) was nothing to the sporting men. Great, heavy, clumsy, long-armed Bill Neate kicked the beam in the scale of the Gas-man's vanity. The amateurs were frightened at his big words, and thought they would make up for the difference of six feet and five feet nine. Truly, the FANCY are not men of imagination. They judge of what has been, and cannot conceive of any thing that is to be. The Gas-man had won hitherto; therefore he must beat a man half as big again as himself – and that to a certainty. Besides, there are as many feuds, factions, prejudices, pedantic notions in the FANCY as in the state or in the schools. Mr Gully is almost the only cool, sensible man among them, who exercises an unbiassed discretion, and is not a slave to his passions in these matters. But enough of reflections, and to our tale. The day, as I have said, was fine for a December morning. The grass was wet and the ground miry, and ploughed up with multitudinous feet, except that, within the ring itself, there was a spot of virgin-green closed in and unprofaned by vulgar tread, that shone with dazzling brightness in the mid-day sun. For it was now noon, and we had an hour to wait. This is the trying time. It is then the heart sickens, as you think what the two champions are about, and how short a time will determine their fate. After the first blow is struck, there is no opportunity for nervous apprehensions; you are swallowed up in the immediate interest of the scene – but

> 'Between the acting of a dreadful thing
> And the first motion, all the interim is
> Like a phantasma, or a hideous dream.'[29]

I found it so as I felt the sun's rays clinging to my back, and saw the white wintry clouds sink below the verge of the horizon. 'So, I thought, my fairest hopes have faded from my sight! – so will the Gas-man's glory, or that of his adversary, vanish in an hour.' The *swells*[30] were parading in their white box-coats, the outer ring was cleared with some bruises on the heads and shins of the rustic assembly (for the *cockneys* had been distanced by the sixty-six miles); the time drew near, I had got a good stand; a bustle, a buzz, ran through the crowd, and, from the opposite side entered Neate, between his second and bottle-holder. He rolled along, swathed in his loose great coat, his knock-knees bending under his huge bulk; and, with a modest cheerful air, threw his hat into the ring. He then just looked round, and began quietly to undress; when from the other side there was a similar rush and an opening made, and the Gas-man came forward with a conscious air of anticipated triumph, too much like the cock-of-the-walk. He strutted about more than became a hero, sucked oranges with a supercilious air, and threw away the skin with a toss of his head, and went up and looked at Neate, which was an act of supererogation. The only sensible thing he did was, as he strode away from the modern Ajax,[31] to fling out his arms, as if he wanted to try whether they would do their work that day. By this time they had stripped, and presented a strong contrast in appearance. If Neate was like Ajax, 'with Atlantean shoulders, fit to bear'[32] the pugilistic reputation of all Bristol, Hickman might be compared to Diomed,[33] light, vigorous, elastic, and his back glistened in the sun, as he moved about, like a panther's hide. There was now a dead pause – attention was awe-struck. Who at that moment, big with a great event, did not draw his breath short – did not feel his heart throb? All was ready. They tossed up for the sun, and the Gas-man won. They were led up to the *scratch*[34] – shook hands, and went at it.

In the first round every one thought it was all over. After making play a short time, the Gas-man flew at his adversary like a tiger, struck five blows in as many seconds, three first, and then following him as he staggered back, two more, right and left, and down he fell, a mighty ruin. There was a shout, and I said, 'There is no standing this.' Neate seemed like a lifeless lump of flesh and bone, round which the Gas-man's blows played with the rapidity of electricity or lightning, and you imagined he would only be lifted up to be knocked down again. It was as if Hickman held a sword or a fire in that right-hand of his, and directed it against an unarmed body. They met again, and Neate seemed, not cowed, but particularly cautious. I saw his teeth clenched together and his brows knit close against the sun. He held out both his arms at full length straight before him, like two sledge-hammers, and raised his left an inch or two higher. The Gas-man could not get over this guard – they struck mutually and fell, but without advantage on either side. It was the same in the next round; but the balance of power was thus restored – the fate of the battle was suspended. No one could tell how it would end. This was the only moment in which opinion was divided; for, in the next, the Gas-man aiming a mortal blow at his adversary's neck, with his right hand, and failing from the length he had to reach, the other returned it with his left at full swing, planted a tremendous blow on his cheek-bone and eye-brow, and made a red ruin of that side of his face. The Gas-man went down, and there was another shout – a roar of triumph as the waves of fortune rolled tumultuously from side to side. This was a settler. Hickman got up, and 'grinned horrible a ghastly smile',[35] yet he was evidently dashed in his opinion of himself; it was the first time he had ever been so punished; all one side of his face was perfect scarlet, and his right eye was closed in dingy blackness, as he advanced to the fight, less confident, but still determined. After one or two rounds, not receiving another such remembrancer, he rallied and went at it with his former impetuosity. But in vain. His strength had been weakened, – his blows could not tell at such a distance, – he was obliged to fling himself at his adversary, and could not strike from his feet; and almost as regularly as he flew at him with his right-hand, Neate warded the blow, or drew back out of its reach, and felled him with the return of his left. There was little cautious sparring – no half-hits – no tapping and trifling, none of the *petit-maîtreship* of the art – they were almost all knock-down blows: – the fight was a good stand-up fight. The wonder was the half-minute-time. If there had been a minute or more allowed between each round, it would have been intelligible how they should by degrees recover strength and resolution; but to see two men smashed to the ground, smeared with gore, stunned, senseless, the breath beaten out of their bodies; and then, before you recover from the shock, to see them rise up with new strength and courage, stand ready to inflict or receive mortal offence, and rush upon each other 'like two clouds over the Caspian'[56] – this is the most astonishing thing of all: – this is the high and heroic state of man! From this time forward the event became more certain every round; and about the twelfth it seemed as if it must have been over. Hickman generally stood with his back to me; but in the scuffle, he had changed positions, and Neate just then made a tremendous lunge at him, and hit him full in the face. It was doubtful whether he would fall backwards or forwards; he hung suspended for a second or two, and then fell back, throwing his hands in the air, and with his face lifted up to the sky. I never saw any thing more terrific than his aspect just before he fell. All traces of life, of natural expression, were gone from him. His face was like a human skull, a death's head, spouting blood. The eyes were filled with blood, the nose streamed with blood, the mouth gaped blood. He was not like an actual man, but like a preternatural, spectral appearance, or like one of the figures in Dante's *Inferno*. Yet he fought on after this for several rounds, still striking the first desperate blow, and Neate standing on the defensive, and using the same cautious guard to the last, as if he had still all his work to do; and it was not till the Gas-man was so stunned in the seventeenth or eighteenth round, that his senses forsook him, and he could not come to time, that the battle was declared over.* Ye who despise the FANCY, do something to shew as much *pluck*, or as much self-possession as this, before you assume a superiority which you have never given a single proof of by any one action in the whole course of your lives! — When the Gas-man came to himself, the first words he uttered were, 'Where am I? What is the matter?' 'Nothing is the matter, Tom, — you have lost the battle, but you are the bravest man alive.' And Jackson whispered to him, 'I am collecting a purse for you, Tom.' — Vain sounds, and unheard at that moment! Neate instantly went up and shook him cordially by the hand, and seeing some old acquaintance, began to flourish with his fists, calling out 'Ah! you always said I couldn't fight — What do you think now?' But all in good humour, and without any appearance of arrogance; only it was evident Bill Neate was pleased that he had won the fight. When it was over, I asked Cribb if he did not think it was a good one? He said, '*Pretty well!*' The carrier-pigeons now mounted into the air, and one of them flew with the news of her husband's victory to the bosom of Mrs Neate. Alas, for Mrs Hickman! —

Mais au revoir, as Sir Fopling Flutter[38] says. I went down with Toms; I returned with Jack Pigott, whom I met on the ground. Toms is a rattle-brain; Pigott is a sentimentalist. Now, under favour, I am a sentimentalist too — therefore I say nothing, but that the interest of the excursion did not flag as I came back. Pigott and I marched along the causeway leading from Hungerford to Newbury, now observing the effect of a brilliant sun on the tawny meads or moss-coloured cottages, now exulting in the fight, now digressing to some topic of general and elegant literature. My friend was dressed in character for the occasion, or like one of the FANCY; that is, with a double portion of great coats, clogs, and overhauls: and just as we had agreed with a couple of country-lads to carry his superfluous wearing-apparel to the next town, we were overtaken by a return

* Scroggins said of the Gas-man, that he thought he was a man of that courage, that if his hands were cut off, he would still fight on with the stumps — like that of Widrington, —

> ——— 'In doleful dumps,
> Who, when his legs were smitten off,
> Still fought upon his stumps.'[37]

post-chaise, into which I got, Pigott preferring a seat on the bar. There were two strangers already in the chaise, and on their observing they supposed I had been to the fight, I said I had, and concluded they had done the same. They appeared, however, a little shy and sore on the subject; and it was not till after several hints dropped, and questions put, that it turned out that they had missed it. One of these friends had undertaken to drive the other there in his gig: they had set out, to make sure work, the day before at three in the afternoon. The owner of the one-horse vehicle scorned to ask his way, and drove right on to Bagshot, instead of turning off at Hounslow: there they stopped all night, and set off the next day across the country to Reading, from whence they took coach, and got down within a mile or two of Hungerford, just half an hour after the fight was over. This might be safely set down as one of the miseries of human life. We parted with these two gentlemen who had been to see the fight, but had returned as they went, at Wolhampton, where we were promised beds (an irresistible temptation, for Pigott had passed the preceding night at Hungerford as we had done at Newbury), and we turned into an old bow-windowed parlour with a carpet and a snug fire; and after devouring a quantity of tea, toast, and eggs, sat down to consider, during an hour of philosophic leisure, what we should have for supper. In the midst of an Epicurean deliberation between a roasted fowl and mutton-chops with mashed potatoes, we were interrupted by an inroad of Goths and Vandals – *O procul este profani*[39] – not real flash-men, but interlopers, noisy pretenders, butchers from Tothill-fields, brokers from Whitechapel, who called immediately for pipes and tobacco, hoping it would not be disagreeable to the gentlemen, and began to insist that it was *a cross*.[40] Pigott withdrew from the smoke and noise into another room, and left me to dispute the point with them for a couple of hours *sans intermission*[41] by the dial. The next morning we rose refreshed; and on observing that Jack had a pocket volume in his hand, in which he read in the intervals of our discourse, I inquired what it was, and learned to my particular satisfaction that it was a volume of the *New Eloise*.[42] Ladies, after this, will you contend that a love for the FANCY is incompatible with the cultivation of sentiment? – We jogged on as before, my friend setting me up in a genteel drab great coat and green silk handkerchief (which I must say became me exceedingly), and after stretching our legs for a few miles, and seeing Jack Randall, Ned Turner, and Scroggins, pass on the top of one of the Bath coaches, we engaged with the driver of the second to take us to London for the usual fee. I got inside, and found three other passengers. One of them was an old gentleman with an aquiline nose, powdered hair, and a pigtail, and who looked as if he had played many a rubber at the Bath rooms. I said to myself, he is very like Mr Windham; I wish he would enter into conversation, that I might hear what fine observations would come from those finely-turned features. However, nothing passed, till, stopping to dine at Reading, some inquiry was made by the company about the fight, and I gave (as the reader may believe) an eloquent and animated description of it. When we got into the coach again, the old gentleman, after a graceful exordium, said, he had, when a boy, been to a fight between the famous Broughton and George Stevenson, who was called the *Fighting Coachman*, in the year 1770, with the late Mr Windham. This beginning flattered the spirit of prophecy within me, and he riveted my attention. He went on – 'George Stevenson was coachman to a friend of my father's. He was an old man when I saw him some years afterwards. He took hold of his own arm and said, "there was muscle here once, but now it is no more than this young gentleman's." He added, "well, no matter; I have been here long, I am willing to go hence, and hope I have done no more harm than another man." Once,' said my unknown companion, 'I asked him if he had ever beat Broughton? He said Yes; that he had fought with him three times, and the last time he fairly beat him, though the world did not allow it. "I'll tell you how it was, master. When the seconds lifted us up in the last round, we were so exhausted that neither of us could stand, and we fell upon one another, and as Master Broughton fell uppermost, the mob gave it in his favour, and he was said to have won the battle. But," says he, "the fact was, that as his second (John Cuthbert) lifted him up, he said to him, 'I'll fight no more, I've had enough'; which," says Stevenson, "you know gave me the victory. And to prove to you that this was the case, when John Cuthbert was on his death-bed, and they asked him if there was any thing on his mind which he wished to confess, he answered, 'Yes, that there was one thing he wished to set right, for that certainly Master Stevenson won that last fight with Master Broughton; for he whispered him as he lifted him up in the last round of all, that he had had enough.'" 'This,' said the Bath gentleman, 'was a bit of human nature'; and I have written this account of the fight on purpose that it might not be lost to the world. He also stated as a proof of the candour of mind in this class of men, that Stevenson acknowledged that Broughton could have beat him in his best day; but that he (Broughton) was getting old in their last rencounter. When we stopped in Piccadilly, I wanted to ask the gentleman some questions about the late Mr Windham, but had not courage. I got out, resigned my coat and green silk handkerchief to Pigott (loth to part with these ornaments of life), and walked home in high spirits.

P. S. Toms called upon me the next day, to ask me if I did not think the fight was a complete thing? I said I thought it was. I hope he will relish my account of it.

'Jack Tars'

*

There are two things that an Englishman understands, hard words and hard blows. Nothing short of this (generally speaking) excites his attention or interests him in the least. His neighbours have the benefit of the one in war time, and his own countrymen of the other in time of peace. The French express themselves astonished at the feats which our Jack Tars[1] have so often performed. A fellow in that class of life in England will strike his hand through a deal board – first, to show his strength, which he is proud of; secondly, to give him a sensation, which he is in want of; lastly to prove his powers of endurance, which he also makes a boast of. So qualified, a controversy with a cannon-ball is not much out of his way: a thirty-two pounder is rather an *ugly customer*, but it presents him with a tangible idea (a thing he is always in search of) – and, should it take off his head or carry away one of his limbs, he does not feel the want of the one or care for that of the other. Naturally obtuse, his feelings become hardened by custom; or if there are any qualms of repugnance or dismay left, a volley of oaths, a few coarse jests, and a double allowance of grog soon turn the affair into a pastime. Stung with wounds, stunned with bruises, bleeding and mangled, an English sailor never finds himself so much alive as when he is flung half dead into the cockpit; for he then perceives the extreme consciousness of his existence in his conflict with external matter, in the violence of his will, and his obstinate contempt for suffering. He feels his personal identity on the side of the disagreeable and repulsive; and it is better to feel it so than to be a stock or a stone, which is his ordinary state. Pain puts life into him; action, soul: otherwise, he is a mere log. The English are not like a nation of women. They are not thin-skinned, nervous, or effeminate, but dull and morbid: they look danger and difficulty in the face, and shake hands with death as with a brother. They do not hold up their heads, but they will turn their backs on no man: they delight in doing and in bearing more than others: what every one else shrinks from through aversion to labour or pain, they are attracted to, and go through with, and so far (and so far only) they are a great people. At least, it cannot be denied that they are a *pugnacious* set. Their heads are so full of this, that if a Frenchman speaks of SCREIB, the celebrated farce-writer, a young Englishman present will suppose he means CRIBB the boxer; and ten thousand people assembled at a prize-fight will witness an exhibition of pugilism with the same breathless attention and delight as the audience at the *Théâtre Français* listen to the dialogue of Racine or Molière. Assuredly, *we* do not pay the same attention to Shakespeare: but at a boxing-match every Englishman feels his power to give and take blows increased by sympathy, as at a French theatre every spectator fancies that the actors on the stage talk, laugh, and make love as he would. A metaphysician might say, that the English perceive objects chiefly by their mere material qualities of solidity, inertness, and impenetrability, or by their own muscular resistance to them; that they do not care about the colour, taste, smell, the sense of luxury or pleasure: — they require the heavy, hard, and tangible only, something for them to grapple with and resist, to try their strength and their unimpressibility upon. They do not like to smell a rose, or to taste of made-dishes, or to listen to soft music, or to look at fine pictures, or to make or hear fine speeches, or to enjoy themselves or amuse others; but they will knock any man down who tells them so, and their sole delight is to be as uncomfortable and disagreeable as possible. To them the greatest labour is to be pleased: they hate to have nothing to find fault with: to expect them to smile or to converse on equal terms, is the heaviest tax you can levy on their want of animal spirits or intellectual resources. A drop of pleasure is the most difficult thing to extract from their hard, dry, mechanical, husky frame; a civil word or look is the last thing they can part with. Hence the *matter-of-factness* of their understandings, their tenaciousness of reason or prejudice, their slowness to distinguish, their backwardness to yield, their mechanical improvements, their industry, their courage, their blunt honesty, their dislike to the frivolous and florid, their love of liberty out of hatred to oppression, and their love of virtue from their antipathy to vice. Hence also their philosophy, from their distrust of appearances and unwillingness to be imposed upon; and even their poetry has its probable source in the same repining, discontented humour, which flings them from cross-grained realities into the region of lofty and eager imaginations.* – A French gentleman, a man of sense and wit, expressed his wonder that all the English did not go and live in the South of France, where they would have a beautiful country, a fine climate, and every comfort almost for nothing. He did not perceive that they would go back in shoals from this scene of fancied contentment to their fogs and sea-coal fires, and that no Englishman can live without something to complain of. Some persons are sorry to see our countrymen abroad cheated, laughed at, quarrelling at all the inns they stop at: – while they are in *hot water*, while they think themselves ill-used and have but the spirit to resent it, they are happy. As long as they can swear, they are excused from being complimentary: if they have to fight, they need not think: while they are provoked beyond measure, they are released from the dreadful obligation of being pleased. Leave them to themselves, and they are dull: introduce them into company, and they are worse. It is the incapacity of enjoyment that makes them sullen and ridiculous; the mortification they feel at not having their own way in every thing, and at seeing others delighted without asking their leave, that makes them haughty and distant. An Englishman is silent abroad from having nothing to say; and he looks stupid, because he is so. It is kind words and graceful acts that afflict his soul – an appearance of happiness, which he

---

* We have five names unrivalled in modern times and in their different ways: – Newton, Locke, Bacon, Shakespeare, and Milton – and if to these we were to add a sixth that could not be questioned in his line, perhaps it would be Hogarth. Our wit is the effect not of gaiety, but spleen – the last result of a pertinacious *reductio ad absurdum*. Our greatest wits have been our gravest men. Fielding seems to have produced his *History of a Foundling* [2] with the same deliberation and forethought that Arkwright did his spinning-jenny. The French have no poetry; that is, no combination of internal feeling with external imagery. Their dramatic dialogue is frothy verbiage or a mucilage[3] of sentiment without natural bones or substance: ours constantly clings to the concrete, and has a *purchase* upon matter. Outward objects interfere with and extinguish the flame of their imagination: with us they are the fuel that kindle it into a brighter and stronger blaze.

suspects to be insincere because he cannot enter into it, and a flow of animal spirits which dejects him the more from making him feel the want of it in himself; pictures that he does not understand, music that he does not feel, love that he cannot make, suns that shine out of England, and smiles more radiant than they! Do not stifle him with roses; do not kill him with kindness:[4] leave him some pretext to grumble, to fret, and torment himself. Point at him as he drives an English mail-coach about the streets of Paris or of Rome, to relieve his despair of *éclat* by affording him a pretence to horsewhip some one. Be disagreeable, surly, lying, knavish, impertinent out of compassion; insult, rob him, and he will thank you; take any thing from him (nay even his life) sooner than his opinion of himself and his prejudices against others, his moody dissatisfaction and his contempt for every one who is not in as ill a humour as he is.

John Bull[5] is certainly a singular animal. It is the being the beast he is that has made a man of him. If he do not take care what he is about, the same ungoverned humour will be his ruin. He must have something to butt at; and it matters little to him whether it be friend or foe, provided only he can *run-a-muck*. He must have a grievance to solace him, a bug-bear of some sort or other to keep himself in breath: otherwise, he droops and hangs the head – he is no longer John Bull, but John Ox, according to a happy allusion of the Poet-laureate's.[6] This necessity of John's to be repulsive (right or wrong) has been lately turned against himself, to the detriment of others, and his proper cost. Formerly, the Pope, the Devil, the Inquisition, and the Bourbons,[7] served the turn, with all of whom he is at present sworn friends, unless Mr Canning should throw out a *tub to a whale*[8] in South America: then Buonaparte took the lead for a while in John's panic-struck brain; and latterly, the Whigs and the *Examiner* newspaper have borne the bell before all other topics of abuse and obloquy. Formerly, liberty was the word with John, – now it has become a bye-word. Whoever is not determined to make a slave and a drudge of him, he defies, he sets at, he tosses in the air, he tramples under foot; and after having mangled and crushed whom he pleases, stands stupid and melancholy (*fœnum in cornu*[9]) over the lifeless remains of his victim. When his fury is over, he repents of what he has done – too late. In his tame fit, and having made a clear stage of all who would or could direct him right, he is led gently by the nose by Mr Croker; and the 'Stout Gentleman'[10] gets upon his back, making a monster of him. Why is there a tablet stuck up in St Peter's at Rome, to the memory of the three last of the Stuarts? Is it a *baisés-mains*[11] to the Pope, or a compromise with legitimacy? Is the dread of usurpation become so strong, that a reigning family are half-ready to acknowledge themselves usurpers, in favour of those who are not likely to come back to assert their claim, and to countenance the principles that may keep them on a throne, in lieu of the paradoxes that placed them there? It is a handsome way of paying for a kingdom with an epitaph, and of satisfying the pretensions of the living and the dead. But we did not expel the slavish and tyrannical Stuarts from our soil by the volcanic eruption of 1688, to send a whining Jesuitical recantation and *writ of error* after them to the other world a hundred years afterwards. But it may be said that the inscription is merely a tribute of respect to misfortune. What! from that quarter? No! it is a 'lily-livered',[12] polished, courtly, pious monument to the fears that have so long beset the hearts of Monarchs, to the pale apparitions of Kings dethroned or beheaded in time past or to come (from that sad example) to the crimson flush of victory, which has put out the light of truth, and to the reviving hope of that deathless night of ignorance and superstition, when they shall once more reign as Gods upon the earth, and make of their enemies their footstool! Foreigners cannot comprehend this bear-garden work of ours at all: they 'perceive a fury, but nothing wherefore'.[13] They cannot reconcile the violence of our wills with the dullness of our apprehensions, nor account for the fuss we make about nothing; our convulsions and throes without end or object, the pains we take to defeat ourselves and others, and to undo all that we have ever done, sooner than any one else should share the benefit of it. They think it is strange, that out of mere perversity and contradiction we would rather be slaves ourselves, than suffer others to be free; that we *back* out of our most heroic acts and disavow our favourite maxims (the blood-stained devices in our national coat of arms) the moment we find others disposed to assent to or imitate us, and that we would willingly see the last hope of liberty and independence extinguished, sooner than give the smallest credit to those who sacrifice every thing to keep the spark alive, or abstain from joining in every species of scurrility, insult, and calumny against them, if the word is once given by the whippers-in of power. The English imagination is not *riante*: [14] it inclines to the gloomy and morbid with a heavy instinctive bias, and when fear and interest are thrown into the scale, down it goes with a vengeance that is not to be resisted, and from the effects of which it is not easy to recover. The enemies of English liberty are aware of this weakness in the public mind, and make a notable use of it.

> 'But that two-handed engine at the door
> Stands ready to smite once and smite no more.'[15]

Give a dog an ill name, and hang him – so says the proverb. The courtiers say, 'Give a *patriot* an ill name, and ruin him' alike with Whig and Tory – with the last, because he hates you as a friend to freedom; with the first, because he is afraid of being implicated in the same obloquy with you. This is the reason why the Magdalen Muse[16] of Mr Thomas Moore finds a taint in the *Liberal*; why Mr Hobhouse visits Pisa, to dissuade Lord Byron from connecting himself with any but gentlemen-born, for the credit of the popular cause. Set about a false report or insinuation, and the effect is instantaneous and universally felt – prove that there is nothing in it, and you are just where you were. Something wrong somewhere, in reality or imagination, in public or in private, is necessary to the minds of the English people: bring a charge against any one, and they hug you to their breasts: attempt to take it from them, and they resist it as they would an attack upon their persons or property: a nickname is to their moody, splenetic humour a freehold estate, from which they will not be ejected by fair means or foul: they conceive they have a *vested right* in calumny. No matter how base the lie, how senseless the jest, it *tells* – because the public appetite greedily swallows whatever is nauseous and disgusting, and refuses, through weakness or obstinacy, to disgorge it again. Therefore Mr Croker plies his dirty task – and is a Privy-councillor; Mr Theodore Hook calls Mr Waithman 'Lord Waithman' once a week, and passes for a wit!

*

On Hogarth's *Marriage à-la-Mode*

The superiority of the pictures of Hogarth, which we have seen in the late collection at the British Institution, to the common prints, is confined chiefly to the *Marriage à-la-Mode*. We shall attempt to illustrate a few of their most striking excellences, more particularly with reference to the expression of character. Their merits are indeed so prominent, and have been so often discussed, that it may be thought difficult to point out any new beauties; but they contain so much truth of nature, they present the objects to the eye under so many aspects and bearings, admit of so many constructions, and are so pregnant with meaning, that the subject is in a manner inexhaustible.

Boccaccio, the most refined and sentimental of all the novel-writers, has been stigmatized as a mere inventor of licentious tales, because readers in general have only seized on those things in his works which were suited to their own taste, and have reflected their own grossness back upon the writer. So it has happened that the majority of critics having been most struck with the strong and decided expression in Hogarth, the extreme delicacy and subtle gradations of character in his pictures have almost entirely escaped them. In the first picture of the *Marriage à-la-Mode*, the three figures of the young Nobleman, his intended Bride, and her inamorato, the Lawyer, show how much Hogarth excelled in the power of giving soft and effeminate expression. They have, however, been less noticed than the other figures, which tell a plainer story, and convey a more palpable moral. Nothing can be more finely managed than the differences of character in these delicate personages. The Beau sits smiling at the looking-glass, with a reflected simper of self-admiration, and a languishing inclination of the head, while the rest of his body is perked up on his high heels with a certain air of tip-toe elevation. He is the Narcissus of the reign of George II, whose powdered peruke, ruffles, gold lace, and patches, divide his self-love unequally with his own person, – the true *Sir Plume* of his day;

> 'Of amber-lidded snuffbox justly vain,
> And the nice conduct of a clouded cane.'[1]

There is the same felicity in the figure and attitude of the Bride, courted by the Lawyer. There is the utmost flexibility, and yielding softness in her whole person, a listless languor and tremulous suspense in the expression of her face. It is the precise look and air which Pope has given to his favourite Belinda, just at the moment of the *Rape of the Lock*.[2] The heightened glow, the forward intelligence, and loosened soul of love in the same face, in the assignation scene before the masquerade, form a fine and instructive contrast to the delicacy, timidity, and coy reluctance expressed in the first. The Lawyer in both pictures is much the same – perhaps too much so – though even this unmoved, unaltered appearance may be designed as characteristic. In both cases he has 'a person, and a smooth dispose, framed to make women false'.[3] He is full of that easy good-humour and easy good opinion of himself, with which the sex are delighted. There is not a sharp angle in his face to obstruct his success, or give a hint of doubt or difficulty. His whole aspect is round and rosy, lively and unmeaning, happy without the least expence of thought, careless and inviting; and conveys a perfect idea of the uninterrupted glide and pleasing murmur of the soft periods that flow from his tongue.

The expression of the Bride in the *Morning Scene* is the most highly seasoned, and at the same time the most vulgar in the series. The figure, face, and attitude of the Husband, are inimitable. Hogarth has with great skill contrasted the pale countenance of the husband with the yellow whitish colour of the marble chimney-piece behind him, in such a manner as to preserve the fleshy tone of the former. The airy splendour of the view of the inner-room in this picture is probably not exceeded by any of the productions of the Flemish School.

The Young Girl in the third picture, who is represented as the victim of fashionable profligacy, is unquestionably one of the Artist's *chef-d'œuvres*. The exquisite delicacy of the painting is only surpassed by the felicity and subtlety of the conception. Nothing can be more striking than the contrast between the extreme softness of her person, and the hardened indifference of her character. The vacant stillness, the docility to vice, the premature suppression of youthful sensibility, the doll-like mechanism of the whole figure, which seems to have no other feeling but a sickly sense of pain, – show the deepest insight into human nature, and into the effects of those refinements in depravity, by which it has been good-naturedly asserted, that 'vice loses half its evil in losing all its grossness'.[4] The story of this picture is in some parts very obscure and enigmatical. It is certain that the Nobleman is not looking straightforward to the Quack, whom he seems to have been threatening with his cane, but that his eyes are turned up with an ironical leer of triumph to the Procuress. The commanding attitude and size of this woman, the swelling circumference of her dress, spread out like a turkey-cock's feathers, – the fierce, ungovernable, inveterate malignity of her countenance, which hardly needs the comment of the clasp-knife to explain her purpose, are all admirable in themselves, and still more so, as they are opposed to the mute insensibility, the elegant negligence of the dress, and the childish figure of the girl, who is supposed to be her *protégée*. – As for the Quack, there can be no doubt entertained about him. His face seems as if it were composed of salve, and his features exhibit all the chaos and confusion of the most gross, ignorant, and impudent empiricism.

The gradations of ridiculous affectation in the *Music Scene* are finely imagined and preserved. The preposterous, overstrained admiration of the Lady of Quality, the sentimental, insipid, patient delight of the Man, with his hair in papers, and sipping his tea, – the pert, smirking, conceited, half-distorted approbation of the figure next to him, the transition to the total insensibility of the round face in profile, and then to the wonder of the Negro-boy at the rapture of his Mistress, form a perfect whole. The sanguine complexion and flame-coloured hair of the female Virtuoso throw an additional light on the character. This is lost in the print. The continuing the red colour of the hair into the back of the chair has been pointed out as one of those instances of alliteration in colouring, of which these pictures are every where full. The gross bloated appearance of the Italian Singer is well relieved by the hard features of the instrumental performer behind him, which might be carved of wood. The Negro-boy, holding the chocolate, both in expression, colour, and execution, is a masterpiece. The gay, lively derision of the other Negro-boy, playing with the Actæon, is an ingenious contrast to the profound amazement of the first. Some account has already been given of the two lovers in this picture. It is curious to observe the infinite activity of mind which the artist displays on every occasion. An instance occurs in the present picture. He has so contrived the papers in the hair of the Bride, as to make them look almost like a wreath of half-blown flowers, while those which he has placed on the head of the musical Amateur very much resemble a *cheveux-de-fris*[5] of horns, which adorn and fortify the lack-lustre expression and mild resignation of the face beneath.

The *Night Scene* is inferior to the rest of the series. The attitude of the Husband, who is just killed, is one in which it would be impossible for him to stand or even to fall. It resembles the loose pasteboard figures they make for children. The characters in the last picture, in which the Wife dies, are all masterly. We would particularly refer to the captious, petulant self-sufficiency of the Apothecary, whose face and figure are constructed on exact physiognomical principles, and to the fine example of passive obedience and non-resistance in the Servant, whom he is taking to task, and whose coat of green and yellow livery is as long and melancholy as his face. The disconsolate look, the haggard eyes, the open mouth, the comb sticking in the hair, the broken, gapped teeth, which, as it were, hitch in an answer, every thing about him denotes the utmost perplexity and dismay. — The harmony and gradations of colour in this picture are uniformly preserved with the greatest nicety, and are well worthy the attention of the artist.

The Subject Continued

It has been observed, that Hogarth's pictures are exceedingly unlike any other representations of the same kind of subjects — that they form a class, and have a character, peculiar to themselves. It may be worth while to consider in what this general distinction consists.

In the first place, they are, in the strictest sense, *Historical* pictures; and if what Fielding says be true,[1] that his novel of *Tom Jones* ought to be regarded as an epic prose-poem, because it contained a regular development of fable, manners, character, and passion, the compositions of Hogarth will, in like manner, be found to have a higher claim to the title of Epic Pictures, than many which have of late arrogated that denomination to themselves. When we say that Hogarth treated his subjects historically, we mean that his works represents the manners and humours of mankind in action, and their characters by varied expression. Every thing in his pictures has life and motion in it. Not only does the business of the scene never stand still, but every feature and muscle is put into full play; the exact feeling of the moment is brought out, and carried to its utmost height, and then instantly seized and stamped on the canvas for ever. The expression is always taken *en passant*, in a state of progress or change, and, as it were, at the salient point. Besides the excellence of each individual face, the reflection of the expression from face to face, the contrast and struggle of particular motives and feelings in the different actors in the scene, as of anger, contempt, laughter, compassion, are conveyed in the happiest and most lively manner. His figures are not like the back-ground on which they are painted: even the pictures on the wall have a peculiar look of their own. — Again, with the rapidity, variety, and scope of history, Hogarth's heads have all the reality and correctness of portraits. He gives the extremes of character and expression, but he gives them with perfect truth and accuracy. This is, in fact, what distinguishes his compositions from all others of the same kind, that they are equally remote from caricature, and from mere still-life. It of course happens in subjects from common life, that the painter can procure real models, and he can get them to sit as long as he pleases. Hence, in general, those attitudes and expressions have been chosen which could be assumed the longest; and in imitating which, the artist, by taking pains and time, might produce almost as complete facsimiles as he could of a flower or a flower-pot, of a damask curtain, or a china vase. The copy was as perfect and as uninteresting in the one case as in the other. On the contrary, subjects of drollery and ridicule affording frequent examples of strange deformity and peculiarity of features, these have been eagerly seized by another class of artists, who, without subjecting themselves to the laborious drudgery of the Dutch School and their imitators, have produced our popular caricatures, by rudely copying or exaggerating the casual irregularities of the human countenance. Hogarth has equally avoided the faults of both these styles, the insipid tameness of the one, and the gross vulgarity of the other, so as to give to the productions of his pencil equal solidity and effect. For his faces go to the very verge of caricature, and yet never (we believe in any single instance) go beyond it: they take the very widest latitude, and yet we always see the links which bind them to nature: they bear all the marks and carry all the conviction of reality with them, as if we had seen the actual faces for the first time, from the precision, consistency, and good sense, with which the whole and every part is made out. They exhibit the most uncommon features with the most uncommon expressions, but which are yet as familiar and intelligible as possible, because with all the boldness they have all the truth of nature. Hogarth has left behind him as many of these memorable faces, in their memorable moments, as perhaps most of us remember in the course of our lives, and has thus doubled the quantity of our observation.

We have, in a former paper, attempted to point out the fund of observation, physical and moral, contained in one set of these pictures, the *Marriage à-la-Mode*. The rest would furnish as many topics to descant upon, were the patience of the reader as inexhaustible as the painter's invention. But as this is not the case, we shall content ourselves with barely referring to some of those figures in the other pictures, which appear the most striking, and which we see not only while we are looking at them, but which we have before us at all other times. – For instance, who having seen can easily forget that exquisite frost-piece of religion and morality, the antiquated Prude in the *Morning Scene*; or that striking commentary on the *good old times*, the little wretched appendage of a Foot-boy, who crawls half famished and half frozen behind her? The French Man and Woman in the *Noon* are the perfection of flighty affectation and studied grimace; the amiable *fraternization* of the two old Women saluting each other is not enough to be admired; and in the little Master, in the same national group, we see the early promise and personification of that eternal principle of wondrous self-complacency, proof against all circumstances, and which makes the French the only people who are vain even of being cuckolded and being conquered! Or shall we prefer to this the outrageous distress and unmitigated terrors of the Boy, who has dropped his dish of meat, and who seems red all over with shame and vexation, and bursting with the noise he makes? Or what can be better than the good housewifery of the Girl underneath, who is devouring the lucky fragments, or than the plump, ripe, florid, luscious look of the Servant-wench embraced by a greasy rascal of an Othello, with her pie-dish tottering like her virtue, and with the most precious part of its contents running over? Just – no, not quite – as good is the joke of the Woman overhead, who, having quarrelled with her husband, is throwing their Sunday's dinner out of the window, to complete this chapter of accidents of baked-dishes. The husband in the *Evening Scene* is certainly as meek as any recorded in history; but we cannot say that we admire this picture, or the *Night Scene* after it. But then, in the Taste in High Life, there is that inimitable pair, differing only in sex, congratulating and delighting one another by 'all the mutually reflected charities'[2] of folly and affectation, with the young Lady coloured like a rose, dandling her little, black, pug-faced, white-teethed, chuckling favourite, and with the portrait of Mons. Des Noyers in the back-ground, dancing in a grand ballet, surrounded by butterflies. And again, in the *Election-*

Dinner, is the immortal Cobbler, surrounded by his Peers, who, 'frequent and full',[3] —

'In *loud* recess and *brawling* conclave sit:' —[4]

the Jew in the second picture, a very Jew in grain — innumerable fine sketches of heads in the Polling for votes, of which the Nobleman overlooking the caricaturist is the best; — and then the irresistible tumultuous display of broad humour in the Chairing the Member, which is, perhaps, of all Hogarth's pictures, the most full of laughable incidents and situations — the yellow, rusty-faced Thresher, with his swinging flail, breaking the head of one of the Chairmen, and his redoubted antagonist, the Sailor, with his oak-stick, and stumping wooden leg, a supplemental cudgel — the persevering ecstasy of the hobbling Blind Fiddler, who, in the fray, appears to have been trod upon by the artificial excrescence of the honest Tar — Monsieur, the Monkey, with piteous aspect, speculating the impending disaster of the triumphant candidate, and his brother Bruin, appropriating the paunch — the precipitous flight of the Pigs, souse over head into the water, the fine Lady fainting, with vermilion lips, and the two Chimney-sweepers, satirical young rogues! We had almost forgot the Politician who is burning a hole through his hat with a candle in reading the newspaper; and the Chickens, in the *March to Finchley*, wandering in search of their lost dam, who is found in the pocket of the Serjeant. Of the pictures in the *Rake's Progress*, in this collection, we shall not here say any thing, because we think them, on the whole, inferior to the prints, and because they have already been criticized by a writer, to whom we could add nothing, in a paper which ought to be read by every lover of Hogarth and of English genius.*

* See an 'Essay on the genius of Hogarth', by C. Lamb, published in a periodical work, called the *Reflector*.

Character of Mr Burke, 1807*

*

The following speech[1] is perhaps the fairest specimen I could give of
Mr Burke's various talents as a speaker. The subject itself is not the
most interesting, nor does it admit of that weight and closeness of
reasoning which he displayed on other occasions. But there is no
single speech which can convey a satisfactory idea of his powers of
mind: to do him justice, it would be necessary to quote all his works;
the only specimen of Burke is, *all that he wrote*. With respect to most
other speakers, a specimen is generally enough, or more than enough.
When you are acquainted with their manner, and see what proficiency
they have made in the mechanical exercise of their profession, with
what facility they can borrow a simile, or round a period, how
dextrously they can argue, and object, and rejoin, you are satisfied;
there is no other difference in their speeches than what arises from
the difference of the subjects. But this was not the case with Burke.
He brought his subjects along with him; he drew his materials from
himself. The only limits which circumscribed his variety were the
stores of his own mind. His stock of ideas did not consist of a few
meagre facts, meagrely stated, of half a dozen commonplaces tortured
in a thousand different ways: but his mine of wealth was a profound
understanding, inexhaustible as the human heart, and various as the
sources of nature. He therefore enriched every subject to which he
applied himself, and new subjects were only the occasions of calling
forth fresh powers of mind which had not been before exerted. It
would therefore be in vain to look for the proof of his powers in any

* This character was written in a fit of extravagant candour, at a time when I thought I
could do justice, or more than justice, to an enemy, without betraying a cause.

one of his speeches or writings: they all contain some additional proof of power. In speaking of Burke, then, I shall speak of the whole compass and circuit of his mind − not of that small part or section of him which I have been able to give: to do otherwise would be like the story of the man who put the brick in his pocket, thinking to show it as the model of a house. I have been able to manage pretty well with respect to all my other speakers, and curtailed them down without remorse. It was easy to reduce them within certain limits, to fix their spirit, and condense their variety; by having a certain quantity given, you might infer all the rest; it was only the same thing over again. But who can bind Proteus,[2] or confine the roving flight of genius?

Burke's writings are better than his speeches, and indeed his speeches are writings. But he seemed to feel himself more at ease, to have a fuller possession of his faculties in addressing the public, than in addressing the House of Commons. Burke was *raised* into public life: and he seems to have been prouder of this new dignity than became so great a man. For this reason, most of his speeches have a sort of parliamentary preamble to them: there is an air of affected modesty, and ostentatious trifling in them: he seems found of coqueting with the House of Commons, and is perpetually calling the Speaker out to dance a minuet with him, before he begins. There is also something like an attempt to stimulate the superficial dullness of his hearers by exciting their surprise, by running into extravagance: and he sometimes demeans himself by condescending to what may be considered as bordering too much upon buffoonery, for the amusement of the company. Those lines of Milton were admirably applied to him by some one − 'The elephant to make them sport wreathed his proboscis lithe.'[3] The truth is, that he was out of his place in the House of Commons; he was eminently qualified to shine as a man of genius, as the instructor of mankind, as the brightest luminary of his age: but he had nothing in common with that motley crew of knights, citizens, and burgesses. He could not be said to be 'native and endued unto that element'.[4] He was above it; and never appeared like himself, but when, forgetful of the idle clamours of party, and of the little views of little men, he appealed to his country, and the enlightened judgment of mankind.

I am not going to make an idle panegyric on Burke (he has no need of it); but I cannot help looking upon him as the chief boast and ornament of the English House of Commons. What has been said of him is, I think, strictly true, that 'he was the most eloquent man of his time: his wisdom was greater than his eloquence'.[5] The only public man that in my opinion can be put in any competition with him, is Lord Chatham: and he moved in a sphere so very remote, that it is almost impossible to compare them. But though it would perhaps be difficult to determine which of them excelled most in his particular way, there is nothing in the world more easy than to point out in what their peculiar excellences consisted. They were in every respect the reverse of each other. Chatham's eloquence was popular: his wisdom was altogether plain and practical. Burke's eloquence was that of the poet; of the man of high and unbounded fancy: his wisdom was profound and contemplative. Chatham's eloquence was calculated to make men *act*; Burke's was calculated to make them *think*. Chatham could have roused the fury of a multitude, and wielded their physical energy as he pleased: Burke's eloquence carried conviction into the mind of the retired and lonely student, opened the recesses of the human breast, and lighted up the face of nature around him. Chatham supplied his hearers with motives to immediate action: Burke furnished them with *reasons* for action which might have little effect upon them at the time, but for which they would be the wiser and better all their lives after. In research, in originality, in variety of knowledge, in richness of invention, in depth and comprehension of mind, Burke had as much the advantage of Lord Chatham as he was excelled by him in plain common sense, in strong feeling, in steadiness of purpose, in vehemence, in warmth, in enthusiasm, and energy of mind. Burke was the man of genius, of fine sense, and subtle reasoning; Chatham was a man of clear understanding, of strong sense, and violent passions. Burke's mind was satisfied with speculation: Chatham's was essentially *active*: it could not rest without an object. The power which governed Burke's mind was his Imagination; that which gave its *impetus* to Chatham's was Will. The one was almost the creature of pure intellect, the other of physical temperament.

There are two very different ends which a man of genius may propose to himself either in writing or speaking, and which will accordingly give birth to very different styles. He can have but one of these two objects; either to enrich or strengthen the mind; either to furnish us with new ideas, to lead the mind into new trains of thought, to which it was before unused, and which it was incapable of striking out for itself; or else to collect and embody what we already knew, to rivet our old impressions more deeply; to make what was before plain still plainer, and to give to that which was familiar all the effect of novelty. In the one case we receive an accession to the stock of our ideas; in the other, an additional degree of life and energy is infused into them: our thoughts continue to flow in the same channels, but their pulse is quickened and invigorated. I do not know how to distinguish these different styles better than by calling them severally the inventive and refined, or the impressive and vigorous styles. It is only the subject-matter of eloquence, however, which is allowed to be remote or obscure. The things in themselves may be subtle and recondite, but they must be dragged out of their obscurity and brought struggling to the light; they must be rendered plain and palpable, (as far as it is in the wit of man to do so) or they are no longer eloquence. That which by its natural impenetrability, and in spite of every effort, remains dark and difficult, which is impervious to every ray, on which the imagination can shed no lustre, which can be clothed with no beauty, is not a subject for the orator or poet. At the same time it cannot be expected that abstract truths or profound observations should ever be placed in the same strong and dazzling points of view as natural objects and mere matters of fact. It is enough if they receive a reflex and borrowed lustre, like that which cheers the first dawn of morning, where the effect of surprise and novelty gilds every object, and the joy of beholding another world gradually emerging out of the gloom of night, 'a new creation rescued from his reign',[6] fills the mind with a sober rapture. Philosophical eloquence is in writing what *chiaro scuro* is in painting; he would be a fool who should object that the colours in the shaded part of a picture were not so bright as those on the opposite side; the eye of the connoisseur receives an equal delight from both, balancing the want of brilliancy and effect with the greater delicacy of the tints, and difficulty of the execution. In judging of Burke, therefore, we are to consider first the style of eloquence which he adopted, and secondly the effects which he produced with it. If he did not produce the same effects on vulgar minds, as some others have done, it was not for want of power, but from the turn and direction of his mind.* It was because his subjects, his ideas, his arguments, were less vulgar. The question is not whether he brought certain truths equally home to us, but how much nearer he brought them than they were before. In my opinion, he united the two extremes of refinement and strength in a higher degree than any other writer whatever.

The subtlety of his mind was undoubtedly that which rendered Burke a less popular writer and speaker than he otherwise would have been. It weakened the impression of his observations upon others, but I cannot admit that it weakened the observations themselves; that it took any thing from their real weight and solidity. Coarse minds think all that is subtle, futile: that because it is not gross and obvious and palpable to the senses, it is therefore light and frivolous, and of no importance in the real affairs of life; thus making their own confined understandings the measure of truth, and supposing that whatever they do not distinctly perceive, is nothing. Seneca, who was not one of the vulgar, also says, that subtle truths are those which have the least substance in them,[7] and consequently approach nearest to nonentity. But for my own part I cannot help thinking that the most important truths must be the most refined and subtle; for that very reason, that they must comprehend a great number of particulars, and instead of referring to any distinct or positive fact, must point out the combined effects of an extensive chain of causes, operating gradually, remotely, and collectively, and therefore imperceptibly. General principles are not the less true or important because from their nature they elude immediate observation; they are like the air, which is not the less necessary because we neither see nor feel it, or like that secret influence which binds the world together, and holds the planets in their orbits. The very same persons who are the most forward to laugh at all systematic reasoning as idle and impertinent, you will the next moment hear exclaiming bitterly against the baleful effects of new-fangled systems of philosophy, or gravely descanting

---

* For instance: he produced less effect on the mob that compose the English House of Commons than Chatham or Fox, or even Pitt.

on the immense importance of instilling sound principles of morality into the mind. It would not be a bold conjecture, but an obvious truism to say, that all the great changes which have been brought about in the moral world, either for the better or worse, have been introduced not by the bare statement of facts, which are things already known, and which must always operate nearly in the same manner, but by the development of certain opinions and abstract principles of reasoning on life and manners, on the origin of society and man's nature in general, which being obscure and uncertain, vary from time to time, and produce correspondent changes in the human mind. They are the wholesome dew and rain, or the mildew and pestilence that silently destroy. To this principle of generalization all religious creeds, the institutions of wise lawgivers, and the systems of philosophers, owe their influence.

It has always been with me a test of the sense and candour of any one belonging to the opposite party, whether he allowed Burke to be a great man. Of all the persons of this description that I have ever known, I never met with above one or two who would make this concession; whether it was that party feelings ran too high to admit of any real candour, or whether it was owing to an essential vulgarity in their habits of thinking, they all seemed to be of opinion that he was a wild enthusiast, or a hollow sophist, who was to be answered by bits of facts, by smart logic, by shrewd questions, and idle songs. They looked upon him as a man of disordered intellect, because he reasoned in a style to which they had not been used and which confounded their dim perceptions. If you said that though you differed with him in sentiment, yet you thought him an admirable reasoner, and a close observer of human nature, you were answered with a loud laugh, and some hackneyed quotation. 'Alas! Leviathan was not so tamed!'[8] They did not know whom they had to contend with. The corner stone,[9] which the builders rejected, became the head-corner, though to the Jews a stumbling block,[10] and to the Greeks foolishness; for indeed I cannot discover that he was much better understood by those of his own party, if we may judge from the little affinity there is between his mode of reasoning and theirs. – The simple clue to all his reasonings on politics is, I think, as follows. He did not agree with some writers, that that mode of government is necessarily the best which is the cheapest. He saw in the construction of society other principles at work, and other capacities of fulfilling the desires, and perfecting the nature of man, besides those of securing the equal enjoyment of the means of animal life, and doing this at as little expence as possible. He thought that the wants and happiness of men were not to be provided for, as we provide for those of a herd of cattle, merely by attending to their physical necessities. He thought more nobly of his fellows. He knew that man had affections and passions and powers of imagination, as well as hunger and thirst and the sense of heat and cold. He took his idea of political society from the pattern of private life, wishing, as he himself expresses it, to incorporate the domestic charities with the orders of the state, and to blend them together. He strove to establish an analogy between the compact that binds together the community at large, and that which binds together the several families that compose it.[11] He knew that the rules that form the basis of private morality are not founded in reason, that is, in the abstract properties of those things which are the subjects of them, but in the nature of man, and his capacity of being affected by certain things from habit, from imagination, and sentiment, as well as from reason.

Thus, the reason why a man ought to be attached to his wife and children is not, surely, that they are better than others, (for in this case every one else ought to be of the same opinion) but because he must be chiefly interested in those things which are nearest to him, and with which he is best acquainted, since his understanding cannot reach equally to every thing; because he must be most attached to those objects which he has known the longest, and which by their situation have actually affected him the most, not those which in themselves are the most affecting, whether they have ever made any impression on him or no; that is, because he is by his nature the creature of habit and feeling, and because it is reasonable that he should act in conformity to his nature. Burke was so far right in saying that it is no objection to an institution, that it is founded in *prejudice*, but the contrary, if that prejudice is natural and right; that is, if it arises from those circumstances which are properly subjects of feeling and association, not from any defect or perversion of the understanding in those things which fall strictly under its jurisdiction.

On this profound maxim he took his stand. Thus he contended, that the prejudice in favour of nobility was natural and proper, and fit to be encouraged by the positive institutions of society; not on account of the real or personal merit of the individuals, but because such an institution has a tendency to enlarge and raise the mind, to keep alive the memory of past greatness, to connect the different ages of the world together, to carry back the imagination over a long tract of time, and feed it with the contemplation of remote events: because it is natural to think highly of that which inspires us with high thoughts, which has been connected for many generations with splendour, and affluence, and dignity, and power, and privilege. He also conceived, that by transferring the respect from the person to the thing, and thus rendering it steady and permanent, the mind would be habitually formed to sentiments of deference, attachment, and fealty, to whatever else demanded its respect: that it would be led to fix its view on what was elevated and lofty, and be weaned from that low and narrow jealousy which never willingly or heartily admits of any superiority in others, and is glad of every opportunity to bring down all excellence to a level with its own miserable standard. Nobility did not therefore exist to the prejudice of the other orders of the state, but by, and for them. The inequality of the different orders of society did not destroy the unity and harmony of the whole. The health and well-being of the moral world was to be promoted by the same means as the beauty of the natural world; by contrast, by change, by light and shade, by variety of parts, by order and proportion. To think of reducing all mankind to the same insipid level, seemed to him the same absurdity as to destroy the inequalities of surface in a country, for the benefit of agriculture and commerce. In short, he believed that the interests of men in society should be consulted, and their several stations and employments assigned, with a view to their nature, not as physical, but as moral beings, so as to nourish their hopes, to lift their imagination, to enliven their fancy, to rouse their activity, to strengthen their virtue, and to furnish the greatest number of objects of pursuit and means of enjoyment to beings constituted as man is, consistently with the order and stability of the whole.

The same reasoning might be extended farther. I do not say that his arguments are conclusive: but they are profound and *true*, as far as they go. There may be disadvantages and abuses necessarily interwoven with his scheme, or opposite advantages of infinitely greater value, to be derived from another order of things and state of society. This however does not invalidate either the truth or importance of Burke's reasoning; since the advantages he points out as connected with the mixed form of government are really and necessarily inherent in it: since they are compatible in the same degree with no other; since the principle itself on which he rests his argument (whatever we may think of the application) is of the utmost weight and moment; and since on whichever side the truth lies, it is impossible to make a fair decision without having the opposite side of the question clearly and fully stated to us. This Burke has done in a masterly manner. He presents to you one view or face of society. Let him, who thinks he can, give the reverse side with equal force, beauty, and clearness. It is said, I know, that truth is *one*; but to this I cannot subscribe, for it appears to me that truth is *many*. There are as many truths as there are things and causes of action and contradictory principles at work in society. In making up the account of good and evil, indeed, the final result must be one way or the other; but the particulars on which that result depends are infinite and various.

It will be seen from what I have said, that I am very far from agreeing with those who think that Burke was a man without understanding, and a merely florid writer. There are two causes which have given rise to this calumny; namely, that narrowness of mind which leads men to suppose that the truth lies entirely on the side of their own opinions, and that whatever does not make for them is absurd and irrational; secondly, a trick we have of confounding reason with judgment, and supposing that it is merely the province of the understanding to pronounce sentence, and not to give in evidence, or argue the case; in short, that it is a passive, not an active faculty. Thus there are persons who never run into any extravagance, because they are so buttressed up with the opinions of others on all sides, that they cannot lean much to one side or the other; they are so little moved with any kind of reasoning, that they remain at an equal distance from every extreme, and are never very far from the truth, because the slowness of their faculties will not suffer them to make much progress in error. These are persons of great judgment. The scales of the mind are pretty sure to remain even, when there is nothing in them. In this sense of the word, Burke must be allowed to have wanted judgment, by all those who think that he was wrong in his conclusions. The accusation of want of judgment, in fact, only means that you yourself are of a different opinion. But if in arriving at one error he discovered a hundred truths, I should consider myself a hundred times more indebted to him than if, stumbling on that which I consider as the right side of the question, he had committed a hundred absurdities in striving to establish his point. I speak of him now merely as an author, or as far as I and other readers are concerned with him; at the same time, I should not differ from any one who may be disposed to contend that the consequences of his writings as instruments of political power have been tremendous, fatal, such as no exertion of wit or knowledge or genius can ever counteract or atone for.

Burke also gave a hold to his antagonists by mixing up sentiment and imagery with his reasoning; so that being unused to such a sight in the region of politics, they were deceived, and could not discern the fruit from the flowers. Gravity is the cloak of wisdom; and those who have nothing else think it an insult to affect the one without the other, because it destroys the only foundation on which their pretensions are built. The easiest part of reason is dullness; the generality of the world are therefore concerned in discouraging any example of unnecessary brilliancy that might tend to show that the two things do not always go together. Burke in some measure dissolved the spell. It was discovered, that his gold was not the less valuable for being wrought into elegant shapes, and richly embossed with curious figures; that the solidity of a building is not destroyed by adding to it beauty and ornament; and that the strength of a man's understanding is not always to be estimated in exact proportion to his want of imagination. His understanding was not the less real, because it was not the only faculty he possessed. He justified the description of the poet, –

> 'How charming is divine philosophy!
> Not harsh and crabbed as dull fools suppose,
> But musical as is Apollo's lute!'[12]

Those who object to this union of grace and beauty with reason, are in fact weak-sighted people, who cannot distinguish the noble and majestic form of Truth from that of her sister Folly, if they are dressed both alike! But there is always a difference even in the adventitious ornaments they wear, which is sufficient to distinguish them.

Burke was so far from being a gaudy or flowery writer, that he was one of the severest writers we have. His words are the most like things; his style is the most strictly suited to the subject. He unites every extreme and every variety of composition; the lowest and the meanest words and descriptions with the highest. He exults in the display of power, in showing the extent, the force, and intensity of his ideas; he is led on by the mere impulse and vehemence of his fancy, not by the affectation of dazzling his readers by gaudy conceits or pompous images. He was completely carried away by his subject. He had no other object but to produce the strongest impression on his reader, by giving the truest, the most characteristic, the fullest, and most forcible description of things, trusting to the power of his own mind to mould them into grace and beauty. He did not produce a splendid effect by setting fire to the light vapours that float in the regions of fancy, as the chemists make fine colours with phosphorus, but by the eagerness of his blows struck fire from the flint, and melted the hardest substances in the furnace of his imagination. The wheels of his imagination did not catch fire from the rottenness of the materials, but from the rapidity of their motion. One would suppose, to hear people talk of Burke, that his style was such as would have suited the *Lady's Magazine*; soft, smooth, showy, tender, insipid, full of fine words, without any meaning. The essence of the gaudy or glittering style consists in producing a momentary effect by fine words and images brought together, without order or connexion. Burke most frequently produced an effect by the remoteness and novelty of his combinations, by the force of contrast, by the striking manner in which the most opposite and unpromising materials were harmoniously blended together; not by laying his hands on all the fine things he could think of, but by bringing together those things which he knew would blaze out into glorious light by their collision. The florid style is a mixture of affectation and common-place. Burke's was an union of untameable vigour and originality.

Burke was not a verbose writer. If he sometimes multiplies words, it is not for want of ideas, but because there are no words that fully express his ideas, and he tries to do it as well as he can by different ones. He had nothing of the *set* or formal style, the measured cadence, and stately phraseology of Johnson, and most of our modern writers. This style, which is what we understand by the *artificial*, is all in one key. It selects a certain set of words to represent all ideas whatever, as the most dignified and elegant, and excludes all others as low and vulgar. The words are not fitted to the things, but the things to the words. Every thing is seen through a false medium. It is putting a mask on the face of nature, which may indeed hide some specks and blemishes, but takes away all beauty, delicacy, and variety. It destroys all dignity or elevation, because nothing can be raised where all is on a level, and completely destroys all force, expression, truth, and character, by arbitrarily confounding the differences of things, and reducing every thing to the same insipid standard. To suppose that this stiff uniformity can add any thing to real grace or dignity, is like supposing that the human body in order to be perfectly graceful, should never deviate from its upright posture. Another mischief of this method is, that it confounds all ranks in literature. Where there is no room for variety, no discrimination, no nicety to be shown in matching the idea with its proper word, there can be no room for taste or elegance. A man must easily learn the art of writing, when every sentence is to be cast in the same mould: where he is only allowed the use of one word, he cannot choose wrong, nor will he be in much danger of making himself ridiculous by affectation or false glitter, when, whatever subject he treats of, he must treat of it in the same way. This indeed is to wear golden chains for the sake of ornament.

Burke was altogether free from the pedantry which I have here endeavoured to expose. His style was as original, as expressive, as rich and varied, as it was possible; his combinations were as exquisite, as playful, as happy, as unexpected, as bold and daring, as his fancy. If any thing, he ran into the opposite extreme of too great an inequality, if truth and nature could ever be carried to an extreme.

Those who are best acquainted with the writings and speeches of Burke will not think the praise I have here bestowed on them exaggerated. Some proof will be found of this in the following extracts.

But the full proof must be sought in his works at large, and particularly in the 'Thoughts on the Discontents'; in his 'Reflections on the French Revolution'; in his 'Letter to the Duke of Bedford'; and in the 'Regicide Peace'. The two last of these are perhaps the most remarkable of all his writings, from the contrast they afford to each other. The one is the most delightful exhibition of wild and brilliant fancy, that is to be found in English prose, but it is too much like a beautiful picture painted upon gauze; it wants something to support it: the other is without ornament, but it has all the solidity, the weight, the gravity of a judicial record. It seems to have been written with a certain constraint upon himself, and to show those who said he could not *reason*, that his arguments might be stripped of their ornaments without losing any thing of their force. It is certainly, of all his works, that in which he has shewn most power of logical deduction, and the only one in which he has made any important use of facts. In general he certainly paid little attention to them: they were the playthings of his mind. He saw them as he pleased, not as they were; with the eye of the philosopher or the poet, regarding them only in their general principle, or as they might serve to decorate his subject. This is the natural consequence of much imagination: things that are probable are elevated into the rank of realities. To those who can reason on the essences of things, or who can invent according to nature, the experimental proof is of little value. This was the case with Burke. In the present instance, however, he seems to have forced his mind into the service of facts: and he succeeded completely. His comparison between our connexion with France or Algiers,[13] and his account of the conduct of the war,[14] are as clear, as convincing, as forcible examples of this kind of reasoning, as are any where to be met with. Indeed I do not think there is any thing in Fox, (whose mind was purely historical) or in Chatham, (who attended to feelings more than facts) that will bear a comparison with them.

Burke has been compared to Cicero — I do not know for what reason. Their excellences are as different, and indeed as opposite, as they well can be. Burke had not the polished elegance; the glossy neatness, the artful regularity, the exquisite modulation of Cicero: he had a thousand times more richness and originality of mind, more strength and pomp of diction.

It has been well observed, that the ancients had no word that properly expresses what we mean by the word *genius*. They perhaps had not the thing. Their minds appear to have been too exact, too retentive, too minute and subtle, too sensible to the external differences of things, too passive under their impressions, to admit of those bold and rapid combinations, those lofty flights of fancy, which, glancing from heaven to earth, unite the most opposite extremes, and draw the happiest illustrations from things the most remote. Their ideas were kept too confined and distinct by the material form or vehicle in which they were conveyed, to unite cordially together, or be melted down in the imagination. Their metaphors are taken from things of the same class, not from things of different classes; the general analogy, not the individual feeling, directs them in their choice. Hence, as Dr Johnson observed,[15] their similes are either repetitions of the same idea, or so obvious and general as not to lend any additional force to it; as when a huntress is compared to Diana, or a warrior rushing into battle to a lion rushing on his prey. Their *forte* was exquisite art and perfect imitation. Witness their statues and other things of the same kind. But they had not that high and enthusiastic fancy which some of our own writers have shown. For the proof of this, let any one compare Milton and Shakespeare with Homer and Sophocles, or Burke with Cicero.

It may be asked whether Burke was a poet. He was so only in the general vividness of his fancy, and in richness of invention. There may be poetical passages in his works, but I certainly think that his writings in general are quite distinct from poetry; and that for the reason before given, namely, that the subject-matter of them is not poetical. The finest parts of them are illustrations or personifications of dry abstract ideas;* and the union between the idea and the illustration is not of that perfect and pleasing kind as to constitute poetry, or indeed to be admissible, but for the effect intended to be produced by it; that is, by every means in our power to give animation and attraction to subjects in themselves barren of ornament, but which at the same time are pregnant with the most important

---

* As in the comparison of the British Constitution to the 'proud keep of Windsor',[16] &c. the most splendid passage in his works.

consequences, and in which the understanding and the passions are equally interested.

I have heard it remarked by a person, to whose opinion I would sooner submit than to a general council of critics, that the sound of Burke's prose is not musical; that it wants cadence; and that instead of being so lavish of his imagery as is generally supposed, he seemed to him to be rather parsimonious in the use of it, always expanding and making the most of his ideas. This may be true if we compare him with some of our poets, or perhaps with some of our early prose writers, but not if we compare him with any of our political writers or parliamentary speakers. There are some very fine things of Lord Bolingbroke's on the same subjects, but not equal to Burke's. As for Junius, he is at the head of his class; but that class is not the highest. He has been said to have more dignity than Burke. Yes – if the stalk of a giant is less dignified than the strut of a *petit-maître*. I do not mean to speak disrespectfully of Junius, but grandeur is not the character of his composition; and if it is not to be found in Burke, it is to be found nowhere.

Character of Mr Burke [1817]

October 5, 1817.

It is not without reluctance that we speak of the vices and infirmities of such a mind as Burke's: but the poison of high example has by far the widest range of destruction: and, for the sake of public honour and individual integrity, we think it right to say, that however it may be defended upon other grounds, the political career of that eminent individual has no title to the praise of consistency. Mr Burke, the opponent of the American war, and Mr Burke, the opponent of the French Revolution, are not the same person, but opposite persons – not opposite persons only, but deadly enemies. In the latter period, he abandoned not only all his practical conclusions, but all the principles on which they were founded. He proscribed all his former sentiments, denounced all his former friends, rejected and reviled all the maxims to which he had formerly appealed as incontestable. In the American war, he constantly spoke of the rights of the people as inherent, and inalienable: after the French Revolution, he began by treating them with the chicanery of a sophist, and ended by raving at them with the fury of a maniac. In the former case, he held out the duty of resistance to oppression, as the palladium and only ultimate resource of natural liberty; in the latter, he scouted, prejudged, vilified and nicknamed, all resistance in the abstract, as a foul and unnatural union of rebellion and sacrilege. In the one case, to answer the purposes of faction, he made it out, that the people are always in the right; in the other, to answer different ends, he made it out that they are always in the wrong – lunatics in the hands of their royal keepers, patients in the sick-wards of an hospital, or felons in the condemned cells of a prison. In the one, he considered that there was a constant tendency on the part of the prerogative to encroach on the rights of the people, which ought always to be the object of the most watchful jealousy, and of resistance, when necessary: in the other, he pretended to regard it as the sole occupation and ruling passion of those in power, to watch over the liberties and happiness of their subjects. The burthen of all his speeches on the American war, was conciliation, concession, timely reform, as the only practicable or desirable alternative of rebellion: the object of all his writings on the French Revolution was, to deprecate and explode all concession and all reform, as encouraging rebellion, and as an irretrievable step to revolution and anarchy. In the one, he insulted kings personally, as among the lowest and worst of mankind; in the other, he held them up to the imagination of his readers, as sacred abstractions. In the one case, he was a partisan of the people, to court popularity; in the other, to gain the favour of the Court, he became the apologist of all courtly abuses. In the one case, he took part with those who were actually rebels against his Sovereign: in the other, he denounced as rebels and traitors, all those of his own countrymen who did not yield sympathetic allegiance to a foreign Sovereign, whom we had always been in the habit of treating as an arbitrary tyrant.

Nobody will accuse the principles of his present Majesty, or the general measures of his reign, of inconsistency. If they had no other merit, they have, at least, that of having been all along actuated by one uniform and constant spirit: yet Mr Burke at one time vehemently opposed, and afterwards most intemperately extolled them: and it was for his recanting his opposition, not for his persevering in it, that he received his pension. He does not himself mention his flaming speeches in the American war, as among the public services which had entitled him to this remuneration.

The truth is, that Burke was a man of fine fancy and subtle reflection; but not of sound and practical judgment, nor of high or rigid principles. – As to his understanding, he certainly was not a great philosopher; for his works of mere abstract reasoning are shallow and inefficient: – nor was he a man of sense and business; for, both in counsel and in conduct, he alarmed his friends as much at least as his opponents: – but he was an acute and accomplished man of letters

– an ingenious political essayist. He applied the habit of reflection, which he had borrowed from his metaphysical studies, but which was not competent to the discovery of any elementary truth in that department, with great facility and success, to the mixed mass of human affairs. He knew more of the political machine than a recluse philosopher; and he speculated more profoundly on its principles and general results than a mere politician. He saw a number of fine distinctions and changeable aspects of things, the good mixed with the ill, and the ill mixed with the good; and with a sceptical indifference, in which the exercise of his own ingenuity was obviously the governing principle, suggested various topics to qualify or assist the judgment of others. But for this very reason, he was little calculated to become a leader or a partisan in any important practical measure. For the habit of his mind would lead him to find out a reason for or against any thing: and it is not on speculative refinements, (which belong to *every* side of a question), but on a just estimate of the aggregate mass and extended combinations of objections and advantages, that we ought to decide or act. Burke had the power of throwing true or false weights into the scales of political casuistry, but not firmness of mind (or, shall we say, honesty enough) to hold the balance. When he took a side, his vanity or his spleen more frequently gave the casting vote than his judgment; and the fieriness of his zeal was in exact proportion to the levity of his understanding, and the want of conscious sincerity.

He was fitted by nature and habit for the studies and labours of the closet; and was generally mischievous when he came out; because the very subtlety of his reasoning, which, left to itself, would have counteracted its own activity, or found its level in the common sense of mankind, became a dangerous engine in the hands of power, which is always eager to make use of the most plausible pretexts to cover the most fatal designs. That which, if applied as a general observation on human affairs, is a valuable truth suggested to the mind, may, when forced into the interested defence of a particular measure or system, become the grossest and basest sophistry. Facts or consequences never stood in the way of this speculative politician. He fitted them to his preconceived theories, instead of conforming his theories to them. They were the playthings of his style, the sport of his fancy. They were the straws of which his imagination made a blaze, and were consumed, like straws, in the blaze they had served to kindle. The fine things he said about Liberty and Humanity, in his speech on the Begum's affairs,[1] told equally well, whether Warren Hastings was a tyrant or not: nor did he care one jot who caused the famine he described, so that he described it in a way that no one else could. On the same principle, he represented the French priests and nobles under the old regime as excellent moral people,[2] very charitable and very religious, in the teeth of notorious facts, — to answer to the handsome things he had to say in favour of priesthood and nobility in general; and, with similar views, he falsifies the records of our English Revolution, and puts an interpretation on the word *abdication*,[3] of which a schoolboy would be ashamed. He constructed his whole theory of government, in short, not on rational, but on picturesque and fanciful principles; as if the king's crown were a painted gewgaw, to be looked at on gala-days; titles an empty sound to please the ear; and the whole order of society a theatrical procession. His lamentations over the age of chivalry,[4] and his projected crusade to restore it, are about as wise as if any one, from reading *The Beggar's Opera*, should take to picking of pockets: or, from admiring the landscapes of Salvator Rosa, should wish to convert the abodes of civilized life into the haunts of wild beasts and banditti. On this principle of false refinement, there is no abuse, nor system of abuses, that does not admit of an easy and triumphant defence; for there is something which a merely speculative inquirer may always find out, good as well as bad, in every possible system, the best or the worst; and if we can once get rid of the restraints of common sense and honesty, we may easily prove, by plausible words, that liberty and slavery, peace and war, plenty and famine, are matters of perfect indifference. This is the school of politics, of which Mr Burke was at the head; and it is perhaps to his example, in this respect, that we owe the prevailing tone of many of those newspaper paragraphs, which Mr Coleridge thinks so invaluable an accession to our political philosophy.[5]

Burke's literary talents were, after all, his chief excellence. His style has all the familiarity of conversation, and all the research of the most elaborate composition. He says what he wants to say, by any means, nearer or more remote, within his reach. He makes use of the most common or scientific terms, of the longest or shortest sentences, of the plainest and most downright, or of the most figurative modes of speech. He gives for the most part loose reins to his imagination, and follows it as far as the language will carry him. As long as the one or the other has any resources in store to make the reader feel and see the thing as he has conceived it, in its nicest shades of difference, in its utmost degree of force and splendour, he never disdains, and never fails to employ them. Yet, in the extremes of his mixed style, there is not much affectation, and but little either of pedantry or of coarseness. He everywhere gives the image he wishes to give, in its true and appropriate colouring: and it is the very crowd and variety of these images that have given to his language its peculiar tone of animation, and even of passion. It is his impatience to transfer his conceptions entire, living, in all their rapidity, strength, and glancing variety, to the minds of others, that constantly pushes him to the verge of extravagance, and yet supports him there in dignified security —

> 'Never so sure our rapture to create,
> As when he treads the brink of all we hate.'[6]

He is the most poetical of our prose writers, and at the same time his prose never degenerates into the mere effeminacy of poetry; for he always aims at overpowering rather than at pleasing; and consequently sacrifices beauty and delicacy to force and vividness. He has invariably a task to perform, a positive purpose to execute, an effect to produce. His only object is therefore to strike hard, and in the right place; if he misses his mark, he repeats his blow; and does not care how ungraceful the action, or how clumsy the instrument, provided it brings down his antagonist.

Character of Mr Fox, 1807*

I shall begin with observing generally, that Mr Fox excelled all his contemporaries in the extent of his knowledge, in the clearness and distinctness of his views, in quickness of apprehension, in plain, practical common sense, in the full, strong, and absolute possession of his subject. A measure was no sooner proposed than he seemed to have an instantaneous and intuitive perception of its various bearings and consequences; of the manner in which it would operate on the different classes of society, on commerce or agriculture, on our domestic or foreign policy; of the difficulties attending its execution; in a word, of all its practical results, and the comparative advantages to be gained either by adopting or rejecting it. He was intimately acquainted with the interests of the different parts of the community, with the minute and complicated details of political economy, with our external relations, with the views, the resources, and the maxims of other states. He was master of all those facts and circumstances which it was necessary to know in order to judge fairly and determine wisely; and he knew them not loosely or lightly, but in number, weight, and measure. He had also stored his memory by reading and general study, and improved his understanding by the lamp of history. He was well acquainted with the opinions and sentiments of the best authors, with the maxims of the most profound politicians, with the causes of the rise and fall of states, with the general passions of men,

---

* If I had to write a character of Mr Fox at present,[1] the praise here bestowed on him would be 'craftily qualified'.[2] His life was deficient in the three principal points, the beginning, the middle, and the end. He began a violent Tory, and became a flaming patriot out of private pique; he afterwards coalesced with Lord North, and died an accomplice with Lord Grenville. But – *what I have written, I have written*.[5] So let it pass.

with the characters of different nations, and the laws and constitution of his own country. He was a man of a large, capacious, powerful, and highly cultivated intellect. No man could know more than he knew; no man's knowledge could be more sound, more plain and useful; no man's knowledge could lie in more connected and tangible masses; no man could be more perfectly master of his ideas, could reason upon them more closely, or decide upon them more impartially. His mind was full, even to overflowing. He was so habitually conversant with the most intricate and comprehensive trains of thought, or such was the natural vigour and exuberance of his mind, that he seemed to recall them without any effort. His ideas quarrelled for utterance. So far from ever being at a loss for them, he was obliged rather to repress and rein them in, lest they should overwhelm and confound, instead of informing the understandings of his hearers.

If to this we add the ardour and natural impetuosity of his mind, his quick sensibility, his eagerness in the defence of truth, and his impatience of every thing that looked like trick or artifice or affectation, we shall be able in some measure to account for the character of his eloquence. His thoughts came crowding in too fast for the slow and mechanical process of speech. What he saw in an instant, he could only express imperfectly, word by word, and sentence after sentence. He would, if he could, 'have bared his swelling heart',[4] and laid open at once the rich treasures of knowledge with which his bosom was fraught. It is no wonder that this difference between the rapidity of his feelings, and the formal round-about method of communicating them, should produce some disorder in his frame; that the throng of his ideas should try to overleap the narrow boundaries which confined them, and tumultuously break down their prison-doors, instead of waiting to be let out one by one, and following patiently at due intervals and with mock dignity, like poor dependants, in the train of words: – that he should express himself in hurried sentences, in involuntary exclamations, by vehement gestures, by sudden starts and bursts of passion. Every thing showed the agitation of his mind. His tongue faltered, his voice became almost suffocated, and his face was bathed in tears. He was lost in the magnitude of his subject. He reeled and staggered under the load of feeling which

oppressed him. He rolled like the sea beaten by a tempest.* Whoever, having the feelings of a man, compared him at these times with his boasted rival, — his stiff, straight, upright figure, his gradual contortions, turning round as if moved by a pivot, his solemn pauses, his deep tones, 'whose sound reverbed their own hollowness',[5] must have said, This is a man; that is an automaton. If Fox had needed grace, he would have had it; but it was not the character of his mind, nor would it have suited with the style of his eloquence. It was Pitt's object to smooth over the abruptness and intricacies of his argument by the gracefulness of his manner, and to fix the attention of his hearers on the pomp and sound of his words. Lord Chatham, again, strove to *command* others; he did not try to convince them, but to overpower their understandings by the greater strength and vehemence of his own; to awe them by a sense of personal superiority: and he therefore was obliged to assume a lofty and dignified manner. It was to him they bowed, not to truth; and whatever related to *himself*, must therefore have a tendency to inspire respect and admiration. Indeed, he would never have attempted to gain that ascendant over men's minds that he did, if either his mind or body had been different from what they were; if his temper had not urged him to control and command others, or if his personal advantages had not enabled him to secure that kind of authority which he coveted. But it would have been ridiculous in Fox to have affected either the smooth plausibility, the stately gravity of the one, or the proud, domineering, imposing dignity of the other; or even if he could have succeeded, it would only have injured the effect of his speeches.†
What he had to rely on was the strength, the solidity of his ideas, his complete and thorough knowledge of his subject. It was his business

---

* See an excellent character of Fox by a celebrated and admirable writer,[6] which appeared in the *Morning Chronicle*, November, 1806, from which this passage is taken as nearly as I could recollect it.

† There is an admirable, judicious, and truly useful remark in the preface to Spenser,[7] (not by Dr Johnson, for he left Spenser out of his poets, but by *one* Upton), that the question was not whether a better poem might not have been written on a different plan, but whether Spenser would have written a better one on a different plan. I wish to apply this to Fox's *ungainly* manner. I do not mean to say, that his manner was the best possible, (for that would be to say that he was the greatest man conceivable), but that it was the best for him.

therefore to fix the attention of his hearers, not on himself, but on his subject; to rivet it there, to hurry it on from words to things: — the only circumstance of which they required to be convinced with respect to himself, was the sincerity of his opinions; and this would be best done by the earnestness of his manner, by giving a loose to his feelings, and by showing the most perfect forgetfulness of himself, and of what others thought of him. The moment a man shews you either by affected words or looks or gestures, that he is thinking of himself, and you, that he is trying either to please or terrify you into compliance, there is an end at once to that kind of eloquence which owes its effect to the force of truth, and to your confidence in the sincerity of the speaker. It was, however, to the confidence inspired by the earnestness and simplicity of his manner, that Mr Fox was indebted for more than half the effect of his speeches. Some others (as Lord Lansdown for instance) might possess nearly as much information, as exact a knowledge of the situation and interests of the country; but they wanted that zeal, that animation, that enthusiasm, that deep sense of the importance of the subject, which removes all doubt or suspicion from the minds of the hearers and communicates its own warmth to every breast. We may convince by argument alone; but it is by the interest we discover in the success of our reasonings, that we persuade others to feel and act with us. There are two circumstances which Fox's speeches and Lord Chatham's had in common: they are alike distinguished by a kind of plain downright common sense, and by the vehemence of their manner. But still there is a great difference between them, in both these respects. Fox in his opinions was governed by facts — Chatham was more influenced by the feelings of others respecting those facts. Fox endeavoured to find out what the consequences of any measure would be; Chatham attended more to what people would think of it. Fox appealed to the practical reason of mankind; Chatham to popular prejudice. The one repelled the encroachments of power by supplying his hearers with arguments against it; the other by rousing their passions and arming their resentment against those who would rob them of their birthright. Their vehemence and impetuosity arose also from very different feelings. In Chatham it was pride, passion, self-will, impatience of control, a determination to have his own way, to carry every thing before him;* in Fox it was pure good nature, a sincere love of truth, an ardent attachment to what he conceived to be right; an anxious concern for the welfare and liberties of mankind. Or if we suppose that ambition had taken a strong hold of both their minds, yet their ambition was of a very different kind: in the one it was the love of power, in the other it was the love of fame. Nothing can be more opposite than these two principles, both in their origin and tendency. The one originates in a selfish, haughty, domineering spirit; the other in a social and generous sensibility, desirous of the love and esteem of others, and anxiously bent upon gaining merited applause. The one grasps at immediate power by any means within its reach; the other, if it does not square its actions by the rules of virtue, at least refers them to a standard which comes the nearest to it — the disinterested applause of our country, and the enlightened judgment of posterity. The love of fame is consistent with the steadiest attachment to principle, and indeed strengthens and supports it; whereas the love of power, where this is the ruling passion, requires the sacrifice of principle at every turn, and is inconsistent even with the shadow of it. I do not mean to say that Fox had no love of power, or Chatham no love of fame, (this would be reversing all we know of human nature), but that the one principle predominated in the one, and the other in the other. My reader will do me great injustice if he supposes that in attempting to describe the characters of different speakers by contrasting their general qualities, I mean any thing beyond the *more* or *less*: but it is necessary to describe those qualities simply and in the abstract, in order to make the distinction intelligible. Chatham resented any attack made upon the cause of liberty, of which he was the avowed champion, as an indignity offered to himself. Fox felt it as a stain upon the honour of his country, and as an injury to the rights of his fellow citizens. The one was swayed by his own passions and purposes, with very little regard to the consequences; the sensibility of the other was roused, and his passions kindled into a generous flame, by a real interest in whatever related to the welfare

* This may seem to contradict what I have before said of Chatham — that he spoke like a man who was discharging a duty, &c. but I there spoke of the tone he assumed, or his immediate feelings at the time, rather than of the real motives by which he was actuated.

of mankind, and by an intense and earnest contemplation of the consequences of the measures he opposed. It was this union of the zeal of the patriot with the enlightened knowledge of the statesman, that gave to the eloquence of Fox its more than mortal energy; that warmed, expanded, penetrated every bosom. He relied on the force of truth and nature alone; the refinements of philosophy, the pomp and pageantry of the imagination were forgotten, or seemed light and frivolous; the fate of nations, the welfare of millions, hung suspended as he spoke; a torrent of manly eloquence poured from his heart, bore down every thing in its course, and surprised into a momentary sense of human feeling the breathing corpses, the wire-moved puppets, the stuffed figures, the flexible machinery, the 'deaf and dumb things'[8] of a court.

I find (I do not know how the reader feels) that it is difficult to write a character of Fox without running into insipidity or extravagance. And the reason of this is, there are no splendid contrasts, no striking irregularities, no curious distinctions to work upon; no 'jutting frieze, buttress, nor coigne of 'vantage',[9] for the imagination to take hold of. It was a plain marble slab, inscribed in plain legible characters, without either hieroglyphics or carving. There was the same directness and manly simplicity in every thing that he did. The whole of his character may indeed be summed up in two words – strength and simplicity. Fox was in the class of common men, but he was the first in that class. Though it is easy to describe the differences of things, nothing is more difficult than to describe their degrees or quantities. In what I am going to say, I hope I shall not be suspected of a design to under-rate his powers of mind, when in fact I am only trying to ascertain their nature and direction. The degree and extent to which he possessed them can only be known by reading, or indeed by having heard his speeches.

His mind, as I have already said, was, I conceive, purely *historical*: and having said this, I have I believe said all. But perhaps it will be necessary to explain a little farther what I mean. I mean, then, that his memory was in an extraordinary degree tenacious of facts; that they were crowded together in his mind without the least perplexity or confusion; that there was no chain of consequences too vast for his powers of comprehension; that the different parts and ramifications of his subject were never so involved and intricate but that they were easily disentangled in the clear prism of his understanding. The basis of his wisdom was experience: however, he not only knew what had happened; but by an exact knowledge of the real state of things, he could always tell what in the common course of events would happen in future. The force of his mind was exerted upon facts: as long as he could lean directly upon these, as long as he had the actual objects to refer to, to steady himself by, he could analyse, he could combine, he could compare and reason upon them, with the utmost exactness; but he could not reason *out of* them. He was what is understood by a *matter-of-fact* reasoner. He was better acquainted with the concrete masses of things, their substantial forms, and practical connexions, than with their abstract nature or general definitions. He was a man of extensive information, of sound knowledge, and clear understanding, rather than the acute observer or profound thinker. He was the man of business, the accomplished statesman, rather than the philosopher. His reasonings were, generally speaking, calculations of certain positive results, which, the *data* being given, must follow as matters of course, rather than unexpected and remote truths drawn from a deep insight into human nature, and the subtle application of general principles to particular cases. They consisted chiefly in the detail and combination of a vast number of items in an account, worked by the known rules of political arithmetic; not in the discovery of bold, comprehensive, and original theorems in the science. They were rather acts of memory, of continued attention, of a power of bringing all his ideas to bear at once upon a single point, than of reason or invention. He was the attentive observer who watches the various effects and successive movements of a machine already constructed, and can tell how to manage it while it goes on as it has always done; but who knows little or nothing of the principles on which it is constructed, nor how to set it right, if it becomes disordered, except by the most common and obvious expedients. Burke was to Fox what the geometrician is to the mechanic. Much has been said of the 'prophetic mind' of Mr Fox. The same epithet has been applied to Mr Burke, till it has become proverbial. It has, I think, been applied without much reason to either. Fox wanted the scientific part, Burke wanted the practical. Fox had too little imagination, Burke had too much: that is, he was careless of facts, and was led away by his passions to look at one side of a question only. He had not that fine sensibility to outward impressions, that nice *tact* of circumstances, which is necessary to the consummate politician. Indeed, his wisdom was more that of the legislator than of the active statesman. They both tried their strength in the Ulysses' bow of politicians, the French Revolution: and they were both foiled. Fox indeed foretold the success of the French in combating with foreign powers. But this was no more than what every friend of the liberty of France foresaw or foretold as well as he. All those on the same side of the question were inspired with the same sagacity on the subject. Burke, on the other hand, seems to have been before-hand with the public in foreboding the internal disorders that would attend the Revolution, and its ultimate failure; but then it is at least a question whether he did not make good his own predictions: and certainly he saw into the causes and connexion of events much more clearly after they had happened than before. He was however undoubtedly a profound commentator on that apocalyptical chapter in the history of human nature, which I do not think Fox was. Whether led to it by the events or not, he saw thoroughly into the principles that operated to produce them; and he pointed them out to others in a manner which could not be mistaken. I can conceive of Burke, as the genius of the storm, perched over Paris, the centre and focus of anarchy, (so he would have us believe) hovering 'with mighty wings outspread over the abyss, and rendering it pregnant',[10] watching the passions of men gradually unfolding themselves in new situations, penetrating those hidden motives which hurried them from one extreme into another, arranging and analysing the principles that alternately pervaded the vast chaotic mass, and extracting the elements of order and the cement of social life from the decomposition of all society: while Charles Fox in the meantime dogged the heels of the Allies, (all the way calling out to them to stop) with his sutler's bag, his muster-roll, and army estimates at his back. He said, You have only fifty thousand troops, the enemy have a hundred thousand: this place is dismantled, it can make no resistance: your troops were beaten last year, they must therefore be disheartened this. This is excellent sense and sound reasoning, but I do not see what it has to do with philosophy. But why was it necessary that Fox should be a philosopher? Why, in the first place, Burke was a philosopher, and Fox, to keep up with him, must be so too. In the second place, it was necessary, in order that his indiscreet admirers, who have no idea of greatness but as it consists in certain names and pompous titles, might be able to talk big about their patron. It is a bad compliment we pay to our idol when we endeavour to make him out something different from himself; it shows that we are not satisfied with what he was. I have heard it said that he had as much imagination as Burke. To this extravagant assertion I shall make what I conceive to be a very cautious and moderate answer: that Burke was as superior to Fox in this respect as Fox perhaps was to the first person you would meet in the street. There is in fact hardly an instance of imagination to be met with in any of his speeches; what there is, is of the rhetorical kind. I may, however, be wrong. He might excel as much in profound thought, and richness of fancy, as he did in other things; though I cannot perceive it. However, when any one publishes a book called *The Beauties of Fox*, containing the original reflections, brilliant passages, lofty metaphors, &c. to be found in his speeches, without the detail or connexion, I shall be very ready to give the point up.

In logic Fox was inferior to Pitt — indeed, in all the formalities of eloquence, in which the latter excelled as much as he was deficient in the soul or substance. When I say that Pitt was superior to Fox in logic, I mean that he excelled him in the formal division of the subject, in always keeping it in view, as far as he chose; in being able to detect any deviation from it in others; in the management of his general topics; in being aware of the mood and figure in which the argument must move, with all its non-essentials, dilemmas, and alternatives; in never committing himself, nor ever suffering his antagonist to occupy an inch of the plainest ground, but under cover of a syllogism. He had more of 'the dazzling fence of argument',[11] as it has been called. He was, in short, better at his weapon. But then, unfortunately, it was only a dagger of lath that the wind could turn aside; whereas Fox wore a good trusty blade, of solid metal, and real execution.

I shall not trouble myself to inquire whether Fox was a man of strict virtue and principle; or in other words, how far he was one of those who screw themselves up to a certain pitch of ideal perfection, who, as it were, set themselves in the stocks of morality, and make mouths at their own situation. He was not one of that tribe, and shall not be tried by their self-denying ordinances. But he was endowed with one of the most excellent natures that ever fell to the lot of any of God's creatures. It has been said, that 'an honest man's the noblest work of God'.[12] There is indeed a purity, a rectitude, an integrity of heart, a freedom from every selfish bias, and sinister motive, a manly simplicity and noble disinterestedness of feeling, which is in my opinion to be preferred before every other gift of nature or art. There is a greatness of soul that is superior to all the brilliancy of the understanding. This strength of moral character, which is not only a more valuable but a rarer quality than strength of understanding (as we are oftener led astray by the narrowness of our feelings, than want of knowledge) Fox possessed in the highest degree. He was superior to every kind of jealousy, of suspicion, of malevolence; to every narrow and sordid motive. He was perfectly above every species of duplicity, of low art and cunning. He judged of every thing in the downright sincerity of his nature, without being able to impose upon himself by any hollow disguise, or to lend his support to any thing unfair or dishonourable. He had an innate love of truth, of justice, of probity, of whatever was generous or liberal. Neither his education, nor his connexions, or his situation in life, nor the low intrigues and virulence of party, could ever alter the simplicity of his taste, nor the candid openness of his nature. There was an elastic force about his heart, a freshness of social feeling, a warm glowing humanity, which remained unimpaired to the last. He was by nature a gentleman. By this I mean that he felt a certain deference and respect for the person of every man; he had an unaffected frankness and benignity in his behaviour to others, the utmost liberality in judging of their conduct and motives. A refined humanity constitutes the character of a gentleman.* He was the true friend of his country, as far as it is possible for a statesman to be so. But his love of his country did not consist in his hatred of the rest of mankind. I shall conclude this account by repeating what

---

* To this character none of those who could be compared with him in talents had the least pretensions, as Chatham, Burke, Pitt, &c. They would *blackguard* and bully any man upon the slightest provocation, or difference of opinion.

Burke said of him at a time when his testimony was of the most value. 'To his great and masterly understanding he joined the utmost possible degree of moderation: he was of the most artless, candid, open, and benevolent disposition; disinterested in the extreme; of a temper mild and placable, even to a fault; and without one drop of gall in his constitution.'[15]

Why the Arts are not Progressive? – A Fragment

It is often made a subject of complaint and surprise, that the arts in this country, and in modern times, have not kept pace with the general progress of society and civilization in other respects, and it has been proposed to remedy the deficiency by more carefully availing ourselves of the advantages which time and circumstances have placed within our reach, but which we have hitherto neglected, the study of the antique, the formation of academies, and the distribution of prizes.

First, the complaint itself, that the arts do not attain that progressive degree of perfection which might reasonably be expected from them, proceeds on a false notion, for the analogy appealed to in support of the regular advances of art to higher degrees of excellence, totally fails; it applies to science, not to art. – Secondly, the expedients proposed to remedy the evil by adventitious means are only calculated to confirm it. The arts hold immediate communication with nature, and are only derived from that source. When that original impulse no longer exists, when the inspiration of genius is fled, all the attempts to recall it are no better than the tricks of galvanism to restore the dead to life. The arts may be said to resemble Antæus in his struggle with Hercules, who was strangled when he was raised above the ground, and only revived and recovered his strength when he touched his mother earth.

Nothing is more contrary to the fact than the supposition that in what we understand by the *fine arts*, as painting and poetry, relative perfection is only the result of repeated efforts, and that what has been once well done constantly leads to something better. What is mechanical, reducible to rule, or capable of demonstration, is progressive, and admits of gradual improvement: what is not mechanical or definite, but depends on genius, taste, and feeling, very soon becomes stationary, or retrograde, and loses more than it gains by transfusion. The contrary opinion is, indeed, a common error, which has grown up, like many others, from transferring an analogy of one kind to something quite distinct, without thinking of the difference in the nature of the things, or attending to the difference of the results. For most persons, finding what wonderful advances have been made in biblical criticism, in chemistry, in mechanics, in geometry, astronomy, &c. *i. e.* in things depending on mere inquiry and experiment, or on absolute demonstration, have been led hastily to conclude, that there was a general tendency in the efforts of the human intellect to improve by repetition, and in all other arts and institutions to grow perfect and mature by time. We look back upon the theological creed of our ancestors, and their discoveries in natural philosophy, with a smile of pity; science, and the arts connected with it, have all had their infancy, their youth, and manhood, and seem to have in them no principle of limitation or decay; and, inquiring no farther about the matter, we infer, in the height of our self-congratulation, and in the intoxication of our pride, that the same progress has been, and will continue to be, made in all other things which are the work of man. The fact, however, stares us so plainly in the face, that one would think the smallest reflection must suggest the truth, and overturn our sanguine theories. The greatest poets, the ablest orators, the best painters, and the finest sculptors that the world ever saw, appeared soon after the birth of these arts, and lived in a state of society, which was, in other respects, comparatively barbarous. Those arts, which depend on individual genius and incommunicable power, have always leaped at once from infancy to manhood, from the first rude dawn of invention to their meridian height and dazzling lustre, and have in general declined ever after. This is the peculiar distinction and privilege of each, of science and of art; of the one, never to attain its utmost summit of perfection, and of the other, to arrive at it almost at once. Homer, Chaucer, Spenser, Shakespeare, Dante, and Ariosto, (Milton alone was of a later age, and not the worse for it), Raphael, Titian, Michael Angelo, Correggio, Cervantes, and Boccaccio – all lived near the beginning of their arts – perfected, and all but created them. These giant sons of genius stand, indeed, upon the earth, but they tower above their fellows, and the long line of their successors does not interpose any thing to obstruct their view, or lessen their brightness. In strength and stature they are unrivalled, in grace and beauty they have never been surpassed. In after-ages, and more refined periods, (as they are called) great men have arisen one by one, as it were by throes and at intervals: though in general the best of these cultivated and artificial minds were of an inferior order, as Tasso and Pope among poets, Guido and Vandyke among painters. But in the earliest stages of the arts, when the first mechanical difficulties had been got over, and the language as it were acquired, they rose by clusters and in constellations, never to rise again.

The arts of painting and poetry are conversant with the world of thought within us, and with the world of sense without us — with what we know, and see, and feel intimately. They flow from the sacred shrine of our own breasts, and are kindled at the living lamp of nature. The pulse of the passions assuredly beat as high, the depths and soundings of the human heart were as well understood three thousand years ago, as they are at present; the face of nature, and 'the human face divine',[1] shone as bright then as they have ever done. It is this light, reflected by true genius on art, that marks out its path before it, and sheds a glory round the Muses' feet, like that which 'circled Una's angel face,

> And made a sunshine in the shady place.'[2]

Nature is the soul of art. There is a strength in the imagination that reposes entirely on nature, which nothing else can supply. There is in the old poets and painters a vigour and grasp of mind, a full possession of their subject, a confidence and firm faith, a sublime simplicity, an elevation of thought, proportioned to their depth of feeling, an increasing force and impetus, which moves, penetrates, and kindles all that comes in contact with it, which seems not theirs, but given to them. It is this reliance on the power of nature which has produced those masterpieces by the Prince of Painters,[3] in which expression is all in all, where one spirit — that of truth — pervades every part, brings down heaven to earth, mingles cardinals and popes with angels and apostles, and yet blends and harmonizes the whole by the true touches and intense feeling of what is beautiful and grand in nature. It was the same trust in nature that enabled Chaucer to describe the patient sorrow of Griselda;[4] or the delight of that young beauty, in *The Flower and the Leaf*,[5] shrouded in her bower, and listening, in the morning of the year, to the singing of the nightingale, while her joy rises with the rising song, and gushes out afresh at every pause, and is borne along with the full tide of pleasure, and still increases and repeats and prolongs itself, and knows no ebb. It is thus that Boccaccio, in the divine story of the Hawk,[6] has represented Frederigo Alberigi steadily contemplating his favourite Falcon, (the wreck and remnant of his fortune), and glad to see how fat and fair a bird she is, thinking what a dainty repast she would make for his Mistress, who had deigned to visit him in his low cell. So Isabella mourns over her pot of Basil,[7] and never asks for any thing but that. So Lear calls out for his poor fool,[8] and invokes the heavens, for they are old like him. So Titian impressed on the countenance of that young Neapolitan nobleman in the Louvre, a look that never passed away. So Nicolas Poussin describes some shepherds wandering out in a morning of the spring, and coming to a tomb with this inscription, 'I ALSO WAS AN ARCADIAN.'

In general, it must happen in the first stages of the Arts, that as none but those who had a natural genius for them would attempt to practise them, so none but those who had a natural taste for them would pretend to judge of or criticize them. This must be an incalculable advantage to the man of true genius, for it is no other than the privilege of being tried by his peers. In an age when connoisseurship had not become a fashion; when religion, war, and intrigue, occupied the time and thoughts of the great, only those minds of superior refinement would be led to notice the works of art, who had a real sense of their excellence; and in giving way to the powerful bent of his own genius, the painter was most likely to consult the taste of his judges. He had not to deal with pretenders to taste, through vanity, affectation, and idleness. He had to appeal to the higher faculties of the soul; to that deep and innate sensibility to truth and beauty, which required only a proper object to have its enthusiasm excited; and to that independent strength of mind, which, in the midst of ignorance and barbarism, hailed and fostered genius, wherever it met with it. Titian was patronized by Charles V. Count Castiglione was the friend of Raphael. These were true patrons, and true critics; and as there were no others, (for the world, in general, merely looked on and wondered), there can be little doubt, that such a period of dearth of factitious patronage would be the most favourable to the full development of the greatest talents, and the attainment of the highest excellence.

The diffusion of taste is not the same thing as the improvement of taste; but it is only the former of these objects that is promoted by public institutions and other artificial means. The number of candidates for fame, and of pretenders to criticism, is thus increased beyond all proportion, while the quantity of genius and feeling remains the same; with this difference, that the man of genius is lost in the crowd of competitors, who would never have become such but from encouragement and example; and that the opinion of those few persons whom nature intended for judges, is drowned in the noisy suffrages of shallow smatterers in taste. The principle of universal suffrage, however applicable to matters of government, which concern the common feelings and common interests of society, is by no means applicable to matters of taste, which can only be decided upon by the most refined understandings. The highest efforts of genius, in every walk of art, can never be properly understood by the generality of mankind: There are numberless beauties and truths which lie far beyond their comprehension. It is only as refinement and sublimity are blended with other qualities of a more obvious and grosser nature, that they pass current with the world. Taste is the highest degree of sensibility, or the impression made on the most cultivated and sensible minds, as genius is the result of the highest powers both of feeling and invention. It may be objected, that the public taste is capable of gradual improvement, because, in the end, the public do justice to works of the greatest merit. This is a mistake. The reputation ultimately, and often slowly affixed to works of genius, is stamped upon them by authority, not by popular consent or the common sense of the world. We imagine that the admiration of the works of celebrated men has become common, because the admiration of their names has become so. But does not every ignorant connoisseur pretend the same veneration, and talk with the same vapid assurance of Michael

Angelo, though he has never seen even a copy of any of his pictures, as if he had studied them accurately, — merely because Sir Joshua Reynolds has praised him? Is Milton more popular now than when the *Paradise Lost* was first published? Or does he not rather owe his reputation to the judgment of a few persons in every successive period, accumulating in his favour, and overpowering by its weight the public indifference? Why is Shakespeare popular? Not from his refinement of character or sentiment, so much as from his power of telling a story, — the variety and invention, — the tragic catastrophe and broad farce of his plays? Spenser is not yet understood. Does not Boccaccio pass to this day for a writer of ribaldry, because his jests and lascivious tales were all that caught the vulgar ear, while the story of the Falcon is forgotten!

Poetry

The Atlas.   *March 8, 1829.*

As there are two kinds of rhyme, one that is rhyme to the ear, and
another to the eye only; so there may be said to be two kinds of
poetry, one that is a description of objects to those who have never
seen or but slightly studied them; the other is a description of objects
addressed to those who have seen and are intimately acquainted with
them, and expressing the feeling which is the result of such knowledge.
It is needless to add that the first kind of poetry is comparatively
superficial and commonplace; the last profound, lofty, nay often
divine. Take an example (one out of a thousand) from Shakespeare.
In enumerating the wished-for contents of her basket of flowers,
Perdita in the *Winter's Tale* mentions among others –

> 'Daffodils
> That come before the swallow dares, and take
> The winds of March with beauty; violets dim,
> But sweeter than the lids of Juno's eyes
> Or Cytherea's breath; pale primroses
> That die unmarried ere they can behold
> Bright Phœbus in his strength, a malady
> Most incident to maids.'[1]

This passage which knocks down John Bull[2] with its perfumed and
melting softness, and savours of 'that fine madness which our first
poets had',[3] is a mystery, an *untranslateable* language, to all France:
Racine could not have conceived what it was about – the stupidest
Englishman feels a certain pride and pleasure in it. What a privilege

(if that were all) to be born on this the cloudy and poetical side of the Channel! We may in part clear up this contradiction in tastes by the clue above given. The French are more apt at taking the patterns of their ideas from words; we, who are slower and heavier, are obliged to look closer at things before we can pronounce upon them at all, which in the end perhaps opens a larger field both of observation and fancy. Thus the phrase 'violets *dim*', to those who have never seen the object, or who, having paid no attention to it, refer to the description for their notion of it, seems to convey a slur rather than a compliment, dimness being no beauty in itself; so this part of the story would not have been ventured upon in French or tinsel poetry. But to those who have seen, and been as it were enamoured of the little hedge-row candidate for applause, looking at it again and again (as misers contemplate their gold – as fine ladies hang over their jewels), till its image has sunk into the soul, what other word is there that (far from putting the reader out of conceit with it) so well recalls its deep purple glow, its retired modesty, its sullen, conscious beauty? Those who have not seen the flower cannot form an idea of its character, nor understand the line without it. Its aspect is dull, obtuse, faint, absorbed; but at the same time soft, luxurious, proud, and full of meaning. People who look at nature without being sensible to these distinctions and contrarieties of feeling, had better (instead of the flower) look only at the label on the stalk. Connoisseurs in French wines pretend to know all these depths and refinements of taste, though connoisseurs in French poetry pretend to know them not. To return to our text –

> 'Violets dim,
> But sweeter than the lids of Juno's eyes
> Or Cytherea's breath.'

How *bizarre*! cries one hypercritic.[4] What far-fetched metaphors! exclaims another. We shall not dwell on the allusion to 'Cytherea's breath', it is obvious enough: but how can the violet's smell be said to be 'sweeter than the lids of Juno's eyes'? Oh! honeyed words, how ill understood! And is there no true and rooted analogy between our different sensations, as well as a positive and literal identity? Is there not a sugared, melting, half-sleepy look in some eyelids, like the luscious, languid smell of flowers? How otherwise express that air of scorn and tenderness which breathes from them? Is there not a balmy dew upon them which one would kiss off? Speak, ye lovers! if any such remain in these degenerate days to take the part of genuine poetry against cold, barren criticism; for poetry is nothing but an intellectual love – Nature is the poet's mistress, and the heart in his case lends words and harmonious utterance to the tongue. – Again, how full of truth and pity is the turn which is given to the description of the pale and faded primrose, watching for the sun's approach as for the torch of Hymen! Milton has imitated this not so well in 'cowslips wan that hang the pensive head'.[5] Cowslips are of a gold colour, rather than wan. In speaking of the daffodils, it seems as if our poet had been struck with these 'lowly children of the ground'[6] on their first appearance, and seeing what bright and unexpected guests they were at that cold, comfortless season, wondered how 'they came before the swallow (the harbinger of summer) dared',[7] and being the only lovely thing in nature, fancied the winds of March were taken with them, and tamed their fury at the sight. No one but a poet who has spent his youth in the company of nature could so describe it, as no reader who has not experienced the same elementary sensations, their combinations and contrasts, can properly enter into it when so described. The finest poetry, then, is not a paradox nor a trite paraphrase; but a bold and happy enunciation of truths and feelings deeply implanted in the mind – Apollo, the god of poetry and day, evolving the thoughts of the breast, as he does the seed from the frozen earth, or enables the flower to burst its folds. Poetry is, indeed, a fanciful structure; but a fanciful structure raised on the groundwork of the strongest and most intimate associations of our ideas: otherwise, it is good for nothing, *vox et preterea nihil*.[8] A literal description goes for nothing in poetry, a pure fiction is of as little worth; but it is the extreme beauty and power of an impression with all its accompaniments, or the very intensity and truth of feeling, that pushes the poet over the verge of matter-of-fact, and justifies him in resorting to the licence of fiction to express what without his 'winged words'[9] must have remained for ever untold. Thus the feeling of the contrast between the roughness and bleakness of the winds of March and the tenderness and beauty of the flowers of spring is already in the reader's mind, if he be an observer of nature: the poet, to show the utmost extent and conceivable effect of this contrast, *feigns* that the winds themselves are sensible of it and smit with the beauty on which they commit such rude assaults. Lord Byron, whose imagination was not of this compound character, and more wilful than natural, produced splendid exaggerations. Mr Shelley, who felt the want of originality without the power to supply it, distorted every thing from what it was, and his pen produced only abortions. The one would say that the sun was a 'ball of dazzling fire';[10] the other, not knowing what to say, but determined 'to elevate and surprise',[11] would swear that it was *black*.[12] This latter class of poetry may be denominated the *Apocalyptical*.

On the Elgin Marbles: The Ilissus

'Who to the life an exact piece would make,
Must not from others' work a copy take;
No, not from Rubens or Vandyke:
Much less content himself to make it like
Th' ideas and the images which lie
In his own Fancy or his Memory.
No: he before his sight must place
The natural and living face;
The real object must command
Each judgment of his eye and motion of his hand.'[1]

The true lesson to be learnt by our students and professors from the Elgin Marbles, is the one which the ingenious and honest Cowley has expressed in the above spirited lines. The great secret is to recur at every step to nature —

'—To learn
Her manner, and with rapture taste her style.'[2]

It is evident to any one who views these admirable remains of Antiquity (nay, it is acknowledged by our artists themselves, in despite of all the melancholy sophistry which they have been taught or have been teaching others for half a century) that the chief excellence of the figures depends on their having been copied from nature, and not from imagination. The communication of art with nature is here everywhere immediate, entire, palpable. The artist gives himself no fastidious airs of superiority over what he sees. He has not arrived at that stage of his progress described at much length in Sir Joshua

Reynolds's *Discourses*, in which having served out his apprenticeship to nature, he can set up for himself in opposition to her. According to the old Greek form of drawing up the indentures in this case, we apprehend they were to last for life. At least, we can compare these Marbles to nothing but human figures petrified: they have every appearance of absolute *facsimiles* or casts taken from nature. The details are those of nature; the masses are those of nature; the forms are from nature; the action is from nature; the whole is from nature. Let any one, for instance, look at the leg of the Ilissus or River-God, which is bent under him — let him observe the swell and undulation of the calf, the inter-texture of the muscles, the distinction and union of all the parts, and the effect of action everywhere impressed on the external form, as if the very marble were a flexible substance, and contained the various springs of life and motion within itself, and he will own that art and nature are here the same thing. It is the same in the back of the Theseus, in the thighs and knees, and in all that remains unimpaired of these two noble figures. It is not the same in the cast (which was shown at Lord Elgin's) of the famous *Torso* by Michael Angelo, the style of which that artist appears to have imitated too well. There every muscle has obviously the greatest prominence and force given to it of which it is capable in itself, not of which it is capable in connexion with others. This fragment is an accumulation of mighty parts, without that play and reaction of each part upon the rest, without that 'alternate action and repose'[3] which Sir Thomas Lawrence speaks of as characteristic of the Theseus and the Ilissus, and which are as inseparable from nature as waves from the sea. The learned, however, here make a distinction, and suppose that the truth of nature is, in the Elgin Marbles, combined with ideal forms. If by *ideal forms* they mean fine natural forms, we have nothing to object; but if they mean that the sculptors of the Theseus and the Ilissus got the forms out of their own heads, and then tacked the truth of nature to them, we can only say, 'Let them look again, let them look again.' We consider the Elgin Marbles as a demonstration of the impossibility of separating art from nature, without a proportionable loss at every remove. The utter absence of all setness of appearance proves that they were done as studies from actual models. The separate parts of the human body may be given from scientific knowledge: — their modifications or inflections can only be learnt by seeing them in action; and the truth of nature is incompatible with ideal form, if the latter is meant to exclude actually existing form. The mutual action of the parts cannot be determined where the object itself is not seen. That the forms of these statues are not common nature, such as we see it every day, we readily allow: that they were not select Greek nature, we see no convincing reason to suppose. That truth of nature, and ideal or fine form, are not always or generally united, we know; but how they can ever be united in art, without being first united in nature, is to us a mystery, and one that we as little believe as understand!

Suppose, for illustration's sake, that these Marbles were originally done as casts from actual nature, and then let us inquire whether they would not have possessed all the same qualities that they now display, granting only, that the forms were in the first instance selected with the eye of taste, and disposed with a knowledge of the art and of the subject.

First, the larger masses and proportions of entire limbs and divisions of the body would have been found in the casts, for they would have been found in nature. The back, and trunk, and arms, and legs, and thighs, would have been there, for these are parts of the natural man, or actual living body, and not inventions of the artist, or *ideal* creations borrowed from the skies. There would have been the same sweep in the back of the Theseus; the same swell in the muscles of the arm on which he leans; the same division of the leg into calf and small, *i.e.* the same general results, or aggregation of parts, in the principal and most striking divisions of the body. The upper part of the arm would have been thicker than the lower, the thighs larger than the legs, the body larger than the thighs, in a cast taken from common nature; and in casts taken from the finest nature they would have been so in the same proportion, form, and manner, as in the statue of the Theseus, if the Theseus answers to the *idea* of the finest nature; for the idea and the reality must be the same; only, we contend that the idea is taken from the reality, instead of existing by itself, or being the creature of fancy. That is, there would be the same grandeur of proportions and parts in a cast taken from finely developed nature, such as the Greek sculptors had constantly before them, naked and in action, that we find in the limbs and masses of bone, flesh, and muscle, in these much and justly admired remains.

Again, and incontestably, there would have been, besides the grandeur of form, all the *minutiæ* and individual details in the cast that subsist in nature, and that find no place in the theory of *ideal* art — in the omission of which, indeed, its very grandeur is made to consist. The Elgin Marbles give a flat contradiction to this gratuitous separation of grandeur of design and exactness of detail, as incompatible in works of art, and we conceive that, with their whole ponderous weight to crush it, it will be difficult to set this theory on its legs again. In these majestic colossal figures, nothing is omitted, nothing is made out by negation. The veins, the wrinkles in the skin, the indications of the muscles under the skin (which appear as plainly to the anatomist, as the expert angler knows from an undulation on the surface of the water what fish is playing with his bait beneath it), the finger-joints, the nails, every the smallest part cognizable to the naked eye, is given here with the same ease and exactness, with the same prominence, and the same subordination, that it would be in a cast from nature, *i.e.* in nature itself. Therefore, so far these things, *viz.* nature, a cast from it, and the Elgin Marbles, are the same; and all three are opposed to the fashionable and fastidious theory of the *ideal*. Look at Sir Joshua's picture of Puck, one of his finest-coloured, and most spirited performances. The fingers are mere *spuds*, and we doubt whether any one can make out whether there are four toes or five allowed to each of the feet. If there had been a young Silenus among the Elgin Marbles, we don't know that in some particulars it would have surpassed Sir Joshua's masterly sketch, but we are sure that the extremities, the nails, &c. would have been studies of natural history. The life, the spirit, the character of the grotesque and imaginary little being would not have made an abortion of any part of his natural growth or form.

Farther, in a cast from nature there would be, as a matter of course, the same play and flexibility of limb and muscle, or, as Sir Thomas Lawrence expresses it, the same 'alternate action and repose', that we find so admirably displayed in the Elgin Marbles. It seems here as if stone could move: where one muscle is strained, another is relaxed, where one part is raised, another sinks in, just as in the ocean, where the waves are lifted up in one place, they sink proportionably low in the next: and all this modulation and affection of the different parts of the form by others arises from an attentive and co-instantaneous observation of the parts of a flexible body, where the muscles and bones act upon, and communicate with, one another like the ropes and pulleys in a machine, and where the action or position given to a particular limb or membrane naturally extends to the whole body. This harmony, this combination of motion, this unity of spirit diffused through the wondrous mass and every part of it, is the glory of the Elgin Marbles: — put a well-formed human body in the same position, and it will display the same character throughout; make a cast from it while in that position and action, and we shall still see the same bold, free, and comprehensive truth of design. There is no alliteration or antithesis in the style of the Elgin Marbles, no setness, squareness, affectation, or formality of appearance. The different muscles do not present a succession of *tumuli*, each heaving with big throes to rival the other. If one is raised, the other falls quietly into its place. Neither do the different parts of the body answer to one another, like shoulder-knots on a lacquey's coat, or the different ornaments of a building. The sculptor does not proceed on architectural principles. His work has the freedom, the variety, and stamp of nature. The form of corresponding parts is indeed the same, but it is subject to inflection from different circumstances. There is no primness or *petit-maîtreship*, as in some of the later antiques; where the artist seemed to think that flesh was glass or some other brittle substance; and that if it were put out of its exact shape it would break in pieces. Here, on the contrary, if the foot of one leg is bent under the body, the leg itself undergoes an entire alteration. If one side of the body is raised above the other, the original, or abstract, or *ideal* form of the two sides is not preserved strict and inviolable, but varies as it necessarily must do in conformity to the law of gravitation, to which all bodies are subject. In this respect, a cast from nature would be the same. Mr Chantrey once made a cast from Wilson the Black.[4] He put him into an attitude at first, and made the cast, but not liking the effect when done, got him to sit again and made use of the plaster of Paris once more. He was satisfied with the result; but Wilson, who was tired with going through the operation, as soon as it was over, went and leaned upon a block of marble with his hands covering his face. The sagacious sculptor was so struck with the superiority of this natural attitude over those into which he had been arbitrarily put, that he begged him (if possible) to continue in it for another quarter of an hour, and another impression was taken off. All three casts remain, and the last is a proof of the superiority of nature over art. The effect of lassitude is visible in every part of the frame, and the strong feeling of this affection, impressed on every limb and muscle, and venting itself naturally in an involuntary attitude which gave immediate relief, is that which strikes every one who has seen this fine study from the life. The casts from this man's figure have been much admired: – it is from no superiority of form: it is merely that, being taken from nature, they bear her 'image and superscription'.[5]

As to expression, the Elgin Marbles (at least the Ilissus and Theseus) afford no examples, the heads being gone.

Lastly, as to the *ideal* form, we contend it is nothing but a selection of fine nature, such as it was seen by the ancient Greek sculptors; and we say that a sufficient approximation to this form may be found in our own country, and still more in other countries, at this day, to warrant the clear conclusion, that under more favourable circumstances of climate, manners, &c. no vain imagination of the human mind could come up to entire natural forms; and that actual casts from Greek models would rival the common Greek statues, or surpass them in the same proportion and manner as the Elgin Marbles do. Or if this conclusion should be doubted, we are ready at any time to produce at least one cast from living nature, which if it does not furnish practical proof of all that we have here advanced, we are willing to forfeit the last thing we can afford to part with – a theory!

If then the Elgin Marbles are to be considered as authority in subjects of art, we conceive the following principles, which have not hitherto been generally received or acted upon in Great Britain, will be found to result from them: –

1. That art is (first and last) the imitation of nature.

2. That the highest art is the imitation of the finest nature, that is to say, of that which conveys the strongest sense of pleasure or power, of the sublime or beautiful.

3. That the *ideal* is only the selecting a particular form which

expresses most completely the idea of a given character or quality, as of beauty, strength, activity, voluptuousness, &c. and which preserves that character with the greatest consistency throughout.

4. That the *historical* is nature in action. With regard to the face, it is expression.

5. That grandeur consists in connecting a number of parts into a whole, and not in leaving out the parts.

6. That as grandeur is the principle of connexion between different parts, beauty is the principle of affinity between different forms, or their gradual conversion into each other. The one harmonizes, the other aggrandizes our impressions of things.

7. That grace is the beautiful or harmonious in what relates to position or motion.

8. That grandeur of motion is unity of motion.

9. That strength is the giving the extremes, softness, the uniting them.

10. That truth is to a certain degree beauty and grandeur, since all things are connected, and all things modify one another in nature. Simplicity is also grand and beautiful for the same reason. Elegance is ease and lightness, with precision.

All this we have, we believe, said before: we shall proceed to such proofs or explanations as we are able to give of it in another article.

On the Elgin Marbles

At the conclusion of a former article on this subject,* we ventured to lay down some general principles, which we shall here proceed to elucidate in such manner as we are able.

1. The first was, that *art is (first and last) the imitation of nature.*

By nature, we mean actually existing nature, or some one object to be found *in rerum natura*,[1] not an idea of nature existing solely in the mind, got from an infinite number of different objects, but which was never yet embodied in an individual instance. Sir Joshua Reynolds may be ranked at the head of those who have maintained the supposition that nature (or the universe of things) was indeed the ground-work or foundation on which art rested; but that the super-structure rose above it, that it towered by degrees above the world of realities, and was suspended in the regions of thought alone — that a middle form, a more refined idea, borrowed from the observation of a number of particulars, but unlike any of them, was the standard of truth and beauty, and the glittering phantom that hovered round the head of the genuine artist:

> '—So from the ground
> Springs lighter the green stalk, from thence the leaves
> More airy, last the bright consummate flower!'[2]

We have no notion of this vague, equivocal theory of art, and contend, on the other hand, that each image in art should have a *tally* or corresponding prototype in some object in nature. Otherwise, we do not see the use of art at all: it is a mere superfluity, an

* ['On the Elgin Marbles: The Ilissus']

incumbrance to the mind, a piece of 'laborious foolery',[3] – for the word, the mere name of any object or class of objects will convey the general idea, more free from particular details or defects than any the most neutral and indefinite representation that can be produced by forms and colours. The word Man, for instance, conveys a more filmy, impalpable, abstracted, and (according to this hypothesis) sublime idea of the species, than Michael Angelo's *Adam*, or any real image can possibly do. If this then is the true object of art, the language of painting, sculpture, &c. becomes quite supererogatory. Sir Joshua and the rest contend, that nature (properly speaking) does not express any single individual, nor the whole mass of things as they exist, but a general principle, a *something common* to all these, retaining the perfections, that is, all in which they are alike, and abstracting the defects, namely, all in which they differ: so that, out of actual nature, we compound an artificial nature, never answering to the former in any one part of its mock-existence, and which last is the true object of imitation to the aspiring artist. Let us adopt this principle of abstraction as the rule of perfection, and see what havoc it will make in all our notions and feelings in such matters. If the *perfect* is the *intermediate*, why not confound all objects, all forms, all colours at once? Instead of painting a landscape with blue sky, or white clouds, or the green earth, or grey rocks and towers; what should we say, if the artist (so named) were to treat all these 'fair varieties'[4] as so many imperfections and mistakes in the creation, and mass them all together, by mixing up the colours on his palette in the same dull leaden tone, and call this the true principle of epic landscape-painting? Would not the thing be abominable, an abortion, and worse than the worst Dutch picture? Variety then is one principle, one beauty in external nature, and not an everlasting source of pettiness and deformity, which must be got rid of at all events, before taste can set its seal upon the work, or fancy own it. But it may be said, it is different in things of the same species, and particularly in man, who is cast in a regular mould, which mould is one. What then, are we, on this pretext, to confound the difference of sex in a sort of hermaphrodite softness, as Mr Westall, Angelica Kauffman, and others, have done in their effeminate performances? Are we to leave out of the scale of legitimate art, the extremes of infancy and old age, as not *middle terms* in man's life? Are we to strike off from the list of available topics and sources of interest, the varieties of character, of passion, of strength, activity, &c.? Is every thing to wear the same form, the same colour, the same unmeaning face? Are we only to repeat the same average idea of perfection, that is, our own want of observation and imagination, for ever, and to melt down the inequalities and excrescences of individual nature in the monotony of abstraction? Oh no! As well might we prefer the cloud to the rainbow; the dead corpse to the living moving body! So Sir Joshua debated upon Rubens's landscapes,[5] and has a whole chapter to inquire whether *accidents in nature*, that is, rainbows, moonlight, sun-sets, clouds and storms, are the proper thing in the classical style of art. Again, it is urged, that this is not what is meant, *viz.* to exclude different classes or characters of things, but that there is in each class or character a *middle point*, which is the point of perfection. What middle point? Or how is it ascertained? What is the middle age of childhood? Or are all children to be alike, dark or fair? Some of Titian's children have black hair, and others yellow or auburn: who can tell which is the most beautiful? May not a St John be older than an infant Christ? Must not a Magdalen be different from a Madonna, a Diana from a Venus? Or may not a Venus have more or less gravity, a Diana more or less sweetness? What then becomes of the abstract idea in any of these cases? It varies as it does in nature; that is, there is indeed a general principle or character to be adhered to, but modified everlastingly by various other given or nameless circumstances. The highest art, like nature, is a living spring of unconstrained excellence, and does not produce a continued repetition of itself, like plaster-casts from the same figure. But once more it may be insisted, that in what relates to mere form or organic structure, there is necessarily a middle line or central point, any thing short of which is deficiency, and any thing beyond it excess, being the average form to which all the other forms included in the same species tend, and approximate more or less. Then this average form as it exists in nature should be taken as the model for art. What occasion to do it out of your own head, when you can bring it under the cognizance of your senses? Suppose a foot of a certain size and shape to be the standard of perfection, or if you will, the *mean proportion* between all other feet. How can you tell this so well as by seeing it? How can you copy it so well as by having it actually before you? But, you will say, there are particular minute defects in the best shaped actual foot which ought not to be transferred to the imitation. Be it so. But are there not also particular minute beauties in the best, or even the worst shaped actual foot, which you will only discover by ocular inspection, which are reducible to no measurement or precepts, and which in finely developed nature outweigh the imperfections a thousand fold, the proper general form being contained there also, and these being only the distinctly articulated parts of it with their inflections which no artist can carry in his head alone? For instance, in the bronze monument of Henry VII and his wife, in Westminster Abbey, by the famous Torregiano, the fingers and finger nails of the woman in particular are made out as minutely, and, at the same time, as beautifully as it is possible to conceive; yet they have exactly the effect that a cast taken from a fine female hand would have, with every natural joint, muscle, and nerve, in complete preservation. Does this take from the beauty or magnificence of the whole? No: it aggrandizes it. What then does it take from? Nothing but the conceit of the artist that he can paint a hand out of his own head (that is, out of nothing, and by reducing it again as near as can be to nothing, to a mere vague image) that shall be better than any thing in nature. A hand, or foot, is not *one thing*, because it is *one word* or name; and the painter of mere abstractions had better lay down his pencil at once, and be contented to write the descriptions or titles under works of art. Lastly, it may be objected that a whole figure can never be found perfect or equal; that the most beautiful arm will not belong to the same figure as the most beautiful leg, and so on. How is this to be remedied? By taking the arm from one, and the leg from the other, and clapping them both on the same body? That will never do; for however admirable in themselves, they will hardly agree together. One will have a different character from the other; and they will form a sort of natural patchwork. Or, to avoid this, will you take neither from actual models, but derive them from the neutralizing medium of your own imagination. Worse and worse. Copy them from the same model, the best in all its parts you can get; so that if you have to alter, you may alter as little as possible, and retain nearly the whole substance of nature.* You may depend upon it that what is so retained, will alone be of any specific value. The rest may have a negative merit, but will be positively good for nothing. It will be to the vital truth and beauty of what is taken from the best nature, like the piecing of an antique statue. It fills a gap, but nothing more. It is, in fact, a mental blank.

2. This leads us to the second point laid down before, which was, that *the highest art is the imitation of the finest nature, or in other words, of that which conveys the strongest sense of pleasure or power, of the sublime or beautiful.*

The artist does not pretend to *invent* an absolutely new class of objects, without any foundation in nature. He does not spread his palette on the canvas, for the mere finery of the thing, and tell us that it makes a brighter show than the rainbow, or even than a bed of tulips. He does not draw airy forms, moving above the earth, 'gay creatures of the element, that play i' th' plighted clouds',[6] and scorn the mere material existences, the concrete descendants of those that came out of Noah's Ark, and that walk, run, or creep upon it. No, he does not paint only what he has seen *in his mind's eye*[7] but the common objects that both he and others daily meet – rocks, clouds, trees, men, women, beasts, fishes, birds, or what he calls such. He is then an imitator by profession. He gives the appearances of things that exist outwardly by themselves, and have a distinct and independent nature of their own. But these know their own nature best; and it is by consulting them that he can alone trace it truly, either in the immediate details, or characteristic essences. Nature is consistent, unaffected, powerful, subtle: art is forgetful, apish, feeble, coarse. Nature is the original, and therefore right: art is the copy, and can but tread lamely in the same steps. Nature penetrates into the parts, and moves the whole mass: it acts with diversity, and in necessary connexion; for real causes never forget to operate, and to contribute their portion. Where, therefore, these causes are called into play to the utmost extent that they ever go to, there we shall have a strength and a refinement, that art may imitate but cannot surpass. But it is said that art can surpass this most perfect image in nature by combining

* I believe this rule will apply to all except grotesques, which are evidently taken from opposite natures.

others with it. What! by joining to the most perfect in its kind something less perfect? Go to, – this argument will not pass. Suppose you have a goblet of the finest wine that ever was tasted: you will not mend it by pouring into it all sorts of samples of an inferior quality. So the best in nature is the stint and limit of what is best in art: for art can only borrow from nature still; and, moreover, must borrow entire objects, for bits only make patches. We defy any landscape-painter to invent out of his own head, and by jumbling together all the different forms of hills he ever saw, by adding a bit to one, and taking a bit from another, any thing equal to Arthur's Seat, with the appendage of Salisbury Crags, that overlook Edinburgh. Why so? Because there are no levers in the mind of man equal to those with which nature works at her utmost need. No imagination can toss and tumble about huge heaps of earth as the ocean in its fury can. A volcano is more potent to rend rocks asunder than the most splashing pencil. The convulsions of nature can make a precipice more frightfully, or heave the backs of mountains more proudly, or throw their sides into waving lines more gracefully than all the *beau idéal* of art. For there is in nature not only greater power and scope, but (so to speak) greater knowledge and unity of purpose. Art is comparatively weak and incongruous, being at once a miniature and caricature of nature. We grant that a tolerable sketch of Arthur's Seat, and the adjoining view, is better than Primrose Hill itself; (dear Primrose Hill! ha! faithless pen, canst thou forget its winding slopes, and valleys green, to which all Scotland can bring no parallel?) but no pencil can transform or dandle Primrose Hill (our favourite Primrose Hill) into a thing of equal character and sublimity with Arthur's Seat. It gives us some pain to make this concession; but in doing it, we flatter ourselves that no Scotchman will have the liberality in any way to return us the compliment. We do not recollect a more striking illustration of the difference between art and nature in this respect, than Mr Martin's very singular, and, in some things, very meritorious pictures. But he strives to outdo nature. He wants to give more than she does, or than his subject requires or admits. He subdivides his groups into infinite littleness, and exaggerates his scenery into absolute immensity. His figures are like rows of shiny pins; his mountains are piled up one upon the back of the other, like the storeys of houses. He has no notion of the moral principle in all art, that a part may be greater than the whole. He reckons that if one range of lofty square hills is good, another range above that with clouds between must be better. He thus wearies the imagination, instead of exciting it. We see no end of the journey, and turn back in disgust. We are tired of the effort, we are tired of the monotony of this sort of reduplication of the same object. We were satisfied before; but it seems the painter was not, and we naturally sympathize with him. This craving after quantity is a morbid affection. A landscape is not an architectural elevation. You may build a house as high as you can lift up stones with pulleys and levers, but you cannot raise mountains into the sky merely with the pencil. They lose probability and effect by striving at too much; and, with their ceaseless throes, oppress the imagination of the spectator, and bury the artist's fame under them. The only error of these pictures is, however, that art here puts on her seven-league boots,[8] and thinks it possible to steal a march upon nature. Mr Martin might make Arthur's Seat sublime, if he chose to take the thing as it is; but he would be for squaring it according to the mould in his own imagination, and for clapping another Arthur's Seat on the top of it, to make the Calton Hill stare! Again, with respect to the human figure. This has an internal structure, muscles, bones, blood-vessels, &c. by means of which the external surface is operated upon according to certain laws. Does the artist, with all his generalizations, understand these, as well as nature does? Can he predict, with all his learning, that if a certain muscle is drawn up in a particular manner, it will present a particular appearance in a different part of the arm or leg, or bring out other muscles, which were before hid, with certain modifications? But in nature all this is brought about by necessary laws, and the effect is visible to those, and those only, who look for it in actual objects. This is the great and master-excellence of the ELGIN MARBLES, that they do not seem to be the outer surface of a hard and immovable block of marble, but to be actuated by an internal machinery, and composed of the same soft and flexible materials as the human body. The skin (or the outside) seems to be protruded or tightened by the natural action of a muscle beneath it. This result is miraculous in art: in nature it is easy and unavoidable. That is to say, art has to imitate or produce

225

certain effects or appearances without the natural causes: but the human understanding can hardly be so true to those causes as the causes to themselves; and hence the necessity (in this sort of *simulated creation*) of recurring at every step to the actual objects and appearances of nature. Having shown so far how indispensable it is for art to identify itself with nature, in order to preserve the truth of imitation, without which it is destitute of value or meaning, it may be said to follow as a necessary consequence, that the only way in which art can rise to greater dignity or excellence is by finding out models of greater dignity and excellence in nature. Will any one, looking at the Theseus, for example, say that it could spring merely from the artist's brain, or that it could be done from a common, ill-made, or stunted body? The fact is, that its superiority consists in this, that it is a perfect combination of art and nature, or an identical, and as it were spontaneous copy of an individual picked out of a finer race of men than generally tread this ball of earth. Could it be made of a Dutchman's trunk-hose? No. Could it be made out of one of Sir Joshua's *Discourses* on the *middle form*? No. How then? Out of an eye, a head, and a hand, with sense, spirit, and energy to follow the finest nature, as it appeared exemplified in sweeping masses, and in subtle details, without pedantry, conceit, cowardice, or affectation! Some one was asking at Mr H—yd—n's[9] one day, as a few persons were looking at the cast from this figure, why the original might not have been done as a cast from nature? Such a supposition would account at least for what seems otherwise unaccountable—the incredible labour and finishing bestowed on the back and other parts of this figure, placed at a prodigious height against the walls of a temple, where they could never be seen after they were once put up there. If they were done by means of a cast in the first instance, the thing appears intelligible, otherwise not. Our host stoutly resisted this imputation, which tended to deprive art of one of its greatest triumphs, and to make it as mechanical as a shaded profile. So far, so good. But the reason he gave was bad, *viz.* that the limbs could not remain in those actions long enough to be cast. Yet surely this would take a shorter time than if the model sat to the sculptor; and we all agreed that nothing but actual, continued, and intense observation of living nature could give the solidity, complexity, and refinement of imitation which we saw in the half animated, almost moving figure before us.* Be this as it may, the principle here stated does not reduce art to the imitation of what is understood by common or low life. It rises to any point of beauty or sublimity you please, but it rises only as nature rises exalted with it too. To hear these critics talk, one would suppose there was nothing in the world really worth looking at. The Dutch pictures were the best that they could paint: they had no other landscapes or faces before them. *Honi soit qui mal y pense.*[11] Yet who is not alarmed at a Venus by Rembrandt? The Greek statues were (*cum grano salis*)[12] Grecian youths and nymphs; and the women in the streets of Rome (it has been remarked†)[13] look to this hour as if they had walked out of Raphael's pictures. Nature is always truth: at its best, it is beauty and sublimity as well; though Sir Joshua tells us[14] in one of the papers in the *Idler* that in itself, or with reference to individuals, it is a mere tissue of meanness and deformity. Luckily, the Elgin Marbles say NO to that conclusion: for they are decidedly *part and parcel thereof.* What constitutes fine nature, we shall inquire under another head. But we would remark here, that it can hardly be the *middle form,* since this principle, however it might determine certain general proportions and outlines, could never be intelligible in the details of nature, or applicable to those of art. Who will say that the form of a finger nail is just midway between a thousand others that he has *not* remarked: we are only struck with it when it is more than ordinarily beautiful, from symmetry, an oblong shape, &c. The staunch partisans of this theory, however, get over the difficulty here spoken of, in practice, by omitting the details altogether, and making their works sketches, or rather what the French call *ébauches,* and the English *daubs.*

3. The IDEAL *is only the selecting a particular form which expresses most completely the idea of a given character or quality, as of beauty, strength, activity, voluptuousness, &c. and which preserves that character with the greatest consistency throughout.*

---

* Some one finely applied to the repose of this figure the words:

> '—Sedet, in eternumque sedebit
> Infelix Theseus.'[10]

† By Mr Coleridge.

Instead of its being true in general that the *ideal* is the *middle point*, it is to be found in the *extremes*; or, it is carrying any *idea* as far as it will go. Thus, for instance, a Silenus is as much an *ideal* thing as an Apollo, as to the principle on which it is done, *viz.* giving to every feature, and to the whole form, the utmost degree of grossness and sensuality that can be imagined, with this exception (which has nothing to do with the understanding of the question), that the *ideal* means by custom this extreme on the side of the good and beautiful. With this reserve, the *ideal* means always the *something more* of any thing which may be anticipated by the fancy, and which must be found in nature (by looking long enough for it) to be expressed as it ought. Suppose a good heavy Dutch face (we speak by the proverb) – this, you will say, is gross; but it is not gross enough. You have an idea of something grosser, that is, you have seen something grosser and must seek for it again. When you meet with it, and have stamped it on the canvas, or carved it out of the block, this is the true *ideal*, namely, that which answers to and satisfies a preconceived idea; not that which is made out of an abstract idea, and answers to nothing. In the Silenus, also, according to the notion we have of the properties and character of that figure, there must be vivacity, slyness, wantonness, &c. Not only the image in the mind, but a real face may express all these combined together; another may express them more, and another most, which last is the *ideal*; and when the image in nature coalesces with, and gives a body, force, and reality to the idea in the mind, then it is that we see the true perfection of art. The forehead should be 'villainous low';[15] the eye-brows bent in; the eyes small and gloating; the nose *pugged*, and pointed at the end, with distended nostrils; the mouth large and shut; the cheeks swollen; the neck thick, &c. There is, in all this process, nothing of softening down, of compromising qualities, of finding out a *mean proportion* between different forms and characters; the sole object is to *intensify* each as much as possible. The only fear is 'to o'erstep the modesty of nature',[16] and run into caricature. This must be avoided; but the artist is only to stop short of this. He must not outrage probability. We must have seen a class of such faces, or something so nearly approaching, as to prevent the imagination from revolting against them. The forehead must be low, but not so low as to lose the character of humanity in the brute. It would thus lose all its force and meaning. For that which is extreme and ideal in one species, is nothing, if, by being pushed too far, it is merged in another. Above all, there should be *keeping* in the whole and every part. In the Pan, the horns and goat's feet, perhaps, warrant the approach to a more *animal* expression than would otherwise be allowable in the human features; but yet this tendency to excess must be restrained within certain limits. If Pan is made into a beast, he will cease to be a God! Let Momus distend his jaws with laughter, as far as laughter can stretch them, but no farther; or the expression will be that of pain and not of pleasure. Besides, the overcharging the expression or action of any one feature will suspend the action of others. The whole face will no longer laugh. But this universal suffusion of broad mirth and humour over the countenance is very different from a placid smile, midway between grief and joy. Yet a classical Momus, by modern theories of the *ideal*, ought to be such a nonentity in expression. The ancients knew better. They pushed art in such subjects to the verge of 'all we hate',[17] while they felt the point beyond which it could not be urged with propriety, *i.e.* with truth, consistency, and consequent effect. – There is no difference, in philosophical reasoning, between the mode of art here insisted on, and the *ideal* regularity of such figures as the Apollo, the Hercules, the Mercury, the Venus, &c. All these are, as it were, *personifications, essences, abstractions* of certain qualities or virtues in human nature, not of human nature in general, which would make nonsense. Instead of being abstractions of all sorts of qualities jumbled together in a neutral character, they are in the opposite sense *abstractions* of some single quality or customary combination of qualities, leaving out all others as much as possible, and imbuing every part with that one predominant character to the utmost. The Apollo is a representation of graceful dignity and mental power; the Hercules of bodily strength; the Mercury of swiftness; the Venus of female loveliness, and so on. In these, in the Apollo, is surely implied and found more grace than usual; in the Hercules more strength than usual; in the Mercury more lightness than usual; in the Venus more softness than usual. Is it not so? What then becomes of the pretended *middle form*? One would think it would be sufficient to prove this, to ask, 'Do not these statues differ from one another? And is this difference a defect?' It would be ridiculous to call them by different names, if they were not supposed to represent different and peculiar characters: sculptors should, in that case, never carve any thing but the statue of *a man*, the statue of *a woman*, &c. and this would be the name of perfection. This theory of art is not at any rate justified by the history of art. An extraordinary quantity of bone and muscle is as proper to the Hercules as his club, and it would be strange if the Goddess of Love had not a more delicately rounded form, and a more languishing look withal, than the Goddess of Hunting. That a form combining and blending the properties of both, the downy softness of the one, with the elastic buoyancy of the other, would be more perfect than either, we no more see than that grey is the most perfect of colours. At any rate, this is the march neither of nature nor of art. It is not denied that these antique sculptures are models of the *ideal*; nay, it is on them that this theory boasts of being founded. Yet they give a flat contradiction to its insipid mediocrity. Perhaps some of them have a slight bias to the false *ideal*, to the smooth and uniform, or the negation of nature: any error on this side is, however, happily set right by the ELGIN MARBLES, which are the paragons of sculpture and the mould of form. – As the *ideal* then requires a difference of character in each figure as a whole, so it expects the same character (or a corresponding one) to be stamped on each part of every figure. As the legs of a Diana should be more muscular and adapted for running, than those of a Venus or a Minerva, so the skin of her face ought to be more tense, bent on her prey, and hardened by being exposed to the winds of heaven. The respective characters of lightness, softness, strength, &c. should pervade each part of the surface of each figure, but still varying according to the texture and functions of the individual part. This can only be learned or practised from an attentive observation of nature in those forms in which any given character or excellence is most strikingly displayed, and which has been selected for imitation and study on that account. – Suppose a dimple in the chin to be a mark of voluptuousness; then the Venus should have a dimple in the chin; and she has one. But this will imply certain correspondent indications in other parts of the features, about the corners of the mouth, a gentle undulation and sinking in of the cheek, as if it had just been pinched, and so on: yet so as to be consistent with the other qualities of roundness, smoothness, &c. which belong to the idea of the character. Who will get all this and embody it out of the idea of a *middle form*, I cannot say: it may be, and has been, got out of the idea of a number of distinct enchanting graces in the mind, and from some heavenly object unfolded to the sight!

4. *That the historical is nature in action. With regard to the face, it is expression.*

Hogarth's pictures are true history. Every feature, limb, figure, group, is instinct with life and motion. He does not take a subject and place it in a position, like a lay figure, in which it stirs neither limb nor joint. The scene moves before you: the face is like a frame-work of flexible machinery. If the mouth is distorted with laughter, the eyes swim in laughter. If the forehead is knit together, the cheeks are puckered up. If a fellow squints most horribly, the rest of his face is awry. The muscles pull different ways, or the same way, at the same time, on the surface of the picture, as they do in the human body. What you see is the reverse of *still-life*. There is a continual and complete action and reaction of one variable part upon another, as there is in the ELGIN MARBLES. If you pull the string of a bow, the bow itself is bent. So it is in the strings and wires that move the human frame. The action of any one part, the contraction or relaxation of any one muscle, extends more or less perceptibly to every other:

'Thrills in each nerve, and lives along the line.'[18]

Thus the celebrated Iö of Correggio is imbued, steeped in a manner in the same voluptuous feeling all over — the same passion languishes in her whole frame, and communicates the infection to the feet, the back, and the reclined position of the head. This is history, not carpenter's work. Some painters fancy that they paint history, if they get the measurement from the foot to the knee, and put four bones where there are four bones. This is not our idea of it; but we think it is to show how one part of the body sways another in action and in passion. The last relates chiefly to the expression of the face, though not altogether. Passion may be shown in a clenched fist as well as in clenched teeth. The face, however, is the throne of expression. Character implies the feeling, which is fixed and permanent; expression that which is occasional and momentary, at least, technically speaking. Portrait treats of objects as they are; history of the events and changes to which they are liable. And so far history has a double superiority; or a double difficulty to overcome, *viz.* in the rapid glance over a number of parts subject to the simultaneous action of the same law, and in the scope of feeling required to sympathize with the critical and powerful movements of passion. It requires greater capacity of muscular motion to follow the progress of a carriage in violent motion, than to lean upon it standing still. If, to describe passion, it were merely necessary to observe its outward effects, these, perhaps, in the prominent points, become more visible and more tangible as the passion is more intense. But it is not only necessary to see the effects, but to discern the cause, in order to make the one true to the other. No painter gives more of intellectual or impassioned appearances than he understands or feels. It is an axiom in painting, that sympathy is indispensable to truth of expression. Without it, you get only caricatures, which are not the thing. But to sympathize with passion, a greater fund of sensibility is demanded in proportion to the strength or tenderness of the passion. And as he feels most of this whose face expresses most passion, so he also feels most by sympathy whose hand can describe most passion. This amounts nearly, we take it, to a demonstration of an old and very disputed point. The same reasoning might be applied to poetry, but this is not the place. – Again, it is easier to paint a portrait than an historical face, because the head *sits* for the first, but the expression will hardly *sit* for the last. Perhaps those passions are the best subjects for painting, the expression of which may be retained for some time, so as to be better caught, which throw out a sort of lambent fire, and leave a reflected glory behind them, as we see in Madonnas, Christ's Heads, and what is understood by sacred subjects in general. The violences of human passion are too soon over to be copied by the hand, and the mere conception of the internal workings is not here sufficient, as it is in poetry. A portrait is to history what still-life is to portraiture: that is, the whole remains the same while you are doing it, or while you are occupied about each part, the rest wait for you. Yet, what a difference is there between taking an original portrait, and making a copy of one! This shows that the face in its most ordinary state is continually varying and in action. So much of history is there in portrait! – No one should pronounce definitively on the superiority of history over portrait, without recollecting Titian's heads. The finest of them are very nearly (say quite) equal to the finest of Raphael's. They have almost the look of *still-life*, yet each part is decidedly influenced by the rest. Every thing is *relative* in them. You cannot put any other eye, nose, lip, in the same face. As is one part, so is the rest. You cannot fix on any particular beauty; the charm is in the whole. They have least action, and the most expression of any portraits. They are doing nothing, and yet all other business seems insipid in comparison of their thoughts. They are silent, retired, and do not court observation; yet you cannot keep your eyes from them. Some one said, that you would be as cautious of your behaviour in a room where a picture of Titian's was hung, as if there was somebody by – so entirely do they look you through. They are the least tiresome *furniture-company* in the world!

5. *Grandeur consists in connecting a number of parts into a whole, and not in leaving out the parts.*

Sir Joshua lays it down[19] that the great style in art consists in the omission of the details. A greater error never man committed. The great style consists in preserving the masses and general proportions; not in omitting the details. Thus, suppose, for illustration's sake, the general form of an eye-brow to be commanding and grand. It is of a certain size, and arched in a particular curve. Now, surely, this general form or outline will be equally preserved, whether the painter daubs it in, in a bold, rough way, as Reynolds or perhaps Rembrandt would, or produces the effect by a number of hairlines arranged in the same form as Titian sometimes did; and in his best pictures. It will not be denied (for it cannot) that the characteristic form of the eye-brow would be the same, or that the effect of the picture at a small distance would be nearly the same in either case; only in the latter, it would be rather more perfect, as being more like nature. Suppose a strong light to fall on one side of a face, and a deep shadow to involve the whole of the other. This would produce two distinct and large masses in the picture; which answers to the conditions of what is called the grand style of composition. Well, would it destroy these masses to give the smallest veins or variation of colour or surface in the light side, or to shade the other with the most delicate and elaborate *chiaro-scuro?* It is evident not; from common sense, from the practice of the best masters, and, lastly, from the example of nature, which contains both the larger masses, the strongest contrasts, and the highest finishing, within itself. The integrity of the whole, then, is not impaired by the indefinite subdivision and smallness of the parts. The grandeur of the ultimate effects depends entirely on the arrangement of these in a certain form or under certain masses. The Ilissus or River-god (of which we have given a print in a former number) is floating in his proper element, and is, in appearance, as firm as a rock, as pliable as a wave of the sea. The artist's breath might be said to mould and play upon the undulating surface. The whole is expanded into noble proportions, and heaves with general effect. What then? Are the parts unfinished; or are they not there? No; they are there with the nicest exactness, but in due subordination; that is, they are there as they are found in fine nature; and float upon the general form, like straw or weeds upon the tide of ocean. Once more: in Titian's portraits we perceive a certain character stamped upon the different features. In the *Hippolito de Medici* the eye-brows are angular, the nose is peaked, the mouth has sharp corners, the face is (so to speak) a pointed oval. The drawing in each of these is as careful and distinct as can be. But the unity of intention in nature, and in the artist, does not the less tend to produce a general grandeur and impressiveness of effect; which at first sight it is not easy to account for. To combine a number of particulars to one end is not to omit them altogether; and is the best way of producing the grand style, because it does this without either affectation or slovenliness.

6. The sixth rule we proposed to lay down was, that *as grandeur is the principle of connexion between different parts; beauty is the principle of affinity between different forms, or their gradual conversion into each other. The one harmonizes, the other aggrandizes, our impressions of things.*

There is a harmony of colours and a harmony of sounds, unquestionably: why then there should be all this squeamishness about admitting an original harmony of forms as the principle of beauty and source of pleasure there we cannot understand. It is true, that there is in organized bodies a certain standard of form to which they approximate more or less, and from which they cannot very widely deviate without shocking the sense of custom, or our settled expectations of what they ought to be. And hence it has been pretended, that there is in all such cases a *middle central form*, obtained by leaving out the peculiarities of all the others, which alone is the pure standard of truth and beauty. A conformity to custom is, we grant, one condition of beauty or source of satisfaction to the eye, because an abrupt transition shocks; but there is a conformity (or correspondence) of colours, sounds, lines, among themselves, which is soft and pleasing for the same reason. The average or customary form merely determines what is *natural*. A thing cannot please, unless it is to be found in nature; but that which is natural is most pleasing, according as it has other properties which in themselves please. Thus the colour of a cheek must be the natural complexion of a human face; − it would not do to make it the colour of a flower or a precious stone; − but among complexions ordinarily to be found in nature, that is most beautiful which would be thought so abstractedly, or in itself. Yellow hair is not the most common, nor is it a *mean proportion* between the different colours of women's hair. Yet, who will say that it is not the most beautiful? Blue or green hair would be a defect and an anomaly, not because it is not the *medium* of nature, but because it is not in nature at all. To say that there is no difference in the sense of form except from custom, is like saying that there is no difference in the sensation of smooth or rough. Judging by analogy, a gradation or symmetry of form must affect the mind in the same manner as a gradation of recurrence at given intervals of tones or sounds; and if it does so in fact, we need not inquire further for the principle. Sir Joshua, (who is the arch-heretic on this subject) makes grandeur or sublimity consist in the middle form, or abstraction of all peculiarities; which is evidently false, for grandeur and sublimity arise from extraordinary strength, magnitude, &c. or in a word, from an excess of power, so as to startle and overawe the mind. But as sublimity is an excess of power, beauty is, we conceive, the blending and harmonizing different powers or qualities together, so as to produce a soft and pleasurable sensation. That it is not the middle form of the species seems proved in various ways. First, because one species is more beautiful than another, according to common sense. A rose is the queen of flowers, in poetry at least; but in this philosophy any other flower is as good. A swan is more beautiful than a goose; a stag, than a goat. Yet if custom were the test of beauty, either we should give no preference, or our preference would be reversed. Again, let us go back to the human face and figure. A straight nose is allowed to be handsome, that is, one that presents nearly a continuation of the line of the forehead, and the sides of which are nearly parallel. Now this cannot be the mean proportion of the form of noses. For, first, most noses are broader at the bottom than at the top, inclining to the negro head, but none are broader at top than at the bottom, to produce the Greek form as a balance between both. Almost all noses sink in immediately under the forehead bone, none ever project there; so that the nearly straight line continued from the forehead cannot be a mean proportion struck between the two extremes of convex and concave form in this feature of the face. There must, therefore, be some other principle of symmetry, continuity, &c. to account for the variation from the prescribed rule. Once more (not to multiply instances tediously), a double calf is undoubtedly the perfection of beauty in the form of the leg. But this is a rare thing. Nor is it the medium between two common extremes. For the muscles seldom swell enough to produce this excrescence, if it may be so called, and never run to an excess there, so as, by diminishing the quantity, to subside into proportion and beauty. But this second or lower calf is a connecting link between the upper calf and the small of the leg, and is just like a second chord or half-note in music. We conceive that any one who does not perceive the beauty of the *Venus de Medicis*, for instance, in this respect, has not the proper perception of form in his mind. As this is the most disputable, or at least the most disputed part of our theory, we may, perhaps, have to recur to it again, and shall leave an opening for that purpose.

7. *That grace is the beautiful or harmonious in what relates to position or motion.*

There needs not much be said on this point; as we apprehend it will be granted, that whatever beauty is as to the form, grace is the same thing in relation to the use that is made of it. Grace, in writing, relates to the transitions that are made from one subject to another, or to the movement that is given to a passage. If one thing leads to another, or an idea or illustration is brought in without effect, or without making a *boggle* in the mind, we call this a graceful style. Transitions must in general be gradual and pieced together. But sometimes the most violent are the most graceful, when the mind is fairly tired out and exhausted with a subject, and is glad to leap to another as a repose and relief from the first. Of these there are frequent instances in Mr Burke's writings, which have something Pindaric in them. That which is not beautiful in itself, or in the mere form, may be made so by position or motion. A figure by no means elegant may be put in an elegant position. Mr Kean's figure is not good; yet we have seen him throw himself into attitudes of infinite spirit, dignity, and grace. John Kemble's figure, on the contrary, is fine in itself; and he has only to show himself to be admired. The direction in which any thing is moved has evidently nothing to do with the shape of the thing moved. The one may be a circle and the other a square. Little and deformed people seem to be well aware of this distinction, who, in spite of their unpromising appearance, usually assume the most imposing attitudes, and give themselves the most extraordinary airs imaginable.

8. *Grandeur of motion is unity of motion.*

This principle hardly needs illustration. Awkwardness is contradictory or disjointed motion.

9. *Strength in art is giving the extremes, softness the uniting them.*

There is no incompatibility between strength and softness, as is sometimes supposed by frivolous people. Weakness is not refinement. A shadow may be twice as deep in a finely coloured picture as in another, and yet almost imperceptible, from the gradations that lead to it, and blend it with the light. Correggio had prodigious strength, and greater softness. Nature is strong and soft, beyond the reach of art to imitate. Softness then does not imply the absence of considerable extremes, but it is the interposing a third thing between them, to break the force of the contrast. Guido is more soft than strong. Rembrandt is more strong than soft.

10. And lastly. *That truth is, to a certain degree, beauty and grandeur, since all things are connected, and all things modify one another in nature. Simplicity is also grand and beautiful for the same reason. Elegance is ease and lightness, with precision.*

This last head appears to contain a number of *gratis dicta*,[20] got together for the sake of completing a decade of propositions. They have, however, some show of truth, and we should add little clearness to them by any reasoning upon the matter. So we will conclude here for the present.

'Prose-Style and the Elgin Marbles'

*

It were to be wished that the French sculptors would come over and look at the Elgin Marbles, as they are arranged with great care and some pomp in the British Museum. They may smile to see that we are willing to remove works of art from their original places of abode, though we will not allow others to do so. These noble fragments of antiquity might startle our fastidious neighbours a little at first from their rude state and their simplicity, but I think they would gain upon them by degrees, and convince their understandings, if they did not subdue their affections. They are indeed an equally instructive lesson and unanswerable rebuke to them and to us – to them for thinking that finishing every part *alike* is perfection, and to us who imagine that to leave every part alike unfinished is grandeur. They are as remote from finicalness as grossness, and combine the parts with the whole in the manner that nature does. Every part is given, but not ostentatiously, and only as it would appear in the circumstances. There is an alternate action and repose. If one muscle is strained, another is proportionably relaxed. If one limb is in action and another at rest, they come under a different law, and the muscles are not brought out nor the skin tightened in the one as in the other. There is a flexibility and sway of the limbs and of the whole body. The flesh has the softness and texture of flesh, not the smoothness or stiffness of stone. There is an undulation and a liquid flow on the surface, as the breath of genius moved the mighty mass: they are the finest forms in the most striking attitudes, and with every thing in its place, proportion, and degree, uniting the ease, truth, force, and delicacy of Nature. They show nothing but the artist's thorough comprehension of, and entire docility to that great teacher. There is no *petit-maîtreship*, no pedantry, no attempt at a display of science, or at forcing the parts into an artificial symmetry, but it is like cutting a human body out of a block of marble, and leaving it to act for itself with all the same springs, levers, and internal machinery. It was said of Shakespeare's dramas, that they were the *logic of passion*; and it may be affirmed of the Elgin Marbles, that they are the *logic of form*. — One part being given, another cannot be otherwise than it is. There is a mutual understanding and reaction throughout the whole frame. The Apollo and other antiques are not equally simple and severe. The limbs have too much an appearance of being cased in marble, of making a display of every recondite beauty, and of balancing and answering to one another, like the rhymes in verse. The Elgin Marbles are harmonious, flowing, varied prose. In a word, they are like casts after the finest nature. Any cast from nature, however inferior, is in the same style. Let the French and English sculptors make casts continually. The one will see in them the parts everywhere given — the other will see them everywhere given in subordination to, and as forming materials for, a whole.

From *A Letter to William Gifford, Esq.*

*

Man is governed by his passions, and not by his interest. – The selfish theory is founded on mixing up vulgar prejudices, and scholastic distinctions; and by being insisted on, tends to debase the mind, and not at all promote the cause of truth.

I do not think I should illustrate the foregoing reasoning so well by any thing I could add on the subject, as by relating the manner in which it first struck me. I remember I had been reading a speech which Mirabaud (the author of the work, called the *System of Nature*) has put into the mouth of a supposed infidel at the day of Judgment; and was afterwards led on by some means or other, to consider the question, whether it could properly be said to be an act of virtue in any one to sacrifice his own final happiness to that of any other person, or number of persons, if it were possible for the one ever to be made the price of the other. Suppose it to be my own case – that it were in my power to save twenty other persons, by voluntarily consenting to suffer for them, why should I not do a generous thing, and never trouble myself about what might be the consequences to myself thousands of years hence? Now the reason, I thought, why a man should prefer his own future welfare to that of others, was, that he has a necessary, or abstract interest in the one, which he cannot have in the other, and this again is the consequence of his being always the same individual, of his continued identity with himself. The distinction is this, that however insensible I may be to my own interest at any future period, yet when the time comes, I shall feel very differently about it. I shall then judge of it from the actual impression of the object, that is, truly and certainly; and as I shall still be conscious of my past feelings, and shall bitterly repent my

own folly and insensibility, I ought, as a rational agent, to be determined now by what I shall then wish I had done, when I shall feel
the consequences of my actions most deeply and sensibly. It is this
continued consciousness of my own feelings which gives me an
immediate interest in whatever relates to my future welfare, and
makes me at all times accountable to myself for my own conduct. As
therefore this consciousness will be renewed in me after death, if I
exist again at all — But stop — As I must be conscious of my past
feelings to be myself, and as this conscious being will be myself, how,
if that consciousness should be transferred to some other being? How
am I to know that I am not imposed upon by a false claim of identity?
But that is impossible, because I shall have no other self than that
which arises from this very consciousness. Why then, if so, this self
may be multiplied in as many different beings as the Deity may
think proper to endue with the same consciousness, which, if it can
be renewed by an act of omnipotence in any one instance, may clearly
be so in a hundred others. Am I to regard all these as equally myself?
Am I equally interested in the fate of all? Or if I must fix upon some
one of them in particular as my representative and other self, how
am I to be determined in my choice? — Here then I saw an end put
to my speculations about absolute self-interest and personal identity.
I saw plainly, that the consciousness of my own feelings, which is
made the foundation of my continued interest in them, could not
extend to what had never been, and might never be, that my identity
with myself must be confined to the connection between my past
and present being, that with respect to my future feelings and interests
they could have no communication with, or influence over my present
feelings and interests, merely because they were future, that I shall
be hereafter affected by the recollection of my former feelings and
actions, and my remorse be equally heightened by reflecting on my
past folly, and late-earned wisdom, whether I am really the same
thinking being, or have only the same consciousness renewed in me;
but that to suppose that this remorse can react in the reverse order
on my present feelings, or create an immediate interest in my future
feelings before it exists, is an express contradiction. For, how can this
pretended unity of consciousness which is only reflected from the
past, which makes me so little acquainted with the future, that I

cannot even tell for a moment how long it will be continued, whether it will be entirely interrupted by, or renewed in me after death, and which might be multiplied in I don't know how many different beings, and prolonged by complicated sufferings, without my being any the wiser for it; how, I ask, can a principle of this sort transfuse my present into my future being, and make me as much a participator in what does not at all affect me as if it were actually impressed upon my senses? I cannot, therefore, have a principle of active self-interest arising out of the connexion between my future and present being, for no such connexion exists or is possible. I am what I am in spite of the future. My feelings, actions, and interests are determined by causes already existing and acting, and cannot depend on any thing else, without a complete transposition of the order in which effects follow one another in nature.

In this manner, Sir, may a man learn to distinguish the limits which circumscribe his identity with himself, and the frail tenure on which he holds his fleeting existence. Here indeed, 'on this bank and shoal of time',[1] we give ourselves credit for a few years, and so far make sure of our continued identity – as far as we can see the horizon before us, while the same busy scene exists, while the same objects, passions, and pursuits engross our attention, we seem to grasp the realities of things; they are incorporated with our imagination and take hold of our affections, and we cannot doubt of our interest in them. Farther than this, we do not go with the same confidence; the indistinctness of another state of being takes away its reality, and we lose the abstract idea of self for want of objects to attach it to. But the reasoning is the same in both cases. The next year, the next hour, the next moment is but a creation of the mind; in all that we hope or fear, love or hate, in all that is nearest and dearest to us, we but mistake the strength of illusion for certainty, and follow the mimic shows of things and catch at a shadow and live in a waking dream. Every thing before us exists in an ideal world. The future is a blank and dreary void, like sleep or death, till the imagination brooding over it with wings outspread,[2] impregnates it with life and motion. The forms and colours it assumes are but the pictures reflected on the eye of fancy, the unreal mockeries of future events. The solid fabric of time and nature moves on, but the future always flies before it. The present moment stands on the brink of nothing. We cannot pass the dread abyss, or make a broad and beaten way over it,[3] or construct a real interest in it, or identify ourselves with what is not, or have a being, sense, and motion, where there are none. Our interest in the future, our identity with it, cannot be substantial; that self which we project before us into it is like a shadow in the water, a bubble of the brain. In becoming the blind and servile drudges of self-interest, we bow down before an idol of our own making, and are spell-bound by a name. Those objects to which we are most attached, make no part of our present sensations or real existence; they are fashioned out of nothing, and riveted to our self-love by the force of a reasoning imagination, (the privilege of our intellectual nature) – and it is the same faculty that carries us out of ourselves as well as beyond the present moment, that pictures the thoughts, passions and feelings of others to us, and interests us in them, that clothes the whole possible world with a borrowed reality, that breathes into all other forms the breath of life, and endows our sympathies with vital warmth, and diffuses the soul of morality through all the relations and sentiments of our social being.

Such, Sir, is the metaphysical discovery of which I spoke; and which I made many years ago. From that time I felt a certain weight and tightness about my heart taken off, and cheerful and confident thoughts springing up in the place of anxious fears and sad forebodings. The plant I had sown and watered with my tears, grew under my eye; and the air about it was wholesome and pleasant. For this cause it is, that I have gone on little discomposed by other things, by good or adverse fortune, by good or ill report, more hurt by public disappointments than my own, and not thrown into the hot or cold fits of a tertian ague, as the *Edinburgh* or *Quarterly Review* damps or raises the opinion of the town in my favour. I have some love of fame, of the fame of a Pascal, a Leibniz, or a Berkeley (none at all of popularity) and would rather that a single inquirer after truth should pronounce my name, after I am dead, with the same feelings that I have thought of theirs, than be puffed in all the newspapers, and praised in all the reviews, while I am living. I myself have been a thinker; and I cannot but believe that there are and will be others, like me. If the few and scattered sparks of truth, which I have been at so much pains to collect, should still be kept alive in the minds of such persons, and not entirely die with me, I shall be satisfied.

My First Acquaintance with Poets

My father was a Dissenting Minister at W—m[1] in Shropshire; and in
the year 1798 (the figures that compose that date are to me like the
'dreaded name of Demogorgon'[2]) Mr Coleridge came to Shrewsbury,
to succeed Mr Rowe in the spiritual charge of a Unitarian Congregation
there. He did not come till late on the Saturday afternoon before he
was to preach; and Mr Rowe, who himself went down to the coach
in a state of anxiety and expectation, to look for the arrival of his
successor, could find no one at all answering the description but a
round-faced man in a short black coat (like a shooting-jacket) which
hardly seemed to have been made for him, but who seemed to be
talking at a great rate to his fellow-passengers. Mr Rowe had scarce
returned to give an account of his disappointment, when the round-
faced man in black entered, and dissipated all doubts on the subject,
by beginning to talk. He did not cease while he stayed; nor has he
since, that I know of. He held the good town of Shrewsbury in
delightful suspense for three weeks that he remained there, 'fluttering
the *proud Salopians* like an eagle in a dove-cote';[3] and the Welsh
mountains that skirt the horizon with their tempestuous confusion,
agree to have heard no such mystic sounds since the days of

'High-born Hoel's harp or soft Llewellyn's lay!'[4]

As we passed along between W—m and Shrewsbury, and I eyed their
blue tops seen through the wintry branches, or the red rustling leaves
of the sturdy oak-trees by the roadside, a sound was in my ears as of
a Siren's song; I was stunned, startled with it, as from deep sleep; but
I had no notion then that I should ever be able to express my
admiration to others in motley imagery or quaint allusion, till the

light of his genius shone into my soul, like the sun's rays glittering in the puddles of the road. I was at that time dumb, inarticulate, helpless, like a worm by the way-side, crushed, bleeding, lifeless; but now, bursting from the deadly bands that 'bound them,

'With Styx nine times round them',[5]

my ideas float on winged words, and as they expand their plumes, catch the golden light of other years. My soul has indeed remained in its original bondage, dark, obscure, with longings infinite and unsatisfied; my heart, shut up in the prison-house of this rude clay, has never found, nor will it ever find, a heart to speak to; but that my understanding also did not remain dumb and brutish, or at length found a language to express itself, I owe to Coleridge. But this is not to my purpose.

My father lived ten miles from Shrewsbury, and was in the habit of exchanging visits with Mr Rowe, and with Mr Jenkins of Whitchurch (nine miles farther on) according to the custom of Dissenting Ministers in each other's neighbourhood. A line of communication is thus established, by which the flame of civil and religious liberty is kept alive, and nourishes its smouldering fire unquenchable; like the fires in the *Agamemnon* of Æschylus,[6] placed at different stations, that waited for ten long years to announce with their blazing pyramids the destruction of Troy. Coleridge had agreed to come over to see my father, according to the courtesy of the country, as Mr Rowe's probable successor; but in the mean time I had gone to hear him preach the Sunday after his arrival. A poet and a philosopher getting up into a Unitarian pulpit to preach the Gospel, was a romance in these degenerate days, a sort of revival of the primitive spirit of Christianity, which was not to be resisted.

It was in January, 1798, that I rose one morning before day-light, to walk ten miles in the mud, to hear this celebrated person preach. Never, the longest day I have to live, shall I have such another walk as this cold, raw, comfortless one, in the winter of the year 1798. – *Il y a des impressions que ni le temps ni les circonstances peuvent effacer. Dusse-je vivre des siècles entiers, le doux temps de ma jeunesse ne peut renaître pour moi, ni s'effacer jamais dans ma mémoire.*[7] When I got there, the organ was playing the 100th psalm, and, when it was done, Mr Coleridge rose and gave out his text, 'And he went up into the mountain to pray, HIMSELF, ALONE.'[8] As he gave out this text, his voice 'rose like a steam of rich distilled perfumes',[9] and when he came to the two last words, which he pronounced loud, deep, and distinct, it seemed to me, who was then young, as if the sounds had echoed from the bottom of the human heart, and as if that prayer might have floated in solemn silence through the universe. The idea of St John came into mind, 'of one crying in the wilderness, who had his loins girt about, and whose food was locusts and wild honey'.[10] The preacher then launched into his subject, like an eagle dallying with the wind. The sermon was upon peace and war; upon church and state − not their alliance, but their separation − on the spirit of the world and the spirit of Christianity, not as the same, but as opposed to one another. He talked of those who had 'inscribed the cross of Christ on banners dripping with human gore'. He made a poetical and pastoral excursion, − and to show the fatal effects of war, drew a striking contrast between the simple shepherd boy, driving his team afield, or sitting under the hawthorn, piping to his flock, 'as though he should never be old', and the same poor country-lad, crimped,[11] kidnapped, brought into town, made drunk at an alehouse, turned into a wretched drummer-boy, with his hair sticking on end with powder and pomatum, a long cue[12] at his back, and tricked out in the loathsome finery of the profession of blood.

'Such were the notes our once-lov'd poet sung.'[13]

And for myself, I could not have been more delighted if I had heard the music of the spheres. Poetry and Philosophy had met together, Truth and Genius had embraced, under the eye and with the sanction of Religion. This was even beyond my hopes. I returned home well satisfied. The sun that was still labouring pale and wan through the sky, obscured by thick mists, seemed an emblem of the *good cause*; and the cold dank drops of dew that hung half melted on the beard of the thistle, had something genial and refreshing in them; for there was a spirit of hope and youth in all nature, that turned every thing into good. The face of nature had not then the brand of JUS DIVINUM[14] on it:

'Like to that sanguine flower inscrib'd with woe.'[15]

On the Tuesday following, the half-inspired speaker came. I was called down into the room where he was, and went half-hoping, half-afraid. He received me very graciously, and I listened for a long time without uttering a word. I did not suffer in his opinion by my silence. 'For those two hours', he afterwards was pleased to say, 'he was conversing with W. H.'s forehead!' His appearance was different from what I had anticipated from seeing him before. At a distance, and in the dim light of the chapel, there was to me a strange wildness in his aspect, a dusky obscurity, and I thought him pitted with the small-pox. His complexion was at that time clear, and even bright —

'As are the children of yon azure sheen.'[16]

His forehead was broad and high, light as if built of ivory, with large projecting eyebrows, and his eyes rolling beneath them like a sea with darkened lustre. 'A certain tender bloom his face o'erspread',[17] a purple tinge as we see it in the pale thoughtful complexions of the Spanish portrait-painters, Murillo and Velázquez. His mouth was gross, voluptuous, open, eloquent; his chin good-humoured and round; but his nose, the rudder of the face, the index of the will, was small, feeble, nothing — like what he has done. It might seem that the genius of his face as from a height surveyed and projected him (with sufficient capacity and huge aspiration) into the world unknown of thought and imagination, with nothing to support or guide his veering purpose, as if Columbus had launched his adventurous course for the New World in a scallop, without oars or compass. So at least I comment on it after the event. Coleridge in his person was rather above the common size, inclining to the corpulent, or like Lord Hamlet, 'somewhat fat and pursy'.[18] His hair (now, alas! grey) was then black and glossy as the raven's, and fell in smooth masses over his forehead. This long pendulous hair is peculiar to enthusiasts, to those whose minds tend heavenward; and is traditionally inseparable (though of a different colour) from the pictures of Christ. It ought to belong, as a character, to all who preach *Christ crucified*, and Coleridge was at that time one of those!

It was curious to observe the contrast between him and my father,

who was a veteran in the cause, and then declining into the vale of
years. He had been a poor Irish lad, carefully brought up by his
parents, and sent to the University of Glasgow (where he studied
under Adam Smith) to prepare him for his future destination. It was
his mother's proudest wish to see her son a Dissenting Minister. So
if we look back to past generations (as far as eye can reach) we see
the same hopes, fears, wishes, followed by the same disappointments,
throbbing in the human heart; and so we may see them (if we look
forward) rising up for ever, and disappearing, like vapourish bubbles,
in the human breast! After being tossed about from congregation to
congregation in the heats of the Unitarian controversy, and squabbles
about the American war, he had been relegated to an obscure village,
where he was to spend the last thirty years of his life, far from the
only converse that he loved, the talk about disputed texts of Scripture
and the cause of civil and religious liberty. Here he passed his days,
repining but resigned, in the study of the Bible, and the perusal of
the Commentators, – huge folios, not easily got through, one of which
would outlast a winter! Why did he pore on these from morn to night
(with the exception of a walk in the fields or a turn in the garden to
gather broccoli-plants or kidney-beans of his own rearing, with no
small degree of pride and pleasure)? – Here were 'no figures nor no
fantasies',[19] – neither poetry nor philosophy – nothing to dazzle,
nothing to excite modern curiosity; but to his lack-lustre eyes there
appeared, within the pages of the ponderous, unwieldy, neglected
tomes, the sacred name of JEHOVAH in Hebrew capitals: pressed
down by the weight of the style, worn to the last fading thinness of
the understanding, there were glimpses, glimmering notions of the
patriarchal wanderings, with palm-trees hovering in the horizon, and
processions of camels at the distance of three thousand years; there
was Moses with the Burning Bush, the number of the Twelve Tribes,
types, shadows, glosses on the law and the prophets; there were
discussions (dull enough) on the age of Methuselah,[20] a mighty
speculation! there were outlines, rude guesses at the shape of Noah's
Ark and of the riches of Solomon's Temple; questions as to the date
of the creation, predictions of the end of all things; the great lapses
of time, the strange mutations of the globe were unfolded with the
voluminous leaf, as it turned over; and though the soul might slumber

with an hieroglyphic veil of inscrutable mysteries drawn over it, yet it was in a slumber ill-exchanged for all the sharpened realities of sense, wit, fancy, or reason. My father's life was comparatively a dream; but it was a dream of infinity and eternity, of death, the resurrection, and a judgment to come!

No two individuals were ever more unlike than were the host and his guest. A poet was to my father a sort of nondescript: yet whatever added grace to the Unitarian cause was to him welcome. He could hardly have been more surprised or pleased, if our visitor had worn wings. Indeed, his thoughts had wings; and as the silken sounds rustled round our little wainscoted parlour, my father threw back his spectacles over his forehead, his white hairs mixing with its sanguine hue; and a smile of delight beamed across his rugged cordial face, to think that Truth had found a new ally in Fancy!* Besides, Coleridge seemed to take considerable notice of me, and that of itself was enough. He talked very familiarly, but agreeably, and glanced over a variety of subjects. At dinner-time he grew more animated, and dilated in a very edifying manner on Mary Wollstonecraft and Mackintosh. The last, he said, he considered (on my father's speaking of his *Vindiciæ Gallicæ* as a capital performance) as a clever scholastic man – a master of the topics, – or as the ready warehouseman of letters, who knew exactly where to lay his hand on what he wanted, though the goods were not his own. He thought him no match for Burke, either in style or matter. Burke was a metaphysician, Mackintosh a mere logician. Burke was an orator (almost a poet) who reasoned in figures, because he had an eye for nature: Mackintosh, on the other hand, was a rhetorician, who had only an eye to common-places. On this I ventured to say that I had always entertained a great opinion of Burke, and that (as far as I could find) the speaking of him with contempt might be made the test of a vulgar democratical mind. This was the first observation I ever made to Coleridge, and he said it was a very just and striking one. I remember the leg of Welsh mutton and the turnips on the table that day had the finest

---

* My father was one of those who mistook his talent after all. He used to be very much dissatisfied that I preferred his *Letters* to his *Sermons*. The last were forced and dry; the first came naturally from him. For ease, half-plays on words, and a supine, monkish, indolent pleasantry, I have never seen them equalled.

flavour imaginable. Coleridge added that Mackintosh and Tom Wedgwood (of whom, however, he spoke highly) had expressed a very indifferent opinion of his friend Mr Wordsworth, on which he remarked to them – 'He strides on so far before you, that he dwindles in the distance!' Godwin had once boasted to him of having carried on an argument with Mackintosh for three hours with dubious success; Coleridge told him – 'If there had been a man of genius in the room, he would have settled the question in five minutes.' He asked me if I had ever seen Mary Wollstonecraft, and I said, I had once for a few moments, and that she seemed to me to turn off Godwin's objections to something she advanced with quite a playful, easy air. He replied, that 'this was only one instance of the ascendancy which people of imagination exercised over those of mere intellect'. He did not rate Godwin very high* (this was caprice or prejudice, real or affected) but he had a great idea of Mrs Wollstonecraft's powers of conversation, none at all of her talent for book-making. We talked a little about Holcroft. He had been asked if he was not much struck *with* him, and he said, he thought himself in more danger of being struck *by* him. I complained that he would not let me get on at all, for he required a definition of every the commonest word, exclaiming, 'What do you mean by a *sensation*, Sir? What do you mean by an *idea*?' This, Coleridge said, was barricadoing the road to truth: – it was setting up a turnpike-gate at every step we took. I forget a great number of things, many more than I remember; but the day passed off pleasantly, and the next morning Mr Coleridge was to return to Shrewsbury. When I came down to breakfast, I found that he had just received a letter from his friend, T. Wedgwood, making him an offer of £150. a-year if he chose to waive his present pursuit, and devote himself entirely to the study of poetry and philosophy. Coleridge seemed to make up his mind to close with this proposal in the act of tying on one of his shoes. It threw an additional damp on his departure. It took the wayward enthusiast quite from us to cast him into Deva's winding vales,[22] or by the shores of old romance.[23] Instead

---

* He complained in particular of the presumption of his attempting to establish the future immortality of man,[21] 'without' (as he said) 'knowing what Death was or what Life was' – and the tone in which he pronounced these two words seemed to convey a complete image of both.

of living at ten miles' distance, of being the pastor of a Dissenting congregation at Shrewsbury, he was henceforth to inhabit the Hill of Parnassus, to be a Shepherd on the Delectable Mountains.[24] Alas! I knew not the way thither, and felt very little gratitude for Mr Wedgwood's bounty. I was presently relieved from this dilemma; for Mr Coleridge, asking for a pen and ink, and going to a table to write something on a bit of card, advanced towards me with undulating step, and giving me the precious document, said that that was his address, *Mr Coleridge, Nether-Stowey, Somersetshire*; and that he should be glad to see me there in a few weeks' time, and, if I chose, would come half-way to meet me. I was not less surprised than the shepherd-boy (this simile is to be found in *Cassandra*[25]) when he sees a thunder-bolt fall close at his feet. I stammered out my acknowledgments and acceptance of this offer (I thought Mr Wedgwood's annuity a trifle to it) as well as I could; and this mighty business being settled, the poet-preacher took leave, and I accompanied him six miles on the road. It was a fine morning in the middle of winter, and he talked the whole way. The scholar in Chaucer is described as going

– 'Sounding on his way'.[26]

So Coleridge went on his. In digressing, in dilating, in passing from subject to subject, he appeared to me to float in air, to slide on ice. He told me in confidence (going along) that he should have preached two sermons before he accepted the situation at Shrewsbury, one on Infant Baptism, the other on the Lord's Supper, showing that he could not administer either, which would have effectually disqualified him for the object in view. I observed that he continually crossed me on the way by shifting from one side of the foot-path to the other. This struck me as an odd movement; but I did not at that time connect it with any instability of purpose or involuntary change of principle, as I have done since. He seemed unable to keep on in a straight line. He spoke slightingly of Hume (whose *Essay on Miracles* he said was stolen from an objection started in one of South's *Sermons – Credat Judæus Apella!*[27]). I was not very much pleased at this account of Hume, for I had just been reading, with infinite relish, that completest of all metaphysical *choke-pears*,[28] his *Treatise on Human Nature*, to which the *Essays*, in point of scholastic subtlety and close reasoning, are mere elegant trifling, light summer-reading. Coleridge even denied the excellence of Hume's general style, which I think betrayed a want of taste or candour. He however made me amends by the manner in which he spoke of Berkeley. He dwelt particularly on his *Essay on Vision* as a masterpiece of analytical reasoning. So it undoubtedly is. He was exceedingly angry with Dr Johnson for striking the stone with his foot, in allusion to this author's Theory of Matter and Spirit, and saying, 'Thus I confute him, Sir.'[29] Coleridge drew a parallel (I don't know how he brought about the connection) between Bishop Berkeley and Tom Paine. He said the one was an instance of a subtle, the other of an acute mind, than which no two things could be more distinct. The one was a shop-boy's quality, the other the characteristic of a philosopher. He considered Bishop Butler as a true philosopher, a profound and conscientious thinker, a genuine reader of nature and of his own mind. He did not speak of his *Analogy*, but of his *Sermons at the Rolls' Chapel*, of which I had never heard. Coleridge somehow always contrived to prefer the *unknown* to the *known*. In this instance he was right. The *Analogy* is a tissue of sophistry, of wire-drawn, theological special-pleading; the *Sermons* (with the Preface to them) are in a fine vein of deep, matured reflection, a candid appeal to our observation of human nature, without pedantry and without bias. I told Coleridge I had written a few remarks, and was sometimes foolish enough to believe that I had made a discovery on the same subject (the *Natural Disinterestedness of the Human Mind*) – and I tried to explain my view of it to Coleridge, who listened with great willingness, but I did not succeed in making myself understood. I sat down to the task shortly afterwards for the twentieth time, got new pens and paper, determined to make clear work of it, wrote a few meagre sentences in the skeleton-style of a mathematical demonstration, stopped half-way down the second page; and, after trying in vain to pump up any words, images, notions, apprehensions, facts, or observations, from that gulf of abstraction in which I had plunged myself for four or five years preceding, gave up the attempt as labour in vain, and shed tears of helpless despondency on the blank unfinished paper. I can write fast enough now. Am I better than I was then? Oh no! One truth discovered, one pang of regret at not being able to express it, is better than all the fluency and flippancy in the world. Would that I could go back to what I then was! Why can we not revive past times as we can revisit old places? If I had the quaint Muse of Sir Philip Sidney to assist me, I would write a Sonnet to the Road between W—m and Shrewsbury, and immortalize every step of it by some fond enigmatical conceit. I would swear that the very milestones had ears, and that Harmer-hill stooped with all its pines, to listen to a poet, as he passed! I remember but one other topic of discourse in this walk. He mentioned Paley, praised the naturalness and clearness of his style, but condemned his sentiments, thought him a mere time-serving casuist, and said that 'the fact of his work on Moral and Political Philosophy being made a text-book in our Universities was a disgrace to the national character'. We parted at the six-mile stone; and I returned homeward, pensive but much pleased. I had met with unexpected notice from a person, whom I believed to have been prejudiced against me. 'Kind and affable to me had been his condescension, and should be honoured ever with suitable regard.'[30] He was the first poet I had known, and he certainly answered to that inspired name. I had heard a great deal of his powers of conversation, and was not disappointed. In fact, I never met with any thing at all like them, either before or since. I could easily credit the accounts which were circulated of his holding forth to a large party of ladies and gentlemen, an evening or two before, on the Berkeleian Theory, when he made the whole material universe look like a transparency of fine words; and another story (which I believe he has somewhere told himself[31]) of his being asked to a party at Birmingham, of his smoking tobacco and going to sleep after dinner on a sofa, where the company found him to their no small surprise, which was increased to wonder when he started up of a sudden, and rubbing his eyes, looked about him, and launched into a three-hours' description of the third heaven, of which he had had a dream, very different from Mr Southey's *Vision of Judgment*, and also from that other *Vision of Judgment*,[32] which Mr Murray, the Secretary of the Bridge-street Junto,[33] has taken into his especial keeping!

On my way back, I had a sound in my ears, it was the voice of Fancy: I had a light before me, it was the face of Poetry. The one still lingers there, the other has not quitted my side! Coleridge in truth met me half-way on the ground of philosophy, or I should not have been won over to his imaginative creed. I had an uneasy, pleasurable sensation all the time, till I was to visit him. During those months the chill breath of winter gave me a welcoming; the vernal air was balm and inspiration to me. The golden sun-sets, the silver star of evening, lighted me on my way to new hopes and prospects. *I was to visit Coleridge in the Spring.* This circumstance was never absent from my thoughts, and mingled with all my feelings. I wrote to him at the time proposed, and received an answer postponing my intended visit for a week or two, but very cordially urging me to complete my promise then. This delay did not damp, but rather increase my ardour. In the mean time, I went to Llangollen Vale, by way of initiating myself in the mysteries of natural scenery; and I must say I was enchanted with it. I had been reading Coleridge's description of England, in his fine *Ode on the Departing Year*, and I applied it, *con amore*, to the objects before me. That valley was to me (in a manner) the cradle of a new existence: in the river that winds through it, my spirit was baptized in the waters of Helicon!

I returned home, and soon after set out on my journey with unworn heart and untired feet. My way lay through Worcester and Gloucester, and by Upton, where I thought of Tom Jones and the adventure of the muff.[34] I remember getting completely wet through one day, and stopping at an inn (I think it was at Tewkesbury) where I sat up all night to read *Paul and Virginia*.[35] Sweet were the showers in early youth that drenched my body, and sweet the drops of pity that fell upon the books I read! I recollect a remark of Coleridge's upon this very book, that nothing could show the gross indelicacy of French manners and the entire corruption of their imagination more strongly than the behaviour of the heroine in the last fatal scene, who turns away from a person on board the sinking vessel, that offers to save her life, because he has thrown off his clothes to assist him in swimming. Was this a time to think of such a circumstance? I once hinted to Wordsworth, as we were sailing in his boat on Grasmere lake, that I thought he had borrowed the idea of his *Poems on the Naming of Places* from the local inscriptions of the same kind in *Paul and Virginia*. He did not own the obligation, and stated some distinction without a difference, in defence of his claim to originality. Any the slightest variation would be sufficient for this purpose in his mind; for whatever *he* added or omitted would inevitably be worth all that any one else had done, and contain the marrow of the sentiment. – I was still two days before the time fixed for my arrival, for I had taken care to set out early enough. I stopped these two days at Bridgwater, and when I was tired of sauntering on the banks of its muddy river, returned to the inn, and read *Camilla*.[36] So have I loitered my life away, reading books, looking at pictures, going to plays, hearing, thinking, writing on what pleased me best. I have wanted only one thing to make me happy; but wanting that, have wanted every thing!

I arrived, and was well received. The country about Nether Stowey is beautiful, green and hilly, and near the sea-shore. I saw it but the other day, after an interval of twenty years, from a hill near Taunton. How was the map of my life spread out before me, as the map of the country lay at my feet! In the afternoon, Coleridge took me over to All-Foxden, a romantic old family-mansion of the St Aubyns, where Wordsworth lived. It was then in the possession of a friend of the poet's, who gave him the free use of it. Somehow that period (the time just after the French Revolution) was not a time when *nothing was given for nothing*.[37] The mind opened, and a softness might be perceived coming over the heart of individuals,[38] beneath 'the scales that fence' our self-interest. Wordsworth himself was from home, but his sister kept house, and set before us a frugal repast; and we had free access to her brother's poems, the *Lyrical Ballads*, which were still in manuscript, or in the form of *Sybilline Leaves*.[39] I dipped into a few of these with great satisfaction, and with the faith of a novice. I slept that night in an old room with blue hangings, and covered with the round-faced family-portraits of the age of George I and II and from the wooded declivity of the adjoining park that overlooked my window, at the dawn of day, could

—'hear the loud stag speak'.[40]

In the outset of life (and particularly at this time I felt it so) our imagination has a body to it. We are in a state between sleeping and waking, and have indistinct but glorious glimpses of strange shapes, and there is always something to come better than what we see. As in our dreams the fullness of the blood gives warmth and reality to the coinage of the brain, so in youth our ideas are clothed, and fed, and pampered with our good spirits; we breathe thick with thoughtless happiness, the weight of future years presses on the strong pulses of the heart, and we repose with undisturbed faith in truth and good. As we advance, we exhaust our fund of enjoyment and of hope. We are no longer wrapped in *lamb's-wool*, lulled in Elysium. As we taste the pleasures of life, their spirit evaporates, the sense palls; and nothing is left but the phantoms, the lifeless shadows of what *has been*!

That morning, as soon as breakfast was over, we strolled out into the park, and seating ourselves on the trunk of an old ash-tree that stretched along the ground, Coleridge read aloud with a sonorous and musical voice, the ballad of *Betty Foy*.[41] I was not critically or sceptically inclined. I saw touches of truth and nature, and took the rest for granted. But in the *Thorn*, the *Mad Mother*, and the *Complaint of a Poor Indian Woman*, I felt that deeper power and pathos which have been since acknowledged,

'In spite of pride, in erring reason's spite',[42]

as the characteristics of this author; and the sense of a new style and a new spirit in poetry came over me. It had to me something of the effect that arises from the turning up of the fresh soil, or of the first welcome breath of Spring,

'While yet the trembling year is unconfirmed'.[43]

Coleridge and myself walked back to Stowey that evening, and his voice sounded high

'Of Providence, foreknowledge, will, and fate,
Fix'd fate, free-will, foreknowledge absolute',[44]

as we passed through echoing grove, by fairy stream or waterfall, gleaming in the summer moonlight! He lamented that Wordsworth was not prone enough to belief in the traditional superstitions of the place, and that there was a something corporeal, a *matter-of-fact-ness*, a clinging to the palpable, or often to the petty, in his poetry, in consequence. His genius was not a spirit that descended to him through the air; it sprung out of the ground like a flower, or unfolded itself from a green spray, on which the gold-finch sang. He said, however (if I remember right) that this objection must be confined to his descriptive pieces, that his philosophic poetry had a grand and comprehensive spirit in it, so that his soul seemed to inhabit the universe like a palace, and to discover truth by intuition, rather than by deduction. The next day Wordsworth arrived from Bristol at Coleridge's cottage. I think I see him now. He answered in some degree to his friend's description of him, but was more gaunt and Don Quixote-like. He was quaintly dressed (according to the *costume* of that unconstrained period) in a brown fustian jacket and striped pantaloons. There was something of a roll, a lounge in his gait, not unlike his own Peter Bell.[45] There was a severe, worn pressure of thought about his temples, a fire in his eye (as if he saw something in objects more than the outward appearance), an intense high narrow forehead, a Roman nose, cheeks furrowed by strong purpose and feeling, and a convulsive inclination to laughter about the mouth, a good deal at variance with the solemn, stately expression of the rest of his face. Chantrey's bust wants the marking traits; but he was teased into making it regular and heavy: Haydon's head of him, introduced into the *Entrance of Christ into Jerusalem*, is the most like his drooping weight of thought and expression. He sat down and talked very naturally and freely, with a mixture of clear gushing accents in his voice, a deep guttural intonation, and a strong tincture of the northern *burr*, like the crust on wine. He instantly began to make havoc of the half of a Cheshire cheese on the table, and said triumphantly that 'his marriage with experience had not been so unproductive as Mr Southey's in teaching him a knowledge of the good things of this life'. He had been to see the *Castle Spectre* by Monk Lewis, while at Bristol, and described it very well. He said 'it fitted the taste of the audience like a glove'. This *ad captandum*[46] merit was however by no means a recommendation of it, according to the severe principles of the new school, which reject rather than court popular effect. Wordsworth, looking out of the low, latticed window, said, 'How beautifully the sun sets on that yellow bank!' I thought within myself, 'With what eyes these poets see nature!' and ever after, when I saw the sun-set stream upon the objects facing it, conceived I had made a discovery, or thanked Mr Wordsworth for having made one for me! We went over to All-Foxden again the day following, and Wordsworth read us the story of Peter Bell in the open air; and the comment made upon it by his face and voice was very different from that of some later critics! Whatever might be thought of the poem, 'his face was as a book where men might read strange matters',[47] and he announced the fate of his hero in prophetic tones. There is a *chaunt* in the recitation both of Coleridge and Wordsworth, which acts as a spell upon the hearer, and disarms the judgment. Perhaps they have deceived themselves by making habitual use of this ambiguous accompaniment. Coleridge's manner is more full, animated, and varied; Wordsworth's more equable, sustained, and internal. The one might be termed more *dramatic*, the other more *lyrical*. Coleridge has told me that he himself liked to compose in walking over uneven ground, or breaking through the straggling branches of a copsewood; whereas Wordsworth always wrote (if he could) walking up and down a straight gravel-walk, or in some spot where the continuity of his verse met with no collateral interruption. Returning that same evening, I got into a metaphysical argument with Wordsworth, while Coleridge was explaining the different notes of the nightingale to his sister, in which we neither of us succeeded in making ourselves perfectly clear and intelligible. Thus I passed three weeks at Nether Stowey and in the neighbourhood, generally devoting the afternoons to a delightful chat in an arbour made of bark by the poet's friend Tom Poole, sitting under two fine elm-trees, and listening to the bees humming round us, while we quaffed our *flip*.[48] It was agreed, among other things, that we should make a jaunt down the Bristol-Channel, as far as Linton. We set off together on foot, Coleridge, John Chester, and I. This Chester was a native of Nether Stowey, one of those who were attracted to Coleridge's discourse as flies are to honey, or bees in swarming-time to the sound of a brass pan. He 'followed in the chace, like a dog who hunts, not like one that made up the cry'.[49] He had on a brown cloth coat, boots, and corduroy breeches, was low in stature, bow-legged, had a drag in his walk like a drover, which he assisted by a hazel switch, and kept on a sort of trot by the side of Coleridge, like a running footman by a state coach, that he might not lose a syllable or sound, that fell from Coleridge's lips. He told me his private opinion, that Coleridge was a wonderful man. He scarcely opened his lips, much less offered an opinion the whole way: yet of the three, had I to choose during that journey, I would be John Chester. He afterwards followed Coleridge into Germany, where the Kantean philosophers were puzzled how to bring him under any of their categories. When he sat down at table with his idol, John's felicity was complete; Sir Walter Scott's, or Mr Blackwood's, when they sat down at the same table with the King, was not more so. We passed Dunster on our right, a small town between the brow of a hill and the sea. I remember eyeing it wistfully as it lay below us: contrasted with the woody scene around, it looked as clear, as pure, as *embrowned* and ideal as any landscape I have seen since, of Gaspard Poussin's or Domenichino's. We had a long day's march – (our feet kept time to the echoes of Coleridge's tongue) – through Minehead and by the Blue Anchor, and on to Linton, which we did not reach till near midnight, and where we had some difficulty in making a lodgment. We however knocked the people of the house up at last, and we were repaid for our apprehensions and fatigue by some excellent rashers of fried bacon and eggs. The view in coming along had been splendid. We walked for miles and miles on dark brown heaths overlooking the channel, with the Welsh hills beyond, and at times descended into little sheltered valleys close by the sea-side, with a smuggler's face scowling by us, and then had to ascend conical hills with a path winding up through a coppice to a barren top, like a monk's shaven crown, from one of which I pointed out to Coleridge's notice the bare masts of a vessel on the very edge of the horizon and within the red-orbed disk of the setting sun, like his own spectre-ship in the *Ancient Mariner*. At Linton the character of the sea-coast becomes more marked and rugged. There is a place called the *Valley of Rocks* (I suspect this was only the poetical name for it) bedded among precipices overhanging the sea, with rocky caverns beneath, into which the waves dash, and where the sea-gull forever wheels its screaming flight. On the tops of these are huge stones thrown transverse, as if an earthquake had tossed them there, and behind these is a fretwork of perpendicular rocks, something like the *Giant's Causeway*. A thunder-storm came on while we were at the inn, and Coleridge was running out bareheaded to enjoy the commotion of the elements in the *Valley of Rocks*, but as if in spite, the clouds only muttered a few angry sounds, and let fall a few refreshing drops. Coleridge told me that he and Wordsworth were to have made this place the scene of a prose-tale, which was to have been in the manner of, but far superior to, the *Death of Abel*,[50] but they had relinquished the design. In the morning of the second day, we breakfasted luxuriously in an old-fashioned parlour, on tea, toast, eggs, and honey, in the very sight of the bee-hives from which it had been taken, and a garden full of thyme and wild flowers that had produced it. On this occasion Coleridge spoke of Virgil's *Georgics*, but not well. I do not think he had much feeling for the classical or elegant. It was in this room that we found a little worn-out copy of the *Seasons*, lying in a window-seat, on which Coleridge exclaimed, '*That* is true fame!' He said Thomson was a great poet, rather than a good one; his style was as meretricious as his thoughts were natural. He spoke of Cowper as the best modern poet. He said the *Lyrical Ballads* were an experiment about to be tried by him and Wordsworth, to see how far the public taste would endure poetry written in a more natural and simple style than had hitherto been attempted; totally discarding the artifices of poetical diction, and making use only of such words as had probably been common in the most ordinary language since the days of Henry II. Some comparison was introduced between Shakespeare and Milton. He said 'he hardly knew which to prefer. Shakespeare seemed to him a mere stripling in the art; he was as tall and as strong, with infinitely more activity than Milton, but he never appeared to have come to man's estate; or if he had, he would not have been a man, but a monster.' He spoke with contempt of Gray, and with intolerance of Pope. He did not like the versification of the latter. He observed that 'the ears of these couplet-writers might be charged with having short memories, that could not retain the harmony of whole passages'. He thought little of Junius as a writer; he had a dislike of Dr Johnson; and a much higher opinion of Burke as an orator and politician, than of Fox or Pitt. He however thought him very inferior in richness of style and imagery to some of our elder prose-writers, particularly Jeremy Taylor. He liked Richardson, but not Fielding; nor could I get him to enter into the merits of *Caleb*

Williams.[51]* In short, he was profound and discriminating with respect to those authors whom he liked, and where he gave his judgment fair play; capricious, perverse, and prejudiced in his antipathies and distastes. We loitered on the 'ribbed sea-sands',[52] in such talk as this, a whole morning, and I recollect met with a curious sea-weed, of which John Chester told us the country name! A fisherman gave Coleridge an account of a boy that had been drowned the day before, and that they had tried to save him at the risk of their own lives. He said 'he did not know how it was that they ventured, but, Sir, we have a *nature* towards one another'. This expression, Coleridge remarked to me, was a fine illustration of that theory of disinterestedness which I (in common with Butler) had adopted. I broached to him an argument of mine to prove that *likeness* was not mere association of ideas. I said that the mark in the sand put one in mind of a man's foot, not because it was part of a former impression of a man's foot (for it was quite new) but because it was like the shape of a man's foot. He assented to the justness of this distinction (which I have explained at length elsewhere, for the benefit of the curious) and John Chester listened; not from any interest in the subject, but because he was astonished that I should be able to suggest any thing to Coleridge that he did not already know. We returned on the third morning, and Coleridge remarked the silent cottage-smoke curling up the valleys where, a few evenings before, we had seen the lights gleaming through the dark.

In a day or two after we arrived at Stowey, we set out, I on my return home, and he for Germany. It was a Sunday morning, and he was to preach that day for Dr Toulmin of Taunton. I asked him if he had prepared any thing for the occasion? He said he had not even thought of the text, but should as soon as we parted. I did not go to hear him, – this was a fault, – but we met in the evening at Bridgwater. The next day we had a long day's walk to Bristol, and sat down, I

---

* He had no idea of pictures, of Claude or Raphael, and at this time I had as little as he. He sometimes gives a striking account at present of the Cartoons at Pisa, by Buffalmacco and others; of one in particular, where Death is seen in the air brandishing his scythe, and the great and mighty of the earth shudder at his approach, while the beggars and the wretched kneel to him as their deliverer. He would of course understand so broad and fine a moral as this at any time.

recollect, by a well-side on the road, to cool ourselves and satisfy our thirst, when Coleridge repeated to me some descriptive lines from his tragedy of *Remorse*; which I must say became his mouth and that occasion better than they, some years after, did Mr Elliston's and the Drury-lane boards, –

> 'Oh memory! shield me from the world's poor strife,
> And give those scenes thine everlasting life.'[55]

I saw no more of him for a year or two, during which period he had been wandering in the Hartz Forest in Germany; and his return was cometary, meteorous, unlike his setting out. It was not till some time after that I knew his friends Lamb and Southey. The last always appears to me (as I first saw him) with a common-place book under his arm, and the first with a *bon-mot* in his mouth. It was at Godwin's that I met him with Holcroft and Coleridge, where they were disputing fiercely which was the best – *Man as he was, or man as he is to be.* 'Give me', says Lamb, 'man as he is *not* to be.' This saying was the beginning of a friendship between us, which I believe still continues. – Enough of this for the present.

> 'But there is matter for another rhyme,
> And I to this may add a second tale.'[54]

Jeremy Bentham

Mr Bentham is one of those persons who verify the old adage, that 'A prophet has no honour, except out of his own country.'[1] His reputation lies at the circumference; and the lights of his understanding are reflected, with increasing lustre, on the other side of the globe. His name is little known in England, better in Europe, best of all in the plains of Chile and the mines of Mexico. He has offered constitutions for the New World, and legislated for future times. The people of Westminster, where he lives, hardly know of such a person; but the Siberian savage has received cold comfort from his lunar aspect, and may say to him with Caliban – 'I know thee, and thy dog and thy bush!'[2] The tawny Indian may hold out the hand of fellowship to him across the GREAT PACIFIC. We believe that the Empress Catherine corresponded with him; and we know that the Emperor Alexander called upon him, and presented him with his miniature in a gold snuff-box, which the philosopher, to his eternal honour, returned. Mr Hobhouse is a greater man at the hustings, Lord Rolle at Plymouth Dock; but Mr Bentham would carry it hollow, on the score of popularity, at Paris or Pegu. The reason is, that our author's influence is purely intellectual. He has devoted his life to the pursuit of abstract and general truths, and to those studies –

'That waft a *thought* from Indus to the Pole' –[3]

and has never mixed himself up with personal intrigues or party politics. He once, indeed, stuck up a hand-bill to say that he (Jeremy Bentham) being of sound mind, was of opinion that Sir Samuel Romilly was the most proper person to represent Westminster; but this was the whim of the moment. Otherwise, his reasonings, if true at all, are true everywhere alike: his speculations concern humanity at large, and are not confined to the hundred or the bills of mortality. It is in moral as in physical magnitude: The little is seen best near: the great appears in its proper dimensions, only from a more commanding point of view, and gains strength with time, and elevation from distance!

Mr Bentham is very much among philosophers what La Fontaine was among poets: — in general habits and in all but his professional pursuits, he is a mere child. He has lived for the last forty years in a house in Westminster, overlooking the Park, like an anchorite in his cell, reducing law to a system, and the mind of man to a machine. He scarcely ever goes out, and sees very little company. The favoured few, who have the privilege of the *entrée*, are always admitted one by one. He does not like to have witnesses to his conversation. He talks a great deal, and listens to nothing but facts. When any one calls upon him, he invites them to take a turn round his garden with him (Mr Bentham is an economist of his time, and sets apart this portion of it to air and exercise) — and there you may see the lively old man, his mind still buoyant with thought and with the prospect of futurity, in eager conversation with some Opposition Member, some expatriated Patriot, or Transatlantic Adventurer, urging the extinction of Close Boroughs, or planning a code of laws for some 'lone island in the watery waste',[4] his walk almost amounting to a run, his tongue keeping pace with it in shrill, cluttering accents, negligent of his person, his dress, and his manner, intent only on his grand theme of UTILITY — or pausing, perhaps, for want of breath and with lack-lustre eye to point out to the stranger a stone in the wall at the end of his garden (overarched by two beautiful cotton-trees) *Inscribed to the Prince of Poets*, which marks the house where Milton formerly lived. To show how little the refinements of taste or fancy enter into our author's system, he proposed at one time to cut down these beautiful trees, to convert the garden where he had breathed the air of Truth and Heaven for near half a century into a paltry *Chreistomathic School*,[5] and to make Milton's house (the cradle of *Paradise Lost*) a thoroughfare, like a three-stalled stable, for the idle rabble of Westminster to pass backwards and forwards to it with their cloven hoofs. Let us not, however, be getting on too fast — Milton himself taught school! There is something not altogether dissimilar between Mr Bentham's appearance, and the portraits of Milton, the same silvery tone, a few dishevelled hairs, a peevish, yet puritanical expression, an irritable temperament corrected by habit and discipline. Or in modern times, he is something between Franklin and Charles Fox, with the comfortable double-chin and sleek thriving look of the one, and the quivering lip, the restless eye, and animated acuteness of the other. His eye is quick and lively; but it glances not from object to object, but from thought to thought. He is evidently a man occupied with some train of fine and inward association. He regards the people about him no more than the flies of a summer. He meditates the coming age. He hears and sees only what suits his purpose, or some 'foregone conclusion';[6] and looks out for facts and passing occurrences in order to put them into his logical machinery and grind them into the dust and powder of some subtle theory, as the miller looks out for grist to his mill! Add to this physiognomical sketch the minor points of costume, the open shirt-collar, the single-breasted coat, the old-fashioned half-boots and ribbed stockings; and you will find in Mr Bentham's general appearance a singular mixture of boyish simplicity and of the venerableness of age. In a word, our celebrated jurist presents a striking illustration of the difference between the *philosophical* and the *regal* look; that is, between the merely abstracted and the merely personal. There is a lackadaisical *bonhomie* about his whole aspect, none of the fierceness of pride or power; an unconscious neglect of his own person, instead of a stately assumption of superiority; a good-humoured, placid intelligence, instead of a lynx-eyed watchfulness, as if it wished to make others its prey, or was afraid they might turn and rend him; he is a beneficent spirit, prying into the universe, not lording it over it; a thoughtful spectator of the scenes of life, or ruminator on the fate of mankind, not a painted pageant, a stupid idol set up on its pedestal of pride for men to fall down and worship with idiot fear and wonder at the thing themselves have made, and which, without that fear and wonder, would in itself be nothing!

Mr Bentham, perhaps, over-rates the importance of his own theories. He has been heard to say (without any appearance of pride or affectation) that 'he should like to live the remaining years of his life, a year at a time at the end of the next six or eight centuries, to see the effect which his writings would by that time have had upon the world'. Alas! his name will hardly live so long! Nor do we think, in point of fact, that Mr Bentham has given any new or decided impulse to the human mind. He cannot be looked upon in the light of a discoverer in legislation or morals. He has not struck out any great leading principle or parent-truth, from which a number of others might be deduced; nor has he enriched the common and established stock of intelligence with original observations, like pearls thrown into wine. One truth discovered is immortal, and entitles its author to be so: for, like a new substance in nature, it cannot be destroyed. But Mr Bentham's *forte* is arrangement; and the form of truth, though not its essence, varies with time and circumstance. He has methodized, collated, and condensed all the materials prepared to his hand on the subjects of which he treats, in a masterly and scientific manner; but we should find a difficulty in adducing from his different works (however elaborate or closely reasoned) any new element of thought, or even a new fact or illustration. His writings are, therefore, chiefly valuable as *books of reference*, as bringing down the account of intellectual inquiry to the present period, and disposing the results in a compendious, connected, and tangible shape; but books of reference are chiefly serviceable for facilitating the acquisition of knowledge, and are constantly liable to be superseded and to grow out of fashion with its progress, as the scaffolding is thrown down as soon as the building is completed. Mr Bentham is not the first writer (by a great many) who has assumed the principle of UTILITY as the foundation of just laws, and of all moral and political reasoning: – his merit is, that he has applied this principle more closely and literally; that he has brought all the objections and arguments, more distinctly labelled and ticketed, under this one head, and made a more constant and explicit reference to it at every step of his progress, than any other writer. Perhaps the weak side of his conclusions also is, that he has carried this single view of his subject too far, and not made sufficient allowance for the varieties of human nature, and the caprices and irregularities of the human will. 'He has not allowed for the *wind*.'7 It is not that you can be said to see his favourite doctrine of Utility glittering everywhere through his system, like a vein of rich, shining ore (that is not the nature of the material) – but it might be plausibly objected that he had struck the whole mass of fancy, prejudice, passion, sense, whim, with his petrific, leaden mace,[8] that he had 'bound volatile Hermes',[9] and reduced the theory and practice of human life to a *caput mortuum*[10] of reason, and dull, plodding, technical calculation. The gentleman is himself a capital logician; and he has been led by this circumstance to consider man as a logical animal. We fear this view of the matter will hardly hold water. If we attend to the *moral* man, the constitution of his mind will scarcely be found to be built up of pure reason and a regard to consequences: if we consider the *criminal* man (with whom the legislator has chiefly to do) it will be found to be still less so.

Every pleasure, says Mr Bentham, is equally a good, and is to be taken into the account as such in a moral estimate, whether it be the pleasure of sense or of conscience, whether it arise from the exercise of virtue or the perpetration of crime. We are afraid the human mind does not readily come into this doctrine, this *ultima ratio philosophorum*,[11] interpreted according to the letter. Our moral sentiments are made up of sympathies and antipathies, of sense and imagination, of understanding and prejudice. The soul, by reason of its weakness, is an aggregating and an exclusive principle; it clings obstinately to some things, and violently rejects others. And it must do so, in a great measure, or it would act contrary to its own nature. It needs helps and stages in its progress, and 'all appliances and means to boot',[12] which can raise it to a partial conformity to truth and good (the utmost it is capable of) and bring it into a tolerable harmony with the universe. By aiming at too much, by dismissing collateral aids, by extending itself to the farthest verge of the conceivable and possible, it loses its elasticity and vigour, its impulse and its direction. The moralist can no more do without the intermediate use of rules and principles, without the 'vantage ground of habit, without the levers of the understanding, than the mechanist can discard the use of wheels and pulleys, and perform every thing by simple motion. If the mind of man were competent to comprehend the whole of truth and good, and act upon it at once, and independently of all other considerations, Mr Bentham's plan would be a feasible one, and *the truth, the whole truth, and nothing but the truth* would be the best possible ground to place morality upon. But it is not so. In ascertaining the rules of moral conduct, we must have regard not merely to the nature of the object, but to the capacity of the agent, and to his fitness for apprehending or attaining it. Pleasure is that which is so in itself: good is that which approves itself as such on reflection, or the idea of which is a source of satisfaction. All pleasure is not, therefore (morally speaking) equally a good; for all pleasure does not equally bear reflecting on. There are some tastes that are sweet in the mouth and bitter in the belly; and there is a similar contradiction and anomaly in the mind and heart of man. Again, what would become of the *Posthæc meminisse juvabit*[13] of the poet, if a principle of fluctuation and reaction is not inherent in the very constitution of our nature, or if all moral truth is a mere literal truism? We are not, then, so much to inquire what certain things are abstractedly or in themselves, as how they affect the mind, and to approve or condemn them accordingly. The same object seen near strikes us more power-fully than at a distance: things thrown into masses give a greater blow to the imagination than when scattered and divided into their component parts. A number of mole-hills do not make a mountain, though a mountain is actually made up of atoms: so moral truth must present itself under a certain aspect and from a certain point of view, in order to produce its full and proper effect upon the mind. The laws of the affections are as necessary as those of optics. A calculation of consequences is no more equivalent to a sentiment, than a *seriatim* enumeration of square yards or feet touches the fancy like the sight of the Alps or Andes!

To give an instance or two of what we mean. Those who on pure cosmopolite principles, or on the ground of abstract humanity affect an extraordinary regard for the Turks and Tartars, have been accused of neglecting their duties to their friends and next-door neighbours. Well, then, what is the state of the question here? One human being is, no doubt, as much worth in himself, independently of the circumstances of time or place, as another; but he is not of so much value to us and our affections. Could our imagination take wing (with our speculative faculties) to the other side of the globe or to the ends of the universe, could our eyes behold whatever our reason teaches us to be possible, could our hands reach as far as our thoughts or wishes, we might then busy ourselves to advantage with the Hottentots, or hold intimate converse with the inhabitants of the Moon; but being as we are, our feelings evaporate in so large a space — we must draw the circle of our affections and duties somewhat closer — the heart hovers and fixes nearer home. It is true, the bands of private, or of local and natural affection are often, nay in general, too tightly strained, so as frequently to do harm instead of good: but the present question is whether we can, with safety and effect, be wholly emancipated from them? Whether we should shake them off at pleasure and without mercy, as the only bar to the triumph of truth and justice? Or whether benevolence, constructed upon a logical scale, would not be merely *nominal*, whether duty, raised to too lofty a pitch of refinement, might not sink into callous indifference or hollow selfishness? Again, is it not to exact too high a strain from humanity, to ask us to qualify the degree of abhorrence we feel against a murderer by taking into our cool consideration the pleasure he may have in committing the deed, and in the prospect of gratifying his avarice or his revenge? We are hardly so formed as to sympathize at the same moment with the assassin and his victim. The degree of pleasure the former may feel, instead of extenuating, aggravates his guilt, and shews the depth of his malignity. Now the mind revolts against this by mere natural antipathy, if it is itself well-disposed; or the slow process of reason would afford but a feeble resistance to violence and wrong. The will, which is necessary to give consistency and promptness to our good intentions, cannot extend so much candour and courtesy to the antagonist principle of evil: virtue, to be sincere and practical, cannot be divested entirely of the blindness and impetuosity of passion! It has been made a plea (half jest, half earnest) for the horrors of war, that they promote trade and manufactures. It has been said, as a set-off for the atrocities practised upon the negro slaves in the West Indies, that without their blood and sweat, so many millions of people could not have sugar to sweeten their tea. Fires and murders have been argued to be beneficial, as they serve to fill the newspapers, and for a subject to talk of — this is a sort of sophistry that it might be difficult to disprove on the bare scheme of contingent utility; but on the ground that we have stated, it must pass for a mere irony. What the proportion between the good and the evil will really be found in any of the supposed cases, may be a question to the understanding;

but to the imagination and the heart, that is, to the natural feelings of mankind, it admits of none!

Mr Bentham, in adjusting the provisions of a penal code, lays too little stress on the co-operation of the natural prejudices of mankind, and the habitual feelings of that class of persons for whom they are more particularly designed. Legislators (we mean writers on legislation) are philosophers, and governed by their reason: criminals, for whose control laws are made, are a set of desperadoes, governed only by their passions. What wonder that so little progress has been made towards a mutual understanding between the two parties! They are quite a different species, and speak a different language, and are sadly at a loss for a common interpreter between them. Perhaps the Ordinary of Newgate[14] bids as fair for this office as any one. What should Mr Bentham, sitting at ease in his arm-chair, composing his mind before he begins to write by a prelude on the organ, and looking out at a beautiful prospect when he is at a loss for an idea, know of the principles of action of rogues, outlaws, and vagabonds? No more than Montaigne[15] of the motions of his cat! If sanguine and tender-hearted philanthropists have set on foot an inquiry into the barbarity and the defects of penal laws, the practical improvements have been mostly suggested by reformed cut-throats, turnkeys, and thief-takers. What even can the Honourable House, who when the Speaker has pronounced the well-known, wished-for sounds 'That this house do now adjourn', retire, after voting a royal crusade or a loan of millions, to lie on down, and feed on plate in spacious palaces, know of what passes in the hearts of wretches in garrets and night-cellars, petty pilferers and marauders, who cut throats and pick pockets with their own hands? The thing is impossible. The laws of the country are, therefore, ineffectual and abortive, because they are made by the rich for the poor, by the wise for the ignorant, by the respectable and exalted in station for the very scum and refuse of the community. If Newgate would resolve itself into a committee of the whole Press-yard, with Jack Ketch at its head, aided by confidential persons from the county prisons or the Hulks,[16] and would make a clear breast, some *data* might be found out to proceed upon; but as it is, the *criminal mind* of the country is a book sealed, no one has been able to penetrate to the inside! Mr Bentham, in his attempts to revise and amend our criminal jurisprudence, proceeds entirely on his favourite principle of Utility. Convince highwaymen and house-breakers that it will be for their interest to reform, and they will reform and lead honest lives; according to Mr Bentham. He says, 'All men act from calculation, even madmen reason.'[17] And, in our opinion, he might as well carry this maxim to Bedlam or St Luke's,[18] and apply it to the inhabitants, as think to coerce or overawe the inmates of a gaol, or those whose practices make them candidates for that distinction, by the mere dry, detailed convictions of the understanding. Criminals are not to be influenced by reason; for it is of the very essence of crime to disregard consequences both to ourselves and others. You may as well preach philosophy to a drunken man, or to the dead, as to those who are under the instigation of any mischievous passion. A man is a drunkard, and you tell him he ought to be sober; he is debauched, and you ask him to reform; he is idle, and you recommend industry to him as his wisest course; he gambles, and you remind him that he may be ruined by this foible; he has lost his character, and you advise him to get into some reputable service or lucrative situation; vice becomes a habit with him, and you request him to rouse himself and shake it off; he is starving, and you warn him that if he breaks the law, he will be hanged. None of this reasoning reaches the mark it aims at. The culprit, who violates and suffers the vengeance of the laws, is not the dupe of ignorance, but the slave of passion, the victim of habit or necessity. To argue with strong passion, with inveterate habit, with desperate circumstances, is to talk to the winds. Clownish ignorance may indeed be dispelled, and taught better; but it is seldom that a criminal is not aware of the consequences of his act, or has not made up his mind to the alternative. They are, in general, *too knowing by half*. You tell a person of this stamp what is his interest; he says he does not care about his interest, or the world and he differ on that particular. But there is one point on which he must agree with them, namely, what *they* think of his conduct, and that is the only hold you have of him. A man may be callous and indifferent to what happens to himself; but he is never indifferent to public opinion, or proof against open scorn and infamy. Shame, then, not fear, is the sheet-anchor of the law. He who is not afraid of being pointed at as a *thief*, will not mind a month's hard labour. He who is prepared to take the life of another, is already reckless of his own. But every one makes a sorry figure in the pillory; and the being launched from the New Drop[19] lowers a man in his own opinion. The lawless and violent spirit, who is hurried by headstrong self-will to break the laws, does not like to have the ground of pride and obstinacy struck from under his feet. This is what gives the *swells* of the metropolis such a dread of the *tread-mill* — it makes them ridiculous. It must be confessed, that this very circumstance renders the reform of criminals nearly hopeless. It is the apprehension of being stigmatized by public opinion, the fear of what will be thought and said of them, that deters men from the violation of the laws, while their character remains unimpeached; but honour once lost, all is lost. The man can never be himself again! A citizen is like a soldier, a part of a machine, who submits to certain hardships, privations, and dangers, not for his own ease, pleasure, profit, or even conscience, but — *for shame*. What is it that keeps the machine together in either case? Not punishment or discipline, but sympathy. The soldier mounts the breach or stands in the trenches, the peasant hedges and ditches, or the mechanic plies his ceaseless task, because the one will not be called a *coward*, the other a *rogue*: but let the one turn deserter and the other vagabond, and there is an end of him. The grinding law of necessity, which is no other than a name, a breath, loses its force; he is no longer sustained by the good opinion of others, and he drops out of his place in society, a useless clog! Mr Bentham takes a culprit, and puts him into what he calls a *Panopticon*,[20] that is, a sort of circular prison, with open cells, like a glass bee-hive. He sits in the middle, and sees all the other does. He gives him work to do, and lectures him if he does not do it. He takes liquor from him, and society, and liberty; but he feeds and clothes him, and keeps him out of mischief; and when he has convinced him, by force and reason together, that this life is for his good, he turns him out upon the world a reformed man, and as confident of the success of his handy-work, as the shoemaker of that which he has just taken off the last, or the Parisian barber in Sterne, of the buckle of his wig. 'Dip it in the ocean,'[21] said the perruquier, 'and it will stand' But we doubt the durability of our projector's patchwork. Will our convert to the great principle of Utility work when he is from under Mr Bentham's eye, because he was forced to work when under it? Will he keep sober, because he has been kept from liquor so long? Will he not return to loose company, because he has had the pleasure of sitting *vis-à-vis* with a philosopher of late? Will he not steal, now that his hands are untied? Will he not take the road, now that it is free to him? Will he not call his benefactor all the names he can set his tongue to, the moment his back is turned? All this is more than to be feared. The charm of criminal life, like that of savage life, consists in liberty, in hardship, in danger, and in the contempt of death, in one word, in extraordinary excitement; and he who has tasted of it, will no more return to regular habits of life, than a man will take to water after drinking brandy, or than a wild beast will give over hunting its prey. Miracles never cease, to be sure; but they are not to be had wholesale, or *to order*. Mr Owen, who is another of these proprietors and patentees of reform, has lately got an American savage with him, whom he carries about in great triumph and complacency, as an antithesis to his *New View of Society*, and as winding up his reasoning to what it mainly wanted, an epigrammatic point. Does the benevolent visionary of the Lanark cotton-mills really think this *natural man* will act as a foil to his *artificial man*? Does he for a moment imagine that his *Address to the higher and middle classes*,[22] with all its advantages of fiction, makes any thing like so interesting a romance as *Hunter's Captivity among the North American Indians*? Has he any thing to show, in all the apparatus of New Lanark and its desolate monotony, to excite the thrill of imagination like the blankets made of wreaths of snow under which the wild wood-rovers bury themselves for weeks in winter? Or the skin of a leopard, which our hardy adventurer slew, and which served him for great coat and bedding? Or the rattle-snake that he found by his side as a bed-fellow? Or his rolling himself into a ball to escape from him? Or his suddenly placing himself against a tree to avoid being trampled to death by the herd of wild buffaloes, that came rushing on like the sound of thunder? Or his account of the huge spiders that prey on blue-bottles and gilded flies in green pathless forests; or of the great Pacific Ocean, that the natives look upon as the gulf that parts time from eternity, and that is to waft them to the spirits of their fathers? After all this, Mr Hunter must find Mr Owen and his parallelograms[23] trite and flat, and will, we suspect, take an opportunity to escape from them!

Mr Bentham's method of reasoning, though comprehensive and exact, labours under the defect of most systems — it is too *topical*. It includes every thing; but it includes every thing alike. It is rather like an inventory, than a valuation of different arguments. Every possible suggestion finds a place, so that the mind is distracted as much as enlightened by this perplexing accuracy. The exceptions seem as important as the rule. By attending to the minute, we overlook the great; and in summing up an account, it will not do merely to insist on the number of items without considering their amount. Our author's page presents a very nicely dove-tailed mosaic pavement of legal common-places. We slip and slide over its even surface without being arrested any where. Or his view of the human mind resembles a map, rather than a picture: the outline, the disposition is correct, but it wants colouring and relief. There is a technicality of manner, which renders his writings of more value to the professional inquirer than to the general reader. Again, his style is unpopular, not to say unintelligible. He writes a language of his own, that *darkens knowledge*. His works have been translated into French — they ought to be translated into English. People wonder that Mr Bentham has not been prosecuted for the boldness and severity of some of his invectives. He might wrap up high treason in one of his inextricable periods, and it would never find its way into Westminster-Hall. He is a kind of Manuscript author — he writes a cypher-hand, which the vulgar have no key to. The construction of his sentences is a curious frame-work with pegs and hooks to hang his thoughts upon, for his own use and guidance, but almost out of the reach of every body else. It is a barbarous philosophical jargon, with all the repetitions, parentheses, formalities, uncouth nomenclature and verbiage of law-Latin; and what makes it worse, it is not mere verbiage, but has a great deal of acuteness and meaning in it, which you would be glad to pick out if you could. In short, Mr Bentham writes as if he was allowed but a single sentence to express his whole view of a subject in, and as if, should he omit a single circumstance or step of the argument, it would be lost to the world for ever, like an estate by a flaw in the title-deeds. This is over-rating the importance of our own discoveries, and mistaking the nature and object of language altogether. Mr Bentham has *acquired* this disability — it is not natural to him. His admirable little work *On Usury*,[24] published forty years ago, is clear, easy, and vigorous. But Mr Bentham has shut himself up since then 'in nook monastic',[25] conversing only with followers of his own, or with 'men of Ind',[26] and has endeavoured to overlay his natural humour, sense, spirit, and style with the dust and cobwebs of an obscure solitude. The best of it is, he thinks his present mode of expressing himself perfect, and that whatever may be objected to his law or logic, no one can find the least fault with the purity, simplicity, and perspicuity of his style.

Mr Bentham, in private life, is an amiable and exemplary character. He is a little romantic, or so; and has dissipated part of a handsome fortune in practical speculations. He lends an ear to plausible projectors, and, if he cannot prove them to be wrong in their premises or their conclusions, thinks himself bound *in reason* to stake his money on the venture. Strict logicians are licensed visionaries. Mr Bentham is half-brother to the late Mr Speaker Abbott* – *Proh pudor!*[27] He was educated at Eton, and still takes our novices to task about a passage in Homer, or a metre in Virgil. He was afterwards at the University, and he has described the scruples of an ingenuous youthful mind about subscribing the Articles, in a passage in his *Church-of-Englandism*, which smacks of truth and honour both, and does one good to read it in an age, when 'to be honest' (or not to laugh at the very idea of honesty) 'is to be one man picked out of ten thousand!'[28] Mr Bentham relieves his mind sometimes, after the fatigue of study, by playing on a fine old organ, and has a relish for Hogarth's prints. He turns wooden utensils in a lathe for exercise, and fancies he can turn men in the same manner. He has no great fondness for poetry, and can hardly extract a moral out of Shakespeare. His house is warmed and lighted by steam. He is one of those who prefer the artificial to the natural in most things, and think the mind of man omnipotent. He has a great contempt for out-of-door prospects, for green fields and trees, and is for referring every thing to Utility. There is a little narrowness in this; for if all the sources of satisfaction are taken away, what is to become of utility itself? It is, indeed, the great

---

* Now Lord Colchester.

fault of this able and extraordinary man, that he has concentrated his faculties and feelings too entirely on one subject and pursuit, and has not 'looked enough abroad into universality'.*[29]

* Lord Bacon's *Advancement of Learning*.

William Godwin

The Spirit of the Age was never more fully shown than in its treatment of this writer — its love of paradox and change, its dastard submission to prejudice and to the fashion of the day. Five-and-twenty years ago he was in the very zenith of a sultry and unwholesome popularity; he blazed as a sun in the firmament of reputation; no one was more talked of, more looked up to, more sought after, and wherever liberty, truth, justice was the theme, his name was not far off: — now he has sunk below the horizon, and enjoys the serene twilight of a doubtful immortality. Mr Godwin, during his lifetime, has secured to himself the triumphs and the mortifications of an extreme notoriety and of a sort of posthumous fame. His bark, after being tossed in the revolutionary tempest, now raised to heaven by all the fury of popular breath, now almost dashed in pieces, and buried in the quicksands of ignorance, or scorched with the lightning of momentary indignation, at length floats on the calm wave that is to bear it down the stream of time. Mr Godwin's person is not known, he is not pointed out in the street, his conversation is not courted, his opinions are not asked, he is at the head of no cabal, he belongs to no party in the State, he has no train of admirers, no one thinks it worth his while even to traduce and vilify him, he has scarcely friend or foe, the world make a point (as Goldsmith used to say[1]) of taking no more notice of him than if such an individual had never existed; he is to all ordinary intents and purposes dead and buried; but the author of *Political Justice* and of *Caleb Williams* can never die, his name is an abstraction in letters, his works are standard in the history of intellect. He is thought of now like any eminent writer a hundred-and-fifty years ago, or just as he will be a hundred-and-fifty years hence. He knows this, and smiles in silent mockery of himself, reposing on the monument of his fame –

> 'Sedet, in eternumque sedebit
> Infelix Theseus.'[2]

No work in our time gave such a blow to the philosophical mind of the country as the celebrated *Enquiry concerning Political Justice.* Tom Paine was considered for the time as a Tom Fool to him; Paley an old woman; Edmund Burke a flashy sophist. Truth, moral truth, it was supposed, had here taken up its abode; and these were the oracles of thought. 'Throw aside your books of chemistry,' said Wordsworth to a young man, a student in the Temple, 'and read Godwin on Necessity.' Sad necessity! Fatal reverse! Is truth then so variable? Is it one thing at twenty, and another at forty? Is it at a burning heat in 1793, and below *zero* in 1814? Not so, in the name of manhood and of common sense! Let us pause here a little. – Mr Godwin indulged in extreme opinions, and carried with him all the most sanguine and fearless understandings of the time. What then? Because those opinions were overcharged, were they therefore altogether groundless? Is the very God of our idolatry all of a sudden to become an abomination and an anathema? Could so many young men of talent, of education, and of principle have been hurried away by what had neither truth, nor nature, not one particle of honest feeling nor the least show of reason in it? Is the *Modern Philosophy* (as it has been called) at one moment a youthful bride, and the next a withered beldame, like the false Duessa[3] in Spenser? Or is the vaunted edifice of Reason, like his House of Pride, gorgeous in front, and dazzling to approach, while 'its hinder parts are ruinous, decayed, and old'?[4] Has the main prop, which supported the mighty fabric, been shaken and given way under the strong grasp of some Samson; or has it not rather been undermined by rats and vermin? At one time, it almost seemed, that 'if this failed,

> The pillar'd firmament was rottenness,
> And earth's base built of stubble':[5]

now scarce a shadow of it remains, it is crumbled to dust, nor is it even talked of! 'What then, went ye forth for to see, a reed shaken with the wind?'[6] Was it for this that our young gownsmen of the greatest expectation and promise, versed in classic lore, steeped in dialectics, armed at all points for the foe, well read, well nurtured, well provided for, left the University and the prospect of lawn sleeves, tearing asunder the shackles of the freeborn spirit, and the cobwebs of school-divinity, to throw themselves at the feet of the new Gamaliel,[7] and learn wisdom from him? Was it for this, that students at the bar, acute, inquisitive, sceptical (here only wild enthusiasts) neglected for a while the paths of preferment and the law as too narrow, tortuous, and unseemly to bear the pure and broad light of reason? Was it for this, that students in medicine missed their way to Lecturerships and the top of their profession, deeming lightly of the health of the body, and dreaming only of the renovation of society and the march of mind? Was it to this that Mr Southey's *Inscriptions*[8] pointed? to this that Mr Coleridge's *Religious Musings* tended? Was it for this, that Mr Godwin himself sat with arms folded, and, 'like Cato, gave his little senate laws'?[9] Or rather, like another Prospero, uttered syllables that with their enchanted breath were to change the world, and might almost stop the stars in their courses? Oh! and is all forgot?[10] Is this sun of intellect blotted from the sky? Or has it suffered total eclipse? Or is it we who make the fancied gloom, by looking at it through the paltry, broken, stained fragments of our own interest and prejudices? Were we fools then, or are we dishonest now? Or was the impulse of the mind less likely to be true and sound when it arose from high thought and warm feeling, than afterwards, when it was warped and debased by the example, the vices, and follies of the world?

The fault, then, of Mr Godwin's philosophy, in one word, was too much ambition – 'by that sin fell the angels'![11] He conceived too nobly of his fellows (the most unpardonable crime against them, for there is nothing that annoys our self-love so much as being complimented on imaginary achievements, to which we are wholly unequal) – he raised the standard of morality above the reach of humanity, and by directing virtue to the most airy and romantic heights, made her path dangerous, solitary, and impracticable. The author of the *Political Justice* took abstract reason for the rule of conduct, and abstract good for its end. He places the human mind on an elevation, from which it commands a view of the whole line of moral consequences; and requires it to conform its acts to the larger and more enlightened conscience which it has thus acquired. He absolves man from the gross and narrow ties of sense, custom, authority, private and local attachment, in order that he may devote himself to the boundless pursuit of universal benevolence. Mr Godwin gives no quarter to the amiable weaknesses of our nature, nor does he stoop to avail himself of the supplementary aids of an imperfect virtue. Gratitude, promises, friendship, family affection give way, not that they may be merged in the opposite vices or in want of principle; but that the void may be filled up by the disinterested love of good, and the dictates of inflexible justice, which is 'the law of laws, and sovereign of sovereigns'.[12] All minor considerations yield, in his system, to the stern sense of duty, as they do, in the ordinary and established ones, to the voice of necessity. Mr Godwin's theory and that of more approved reasoners differ only in this, that what are with them the exceptions, the extreme cases, he makes the every-day rule. No one denies that on great occasions, in moments of fearful excitement, or when a mighty object is at stake, the lesser and merely instrumental points of duty are to be sacrificed without remorse at the shrine of patriotism, of honour, and of conscience. But the disciple of the *New School* (no wonder it found so many impugners, even in its own bosom!) is to be always the hero of duty; the law to which he has bound himself never swerves nor relaxes; his feeling of what is right is to be at all times wrought up to a pitch of enthusiastic self-devotion; he must become the unshrinking martyr and confessor of the public good. If it be said that this scheme is chimerical and impracticable on ordinary occasions, and to the generality of mankind, well and good; but those who accuse the author of having trampled on the common feelings and prejudices of mankind in wantonness or insult, or without wishing to substitute something better (and only unattainable, because it is better) in their stead, accuse him wrongfully. We may not be able to launch the bark of our affections on the ocean-tide of humanity, we may be forced to paddle along its shores, or shelter in its creeks and rivulets: but we have no right to reproach the bold and adventurous pilot, who dared us to tempt the uncertain abyss, with our own want of courage or of skill, or with the jealousies and impatience, which deter us from undertaking, or might prevent us from accomplishing the voyage!

The *Enquiry concerning Political Justice* (it was urged by its favourers and defenders at the time, and may still be so, without either profaneness or levity) is a metaphysical and logical commentary on some of the most beautiful and striking texts of Scripture. Mr Godwin is a mixture of the Stoic and of the Christian philosopher. To break the force of the vulgar objections and outcry that have been raised against the *Modern Philosophy*, as if it were a new and monstrous birth in morals, it may be worth noticing, that volumes of sermons have been written to excuse the founder of Christianity for not including friendship and private affection among its golden rules, but rather excluding them.* Moreover, the answer to the question, 'Who is thy neighbour?'[13] added to the divine precept, 'Thou shalt love thy neighbour as thyself',[14] is the same as in the exploded pages of our author, – 'He to whom we can do most good'. In determining this point, we were not to be influenced by any extrinsic or collateral considerations, by our own predilections, or the expectations of others, by our obligations to them or any services they might be able to render us, by the climate they were born in, by the house they lived in, by rank or religion, or party, or personal ties, but by the abstract merits, the pure and unbiassed justice of the case. The artificial helps and checks to moral conduct were set aside as spurious and unnecessary, and we came at once to the grand and simple question – 'In what manner we could best contribute to the greatest possible good?' This was the paramount obligation in all cases whatever, from which we had no right to free ourselves upon any idle or formal pretext, and of which each person was to judge for himself, under the infallible authority of his own opinion and the inviolable sanction of his self-approbation. 'There was the rub that made *philosophy* of so short life!'[15] Mr Godwin's definition of morals was the same as the admired one of law, *reason without passion*; but with the unlimited scope of private opinion, and in a boundless field of speculation (for nothing less would satisfy the pretensions of the New School), there was danger that the unseasoned novice might substitute

---

* Shaftesbury made this an objection to Christianity, which was answered by Foster, Leland, and other eminent divines, on the ground that Christianity had a higher object in view, namely, general philanthropy.

some pragmatical conceit of his own for the rule of right reason, and mistake a heartless indifference for a superiority to more natural and generous feelings. Our ardent and dauntless reformer followed out the moral of the parable of the Good Samaritan into its most rigid and repulsive consequences with a pen of steel, and let fall his 'trenchant blade'[16] on every vulnerable point of human infirmity; but there is a want in his system of the mild and persuasive tone of the Gospel, where 'all is conscience and tender heart'.[17] Man was indeed screwed up, by mood and figure, into a logical machine, that was to forward the public good with the utmost punctuality and effect, and it might go very well on smooth ground and under favourable circumstances; but would it work up-hill or *against the grain*? It was to be feared that the proud Temple of Reason, which at a distance and in stately supposition shone like the palaces of the New Jerusalem, might (when placed on actual ground) be broken up into the sordid styes of sensuality, and the petty huckster's shops of self-interest! Every man (it was proposed – 'so ran the tenour of the bond'[18]) was to be a Regulus, a Codrus, a Cato, or a Brutus – every woman a Mother of the Gracchi.

> '——— It was well said,
> And 'tis a kind of good deed to say well.'[19]

But heroes on paper might degenerate into vagabonds in practice, Corinnas into courtesans. Thus a refined and permanent individual attachment is intended to supply the place and avoid the inconveniences of marriage; but vows of eternal constancy, without church security, are found to be fragile. A member of the *ideal* and perfect commonwealth of letters lends another a hundred pounds for immediate and pressing use; and when he applies for it again, the borrower has still more need of it than he, and retains it for his own especial, which is tantamount to the public good. The Exchequer of pure reason, like that of the State, never refunds. The political as well as the religious fanatic appeals from the over-weening opinion and claims of others to the highest and most impartial tribunal, namely, his own breast. Two persons agree to live together in Chambers on principles of pure equality and mutual assistance – but when it comes to the push, one of them finds that the other always insists on his fetching water from the pump in Hare-court, and cleaning his shoes for him. A modest assurance was not the least indispensable virtue in the new perfectibility code; and it was hence discovered to be a scheme, like other schemes where there are all prizes and no blanks, for the accommodation of the enterprising and cunning, at the expense of the credulous and honest. This broke up the system, and left no good odour behind it! Reason has become a sort of bye-word, and philosophy has 'fallen first into a fasting, then into a sadness, then into a decline, and last, into the dissolution of which we all complain!'[20] This is a worse error than the former: we may be said to have 'lost the immortal part of ourselves, and what remains is beastly!'[21]

The point of view from which this matter may be fairly considered, is two-fold, and may be stated thus: — In the first place, it by no means follows, because reason is found not to be the only infallible or safe rule of conduct, that it is no rule at all; or that we are to discard it altogether with derision and ignominy. On the contrary, if not the sole, it is the principal ground of action; it is 'the guide, the stay and anchor of our purest thoughts, and soul of all our moral being'.[22] In proportion as we strengthen and expand this principle, and bring our affections and subordinate, but perhaps more powerful motives of action into harmony with it, it will not admit of a doubt that we advance to the goal of perfection, and answer the ends of our creation, those ends which not only morality enjoins, but which religion sanctions. If with the utmost stretch of reason, man cannot (as some seemed inclined to suppose) soar up to the God, and quit the ground of human frailty, yet, stripped wholly of it, he sinks at once into the brute. If it cannot stand alone, in its naked simplicity, but requires other props to buttress it up, or ornaments to set it off; yet without it the moral structure would fall flat and dishonoured to the ground. Private reason is that which raises the individual above his mere animal instincts, appetites and passions: public reason in its gradual progress separates the savage from the civilized state. Without the one, men would resemble wild beasts in their dens; without the other, they would be speedily converted into hordes of barbarians or banditti. Sir Walter Scott, in his zeal to restore the spirit of loyalty, of passive obedience and non-resistance as an acknowledgment for his having been created a Baronet by a Prince of the House of

Brunswick, may think it a fine thing to return in imagination to the good old times, 'when in Auvergne alone, there were three hundred nobles whose most ordinary actions were robbery, rape, and murder',[23] when the castle of each Norman baron was a stronghold from which the lordly proprietor issued to oppress and plunder the neighbouring districts, and when the Saxon peasantry were treated by their gay and gallant tyrants as a herd of loathsome swine – but for our own parts we beg to be excused; we had rather live in the same age with the author of *Waverley* and *Blackwood's Magazine*. Reason is the meter and alnager in civil intercourse, by which each person's upstart and contradictory pretensions are weighed and approved or found wanting, and without which it could not subsist, any more than traffic or the exchange of commodities could be carried on without weights and measures. It is the medium of knowledge, and the polisher of manners, by creating common interests and ideas. Or in the words of a contemporary writer, 'Reason is the queen of the moral world, the soul of the universe, the lamp of human life, the pillar of society, the foundation of law, the beacon of nations, the golden chain let down from heaven, which links all accountable and all intelligent natures in one common system – and in the vain strife between fanatic innovation and fanatic prejudice, we are exhorted to dethrone this queen of the world, to blot out this light of the mind, to deface this fair column, to break in pieces this golden chain! We are to discard and throw from us with loud taunts and bitter execrations that reason, which has been the lofty theme of the philosopher, the poet, the moralist, and the divine, whose name was not first named to be abused by the enthusiasts of the French Revolution, or to be blasphemed by the madder enthusiasts, the advocates of Divine Right, but which is coeval with, and inseparable from the nature and faculties of man – is the image of his Maker stamped upon him at his birth, the understanding breathed into him with the breath of life, and in the participation and improvement of which alone he is raised above the brute creation and his own physical nature!'[24] – The overstrained and ridiculous pretensions of monks and ascetics were never thought to justify a return to unbridled licence of manners, or the throwing aside of all decency. The hypocrisy, cruelty, and fanaticism, often attendant on peculiar professions of sanctity, have not banished the name of religion from the world. Neither can 'the unreasonableness of the reason'[25] of some modern sciolists 'so unreason our reason', as to debar us of the benefit of this principle in future, or to disfranchise us of the highest privilege of our nature. In the second place, if it is admitted that Reason alone is not the sole and self-sufficient ground of morals, it is to Mr Godwin that we are indebted for having settled the point. No one denied or distrusted this principle (before his time) as the absolute judge and interpreter in all questions of difficulty; and if this is no longer the case, it is because he has taken this principle, and followed it into its remotest consequences with more keenness of eye and steadiness of hand than any other expounder of ethics. His grand work is (at least) an *experimentum crucis*[26] to show the weak sides and imperfections of human reason as the sole law of human action. By overshooting the mark, or by 'flying an eagle flight, forth and right on',[27] he has pointed out the limit or line of separation, between what is practicable and what is barely conceivable — by imposing impossible tasks on the naked strength of the will, he has discovered how far it is or is not in our power to dispense with the illusions of sense, to resist the calls of affection, to emancipate ourselves from the force of habit; and thus, though he has not said it himself, has enabled others to say to the towering aspirations after good, and to the over-bearing pride of human intellect — 'Thus far shalt thou come, and no farther!'[28] Captain Parry would be thought to have rendered a service to navigation and his country, no less by proving that there is no North-West Passage, than if he had ascertained that there is one: so Mr Godwin has rendered an essential service to moral science, by attempting (in vain) to pass the Arctic Circle and Frozen Regions, where the understanding is no longer warmed by the affections, nor fanned by the breeze of fancy! This is the effect of all bold, original, and powerful thinking, that it either discovers the truth, or detects where error lies; and the only crime with which Mr Godwin can be charged as a political and moral reasoner is, that he has displayed a more ardent spirit, and a more independent activity of thought than others, in establishing the fallacy (if fallacy it be) of an old popular prejudice that *the Just and True were one*, by 'championing it to the Outrance',[29] and in the final result placing the Gothic structure of human virtue on an humbler, but a wider and safer foundation than it had hitherto occupied in the volumes and systems of the learned.

Mr Godwin is an inventor in the regions of romance, as well as a skilful and hardy explorer of those of moral truth. *Caleb Williams* and *St Leon* are two of the most splendid and impressive works of the imagination that have appeared in our times. It is not merely that these novels are very well for a philosopher to have produced – they are admirable and complete in themselves, and would not lead you to suppose that the author, who is so entirely at home in human character and dramatic situation, had ever dabbled in logic or metaphysics. The first of these, particularly, is a master-piece, both as to invention and execution. The romantic and chivalrous principle of the love of personal fame is embodied in the finest possible manner in the character of Falkland;* as in Caleb Williams (who is not the first, but the second character in the piece) we see the very demon of curiosity personified. Perhaps the art with which these two characters are contrived to relieve and set off each other, has never been surpassed in any work of fiction, with the exception of the immortal satire of Cervantes. The restless and inquisitive spirit of Caleb Williams, in search and in possession of his patron's fatal secret, haunts the latter like a second conscience, plants stings in his tortured mind, fans the flame of his jealous ambition, struggling with agonized remorse; and the hapless but noble-minded Falkland at length falls a martyr to the persecution of that morbid and overpowering interest, of which his mingled virtues and vices have rendered him the object. We conceive no one ever began *Caleb Williams* that did not read it through: no one that ever read it could possibly forget it, or speak of it after any length of time, but with an impression as if the events and feelings had been personal to himself. This is the case also with the story of St Leon, which, with less dramatic interest and intensity of purpose, is set off by a more gorgeous and flowing eloquence, and by a crown of preternatural imagery, that waves over it like a palm-tree! It is the beauty and the charm of Mr Godwin's descriptions

---

* Mr Fuseli used to object to this striking delineation a want of historical correctness, inasmuch as the animating principle of the true chivalrous character was the sense of honour, not the mere regard to, or saving of, appearances. This, we think, must be an hypercriticism, from all we remember of books of chivalry and heroes of romance.

that the reader identifies himself with the author; and the secret of this is, that the author has identified himself with his personages. Indeed, he has created them. They are the proper issue of his brain, lawfully begot, not foundlings, nor the 'bastards of his art'.[50] He is not an indifferent, callous spectator of the scenes which he himself portrays, but without seeming to feel them. There is no look of patch-work and plagiarism,[51] the beggarly copiousness of borrowed wealth; no tracery-work from worm-eaten manuscripts, from forgotten chronicles, nor piecing out of vague traditions with fragments and snatches of old ballads, so that the result resembles a gaudy, staring transparency, in which you cannot distinguish the daubing of the painter from the light that shines through the flimsy colours and gives them brilliancy. Here all is fairly made out with strokes of the pencil, by fair, not by factitious means. Our author takes a given subject from nature or from books, and then fills it up with the ardent workings of his own mind, with the teeming and audible pulses of his own heart. The effect is entire and satisfactory in proportion. The work (so to speak) and the author are one. We are not puzzled to decide upon their respective pretensions. In reading Mr Godwin's novels, we know what share of merit the author has in them. In reading the *Scotch Novels*, we are perpetually embarrassed in asking ourselves this question; and perhaps it is not altogether a false modesty that prevents the editor from putting his name in the title-page – he is (for any thing we know to the contrary) only a more voluminous sort of Allen-a-Dale.[52] At least, we may claim this advantage for the English author, that the chains with which he rivets our attention are forged out of his own thoughts, link by link, blow for blow, with glowing enthusiasm: we see the genuine ore melted in the furnace of fervid feeling, and moulded into stately and *ideal* forms; and this is so far better than peeping into an old iron shop, or pilfering from a dealer in marine stores! There is one drawback, however, attending this mode of proceeding, which attaches generally, indeed, to all originality of composition; namely, that it has a tendency to a certain degree of monotony. He who draws upon his own resources, easily comes to an end of his wealth. Mr Godwin, in all his writings, dwells upon one idea or exclusive view of a subject, aggrandizes a sentiment, exaggerates a character, or pushes an argument to extremes, and makes up by the force of style and continuity of feeling for what he wants in variety of incident or ease of manner. This necessary defect is observable in his best works, and is still more so in Fleetwood and Mandeville; the one of which, compared with his more admired performances, is mawkish, and the other morbid. Mr Godwin is also an essayist, an historian — in short, what is he not, that belongs to the character of an indefatigable and accomplished author? His *Life of Chaucer* would have given celebrity to any man of letters possessed of three thousand a year, with leisure to write quartos: as the legal acuteness displayed in his *Remarks on Judge Eyre's Charge to the Jury* would have raised any briefless barrister to the height of his profession. This temporary effusion did more — it gave a turn to the trials for high treason in the year 1794, and possibly saved the lives of twelve innocent individuals, marked out as political victims to the Moloch of Legitimacy, which then skulked behind a British throne, and had not yet dared to stalk forth (as it has done since) from its lurking-place, in the face of day, to brave the opinion of the world. If it had then glutted its maw with its intended prey (the sharpness of Mr Godwin's pen cut the legal cords with which it was attempted to bind them), it might have done so sooner, and with more lasting effect. The world do not know (and we are not sure but the intelligence may startle Mr Godwin himself), that he is the author of a volume of *Sermons*, and of a *Life of Chatham.**

Mr Fawcett (an old friend and fellow-student of our author, and who always spoke of his writings with admiration, tinctured with wonder) used to mention a circumstance with respect to the last-mentioned work, which may throw some light on the history and progress of Mr Godwin's mind. He was anxious to make his biographical account as complete as he could, and applied for this purpose to many of his acquaintance to furnish him with anecdotes or to suggest criticisms. Amongst others Mr Fawcett repeated to him what he thought a striking passage in a speech on *General Warrants* [35] delivered by Lord Chatham, at which he (Mr Fawcett) had been present. 'Every man's house' (said this emphatic thinker and speaker) 'has been called his castle. And why is it called his castle? Is it because it is defended

---

* We had forgotten the tragedies of Antonio and Ferdinand. Peace be with their *manes*!

by a wall, because it is surrounded with a moat? No, it may be nothing more than a straw-built shed. It may be open to all the elements: the wind may enter in, the rain may enter in — but the king *cannot* enter in!' His friend thought that the point was here palpable enough: but when he came to read the printed volume,[34] he found it thus *transposed*: 'Every man's house is his castle. And why is it called so? Is it because it is defended by a wall, because it is surrounded with a moat? No, it may be nothing more than a straw-built shed. It may be exposed to all the elements: the rain may enter into it, *all the winds of Heaven may whistle round it*, but the king cannot, &c.' This was what Fawcett called a defect of *natural imagination*. He at the same time admitted that Mr Godwin had improved his native sterility in this respect; or atoned for it by incessant activity of mind and by accumulated stores of thought and powers of language. In fact, his *forte* is not the spontaneous, but the voluntary exercise of talent. He fixes his ambition on a high point of excellence, and spares no pains or time in attaining it. He has less of the appearance of a man of genius, than any one who has given such decided and ample proofs of it. He is ready only on reflection: dangerous only at the rebound. He gathers himself up, and strains every nerve and faculty with deliberate aim to some heroic and dazzling achievement of intellect: but he must make a career before he flings himself, armed, upon the enemy, or he is sure to be unhorsed. Or he resembles an eight-day clock that must be wound up long before it can strike. Therefore, his powers of conversation are but limited. He has neither acuteness of remark, nor a flow of language, both which might be expected from his writings, as these are no less distinguished by a sustained and impassioned tone of declamation than by novelty of opinion or brilliant tracks of invention. In company, Horne Tooke used to make a mere child of him — or of any man! Mr Godwin liked this treatment,* and indeed it is his foible to fawn on those who use him *cavalierly*, and to be cavalier to those

* To be sure, it was redeemed by a high respect, and by some magnificent compliments. Once in particular, at his own table, after a good deal of *badinage* and cross-questioning about his being the author of the *Reply to Judge Eyre's Charge*, on Mr Godwin's acknowledging that he was, Mr Tooke said, 'Come here then', — and when his guest went round to his chair, he took his hand, and pressed it to his lips, saying — 'I can do no less for the hand that saved my life!'

who express an undue or unqualified admiration of him. He looks up with unfeigned respect to acknowledged reputation (but then it must be very well ascertained before he admits it) – and has a favourite hypothesis that Understanding and Virtue are the same thing. Mr Godwin possesses a high degree of philosophical candour, and studiously paid the homage of his pen and person to Mr Malthus, Sir James Mackintosh, and Dr Parr, for their unsparing attacks on him; but woe to any poor devil who had the hardihood to defend him against them! In private, the author of *Political Justice* at one time reminded those who knew him of the metaphysician engrafted on the Dissenting Minister. There was a dictatorial, captious, quibbling pettiness of manner. He lost this with the first blush and awkwardness of popularity, which surprised him in the retirement of his study; and he has since, with the wear and tear of society, from being too pragmatical, become somewhat too careless. He is, at present, as easy as an old glove. Perhaps there is a little attention to effect in this, and he wishes to appear a foil to himself. His best moments are with an intimate acquaintance or two, when he gossips in a fine vein about old authors, Clarendon's *History of the Rebellion*, or Burnet's *History of his own Times*; and you perceive by your host's talk, as by the taste of seasoned wine, that he has a *cellarage* in his understanding! Mr Godwin also has a correct *acquired* taste in poetry and the drama. He relishes Donne and Ben Jonson, and recites a passage from either with an agreeable mixture of pedantry and *bonhomie*. He is not one of those who do not grow wiser with opportunity and reflection: he changes his opinions, and changes them for the better. The alteration of his taste in poetry, from an exclusive admiration of the age of Queen Anne to an almost equally exclusive one of that of Elizabeth, is, we suspect, owing to Mr Coleridge, who some twenty years ago, threw a great stone into the standing pool of criticism, which splashed some persons with the mud, but which gave a motion to the surface and a reverberation to the neighbouring echoes, which has not since subsided. In common company, Mr Godwin either goes to sleep himself, or sets others to sleep. He is at present engaged in a History of the Commonwealth of England. – *Esto perpetua!*[55] In size Mr Godwin is below the common stature, nor is his deportment graceful or animated. His face is, however, fine, with an expression of placid temper and recondite thought. He is not unlike the common portraits of Locke. There is a very admirable likeness of him by Mr Northcote, which with a more heroic and dignified air, only does justice to the profound sagacity and benevolent aspirations of our author's mind. Mr Godwin has kept the best company of his time, but he has survived most of the celebrated persons with whom he lived in habits of intimacy. He speaks of them with enthusiasm and with discrimination; and sometimes dwells with peculiar delight on a day passed at John Kemble's in company with Mr Sheridan, Mr Curran, Mrs Wollstonecraft and Mrs Inchbald, when the conversation took a most animated turn and the subject was of Love. Of all these our author is the only one remaining. Frail tenure, on which human life and genius are lent us for a while to improve or to enjoy!

Mr Coleridge

The present is an age of talkers, and not of doers; and the reason is, that the world is growing old. We are so far advanced in the Arts and Sciences, that we live in retrospect, and dote on past achievements. The accumulation of knowledge has been so great, that we are lost in wonder at the height it has reached, instead of attempting to climb or add to it; while the variety of objects distracts and dazzles the looker-on. What *niche* remains unoccupied? What path untried? What is the use of doing anything, unless we could do better than all those who have gone before us? What hope is there of this? We are like those who have been to see some noble monument of art, who are content to admire without thinking of rivalling it; or like guests after a feast, who praise the hospitality of the donor 'and thank the bounteous Pan'[1] – perhaps carrying away some trifling fragments; or like the spectators of a mighty battle, who still hear its sound afar off, and the clashing of armour and the neighing of the war-horse and the shout of victory is in their ears, like the rushing of innumerable waters!

Mr Coleridge has 'a mind reflecting ages past':[2] his voice is like the echo of the congregated roar of the 'dark rearward and abyss'[3] of thought. He who has seen a mouldering tower by the side of a crystal lake, hid by the mist, but glittering in the wave below, may conceive the dim, gleaming, uncertain intelligence of his eye: he who has marked the evening clouds uprolled (a world of vapours), has seen the picture of his mind, unearthly, unsubstantial, with gorgeous tints and ever-varying forms –

'That which was now a horse, even with a thought
The rack dislimns, and makes it indistinct
As water is in water.'[4]

Our author's mind is (as he himself might express it) *tangential*. There is no subject on which he has not touched, none on which he has rested. With an understanding fertile, subtle, expansive, 'quick, forgetive, apprehensive',[5] beyond all living precedent, few traces of it will perhaps remain. He lends himself to all impressions alike; he gives up his mind and liberty of thought to none. He is a general lover of art and science, and wedded to no one in particular. He pursues knowledge as a mistress, with outstretched hands and winged speed; but as he is about to embrace her, his Daphne turns[6] – alas! not to a laurel! Hardly a speculation has been left on record from the earliest time, but it is loosely folded up in Mr Coleridge's memory, like a rich, but somewhat tattered piece of tapestry: we might add (with more seeming than real extravagance), that scarce a thought can pass through the mind of man, but its sound has at some time or other passed over his head with rustling pinions. On whatever question or author you speak, he is prepared to take up the theme with advantage – from Peter Abelard down to Thomas Moore, from the subtlest metaphysics to the politics of the *Courier*. There is no man of genius, in whose praise he descants, but the critic seems to stand above the author, and 'what in him is weak, to strengthen, what is low, to raise and support':[7] nor is there any work of genius that does not come out of his hands like an Illuminated Missal, sparkling even in its defects. If Mr Coleridge had not been the most impressive talker of his age, he would probably have been the finest writer; but he lays down his pen to make sure of an auditor, and mortgages the admiration of posterity for the stare of an idler. If he had not been a poet, he would have been a powerful logician; if he had not dipped his wing in the Unitarian controversy, he might have soared to the very summit of fancy. But in writing verse, he is trying to subject the Muse to *transcendental* theories: in his abstract reasoning, he misses his way by strewing it with flowers. All that he has done of moment, he had done twenty years ago: since then, he may be said to have lived on the sound of his own voice. Mr Coleridge is too rich in intellectual wealth, to need to task himself to any drudgery: he has only to draw the sliders of his imagination, and a thousand subjects expand before him, startling him with their brilliancy, or losing themselves in endless obscurity –

> 'And by the force of blear illusion,
> They draw him on to his confusion.'[8]

What is the little he could add to the stock, compared with the countless stores that lie about him, that he should stoop to pick up a name, or to polish an idle fancy? He walks abroad in the majesty of an universal understanding, eyeing the 'rich strond',[9] or golden sky above him, and 'goes sounding on his way',[10] in eloquent accents, uncompelled and free!

Persons of the greatest capacity are often those, who for this reason do the least; for surveying themselves from the highest point of view, amidst the infinite variety of the universe, their own share in it seems trifling, and scarce worth a thought, and they prefer the contemplation of all that is, or has been, or can be, to the making a coil about doing what, when done, is no better than vanity. It is hard to concentrate all our attention and efforts on one pursuit, except from ignorance of others; and without this concentration of our faculties, no great progress can be made in any one thing. It is not merely that the mind is not capable of the effort; it does not think the effort worth making. Action is one; but thought is manifold. He whose restless eye glances through the wide compass of nature and art, will not consent to have 'his own nothings monstered':[11] but he must do this, before he can give his whole soul to them. The mind, after 'letting contemplation have its fill',[12] or

> 'Sailing with supreme dominion
> Through the azure deep of air',[13]

sinks down on the ground, breathless, exhausted, powerless, inactive; or if it must have some vent to its feelings, seeks the most easy and obvious; is soothed by friendly flattery, lulled by the murmur of immediate applause, thinks as it were aloud, and babbles in its dreams! A scholar (so to speak) is a more disinterested and abstracted character than a mere author. The first looks at the numberless volumes of a library, and says, 'All these are mine': the other points to a single volume (perhaps it may be an immortal one) and says, 'My name is written on the back of it.' This is a puny and grovelling ambition, beneath the lofty amplitude of Mr Coleridge's mind. No, he revolves in his wayward soul, or utters to the passing wind, or discourses to his own shadow, things mightier and more various! – Let us draw the curtain, and unlock the shrine.

Learning rocked him in his cradle, and, while yet a child,

'He lisped in numbers, for the numbers came.'[14]

At sixteen he wrote his *Ode on Chatterton*, and he still reverts to that period with delight, not so much as it relates to himself (for that string of his own early promise of fame rather jars than otherwise) but as exemplifying the youth of a poet. Mr Coleridge talks of himself, without being an egotist, for in him the individual is always merged in the abstract and general. He distinguished himself at school and at the University by his knowledge of the classics, and gained several prizes for Greek epigrams. How many men are there (great scholars, celebrated names in literature) who having done the same thing in their youth, have no other idea all the rest of their lives but of this achievement, of a fellowship and dinner, and who, installed in academic honours, would look down on our author as a mere strolling bard! At Christ's Hospital, where he was brought up, he was the idol of those among his school-fellows, who mingled with their bookish studies the music of thought and of humanity; and he was usually attended round the cloisters by a group of these (inspiring and inspired) whose hearts, even then, burnt within them as he talked,[15] and where the sounds yet linger to mock ELIA[16] on his way, still turning pensive to the past! One of the finest and rarest parts of Mr Coleridge's conversation, is when he expatiates on the Greek tragedians (not that he is not well acquainted, when he pleases, with the epic poets, or the philosophers, or orators, or historians of antiquity) – on the subtle reasonings and melting pathos of Euripides, on the harmonious gracefulness of Sophocles, tuning his love-laboured song, like sweetest warblings from a sacred grove; on the high-wrought trumpet-tongued eloquence of Æschylus, whose Prometheus, above all, is like an Ode to Fate, and a pleading with Providence, his thoughts being let loose as his body is chained on his solitary rock, and his afflicted will (the emblem of mortality)

'Struggling in vain with ruthless destiny.'[17]

As the impassioned critic speaks and rises in his theme, you would think you heard the voice of the Man hated by the Gods, contending with the wild winds as they roar, and his eye glitters with the spirit of Antiquity!

Next, he was engaged with Hartley's tribes of mind, 'etherial braid, thought-woven',[18] – and he busied himself for a year or two with vibrations and vibratiuncles and the great law of association that binds all things in its mystic chain, and the doctrine of Necessity (the mild teacher of Charity) and the Millennium, anticipative of a life to come – and he plunged deep into the controversy on Matter and Spirit, and, as an escape from Dr Priestley's Materialism, where he felt himself imprisoned by the logician's spell, like Ariel[19] in the cloven pine-tree, he became suddenly enamoured of Bishop Berkeley's fairy-world,* and used in all companies to build the universe, like a brave poetical fiction, of fine words – and he was deep-read in Malebranche, and in Cudworth's *Intellectual System* (a huge pile of learning, unwieldy, enormous) and in Lord Brook's hieroglyphic theories, and in Bishop Butler's *Sermons*, and in the Duchess of Newcastle's fantastic folios, and in Clarke and South and Tillotson, and all the fine thinkers and masculine reasoners of that age – and Leibniz's *Pre-established Harmony* reared its arch above his head, like the rainbow in the cloud, covenanting with the hopes of man – and then he fell plump, ten thousand fathoms down[21] (but his wings saved him harmless) into the *hortus siccus*[22] of Dissent, where he pared religion down to the standard of reason and stripped faith of mystery, and preached Christ crucified and the Unity of the Godhead, and so dwelt for a while in the spirit with John Huss and Jerome of

---

* Mr Coleridge named his eldest son (the writer of some beautiful Sonnets) after Hartley, and the second after Berkeley. The third was called Derwent, after the river of that name. Nothing can be more characteristic of his mind than this circumstance. All his ideas indeed are like a river, flowing on for ever, and still murmuring as it flows, discharging its waters and still replenished –

'And so by many winding nooks it strays,
With willing sport to the wild ocean!'[20]

Prague and Socinus and old John Zisca, and ran through Neal's *History of the Puritans*, and Calamy's *Non-Conformists' Memorial*, having like thoughts and passions with them – but then Spinoza became his God, and he took up the vast chain of being in his hand, and the round world became the centre and the soul of all things in some shadowy sense, forlorn of meaning, and around him he beheld the living traces and the sky-pointing proportions of the mighty Pan – but poetry redeemed him from this spectral philosophy, and he bathed his heart in beauty, and gazed at the golden light of heaven, and drank of the spirit of the universe, and wandered at eve by fairy-stream or fountain,

> '—— When he saw nought but beauty,
> When he heard the voice of that Almighty One
> In every breeze that blew, or wave that murmured' —[23]

and wedded with truth in Plato's shade, and in the writings of Proclus and Plotinus saw the ideas of things in the eternal mind, and unfolded all mysteries with the Schoolmen and fathomed the depths of Duns Scotus and Thomas Aquinas, and entered the third heaven with Jacob Behmen, and walked hand in hand with Swedenborg through the pavilions of the New Jerusalem, and sung his faith in the promise and in the word in his *Religious Musings* – and lowering himself from that dizzy height, poised himself on Milton's wings, and spread out his thoughts in charity with the glad prose of Jeremy Taylor, and wept over Bowles's *Sonnets*, and studied Cowper's blank verse, and betook himself to Thomson's Castle of Indolence, and sported with the wits of Charles the Second's days and of Queen Anne, and relished Swift's style and that of the John Bull (Arbuthnot's we mean, not Mr Croker's) and dallied with the British Essayists and Novelists, and knew all qualities of more modern writers with a learned spirit, Johnson, and Goldsmith, and Junius, and Burke, and Godwin, and the *Sorrows of Werter*,[24] and Jean Jacques Rousseau, and Voltaire, and Marivaux, and Crébillon, and thousands more – now 'laughed with Rabelais in his easy chair'[25] or pointed to Hogarth, or afterwards dwelt on Claude's classic scenes or spoke with rapture of Raphael, and compared the women at Rome to figures that had walked out of his pictures, or visited the Oratory of Pisa, and described the works of Giotto and Ghirlandaio and Masaccio, and gave the moral of the picture of the *Triumph of Death*,[26] where the beggars and the wretched invoke his dreadful dart, but the rich and mighty of the earth quail and shrink before it; and in that land of siren sights and sounds, saw a dance of peasant girls, and was charmed with lutes and gondolas, – or wandered into Germany and lost himself in the labyrinths of the Hartz Forest and of the Kantean philosophy, and amongst the cabalistic names of Fichte and Schelling and Lessing, and God knows who – this was long after, but all the former while, he had nerved his heart and filled his eyes with tears, as he hailed the rising orb of liberty, since quenched in darkness and in blood, and had kindled his affections at the blaze of the French Revolution, and sang for joy when the towers of the Bastille and the proud places of the insolent and the oppressor fell, and would have floated his bark,[27] freighted with fondest fancies, across the Atlantic wave with Southey and others to seek for peace and freedom –

'In Philarmonia's undivided dale!'[28]

Alas! 'Frailty, thy name is *Genius*!'[29] – What is become of all this mighty heap of hope, of thought, of learning, and humanity? It has ended in swallowing doses of oblivion[30] and in writing paragraphs in the *Courier*. – Such, and so little is the mind of man!

It was not to be supposed that Mr Coleridge could keep on at the rate he set off; he could not realize all he knew or thought, and less could not fix his desultory ambition; other stimulants supplied the place, and kept up the intoxicating dream, the fever and the madness of his early impressions. Liberty (the philosopher's and the poet's bride) had fallen a victim, meanwhile, to the murderous practices of the hag, Legitimacy. Proscribed by court-hirelings, too romantic for the herd of vulgar politicians, our enthusiast stood at bay, and at last turned on the pivot of a subtle casuistry to the *unclean side*: but his discursive reason would not let him trammel himself into a Poet-laureate or stamp-distributor,[31] and he stopped, ere he had quite passed that well-known 'bourne from whence no traveller returns'[32] – and so has sunk into torpid, uneasy repose, tantalized by useless resources, haunted by vain imaginings, his lips idly moving, but his heart forever still, or, as the shattered chords vibrate of themselves, making melancholy music to the ear of memory! Such is the fate of genius in an age, when in the unequal contest with sovereign wrong, every man is ground to powder who is not either a born slave, or who does not willingly and at once offer up the yearnings of humanity and the dictates of reason as a welcome sacrifice to besotted prejudice and loathsome power.

Of all Mr Coleridge's productions, the *Ancient Mariner* is the only one that we could with confidence put into any person's hands, on whom we wished to impress a favourable idea of his extraordinary powers. Let whatever other objections be made to it, it is unquestionably a work of genius – of wild, irregular, overwhelming imagination, and has that rich, varied movement in the verse, which gives a distant idea of the lofty or changeful tones of Mr Coleridge's voice. In the *Christobel*, there is one splendid passage on divided friendship. The *Translation of Schiller's Wallenstein* is also a masterly production in its kind, faithful and spirited. Among his smaller pieces there are occasional bursts of pathos and fancy, equal to what we might expect from him; but these form the exception, and not the rule. Such, for instance, is his affecting Sonnet to the author of *The Robbers*.

> 'Schiller! that hour I would have wish'd to die,
> If through the shudd'ring midnight I had sent
> From the dark dungeon of the tower time-rent,
> That fearful voice, a famish'd father's cry –
>
> That in no after-moment aught less vast
> Might stamp me mortal! A triumphant shout
> Black horror scream'd, and all her goblin rout
> From the more with'ring scene diminish'd pass'd.
>
> Ah! Bard tremendous in sublimity!
> Could I behold thee in thy loftier mood,
> Wand'ring at eve, with finely frenzied eye,
> Beneath some vast old tempest-swinging wood!
> Awhile, with mute awe gazing, I would brood,
> Then weep aloud in a wild ecstasy.'

His Tragedy, entitled *Remorse*, is full of beautiful and striking passages, but it does not place the author in the first rank of dramatic writers. But if Mr Coleridge's works do not place him in that rank, they injure instead of conveying a just idea of the man, for he himself is certainly in the first class of general intellect.

If our author's poetry is inferior to his conversation, his prose is utterly abortive. Hardly a gleam is to be found in it of the brilliancy and richness of those stores of thought and language that he pours out incessantly, when they are lost like drops of water in the ground. The principal work, in which he has attempted to embody his general views of things, is the FRIEND, of which, though it contains some noble passages and fine trains of thought, prolixity and obscurity are the most frequent characteristics.

No two persons can be conceived more opposite in character or genius than the subject of the present and of the preceding sketch. Mr Godwin, with less natural capacity, and with fewer acquired advantages, by concentrating his mind on some given object, and doing what he had to do with all his might, has accomplished much, and will leave more than one monument of a powerful intellect behind him; Mr Coleridge, by dissipating his, and dallying with every subject by turns, has done little or nothing to justify to the world or to posterity, the high opinion which all who have ever heard him converse, or known him intimately, with one accord entertain of him. Mr Godwin's faculties have kept house, and plied their task in the work-shop of the brain, diligently and effectually: Mr Coleridge's have gossipped away their time, and gadded about from house to house, as if life's business[33] were to melt the hours in listless talk. Mr Godwin is intent on a subject, only as it concerns himself and his reputation; he works it out as a matter of duty, and discards from his mind whatever does not forward his main object as impertinent and vain. Mr Coleridge, on the other hand, delights in nothing but episodes and digressions, neglects whatever he undertakes to perform, and can act only on spontaneous impulses, without object or method. 'He cannot be constrained by mastery.'[34] While he should be occupied with a given pursuit, he is thinking of a thousand other things; a thousand tastes, a thousand objects tempt him, and distract his mind, which keeps open house, and entertains all comers; and after being fatigued and amused with morning calls from idle visitors,[35] finds the day consumed and its business unconcluded. Mr Godwin, on the contrary, is somewhat exclusive and unsocial in his habits of mind, entertains no company but what he gives his whole time and attention to, and wisely writes over the doors of his understanding, his fancy, and his senses – 'No admittance except on business'. He has none of that fastidious refinement and false delicacy, which might lead him to balance between the endless variety of modern attainments. He does not throw away his life (nor a single half-hour of it) in adjusting the claims of different accomplishments, and in choosing between them or making himself master of them all. He sets about his task, (whatever it may be) and goes through it with spirit and fortitude. He has the happiness[36] to think an author the greatest character in the world, and himself the greatest author in it. Mr Coleridge, in writing an harmonious stanza, would stop to consider whether there was not more grace and beauty in a *Pas de trois*,[37] and would not proceed till he had resolved this question by a chain of metaphysical reasoning without end. Not so Mr Godwin. That is best to him, which he can do best. He does not waste himself in vain aspirations and effeminate sympathies. He is blind, deaf, insensible to all but the trump of Fame. Plays, operas, painting, music, ball-rooms, wealth, fashion, titles, lords, ladies, touch him not – all these are no more to him than to the anchorite in his cell, and he writes on to the end of the chapter, through good report and evil report. *Pingo in eternitatem*[38] – is his motto. He neither envies nor admires what others are, but is contented to be what he is, and strives to do the utmost he can. Mr Coleridge has flirted with the Muses as with a set of mistresses: Mr Godwin has been married twice, to Reason and to Fancy, and has to boast no short-lived progeny by each. So to speak, he has *valves* belonging to his mind, to regulate the quantity of gas admitted into it, so that like the bare, unsightly, but well-compacted steam-vessel, it cuts its liquid way, and arrives at its promised end: while Mr Coleridge's bark, 'taught with the little nautilus to sail',[39] the sport of every breath, dancing to every wave,

'Youth at its prow, and Pleasure at its helm',[40]

flutters its gaudy pennons in the air, glitters in the sun, but we wait in vain to hear of its arrival in the destined harbour. Mr Godwin, with less variety and vividness, with less subtlety and susceptibility both of thought and feeling, has had firmer nerves, a more determined purpose, a more comprehensive grasp of his subject, and the results are as we find them. Each has met with his reward: for justice has, after all, been done to the pretensions of each; and we must, in all cases, use means to ends!

Mr Wordsworth

Mr Wordsworth's genius is a pure emanation of the Spirit of the Age. Had he lived in any other period of the world, he would never have been heard of. As it is, he has some difficulty to contend with, the hebetude of his intellect, and the meanness of his subject. With him 'lowliness is young ambition's ladder':[1] but he finds it a toil to climb in this way the steep of Fame. His homely Muse can hardly raise her wing from the ground, nor spread her hidden glories to the sun. He has 'no figures nor no fantasies, which busy *passion* draws in the brains of men':[2] neither the gorgeous machinery of mythologic lore, nor the splendid colours of poetic diction. His style is vernacular: he delivers household truths. He sees nothing loftier than human hopes; nothing deeper than the human heart. This he probes, this he tampers with, this he poises, with all its incalculable weight of thought and feeling, in his hands; and at the same time calms the throbbing pulses of his own heart, by keeping his eye ever fixed on the face of nature. If he can make the life-blood flow from the wounded breast, this is the living colouring with which he paints his verse: if he can assuage the pain or close up the wound with the balm of solitary musing, or the healing powers of plants and herbs and 'skyey influences',[3] this is the sole triumph of his art. He takes the simplest elements of nature and of the human mind, the mere abstract conditions inseparable from our being, and tries to compound a new system of poetry from them; and has perhaps succeeded as well as any one could. '*Nihil humani a me alienum puto*'[4] – is the motto of his works. He thinks nothing low or indifferent of which this can be affirmed: every thing that professes to be more than this, that is not an absolute essence of truth and feeling, he holds to be vitiated, false, and spurious. In a word, his poetry is founded on setting up an opposition (and pushing it to the utmost length) between the natural and the artificial: between the spirit of humanity, and the spirit of fashion and of the world!

It is one of the innovations of the time. It partakes of, and is carried along with, the revolutionary movement of our age: the political changes of the day were the model on which he formed and conducted his poetical experiments. His Muse (it cannot be denied, and without this we cannot explain its character at all) is a levelling one. It proceeds on a principle of equality, and strives to reduce all things to the same standard. It is distinguished by a proud humility. It relies upon its own resources, and disdains external show and relief. It takes the commonest events and objects, as a test to prove that nature is always interesting from its inherent truth and beauty, without any of the ornaments of dress or pomp of circumstances to set it off. Hence the unaccountable mixture of seeming simplicity and real abstruseness in the *Lyrical Ballads*. Fools have laughed at, wise men scarcely understand them. He takes a subject or a story merely as pegs or loops to hang thought and feeling on;[5] the incidents are trifling, in proportion to his contempt for imposing appearances; the reflections are profound, according to the gravity and the aspiring pretensions of his mind.

His popular, inartificial style gets rid (at a blow) of all the trappings of verse, of all the high places of poetry: 'the cloud-capt towers, the solemn temples, the gorgeous palaces', are swept to the ground, and 'like the baseless fabric of a vision, leave not a wreck behind'.[6] All the traditions of learning, all the superstitions of age, are obliterated and effaced. We begin *de novo*,[7] on a *tabula rasa*[8] of poetry. The purple pall, the nodding plume of tragedy are exploded as mere pantomime and trick, to return to the simplicity of truth and nature. Kings, queens, priests, nobles, the altar and the throne, the distinctions of rank, birth, wealth, power, 'the judge's robe, the marshall's truncheon, the ceremony that to great ones 'longs',[9] are not to be found here. The author tramples on the pride of art with greater pride. The Ode and Epode, the Strophe and the Antistrophe, he laughs to scorn. The harp of Homer, the trump of Pindar and of Alcæus are still. The decencies of costume, the decorations of vanity are stripped off without mercy as barbarous, idle, and Gothic. The jewels in the crisped hair,[10] the diadem on the polished brow are thought meretricious, theatrical, vulgar; and nothing contents his fastidious taste beyond a simple garland of flowers. Neither does he avail himself of the advantages which nature or accident holds out to him. He chooses to have his subject a foil to his invention, to owe nothing but to himself. He gathers manna in the wilderness, he strikes the barren rock for the gushing moisture.[11] He elevates the mean by the strength of his own aspirations; he clothes the naked with beauty and grandeur from the store of his own recollections. No cypress-grove loads his verse with perfumes: but his imagination lends 'a sense of joy

> To the bare trees and mountains bare,
> And grass in the green field.'[12]

No storm, no shipwreck startles us by its horrors: but the rainbow lifts its head in the cloud, and the breeze sighs through the withered fern. No sad vicissitude of fate,[13] no overwhelming catastrophe in nature deforms his page: but the dew-drop glitters on the bending flower, the tear collects in the glistening eye.

> 'Beneath the hills, along the flowery vales,
> The generations are prepared; the pangs,
> The internal pangs are ready; the dread strife
> Of poor humanity's afflicted will,
> Struggling in vain with ruthless destiny.'[14]

As the lark ascends from its low bed on fluttering wing, and salutes the morning skies; so Mr Wordsworth's unpretending Muse, in russet guise, scales the summits of reflection, while it makes the round earth its footstool,[15] and its home!

Possibly a good deal of this may be regarded as the effect of disappointed views and an inverted ambition. Prevented by native pride and indolence from climbing the ascent of learning or greatness, taught by political opinions to say to the vain pomp and glory of the world,[16] 'I hate ye', seeing the path of classical and artificial poetry blocked up by the cumbrous ornaments of style and turgid *common-places*, so that nothing more could be achieved in that direction but by the most ridiculous bombast or the tamest servility; he has turned back partly from the bias of his mind, partly perhaps from a judicious policy – has struck into the sequestered vale of humble life, sought out the Muse among sheep-cotes and hamlets and the peasant's mountain-haunts, has discarded all the tinsel pageantry of verse, and endeavoured (not in vain) to aggrandize the trivial and add the charm of novelty to the familiar. No one has shown the same imagination in raising trifles into importance: no one has displayed the same pathos in treating of the simplest feelings of the heart. Reserved, yet haughty, having no unruly or violent passions, (or those passions having been early suppressed), Mr Wordsworth has passed his life in solitary musing, or in daily converse with the face of nature. He exemplifies in an eminent degree the power of *association*; for his poetry has no other source or character. He has dwelt among pastoral scenes, till each object has become connected with a thousand feelings, a link in the chain of thought, a fibre of his own heart. Every one is by habit and familiarity strongly attached to the place of his birth, or to objects that recall the most pleasing and eventful circumstances of his life. But to the author of the *Lyrical Ballads*, nature is a kind of home; and he may be said to take a personal interest in the universe. There is no image so insignificant that it has not in some mood or other found the way into his heart: no sound that does not awaken the memory of other years. –

> 'To him the meanest flower that blows can give
> Thoughts that do often lie too deep for tears.'[17]

The daisy looks up to him[18] with sparkling eye as an old acquaintance: the cuckoo haunts him with sounds of early youth not to be expressed: a linnet's nest startles him with boyish delight: an old withered thorn is weighed down with a heap of recollections: a grey cloak, seen on some wild moor, torn by the wind, or drenched in the rain, afterwards becomes an object of imagination to him: even the lichens on the rock have a life and being in his thoughts. He has described all these objects in a way and with an intensity of feeling that no one else had done before him, and has given a new view or aspect of nature. He is in this sense the most original poet now living, and the one whose writings could the least be spared: for they have no substitute elsewhere. The vulgar do not read them, the learned, who see all things through books, do not understand them, the great despise, the

fashionable may ridicule them: but the author has created himself
an interest in the heart of the retired and lonely student of nature,
which can never die. Persons of this class will still continue to feel
what he has felt: he has expressed what they might in vain wish to
express, except with glistening eye and faltering tongue! There is a
lofty philosophic tone, a thoughtful humanity, infused into his pastoral
vein. Remote from the passions and events of the great world, he has
communicated interest and dignity to the primal movements of the
heart of man, and ingrafted his own conscious reflections on the
casual thoughts of hinds and shepherds. Nursed amidst the grandeur
of mountain scenery, he has stooped to have a nearer view of the
daisy under his feet, or plucked a branch of white-thorn from the
spray: but in describing it, his mind seems imbued with the majesty
and solemnity of the objects around him – the tall rock lifts its head
in the erectness of his spirit; the cataract roars in the sound of his
verse; and in its dim and mysterious meaning, the mists seem to
gather in the hollows of Helvellyn, and the forked Skiddaw hovers
in the distance. There is little mention of mountainous scenery in
Mr Wordsworth's poetry; but by internal evidence one might be
almost sure that it was written in a mountainous country, from its
bareness, its simplicity, its loftiness and its depth!

His later philosophic productions have a somewhat different character. They are a departure from, a dereliction of his first principles.
They are classical and courtly. They are polished in style, without
being gaudy; dignified in subject, without affectation. They seem to
have been composed not in a cottage at Grasmere, but among the
half-inspired groves and stately recollections of Cole-Orton.[19] We
might allude in particular, for examples of what we mean, to the
lines on a Picture by Claude Lorraine, and to the exquisite poem,
entitled *Laodamia*. The last of these breathes the pure spirit of the
finest fragments of antiquity – the sweetness, the gravity, the strength,
the beauty and the languor of death –

'Calm contemplation and majestic pains.'[20]

Its glossy brilliancy arises from the perfection of the finishing, like
that of careful sculpture, not from gaudy colouring – the texture of
the thoughts has the smoothness and solidity of marble. It is a poem

that might be read aloud in Elysium, and the spirits of departed heroes and sages would gather round to listen to it! Mr Wordsworth's philosophic poetry, with a less glowing aspect and less tumult in the veins than Lord Byron's on similar occasions, bends a calmer and keener eye on mortality; the impression, if less vivid, is more pleasing and permanent; and we confess it (perhaps it is a want of taste and proper feeling) that there are lines and poems of our author's that we think of ten times for once that we recur to any of Lord Byron's. Or if there are any of the latter's writings, that we can dwell upon in the same way, that is, as lasting and heart-felt sentiments, it is when laying aside his usual pomp and pretension, he descends with Mr Wordsworth to the common ground of a disinterested humanity. It may be considered as characteristic of our poet's writings, that they either make no impression on the mind at all, seem mere *nonsense-verses*, or that they leave a mark behind them that never wears out. They either

'Fall blunted from the indurated breast' — [21]

without any perceptible result, or they absorb it like a passion. To one class of readers he appears sublime, to another (and we fear the largest) ridiculous. He has probably realized Milton's wish, — 'and fit audience found, though few':[22] but we suspect he is not reconciled to the alternative. There are delightful passages in the EXCURSION, both of natural description and of inspired reflection (passages of the latter kind that in the sound of the thoughts and of the swelling language resemble heavenly symphonies, mournful *requiems* over the grave of human hopes); but we must add, in justice and in sincerity, that we think it impossible that this work should ever become popular, even in the same degree as the *Lyrical Ballads*. It affects a system without having any intelligible clue to one; and instead of unfolding a principle in various and striking lights, repeats the same conclusions till they become flat and insipid. Mr Wordsworth's mind is obtuse, except as it is the organ and the receptacle of accumulated feelings: it is not analytic, but synthetic; it is reflecting, rather than theoretical. The EXCURSION, we believe, fell still-born from the press.[23] There was something abortive, and clumsy, and ill-judged in the attempt. It was long and laboured. The personages, for the most part, were low, the fare rustic: the plan raised expectations which were not fulfilled, and the effect was like being ushered into a stately hall and invited to sit down to a splendid banquet in the company of clowns, and with nothing but successive courses of apple-dumplings served up. It was not even *toujours perdrix*![24]

Mr Wordsworth, in his person, is above the middle size, with marked features, and an air somewhat stately and Quixotic. He reminds one of some of Holbein's heads, grave, saturnine, with a slight indication of sly humour, kept under by the manners of the age or by the pretensions of the person. He has a peculiar sweetness in his smile, and great depth and manliness and a rugged harmony, in the tones of his voice. His manner of reading his own poetry is particularly imposing; and in his favourite passages his eye beams with preternatural lustre, and the meaning labours slowly up from his swelling breast. No one who has seen him at these moments could go away with an impression that he was a 'man of no mark or likelihood'.[25] Perhaps the comment of his face and voice is necessary to convey a full idea of his poetry. His language may not be intelligible, but his manner is not to be mistaken. It is clear that he is either mad or inspired. In company, even in a *tête-à-tête*, Mr Wordsworth is often silent, indolent, and reserved. If he is become verbose and oracular of late years, he was not so in his better days. He threw out a bold or an indifferent remark without either effort or pretension, and relapsed into musing again. He shone most (because he seemed most roused and animated) in reciting his own poetry, or in talking about it. He sometimes gave striking views of his feelings and trains of association in composing certain passages; or if one did not always understand his distinctions, still there was no want of interest – there was a latent meaning worth inquiring into, like a vein of ore that one cannot exactly hit upon at the moment, but of which there are sure indications. His standard of poetry is high and severe, almost to exclusiveness. He admits of nothing below, scarcely of any thing above himself. It is fine to hear him talk of the way in which certain subjects should have been treated by eminent poets, according to his notions of the art. Thus he finds fault with Dryden's description of Bacchus in the *Alexander's Feast*, as if he were a mere good-looking youth, or boon companion –

'Flushed with a purple grace,
He shews his honest face' — [26]

instead of representing the God returning from the conquest of India,
crowned with vine-leaves, and drawn by panthers, and followed by
troops of satyrs, of wild men and animals that he had tamed. You
would think, in hearing him speak on this subject, that you saw
Titian's picture of the meeting of *Bacchus and Ariadne* — so classic
were his conceptions, so glowing his style. Milton is his great idol,
and he sometimes dares to compare himself with him. His Sonnets,
indeed, have something of the same high-raised tone and prophetic
spirit. Chaucer is another prime favourite of his, and he has been at
the pains to modernize some of the *Canterbury Tales*. Those persons
who look upon Mr Wordsworth as a merely puerile writer, must be
rather at a loss to account for his strong predilection for such geniuses
as Dante and Michael Angelo. We do not think our author has any
very cordial sympathy with Shakespeare. How should he? Shakespeare
was the least of an egotist of any body in the world. He does not
much relish the variety and scope of dramatic composition. 'He hates
those interlocutions between Lucius and Caius.'[27] Yet Mr Wordsworth
himself wrote a tragedy when he was young; and we have heard the
following energetic lines quoted from it, as put into the mouth of a
person smit with remorse for some rash crime:

—— 'Action is momentary,
The motion of a muscle this way or that;
Suffering is long, obscure, and infinite!'[28]

Perhaps for want of light and shade, and the unshackled spirit of the
drama, this performance was never brought forward. Our critic has
a great dislike to Gray, and a fondness for Thomson and Collins. It
is mortifying to hear him speak of Pope and Dryden, whom, because
they have been supposed to have all the possible excellences of poetry,
he will allow to have none. Nothing, however, can be fairer, or more
amusing, than the way in which he sometimes exposes the unmeaning
verbiage of modern poetry. Thus, in the beginning of Dr Johnson's
Vanity of Human Wishes —

'Let observation with extensive view
Survey mankind from China to Peru' –

he says there is a total want of imagination accompanying the words, the same idea is repeated three times under the disguise of a different phraseology: it comes to this – 'let *observation*, with extensive *observation*, *observe* mankind'; or take away the first line, and the second,

'Survey mankind from China to Peru',

literally conveys the whole. Mr Wordsworth is, we must say, a perfect Drawcansir[29] as to prose writers. He complains of the dry reasoners and matter-of-fact people for their want of *passion*; and he is jealous of the rhetorical declaimers and rhapsodists as trenching on the province of poetry. He condemns all French writers (as well of poetry as prose) in the lump. His list in this way is indeed small. He approves of Walton's *Angler*, Paley, and some other writers of an inoffensive modesty of pretension. He also likes books of voyages and travels, and *Robinson Crusoe*. In art, he greatly esteems Bewick's wood-cuts, and Waterloo's sylvan etchings. But he sometimes takes a higher tone, and gives his mind fair play. We have known him enlarge with a noble intelligence and enthusiasm on Nicolas Poussin's fine landscape-compositions, pointing out the unity of design that pervades them, the superintending mind, the imaginative principle that brings all to bear on the same end; and declaring he would not give a rush for any landscape that did not express the time of day, the climate, the period of the world it was meant to illustrate, or had not this character of *wholeness* in it. His eye also does justice to Rembrandt's fine and masterly effects. In the way in which that artist works something out of nothing, and transforms the stump of a tree, a common figure into an *ideal* object, by the gorgeous light and shade thrown upon it, he perceives an analogy to his own mode of investing the minute details of nature with an atmosphere of sentiment; and in pronouncing Rembrandt to be a man of genius, feels that he strengthens his own claim to the title. It has been said of Mr Wordsworth, that 'he hates conchology, that he hates the Venus of Medicis'.[30] But these, we hope, are mere epigrams and *jeux-d'esprit*, as far from truth as they are free from malice; a sort of running satire or critical clenches –

> 'Where one for sense and one for rhyme
> Is quite sufficient at one time.'[51]

We think, however, that if Mr Wordsworth had been a more liberal and candid critic, he would have been a more sterling writer. If a greater number of sources of pleasure had been open to him, he would have communicated pleasure to the world more frequently. Had he been less fastidious in pronouncing sentence on the works of others, his own would have been received more favourably, and treated more leniently. The current of his feelings is deep, but narrow; the range of his understanding is lofty and aspiring rather than discursive. The force, the originality, the absolute truth and identity with which he feels some things, makes him indifferent to so many others. The simplicity and enthusiasm of his feelings, with respect to nature, renders him bigoted and intolerant in his judgments of men and things. But it happens to him, as to others, that his strength lies in his weakness; and perhaps we have no right to complain. We might get rid of the cynic and the egotist, and find in his stead a common-place man. We should 'take the good the Gods provide us':[52] a fine and original vein of poetry is not one of their most contemptible gifts, and the rest is scarcely worth thinking of, except as it may be a mortification to those who expect perfection from human nature; or who have been idle enough at some period of their lives, to deify men of genius as possessing claims above it. But this is a chord that jars, and we shall not dwell upon it.

Lord Byron we have called, according to the old proverb, 'the spoiled child of fortune':[53] Mr Wordsworth might plead, in mitigation of some peculiarities, that he is 'the spoiled child of disappointment'. We are convinced, if he had been early a popular poet, he would have borne his honours meekly, and would have been a person of great *bonhomie* and frankness of disposition. But the sense of injustice and of undeserved ridicule sours the temper and narrows the views. To have produced works of genius, and to find them neglected or treated with scorn, is one of the heaviest trials of human patience. We exaggerate our own merits when they are denied by others, and

are apt to grudge and cavil at every particle of praise bestowed on
those to whom we feel a conscious superiority. In mere self-defence
we turn against the world, when it turns against us; brood over the
undeserved slights we receive; and thus the genial current of the soul[34]
is stopped, or vents itself in effusions of petulance and self-conceit.
Mr Wordsworth has thought too much of contemporary critics and
criticism; and less than he ought of the award of posterity, and of the
opinion, we do not say of private friends, but of those who were made
so by their admiration of his genius. He did not court popularity by
a conformity to established models, and he ought not to have been
surprised that his originality was not understood as a matter of course.
He has *gnawed too much on the bridle*; and has often thrown out
crusts to the critics, in mere defiance or as a point of honour when
he was challenged, which otherwise his own good sense would have
withheld. We suspect that Mr Wordsworth's feelings are a little
morbid in this respect, or that he resents censure more than he is
gratified by praise. Otherwise, the tide has turned much in his favour
of late years – he has a large body of determined partisans – and is
at present sufficiently in request with the public to save or relieve
him from the last necessity to which a man of genius can be reduced
– that of becoming the God of his own idolatry![35]

'Venice'

*

The traveller to Venice (who goes there to see the masterpieces of
Titian or Palladio's admired designs), runs the gauntlet all the way
along at every town or villa he passes, of the most clumsy, affected,
paltry, sprawling figures, cut in stone, that ever disgraced the chisel.
Even their crucifixes and common Madonnas are in bad taste and
proportion. This inaptitude for the representation of forms in a people,
whose eye for colours transcended that of all the world besides, is
striking as it is curious: and it would be worth the study of a man's
whole life to give a true and satisfactory solution of the mystery.
Padua, though one of the oldest towns in Italy, is still a place of some
resort and bustle; among other causes, from the number of Venetian
families who are in the habit of spending the summer months there.
Soon after leaving it, you begin to cross the canals and rivers which
intersect this part of the country bordering upon the sea, and for
some miles you follow the course of the Brenta along a flat, dusty,
and unprofitable road. This is a period of considerable and painful
suspense, till you arrive at Fusina, where you are put into a boat and
rowed down one of the *Lagunes*, where over banks of high rank grass
and reeds, and between solitary sentry-boxes at different intervals,
you see Venice rising from the sea. For an hour and a half, that it
takes you to cross from the last point of land to this Spouse of the
Adriatic, its long line of spires, towers, churches, wharfs is stretched
along the water's edge, and you view it with a mixture of awe and
incredulity. A city built in the air would be something still more
wonderful; but any other must yield the palm to this for singularity
and imposing effect. If it were on the firm land, it would rank as one

of the first cities in Europe for magnificence, size, and beauty; as it is, it is without a rival. I do not know what Lord Byron and Lady Morgan could mean by quarrelling[1] about the question who first called Venice 'the Rome of the sea' — since it is perfectly unique in its kind. If a parallel must be found for it, it is more like Genoa shoved into the sea. Genoa stands *on* the sea, this *in* it. The effect is certainly magical, dazzling, perplexing. You feel at first a little giddy: you are not quite sure of your footing as on the deck of a vessel. You enter its narrow, cheerful canals, and find that instead of their being scooped out of the earth, you are gliding amidst rows of palaces and under broad-arched bridges, piled on the sea-green wave. You begin to think that you must cut your liquid way in this manner through the whole city, and use oars instead of feet. You land, and visit quays, squares, market-places, theatres, churches, halls, palaces; ascend tall towers, and stroll through shady gardens, without being once reminded that you are not on *terra firma*. The early inhabitants of this side of Italy, drive by Attila and his hordes of Huns from the land, sought shelter in the sea, built there for safety and liberty, laid the first foundations of Venice in the rippling wave, and commerce, wealth, luxury, arts, and crimson conquest crowned the growing Republic; —

'And Ocean smil'd,
Well pleased to see his wondrous child.'[2]

Man, proud of his amphibious creation, spared no pains to aggrandize and embellish it, even to extravagance and excess. The piles and blocks of wood on which it stands are brought from the huge forests at Treviso and Cadore: the stones that girt its circumference, and prop its walls, are dug from the mountains of Istria and Dalmatia: the marbles that inlay its palace-floors are hewn from the quarries near Verona. Venice is loaded with ornament, like a rich city-heiress with jewels. It seems the natural order of things. Her origin was a wonder: her end is to surprise. The strong, implanted tendency of her genius must be to the showy, the singular, the fantastic. Herself an anomaly, she reconciles contradictions, liberty with aristocracy, commerce with nobility, the want of titles with the pride of birth and heraldry. A violent birth in nature, she lays greedy, perhaps ill-advised, hands on all the artificial advantages that can supply her original defects. Use turns to gaudy beauty; extreme hardship to intemperance in pleasure. From the level uniform expanse that forever encircles her, she would obviously affect the aspiring in forms, the quaint, the complicated, relief and projection. The richness and foppery of her architecture arise from this: its stability and excellence probably from another circumstance counteracting this tendency to the buoyant and fluttering, *viz.*, the necessity of raising solid edifices on such slippery foundations, and of not playing tricks with stone-walls upon the water. Her eye for colours and costume she would bring with conquest from the East. The spirit, intelligence, and activity of her men, she would derive from their ancestors: the grace, the glowing animation and bounding step of her women, from the sun and mountain-breeze! The want of simplicity and severity in Venetian taste seems owing to this, that all here is factitious and the work of art: redundancy again is an attribute of commerce, whose eye is gross and large, and does not admit of the *too much*; and as to irregularity and want of fixed principles, we may account by analogy at least for these, from that element of which Venice is the nominal bride, to which she owes her all, and the very essence of which is caprice, uncertainty, and vicissitude!

> 'And now from out the watery floor
> A city rose, and well she wore
> Her beauty, and stupendous walls,
> And towers that touched the stars, and halls
> Pillar'd with whitest marble, whence
> Palace on lofty palace sprung:
> And over all rich gardens hung,
> Where, amongst silver water-falls,
> Cedars and spice-trees, and green bowers,
> And sweet winds playing with all the flowers
> Of Persia and of Araby,
> Walked princely shapes; some with an air
> Like warriors; some like ladies fair
> Listening . . . .
> In supreme magnificence.'[5]

This, which is a description of a dream of Babylon of old, by a living poet, is realized almost literally in modern Venice.

On the Present State of Parliamentary Eloquence

It was a fine impertinence of the younger Pliny, to try to persuade Tacitus, in one of his epistles, that the diffuse style was better than the concise. 'Such a one', says he, 'aims at the throat of his adversary: now I like to strike him wherever I can.'[1] I may be thought guilty of a like piece of officiousness in the remarks here offered on several of the most prominent of our parliamentary speakers. In general, to suggest advice, or hazard criticism, is to recommend it to others to do something, which we know they either will not or cannot do: or it is to desire them either to please us, or do nothing. The present article may be considered as a marginal note or explanatory addition to a former one, on nearly the same subject – like one of Lord Castlereagh's long parentheses: but I hope there will be more in it. It is a subject of which I wish to make clear work as I go; for it is one to which, if I can once get rid of it, I am not likely to recur.

The haughty tone of invective which I have already ascribed to Lord Chatham, was very different from that didactic style of parliamentary oratory which has since been imported from northern colleges and lecture-rooms. Of this school Sir James Mackintosh and Mr Brougham may be reckoned at the head. This method consists, not so much in taking a side, as in stating a question. The speaker takes upon him to be the judge rather than the advocate; and if he had the authority of a judge, or could direct the decision, as well as sum up the evidence, it would be all very well. An orator of this stamp does not seat himself on the Opposition side of the House to urge or to reply to particular points, but in a Professor's chair of Humanity, to read a lecture to the tyros of the Treasury-Bench, on the elementary principles and all the possible bearings, the objections and answers, the difficulties and the solutions of every question in philosophy, jurisprudence, politics, and political economy, – on war, peace, 'domestic treason, foreign levy',[2] colonial produce, copy-right of authors, prison discipline, the hulks, the corn-bill, the penitentiary, prostitutes, and pick-pockets. Nothing comes amiss to him that can puzzle himself or *pose* his hearers; and he lets out all his knowledge indiscriminately, whether it makes for or against him, with deliberate impartiality and scrupulous exactness. Such persons might be called *Orators of the Human Mind.* They are a little out of their place, it must be owned, in the House of Commons. The object there is – not to put the majority in possession of the common grounds of judging, as in a class of students – (these are taken for granted as already known) – but to carry a point, to gain a verdict for yourself or for truth, by throwing the weight of eloquence and argument into the scale against interest, prejudice, or sophistry. There are retainers enough on the other side to manage for the crown, who are ready to take all advantages without your volunteering to place yourself in their power, or to put excuses in their mouths, to help them out at a dead-lift. If they were candid, if they were disinterested, if they were not hostilely disposed, it might be a feasible scheme to consider a debate as an amicable communication of doubts and lights, as a comparison of strength or a confession of weakness: but why hint a doubt, or start a difficulty needlessly in your own path, which will be eagerly caught at, and made use of in the most insulting manner to defeat a host of real proofs, and overturn the most legitimate conclusions? Why tamper with your own cause? Why play at fast and loose with your object? Why restore the weapons into your enemies' hands, which you have just wrested from them? Why 'make a wanton'[3] of the First Minister of State? It is either vanity, weakness, or indiffer-ence to do so. You might as well in confidence tell an adversary where you meant to strike him, point out to him your own weak sides, or wait in courtesy for the blow. Gamesters do not show one another their hands: neither should politicians, who understand what they are about – that is, knaves *will* not, and honest men *ought* not. Others will find out the rotten parts of a question: do you stick to the sound – knowledge is said to be power: but knowledge, applied as we have seen it, neutralizes itself. Mere knowledge, to be effectual, must act *in vacuo*: but the House of Commons is by no means a vacuum, an empty receiver for abstract truth and airy speculation. There is the resistance, the refrangibility of dense prejudice and crooked policy: you must concentrate, you must enforce, you must urge to glowing sympathy: and enthusiasm, zeal, perfect conviction on your part, is the only principle that can be brought into play against the cool calculations or gross incentives of selfishness and servility on the opposite side. A middle line of conduct does not excite respect, but contempt. They do not think you sincere, but lukewarm. They give you credit for affectation or timidity, but none for heartiness in a cause, or fidelity to a party. They have more hopes of you than fears. By everlasting subtle distinctions, and hesitating, qualified, retracting dissent from measures you would be thought most to reprobate, you do more harm than good. In theory there are infinite shades of difference, but in practice the question must be decided one way or other: either the Ayes or the Noes must have it. In all such cases, those who are not for us are against us. In political controversy, as in a battle, there are but two sides to choose between; and those who create a diversion in favour of established abuses by setting up a third, fanciful, impracticable standard of perfection of their own, in the most critical circumstances, betray the cause they pretend to espouse with such overweening delicacy. For my own part, I hate a fellow who picks a hole in his own coat, who finds a flaw in his own argument, who treats his enemies as if they might become friends, or his friends as if they might become enemies. I hate your shuffling, *shilly-shally* proceedings, and diagonal side-long movements between right and wrong. Fling yourself into the gap at once – either into the arms, or at the heads of Ministers! –

I remember hearing, with some pain and uneasiness, Sir James Mackintosh's maiden speech on the Genoa business. It was a great, but ineffectual effort. The mass of information, of ingenuity, and reasoning, was very prodigious; but the whole was misdirected, no impression whatever was made. It was like an inaugural dissertation on the general principles of ethics, on the laws of nature and nations, on ancient and modern history – a laboured treatise *de omnibus rebus et quibusdam aliis.*[4] There were all the rules of moral arithmetic, all the items in a profligate political account; but the bill was not properly cast up, the case was not distinctly made out, the counsel got no damages for his client. Nothing was gained by this motion, nor could there be. When he had brought his heaviest artillery to bear with probable success upon a certain point, he stopped short like a scientific demonstrator (not like a skilful engineer) to show how it might be turned against himself. When he had wound up the charge of treachery or oppression to a climax, he gratuitously suggested a possible plea of necessity, accident, or some other topic, to break the force of his inference; or he anticipated the answers that might be made to it, as if he was afraid he should not be thought to know all that could be said on both sides of the question. This enlarged knowledge of good and evil may be very necessary to a philosopher, but it is very prejudicial to an orator. No man can play the whole game in this manner, blow hot and cold in a breath, or take an entire debate into his own hands, and wield it in which way he pleases. He will find his own load enough for his own shoulders to bear. The exceptions, if you choose to go into them, multiply faster than the rules: the various complications of the subject distract, instead of convincing: you do your adversary's work for him; the battle is lost without a blow being struck; and a speech of this sceptical kind requires and receives no answer. It falls by its own weight, and buries any body but the Minister under its ruins — or it is left, not a triumphal arch, but a splendid mausoleum of the learning, genius, and eloquence of the speaker. — The Cock-pit of St Stephen's does not relish this scholastic refinement, this method of holding an argument with a man's self: a little bear-garden, cut-and-thrust work would be much better understood. Sir James has of late improved his tact and knowledge of the House. He has taken up Sir Samuel Romilly's department of questions relating to the amelioration of the penal code and general humanity, and I have no doubt Government will leave him in quiet possession of it. They concede these sort of questions as an amiable diversion, or friendly *bonus*, to the indefatigable spirit of Opposition.

Mr Brougham is, I conceive, another instance of this analytical style of debating, which 'plays round the head, but does not reach the heart'.[5] There is a want of warmth, of *momentum*, of impulse in his speeches. He loses himself in an infinity of details, as his learned and honourable friend does in a wide sea of speculation.[6] He goes picking up a number of curious pebbles on the shore, and at the outlets of a question — but he does not 'roll all his strength and all his sharpness up into one ball',[7] to throw at and crush his enemies beneath his feet. He enters into statistics, he calls for documents, he examines accounts. This method is slow, perplexing, circuitous, and not sure. While the evidence is collecting, the question is lost. While one thing is substantiating, another goes out of your mind. These little detached multifarious particulars, which require such industry and sagacity in the speaker to bring them forward, have no clue in the minds of the hearers to connect them together. There is no substratum of prejudice, no cement of interest. They do not grow out of the soil of common feeling and experience, but are set in it; nor do they bear the fruits of conviction. Mr Brougham can follow the ramifications of an intricate subject, but he is not so well acquainted with the springs of the human mind. He finds himself at the end of his speech, — in the last sentence of it, — just where he was at the beginning, or in any other given part of it. He has not acquired any additional *impetus*, is not projected forward with any new degree of warmth or vigour. He was cold, correct, smart, pointed at first, and he continues so still. A repetition of blows, however, is of no use, unless they are struck in the same place: a change of position is not progression. As Sir James Mackintosh's speeches are a decomposition of the moral principles of society, so Mr Brougham's are an ingenious taking in pieces of its physical mechanism. While they are at work with their experiments, their antagonists are putting in motion the passions, the fears, and antipathies of mankind, and blowing their schemes of reform above the moon.

Talent alone, then, is not sufficient to support a successful Opposition. There is talent on the other side too, of some sort or other; and, in addition, there is another weight, that of influence, which requires a counterpoise. This can be nothing else but fixed principle, but naked honesty, but undisguised enthusiasm. That is the expansive force that must shatter the strongholds of corruption if ever they are shattered, that must make them totter, if ever they are made to totter, about the heads of their possessors. Desire to expose a ministry, and you will do it — if it be, like ours, vulnerable all over. Desire to make a display of yourself, and you will do it, if you have a decent stock of acquirements. Mr Brougham has a great quantity of combustible materials constantly passing through his hands, but he has not the warmth in his own heart to 'kindle them into a flame of sacred vehemence'.[8] He is not a good hater.[9] He is not an impassioned lover of the popular cause. He is not a Radical orator: he is not a Back-bone debater. He wants nerve, he wants impetuosity. He may divide on a question, but he will never carry it. His circumspection, which he thinks his strength, is in reality his weakness. He makes paltry excuses, unmanly concessions. His political warfare is not a *bellum internecinum*.[10] He commits no mortal offences. He has not yet cut off his retreat. In a word, he trims too much between all parties. A person who does this too long, loses the confidence, loses the cordiality of all parties; loses his character; and when he has once lost that, there is nothing to stand in his way to office and the first honours of the State! —

He who is not indifferent himself will find out, from his own feelings, what it is that interests others in a cause. An honest man is an orator by nature. The late Mr Whitbread was an honest man, and a true parliamentary speaker. He had no artifices, no tricks, no reserve about him. He spoke point-blank what he thought, and his heart was in his broad, honest, English face. He had as much activity of mind as Mr Brougham, and paid the same attention to business as that gentleman does; but it was with him a matter of feeling, and had nothing of a professional look. His objects were open and direct; and he had a sufficient stock of natural good sense and practical information, not to be made the dupe of sophistry and chicane. He was always in his place, and ready to do his duty. If a falsehood was stated, he contradicted it instantly in a few plain words: if an act of injustice was palliated, it excited his contempt; if it was justified, it roused his indignation: he retorted a mean insinuation with manly spirit, and never shrunk from a frank avowal of his sentiments. He presented a petition or complaint against some particular grievance better than any one else I ever saw. His manner seemed neither to implicate him in the truth of the charge, nor to signify a wish to disclaim it beforehand. He was merely the organ through which any alleged abuse of power might meet the public ear, and he either answered or redressed, according to the merits of the case upon inquiry. In short, he was the representative of the spontaneous, unsophisticated sense of the English people on public men and public measures. Any plain, well-meaning man, on hearing him speak, would say, 'That is just what I think'; or from observing his manner, would say, 'That is just what I feel.' He was not otherwise a powerful debater or an accomplished speaker. He could not master a general view of any subject, or get up a set speech with effect. One or two that I heard him make (particularly one on the Princess of Wales and the situation of her affairs in 1813, in which he grew pathetic) were complete failures. He could pull down better than he could build up. The irritation of constant contradiction was necessary to his full possession of himself: – give him 'ample scope and verge enough',[11] and he lost his way. He stuck close to the skirts of Ministry, but he was not qualified to originate or bring to a triumphant conclusion any great political movement. His enthusiasm ran away with his judgment, and was not *backed* by equal powers of reasoning or imagination. He was a sanguine, high-spirited man, but not a man of genius, or a deep thinker; and his fortitude failed him, when the last fatal blow was given to himself and his party. He could not have drawn up so able a political statement as Mr Brougham; but he would have more personal adherents in the House of Commons, for he was himself the adherent of a cause.

Mr Tierney is certainly a better speaker and a cleverer man. But he can never make a leader for want of earnestness. He has no Quixotic enthusiasm in himself; much less any to spare for his followers. He cares nothing (or seems to care nothing) about a question; but he is impatient of absurdity, and has a thorough contempt for the understandings of his opponents. Sharpened by his spleen, nothing escapes his acuteness. He makes fine sport for the spectators. He takes up Lord Castlereagh's blunders, and Mr Vansittart's no-meanings; and retorts them on their heads in the finest style of execution imaginable. It is like being present on a Shrove-Tuesday, and seeing a set of mischievous unfeeling boys throwing at a brace of cocks, and breaking their shins. Mr Tierney always brings down his man: but beyond this you feel no confidence in him; you take no interest in his movements but as he is instrumental in annoying other people. He (to all appearance) has no great point to carry himself, and no wish to be thought to have any important principle at stake. He is by much too sincere for a hypocrite, but is not enough in earnest for a parliamentary leader. For others to sympathize with you, you must first sympathize with them. When Mr Whitbread got up to speak, you felt an interest in what he was going to say, in the success of his arguments: when you hear that Mr Tierney is on his legs, you feel that you shall be amused with an admirable display of dexterity and talent, but are nearly indifferent as to the result. You look on as at an exhibition of extraordinary skill in fencing or prize-fighting.

Of all those who have for some years past aspired by turns to be leaders of the Opposition, Mr Ponsonby was the person who had the fewest pretensions. He was a literal arguer. He affected great sagacity and judgment, and referred every thing, in a summary way, to the principles of common sense, and the reason of the case. He abounded in truisms, which seldom go far in deciding disputable points. He generally reduced the whole range of the debate into the narrow compass of a self-evident proposition: – to make sure of his object, he began by taking the question for granted, and necessarily failed when he came to the particular application. He was not aware of the maxim, that he who proves too much, proves nothing. His turn of observation was legal, not acute: his manner was dry, but his blows were not hard: his features were flat on his face, and his arguments did not stand out from the question. He might have been a tolerable special-pleader, but he was a bad orator, and, I think, a worse politician. Any one who argues on strict logical grounds must be prepared to go all lengths, or he will be sure to be defeated at every step he takes: but the gentleman's principles were of a very cautious and temporizing cast. I have seen him, more than once, give himself great airs over those who took more general views of the subject; and he was very fastidious in the choice of associates, with whom he would condescend to act.

Mr Ponsonby's style of speaking was neither instructive nor entertaining. In this respect, it was the reverse of Mr Grattan's, which was both. To see the latter make one of his promised motions on Catholic Emancipation, was one of the most extraordinary exhibitions, both bodily and mental, which could possibly be witnessed. You saw a little oddly-compacted figure of a man, with a large head and features,

— such as they give to pasteboard masks, or stick upon the shoulders of Punch in the puppet-show, — rolling about like a Mandarin — sawing the air with his whole body from head to foot, sweeping the floor with a roll of parchment, which he held in one hand, and throwing his legs and arms about like the branches of trees tossed by the wind: — every now and then striking the table with impatient vehemence, and, in a sharp, slow, nasal, guttural tone, drawling out, with due emphasis and discretion, a set of little smart antithetical sentences, — all ready-cut and dry, polished and pointed; — that seemed as if they 'would lengthen out in succession to the crack of doom'.[12] Alliterations were tacked to alliterations, — inference was dove-tailed into inference, — and the whole derived new brilliance and piquancy from the contrast it presented to the uncouthness of the speaker, and the monotony of his delivery. His were compositions that would have done equally well to be said or sung. The rhyme was placed at the beginning instead of the end of each line; he sharpened the sense on the sound, and clenched an argument by corresponding letters of the alphabet. It must be confessed, that there was something meretricious, as well as alluring, in this style. After the first surprise and startling effect is over, and the devoted champion of his country's cause goes on ringing the changes on 'the Irish People and the Irish Parliament' — on 'the Guinea and the Gallows', as the ultimate resources of the English government, — on 'ministerial mismanagement, and privileged profligacy', — we begin to feel that there is nothing in these quaint and affected verbal coincidences more nearly allied to truth than falsehood: — there is a want of directness and simplicity in this warped and garbled style; and our attention is drawn off from the importance of the subject by a shower of epigrammatic conceits, and fanciful phraseology, in which the orator chooses to veil it. It is hardly enough to say, in defence of this jingle of words, (as well as of the overstrained hyperbolical tone of declamation which accompanies it) that 'it is a custom of Ireland'.* The same objection may be made to it in point of taste that has been made to the old-fashioned, obsolete practice of cutting trees into the shape of

---

* 'Liberty is a custom of England,' said a Member of Congress;[15] who seems also to be of opinion, that *it is a custom more honoured in the breach than the observance.*[14]

arm-chairs and peacocks, or to that style of landscape-gardening, where

> 'Grove nods to grove, each alley has a brother,
> And half the platform just reflects the other −'[15]

and I am afraid that this objection cannot be got over, at least, on this side the water.*

The best Irish speaker I ever heard (indeed the best speaker without any exception whatever) is Mr Plunkett; who followed Mr Grattan in one of the debates on the Catholic question above alluded to. The contrast was not a little striking; and it was certainly in favour of Mr Plunkett. His style of workmanship was more manly and more masterly. There were no little Gothic ornaments or fantastic excrescences to catch and break the attention: no quaintness, witticism, or conceit. Roubiliac, after being abroad, said, that 'what he had seen there made his own work in Westminster Abbey look like tobacco-pipes'.[17] You had something of the same sort of feeling with respect to Mr Grattan's artificial and frittered style, after hearing Mr Plunkett's defence of the same side of the question. He went straight forward to his end with a force equal to his rapidity. He removed all obstacles, as he advanced. He overturned Mr Banks with his right hand, and Mr Charles Yorke with his left − the one on a chronological question of the Concordat, and the other as to the origin of the Corporation and Test Acts. One wonders how they ever got up again, or trusted themselves on a ground of matter-of-fact ever after. Mr Secretary Peel did not offer to put himself in his way. No part of the subject could come amiss to him − history, law, constitutional principle, common feeling, local prejudices, general theory, − all was alike within his reach and his control. Having settled one point, he passed

---

* I by no means wish to preclude Mr Phillips from trying annually to naturalize his favourite mode of oratory at watering-places in this country, or in Evangelical Societies held at the Egyptian-hall, where it is not out of character. He may there assure his hearers, with great impunity, that Dr Franklin's orthodoxy was never called in question; and rank Moses and Mahomet together as true prophets (by virtue of the first letter of their names), in opposition to the infidelity of Paine and Priestley, who go together for the same reason −

'Like Juno's Swans, link'd and inseparable'.[16]

on to another, carrying his hearers with him: — it was as if he knew all that could be said on the question, and was anxious to impart his knowledge without any desire of shining. There was no affectation, no effort, but equal ease and earnestness. Every thing was brought to bear that could answer his purpose, and there was nothing superfluous. His eloquence swept along like a river,

'Without o'erflowing, full'.[18]

Every step told: every sentence went to account. I cannot say that there was any thing very profound or original in argument, imposing in imagination, or impassioned in sentiment, in any part of this address — but it was throughout impregnated with as much thought, imagination and passion as the House would be likely to understand or sympathize with. It acted like a loadstone to the feelings of the House; and the speaker raised their enthusiasm, and carried their convictions as far as he wished, or as it was practicable. The effect was extraordinary: the impression grew stronger from first to last. No one stirred the whole time, and, at the end, the lobbies were crowded with members going up stairs and saying, 'Well, this is a speech worth going without one's dinner to hear,' (Oh, unequivocal testimony of applause!) 'there has been nothing like this since the time of Fox,' &c. For myself, I never heard any other speech that I would have given three farthings to have made. It did not make the same figure in the newspapers the next day; for it was but indifferently reported, owing to the extreme fluency with which it was delivered. There was no boggling, no straggling, irrelevant matter; — you could not wait for him at the end of a long parenthesis, and go on with your report as if nothing had happened in the interval, as is sometimes the case,* — and besides, for the reason above given, it was a speech better calculated to strike in the hearing than the perusal; for though it was fully up to the tone of the House, the public mind can bear stronger meats. Another such speech would have decided the question, and made the difference of four votes by which it was lost. While the impression was fresh in the mind, it was not easy for any one,

* The best speeches are the worst reported, the worst are made better than they are. They both find a convenient newspaper level.

pretending to honesty, to look his neighbour in the face and vote against the motion. But Mr Plunkett, in the mean time, sailed for Ireland. Any one who can speak as he can, and is a friend to his own, or any other country, ought not to let the present men retain their seats six months longer. Nothing but the will is wanting. – The ability, I will venture to say, is there.

And what shall I say of Lord Castlereagh – that spouter without beginning, middle, or end – who has not an idea in his head, nor a word to say for himself – who carries the House of Commons by his manner alone – who bows and smiles assent and dissent – who makes a dangling proposition of his person, and is himself a drooping figure of speech – what shall I say of this inanimate automaton? Nothing! For what can be said of him?

'Come then, expressive silence, muse his praise.'*[19]

Neither have I any thing to say of the style of eloquence of Mr Alderman Wood, or Mr Waithman, or Sir W. Curtis – except that the latter always appears to me a very fit and lively representative of the good living, drinking, and eating of the city. This is but reasonable. The bodies of the city, not their minds, should be represented. A large turtle in the House (with a proxy to the minister) would answer the purpose just as well.

Mr Wilberforce is a speaker whom it is difficult to class either with ministers or opposition. His character and his pretensions are altogether equivocal. He is a man of some ability, and, at one time, had considerable influence. He is what might be called 'a sweet speaker': his silver voice floats and glides up and down in the air, as if it was avoiding every occasion of offence, and dodging the question through its various avenues of reason and interest.

---

* His Lordship is said to speak French with as little hesitation as he does his native tongue; and once made a speech in that language to the Congress for three hours without interruption. The sentiments, we may be sure, were not English. Or was it on that occasion that Prince Talleyrand made his observation, 'that speech was given to man to conceal his thoughts'?[20] I cannot agree with Mr Hobhouse in his compliment to the expression which Isabey has given[21] to Lord Castlereagh's face in the *insulated* figure of him in the picture of the Congress. An old classical friend of Mr Hobhouse's would have supplied a better interpretation of it. But I do not think the French artist has done his Lordship justice. His features are marked, but the expression is dormant.

— 'In many a winding bout
Of melting softness long drawn out.'[22]

There is a finical flexibility of purpose, and a cautious curiosity of research, that would put you in pain for him, if the want of proper self-respect did not take away all common fellow-feeling. His stratagems are so over-wrought that you wish them to fail: his evasions are so slippery and yet so palpable that you laugh in his face. Mr Wilberforce is a man that has always two strings to his bow: as an orator, he is a kind of lay-preacher in parliament. He is at continual *hawk and buzzard*[23] between character and conscience, between popularity and court favour, between his loyalty and his religion, between this world and the next. Is not this something like trying to serve God and Mammon? He is anxious to stand fair with the reflecting part of the community, without giving umbrage to power. He is shocked at vice in low stations:

'But 'tis the fall degrades her to a whore;
Let greatness own her, and she's mean no more.'[24]

He would go with the popular cause as long as it was popular, and gave him more weight than he lost by it; but would desert it the instant it became obnoxious, and that an obstinate adherence to it was likely to deprive him of future opportunities of doing good. He had rather be on the right side than the wrong, if he loses nothing by it. His reputation costs him nothing; though he always takes care to save appearances. His virtues compound for his vices in a very amicable manner. His humanity is at the horizon, three thousand miles off, – his servility stays at home, at the beck of the minister. He unbinds the chains of Africa, and helps (we trust without meaning it) to rivet those of his own country, and of Europe. As a general truth, – (not meaning any undue application in the present instance), it may be affirmed, that there is not a more insignificant as well as a dangerous character crawling between heaven and earth, than that of the pretended patriot, and philanthropist, who has not courage to take the plain reward of vice or virtue – who crouches to authority, and yet dreads the censure of the world, who gives a sneaking casting vote on the side of conscience only when he can do it with impunity,

– or else throws the weight of his reputation into the scale of his interest and the profligacy of others – who makes an affectation of principle a stalking-horse to his pitiful desire of distinction, and betrays a cause, sooner than commit himself.

'Out upon such half-faced fellowship.'[25] We have another example of trumpery ambition in the person of Mr C. Wynn; who, officious, indefatigable in his petty warfare with the abuses of power, is chiefly anxious to stand well with those who sanction them. He interprets the text literally, *not to do evil that good may come*. He is so fearful of the imputation of the least wrong, that he will never do or let any one else do the greatest right. *Summum jus summa injuria*,[26] has never entered his head. He is the dog in the political manger: a technical marplot. He takes a systematic delight in giving a lift to his enemies, and in hampering his friends. He is a regular whipper-in on the side of opposition, to all those who go but a hair's-breadth beyond his pragmatical notions of discretion and propriety. He sets up for a balance-master of the constitution and, by insisting on its never deviating from its erect, perpendicular position, is sure to have it overturned. He professes to be greatly scandalized at the abuses and corruptions in our ancient institutions, which are 'as notorious as the sun at noon-day',[27] and would have them removed – but he is much more scandalized at those indiscreet persons who bring to light any of these notorious abuses, in order to have them remedied. He is more angry at those with whom he differs in the smallest iota than at those who differ from him *toto cælo*:[28] and is at mortal enmity with every antiministerial measure that is not so clogged with imbecility and objections as to be impracticable or absolutely unavailing. He is therefore a bad partisan, and does little mischief, only because he is little attended to. Indeed, his voice is against him.

I did not much like Sir Samuel Romilly's significant, oracular way of laying down the law in the House: – his self-important assumption of second-hand truths, and his impatience of contradiction, as if he gave his time there to humanity for *nothing*. He was too solemn a speaker: as Garrow was too flippant and fluent. The latter appeared to have nothing to do but to talk nonsense *by the yard*, for the pleasure of exposing himself or being exposed by others. He might be said to hold in his hand a general retainer for absurdity, and to hold his head up in the pillory of his own folly with a very unabashed and unblushing gaiety of demeanour. Lawyers, as a general rule, are the very worst speakers in the House: if there are a few nominal exceptions, it is because they are not lawyers.

I do not recollect any other speaker of importance but Mr Canning; and he requires a chapter by himself. Thus then I would try to estimate him. – The orator and the writer do not always belong to the same class of intellectual character; nor is it, I think, in general, fair to judge of the merit of popular harangues by reducing them to the standard of literary compositions. Something, – a great deal, – is to be given to the suddenness of the emergency, the want of preparation, the instantaneous and effectual, but passing appeal to individual characters, feelings, and events. The speaker has less time allowed him to enforce his purpose, and to procure the impression he aims at than the writer; and he is therefore entitled to produce it by less scrupulous, by more obvious and fugitive means. He must strike the iron while it is hot. The blow must be prompt and decisive. He must mould the convictions and purposes of his hearers while they are under the influence of passion and circumstances, – as the glass-blower moulds the vitreous fluid with his breath. If he can take the popular mind by surprise, and stamp on it, while warm, the impression desired, it is not to be demanded whether the same means would have been equally successful on cool reflection or after the most mature deliberation. That is not the question at issue. At a moment's notice the expert debater is able to start some topic, some view of a subject, which answers the purpose of the moment. He can suggest a dextrous evasion of his adversaries' objections, he knows when to seize and take advantage of the impulse of popular feeling, he is master of the dazzling fence of argument, 'the punto, the stoccado, the reverso',[29] the shifts, and quirks, and palpable topics of debate; he can wield these at pleasure, and employ them to advantage on the spur of the occasion – this is all that can be required of him; for it is all that is necessary, and all that he undertakes to do. That another could bring forward more weighty reasons, offer more wholesome advice, convey more sound and extensive information in an indefinite period, is nothing to the purpose; for all this wisdom and knowledge would be of no avail in the supposed circumstances; the critical opportunity for action would be lost, before any use could be made of it. The one thing needful in public speaking is not to say what is best, but the best that can be said in a given time, place, and circumstance. The great qualification therefore of a leader in debate (as of a leader in fight) is presence of mind: he who has not this, wants every thing, and he who has it, may be forgiven almost all other deficiencies. The current coin of his discourses may be light and worthless in itself; but if it is always kept bright and ready for immediate use, it will pass unquestioned; and the public voice will affix to his name the praise of a sharp-witted, able, fluent, and eloquent speaker. We 'no further seek his merits to disclose, or scan his frailties in their brief abode',[30] – the popular ear and echo of popular applause. What he says may be trite, pert, shallow, contradictory, false, unfounded, and sophistical; but it was what was wanted for the occasion, and it told with those who heard it. Let it stop there, and all is well. The rest is forgotten; nor is it worth remembering.

But Mr Canning has an ill habit of printing his speeches: and I doubt whether the same oratorical privileges can be extended to *printed* speeches; or to this gentleman's speeches in general, even though they should not be printed. Whether afterwards committed to the press or not, they have evidently, I think, been first committed, with great care, to paper or to memory. They have all the marks, and are chargeable with all the *malice prepense*[31] of written compositions. They are not occasional effusions, but set harangues. They are elaborate *impromptus*; deeply concerted and highly polished pieces of extempore ingenuity. The repartee has been conceived many months before the luckless observation which gives ostensible birth to it; and an argument woven into a debate is sure to be the counterpart or fag-end of some worn-out sophism of several years' standing. Mr Canning is not so properly an orator as an author reciting his own compositions. He foresees (without much of the spirit of prophecy) what will, may, or can be said on some well-conned subject, and gets up, by anticipation, a tissue of excellent good conceits, indifferent bad arguments, classical quotations, and showy similes, which he contrives, by a sort of rhetorical join-hand, to tack on to some straggling observation dropped by some Honourable Member, – and so goes on, with folded arms and sonorous voice, neither quickened nor retarded, neither elevated nor depressed by the '*hear him*'s that now rise on the one side, or are now echoed from the other';[32] – never diverted into laughing gaiety, never hurried into incontrollable passion – till he is regularly delivered in the course of the same number of hours of the labour of weeks and months. To those who are in the secret of the arts of debating, who are versed in the complicated tactics of parliamentary common-place, there is nothing very mysterious in the process, though it startles the uninitiated. The fluency, the monotony, the unimpressible, imposing style of his elocution, – 'swinging slow with sullen roar',[33] like the alternate oscillation of a pendulum – afraid of being thrown off his balance – never trusting himself with the smallest inflection of tone or manner from the impulse of the moment, – all show that the speaker relies on the tenaciousness of his memory, not on the quickness and fertility of his invention. Mr Canning, I apprehend, never answered a speech: he answers, or affects to answer some observation in a speech, and then manufactures a long *tirade* out of his own 'mother-wit and arts *well-known* before'.[34] He *caps* an oration, as school-boys cap verses; and gets up his oracular responses, as Sidrophel and Whackum[35] did theirs, by having met with his customers of old. From that time he has the debate entirely in his own hands, and exercises over it 'sole sovereign sway and masterdom'.[36] One of these spontaneous mechanical sallies of his resembles a *voluntary* played on a barrel-organ: it is a kind of Panharmonic display of wit and wisdom – such as Mr Canning possesses! The amplest stores of his mind are unfolded to their inmost source – the classic lore, the historic page, the philosophic doubt, the sage reply, the sprightly allusion, the delicate irony, the happy turning of a period or insinuation of a paragraph with senatorial dignity and Ovidian grace – are all here concocted, studied, revised, varnished over, till the sense aches at their glossy beauty and sickens at hopeless perfection. Our modern orator's thoughts have been declared by some to have all the elegance of the antique; I should say, they have only the fragility and smoothness of plaster-cast copies!

If I were compelled to characterize Mr Canning's style by a single trait, I should say that he is a mere *parodist* in verse or prose, in reasoning or in wit. He transposes arguments as he does images, and makes sophistry of the one, and burlesque of the other. 'What's serious, he turns to farce.'[37] This is perhaps, not art in him, so much as nature. The specific levity of his mind causes it to subsist best in the rarefied atmosphere of indifference and scorn: it attaches most interest and importance to the slight and worthless. There is a striking want of solidity and keeping in this person's character. The frivolous, the equivocal, is his delight – the element in which he speaks, and writes,[38] and has his being, as an orator and poet. By applying to low and contemptible objects the language or ideas which have been appropriated to high and swelling contemplations, he reduces the latter to the same paltry level, or renders the former doubly ridiculous. On the same principle, or from not feeling the due force and weight of different things, as they affect either the imagination or the understanding, he brings the slenderest and most evanescent analogies to bear out the most important conclusions; establishes some fact in history by giving it the form of an idle interrogation, like a schoolboy declaiming on he knows not what; and thinks to overturn the fixed sentiment of a whole people by an interjection of surprise at what he knows to be unavoidable and unanswerable. There is none of the gravity of the statesman, of the enthusiasm of the patriot, the impatient zeal of the partisan, in Mr. Canning. We distinguish through the disguise of pompous declamation, or the affectation of personal consequence, only the elegant trifler, the thoughtless epigrammatist, spreading 'a windy fan of painted plumes',[39] to catch the breath of popular applause, or to flutter in the tainted breeze of court-favour. 'As those same plumes, so seems he vain and light',[40] – never applying his hand to useful action, or his mind to sober truth. A thing's being evident, is to him a reason for attempting to falsify it: its being right is a reason for straining every nerve to evade or defeat it at all events. It might appear, that with him inversion is the order of nature. 'Trifles light as air, are' to his understanding, 'confirmations strong as proofs of holy writ':[41] and he winks and shuts his apprehension up to the most solemn and momentous truths as gross and vulgar errors. His political creed is of an entirely fanciful and fictitious texture – a kind of moral, religious, political, and sentimental *filigree-work*: or it is made up of monstrous pretexts, and idle shadows, and spurious theories, and mock-alarms. Hence his gravest reasonings have very much an air of concealed irony; and it might sometimes almost be suspected that, by his partial, loose, and unguarded sophisms, he meant to abandon the very cause he professes to magnify and extol.* It is indeed, his boast, his pride, his pleasure, 'to make the worse appear the better reason',[42] which he does with the pertness of a school-boy and the effrontery of a prostitute: he assumes indecent postures in the debate, confounds the sense of right and wrong by his licentious disregard of both, puts honesty out of countenance by the familiarity of his proposals, makes a jest of principle, — 'takes the rose from the fair forehead of a virtuous cause, and plants a blister there'.[43]

The House of Lords does not at present display much of the aristocracy of talent. The scene is by no means so amusing or dramatic here as in the House of Commons. Every speaker seems to claim his privilege of peerage in the awful attention of his auditors, which is granted while there is any reasonable hope of a return: but it is not easy to hear Lord Grenville repeat the same thing regularly four times over, in different words — to listen to the Marquis of Wellesley, who never lowers his voice for four hours from the time he begins, nor utters the commonest syllable in a tone below that in which Pierre curses the Senate[44] — Lord Holland might have other pretensions to alacrity of mind than an impediment of speech, and Lord Liverpool might introduce less of the *vis inertiæ*[45] of office into his official harangues, than he does. Lord Ellenborough was great 'in the extremity of an oath'.[46] Lord Eldon, 'his face 'twixt tears and smiles contending',[47] never loses his place or his temper. It is a pity to see Lord Erskine sit silent, who was once a popular and powerful speaker; and when he does get up to speak, you wish he had said nothing. This nobleman, the other day, on his return to Scotland after an absence of fifty years, made a striking speech on the instinctive and indissoluble attachment of all persons to the country where they are born, — which he considered as an innate and unerring principle of the human mind; and, in expatiating on the advantages of patriotism, argued by way of illustration, that if it were not for this original dispensation of Providence, attaching and, as it were, *rooting* every one to the spot

* See his panegyric on the late King, his defence of the House of Commons, and his eulogy on the practical liberty of the English Constitution in his Liverpool Dinner Speech.

where he was bred and born, – civil society should never have existed, nor mankind have been reclaimed from the barbarous and wandering way of life, to which they were in the first instance addicted! How these persons should become attached by habit to places where it appears, from their vagabond dispositions, they never stayed at all, is an over-sight of the speaker which remains unexplained. On the same occasion, the learned Lord, in order to produce an effect, observed that when, advancing farther north, he should come to the old playground near his father's mansion, where he used to play at ball when a child, his sensations would be of a most affecting description. This is possible; but his Lordship returned homewards the next day, thinking, no doubt, he had anticipated all the sentiment of the situation. This puts one in mind of the story one has heard of Tom Sheridan, who told his father he had been down to the bottom of a coal-pit. 'Then, you are a fool, Tom,' said the father. 'Why so, Sir?' 'Because', said the other, 'it would have answered all the same purpose *to have said you had been down!*'

On the Spirit of Monarchy

'Strip it of its externals, and what is it but *a jest?*'

Charade on the word MAJESTY.

'As for politics, I think poets are *Tories* by nature, supposing them to be by nature poets. The love of an individual person or family, that has worn a crown for many successions, is an inclination greatly adapted to the fanciful tribe. On the other hand, mathematicians, abstract reasoners, of no manner of attachment to persons, at least to the visible part of them, but prodigiously devoted to the ideas of virtue, liberty, and so forth, are generally *Whigs.* It happens agreeably enough to this maxim, that the Whigs are friends to that wise, plodding, unpoetical people, the Dutch.' – *Shenstone's Letters,* 1746.

The Spirit of Monarchy, then, is nothing but the craving in the human mind after the Sensible and the One. It is not so much a matter of state-necessity or policy, as a natural infirmity, a disease, a false appetite in the popular feeling, which must be gratified. Man is an individual animal with narrow faculties, but infinite desires, which he is anxious to concentrate in some one object within the grasp of his imagination, and where, if he cannot be all that he wishes himself, he may at least contemplate his own pride, vanity, and passions, displayed in their most extravagant dimensions in a being no bigger and no better than himself. Each individual would (were it in his power) be a king, a God: but as he cannot, the next best thing is to see this reflex image of his self-love, the darling passion of his breast, realized, embodied out of himself in the first object he can lay his hands on for the purpose. The slave admires the tyrant because the last *is*, what the first *would be*. He surveys himself all over in the glass of royalty. The swelling bloated, self-importance of the one is the very counter-part and ultimate goal of the abject servility of the other. But both hate mankind for the same reason, because a respect for humanity is a diversion to their inordinate self-love, and the idea of the general good is a check to the gross intemperance of passion. The worthlessness of the object does not diminish but irritate the propensity to admire. It serves to pamper our imagination equally, and does not provoke our envy. All we want is to aggrandize our own vain-glory at second hand; and the less of real superiority or excellence there is in the person we fix upon as our proxy in this dramatic exhibition, the more easily can we change places with him, and fancy ourselves as good as he. Nay, the descent favours the rise; and we heap our tribute of applause the higher, in proportion as it is a free gift. An idol is not the worse for being of coarse materials; a king should be a common-place man. Otherwise, he is superior in his own nature, and not dependent on our bounty or caprice. Man is a poetical animal, and delights in fiction. We like to have scope for the exercise of our mere will. We make kings of men, and Gods of stocks and stones: we are not jealous of the creatures of our own hands. We only want a peg or loop to hang our idle fancies on, a puppet to dress up, a lay-figure to paint from. It is 'THING Ferdinand, and not KING Ferdinand',[1] as it was wisely and wittily observed. We ask only for the stage effect; we do not go behind the scenes, or it would go hard with many of our prejudices! We see the symbols of Majesty, we enjoy the pomp, we crouch before the power, we walk in the procession, and make part of the pageant, and we say in our secret hearts, there is nothing but accident that prevents us from being at the head of it. There is something in the mock-sublimity of thrones, wonderfully congenial to the human mind. Every man feels that he could sit there; every man feels that he could look big there; every man feels that he could bow there; every man feels that he could play the monarch there. The transition is so easy, and so delightful! The imagination keeps pace with royal state,

'And by the vision splendid
Is on its way attended'.[2]

The Madman in Hogarth[3] who fancies himself a king, is not a solitary
instance of this species of hallucination. Almost every true and loyal
subject holds such a barren sceptre in his hand; and the meanest of
the rabble, as he runs by the monarch's side, has wit enough to think
– 'There goes my *royal* self!' From the most absolute despot to the
lowest slave there is but one step (no, not one) in point of real merit.
As far as truth or reason is concerned, they might change situations
to-morrow – nay, they constantly do so without the smallest loss or
benefit to mankind! Tyranny, in a word, is a farce got up for the
entertainment of poor human nature; and it might pass very well, if
it did not so often turn into a tragedy.

We once heard a celebrated and elegant historian and a hearty
Whig[4] declare, he liked a king like George III better than such a one
as Buonaparte; because, in the former case, there was nothing to
overawe the imagination but birth and situation; whereas he could
not so easily brook the double superiority of the other, mental as well
as adventitious. So does the spirit of independence and the levelling
pride of intellect join in with the servile rage of the vulgar! This is
the advantage which an hereditary has over an elective monarchy:
for there is no end of the dispute about precedence while merit is
supposed to determine it, each man laying claim to this in his own
person; so that there is no other way to set aside all controversy and
heart-burnings, but by precluding moral and intellectual qualifications
altogether, and referring the choice to accident, and giving the
preference to a nonentity. 'A good king', says Swift, 'should be, in all
other respects, a mere cypher.'[5]

It has been remarked, as a peculiarity in modern criticism, that
the courtly and loyal make a point of crying up Mr Young, as an
actor, and equally running down Mr Kean; and it has been conjectured
in consequence that Mr Kean was a *radical*. Truly, he is not a radical
politician; but what is as bad, he is a radical actor. He savours too
much of the reality. He is not a mock-tragedian, an automaton player
– he is something besides his paraphernalia. He has 'that within
which passes show'.[6] There is not a particle of affinity between him

and the patrons of the court-writers. Mr Young, on the contrary, is the very thing – all assumption and strut and measured pomp, full of self-importance, void of truth and nature, the mask of the characters he takes, a pasteboard figure, a stiff piece of wax-work. He fills the throne of tragedy, not like an upstart or usurper, but as a matter of course, decked out in his plumes of feathers, and robes of state, stuck into a posture, and repeating certain words by rote. Mr Kean has a heart in his bosom, beating with human passion (a thing for the great 'to fear, not to delight in!'[7]); he is a living man, and not an artificial one. How should those, who look to the surface, and never probe deeper, endure him? He is the antithesis of a court-actor. It is the object there to suppress and varnish over the feelings, not to give way to them. His *overt* manner must shock them, and be thought a breach of all decorum. They are in dread of his fiery humours, of coming near his Voltaic Battery[8] – they choose rather to be roused gently from their self-complacent apathy by the application of Metallic Tractors.[9] They dare not trust their delicate nerves within the estuary of the passions, but would slumber out their torpid existence in a calm, a Dead Sea – the air of which extinguishes life and motion!

Would it not be hard upon a little girl, who is busy in dressing up a favourite doll, to pull it in pieces before her face in order to show her the bits of wood, the wool, and rags it is composed of? So it would be hard upon that great baby, the world, to take any of its idols to pieces, and show that they are nothing but painted wood. Neither of them would thank you, but consider the offer as an insult. The little girl knows as well as you do that her doll is a cheat; but she shuts her eyes to it, for she finds her account in keeping up the deception. Her doll is her pretty little self. In its glazed eyes, its cherry cheeks, its flaxen locks, its finery and its baby-house, she has a fairy vision of her own future charms, her future triumphs, a thousand hearts led captive, and an establishment for life. Harmless illusion! that can create something out of nothing, can make that which is good for nothing in itself so fine in appearance, and clothe a shapeless piece of deal-board with the attributes of a divinity! But the great world has been doing little else but playing at *make-believe* all its life-time. For several thousand years its chief rage was to paint larger pieces of wood and smear them with gore and call them Gods and offer victims to them – slaughtered hecatombs, the fat of goats and oxen, or human sacrifices – shewing in this its love of shew, of cruelty, and imposture; and woe to him who should 'peep through the blanket of the dark to cry, *Hold, hold*'.[10] – *Great is Diana of the Ephesians,*[11] was the answer in all ages. It was in vain to represent to them, 'Your Gods have eyes but they see not, ears but they hear not, neither do they understand'[12] – the more stupid, brutish, helpless, and contemptible they were, the more furious, bigoted, and implacable were their votaries in their behalf.* The more absurd the fiction, the louder was the noise made to hide it – the more mischievous its tendency, the more did it excite all the frenzy of the passions. Superstition nursed, with peculiar zeal, her rickety, deformed, and preposterous offspring. She passed by the nobler races of animals even, to pay divine honours to the odious and unclean – she took toads and serpents, cats, rats, dogs, crocodiles, goats and monkeys, and hugged them to her bosom, and dandled them into deities, and set up altars to them, and drenched the earth with tears and blood in their defence; and those who did not believe in them were cursed, and were forbidden the use of bread, of fire, and water, and to worship them was piety, and their images were held sacred, and their race became Gods in perpetuity and by divine right. To touch them, was sacrilege: to kill them, death, even in your own defence. If they stung you, you must die: if they infested the land with their numbers and their pollutions, there was no remedy. The nuisance was intolerable, impassive, immortal. Fear, religious horror, disgust, hatred, heightened the flame of bigotry and intolerance. There was nothing so odious or contemptible but it found a sanctuary in the more odious and contemptible perversity of human nature. The barbarous Gods of antiquity reigned *in contempt of their worshippers*!

This game was carried on through all the first ages of the world, and is still kept up in many parts of it; and it is impossible to describe the wars, massacres, horrors, miseries and crimes, to which it gave

'Of whatsoe'er descent his Godhead be,
Stock, stone, or other homely pedigree,
In his defence his servants are as bold
As if he had been made of beaten gold.' – DRYDEN.[13]

343

colour, sanctity, and sway. The idea of a God, beneficent and just, the invisible maker of all things, was abhorrent to their gross, material notions. No, they must have Gods of their own making, that they could see and handle, that they knew to be nothing in themselves but senseless images, and these they daubed over with the gaudy emblems of their own pride and passions, and these they lauded to the skies, and grew fierce, obscene, frantic before them, as the representatives of their sordid ignorance and barbaric vices. TRUTH, GOOD, were idle names to them, without a meaning. They must have a lie, a palpable, pernicious lie, to pamper their crude, unhallowed conceptions with, and to exercise the untameable fierceness of their wills. The Jews were the only people of antiquity who were withheld from running headlong into this abomination; yet so strong was the propensity in them (from inherent frailty as well as neighbour-ing example) that it could only be curbed and kept back by the hands of Omnipotence.* At length, reason prevailed over imagination so far, that these brute idols and their altars were overturned: it was thought too much to set up stocks and stones, Golden Calves and Brazen Serpents, as *bona fide* Gods and Goddesses, which men were to fall down and worship at their peril – and Pope long after sum-med up the merits of the whole mythologic tribe in a handsome distich –

> 'Gods partial, changeful, passionate, unjust,
> Whose attributes were rage, revenge, or lust.'[14]

It was thought a bold stride to divert the course of our imaginations, the overflowings of our enthusiasm, our love of the mighty and the marvellous, from the dead to the living *subject*, and there we stick. We have got living idols, instead of dead ones; and we fancy that they are real, and put faith in them accordingly. Oh, Reason! when will thy long minority expire? It is not now the fashion to make Gods of wood and stone and brass, but we make kings of common men, and are proud of our own handy-work. We take a child from his

---

* They *would* have a king in spite of the devil. The image-worship of the Papists is a batch of the same leaven. The apishness of man's nature would not let even the Christian religion escape.

birth, and we agree, when he grows up to be a man, to heap the highest honours of the state upon him, and to pay the most devoted homage to his will. Is there any thing in the person, 'any mark, any likelihood',[15] to warrant this sovereign awe and dread? No: he may be little better than an idiot, little short of a madman, and yet he is no less qualified for king.* If he can contrive to pass the College of Physicians, the Heralds' College dub him divine. Can we make any given individual taller or stronger or wiser than other men, or different in any respect from what nature intended him to be? No; but we can make a king of him. We cannot add a cubit to the stature, or instil a virtue into the minds of monarchs – but we can put a sceptre into their hands, a crown upon their heads, we can set them on an eminence, we can surround them with circumstance, we can aggrandize them with power, we can pamper their appetites, we can pander to their wills. We can do every thing to exalt them in external rank and station – nothing to lift them one step higher in the scale of moral or intellectual excellence. Education does not give capacity or temper; and the education of kings is not especially directed to useful knowledge or liberal sentiment. What then is the state of the case? The highest respect of the community and of every individual in it is paid and is due of right there, where perhaps not an idea can take root, or a single virtue be engrafted. Is not this to erect a standard of esteem directly opposite to that of mind and morals? The lawful monarch may be the best or the worst man in his dominions, he may be the

---

* 'In fact, the argument drawn from the supposed incapacity of the people against a representative Government, comes with the worst grace in the world from the patrons and admirers of hereditary government. Surely, if government were a thing requiring the utmost stretch of genius, wisdom, and virtue, to carry it on, the office of King would never even have been dreamt of as hereditary, any more than that of poet, painter, or philosopher. It is easy here 'for the son to tread in the Sire's steady steps'. It requires nothing but the will to do it. Extraordinary talents are not once looked for. Nay, a person, who would never have risen by natural abilities to the situation of churchwarden or parish beadle, succeeds by unquestionable right to the possession of a throne, and wields the energies of an empire, or decides the fate of the world, with the smallest possible share of human understanding. The line of distinction which separates the regal purple from the slabbering-bib, is sometimes fine indeed; as we see in the case of the two Ferdinands. Any one above the rank of an idiot is supposed capable of exercising the highest functions of royal state. Yet these are the persons who talk of the people as a swinish multitude, and taunt them with their want of refinement and philosophy.' – *Yellow Dwarf*, p. 84.[16]

wisest or the weakest, the wittiest or the stupidest: still he is equally entitled to our homage as king, for it is the place and power we bow to, and not the man. He may be a sublimation of all the vices and diseases of the human heart; yet we are not to say so, we dare not even think so. 'Fear God, and honour the King', is equally a maxim at all times and seasons. The personal character of the king has nothing to do with the question. Thus the extrinsic is set up over the intrinsic by authority: wealth and interest lend their countenance to gilded vice and infamy on principle, and outward show and advantages become the symbols and the standard of respect in despite of useful qualities or well-directed efforts through all ranks and gradations of society. 'From the crown of the head to the sole of the foot there is no soundness left.'[17] The whole style of moral thinking, feeling, acting, is in a false tone − is hollow, spurious, meretricious. Virtue, says Montesquieu,[18] is the principle of republics; honour, of a monarchy. But it is 'honour dishonourable, sin-bred'[19] − it is the honour of trucking a principle for a place, of exchanging our honest convictions for a ribbon or a garter. The business of life is a scramble for unmerited precedence. Is not the highest respect entailed, the highest station filled without any possible proofs or pretensions to public spirit or public principle? Shall not the next places to it be secured by the sacrifice of them? It is the order of the day, the understood etiquette of courts and kingdoms. For the servants of the crown to presume on merit, when the crown itself is held as an heir-loom by prescription, is a kind of *lèse majesté*, an indirect attainder of the title to the succession. Are not all eyes turned to the sun of court-favour? Who would not then reflect its smile by the performance of any acts which can avail in the eye of the great, and by the surrender of any virtue, which attracts neither notice nor applause? The stream of corruption begins at the fountainhead of court-influence. The sympathy of mankind is that on which all strong feeling and opinion floats; and this sets in full in every absolute monarchy to the side of tinsel show and iron-handed power, in contempt and defiance of right and wrong. The right and the wrong are of little consequence, compared to the *in* and the *out*. The distinction between Whig and Tory is merely nominal: neither have their country one bit at heart. Phaw! we had forgot − Our British monarchy is a mixed, and the only perfect form of government; and therefore what is here said cannot properly apply to it. But MIGHT BEFORE RIGHT is the motto blazoned on the front of unimpaired and undivided Sovereignty! –

A court is the centre of fashion; and no less so, for being the sink of luxury and vice –

> – 'Of outward shew
> Elaborate, of inward less exact'.[20]

The goods of fortune, the baits of power, the indulgences of vanity, may be accumulated without end, and the taste for them increases as it is gratified: the love of virtue, the pursuit of truth, grow stale and dull in the dissipation of a court. Virtue is thought crabbed and morose, knowledge pedantic, while every sense is pampered, and every folly tolerated. Every thing tends naturally to personal aggrandizement and unrestrained self-will. It is easier for monarchs as well as other men 'to tread the primrose path of dalliance'[21] than 'to scale the steep and thorny road to heaven'.[22] The vices, when they have leave from power and authority, go greater lengths than the virtues; example justifies almost every excess, and 'nice customs curtsy to great kings'.[23] What chance is there that monarchs should not yield to the temptations of gallantry then, when youth and beauty are as wax? What female heart can indeed withstand the attractions of a throne – the smile that melts all hearts, the air that awes rebellion, the frown that kings dread, the hand that scatters fairy wealth, that bestows titles, places, honour, power, the breast on which the star glitters, the head circled with a diadem, whose dress dazzles with its richness and its taste, who has nations at his command, senates at his control, 'in form and motion so express and admirable, in action how like an angel, in apprehension how like a God; the beauty of the world, the paragon of animals'![24] The power of resistance is so much the less, where fashion extends impunity to the frail offender, and screens the loss of character.

> 'Vice is undone, if she forgets her birth,
> And stoops from angels to the dregs of earth;
> But 'tis the fall degrades her to a whore:
> Let greatness own her, and she's mean no more.

347

Her birth, her beauty, crowds and courts confess,
Chaste matrons praise her, and grave bishops bless.
In golden chains the willing world she draws,
And hers the Gospel is, and hers the laws.'*[25]

The air of a court is not assuredly that which is most favourable
to the practice of self-denial and strict morality. We increase the
temptations of wealth, of power, and pleasure a thousand-fold, while
we can give no additional force to the antagonist principles of reason,
disinterested integrity and goodness of heart. Is it to be wondered at
that courts and palaces have produced so many monsters of avarice,
cruelty, and lust? The adept in voluptuousness is not likely to be a
proportionable proficient in humanity. To feed on plate or be clothed
in purple, is not to feel for the hungry and the naked. He who has
the greatest power put into his hands, will only become more impatient
of any restraint in the use of it. To have the welfare and the lives of
millions placed at our disposal, is a sort of warrant, a challenge to
squander them without mercy. An arbitrary monarch set over the
heads of his fellows does not identify himself with them, or learn to
comprehend their rights or sympathize with their interests, but looks
down upon them as of a different species from himself, as insects
crawling on the face of the earth, that he may trample on at his

---

* A lady of quality abroad, in allusion to the gallantries of the reigning Prince, being told,
'I suppose it will be your turn next?' said, 'No, I hope not; for you know it is impossible to
refuse!' What a satire on the court and fashionables! If this be true, female virtue in the
blaze of royalty is no more than the moth in the candle, or ice in the sun's ray. What will
the great themselves say to it, in whom at that rate,

– 'the same luck holds,
They all are subjects, courtiers, and cuckolds!'[26]

Out upon it! We'll not believe it. Alas! poor virtue, what is to become of the very idea of
it, if we are to be told that every man within the precincts of a palace is an *hypothetical*
cuckold, or holds his wife's virtue in trust for the Prince? We entertain no doubt that many
ladies of quality have resisted the importunities of a throne, and that many more would
do so in private life, if they had the desired opportunity: nay, we have been assured by
several that a king would no more be able to prevail with them than any other man! If
however there is any foundation for the above insinuation, it throws no small light on the
Spirit of Monarchy, which by the supposition implies in it the *virtual* surrender of the
whole sex at discretion; and at the same time accounts perhaps for the indifference shown
by some monarchs in availing themselves of so mechanical a privilege.

pleasure, or if he spares them, it is an act of royal grace; — he is besotted with power, blinded with prerogative, an alien to his nature, a traitor to his trust, and instead of being the organ of public feeling and public opinion, is an excrescence and an anomaly in the state, a bloated mass of morbid humours and proud flesh! A constitutional king, on the other hand, is a servant of the public, a representative of the people's wants and wishes, dispensing justice and mercy according to law. Such a monarch is the King of England! Such was his late, and such is his present Majesty George the IVth! —

Let us take the Spirit of Monarchy in its highest state of exaltation, in the moment of its proudest triumph — a Coronation-day. We now see it in our mind's eye; the preparation of weeks — the expectation of months — the seats, the privileged places, are occupied in the obscurity of night, and in silence — the day dawns slowly, big with the hope of Cæsar and of Rome — the golden censers are set in order, the tables groan with splendour and with luxury — within the inner space the rows of peeresses are set, and revealed to the eye decked out in ostrich feathers and pearls, like beds of lilies sparkling with a thousand dew-drops — the marshals and the heralds are in motion — the full organ, majestic, peals forth the Coronation Anthem — every thing is ready — and all at once the Majesty of kingdoms bursts upon the astonished sight — his person is swelled out with all the gorgeousness of dress, and swathed in bales of silk and golden tissues — the bow with which he greets the assembled multitude, and the representatives of foreign kings, is the climax of conscious dignity, bending gracefully on its own bosom, and instantly thrown back into the sightless air, as if asking no recognition in return — the oath of mutual fealty between him and his people is taken — the fairest flowers of female beauty precede the Sovereign, scattering roses; the sons of princes page his heels, holding up the robes of crimson and ermine — he staggers and reels under the weight of royal pomp, and of a nation's eyes; and thus the pageant is launched into the open day, dazzling the sun, whose beams seem beaten back by the sun of royalty — there were the warrior, the statesman, and the mitred head — there was Prince Leopold, like a panther in its dark glossy pride, and Castlereagh, clad in triumphant smiles and snowy satin, unstained with his own blood — the loud trumpet brays, the cannon roars, the spires are mad with music, the stones in the street are startled at the presence of a king: – the crowd press on, the metropolis heaves like a sea in restless motion, the air is thick with loyalty's quick pants in its monarch's arms – all eyes drink up the sight, all tongues reverberate the sound –

> 'A present deity they shout around,
> A present deity the vaulted roofs rebound!'[27]

What does it all amount to? A show – a theatrical spectacle! What does it prove? That a king is crowned, that a king is dead! What is the moral to be drawn from it, that is likely to sink into the heart of a nation? That greatness consists in finery, and that supreme merit is the dower of birth and fortune! It is a form, a ceremony to which each successor to the throne is entitled in his turn as a matter of right. Does it depend on the inheritance of virtue, on the acquisition of knowledge in the new monarch, whether he shall be thus exalted in the eyes of the people? No: – to say so is not only an offence in manners, but a violation of the laws. The king reigns in contempt of any such pragmatical distinctions. They are set aside, proscribed, treasonable, as it relates to the august person of the monarch; what is likely to become of them in the minds of the people? A Coronation overlays and drowns all such considerations for a generation to come, and so far it serves its purpose well. It debauches the understandings of the people, and makes them the slaves of sense and show. It laughs to scorn and tramples upon every other claim to distinction or respect. Is the chief person in the pageant a tyrant? It does not lessen, but aggrandize him to the imagination. Is he the king of a free people? We make up in love and loyalty what we want in fear. Is he young? He borrows understanding and experience from the learning and tried wisdom of councils and parliaments. Is he old? He leans upon the youth and beauty that attend his triumph. Is he weak? Armies support him with their myriads. Is he diseased? What is health to a staff of physicians? Does he die? The truth is out, and he is then – nothing!

There is a cant among court-sycophants of calling all those who are opposed to them 'the *rabble*', '*fellows*', '*miscreants*', &c. This shows the grossness of their ideas of all true merit, and the false standard of rank and power by which they measure every thing; like footmen, who suppose their masters must be gentlemen, and that the rest of the world are low people. Whatever is opposed to power, they think despicable; whatever suffers oppression, they think deserves it. They are ever ready to side with the strong, to insult and trample on the weak. This is with us a pitiful fashion of thinking. They are not of the mind of Pope, who was so full of the opposite conviction, that he has even written a bad couplet to express it: —

> 'Worth makes the man, and want of it the fellow:
> The rest is all but leather and prunella.'[28]

Those lines in Cowper also must sound very puerile or old-fashioned to courtly ears: —

> 'The only amaranthine flower on earth
> Is virtue; the only lasting treasure, truth.'[29]

To this sentiment, however, we subscribe our hearts and hands. There is nothing truly liberal but that which postpones its own claims to those of propriety — or great, but that which looks out of itself to others. All power is but an unabated nuisance, a barbarous assumption, an aggravated injustice, that is not directed to the common good: all grandeur that has not something corresponding to it in personal merit and heroic acts, is a deliberate burlesque, and an insult on common sense and human nature. That which is true, the understanding ratifies: that which is good, the heart owns: all other claims are spurious, vitiated, mischievous, false — fit only for those who are sunk below contempt, or raised above opinion. We hold in scorn all right-lined pretensions but those of rectitude. If there is offence in this, we are ready to abide by it. If there is shame, we take it to ourselves: and we hope and hold that the time will come, when all other idols but those which represent pure truth and real good, will be looked upon with the same feelings of pity and wonder that we now look back to the images of Thor and Woden!

Really, that men born to a throne (limited or unlimited) should employ the brief span of their existence here in doing all the mischief in their power, in levying cruel wars and undermining the liberties of the world, to prove to themselves and others that their pride and passions are of more consequence than the welfare of mankind at large, would seem a little astonishing, but that the fact is so. It is not our business to preach lectures to monarchs, but if we were at all disposed to attempt the ungracious task, we should do it in the words of an author who often addressed the ear of monarchs.

'A man may read a sermon,'[30] says Jeremy Taylor, 'the best and most passionate that ever man preached, if he shall but enter into the sepulchres of kings. In the same Escorial where the Spanish princes live in greatness and power, and decree war or peace, they have wisely placed a cemetery where their ashes and their glory shall sleep till time shall be no more: and where *our* kings have been crowned, their ancestors lie interred, and they must walk over their grandsire's head to take his crown. There is an acre sown with royal seed, the copy of the greatest change from rich to naked, from ceiled roofs to arched coffins, from living like Gods to die like men. There is enough to cool the flames of lust, to abate the height of pride, to appease the itch of covetous desires, to sully and dash out the dissembling colours of a lustful, artificial, and imaginary beauty. There the warlike and the peaceful, the fortunate and the miserable, the beloved and the despised princes mingle their dust, and pay down their symbol of mortality, and tell all the world, that when we die our ashes shall be equal to kings, and our accounts shall be easier, and our pains for our crimes shall be less. To my apprehension, it is a sad record which is left by Athenæus concerning Ninus, the great Assyrian monarch, whose life and death is summed up in these words: "Ninus, the Assyrian, had an ocean of gold, and other riches more than the sand in the Caspian sea; he never saw the stars, and perhaps he never desired it; he never stirred up the holy fire among the Magi; nor touched his God with the sacred rod, according to the laws; he never offered sacrifice, nor worshipped the Deity, nor administered justice, nor spake to the people, nor numbered them; but he was most valiant to eat and drink, and having mingled his wines, he threw the rest upon the stones. This man is dead: behold his sepulchre, and now hear where Ninus is. *Sometime I was Ninus, and drew the breath of a living man, but now am nothing but clay. I have nothing but what I did eat, and what I served to myself in lust is all my portion: the wealth with which I was blest, my enemies meeting together shall carry away, as the mad Thyades carry a raw goat. I am gone to Hell; and when I went thither, I carried neither gold nor horse, nor a silver chariot. I that wore a mitre, am now a little heap of dust!"'* – Taylor's *Holy Living and Dying.*

On the Connexion Between
Toad-Eaters and Tyrants

'Doubtless, the pleasure is as great
In being cheated as to cheat.'[1]

Jan. 12, 1817.

We some time ago promised our friend, Mr Robert Owen, an explanation of some of the causes which impede the natural progress of
liberty and human happiness. We have in part redeemed this pledge
in what we said about *Coriolanus*,[2] and we shall try in this article to
redeem it still more. We grant to our ingenious and romantic friend,
that the progress of knowledge and civilization is in itself favourable
to liberty and equality, and that the general stream of thought and
opinion constantly sets in this way, till power finds the tide of public
feeling becoming too strong for it, ready to sap its rotten foundations,
and 'bore through its castle-walls';[3] and then it contrives to turn the
tide of knowledge and sentiment clean the contrary way, and either
bribes human reason to take part against human nature, or knocks it
on the head by a more summary process. Thus, in the year 1792, Mr
Burke became a pensioner for writing his book against the French
Revolution, and Mr Thomas Paine was outlawed for his *Rights of
Man*. Since that period, the press has been the great enemy of freedom,
the whole weight of that immense engine (for the purposes of good
or ill) having a fatal bias given to it by the two main springs of fear
and favour.

The weak sides of human intellect, by which power effects its
conversion to the worst purposes, when it finds the exercise of free
opinion inconsistent with the existence and uncontrolled exercise of

arbitrary power, are these four, *viz.* the grossness of the imagination, which is seduced by outward appearances from the pursuit of real ultimate good; the subtlety of the understanding itself, which palliates by flimsy sophistry the most flagrant abuses; interest and advancement in the world; and lastly, the feuds and jealousies of literary men among one another. There is no class of persons so little calculated to act in *corps* as literary men. All their views are recluse and separate (for the mind acts by individual energy, and not by numbers): their motives, whether good or bad, are personal to themselves, their vanity exclusive, their love of truth independent; they exist not by the preservation, but the destruction of their own species; they are governed not by the spirit of unanimity, but of contradiction. They will hardly allow any thing to be right or any thing to be wrong, unless they are the first to find out that it is so; and are ready to prove the best things in the world the worst, and the worst the best, from the pure impulse of splenetic over-weening self-opinion, much more if they are likely to be well paid for it − not that interest is their ruling passion, but still it operates, silent and unseen, with them as with other men, when it can make a compromise with their vanity. This part of the character of men of letters is so well known, that Shakespeare makes *Brutus* protest against the fitness of *Cicero* to be included in their enterprise on this very principle: −

> 'Oh, name him not: let us not break with him;
> For he will never follow any thing,
> That other men begin.'[4]

The whole of Mr Burke's *Reflections on the French Revolution** is but an elaborate and damning comment on this short text. He quarrelled with the French Revolution out of spite to Rousseau, the spark of whose genius had kindled the flame of liberty in a nation. He therefore endeavoured to extinguish the flame − to put out the light; and he succeeded, because there were others like himself, ready to sacrifice every manly and generous principle to the morbid, sickly, effeminate,

* When this work was first published, the King had copies of it bound in Morocco, and gave them away to his favourite courtiers, saying, 'It was a book which every gentleman ought to read.'

little, selfish, irritable, dirty spirit of authorship. Not only did such persons, according to Mr Coleridge's valuable and competent testimony (see his *Lay-Sermon*)[5] make the distinction between Atheism and Religion a mere stalking-horse for the indulgence of their idle vanity, but they made the other questions of Liberty and Slavery, of the Rights of Man, or the Divine Right of Kings to rule millions of men as their Slaves for ever, they made these vital and paramount questions (which whoever wilfully and knowingly compromises, is a traitor to himself and his species), subordinate to the low, whiffling, contemptible gratification of their literary jealousy. We shall not go over the painful list of instances; neither can we forget them. But they all or almost all contrived to sneak over one by one to the side on which 'empty praise or solid pudding'[6] was to be got; they could not live without the smiles of the great (not they), nor provide for an increasing establishment without a loss of character; instead of going into some profitable business and exchanging their lyres for ledgers, their pens for the plough (the honest road to riches), they chose rather to prostitute their pens to the mock-heroic defence of the most bare-faced of all mummeries, the pretended alliance of kings and people! We told them how it would be, if they succeeded; it has turned out just as we said; and a pretty figure do these companions of Ulysses (*Compagnons du Lys*),[7] these gaping converts to despotism, these well-fed victims of the charms of the Bourbons, now make, nestling under their laurels in the stye of Corruption, and sunk in torpid repose (from which they do not like to be disturbed by calling on their former names or professions), in lazy sinecures and good warm berths! Such is the history and mystery of literary patriotism and prostitution for the last twenty years. – Power is subject to none of these disadvantages. It is one and indivisible; it is self-centred, self-willed, incorrigible, inaccessible to temptation or entreaty; interest is on its side, passion is on its side, prejudice is on its side, the name of religion is on its side; the qualms of conscience it is not subject to, for it is iron-nerved; humanity it is proof against, for it sets itself up above humanity; reason it does not hearken to, except that reason which panders to its will and flatters its pride. It pursues its steady way, its undeviating everlasting course, 'unslacked of motion',[8] like that foul Indian idol, the Jaggernaut,[9] and crushes poor upstart poets, patriots, and philosophers (the beings of an hour) and the successive never-ending generations of fools and knaves, beneath its feet; and mankind bow their willing necks to the yoke, and eagerly consign their children and their children's children to be torn in pieces by its scythe, or trampled to death by the gay, gaudy, painted, blood-stained wheels of the grim idol of power!

Such is the state of the Eastern world, where the inherent baseness of man's nature, and his tendency to social order, to tyrannize and to be tyrannized over, has had full time to develop itself. Our turn seems next. We are but just setting out, it is true, in this bye-nook and corner of the world – but just recovering from the effects of the Revolution of 1688, and the defeated Rebellions of the years 1715 and 1745, but we need hardly despair under the auspices of the Editor of *The Times*, and with the example of the defeat 'of the last successful instance of a democratic rebellion',[10] by the second restoration of the Bourbons, before our eyes and close under our noses. Mr Owen may think the example of New Lanark more inviting, but the persons to whom he has dedicated his work turn their eyes another way!*[11]

Man is a toad-eating animal. The admiration of power in others is as common to man as the love of it in himself: the one makes him a tyrant, the other a slave. It is not he alone, who wears the golden crown, that is proud of it: the wretch who pines in a dungeon, and in chains, is dazzled with it; and if he could but shake off his own fetters, would care little about the wretches whom he left behind him, so that he might have an opportunity, on being set free himself, of gazing at this glittering gew-gaw 'on some high holiday of once a year'.[13] The slave, who has no other hope or consolation, clings to the apparition of royal magnificence, which insults his misery and his despair; stares through the hollow eyes of famine at the insolence of pride and luxury which has occasioned it, and hugs his chains the closer, because he has nothing else left. The French, under the old

---

* Our loyal Editor used to bluster a great deal some time ago about putting down James Madison, and 'the last example of democratic rebellion in America'. In this he was consistent and logical. Could he not, however, find out another example of this same principle, by going a little farther back in history, and coming a little nearer home? If he has forgotten this chapter in our history, others who have profited more by it have not. He may understand what we mean, by turning to the story of the two elder Blifils[12] in *Tom Jones*.

regime, made the glory of their *Grand Monarque* a set-off against rags and hunger, equally satisfied with *shows or bread*; and the poor Spaniard, delivered from temporary to permanent oppression, looks up once more with pious awe, to the time-hallowed towers of the Holy Inquisition. As the herd of mankind are stripped of every thing, in body and mind, so are they thankful for what is left; as is the desolation of their hearts and the wreck of their little all, so is the pomp and pride which is built upon their ruin, and their fawning admiration of it.

> 'I've heard of hearts unkind, kind deeds
> With coldness still returning:
> Alas! the gratitude of men
> Has oftener set me mourning.'[14]*

There is something in the human mind, which requires an object for it to repose on; and, driven from all other sources of pride or pleasure, it falls in love with misery, and grows enamoured of oppression. It gazes after the liberty, the happiness, the comfort, the knowledge, which have been torn from it by the unfeeling gripe of wealth and power, as the poor debtor gazes with envy and wonder at the Lord Mayor's show. Thus is the world by degrees reduced to a spital or lazar-house, where the people waste away with want and disease, and are thankful if they are only suffered to crawl forgotten to their graves. Just in proportion to the systematic tyranny exercised over a nation, to its loss of a sense of freedom and the spirit of resistance, will be its loyalty; the most abject submission will always be rendered to the most confirmed despotism. The most wretched slaves are the veriest sycophants. The lackey, mounted behind his master's coach, looks down with contempt upon the mob, forgetting his own origin and his actual situation, and comparing them only with that standard of gentility which he has perpetually in his eye. The hireling of the press (a still meaner slave) wears his livery, and is proud of it. He

---

* *Simon Lee, the old Huntsman*, a tale by Mr Wordsworth, of which he himself says,

> 'It is no tale, but if you think,
> Perhaps a tale you'll make it.'[15]

In this view it is a tale indeed, not 'of other times',[16] but of these.

measures the greatness of others by his own meanness; their lofty pretensions indemnify him for his servility; he magnifies the sacredness of their persons to cover the laxity of his own principles. He offers up his own humanity, and that of all men, at the shrine of royalty. He sneaks to court; and the bland accents of power close his ears to the voice of freedom ever after; its velvet touch makes his heart marble to a people's sufferings. He is the intellectual pimp of power, as others are the practical ones of the pleasures of the great, and often on the same disinterested principle. For one tyrant, there are a thousand ready slaves. Man is naturally a worshipper of idols and a lover of kings. It is the excess of individual power, that strikes and gains over his imagination: the general misery and degradation which are the necessary consequences of it, are spread too wide, they lie too deep, their weight and import are too great, to appeal to any but the slow, inert, speculative, imperfect faculty of reason. The cause of liberty is lost in its own truth and magnitude; while the cause of despotism flourishes, triumphs, and is irresistible in the gross mixture, the *Belle Alliance*, of pride and ignorance.

Power is the grim idol that the world adore; that arms itself with destruction, and reigns by terror in the coward heart of man; that dazzles the senses, haunts the imagination, confounds the understanding, and tames the will, by the vastness of its pretensions, and the very hopelessness of resistance to them. Nay more, the more mischievous and extensive the tyranny – the longer it has lasted, and the longer it is likely to last – the stronger is the hold it takes of the minds of its victims, the devotion to it increasing with the dread. It does not satisfy the enormity of the appetite for servility, till it has slain the mind of a nation, and becomes like the evil principle of the universe, from which there is no escape. So in some countries, the most destructive animals are held sacred, despair and terror completely overpowering reason. The prejudices of superstition (religion is another name for fear) are always the strongest in favour of those forms of worship which require the most bloody sacrifices; the foulest idols are those which are approached with the greatest awe; for it should seem that those objects are the most sacred to passion and imagination, which are the most revolting to reason and common sense. No wonder that the Editor of *The Times* bows his head before the idol of Divine Right, or of Legitimacy, (as he calls it) which has had more lives sacrificed to its ridiculous and unintelligible pretensions, in the last twenty-five years, than were ever sacrificed to any other idol in all preceding ages. Never was there any thing so well contrived as this fiction of Legitimacy, to suit the fastidious delicacy of modern sycophants. It hits their grovelling servility and petulant egotism exactly between wind and water.[17] The contrivers or re-modellers of this idol, beat all other idol-mongers, whether Jews, Gentiles or Christians, hollow. The principle of all idolatry is the same: it is the want of something to admire, without knowing what or why: it is the love of an effect without a cause; it is a voluntary tribute of admiration which does not compromise our vanity: it is setting something up over all the rest of the world, to which we feel ourselves to be superior, for it is our own handy-work; so that the more perverse the homage we pay to it, the more it pampers our self-will: the meaner the object, the more magnificent and pompous the attributes we bestow upon it; the greater the lie, the more enthusiastically it is believed and greedily swallowed: —

> 'Of whatsoever race his godhead be,
> Stock, stone, or other homely pedigree,
> In his defence his servants are as bold
> As if he had been made of beaten gold.'[18]

In this inverted ratio, the bungling impostors of former times, and less refined countries, got no further than stocks and stones: their utmost stretch of refinement in absurdity went no further than to select the most mischievous animals or the most worthless objects for the adoration of their besotted votaries: but the framers of the new law-fiction of legitimacy have started a nonentity. The ancients sometimes worshipped the sun or stars, or deified heroes and great men: the moderns have found out the image of the divinity in Louis XVIII! They have set up an object for their idolatry, which they themselves must laugh at, if hypocrisy were not with them the most serious thing in the world. They offer up thirty millions of men to it as its victims, and yet they know that it is nothing but a scare-crow to keep the world in subjection to their renegado whimsies and preposterous hatred of the liberty and happiness of mankind. They do not think kings gods, but they make believe that they do so, to degrade their fellows to the rank of brutes. Legitimacy answers every object of their meanness and malice – *omne tulit punctum*[19] – This mock-doctrine, this little Hunchback, which our resurrection-men, the Humane Society of Divine Right, have foisted on the altar of Liberty, is not only a phantom of the imagination, but a contradiction in terms; it is a prejudice, but an exploded prejudice; it is an imposture, that imposes on nobody; it is powerful only in impotence, safe in absurdity, courted from fear and hatred, a dead prejudice linked to the living mind; the sink of honour, the grave of liberty, a palsy in the heart of a nation; it claims the species as its property, and derives its right neither from God nor man; not from the authority of the Church, which it treats cavalierly, and yet in contempt of the will of the people, which it scouts as opposed to its own: its two chief supporters are, the sword of the Duke of Wellington and the pen of the Editor of *The Times*! The last of these props has, we understand, just failed[20] it.

We formerly gave the Editor of *The Times* a definition of a true Jacobin, as one 'who had seen the evening star set over a poor man's cottage, and connected it with the hope of human happiness'.[21] The city-politician laughed this pastoral definition to scorn, and nicknamed the person who had very innocently laid it down, 'the true Jacobin who writes in the *Chronicle*',[22] – a nickname by which we profited as little as he has by our Illustrations. Since that time our imagination has grown a little less romantic: so we will give him another, which he may chew the cud upon at his leisure. A true Jacobin, then, is one who does not believe in the divine right of kings, or in any other *alias* for it, which implies that they reign 'in contempt of the will of the people';[23] and he holds all such kings to be tyrants, and their subjects slaves. To be a true Jacobin, a man must be a good hater;[24] but this is the most difficult and the least amiable of all the virtues: the most trying and the most thankless of all tasks. The love of liberty consists in the hatred of tyrants. The true Jacobin hates the enemies of liberty as they hate liberty, with all his strength and with all his might, and with all his heart and with all his soul. His memory is as long, and his will as strong as theirs, though his hands are shorter. He never forgets or forgives an injury done to the people, for tyrants never forget or forgive one done to themselves. There is no love lost between them. He does not leave them the sole benefit of their old motto, *Odia in longum jaciens quæ conderet auctaque promeret.*[25] He makes neither peace nor truce with them. His hatred of wrong only ceases with the wrong. The sense of it, and of the barefaced assumption of the right to inflict it, deprives him of his rest. It stagnates in his blood. It loads his heart with aspics' tongues, deadly to venal pens. It settles in his brain — it puts him beside himself. Who will not feel all this for a girl, a toy, a turn of the dice, a word, a blow, for any thing relating to himself; and will not the friend of liberty feel as much for mankind? The love of truth is a passion in his mind, as the love of power is a passion in the minds of others. Abstract reason, unassisted by passion, is no match for power and prejudice, armed with force and cunning. The love of liberty is the love of others; the love of power is the love of ourselves. The one is real; the other often but an empty dream. Hence the defection of modern apostates. While they are looking about, wavering and distracted, in pursuit of universal good or universal fame, the eye of power is upon them, like the eye of Providence, that neither slumbers nor sleeps, and that watches but for one object, its own good. They take no notice of it at first, but it is still upon them, and never off them. It at length catches theirs, and they bow to its sacred light; and like the poor fluttering bird, quail beneath it, are seized with a vertigo, and drop senseless into its jaws, that close upon them for ever, and so we see no more of them, which is well.

'And we saw three poets[26] in a dream, walking up and down on the face of the earth, and holding in their hands a human heart, which, as they raised their eyes to heaven, they kissed and worshipped; and a mighty shout arose and shook the air, for the towers of the Bastille had fallen, and a nation had become, of slaves, freemen; and the three poets, as they heard the sound, leaped and shouted, and made merry, and their voice was choked with tears of joy, which they shed over the human heart, which they kissed and worshipped. And not long after, we saw the same three poets, the one with a receipt-stamp in his hand, the other with a laurel on his head, and the third with a symbol which we could make nothing of, for it was neither literal nor allegorical, following in the train of the Pope and the Inquisition and the Bourbons, and worshipping the mark of the Beast, with the emblem of the human heart thrown beneath their feet, which they trampled and spit upon!' – This apologue is not worth finishing, nor are the people to whom it relates worth talking of. We have done with them.

What is the People?

March 7, 1818.

And who are you that ask the question? One of the people. And yet you would be something! Then you would not have the People nothing. For what is the People? Millions of men, like you, with hearts beating in their bosoms, with thoughts stirring in their minds, with the blood circulating in their veins, with wants and appetites, and passions and anxious cares, and busy purposes and affections for others and a respect for themselves, and a desire of happiness, and a right to freedom, and a will to be free. And yet you would tear out this mighty heart of a nation, and lay it bare and bleeding at the foot of despotism: you would slay the mind of a country to fill up the dreary aching void with the old, obscene, drivelling prejudices of superstition and tyranny: you would tread out the eye of Liberty (the light of nations) like 'a vile jelly',[1] that mankind may be led about darkling to its endless drudgery, like the Hebrew Samson (shorn of his strength and blind), by his insulting taskmasters: you would make the throne every thing, and the people nothing, to be yourself less than nothing, a very slave, a reptile, a creeping, cringing sycophant, a court favourite, a pander to Legitimacy – that detestable fiction, which would make you and me and all mankind its slaves or victims; which would, of right and with all the sanctions of religion and morality, sacrifice the lives of millions to the least of its caprices; which subjects the rights, the happiness, and liberty of nations, to the will of some of the lowest of the species; which rears its bloated hideous form to brave the will of a whole people; that claims mankind as its property, and allows human nature to exist only upon sufferance;

that haunts the understanding like a frightful spectre, and oppresses the very air with a weight that is not to be borne; that like a witch's spell covers the earth with a dim and envious mist, and makes us turn our eyes from the light of heaven, which we have no right to look at without its leave: robs us of 'the unbought grace of life',[2] the pure delight and conscious pride in works of art or nature; leaves us no thought or feeling that we dare call our own; makes genius its lackey, and virtue its easy prey; sports with human happiness, and mocks at human misery; suspends the breath of liberty, and almost of life; exenterates us of our affections, blinds our understandings, debases our imaginations, converts the very hope of emancipation from its yoke into sacrilege, binds the successive countless generations of men together in its chains like a string of felons or galley-slaves, lest they should 'resemble the flies of a summer',[3] considers any remission of its absolute claims as a gracious boon, an act of royal clemency and favour, and confounds all sense of justice, reason, truth, liberty, humanity, in one low servile deathlike dread of power without limit and without remorse!*

Such is the old doctrine of Divine Right, new-vamped up under the style and title of Legitimacy. 'Fine word, Legitimate!'[4] We wonder where our English politicians picked it up. Is it an echo from the tomb of the martyred monarch, Charles the First? Or was it the last word which his son, James the Second, left behind him in his flight, and bequeathed with his *abdication*, to his legitimate successors? It is not written in our annals in the years 1688, in 1715, or 1745. It was not sterling then, which was only fifteen years before his present Majesty's accession to the throne. Has it become so since? Is the Revolution of 1688 at length acknowledged to be a blot in the family escutcheon of the Prince of Orange or the Elector of Hanover? Is the choice of the people, which raised them to the throne, found to be the only flaw in their title to the succession; the weight of royal gratitude growing more uneasy with the distance of the obligation? Is the alloy of liberty, mixed up with it, thought to debase that *fine carat*, which should compose the regal diadem? Are the fire-new

---

* This passage is nearly a repetition of what was said before; but as it contains the sum and substance of all I have ever said on such subjects, I have let it stand.

specimens of the principles of the Right-Liners, and of Sir Robert Filmer's patriarchal scheme, to be met with in *The Courier*, *The Day*, *The Sun*, and some time back, in *The Times*, handed about to be admired in the highest circle, like the new gold coinage of sovereigns and half-sovereigns? We do not know. It may seem to be *Latter Lammas*[5] with the doctrine at this time of day; but better late than never. By taking root in the soil of France, from which it was expelled (not quite so long as from our own), it may in time stretch out its feelers and strong suckers to this country; and present an altogether curious and novel aspect, by ingrafting the principles of the House of Stuart on the illustrious stock of the House of Brunswick.

'Miraturque novas frondes, et non sua poma.'[6]

What then is the People? We will answer first, by saying what it is not; and this we cannot do better than in the words of a certain author,[7] whose testimony on the subject is too important not to avail ourselves of it again in this place. That infatuated drudge of despotism, who at one moment asks, 'Where is the madman that maintains the doctrine of divine right?' and the next affirms, that 'Louis XVIII has the same right to the throne of France, independently of his merits or conduct, that Mr Coke of Norfolk has to his estate at Holkham',* has given us a tolerable clue to what we have to expect from that mild paternal sway to which he would so kindly make us and the rest of the world over, in hopeless perpetuity. In a violent philippic against the author of the *Political Register*, he thus inadvertently expresses himself: – 'Mr Cobbett had been sentenced to two years' imprisonment for a libel, and during the time that he was in Newgate, it was discovered that he had been in treaty with Government to avoid the sentence passed upon him; and that he had proposed to certain of the agents of Ministers, that if they would let him off, they might make what future use they pleased of him; *he would entirely*

---

* What is the amount of this right of Mr Coke's? It is not greater than that of the Lords Balmerino and Lovat to their estates in Scotland, or to the heads upon their shoulders, the one of which however were forfeited, and the other stuck upon Temple Bar, for maintaining, in theory and practice, that James II had the same right to the throne of these realms, independently of his merits or conduct, that Mr Coke has to his estate at Holkham. So thought they. So did not think George II.

betray the cause of the people; he would either write or not write, or *write against them*, as he had once done before, just as Ministers thought proper. To this, however, it was replied, that "Cobbett had written on too many sides already *to be worth a groat for the service of Government*"; and he accordingly suffered his confinement!' – We here then see plainly enough what it is that, in the opinion of this very competent judge, alone renders any writer 'worth a groat for the service of Government', *viz.* that he shall be able and willing entirely to betray the cause of the people. It follows from this principle (by which he seems to estimate the value of his lucubrations in the service of Government – we do not know whether the Government judge of them in the same way), that the cause of the people and the cause of the Government, who are represented as thus anxious to suborn their creatures to write against the people, are not the same but the reverse of one another. This slip of the pen in our professional retainer of legitimacy, though a libel on our own Government, is, notwithstanding, a general philosophic truth (the only one he ever hit upon), and an axiom in political mechanics, which we shall make the text of the following commentary.

What are the interests of the people? Not the interests of those who would betray them. Who is to judge of those interests? Not those who would suborn others to betray them. That Government is instituted for the benefit of the governed, there can be little doubt; but the interests of the Government (when once it becomes absolute and independent of the people) must be directly at variance with those of the governed. The interests of the one are common and equal rights: of the other, exclusive and invidious privileges. The essence of the first is to be shared alike by all, and to benefit the community in proportion as they are spread: the essence of the last is to be destroyed by communication, and to subsist only – in wrong of the people. Rights and privileges are a contradiction in terms: for if one has more than his right, others must have less. The latter are the deadly nightshade of the commonwealth, near which no wholesome plant can thrive, – the ivy clinging round the trunk of the British oak, blighting its verdure, drying up its sap, and oppressing its stately growth. The insufficient checks and balances opposed to the overbearing influence of hereditary rank and power in our own

Constitution, and in every Government which retains the least trace
of freedom, are so many illustrations of this principle, if it needed
any. The tendency in arbitrary power to encroach upon the liberties
and comforts of the people, and to convert the public good into a
stalking-horse to its own pride and avarice, has never (that we know)
been denied by any one but 'the professional gentleman',[8] who writes
in *The Day* and *New Times*. The great and powerful, in order to be
what they aspire to be, and what this gentleman would have them,
perfectly independent of the will of the people, ought also to be
perfectly independent of the assistance of the people. To be formally
invested with the attributes of Gods upon earth, they ought first to
be raised above its petty wants and appetites: they ought to give
proofs of the beneficence and wisdom of Gods, before they can be
trusted with the power. When we find them seated above the world,
sympathizing with the welfare, but not feeling the passions of men,
receiving neither good nor hurt, neither tilth nor tithe from them,
but bestowing their benefits as free gifts on all, they may then be
expected, but not till then, to rule over us like another Providence.
We may make them a present of all the taxes they do not apply to
their own use: they are perfectly welcome to all the power, to the
possession of which they are perfectly indifferent, and to the abuse
of which they can have no possible temptation. But Legitimate
Governments (flatter them as we will) are not another Heathen
mythology. They are neither so cheap nor so splendid as the Delphin
edition of Ovid's *Metamorphoses*. They are indeed 'Gods to punish',
but in other respects 'men of our infirmity'.[9] They do not feed on
ambrosia or drink nectar; but live on the common fruits of the earth,
of which they get the largest share, and the best. The wine they drink
is made of grapes: the blood they shed is that of their subjects: the
laws they make are not against themselves: the taxes they vote, they
afterwards devour. They have the same wants that we have: and
having the option, very naturally help themselves first, out of the
common stock, without thinking that others are to come after them.
With the same natural necessities, they have a thousand artificial
ones besides; and with a thousand times the means to gratify them,
they are still voracious, importunate; unsatisfied. Our State-paupers
have their hands in every man's dish, and fare sumptuously every

day. They live in palaces, and loll in coaches. In spite of Mr Malthus, their studs of horses consume the produce of our fields, their dog-kennels are glutted with the food which would maintain the children of the poor. They cost us so much a year in dress and furniture, so much in stars and garters, blue ribbons, and grand crosses, – so much in dinners, breakfasts, and suppers, and so much in suppers, breakfasts, and dinners.* These heroes of the Income-tax, Worthies of the Civil List, Saints of the Court-calendar (*compagnons du lys*[10]), have their naturals and non-naturals, like the rest of the world, but at a dearer rate. They are real *bona fide* personages, and do not live upon air. You will find it easier to keep them a week than a month; and at the end of that time, waking from the sweet dream of Legitimacy, you may say with Caliban, 'Why, what a fool was I to take this drunken monster for a God!'[11] In fact, the case on the part of the people is so far self-evident. There is but a limited earth and a limited fertility to supply the demands both of Government and people; and what the one gains in the division of the spoil, beyond its average proportion, the other must needs go without. Do you suppose that our gentlemen-placemen and pensioners would suffer so many wretches to be perishing in our streets and highways, if they could relieve their extreme misery without parting with any of their own superfluities? If the Government take a fourth of the produce of the poor man's labour, they will be rich, and he will be in want. If they can contrive to take one half of it by legal means, or by a stretch of arbitrary power, they will be just twice as rich, twice as insolent and tyrannical, and he will be twice as poor, twice as miserable and oppressed, in a mathematical ratio to the end of the chapter, that is, till the one can extort and the other endure no more. It is the same with respect to power. The will and passions of the great are not exerted in regulating the seasons, or rolling the planets round their orbits for our good, without fee or reward, but in controlling the will and passions of others, in making the follies and vices of mankind subservient to their own, and marring,

'Because men suffer it, their toy, the world'.[12]

---

* See the description of Gargantua in Rabelais.

This is self-evident, like the former. Their will cannot be paramount, while any one in the community, or the whole community together, has the power to thwart it. A King cannot attain absolute power, while the people remain perfectly free; yet what King would not attain absolute power? While any trace of liberty is left among a people, ambitious Princes will never be easy, never at peace, never of sound mind; nor will they ever rest or leave one stone unturned, till they have succeeded in destroying the very name of liberty, or making it into a bye-word, and in rooting out the germs of every popular right and liberal principle from a soil once sacred to liberty. It is not enough that they have secured the whole power of the state in their hands, – that they carry every measure they please without the chance of an effectual opposition to it: but a word uttered against it is torture to their ears, – a thought that questions their wanton exercise of the royal prerogative rankles in their breasts like poison. Till all distinctions of right and wrong, liberty and slavery, happiness and misery, are looked upon as matters of indifference, or as saucy, insolent pretensions, – are sunk and merged in their idle caprice and pampered self-will, they will still feel themselves 'cribbed, confined, and cabin'd in':[13] but if they can once more set up the doctrine of Legitimacy, 'the right divine of Kings to govern wrong',[14] and set mankind at defiance with impunity, they will then be 'broad and casing as the general air, whole as the rock'.[15] This is the point from which they set out, and to which by the grace of God and the help of man they may return again. Liberty is short and fleeting, a transient grace that lights upon the earth by stealth and at long intervals –

> 'Like the rainbow's lovely form,
> Evanishing amid the storm;
> Or like the Borealis race,
> That shift ere you can point their place;
> Or like the snow falls in the river,
> A moment white, then melts for ever'.[16]

But power is eternal; it is 'enthroned in the hearts of Kings'.[17] If you want the proofs, look at history, look at geography, look abroad; but do not look at home!

The power of an arbitrary King or an aspiring Minister does not increase with the liberty of the subject, but must be circumscribed by it. It is aggrandized by perpetual, systematic, insidious, or violent encroachments on popular freedom and natural right, as the sea gains upon the land by swallowing it up. – What then can we expect from the mild paternal sway of absolute power, and its sleek minions? What the world has always received at its hands, an abuse of power as vexatious, cowardly, and unrelenting, as the power itself was unprincipled, preposterous, and unjust. They who get wealth and power from the people, who drive them like cattle to slaughter or to market, 'and levy cruel wars, wasting the earth',[18] they who wallow in luxury, while the people are 'steeped in poverty to the very lips',[19] and bowed to the earth with unremitting labour, can have but little sympathy with those whose loss of liberty and property is their gain. What is it that the wealth of thousands is composed of? The tears, the sweat, and blood of millions. What is it that constitutes the glory of the Sovereigns of the earth? To have millions of men their slaves. Wherever the Government does not emanate (as in our own excellent Constitution) from the people, the principle of the Government, the *esprit de corps*, the point of honour, in all those connected with it, and raised by it to privileges above the law and above humanity, will be hatred to the people. Kings who would be thought to reign in contempt of the people, will show their contempt of them in every act of their lives. Parliaments, not chosen by the people, will only be the instruments of Kings, who do not reign in the hearts of the people, 'to betray the cause of the people'.[20] Ministers, not responsible to the people, will squeeze the last shilling out of them. *Charity begins at home*, is a maxim as true of Governments as of individuals. When the English Parliament insisted on its right of taxing the Americans without their consent, it was not from an apprehension that the Americans would, by being left to themselves, lay such heavy duties on their own produce and manufactures, as would afflict the generosity of the mother-country, and put the mild paternal sentiments of Lord North to the blush. If any future King of England should keep a wistful eye on the map of that country, it would rather be to hang it up as a trophy of legitimacy, and to 'punish the last successful example of a democratic rebellion', than from any yearnings of fatherly goodwill to the American people, or from finding his 'large heart' and capacity for good government, 'confined in too narrow room'[21] in the united kingdoms of Great Britain, Ireland, and Hanover. If Ferdinand VII refuses the South American patriots leave to plant the olive or the vine, throughout that vast continent, it is his pride, not his humanity, that steels his royal resolution.*

In 1781, the Controller-general of France, under Louis XVI, Monsieur Joly de Fleury, defined the people of France to be *un peuple serf, corvéable et baillable, à merci et miséricorde.*[22] When Louis XVIII as the Count de Lille, protested against his brother's accepting the Constitution of 1792 (he has since become an accepter of Constitutions himself, if not an observer of them), as compromising the rights and privileges of the noblesse and clergy as well as of the crown, he was right in considering the Bastille, or 'King's castle',[23] with the picturesque episode of the Man in the Iron Mask, the fifteen thousand *lettres de cachet,*[24] issued in the mild reign of Louis XV, *corvées,*[25] tithes, game-laws, holy water, the right of pillaging, imprisoning, massacring, persecuting, harassing, insulting, and ingeniously tormenting the minds and bodies of the whole French people at every moment of their lives, on every possible pretence, and without any check or control but their own mild paternal sentiments towards them, as among the *menus plaisirs,*[26] the chief points of etiquette, the immemorial privileges, and favourite amusements of Kings, Priests, and Nobles, from the beginning to the end of time, without which the bare title of King, Priest, or Noble, would not have been worth a groat.

The breasts of Kings and Courtiers then are not the safest depository of the interests of the people. But they know best what is for their good! Yes – to prevent it! The people may indeed feel their grievance, but their betters, it is said, must apply the remedy – which they take good care never to do! If the people want judgment in their own affairs (which is not certain, for they only meddle with their own

---

* The Government of Ovando, a Spanish Grandee and Knight of Alcantara, who had been sent over to Mexico soon after its conquest, exceeded in treachery, cruelty, wanton bloodshed, and deliberate extortion, that of all those who had preceded him; and the complaints became so loud, that Queen Isabel on her death-bed requested that he might be recalled; but Ferdinand found that Ovando had sent home *much gold,* and he retained him in his situation. – See Capt. Burney's *History of the Buccaneers.*

affairs when they are forcibly brought home to them in a way which they can hardly misunderstand), this is at any rate better than the want of sincerity, which would constantly and systematically lead their superiors to betray those interests, from their having other ends of their own to serve. It is better to trust to ignorance than to malice – to run the risk of sometimes miscalculating the odds than to play against loaded dice. The people would in this way stand as little chance in defending their purses or their persons against Mr C— or Lord C—, as an honest country gentleman would have had in playing at put or hazard with Count Fathom or Jonathan Wild.[27] A certain degree of folly, or rashness, or indecision, or even violence in attaining an object, is surely less to be dreaded than a malignant, deliberate, mercenary intention in others to deprive us of it. If the people must have attorneys, and the advice of counsel, let them have attorneys and counsel of their own choosing, not those who are employed by special retainer against them, or who regularly hire others *to betray their cause.*

— 'O silly sheep,
Come ye to seek the lamb here of the wolf?'[28]

This then is the cause of the people, the good of the people, judged of by common feeling and public opinion. Mr Burke contemptuously defines the people to be 'any faction that at the time can get the power of the sword into its hands'.[29] No: that may be a description of the Government, but it is not of the people. The people is the hand, heart, and head of the whole community acting to one purpose, and with a mutual and thorough consent. The hand of the people so employed to execute what the heart feels, and the head thinks, must be employed more beneficially for the cause of the people, than in executing any measures which the cold hearts, and contriving heads of any faction, with distinct privileges and interests, may dictate to betray their cause. The will of the people necessarily tends to the general good as its end; and it must attain that end, and can only attain it, in proportion as it is guided – First, by popular feeling, as arising out of the immediate wants and wishes of the great mass of the people, – secondly, by public opinion, as arising out of the impartial reason and enlightened intellect of the community. What is it that determines the opinion of any number of persons in things they actually feel in their practical and home results? Their common interest. What is it that determines their opinion in things of general inquiry, beyond their immediate experience or interest? Abstract reason. In matters of feeling and common sense, of which each individual is the best judge, the majority are in the right; in things requiring a greater strength of mind to comprehend them, the greatest power of understanding will prevail, if it has but fair play. These two, taken together, as the test of the practical measures or general principles of Government, must be right, cannot be wrong. It is an absurdity to suppose that there can be any better criterion of national grievances, or the proper remedies for them, than the aggregate amount of the actual, dear-bought experience, the honest feelings, and heart-felt wishes of a whole people, informed and directed by the greatest power of understanding in the community, unbiased by any sinister motive. Any other standard of public good or ill must, in proportion as it deviates from this, be vitiated in principle, and fatal in its effects. *Vox populi vox Dei*,[30] is the rule of all good Government: for in that voice, truly collected and freely expressed (not when it is made the servile echo of a corrupt Court, or a designing Minister), we have all the sincerity and all the wisdom of the community. If we could suppose society to be transformed into one great animal (like Hobbes's *Leviathan*[31]), each member of which had an intimate connexion with the head or Government, so that every want or intention of every individual in it could be made known and have its due weight, the State would have the same consciousness of its own wants and feelings, and the same interest in providing for them, as an individual has with respect to his own welfare. Can any one doubt that such a state of society in which the greatest knowledge of its interests was thus combined with the greatest sympathy with its wants, would realize the idea of a perfect Commonwealth? But such a Government would be the precise idea of a truly popular or *representative* Government. The opposite extreme is the purely hereditary and despotic form of Government, where the people are an inert, torpid mass, without the power, scarcely with the will, to make its wants or wishes known: and where the feelings of those who are at the head of the State, centre in their own exclusive interests, pride, passions, prejudices; and all their thoughts are employed in defeating the happiness and undermining the liberties of a country.

What is the People?
(Concluded)

March 14, 1818.

It is not denied that the people are best acquainted with their own wants, and most attached to their own interests. But then a question is started, as if the persons asking it were at a great loss for the answer, – Where are we to find the intellect of the people? Why, all the intellect that ever was is theirs. The public opinion expresses not only the collective sense of the whole people, but of all ages and nations, of all those minds that have devoted themselves to the love of truth and the good of mankind, – who have bequeathed their instructions, their hopes, and their example to posterity, – who have thought, spoke, written, acted, and suffered in the name and on the behalf of our common nature. All the greatest poets, sages, heroes, are ours originally, and by right. But surely Lord Bacon was a great man? Yes; but not because he was a lord. There is nothing of hereditary growth but pride and prejudice. That 'fine word Legitimate'[1] never produced any thing but bastard philosophy and patriotism! Even Burke was one of the people, and would have remained with the people to the last, if there had been no court-side for him to go over to. The King gave him his pension, not his understanding or his eloquence. It would have been better for him and for mankind if he had kept to his principles, and gone without his pension. It is thus that the tide of power constantly setting in against the people, swallows up natural genius and acquired knowledge in the vortex of corruption, and then they reproach us with our want of leaders of weight and influence, to stem the torrent. All that has ever been done for society, has, however, been done for it by this intellect, before it was cheapened

376

to be a cat's-paw of divine right. All discoveries and all improvements in arts, in science, in legislation, in civilization, in every thing dear and valuable to the heart of man, have been made by this intellect – all the triumphs of human genius over the rudest barbarism, the darkest ignorance, the grossest and most inhuman superstition, the most unmitigated and remorseless tyranny, have been gained for themselves by the people. Great Kings, great law-givers, great founders, and great reformers of religion, have almost all arisen from among the people. What have hereditary Monarchs, or regular Governments, or established priesthoods, ever done for the people? Did the Pope and Cardinals first set on foot the Reformation? Did the Jesuits attempt to abolish the Inquisition? For what one measure of civil or religious liberty did our own Bench of Bishops ever put themselves forward? What judge ever proposed a reform in the laws? Have not the House of Commons, with all their 'tried wisdom',[2] voted for every measure of Ministers for the last twenty-five years, except the Income-tax? It is the press that has done every thing for the people, and even for Governments. – 'If they had not ploughed with our heifer, they would not have found out our riddle.'[3] And it has done this by slow degrees, by repeated, incessant, and incredible struggles with the oldest, most inveterate, powerful, and active enemies of the freedom of the press and of the people, who wish, in spite of the nature of things and of society, to retain the idle and mischievous privileges they possess as the relics of barbarous and feudal times, who have an exclusive interest as a separate caste in the continuance of all existing abuses, and who plead a permanent *vested right* in the prevention of the progress of reason, liberty, and civilization. Yet they tax us with our want of intellect; and *we* ask them in return for their court-list of great names in arts or philosophy, for the coats of arms of their heroic vanquishers of error and intolerance, for their devout benefactors and royal martyrs of humanity. What are the claims of the people – the obvious, undoubted rights of common justice and humanity, forcibly withheld from them by pride, bigotry, and selfishness, – demanded for them, age after age, year after year, by the wisdom and virtue of the enlightened and disinterested part of mankind, and only grudgingly yielded up, with indecent, disgusting excuses, and sickening delays, when the burning

shame of their refusal can be no longer concealed by fear of favour
from the whole world. What did it not cost to abolish the Slave Trade?
How long will the Catholic Claims be withheld by our State-jugglers?
How long, and for what purpose? We may appeal, in behalf of the
people, from the interested verdict of the worst and weakest men
now living, to the disinterested reason of the best and wisest men
among the living and the dead. We appeal from the corruption of
Courts, the hypocrisy of zealots, and the dotage of hereditary imbecility, to the innate love of liberty in the human breast, and to the
growing intellect of the world. We appeal to the pen, and they answer
us with the point of the bayonet; and, at one time, when that had
failed, they were for recommending the dagger.* They quote Burke,
but rely on the Attorney-General. They hold Universal Suffrage to
be the most dreadful of all things, and a Standing Army the best
representatives of the people abroad and at home. They think Church-
and-King mobs good things, for the same reason that they are alarmed
at a meeting to petition for a Reform of Parliament. They consider
the cry of 'No Popery' a sound, excellent, and constitutional cry, –
but the cry of a starving population for food, strange and unnatural.
They exalt the war-whoop of the Stock Exchange into the voice of
undissembled patriotism, while they set down the cry for peace as
the work of the Jacobins, the ventriloquism of the secret enemies of
their country. The writers on the popular side of the question are
factious, designing demagogues, who delude the people to make tools
of them: but the government-writers, who echo every calumny, and
justify every encroachment on the people, are profound philosophers
and very honest men. Thus when Mr John Gifford, the Editor of the
Anti-Jacobin (not Mr William Gifford, who at present holds the same
office under Government, as the Editor of the *Quarterly Review*),
denounced Mr Coleridge as a person who had 'left his wife destitute
and his children fatherless',⁴ and proceeded to add – '*Ex hoc disce* his
friends Lamb and Southey' – we are to suppose that he was influenced
in this gratuitous statement purely by his love for his King and
country. Loyalty, patriotism, and religion, are regarded as the natural
virtues and plain unerring instincts of the common people: the mixture

* See Coleridge's *Friend*, No. 15.

of ignorance or prejudice is never objected to in these: it is only their love of liberty or hatred of oppression that are discovered, by the same liberal-minded junto, to be proofs of a base and vulgar disposition. The Bourbons are set over the immense majority of the French people against their will, because a talent for governing does not go with numbers. This argument was not thought of when Buonaparte tried to show his talent for governing the people of the Continent against their will, though he had quite as much talent as the Bourbons. Mr Canning rejoiced that the first successful resistance to Buonaparte was made in Russia, a country of barbarians and slaves. The heroic struggles of 'the universal Spanish nation'[5] in the cause of freedom and independence, have ended in the destruction of the Cortes and the restoration of the Inquisition, but without making the Duke of Wellington look thoughtful: – not a single renegado poet has vented his indignation in a single ode, elegy, or sonnet;[6] nor does Mr Southey 'make him a willow cabin at its gate, write loyal cantos of contemned love, and sing them loud even in the dead of the night!'[7] He indeed assures us[8] in the *Quarterly Review*, that the Inquisition was restored by the voice of the Spanish people. He also asks, in the same place, 'whether the voice of God was heard in the voice of the people at Jerusalem, when they cried, "Crucify him, crucify him"?'[9] We do not know; but we suppose, he would hardly go to the Chief Priests and Pharisees to find it. This great historian, politician, and logician, breaks out into a rhapsody against the old maxim, *vox populi vox Dei*, in the midst of an article of 55 pages, written expressly to prove that the last war was 'the most popular, *because* the most just and necessary war that ever was carried on'. He shrewdly asks, 'Has the *vox populi* been the *vox Dei* in France for the last twenty-five years?' But, at least, according to his own showing, it has been so in this country for all that period. We, however, do not think so. The voice of the country has been for war, because the voice of the King was for it, which was echoed by Parliament, both Lords and Commons, by Clergy and Gentry, and by the populace, till, as Mr Southey himself states in the same connected chain of reasoning, the cry for war became *so* popular, that all those who did not join in it (of which number the Poet-laureate himself was one) were 'persecuted, insulted, and injured in their persons, fame, and fortune'.[10] This is the true way of accounting for the fact, but it unfortunately knocks the Poet's inference on the head. Mr Locke has observed,[11] that there are not so many wrong opinions in the world as we are apt to believe, because most people take their opinions on trust from others. Neither are the opinions of the people their own, when they have been bribed or bullied into them by a mob of Lords and Gentlemen, following in full cry at the heels of the Court. The *vox populi* is the *vox Dei* only when it springs from the individual, unbiased feelings, and unfettered, independent opinion of the people. Mr Southey does not understand the terms of this good old adage, now that he is so furious against it: we fear, he understood them no better when he was as loudly in favour of it.

All the objections, indeed, to the voice of the people being the best rule for Government to attend to, arise from the stops and impediments to the expression of that voice, from the attempts to stifle or to give it a false bias, and to cut off its free and open communication with the head and heart of the people – by the Government itself. The sincere expression of the feelings of the people must be true; the full and free development of the public opinion must lead to truth, to the gradual discovery and diffusion of knowledge in this, as in all other departments of human inquiry. It is the interest of Governments in general to keep the people in a state of vassalage as long as they can – to prevent the expression of their sentiments, and the exercise and improvement of their understandings, by all the means in their power. They have a patent, and a monopoly, which they do not like to have looked into or to share with others. The argument for keeping the people in a state of lasting wardship, or for treating them as lunatics, incapable of self-government, wears a very suspicious aspect, as it comes from those who are trustees to the estate, or keepers of insane asylums. The long minority of the people would, at this rate, never expire, while those who had an interest had also the power to prevent them from arriving at years of discretion: their government-keepers have nothing to do but to drive the people mad by ill-treatment, and to keep them so by worse, in order to retain the pretence for applying the gag, the strait waistcoat, and the whip as long as they please. It is like the dispute between Mr Epps, the angry shopkeeper in the Strand, and his journeyman, whom he would restrict from setting up for himself. Shall we never serve out our apprenticeship to liberty? Must our indentures to slavery bind us for life? It is well, it is perfectly well. You teach us nothing, and you will not let us learn. You deny us education, like Orlando's eldest brother, and then 'stying us'[12] in the den of legitimacy, you refuse to let us take the management of our own affairs into our own hands, or to seek our fortunes in the world ourselves. You found a right to treat us with indignity on the plea of your own neglect and injustice. You abuse a trust in order to make it perpetual. You profit of our ignorance and of your own wrong. You degrade, and then enslave us; and by enslaving, you degrade us more, to make us more and more incapable of ever escaping from your selfish, sordid yoke. There is no end of this. It is the fear of the progress of knowledge and a *Reading Public*, that has produced all the fuss and bustle and cant about Bell and Lancaster's plans, Bible and Missionary, and Auxiliary and Cheap Tract Societies, and that when it was impossible to prevent our reading something, made the Church and State so anxious to provide us with that sort of food for our stomachs, which they thought best. The Bible is an excellent book; and when it becomes the Statesman's Manual, in its precepts of charity – not of beggarly alms-giving, but of peace on earth and good will to man, the people may read nothing else. It reveals the glories of the world to come, and records the preternatural dispensations of Providence to mankind two thousand years ago. But it does not describe the present state of Europe, or give an account of the measures of the last or of the next reign, which yet it is important the people of England should look to. We cannot learn from Moses and the Prophets what Mr Vansittart and the Jews are about in 'Change-alley. Those who prescribe us the study of the miracles and prophecies, themselves laugh to scorn the promised deliverance of Joanna Southcott and the Millennium. Yet they would have us learn patience and resignation from the miraculous interpositions of Providence recorded in the Scriptures. '*When the sky falls*'[13] – the proverb is somewhat musty.[14] The worst compliment ever paid to the Bible was the recommendation of it as a political palliative by the Lay Preachers of the day.

To put this question in a different light, we might ask, What is the public? and examine what would be the result of depriving the people of the use of their understandings in other matters as well as government – to subject them to the trammels of prescriptive prejudice and hereditary pretension. Take the stage as an example. Suppose Mr Kean should have a son, a little crook-kneed, raven-voiced, disagreeable, mischievous, stupid urchin, with the faults of his father's acting exaggerated tenfold, and none of his fine qualities, – what if Mr Kean should take it into his head to get out letters-patent to empower him and his heirs for ever, with this hopeful commencement, to play all the chief parts in tragedy, by the grace of God and the favour of the Prince Regent! What a precious race of tragedy kings and heroes we should have! They would not even play the villain with a good grace. The theatres would soon be deserted, and the race of the Keans would 'hold a barren sceptre' over empty houses, to be 'wrenched from them by an unlineal hand'![15] – But no! For it would be necessary to uphold theatrical order, the cause of the legitimate drama, and so to levy a tax on all those who stayed away from the theatre, or to drag them into it by force. Every one seeing the bayonet at the door, would be compelled to applaud the hoarse tones and lengthened pauses of the illustrious house of Kean; the newspaper critics would grow wanton in their praise, and all those would be held as rancorous enemies of their country, and of the prosperity of the stage, who did not join in the praises of the best of actors. What a falling off would there be from the present system of universal suffrage and open competition among the candidates, the frequency of rows in the pit, the noise in the gallery, the whispers in the boxes, and the lashing in the newspapers the next day!

In fact, the argument drawn from the supposed incapacity of the people against a representative Government, comes with the worst grace in the world from the patrons and admirers of hereditary government. Surely, if government were a thing requiring the utmost stretch of genius, wisdom, and virtue, to carry it on, the office of King would never even have been dreamt of as hereditary, any more than that of poet, painter, or philosopher. It is easy here 'for the Son to tread in the Sire's steady steps'.[16] It requires nothing but the will to do it. Extraordinary talents are not once looked for. Nay, a person, who would never have risen by natural abilities to the situation of churchwarden or parish beadle, succeeds by unquestionable right to the possession of a throne, and wields the energies of an empire, or decides the fate of the world, with the smallest possible share of human understanding. The line of distinction which separates the regal purple from the slabbering-bib, is sometimes fine indeed; as we see in the case of the two Ferdinands.[17] Any one above the rank of an idiot is supposed capable of exercising the highest functions of royal state. Yet these are the persons who talk of the people as a swinish multitude,[18] and taunt them with their want of refinement and philosophy.

*

The great problem of political science is not of so profoundly metaphysical or highly poetical a cast as Mr Burke represents it. It is simply a question on the one part, with how little expense of liberty and property the Government, 'that complex constable',[19] as it has been quaintly called, can keep the peace; and on the other part, for how great a sacrifice of both, the splendour of the throne and the safety of the state can be made a pretext. Kings and their Ministers generally strive to get their hands in our pockets, and their feet on our necks; the people and their representatives will be wise enough, if they can only contrive to prevent them; but this, it must be confessed, they do not always succeed in. For a people to be free, it is sufficient that they will to be free. But the love of liberty is less strong than the love of power, and is guided by a less sure instinct in attaining its object. Milton only spoke the sentiments of the English people of his day (sentiments too which they had acted upon), in strong language, when he said, in answer to a foreign pedant: – 'Liceat, quæso, populo qui servitutis jugum in cervicibus grave sentit, tam sapienti esse, tam docto, tamque nobili, ut sciat quid tyranno suo faciendum sit, etiamsi neque exteros neque grammaticos sciscitatum mittat.'[20] (Defensio pro populo Anglicano.) Happily the whole of the passage is not applicable to their descendants in the present day; but at all times a people may be allowed to know when they are oppressed, enslaved, and miserable, to feel their wrongs and to demand a remedy – from the superior knowledge and humanity of Ministers, who, if they cannot cure the State-malady, ought in decency, like other doctors, to resign their

authority over the patient. The people are not subject to fanciful
wants, speculative longings, or hypochondriacal complaints. Their
disorders are real, their complaints substantial and well-founded.
Their grumblings are in general seditions of the belly. They do not
cry out till they are hurt. They do not stand upon nice questions, or
trouble themselves with Mr Burke's Sublime and Beautiful; but when
they find the money conjured clean out of their pockets, and the
Constitution suspended over their heads, they think it time to look
about them. For example, poor Evans, that amateur of music and
politics (strange combination of tastes), thought it hard, no doubt, to
be sent to prison and deprived of his flute by a State-warrant, because
there was no ground for doing it by law; and Mr Hiley Addington,
being himself a flute-player, thought so too: though, in spite of this
romantic sympathy, the Minister prevailed over the musician, and
Mr Evans has, we believe, never got back his flute. For an act of
injustice, by the new system, if complained of 'forsooth',[21] becomes
justifiable by the very resistance to it: if not complained of, nobody
knows any thing about it, and so it goes equally unredressed in either
way. Or to take another obvious instance and sign of the times: a
tenant or small farmer who has been distrained upon and sent to
gaol or to the workhouse, probably thinks, and with some appearance
of reason, that he was better off before this change of circumstances;
and Mr Cobbett, in his twopenny *Registers*, proves to him so clearly,
that this change for the worse is owing to the war and taxes, which
have driven him out of his house and home, that Mr Cobbett himself
has been forced to quit the country to argue the question, whether
two and two make four, with Mr Vansittart, upon safer ground to
himself, and more equal ground to the Chancellor of the Exchequer.
Such questions as these are, one would think, within the verge of
common sense and reason. For any thing we could ever find, the
people have as much common sense and sound judgment as any other
class of the community. Their folly is second-hand, derived from
their being the dupe of the passions, interests, and prejudices of their
superiors. When they judge for themselves, they in general judge
right. At any rate, the way to improve their judgment in their own
concerns (and if they do not judge for themselves, they will infallibly
be cheated both of liberty and property, by those who kindly insist

on relieving them of that trouble) is not to deny them the use and exercise of their judgment altogether. Nothing can be pleasanter than one of the impositions of late attempted to be put upon the people, by persuading them that economy is no part of a wise Government. The people must be pretty competent judges of the cheapness of a Government. But it is pretended by our high-flying sinecurists and pensioners, that this is a low and vulgar view of the subject, taken up by interested knaves, like Paine and Cobbett, to delude, and, in the end, make their market of the people. With all the writers and orators who compose the band of gentlemen pensioners and their patrons, politics is entirely a thing of sentiment and imagination. To speak of the expenses of Government, as if it were a little paltry huckstering calculation of profit and loss, quite shocks their lofty, liberal, and disinterested notions. They have no patience with the people if they are not ready to sacrifice their all for the public good! This is something like a little recruiting cavalry-lieutenant we once met with, who, sorely annoyed at being so often dunned for the arrears of board and lodging by the people where he took up his quarters, exclaimed with the true broad Irish accent and emphasis − *'Vulgar ideas! These wretches always expect one to pay for what one has of them!'* Our modest lieutenant thought, that while he was employed on his Majesty's service, he had a right to pick the pockets of his subjects, and that if they complained of being fobbed of what was their own, they were blackguards and *no gentlemen*! Mr Canning hit upon nothing so good as this, in his luminous defence of his Lisbon Job![22]

But allow the people to be as gross and ignorant as you please, as base and stupid as you can make them or keep them, 'duller than the fat weed that roots itself at ease on Lethe's wharf',[23] − is nothing ever to rouse them? Grant that they are slow of apprehension − that they do not see till they feel. Is that a reason that they are not to feel then, neither? Would you blindfold them with the double bandages of bigotry, or quench their understandings with 'the dim suffusion',[24] 'the drop serene',[25] of Legitimacy, that 'they may roll in vain and find no dawn'[26] of liberty, no ray of hope? Because they do not see tyranny till it is mountain high, 'making Ossa like a wart',[27] are they not to feel its weight when it is heaped upon them, or to throw it off with giant strength and a convulsive effort? If they do not see the evil till it has grown enormous, palpable, and undeniable, is that a reason why others should then deny that it exists, or why it should not be removed? They do not snuff arbitrary power a century off: they are not shocked at it on the other side of the globe, or of the Channel: are they not therefore to see it, could it in time be supposed to stalk over their heads, to trample and grind them to the earth? If in their uncertainty how to deal with it, they sometimes strike random blows, if their despair makes them dangerous, why do not they, who, from their elevated situation, see so much farther and deeper into the principles and consequences of things – in their boasted wisdom prevent the causes of complaint in the people before they accumulate to a terrific height, and burst upon the heads of their oppressors? The higher classes, who would disqualify the people from taking the cure of their disorders into their own hands, might do this very effectually, by preventing the first symptoms of their disorders. They would do well, instead of abusing the blunders and brutishness of the multitude, to show their superior penetration and zeal in detecting the first approaches of mischief, in withstanding every encroachment on the comforts and rights of the people, in guarding every bulwark against the influence and machinations of arbitrary power, as a precious, inviolable, sacred trust. Instead of this, they are the first to be lulled into security, a security 'as gross as ignorance made drunk'[28] – the last to believe the consequences, because they are the last to feel them. Instead of this, the patience of the lower classes, in submitting to privations and insults, is only surpassed by the callousness of their betters in witnessing them. The one never set about the redress of grievances or the reform of abuses, till they are no longer to be borne; the others will not hear of it even then. It is for this reason, among others, that the *vox populi* is the *vox Dei*, that it is the agonizing cry of human nature raised, and only raised, against intolerable oppression and the utmost extremity of human suffering. The people do not rise up till they are trod down. They do not turn upon their tormentors till they are goaded to madness. They do not complain till the thumbscrews have been applied, and have been strained to the last turn. Nothing can ever wean the affections or confidence of a people from a Government (to which habit, prejudice, natural pride, perhaps old benefits and joint struggles for liberty have attached them) but an excessive degree of irritation and disgust, occasioned either by a sudden and violent stretch of power, contrary to the spirit and forms of the established Government, or by a blind and wilful adherence to old abuses and established forms, when the changes in the state of manners and opinion have rendered them as odious as they are ridiculous. The Revolutions of Switzerland, the Low Countries, and of America, are examples of the former – the French Revolution of the latter: our own Revolution of 1688 was a mixture of the two. As a general rule, it might be laid down, that for every instance of national resistance to tyranny, there ought to have been hundreds, and that all those which have been attempted ought to have succeeded. In the case of Wat Tyler, for instance, which has been so naturally dramatized by the Poet-laureate,[29] the rebellion was crushed, and the ringleaders hanged by the treachery of the Government; but the grievances of which they had complained were removed a few years after, and the rights they had claimed granted to the people, from the necessary progress of civilization and knowledge. Did not Mr Southey know, when he applied for an injunction against Wat Tyler, that the feudal system had been abolished long ago? – Again, as nothing rouses the people to resistance but extreme and aggravated injustice, so nothing can make them persevere in it, or push their efforts to a successful and triumphant issue, but the most open and unequivocal determination to brave their cries and insult their misery. They have no principle of union in themselves, and nothing brings or holds them together but the strong pressure of want, the stern hand of necessity – 'a necessity that is not chosen, but chooses, – a necessity paramount to deliberation, that admits of no discussion and demands no evidence, that can alone, [according to Mr Burke's theory] justify a resort to anarchy',[30] and that alone ever did or can produce it. In fine, there are but two things in the world, might and right. Whenever one of these is overcome, it is by the other. The triumphs of the people, or the stand which they at any time make against arbitrary sway, are the triumphs of reason and justice over the insolence of individual power and authority, which, unless as it is restrained, curbed, and corrected by popular feeling or public opinion, can be guided only by its own drunken, besotted, mad pride, selfishness and caprice, and must be productive of all the mischief, which it can wantonly or deliberately commit with impunity.

The people are not apt, like a fine lady, to affect the vapours of discontent; nor to volunteer a rebellion for the theatrical éclat of the thing. But the least plausible excuse, one kind word, one squeeze of the hand, one hollow profession of good will, subdues the soft heart of rebellion, (which is 'too foolish fond and pitiful'[31] to be a match for the callous hypocrisy opposed to it) dissolves and melts the whole fabric of popular innovation like butter in the sun. Wat Tyler is a case in point again. The instant the effeminate king and his unprincipled courtiers gave them fair words, they dispersed, relying in their infatuation on the word of the King as binding, on the oath of his officers as sincere; and no sooner were they dispersed than they cut off their leaders' heads, and poor John Ball's along with them, in spite of all his texts of Scripture. The story is to be seen in all the shop-windows, *written in very choice blank verse!*[32] – That the people are rash in trusting to the promises of their friends, is true; they are more rash in believing their enemies. If they are led to expect too much in theory, they are satisfied with too little in reality. Their anger is sometimes fatal while it lasts, but it is not roused very soon, nor does it last very long. Of all dynasties, anarchy is the shortest lived. They are violent in their revenge, no doubt; but it is because justice has been long denied them, and they have to pay off a very long score at a very short notice. What Cæsar says of himself, might be applied well enough to the people, that they 'did never wrong but with just cause'.[33] The errors of the people are the crimes of Governments. They apply sharp remedies to lingering diseases, and when they get sudden power in their hands, frighten their enemies, and wound themselves with it. They rely on brute force and the fury of despair, in proportion to the treachery which surrounds them, and to the degradation, the want of general information and mutual co-operation, in which they have been kept, on purpose to prevent them from ever acting in concert, with wisdom, energy, confidence, and calmness, for the public good. The American Revolution produced no horrors, because its enemies could not succeed in sowing the seeds of terror, hatred, mutual treachery, and universal dismay in the hearts of the people. The French Revolution, under the auspices of Mr Burke, and other friends of social order, was tolerably prolific of these horrors. But that should not be charged as the fault of the Revolution or of the people. Timely Reforms are the best preventives of violent Revolutions. If Governments are determined that the people shall have no redress, no remedies for their acknowledged grievances, but violent and desperate ones, they may thank themselves for the obvious consequences. Despotism must always have the most to fear from the reaction of popular fury, where it has been guilty of the greatest abuses of power, and where it has shown the greatest tenaciousness of those abuses, putting an end to all prospect of amicable arrangement, and provoking the utmost vengeance of its oppressed and insulted victims. This tenaciousness of power is the chief obstacle to improvement, and the cause of the revulsions which follow the attempts at it. In America, a free Government was easy of accomplishment, because it was not necessary, in building up, to pull down: there were no nuisances to abate. The thing is plain. Reform in old Governments is just like the new improvements in the front of Carlton House, that would go on fast enough but for the vile, old, dark, dirty, crooked streets, which cannot be removed without giving the inhabitants notice to quit. Mr Burke, in regretting these old institutions as the result of the wisdom of ages,[34] and not the remains of Gothic ignorance and barbarism, played the part of *Crockery*, in the farce of *Exit by Mistake*,[35] who sheds tears of affection over the loss of the old windows and buttresses of the houses that no longer jut out to meet one another, and stop up the way.

There is one other consideration which may induce hereditary Sovereigns to allow some weight to the arguments in favour of popular feeling and public opinion. They are the only security which they themselves possess individually for the continuance of their splendour and power. Absolute monarchs have nothing to fear from the people, but they have every thing to fear from their slaves and one another. Where power is lifted beyond the reach of the law or of public opinion, there is no principle to oppose it, and he who can obtain possession of the throne (by whatever means) is always the rightful possessor of it, till he is supplanted by a more fortunate or artful successor, and so on in a perpetual round of treasons, conspiracies, murders, usurpations, regicides, and rebellions, with which the people have nothing to do, but as passive, unconcerned spectators. — Where the son succeeds to the father's throne by assassination, without being amenable to public justice, he is liable to be cut off himself by the same means, and with the same impunity. The only thing that can give stability or confidence to power, is that very will of the people, and public censure exercised upon public acts, of which legitimate Sovereigns are so disproportionately apprehensive. For one regicide committed by the people, there have been thousands committed by Kings themselves. A Constitutional King of England reigns in greater security than the Persian Sophi, or the Great Mogul; and the Emperor of Turkey, or the Autocrat of all the Russias, has much more to fear from a cup of coffee or the bowstring, than the Prince Regent from the speeches and writings of all the Revolutionists in Europe. By removing the barrier of public opinion, which interferes with their own lawless acts, despotic Kings lay themselves open to the hand of the assassin, — and while they reign in contempt of the will, the voice, the heart and mind of a whole people, hold their crowns, and every moment of their lives at the mercy of the meanest of their slaves.

'Portrait of Croker'

*

Who is it that you meet sauntering along Pall-mall with fleering eyes, and nose turned up, as if the mud and the people offended him, – that has the look of an informer, or the keeper of a bagnio, or a dealer in marine stores, or an attorney struck off the list, – a walking nuisance, with the sense of smell added to it, a moving *nausea*, with whose stomach nothing agrees, and that seeks some object to vent its spleen and ill-humour upon, that turns another way, afraid to express it –

'A dog, in forehead; and in heart, a deer';[1]

that stops to look at a print shop with a supercilious air of indifference, as if he would be thought to understand, but scorned to approve any thing – that finds fault with Hogarth, and can see no grace in Raphael; with his round shoulders, *hulking* stoop, slouching greatcoat, and unwashed face, like the smut of his last night's conversation – that's let in and out of —— House,[2] like a night-cart, full of filth, and crawling with lies – the Thersites[3] of modern politics, the ring-leader of the Yahoos of the Press, the *ghoul* of the Boroughmongers; that preys on the carcase of patriot reputation; the Probert of the Allies, that 'bags the game' of liberty in the *Quarterly* that Duke Humphrey[4] slew in the field – a Jack-pudding in wit, a pretender to sense, a tool of power, who thinks that a nickname implies disgrace, as a title confers honour, that to calumniate is to convince, and whose genius is on an exact par with the taste and understanding of his employers; – whose highest ambition is to be a *cat's-paw*, whose leading principle is to advocate his own interest by betraying his country and his species; to whom the very names of LIBERTY, HUMANITY, VIRTUE, PATRIOT-

ISM, are a bye-word from the want of a single generous or manly feeling in his own breast; whose only pleasure is in malignity, and whose only pride is in degrading others to his own level; who affects literature, and fancies he writes like Tacitus, by leaving out the conjunction *and*; who helps himself to English out of Lindley Murray's *Grammar*, and maintains, with a pragmatical air, that no one writes it but himself; who conceals his own writings and publishes those of other people, which he procures from his relations at a lodging-house; who frightens elderly gentlewomen who ask him to dinner, by pleasantly offering to carve a 'Holy-Ghost Pye', that is, a Pigeon-Pye, and gallantly calling for a bit of the 'Leg of the Saviour', that is, a leg of Lamb; who afterwards props the Bible and the Crown with ribaldry and slander, but who has no objection to the Pope, the Turk or the Devil, provided they are on the side of his LEGITIMATE Patrons, and who keeps a fellow[5] even more impudent than himself, who, whenever the cause of humanity is mentioned, sticks his hands in his sides, and cries HUMBUG, and while nations are massacring, and the hopes of earth withered, plays a tune on the salt-box for the amusement of the Ladies and Gentlemen of Great Britain, and in honour of the Great Fûm?[6]

On the Prose-Style of Poets

I have but an indifferent opinion of the prose-style of poets: not that it is not sometimes good, nay, excellent; but it is never the better, and generally the worse from the habit of writing verse. Poets are winged animals, and can cleave the air, like birds, with ease to themselves and delight to the beholders; but like those 'feathered, two-legged things',[1] when they light upon the ground of prose and matter-of-fact, they seem not to have the same use of their feet.

What is a little extraordinary, there is a want of *rhythmus* and cadence in what they write without the help of metrical rules. Like persons who have been accustomed to sing to music, they are at a loss in the absence of the habitual accompaniment and guide to their judgment. Their style halts, totters, is loose, disjointed, and without expressive pauses or rapid movements. The measured cadence and regular *sing-song* of rhyme or blank verse have destroyed, as it were, their natural ear for the mere characteristic harmony which ought to subsist between the sound and the sense. I should almost guess the Author of *Waverley*[2] to be a writer of ambling verses from the desultory vacillation and want of firmness in the march of his style. There is neither *momentum* nor elasticity in it; I mean as to the *score*, or effect upon the ear. He has improved since in his other works: to be sure, he has had practice enough.* Poets either get into this incoherent, undetermined, shuffling style, made up of 'unpleasing flats and sharps',[3] of unaccountable starts and pauses, of doubtful odds

---

* Is it not a collateral proof that Sir Walter Scott is the Author of *Waverley*, that ever since these Novels began to appear, his Muse has been silent, till the publication of *Halidon-Hill*?

and ends, flirted about like straws in a gust of wind; or, to avoid it and steady themselves, mount into a sustained and measured prose (like the translation of Ossian's *Poems*, or some parts of Shaftesbury's *Characteristics*) which is more odious still, and as bad as being at sea in a calm. Dr Johnson's style (particularly in his *Rambler*), is not free from the last objection. There is a tune in it, a mechanical recurrence of the same rise and fall in the clauses of his sentences, independent of any reference to the meaning of the text, or progress or inflection of the sense. There is the alternate roll of his cumbrous cargo of words; his periods complete their revolutions at certain stated intervals, let the matter be longer or shorter, rough or smooth, round or square, different or the same. This monotonous and balanced mode of composition may be compared to that species of portrait-painting which prevailed about a century ago, in which each face was cast in a regular and preconceived mould. The eye-brows were arched mathematically as if with a pair of compasses, and the distances between the nose and mouth, the forehead and chin, determined according to a 'foregone conclusion',* and the features of the identical individual were afterwards accommodated to them, how they could!*

Horne Tooke used to maintain that no one could write a good prose-style, who was not accustomed to express himself *viva voce*, or to talk in company. He argued that this was the fault of Addison's prose, and that its smooth, equable uniformity, and want of sharpness and spirit, arose from his not having familiarized his ear to the sound of his own voice, or at least only among friends and admirers, where there was but little collision, dramatic fluctuation, or sudden contrariety of opinion to provoke animated discussion, and give birth to different intonations and lively transitions of speech. His style (in this view of it) was not indented, nor did it project from the surface. There was no stress laid on one word more than another — it did not hurry on or stop short, or sink or swell with the occasion: it was throughout equally insipid, flowing, and harmonious, and had the effect of a studied recitation rather than of a natural discourse. This would not have happened (so the Member for Old Sarum contended) had Addison laid himself out to argue at his club, or to speak in

* See the Portraits of Kneller, Richardson, and others.

public; for then his ear would have caught the necessary modulations of sound arising out of the feeling of the moment, and he would have transferred them unconsciously to paper. Much might be said on both sides of this question:* but Mr Tooke was himself an unintentional confirmation of his own argument; for the tone of his written compositions is as flat and unraised as his manner of speaking was hard and dry. Of the poet it is said by some one, that

> 'He murmurs by the running brooks
> A music sweeter than their own.'[5]

On the contrary, the celebrated person just alluded to might be said to grind the sentences between his teeth, which he afterwards committed to paper, and threw out crusts to the critics, or *bon-mots* to the Electors of Westminster (as we throw bones to the dogs), without altering a muscle, and without the smallest tremulousness of voice or eye!† I certainly so far agree with the above theory as to conceive that no style is worth a farthing that is not calculated to be read out, or that is not allied to spirited conversation: but I at the same time think the process of modulation and inflection may be quite as complete, or more so, without the external enunciation; and that an author had better try the effect of his sentences on his stomach than on his ear. He may be deceived by the last, not by the first. No person, I imagine, can dictate a good style; or spout his own compositions with impunity. In the former case, he will flounder on before the sense or words are ready, sooner than suspend his voice in air; and in the latter, he can supply what intonation he pleases, without consulting his readers. Parliamentary speeches sometimes read well aloud; but we do not find, when such persons sit down to write, that the prose-style of public speakers and great orators is the best, most

* Goldsmith was not a talker, though he blurted out his good things now and then: yet his style is gay and voluble enough. Pope was also a silent man; and his prose is timid and constrained, and his verse inclining to the monotonous.

† As a singular example of steadiness of nerves, Mr Tooke on one occasion had got upon the table at a public dinner to return thanks for his health having been drunk. He held a bumper of wine in his hand, but he was received with considerable opposition by one party, and at the end of the disturbance, which lasted for a quarter of an hour, he found the wine glass still full to the brim.

natural, or varied of all others. It has almost always either a professional twang, a mechanical rounding off, or else is stunted and unequal. Charles Fox was the most rapid and even *hurried* of speakers; but his written style halts and creeps slowly along the ground* – A speaker is necessarily kept within bounds in expressing certain things, or in pronouncing a certain number of words, by the limits of the breath or power of respiration: certain sounds are observed to join in harmoniously or happily with others: an emphatic phrase must not be placed, where the power of utterance is enfeebled or exhausted, &c. All this must be attended to in writing, (and will be so unconsciously by a practised hand), or there will be *hiatus in manuscriptis*. The words must be so arranged, in order to make an efficient readable style, as 'to come trippingly off the tongue'.[6] Hence it seems that there is a natural measure of prose in the feeling of the subject and the power of expression in the voice, as there is an artificial one of verse in the number and co-ordination of the syllables; and I conceive that the trammels of the last do not (where they have been long worn) greatly assist the freedom or the exactness of the first.

Again, in poetry, from the restraints in many respects, a greater number of inversions, or a latitude in the transposition of words is allowed, which is not conformable to the strict laws of prose. Consequently, a poet will be at a loss, and flounder about for the common or (as we understand it) *natural* order of words in prose-composition. Dr Johnson endeavoured to give an air of dignity and novelty to his diction by affecting the order of words usual in poetry. Milton's prose has not only this draw-back, but it has also the

---

* I have been told, that when Sheridan was first introduced to Mr Fox, what cemented an immediate intimacy between them was the following circumstance. Mr Sheridan had been the night before to the House of Commons; and being asked what his impression was, said he had been principally struck with the difference of manner between Mr Fox and Lord Stormont. The latter began by declaring in a slow, solemn, drawling, nasal tone that 'when he considered the enormity and the unconstitutional tendency of the measures just proposed, he was hurried away in a torrent of passion and a whirlwind of impetuosity', pausing between every word and syllable; while the first said (speaking with the rapidity of lightning, and with breathless anxiety and impatience), that 'such was the magnitude, such the importance, such the vital interest of this question, that he could not help imploring, he could not help adjuring the House to come to it with the utmost calmness, the utmost coolness, the utmost deliberation'. This trait of discrimination instantly won Mr Fox's heart.

disadvantage of being formed on a classic model. It is like a fine translation from the Latin; and indeed, he wrote originally in Latin. The frequency of epithets and ornaments, too, is a resource for which the poet finds it difficult to obtain an equivalent. A direct, or simple prose-style seems to him bald and flat; and, instead of forcing an interest in the subject by severity of description and reasoning, he is repelled from it altogether by the absence of those obvious and meretricious allurements, by which his senses and his imagination have been hitherto stimulated and dazzled. Thus there is often at the same time a want of splendour and a want of energy in what he writes, without the invocation of the Muse – *invita Minerva*.[7] It is like setting a rope-dancer to perform a tumbler's tricks – the hardness of the ground jars his nerves; or it is the same thing as a painter's attempting to carve a block of marble for the first time – the coldness chills him, the colourless uniformity distracts him, the precision of form demanded disheartens him. So in prose-writing, the severity of composition required damps the enthusiasm, and cuts off the resources of the poet. He is looking for beauty, when he should be seeking for truth; and aims at pleasure, which he can only communicate by increasing the sense of power in the reader. The poet spreads the colours of fancy, the illusions of his own mind, round every object, *ad libitum*;[8] the prose-writer is compelled to extract his materials patiently and bit by bit, from his subject. What he adds of ornament, what he borrows from the pencil, must be sparing, and judiciously inserted. The first pretends to nothing but the immediate indulgence of his feelings: the last has a remote practical purpose. The one strolls out into the adjoining fields or groves to gather flowers: the other has a journey to go, sometimes through dirty roads, and at others through untrodden and difficult ways. It is this effeminacy, this immersion in sensual ideas, or craving after continual excitement, that spoils the poet for his prose-tasks. He cannot wait till the effect comes of itself, or arises out of the occasion: he must force it upon all occasions, or his spirit droops and flags under a supposed imputation of dullness. He can never drift with the current, but is always hoisting sail, and has his streamers flying. He has got a striking simile on hand; he *lugs* it in with the first opportunity, and with little connexion, and so defeats his object. He has a story to tell: he tells it in the first page, and where it would come in well, has nothing to say; like Goldsmith,[9] who having to wait upon a Noble Lord, was so full of himself and of the figure he should make, that he addressed a set speech, which he had studied for the occasion, to his Lordship's butler, and had just ended as the nobleman made his appearance. The prose ornaments of the poet are frequently beautiful in themselves, but do not assist the subject. They are pleasing excrescences — hindrances, not helps in an argument. The reason is, his embellishments in his own walk grow out of the subject by natural association; that is, beauty gives birth to kindred beauty, grandeur leads the mind on to greater grandeur. But in treating a common subject, the link is truth, force of illustration, weight of argument, not a graceful harmony in the immediate ideas; and hence the obvious and habitual clue which before guided him is gone, and he hangs on his patch-work, tinsel finery at random, in despair, without propriety, and without effect. The poetical prose-writer stops to describe an object, if he admires it, or thinks it will bear to be dwelt on: the genuine prose-writer only alludes to or characterizes it in passing, and with reference to his subject. The prose-writer is master of his materials: the poet is the slave of his style. Every thing showy, every thing extraneous tempts him, and he reposes idly on it: he is bent on pleasure, not on business. He aims at effect, at captivating the reader, and yet is contented with common-place ornaments, rather than none. Indeed, this last result must necessarily follow, where there is an ambition to shine, without the effort to dig for jewels in the mine of truth. The habits of a poet's mind are not those of industry or research: his images come to him, he does not go to them; and in prose-subjects, and dry matters-of-fact and close reasoning, the natural stimulus that at other times warms and rouses, deserts him altogether. He sees no unhallowed visions, he is inspired by no day-dreams. All is tame, literal, and barren, without the Nine. Nor does he collect his strength to strike fire from the flint by the sharpness of collision, by the eagerness of his blows. He gathers roses, he steals colours from the rainbow. He lives on nectar and ambrosia. He 'treads the primrose path of dalliance',[10] or ascends 'the highest heaven of invention',[11] or falls flat to the ground. *He is nothing, if not fanciful!*[12]

I shall proceed to explain these remarks, as well as I can, by a few instances in point.

It has always appeared to me that the most perfect prose-style, the most powerful, the most dazzling, the most daring, that which went the nearest to the verge of poetry, and yet never fell over, was Burke's. It has the solidity, and sparkling effect of the diamond: all other *fine writing* is like French paste or Bristol-stones[13] in the comparison. Burke's style is airy, flighty, adventurous, but it never loses sight of the subject; nay, is always in contact with, and derives its increased or varying impulse from it. It may be said to pass yawning gulfs 'on the unsteadfast footing of a spear':[14] still it has an actual resting-place and tangible support under it — it is not suspended on nothing. It differs from poetry, as I conceive, like the chamois from the eagle: it climbs to an almost equal height, touches upon a cloud, overlooks a precipice, is picturesque, sublime — but all the while, instead of soaring through the air, it stands upon a rocky cliff, clambers up by abrupt and intricate ways, and browses on the roughest bark,[15] or crops the tender flower. The principle which guides his pen is truth, not beauty — not pleasure, but power. He has no choice, no selection of subject to flatter the reader's idle taste, or assist his own fancy: he must take what comes, and make the most of it. He works the most striking effects out of the most unpromising materials, by the mere activity of his mind. He rises with the lofty, descends with the mean, luxuriates in beauty, gloats over deformity. It is all the same to him, so that he loses no particle of the exact, characteristic, extreme impression of the thing he writes about, and that he communicates this to the reader, after exhausting every possible mode of illustration, plain or abstracted, figurative or literal. Whatever stamps the original image more distinctly on the mind, is welcome. The nature of his task precludes continual beauty; but it does not preclude continual ingenuity, force, originality. He had to treat of political questions, mixed modes, abstract ideas, and his fancy (or poetry, if you will) was ingrafted on these artificially, and as it might sometimes be thought, violently, instead of growing naturally out of them, as it would spring of its own accord from individual objects and feelings. There is a resistance in the *matter* to the illustration applied to it — the concrete and abstract are hardly co-ordinate; and therefore it is that, when the first difficulty is overcome, they must agree more closely in the essential qualities, in order that the coincidence may be complete. Otherwise, it is good for nothing; and you justly charge the author's style with being loose, vague, flaccid, and imbecile. The poet has been said

'To make us heirs
Of truth and pure delight in endless lays.'[16]

Not so the prose-writer, who always mingles clay with his gold, and often separates truth from mere pleasure. He can only arrive at the last through the first. In poetry, one pleasing or striking image obviously suggests another: the increasing the sense of beauty or grandeur is the principle of composition: in prose, the professed object is to impart conviction, and nothing can be admitted by way of ornament or relief, that does not add new force or clearness to the original conception. The two classes of ideas brought together by the orator or impassioned prose-writer, to wit, the general subject and the particular image, are so far incompatible, and the identity must be more strict, more marked, more determinate, to make them coalesce to any practical purpose. Every word should be a blow: every thought should instantly grapple with its fellow. There must be a weight, a precision, a conformity from association in the tropes and figures of animated prose to fit them to their place in the argument, and make them *tell*, which may be dispensed with in poetry, where there is something much more congenial between the subject-matter and the illustration —

'Like beauty making beautiful old rime!'[17]

What can be more remote, for instance, and at the same time more apposite, more *the same*, than the following comparison of the English Constitution to 'the proud Keep of Windsor',[18] in the celebrated *Letter to a Noble Lord*?

'Such are *their* ideas;[19] such *their* religion, and such *their* law. But as to *our* country and *our* race, as long as the well-compacted structure of our church and state, the sanctuary, the holy of holies of that ancient law, defended by reverence, defended by power — a fortress at once and a temple* — shall stand inviolate on the brow of the British Sion; as long as the British Monarchy — not more limited than

*   *'Templum in modum arcis.'*

                TACITUS of the Temple of Jerusalem.

fenced by the orders of the State — shall, like the proud Keep of Windsor, rising in the majesty of proportion, and girt with the double belt of its kindred and coeval towers; as long as this awful structure shall oversee and guard the subjected land, so long the mounds and dykes of the low, fat, Bedford level will have nothing to fear from all the pickaxes of all the levellers of France. As long as our Sovereign Lord the King, and his faithful subjects, the Lords and Commons of this realm — the triple cord which no man can break; the solemn, sworn, constitutional frank-pledge of this nation; the firm guarantees of each other's being, and each other's rights; the joint and several securities, each in its place and order, for every kind and every quality of property and of dignity — As long as these endure, so long the Duke of Bedford is safe: and we are all safe together — the high from the blights of envy and the spoliations of rapacity; the low from the iron hand of oppression and the insolent spurn of contempt. Amen! and so be it: and so it will be,

> "*Dum domus Æneæ Capitoli immobile saxum*
> *Accolet; imperiumque pater Romanus habebit*".'[20]

Nothing can well be more impracticable to a simile than the vague and complicated idea which is here embodied in one; yet how finely, how nobly it stands out, in natural grandeur, in royal state, with double barriers round it to answer for its identity, with 'buttress, frieze, and coigne of 'vantage' for the imagination to 'make its pendant bed and procreant cradle',[21] till the idea is confounded with the object representing it — the wonder of a kingdom; and then how striking, how determined the descent, 'at one fell swoop',[22] to the 'low, fat, Bedford level'! Poetry would have been bound to maintain a certain decorum, a regular balance between these two ideas; sterling prose throws aside all such idle respect to appearances, and with its pen, like a sword, 'sharp and sweet',[23] lays open the naked truth! The poet's Muse is like a mistress, whom we keep only while she is young and beautiful, *durante bene placito*;[24] the Muse of prose is like a wife, whom we take during life, *for better for worse*. Burke's execution, like that of all good prose, savours of the texture of what he describes, and his pen slides or drags over the ground of his subject, like the painter's pencil. The most rigid fidelity and the most fanciful extravagance meet, and are reconciled in his pages. I never pass Windsor but I think of this passage in Burke, and hardly know to which I am indebted most for enriching my moral sense, that or the fine picturesque stanza in Gray,

> 'From Windsor's heights the expanse below
> Of mead, of lawn, of wood survey', &c.[25]

I might mention that the so much admired description in one of the India speeches, of Hyder Ally's army (I think it is) which 'now hung like a cloud upon the mountain, and now burst upon the plain like a thunder-bolt',[26] would do equally well for poetry or prose. It is a bold and striking illustration of a naturally impressive object. This is not the case with the Abbé Sieyès's far-famed 'pigeon-holes',[27] nor with the comparison of the Duke of Bedford to 'the Leviathan, tumbling about his unwieldy bulk in the ocean of royal bounty'.[28] Nothing here saves the description but the force of the invective; the startling truth, the vehemence, the remoteness, the aptitude, the perfect peculiarity and coincidence of the allusion. No writer would ever have thought of it but himself; no reader can ever forget it. What is there in common, one might say, between a Peer of the Realm, and 'that sea-beast', of those

> 'Created hugest that swim the ocean-stream'?[29]

Yet Burke has knit the two ideas together, and no man can put them asunder. No matter how slight and precarious the connection, the length of line it is necessary for the fancy to give out in keeping hold of the object on which it has fastened, he seems to have 'put his hook in the nostrils'[30] of this enormous creature of the crown, that empurples all its track through the glittering expanse of a profound and restless imagination!

In looking into the *Iris* of last week, I find the following passages, in an article on the death of Lord Castlereagh.

'The splendour of Majesty leaving the British metropolis, careering along the ocean, and landing in the capital of the North, is distinguished only by glimpses through the dense array of clouds in which Death hid himself, while he struck down to the dust the stateliest courtier near the throne, and the broken train of which pursues and crosses the Royal progress wherever its glories are presented to the eye of imagination . . .

'The same indefatigable mind – a mind of all work – which thus ruled the Continent with a rod of iron, the sword – within the walls of the House of Commons ruled a more distracted region with a more subtle and finely-tempered weapon, the tongue; and truly, if this *was* the only weapon his Lordship wielded there, where he had daily to encounter, and frequently almost alone, enemies more formidable than Buonaparte, it must be acknowledged that he achieved greater victories than Demosthenes or Cicero ever gained in far more easy fields of strife; nay, he wrought miracles of speech, outvying those miracles of song, which Orpheus is said to have performed, when not only men and brutes, but rocks, woods, and mountains, followed the sound of his voice and lyre . . .

'But there was a worm at the root of the gourd that flourished over his head in the brightest sunshine of a court; both perished in a night, and in the morning, that which had been his glory and his shadow, covered him like a shroud; while the corpse, notwithstanding all his honours, and titles, and offices, lay unmoved in the place where it fell, till a judgment had been passed upon him, which the poorest peasant escapes when he dies in the ordinary course of nature.'

Sheffield Advertiser, Aug. 20, 1822.

This, it must be confessed, is very unlike Burke: yet Mr Montgomery is a very pleasing poet, and a strenuous politician. The whole is *travelling out of the record*,[31] and to no sort of purpose. The author is constantly getting away from the impression of his subject, to envelop himself in a cloud of images, which weaken and perplex, instead of adding force and clearness to it. Provided he is figurative, he does not care how common-place or irrelevant the figures are, and he wanders on, delighted in a labyrinth of words, like a truant school-boy, who is only glad to have escaped from his task. He has a very slight hold of his subject, and is tempted to let it go for any fallacious ornament of style. How obscure and circuitous is the allusion to 'the clouds in which Death hid himself, to strike down the stateliest courtier near the throne'! How hackneyed is the reference to Demosthenes and Cicero, and how utterly quaint and unmeaning is the ringing the changes upon Orpheus and his train of men, beasts, woods, rocks, and mountains in connection with Lord Castlereagh! But he is better pleased with this classical fable than with the death of the Noble Peer, and delights to dwell upon it, to however little use. So he is glad to take advantage of the scriptural idea of a gourd; not to enforce, but as a relief to his reflections; and points his conclusion with a puling sort of common-place, that a peasant, who dies a natural death, has no Coroner's Inquest to sit upon him. All these are the faults of the ordinary poetical style. Poets think they are bound, by the tenor of their indentures to the Muses, to 'elevate and surprise'[32] in every line; and not having the usual resources at hand in common or abstracted subjects, aspire to the end without the means. They make, or pretend, an extraordinary interest where there is none. They are ambitious, vain, and indolent — more busy in preparing idle ornaments, which they take their chance of bringing in somehow or other, than intent on eliciting truths by fair and honest inquiry. It should seem as if they considered prose as a sort of waiting-maid to poetry, that could only be expected to wear her mistress's cast-off finery. Poets have been said to succeed best in fiction; and the account here given may in part explain the reason. That is to say, they must choose their own subject, in such a manner as to afford them continual opportunities of appealing to the senses and exciting the fancy. Dry details, abstruse speculations, do not give scope to vividness of description; and, as they cannot bear to be considered dull, they become too often affected, extravagant, and insipid.

I am indebted to Mr Coleridge[33] for the comparison of poetic prose to the second-hand finery of a lady's maid (just made use of). He himself is an instance of his own observation, and (what is even worse) of the opposite fault — an affectation of quaintness and originality. With bits of tarnished lace and worthless frippery, he assumes a sweeping oriental costume, or borrows the stiff dresses of our ancestors, or starts an eccentric fashion of his own. He is swelling and turgid — everlastingly aiming to be greater than his subject; filling his fancy with fumes and vapours in the pangs and throes of miraculous parturition, and bringing forth only *still births*. He has an incessant craving, as it were, to exalt every idea into a metaphor, to expand every sentiment into a lengthened mystery, voluminous and vast, confused and cloudy. His style is not succinct, but incumbered with a train of words and images that have no practical, and only a possible relation to one another – that add to its stateliness, but impede its march. One of his sentences winds its 'forlorn way obscure'[34] over the page like a patriarchal procession with camels laden, wreathed turbans, household wealth, the whole riches of the author's mind poured out upon the barren waste of his subject. The palm-tree spreads its sterile branches overhead, and the land of promise is seen in the distance. All this is owing to his wishing to overdo every thing – to make something more out of every thing than it is, or than it is worth. The simple truth does not satisfy him – no direct proposition fills up the moulds of his understanding. All is foreign, far-fetched, irrelevant, laboured, unproductive. To read one of his disquisitions is like hearing the variations to a piece of music without the score. Or, to vary the simile, he is not like a man going a journey by the stage-coach along the high-road, but is always getting into a balloon, and mounting into the air, above the plain ground of prose. Whether he soars to the empyrean, or dives to the centre (as he sometimes does), it is equally to get away from the question before him, and to prove that he owes every thing to his own mind. His object is to invent; he scorns to imitate. The business of prose is the contrary. But Mr Coleridge is a poet, and his thoughts are free.

I think the Poet-laureate is a much better prose-writer. His style has an antique quaintness, with a modern familiarity. He has just a sufficient sprinkling of *archaisms*, of allusions to old Fuller, and Burton, and Latimer, to set off or qualify the smart flippant tone of his apologies for existing abuses, or the ready, galling virulence of his personal invectives. Mr Southey is a faithful historian, and no inefficient partisan. In the former character, his mind is tenacious of facts; and in the latter, his spleen and jealousy prevent the 'extravagant and erring spirit'[35] of the poet from losing itself in Fancy's endless maze. He 'stoops to *earth*',[36] at least, and prostitutes his pen to some purpose (not at the same time losing his own soul, and gaining nothing by it) – and he vilifies Reform, and praises the reign of George III in good set terms, in a straightforward, intelligible, practical, pointed way. He is not buoyed up by conscious power out of the reach of common apprehensions, but makes the most of the obvious advantages he possesses. You may complain of a pettiness and petulance of manner, but certainly there is no want of spirit or facility of execution. He does not waste powder and shot in the air, but loads his piece, takes a level aim, and hits his mark. One would say (though his Muse is ambidexter) that he wrote prose with his right hand; there is nothing awkward, circuitous, or feeble in it. 'The words of Mercury are harsh after the songs of Apollo':[37] but this would not apply to him. His prose-lucubrations are pleasanter reading than his poetry. Indeed, he is equally practised and voluminous in both; and it is no improbable conjecture, that Mr Southey may have had some idea of rivalling the reputation of Voltaire in the extent, the spirit, and the versatility of his productions in prose and verse, except that he has written no tragedies but *Wat Tyler*!

To my taste, the Author of *Rimini*,[38] and Editor of the *Examiner*, is among the best and least corrupted of our poetical prose-writers. In his light but well-supported columns we find the raciness, the sharpness, and sparkling effect of poetry, with little that is extravagant or far-fetched, and no turgidity or pompous pretension. Perhaps there is too much the appearance of relaxation and trifling (as if he had escaped the shackles of rhyme), a caprice, a levity, and a disposition to innovate in words and ideas. Still the genuine master-spirit of the prose-writer is there; the tone of lively, sensible conversation; and this may in part arise from the author's being himself an animated talker. Mr Hunt wants something of the heat and earnestness of the political partisan; but his familiar and miscellaneous papers have all the ease, grace, and point of the best style of Essay-writing. Many of his effusions in the *Indicator* show, that if he had devoted himself exclusively to that mode of writing, he inherits more of the spirit of Steele than any man since his time.

Lord Byron's prose is bad; that is to say, heavy, laboured, and coarse: he tries to knock some one down with the butt-end of every line, which defeats his object — and the style of the Author of *Waverley* (if he comes fairly into this discussion) as mere style, is villainous. It is pretty plain he is a poet; for the sound of names runs mechanically in his ears, and he rings the changes unconsciously on the same words in a sentence, like the same rhymes in a couplet.

Not to spin out this discussion too much, I would conclude by observing, that some of the old English prose-writers (who were not poets) are the best, and, at the same time, the most *poetical* in the favourable sense. Among these we may reckon some of the old divines, and Jeremy Taylor at the head of them. There is a flush like the dawn over his writings; the sweetness of the rose, the freshness of the morning-dew. There is a softness in his style, proceeding from the tenderness of his heart: but his head is firm, and his hand is free. His materials are as finely wrought up as they are original and attractive in themselves. Milton's prose-style savours too much of poetry, and, as I have already hinted, of an imitation of the Latin. Dryden's is perfectly unexceptionable, and a model, in simplicity, strength, and perspicuity, for the subjects he treated of.

On Reason and Imagination

I hate people who have no notion of any thing but generalities, and forms, and creeds, and naked propositions, even worse than I dislike those who cannot for the soul of them arrive at the comprehension of an abstract idea. There are those (even among philosophers) who, deeming that all truth is contained within certain outlines and common topics, if you proceed to add colour or relief from individuality, protest against the use of rhetoric as an illogical thing; and if you drop a hint of pleasure or pain as ever entering into 'this breathing world',[1] raise a prodigious outcry against all appeals to the passions.

It is, I confess, strange to me that men who pretend to more than usual accuracy in distinguishing and analysing, should insist that in treating of human nature, of moral good and evil, the nominal differences are alone of any value, or that in describing the feelings and motives of men, any thing that conveys the smallest idea of what those feelings are in any given circumstances, or can by parity of reason ever be in any others, is a deliberate attempt at artifice and delusion — as if a knowledge or representation of things as they really exist (rules and definitions apart) was a proportionable departure from the truth. They stick to the table of contents, and never open the volume of the mind. They are for having maps, not pictures of the world we live in: as much as to say that a bird's-eye view of things contains the truth, the whole truth, and nothing but the truth. If you want to look for the situation of a particular spot, they turn to a pasteboard globe, on which they fix their wandering gaze; and because you cannot find the object of your search in their bald 'abridgements', tell you there is no such place, or that it is not worth inquiring after. They had better confine their studies to the celestial sphere and the signs of the zodiac; for there they will meet with no petty details to boggle at, or contradict their vague conclusions. Such persons would make excellent theologians, but are very indifferent philosophers. — To pursue this geographical reasoning a little farther. They may say that the map of a county or shire, for instance, is too large, and conveys a disproportionate idea of its relation to the whole. And we say that their map of the globe is too small, and conveys no idea of it at all.

—'In the world's volume
Our Britain shows as of it, but not in it;
In a great pool a swan's nest:'[2]

but is it really so? What! the county is bigger than the map at any rate: the representation falls short of the reality, by a million degrees, and you would omit it altogether in order to arrive at a balance of power in the nonentities of the understanding, and call this keeping within the bounds of sense and reason; and whatever does not come within those self-made limits is to be set aside as frivolous or monstrous. But 'there are more things between heaven and earth than were ever dreamt of in this philosophy'.[3] They cannot get them all in, *of the size of life*, and therefore they reduce them on a graduated scale, till they think they can. So be it, for certain necessary and general purposes, and in compliance with the infirmity of human intellect: but at other times, let us enlarge our conceptions to the dimensions of the original objects; nor let it be pretended that we have outraged truth and nature, because we have encroached on your diminutive mechanical standard. There is no language, no description that can strictly come up to the truth and force of reality: all we have to do is to guide our descriptions and conclusions by the reality. A certain proportion must be kept: we must not invert the rules of moral perspective. Logic should enrich and invigorate its decisions by the use of imagination; as rhetoric should be governed in its application, and guarded from abuse by the checks of the understanding. Neither, I apprehend, is sufficient alone. The mind can conceive only one or a few things in their integrity: if it proceeds to more, it must have recourse to artificial substitutes, and judge by comparison merely. In the former case, it may select the least worthy, and so distort the truth of things, by giving a hasty preference: in the latter, the danger is that it may refine and abstract so much as to attach no idea at all to them, corresponding with their practical value, or their influence on the minds of those concerned with them. Men act from individual impressions; and to know mankind, we should be acquainted with nature. Men act from passion; and we can only judge of passion by sympathy. Persons of the dry and husky class above spoken of, often seem to think even nature itself an interloper on their flimsy theories. They prefer the shadows in Plato's cave to the actual objects without it. They consider men 'as mice in an air-pump',[4] fit only for their experiments; and do not consider the rest of the universe, or 'all the mighty world of eye and ear',[5] as worth any notice at all. This is making short, but not sure work. Truth does not lie *in vacuo*,[6] any more than in a well. We must improve our concrete experience of persons and things into the contemplation of general rules and principles; but without being grounded in individual facts and feelings, we shall end as we began, in ignorance.

It is mentioned in a short account[7] of the *Last Moments of Mr Fox*, that the conversation at the house of Lord Holland (where he died) turning upon Mr Burke's style, that Noble Person objected to it as too gaudy and meretricious, and said that it was more profuse of flowers than fruit. On which Mr Fox observed, that though this was a common objection, it appeared to him altogether an unfounded one; that on the contrary, the flowers often concealed the fruit beneath them, and the ornaments of style were rather an hindrance than an advantage to the sentiments they were meant to set off. In confirmation of this remark, he offered to take down the book, and translate a page any where into his own plain, natural style; and by his doing so, Lord Holland was convinced that he had often missed the thought from having his attention drawn off to the dazzling imagery. Thus people continually find fault with the colours of style as incompatible with the truth of the reasoning, but without any foundation whatever. If it were a question about the figure of two triangles, and any person were to object that one triangle was green and the other yellow, and bring this to bear upon the acuteness or obtuseness of the angles, it would be obvious to remark that the colour had nothing to do with the question. But in a dispute whether two objects are coloured alike, the discovery, that one is green and the other yellow, is fatal. So with respect to moral truth (as distinct from mathematical), whether a thing is good or evil, depends on the quantity of passion, of feeling, of pleasure and pain connected with it, and with which we must be made acquainted in order to come to a sound conclusion, and not on the inquiry, whether it is round or square. Passion, in short, is the essence, the chief ingredient in moral truth; and the warmth of passion is sure to kindle the light of imagination on the objects around it. The 'words that glow' are almost inseparable from the 'thoughts that burn'.[8] Hence logical reason and practical truth are *disparates*. It is easy to raise an outcry against violent invectives, to talk loud against extravagance and enthusiasm, to pick a quarrel with every thing but the most calm, candid, and qualified statement of facts: but there are enormities to which no words can do adequate justice. Are we then, in order to form a complete idea of them, to omit every circumstance of aggravation, or to suppress every feeling of impatience that arises out of the details, lest we should be accused of giving way to the influence of prejudice and passion? This would be to falsify the impression altogether, to misconstrue reason, and fly in the face of nature. Suppose, for instance, that in the discussions on the Slave-Trade, a description to the life was given of the horrors of the *Middle Passage* (as it was termed), that you saw the manner in which thousands of wretches, year after year, were stowed together in the hold of a slave-ship, without air, without light, without food, without hope, so that what they suffered in reality was brought home to you in imagination, till you felt in sickness of heart as one of them, could it be said that this was a prejudging of the case, that your knowing the extent of the evil disqualified you from pronouncing sentence upon it, and that your disgust and abhorrence were the effects of a heated imagination? No. Those evils that inflame the imagination and make the heart sick, ought not to leave the head cool. This is the very test and measure of the degree of the enormity, that it involuntarily staggers and appals the mind. If it were a common iniquity, if it were slight and partial, or necessary, it would not have this effect; but it very properly carries away the feelings, and (if you will) overpowers the judgment, because it is a mass of evil so monstrous and unwarranted as not to be endured, even in thought. A man on the rack does not suffer the less, because the extremity of anguish takes away his command of feeling and attention to appearances. A pang inflicted on humanity is not the less real, because it stirs up sympathy in the breast of humanity. Would you tame down the glowing language of justifiable passion into that of cold indifference, of self-complacent, sceptical reasoning, and thus take out the sting of indignation from the mind of the spectator? Not, surely, till you have removed the nuisance by the levers that strong feeling alone can set at work, and have thus taken away the pang of suffering that caused it! Or say that the question were proposed to you, whether, on some occasion, you should thrust your hand into the flames, and were coolly told that you were not at all to consider the pain and anguish it might give you, nor suffer yourself to be led away by any such idle appeals to natural sensibility, but to refer the decision to some abstract, technical ground of propriety, would you not laugh in your adviser's face? Oh! no; where our own interests are concerned, or where we are sincere in our professions of regard, the pretended distinction between sound judgment and lively imagination is quickly done away with. But I would not wish a better or more philosophical standard of morality, than that we should think and feel towards others as we should, if it were our own case. If we look for a higher standard than this, we shall not find it; but shall lose the substance for the shadow! Again, suppose an extreme or individual instance is brought forward in any general question, as that of the cargo of sick slaves that were thrown overboard as so much *live lumber* by the captain of a Guinea vessel, in the year 1775, which was one of the things that first drew the attention of the public to this nefarious traffic,* or the practice of suspending contumacious negroes in cages to have their eyes pecked out, and to be devoured alive by birds of prey — Does this form no rule, because the mischief is solitary or excessive? The rule is absolute; for we feel that nothing of the kind could take place, or be tolerated for an instant, in any system that was not rotten at the core. If such things are ever done in any circumstances with impunity, we know what must be done every day under the same sanction. It shows that there is an utter deadness to every principle of justice or feeling of

* See *Memoirs of Granville Sharp*, by Prince Hoare, Esq.

humanity; and where this is the case, we may take out our tables of abstraction, and set down what is to follow through every gradation of petty, galling vexation, and wanton, unrelenting cruelty. A state of things, where a single instance of the kind can possibly happen without exciting general consternation, ought not to exist for half an hour. The parent, hydra-headed injustice ought to be crushed at once with all its viper brood. Practices, the mention of which makes the flesh creep, and that affront the light of day, ought to be put down the instant they are known, without inquiry and without repeal.

There was an example of eloquent moral reasoning connected with this subject, given in the work just referred to, which was not the less solid and profound, because it was produced by a burst of strong personal and momentary feeling. It is what follows: – 'The name of a person having been mentioned in the presence of Naimbanna (a young African chieftain), who was understood by him to have publicly asserted something very degrading to the general character of Africans, he broke out into violent and vindictive language. He was immediately reminded of the Christian duty of forgiving his enemies; upon which he answered nearly in the following words: – "If a man should rob me of my money, I can forgive him; if a man should shoot at me, or try to stab me, I can forgive him; if a man should sell me and all my family to a slave-ship, so that we should pass all the rest of our days in slavery in the West Indies, I can forgive him; but" (added he, rising from his seat with much emotion) "if a man takes away the character of the people of my country, I never can forgive him." Being asked why he would not extend his forgiveness to those who took away the character of the people of his country, he answered: "If a man should try to kill me, or should sell me and my family for slaves, he would do an injury to as many as he might kill or sell; but if any one takes away the character of Black people, that man injures Black people all over the world; and when he has once taken away their character, there is nothing which he may not do to Black people ever after. That man, for instance, will beat Black men, and say, *Oh, it is only a Black man, why should not I beat him?* That man will make slaves of Black people; for, when he has taken away their character, he will say, *Oh, they are only Black people, why should not I make them slaves?* That man will take away all the people of Africa if he can catch them; and if you ask him, But why do you take away all these people? he will say, *Oh! they are only Black people – they are not like White people – why should I not take them?* That is the reason why I cannot forgive the man who takes away the character of the people of my country." ' – *Memoirs of Granville Sharpe.*

I conceive more real light and vital heat is thrown into the argument by this struggle of natural feeling to relieve itself from the weight of a false and injurious imputation, than would be added to it by twenty volumes of tables and calculations of the *pros* and *cons* of right and wrong, of utility and inutility, in Mr Bentham's hand-writing. In allusion to this celebrated person's theory of morals, I will here go a step farther, and deny that the dry calculation of consequences is the sole and unqualified test of right and wrong; for we are to take into the account (as well) the reaction of these consequences upon the mind of the individual and the community. In morals, the cultivation of a *moral sense* is not the last thing to be attended to – nay, it is the first. Almost the only unsophisticated or spirited remark that we meet with in Paley's *Moral Philosophy,*[9] is one which is also to be found in Tucker's *Light of Nature* – namely, that in dispensing charity to common beggars we are not to consider so much the good it may do the object of it, as the harm it will do the person who refuses it. A sense of compassion is involuntarily excited by the immediate appearance of distress, and a violence and injury is done to the kindly feelings by withholding the obvious relief, the trifling pittance in our power. This is a remark, I think, worthy of the ingenious and amiable author from whom Paley borrowed it. So with respect to the atrocities committed in the Slave-Trade, it could not be set up as a doubtful plea in their favour, that the actual and intolerable sufferings inflicted on the individuals were compensated by certain advantages in a commercial and political point of view – in a moral sense they *cannot* be compensated. They hurt the public mind: they harden and sear the natural feelings. The evil is monstrous and palpable; the pretended good is remote and contingent. In morals, as in philosophy, *De non apparentibus et non existentibus eadem est ratio.*[10] What does not touch the heart, or come home to the feelings, goes comparatively for little or nothing. A benefit that exists merely in possibility, and is judged of only by the forced dictates of the understanding, is not a set-off against an evil (say of equal magnitude in itself) that strikes upon the senses, that haunts the imagination, and lacerates the human heart. A spectacle of deliberate cruelty, that shocks every one that sees and hears of it, is not to be justified by any calculations of cold-blooded self-interest − is not to be permitted in any case. It is prejudged and self-condemned. Necessity has been therefore justly called 'the tyrant's plea'.[11] It is no better with the mere doctrine of utility, which is the sophist's plea. Thus, for example, an infinite number of lumps of sugar put into Mr Bentham's artificial ethical scales would never weigh against the pounds of human flesh, or drops of human blood, that are sacrificed to produce them. The taste of the former on the palate is evanescent; but the others sit heavy on the soul. The one is an object to the imagination: the others only to the understanding. But man is an animal compounded both of imagination and understanding; and, in treating of what is good for man's nature, it is necessary to consider both. A calculation of the mere ultimate advantages, without regard to natural feelings and affections, may improve the external face and physical comforts of society, but will leave it heartless and worthless in itself. In a word, the sympathy of the individual with the consequences of his own act is to be attended to (no less than the consequences themselves) in every sound system of morality; and this must be determined by certain natural laws of the human mind, and not by rules of logic or arithmetic.

The aspect of a moral question is to be judged of very much like the face of a country, by the projecting points, by what is striking and memorable, by that which leaves traces of itself behind, or 'casts its shadow before'.[12] Millions of acres do not make a picture; nor the calculation of all the consequences in the world a sentiment. We must have some outstanding object for the mind, as well as the eye, to dwell on and recur to − something marked and decisive to give a tone and texture to the moral feelings. Not only is the attention thus roused and kept alive; but what is most important as to the principles of action, the desire of good or hatred of evil is powerfully excited. But all individual facts and history come under the head of what these people call *Imagination*. All full, true, and particular accounts they consider as romantic, ridiculous, vague, inflammatory. As a case in point, one of this school of thinkers[13] declares that he was qualified to write a better History of India from having never been there than if he had, as the last might lead to local distinctions or party-prejudices; that is to say, that he could describe a country better at second-hand than from original observation, or that from having seen no one object, place, or person, he could do ampler justice to the whole. It might be maintained, much on the same principle, that an artist would paint a better likeness of a person after he was dead, from description or different sketches of the face, than from having seen the individual living man. On the contrary, I humbly conceive that the seeing half a dozen wandering Lascars in the streets of London gives one a better idea of the soul of India, that cradle of the world, and (as it were) garden of the sun, than all the charts, records, and statistical reports that can be sent over, even under the clerical administration of Mr Canning. *Ex uno omnes.*[14] One Hindoo differs more from a citizen of London than he does from all other Hindoos; and by seeing the two first, man to man, you know comparatively and essentially what they are, nation to nation. By a very few specimens you fix the great leading differences, which are nearly the same throughout. Any one thing is a better representative of its kind, than all the words and definitions in the world can be. The sum total is indeed different from the particulars; but it is not easy to guess at any general result, without some previous induction of particulars and appeal to experience.

'What can we reason, but from what we know?'[15]

Again, it is quite wrong, instead of the most striking illustrations of human nature, to single out the stalest and tritest, as if they were most authentic and infallible; not considering that from the extremes you may infer the means, but you cannot from the means infer the extremes in any case. It may be said that the extreme and individual cases may be retorted upon us: − I deny it, unless it be with truth. The imagination is an *associating* principle; and has an instinctive perception when a thing belongs to a system, or is only an exception to it. For instance, the excesses committed by the victorious besiegers of a town do not attach to the nation committing them, but to the nature of that sort of warfare, and are common to both sides. They may be struck off the score of national prejudices. The cruelties exercised upon slaves, on the other hand, grow out of the relation between master and slave; and the mind intuitively revolts at them as such. The cant about the horrors of the French Revolution is mere cant — every body knows it to be so: each party would have retaliated upon the other: it was a civil war, like that for a disputed succession: the general principle of the right or wrong of the change remained untouched. Neither would these horrors have taken place, except from Prussian manifestos, and treachery within: there were none in the American, and have been none in the Spanish Revolution. The massacre of St Bartholomew arose out of the principles of that religion which exterminates with fire and sword, and keeps no faith with heretics. — If it be said that nicknames, party watch-words, bugbears, the cry of 'No Popery', &c. are continually played off upon the imagination with the most mischievous effect, I answer that most of these bugbears and terms of vulgar abuse have arisen out of abstruse speculation or barbarous prejudice, and have seldom had their root in real facts or natural feelings. Besides, are not general topics, rules, exceptions, endlessly bandied to and fro, and balanced one against the other by the most learned disputants? Have not three-fourths of all the wars, schisms, heart-burnings in the world begun on mere points of controversy? — There are two classes whom I have found given to this kind of reasoning against the use of our senses and feelings in what concerns human nature, *viz.* knaves and fools. The last do it, because they think their own shallow dogmas settle all questions best without any farther appeal; and the first do it, because they know that the refinements of the head are more easily got rid of than the suggestions of the heart, and that a strong sense of injustice, excited by a particular case in all its aggravations, tells more against them than all the distinctions of the jurists. Facts, concrete existences, are stubborn things, and are not so soon tampered with or turned about to any point we please, as mere names and abstractions. Of these last it may be said,

'A breath can *mar* them, as a breath has made':[16]

and they are liable to be puffed away by every wind of doctrine, or baffled by every plea of convenience. I wonder that Rousseau gave in to this cant about the want of soundness in rhetorical and imaginative reasoning; and was so fond of this subject, as to make an abridgement of Plato's rhapsodies upon it, by which he was led to expel poets from his commonwealth. Thus two of the most flowery writers are those who have exacted the greatest severity of style from others. Rousseau was too ambitious of an exceedingly technical and scientific mode of reasoning, scarcely attainable in the mixed questions of human life, (as may be seen in his *Social Contract* – a work of great ability, but extreme formality of structure) and it is probable he was led into this error in seeking to overcome his too great warmth of natural temperament and a tendency to indulge merely the impulses of passion. Burke, who was a man of fine imagination, had the good sense (without any of this false modesty) to defend the moral uses of the imagination, and is himself one of the grossest instances of its abuse.

It is not merely the fashion among philosophers – the poets also have got into a way of scouting individuality as beneath the sublimity of their pretensions, and the universality of their genius. The philosophers have become mere logicians, and their rivals mere rhetoricians; for as these last must float on the surface, and are not allowed to be harsh and crabbed and recondite like the others, by leaving out the individual, they become common-place. They cannot reason, and they must declaim. Modern tragedy, in particular, is no longer like a vessel making the voyage of life, and tossed about by the winds and waves of passion, but is converted into a handsomely-constructed steam-boat, that is moved by the sole expansive power of words. Lord Byron has launched several of these ventures lately (if ventures they may be called) and may continue in the same strain as long as he pleases. We have not now a number of *dramatis personæ* affected by particular incidents and speaking according to their feelings, or as the occasion suggests, but each mounting the rostrum, and delivering his opinion on fate, fortune, and the entire consummation of things. The individual is not of sufficient importance to occupy his own thoughts or the thoughts of others. The poet fills his page with *grandes pensées*. He covers the face of nature with the beauty of his sentiments and the brilliancy of his paradoxes. We have the subtleties of the head, instead of the workings of the heart, and possible justifications instead of the actual motives of conduct. This all seems to proceed on a false estimate of individual nature and the value of human life. We have been so used to count by millions of late, that we think the units that compose them nothing; and are so prone to trace remote principles, that we neglect the immediate results. As an instance of the opposite style of dramatic dialogue, in which the persons speak for themselves, and to one another, I will give, by way of illustration, a passage from an old tragedy, in which a brother has just caused his sister to be put to a violent death.

> '*Bosola.* Fix your eye here.
> *Ferdinand.* Constantly.
> *Bosola.* Do you not weep?
> Other sins only speak; murther shrieks out:
> The element of water moistens the earth;
> But blood flies upwards, and bedews the heavens.
> *Ferdinand.* Cover her face: mine eyes dazzle; she died young.
> *Bosola.* I think not so: her infelicity
> Seem'd to have years too many.
> *Ferdinand.* She and I were twins:
> And should I die this instant, I had lived
> Her time to a minute.'

DUCHESS OF MALFI, Act IV. Scene 2.

How fine is the constancy with which he first fixes his eye on the dead body, with a forced courage, and then, as his resolution wavers, how natural is his turning his face away, and the reflection that strikes him on her youth and beauty and untimely death, and the thought that they were twins, and his measuring his life by hers up to the present period, as if all that was to come of it were nothing! Now, I would fain ask whether there is not in this contemplation of the interval that separates the beginning from the end of life, of a life too so varied from good to ill, and of the pitiable termination of which the person speaking has been the wilful and guilty cause, enough to 'give the mind pause'?[17] Is not that revelation as it were of the whole extent of our being which is made by the flashes of passion and stroke of calamity, a subject sufficiently staggering to have place in legitimate tragedy? Are not the struggles of the will with untoward events and the adverse passions of others as interesting and instructive in the representation as reflections on the mutability of fortune or inevitableness of destiny, or on the passions of men in general? The tragic Muse does not merely utter muffled sounds: but we see the paleness on the cheek, and the life-blood gushing from the heart! The interest we take in our own lives, in our successes or disappointments, and the *home* feelings that arise out of these, when well described, are the clearest and truest mirror in which we can see the image of human nature. For in this sense each man is a microcosm. What he is, the rest are — whatever his joys and sorrows are composed of, theirs are the same — no more, no less.

'One touch of nature makes the whole world kin.'[18]

But it must be the genuine touch of nature, not the outward flourishes and varnish of art. The spouting, oracular, didactic figure of the poet no more answers to the living man, than the lay-figure of the painter does. We may well say to such a one,

'Thou hast no speculation in those eyes
That thou dost glare with: thy bones are marrowless,
Thy blood is cold'![19]

Man is (so to speak) an endless and infinitely varied repetition: and if we know what one man feels, we so far know what a thousand feel in the sanctuary of their being. Our feeling of general humanity is at once an aggregate of a thousand different truths, and it is also the same truth a thousand times told. As is our perception of this original truth, the root of our imagination, so will the force and richness of the general impression proceeding from it be. The boundary of our sympathy is a circle which enlarges itself according to its propulsion from the centre — the heart. If we are imbued with a deep sense of individual weal or woe, we shall be awe-struck at the idea of humanity in general. If we know little of it but its abstract and common properties, without their particular application, their force or degrees, we shall care just as little as we know either about the whole or the individuals. If we understand the texture and vital feeling, we then can fill up the outline, but we cannot supply the former from having the latter given. Moral and poetical truth is like expression in a picture — the one is not to be attained by smearing over a large canvas, nor the other by bestriding a vague topic. In such matters, the most pompous sciolists are accordingly found to be the greatest contemners of human life. But I defy any great tragic writer to despise that nature which he understands, or that heart which he has probed, with all its rich bleeding materials of joy and sorrow. The subject may not be a source of much triumph to him, from its alternate light and shade, but it can never become one of supercilious indifference. He must feel a strong reflex interest in it, corresponding to that which he has depicted in the characters of others. Indeed, the object and end of playing, 'both at the first and now, is to hold the mirror up to nature',[20] to enable us to feel for others as for ourselves, or to embody a distinct interest out of ourselves by the force of imagination and passion. This is summed up in the wish of the poet —

'To feel what others are, and know myself a man'.[21]

If it does not do this, it loses both its dignity and its proper use.

Whether Genius is Conscious of its Powers?

No really great man ever thought himself so. The idea of greatness in the mind answers but ill to our knowledge — or to our ignorance of ourselves. What living prose-writer, for instance, would think of comparing himself with Burke? Yet would it not have been equal presumption or egotism in him to fancy himself equal to those who had gone before him — Bolingbroke or Johnson or Sir William Temple? Because his rank in letters is become a settled point with us, we conclude that it must have been quite as self-evident to him, and that he must have been perfectly conscious of his vast superiority to the rest of the world. Alas! not so. No man is truly himself, but in the idea which others entertain of him. The mind, as well as the eye, 'sees not itself, but by reflection from some other thing'.[1] What parity can there be between the effect of habitual composition on the mind of the individual, and the surprise occasioned by first reading a fine passage in an admired author; between what we do with ease, and what we thought it next to impossible ever to be done; between the reverential awe we have for years encouraged, without seeing reason to alter it, for distinguished genius, and the slow, reluctant, unwelcome conviction that after infinite toil and repeated disappointments, and when it is too late and to little purpose, we have ourselves at length accomplished what we at first proposed; between the insignificance of our petty, personal pretensions, and the vastness and splendour which the atmosphere of imagination lends to an illustrious name? He who comes up to his own idea of greatness, must always have had a very low standard of it in his mind. 'What a pity', said some one, 'that Milton had not the pleasure of reading *Paradise Lost*!'[2] He could not read it, as we do, with the weight of impression that a hundred years of admiration have added to it — 'a phœnix gazed by all'[5] — with the sense of the number of editions it has passed through with still increasing reputation, with the tone of solidity, time-proof, which it has received from the breath of cold, envious maligners, with the sound which the voice of Fame has lent to every line of it! The writer of an ephemeral production may be as much dazzled with it as the public: it may sparkle in his own eyes for a moment, and be soon forgotten by every one else. But no one can anticipate the suffrages of posterity. Every man, in judging of himself, is his own contemporary. He may feel the gale of popularity, but he cannot tell how long it will last. His opinion of himself wants distance, wants time, wants numbers, to set it off and confirm it. He must be indifferent to his own merits, before he can feel a confidence in them. Besides, every one must be sensible of a thousand weaknesses and deficiencies in himself; whereas Genius only leaves behind it the monuments of its strength. A great name is an abstraction of some one excellence: but whoever fancies himself an abstraction of excellence, so far from being great, may be sure that he is a blockhead, equally ignorant of excellence or defect, of himself or others. Mr Burke, besides being the author of the *Reflections*, and the *Letter to a Noble Lord*, had a wife and son; and had to think as much about them as we do about him. The imagination gains nothing by the minute details of personal knowledge.

On the other hand, it may be said that no man knows so well as the author of any performance what it has cost him, and the length of time and study devoted to it. This is one, among other reasons, why no man can pronounce an opinion upon himself. The happiness of the result bears no proportion to the difficulties overcome or the pains taken. *Materiam superabat opus*,[4] is an old and fatal complaint. The definition of genius is that it acts unconsciously; and those who have produced immortal works, have done so without knowing how or why. The greatest power operates unseen, and executes its appointed task with as little ostentation as difficulty. Whatever is done best, is done from the natural bent and disposition of the mind. It is only where our incapacity begins, that we begin to feel the obstacles, and to set an undue value on our triumph over them. Correggio, Michael Angelo, Rembrandt, did what they did without premeditation or effort – their works came from their minds as a natural birth – if you had asked them why they adopted this or that style, they would have answered, *because they could not help it*, and because they knew of no other. So Shakespeare says:

> 'Our poesy is as a gum which issues
> From whence 'tis nourish'd. The fire i' th' flint
> Shows not till it be struck: our gentle flame
> Provokes itself; and, like the current, flies
> Each bound it chafes.'[5]

Shakespeare himself was an example of his own rule, and appears to have owed almost every thing to chance, scarce any thing to industry or design. His poetry flashes from him, like the lightning from the summer-cloud, or the stroke from the sun-flower. When we look at the admirable comic designs of Hogarth, they seem, from the unfinished state in which they are left, and from the freedom of the pencilling, to have cost him little trouble; whereas the *Sigismunda* is a very laboured and comparatively feeble performance, and he accordingly set great store by it. He also thought highly of his portraits, and boasted that 'he could paint equal to Vandyke, give him his time and let him choose his subject'.[6] This was the very reason why he could not. Vandyke's excellence consisted in this, that he could paint a fine portrait of any one at sight: let him take ever so much pains or choose ever so bad a subject, he could not help making something of it. His eye, his mind, his hand was cast in the mould of grace and delicacy. Milton again is understood to have preferred *Paradise Regained* to his other works. This, if so, was either because he himself was conscious of having failed in it; or because others thought he had. We are willing to think well of that which we know wants our favourable opinion, and to prop the rickety bantling. Every step taken, *invitâ Minervâ*,[7] costs us something, and is set down to account; whereas we are borne on the full tide of genius and success into the very haven of our desires, almost imperceptibly. The strength of the impulse by which we are carried along prevents the sense of difficulty or resistance: the true inspiration of the Muse is soft and balmy as the air we breathe; and indeed, leaves us little to boast of, for the effect hardly seems to be our own.

There are two persons who always appear to me to have worked under this involuntary, silent impulse more than any others; I mean Rembrandt and Correggio. It is not known that Correggio ever saw a picture of any great master. He lived and died obscurely in an obscure village. We have few of his works, but they are all perfect. What truth, what grace, what angelic sweetness are there! Not one line or tone that is not divinely soft or exquisitely fair; the painter's mind rejecting, by a natural process, all that is discordant, coarse, or unpleasing. The whole is an emanation of pure thought. The work grew under his hand as if of itself, and came out without a flaw, like the diamond from the rock. He knew not what he did; and looked at each modest grace as it stole from the canvas with anxious delight and wonder. Ah! gracious God! not he alone; how many more in all time have looked at their works with the same feelings, not knowing but they too may have done something divine, immortal, and finding in that sole doubt ample amends for pining solitude, for want, neglect, and an untimely fate. Oh! for one hour of that uneasy rapture, when the mind first thinks it has struck out something that may last for ever; when the germ of excellence bursts from nothing on the startled sight! Take, take away the gaudy triumphs of the world, the long deathless shout of fame, and give back that heart-felt sigh with which the youthful enthusiast first weds immortality as his secret bride! And thou too, Rembrandt! who wert a man of genius, if ever painter was a man of genius, did this dream hang over you as you painted that strange picture of *Jacob's Ladder*?[8] Did your eye strain over those gradual dusky clouds into futurity, or did those white-vested, beaked figures babble to you of fame as they approached? Did you know what you were about, or did you not paint much as it happened? Oh! if you had thought once about yourself, or any thing but the subject, it would have been all over with 'the glory, the intuition, the amenity',[9] the dream had fled, the spell had been broken. The hills would not have looked like those we see in sleep – that tatterdemalion figure of Jacob, thrown on one side, would not have slept as if the breath was fairly taken out of his body. So much do Rembrandt's pictures savour of the soul and body of reality, that the thoughts seem identical with the objects – if there had been the least question what he should have done, or how he should do it, or how far he had succeeded, it would have spoiled every thing. Lumps of light hung upon his pencil and fell upon his canvas like dew-drops: the shadowy veil was drawn over his backgrounds by the dull, obtuse finger of night, making darkness visible by still greater darkness that could only be felt!

Cervantes is another instance of a man of genius, whose work may be said to have sprung from his mind, like Minerva from the head of Jupiter. Don Quixote and Sancho were a kind of twins; and the jests of the latter, as he says, fell from him like drops of rain when he least thought of it.[10] Shakespeare's creations were more multiform, but equally natural and unstudied. Raphael and Milton seem partial exceptions to this rule. Their productions were of the *composite order*; and those of the latter sometimes even amount to centos. Accordingly, we find Milton quoted among those authors, who have left proofs of their entertaining a high opinion of themselves, and of cherishing a strong aspiration after fame. Some of Shakespeare's *Sonnets* have been also cited to the same purpose; but they seem rather to convey wayward and dissatisfied complaints of his untoward fortune than any thing like a triumphant and confident reliance on his future renown. He appears to have stood more alone and to have thought less about himself than any living being. One reason for this indifference may have been, that as a writer he was tolerably successful in his life-time, and no doubt produced his works with very great facility.

I hardly know whether to class Claude Lorraine as among those who succeeded most 'through happiness or pains'.[11] It is certain that he imitated no one, and has had no successful imitator. The perfection of his landscapes seems to have been owing to an inherent quality of harmony, to an exquisite sense of delicacy in his mind. His monotony has been complained of, which is apparently produced from a preconceived idea in his mind; and not long ago I heard a person, not more distinguished for the subtlety than the *naïveté* of his sarcasms, remark, 'Oh! I never look at Claude: if one has seen one of his pictures, one has seen them all; they are every one alike: there is the same sky, the same climate, the same time of day, the same tree, and that tree is like a cabbage. To be sure, they say he did pretty well; but when a man is always doing one thing, he ought to do it pretty well.'[12] There is no occasion to write the name under this criticism, and the best answer to it is that it is true – his pictures always are the same, but we never wish them to be otherwise. Perfection is one thing. I confess I think that Claude knew this, and felt that his were the finest landscapes in the world – that ever had been, or would ever be.

I am not in the humour to pursue this argument any farther at present, but to write a digression. If the reader is not already apprised of it, he will please to take notice that I write this at Winterslow. My style there is apt to be redundant and excursive. At other times it may be cramped, dry, abrupt; but here it flows like a river, and overspreads its banks. I have not to seek for thoughts or hunt for images: they come of themselves, I inhale them with the breeze, and the silent groves are vocal with a thousand recollections –

> 'And visions, as poetic eyes avow,
> Hang on each leaf, and cling to ev'ry bough.'[13]

Here I came fifteen years ago, a willing exile; and as I trod the lengthened greensward by the low wood-side, repeated the old line,

> 'My mind to me a kingdom is'![14]

I found it so then, before, and since; and shall I faint, now that I have poured out the spirit of that mind to the world, and treated many subjects with truth, with freedom, and power, because I have been followed with one cry of abuse ever since *for not being a government-tool*? Here I returned a few years after to finish some works I had undertaken, doubtful of the event, but determined to do my best; and wrote that character of Millamant[15] which was once transcribed by fingers fairer than Aurora's, but no notice was taken of it, because I was not a government-tool, and must be supposed devoid of taste and elegance by all who aspired to these qualities in their own persons. Here I sketched my account of that old honest Signior Orlando Friscobaldo,[16] which with its fine, racy, acrid tone that old crab-apple, G*ff***d,[17] would have relished or pretended to relish, had I been a government-tool! Here too I have written *Table-Talks* without number, and as yet without a falling-off, till now that they are nearly done, or I should not make this boast. I could swear (were they not mine) the thoughts in many of them are founded as the rock,[18] free as air, the tone like an Italian picture.

What then? Had the style been like polished steel, as firm and as bright, it would have availed me nothing, for I am not a government-tool! I had endeavoured to guide the taste of the English people to the best old English writers; but I had said that English kings did not reign by right divine, and that his present majesty was descended from an elector of Hanover in a right line; and no loyal subject would after this look into Webster or Dekker because I had pointed them out. I had done something (more than any one except Schlegel) to vindicate the *Characters of Shakespeare's Plays* from the stigma of French criticism: but our Anti-Jacobin and Anti-Gallican writers soon found out that I had said and written that Frenchmen, Englishmen, men were not slaves by birth-right. This was enough to *damn* the work. Such has been the head and front[19] of my offending. While my friend Leigh Hunt was writing the *Descent of Liberty*, and strewing the march of the Allied Sovereigns with flowers,[20] I sat by the waters of Babylon[21] and hung my harp upon the willows. I knew all along there was but one alternative – the cause of kings or of mankind. This I foresaw, this I feared; the world see it now, when it is too late. Therefore I lamented, and would take no comfort when the Mighty[22] fell, because we, all men, fell with him, like lightning from heaven, to grovel in the grave of Liberty, in the style of Legitimacy! There is but one question in the hearts of monarchs, whether mankind are their property or not. There was but this one question in mine. I had made an abstract, metaphysical principle of this question. I was not the dupe of the voice of the charmers. By my hatred of tyrants I knew what their hatred of the freeborn spirit of man must be, of the semblance, of the very name of Liberty and Humanity. And while others bowed their heads to the image of the BEAST,[23] I spit upon it and buffeted it, and made mouths at it, and pointed at it, and drew aside the veil that then half concealed it, but has been since thrown off, and named it by its right name; and it is not to be supposed that my having penetrated their mystery would go unrequited by those whose darling and whose delight the idol, half-brute, half-demon, was, and who were ashamed to acknowledge the image and superscription[24] as their own! Two half-friends of mine, who would not make a whole one between them, agreed the other day that the indiscriminate, incessant abuse of what I write was mere prejudice and party-spirit, and that what I do in periodicals and without a name does well, pays well, and is 'cried out upon in the top of the compass'.[25] It is this indeed that has saved my shallow skiff from quite foundering on Tory spite and rancour; for when people have been reading and approving an article in a miscellaneous journal, it does not do to say when they discover the author afterwards (whatever might have been the case before) it is written by a blockhead; and even Mr Jerdan recommends the volume of *Characteristics* as an excellent little work,[26] because it has no cabalistic name in the title-page, and swears 'there is a first-rate article of forty pages in the last number of the *Edinburgh* from Jeffrey's own hand', though when he learns against his will that it is mine, he devotes three successive numbers of the *Literary Gazette* to abuse 'that *strange* article in the last number of the *Edinburgh Review*'. Others who had not this advantage have fallen a sacrifice to the obloquy attached to the suspicion of doubting, or of being acquainted with any one who is known to doubt, the divinity of kings. Poor Keats paid the forfeit of this *lèse majesté* with his health and life. What, though his Verses were like the breath of spring, and many of his thoughts like flowers – would this, with the circle of critics that beset a throne, lessen the crime of their having been praised in the *Examiner*? The lively and most agreeable Editor of that paper[27] has in like manner been driven from his country and his friends who delighted in him, for no other reason that having written the *Story of Rimini*, and asserted ten years ago, 'that the most accomplished prince in Europe was an Adonis of fifty'![28]

> 'Return, Alpheus, the dread voice is past,
> That shrunk thy streams; return, Sicilian Muse'![29]

I look out of my window and see that a shower has just fallen: the fields look green after it, and a rosy cloud hangs over the brow of the hill; a lily expands its petals in the moisture, dressed in its lovely green and white; a shepherd-boy has just brought some pieces of turf with daisies and grass for his young mistress to make a bed for her sky-lark, not doomed to dip his wings in the dappled dawn – my cloudy thoughts draw off, the storm of angry politics has blown over – Mr Blackwood, I am yours – Mr Croker, my service to you – Mr T. Moore, I am alive and well – Really, it is wonderful how little the worse I am for fifteen years' wear and tear, how I come upon my legs again on the ground of truth and nature, and 'look abroad into universality',[30] forgetting that there is any such person as myself in the world!

I have let this passage stand (however critical) because it may serve as a practical illustration to show what authors really think of themselves when put upon the defensive – (I confess, the subject has nothing to do with the title at the head of the Essay!) – and as a warning to those who may reckon upon their fair portion of popularity as the reward of the exercise of an independent spirit and such talents as they possess. It sometimes seems at first sight as if the low scurrility and jargon of abuse by which it is attempted to overlay all common sense and decency by a tissue of lies and nicknames, everlastingly repeated and applied indiscriminately to all those who are not of the regular government-party, was peculiar to the present time, and the anomalous growth of modern criticism; but if we look back, we shall find the same system acted upon, as often as power, prejudice, dullness, and spite found their account in playing the game into one another's hands – in decrying popular efforts, and in giving currency to every species of base metal that had their own conventional stamp upon it. The names of Pope and Dryden were assailed with daily and unsparing abuse – the epithet A.P.E. was levelled at the sacred head of the former – and if even men like these, having to deal with the consciousness of their own infirmities and the insolence and spurns of wanton enmity, must have found it hard to possess their souls in patience, any living writer amidst such contradictory evidence can scarcely expect to retain much calm, steady conviction of his own merits, or build himself a secure reversion in immortality.

However one may in a fit of spleen and impatience turn round and assert one's claims in the face of low-bred, hireling malice, I will here repeat what I set out with saying, that there never yet was a man of sense and proper spirit, who would not decline rather than court a comparison with any of those names, whose reputation he really emulates – who would not be sorry to suppose that any of the great heirs of memory had as many foibles as he knows himself to possess – and who would not shrink from including himself or being included by others in the same praise, that was offered to long-established and universally acknowledged merit, as a kind of profanation. Those who are ready to fancy themselves Raphaels and Homers are very inferior men indeed – they have not even an idea of the mighty names that 'they take in vain'.[31] They are as deficient in pride as in modesty, and have not so much as served an apprenticeship to a true and honourable ambition. They mistake a momentary popularity for lasting renown, and a sanguine temperament for the inspirations of genius. The love of fame is too high and delicate a feeling in the mind to be mixed up with realities – it is a solitary abstraction, the secret sigh of the soul –

> 'It is all one as we should love
> A bright particular star, and think to wed it.'[32]

A name 'fast-anchored in the deep abyss of time'[33] is like a star twinkling in the firmament, cold, silent, distant, but eternal and sublime; and our transmitting one to posterity is as if we should contemplate our translation to the skies. If we are not contented with this feeling on the subject, we shall never sit in Cassiopeia's chair,[34] nor will our names, studding Ariadne's crown or streaming with Berenice's locks,[35] ever make

> 'the face of heaven so bright,
> That birds shall sing, and think it were not night.'[36]

Those who are in love only with noise and show, instead of devoting themselves to a life of study, had better hire a booth at Bartlemy-Fair, or march at the head of a recruiting regiment with drums beating and colours flying!

It has been urged, that however little we may be disposed to indulge the reflection at other times or out of mere self-complacency, yet the mind cannot help being conscious of the effort required for any great work while it is about it, of

> 'The high endeavour and the glad success'.[37]

I grant that there is a sense of power in such cases, with the exception before stated; but then this very effort and state of excitement engrosses the mind at the time, and leaves it listless and exhausted afterwards. The energy we exert, or the high state of enjoyment we feel, puts us out of conceit with ourselves at other times: compared to what we are in the act of composition, we seem dull, common-place people, generally speaking; and what we have been able to perform is rather matter of wonder than of self-congratulation to us. The stimulus of writing is like the stimulus of intoxication, with which we can hardly sympathize in our sober moments, when we are no longer under the inspiration of the demon, or when the virtue is gone out of us. While we are engaged in any work, we are thinking of the subject, and cannot stop to admire ourselves; and when it is done, we look at it with comparative indifference. I will venture to say, that no one but a pedant ever read his own works regularly through. They are not *his* — they are become mere words, waste-paper, and have none of the glow, the creative enthusiasm, the vehemence, and natural spirit with which he wrote them. When we have once committed our thoughts to paper, written them fairly out, and seen that they are right in the printing, if we are in our right wits, we have done with them for ever. I sometimes try to read an article I have written in some magazine or review — (for when they are bound up in a volume, I dread the very sight of them) — but stop after a sentence or two, and never recur to the task. I know pretty well what I have to say on the subject, and do not want to go to school to myself. It is the worst instance of the *bis repetita crambe* [38] in the world. I do not think that even painters have much delight in looking at their works after they are done. While they are in progress, there is a great degree of satisfaction in considering what has been done, or what is still to do — but this is hope, is reverie, and ceases with the completion of our efforts. I should not imagine Raphael or Correggio would have much pleasure in looking at their former works, though they might recollect the pleasure they had had in painting them; they might spy defects in them (for the idea of unattainable perfection still keeps pace with our actual approaches to it), and fancy that they were not worthy of immortality. The greatest portrait-painter the world ever saw used to write under his pictures, '*Titianus faciebat*', [39] signifying that they were imperfect; and in his letter to Charles V accompanying one of his most admired works, he only spoke of the time he had been about it. Annibal Caracci boasted that he could do like Titian and Correggio, and, like most boasters, was wrong. (*See his spirited Letter to his cousin Ludovico, on seeing the pictures at Parma.*)

The greatest pleasure in life is that of reading, while we are young. I have had as much of this pleasure as perhaps any one. As I grow older, it fades; or else, the stronger stimulus of writing takes off the edge of it. At present, I have neither time nor inclination for it: yet I should like to devote a year's entire leisure to a course of the English Novelists; and perhaps clap on that old sly knave, Sir Walter, to the end of the list. It is astonishing how I used formerly to relish the style of certain authors, at a time when I myself despaired of ever writing a single line. Probably this was the reason. It is not in mental as in natural ascent – intellectual objects seem higher when we survey them from below, than when we look down from any given elevation above the common level. My three favourite writers about the time I speak of were Burke, Junius, and Rousseau. I was never weary of admiring and wondering at the felicities of the style, the turns of expression, the refinements of thought and sentiment: I laid the book down to find out the secret of so much strength and beauty, and took it up again in despair, to read on and admire. So I passed whole days, months, and I may add, years; and have only this to say now, that as my life began, so I could wish that it may end. The last time I tasted this luxury in its full perfection was one day after a sultry day's walk in summer between Farnham and Alton. I was fairly tired out; I walked into an inn-yard (I think at the latter place); I was shown by the waiter to what looked at first like common out-houses at the other end of it, but they turned out to be a suite of rooms, probably a hundred years old – the one I entered opened into an old-fashioned garden, embellished with beds of larkspur and a leaden Mercury; it was wainscoted, and there was a grave-looking, dark-coloured portrait of Charles II hanging up over the tiled chimney-piece. I had *Love for Love* in my pocket, and began to read; coffee was brought in in a silver coffee-pot; the cream, the bread and butter, every thing was excellent, and the flavour of Congreve's style prevailed over all. I prolonged the entertainment till a late hour, and relished this divine comedy better even than when I used to see it played by Miss Mellon, as *Miss Prue*; Bob Palmer, as *Tattle*; and Bannister, as honest *Ben.* This circumstance happened just five years ago, and it seems like yesterday. If I count my life so by lustres, it will soon glide away; yet I shall not have to repine, if, while it lasts, it is enriched with a few such recollections!

On the Pleasure of Hating

There is a spider crawling along the matted floor of the room where I sit (not the one which has been so well allegorized in the admirable *Lines to a Spider*,[1] but another of the same edifying breed) – he runs with heedless, hurried haste, he hobbles awkwardly towards me, he stops – he sees the giant shadow before him, and, at a loss whether to retreat or proceed, meditates his huge foe – but as I do not start up and seize upon the straggling caitiff, as he would upon a hapless fly within his toils, he takes heart, and ventures on, with mingled cunning, impudence, and fear. As he passes me, I lift up the matting to assist his escape, am glad to get rid of the unwelcome intruder, and shudder at the recollection after he is gone. A child, a woman, a clown, or a moralist a century ago, would have crushed the little reptile to death – my philosophy has got beyond that – I bear the creature no ill-will, but still I hate the very sight of it. The spirit of malevolence survives the practical exertion of it. We learn to curb our will and keep our overt actions within the bounds of humanity, long before we can subdue our sentiments and imaginations to the same mild tone. We give up the external demonstration, the *brute* violence, but cannot part with the essence or principle of hostility. We do not tread upon the poor little animal in question (that seems barbarous and pitiful!) but we regard it with a sort of mystic horror and superstitious loathing. It will ask another hundred years of fine writing and hard thinking to cure us of the prejudice, and make us feel towards this ill-omened tribe with something of 'the milk of human kindness',[2] instead of their own shyness and venom.

Nature seems (the more we look into it) made up of antipathies: without something to hate, we should lose the very spring of thought and action. Life would turn to a stagnant pool, were it not ruffled by the jarring interests, the unruly passions of men. The white streak in our own fortunes is brightened (or just rendered visible) by making all around it as dark as possible; so the rainbow paints its form upon the cloud. Is it pride? Is it envy? Is it the force of contrast? Is it weakness or malice? But so it is, that there is a secret affinity, a *hankering* after evil in the human mind, and that it takes a perverse, but a fortunate delight in mischief, since it is a never-failing source of satisfaction. Pure good soon grows insipid, wants variety and spirit. Pain is a bitter-sweet, which never surfeits. Love turns, with a little indulgence, to indifference or disgust: hatred alone is immortal. – Do we not see this principle at work every where? Animals torment and worry one another without mercy: children kill flies for sport: every one reads the accidents and offences in a newspaper, as the cream of the jest: a whole town runs to be present at a fire, and the spectator by no means exults to see it extinguished. It is better to have it so, but it diminishes the interest; and our feelings take part with our passions, rather than with our understandings. Men assemble in crowds, with eager enthusiasm, to witness a tragedy: but if there were an execution going forward in the next street, as Mr Burke observes,[3] the theatre would be left empty. A strange cur in a village, an idiot, a crazy woman, are set upon and baited by the whole community. Public nuisances are in the nature of public benefits. How long did the Pope, the Bourbons, and the Inquisition keep the people of England in breath, and supply them with nicknames to vent their spleen upon! Had they done us any harm of late? No: but we have always a quantity of superfluous bile upon the stomach, and we wanted an object to let it out upon. How loth were we to give up our pious belief in ghosts and witches, because we liked to persecute the one, and frighten ourselves to death with the other! It is not the quality so much as the quantity of excitement that we are anxious about: we cannot bear a state of indifference and *ennui*: the mind seems to abhor a *vacuum*[4] as much as ever matter was supposed to do. Even when the spirit of the age (that is, the progress of intellectual refinement, warring with our natural infirmities) no longer allows us to carry our vindictive and headstrong humours into effect, we try to revive them in description, and keep up the old bugbears, the phantoms of our terror and our hate, in imagination. We burn Guy Faux in effigy, and the hooting and buffeting and maltreating that poor tattered figure of rags and straw makes a festival in every village in England once a year. Protestants and Papists do not now burn one another at the stake: but we subscribe to new editions of *Fox's Book of Martyrs*; and the secret of the success of the *Scotch Novels* [5] is much the same — they carry us back to the feuds, the heart-burnings, the havoc, the dismay, the wrongs and the revenge of a barbarous age and people — to the rooted prejudices and deadly animosities of sects and parties in politics and religion, and of contending chiefs and clans in war and intrigue. We feel the full force of the spirit of hatred with all of them in turn. As we read, we throw aside the trammels of civilization, the flimsy veil of humanity. 'Off, you lendings!' [6] The wild beast resumes its sway within us, we feel like hunting-animals, and as the hound starts in his sleep and rushes on the chase in fancy, the heart rouses itself in its native lair, and utters a wild cry of joy, at being restored once more to freedom and lawless, unrestrained impulses. Every one has his full swing, or goes to the Devil his own way. Here are no Jeremy Bentham Panopticons, [7] none of Mr Owen's impassable Parallelograms, [8] (Rob Roy would have spurned and poured a thousand curses on them), no long calculations of self-interest — the will takes its instant way to its object; as the mountain-torrent flings itself over the precipice, the greatest possible good of each individual consists in doing all the mischief he can to his neighbour: that is charming, and finds a sure and sympathetic chord in every breast! So Mr Irving, the celebrated preacher, has rekindled the old, original, almost exploded hell-fire in the aisles of the Caledonian Chapel, as they introduce the real water of the New River at Sadler's Wells, to the delight and astonishment of his fair audience. *'Tis pretty, though a plague*, [9] to sit and peep into the pit of Tophet, to play at *snap-dragon* [10] with flames and brimstone (it gives a smart electrical shock, a lively fillip to delicate constitutions), and to see Mr Irving, like a huge Titan, looking as grim and swarthy as if he had to forge tortures for all the damned! What a strange being man is! Not content with doing all he can to vex and hurt his fellows here, 'upon this bank and shoal of time', [11] where one would think there were heart-aches, pain, disappointment, anguish, tears, sighs, and groans enough, the bigoted

437

maniac takes him to the top of the high peak of school divinity to hurl him down the yawning gulf of penal fire; his speculative malice asks eternity to wreak its infinite spite in, and calls on the Almighty to execute its relentless doom! The cannibals burn their enemies and eat them, in good-fellowship with one another: meek Christian divines cast those who differ from them but a hair's-breadth, body and soul, into hell-fire, for the glory of God and the good of his creatures! It is well that the power of such persons is not co-ordinate with their wills: indeed, it is from the sense of their weakness and inability to control the opinions of others, that they thus 'outdo termagant',[12] and endeavour to frighten them into conformity by big words and monstrous denunciations.

The pleasure of hating, like a poisonous mineral, eats into the heart of religion, and turns it to rankling spleen and bigotry; it makes patriotism an excuse for carrying fire, pestilence, and famine into other lands: it leaves to virtue nothing but the spirit of censoriousness, and a narrow, jealous, inquisitorial watchfulness over the actions and motives of others. What have the different sects, creeds, doctrines in religion been but so many pretexts set up for men to wrangle, to quarrel, to tear one another in pieces about, like a target as a mark to shoot at? Does any one suppose that the love of country in an Englishman implies any friendly feeling or disposition to serve another, bearing the same name? No, it means only hatred to the French, or the inhabitants of any other country that we happen to be at war with for the time. Does the love of virtue denote any wish to discover or amend our own faults? No, but it atones for an obstinate adherence to our own vices by the most virulent intolerance to human frailties. This principle is of a most universal application. It extends to good as well as evil: if it makes us hate folly, it makes us no less dissatisfied with distinguished merit. If it inclines us to resent the wrongs of others, it impels us to be as impatient of their prosperity. We revenge injuries: we repay benefits with ingratitude. Even our strongest partialities and likings soon take this turn. 'That which was luscious as locusts, anon becomes bitter as coloquintida';[13] and love and friendship melt in their own fires. We hate old friends: we hate old books: we hate old opinions; and at last we come to hate ourselves.

I have observed that few of those, whom I have formerly known

most intimate, continue on the same friendly footing, or combine the
steadiness with the warmth of attachment. I have been acquainted
with two or three knots of inseparable companions, who saw each
other 'six days in the week',[14] that have broken up and dispersed. I
have quarrelled with almost all my old friends, (they might say this
is owing to my bad temper, but) they have also quarrelled with one
another. What is become of 'that set of whist-players', celebrated by
ELIA[15] in his notable *Epistle to Robert Southey, Esq.* (and now I think
of it – that I myself have celebrated in this very volume) 'that for so
many years called Admiral Burney friend'? They are scattered, like
last year's snow. Some of them are dead – or gone to live at a distance
– or pass one another in the street like strangers; or if they stop to
speak, do it as coolly and try to *cut* one another as soon as possible.
Some of us have grown rich – others poor. Some have got places
under Government – others a *niche* in the *Quarterly Review.* Some
of us have dearly earned a name in the world; whilst others remain
in their original privacy. We despise the one; and envy and are glad
to mortify the other. Times are changed; we cannot revive our old
feelings; and we avoid the sight and are uneasy in the presence of
those, who remind us of our infirmity, and put us upon an effort at
seeming cordiality, which embarrasses ourselves and does not impose
upon our *quondam* associates. Old friendships are like meats served
up repeatedly, cold, comfortless, and distasteful. The stomach turns
against them. Either constant intercourse and familiarity breed weariness and contempt; or if we meet again after an interval of absence,
we appear no longer the same. One is too wise, another too foolish
for us; and we wonder we did not find this out before. We are
disconcerted and kept in a state of continual alarm by the wit of one,
or tired to death of the dullness of another. The *good things* of the
first (besides leaving stings behind them) by repetition grow stale,
and lose their startling effect; and the insipidity of the last becomes
intolerable. The most amusing or instructive companion is at best
like a favourite volume, that we wish after a time to *lay upon the
shelf*; but as our friends are not willing to be laid there, this produces
a misunderstanding and ill-blood between us. – Or if the zeal and
integrity of friendship is not abated, or its career interrupted by any
obstacle arising out of its own nature, we look out for other subjects

of complaint and sources of dissatisfaction. We begin to criticize each other's dress, looks, and general character. 'Such a one is a pleasant fellow, but it is a pity he sits so late!' Another fails to keep his appointments, and that is a sore that never heals. We get acquainted with some fashionable young men or with a mistress, and wish to introduce our friend; but he is awkward and a sloven, the interview does not answer, and this throws cold water on our intercourse. Or he makes himself obnoxious to opinion – and we shrink from our own convictions on the subject as an excuse for not defending him. All or any of these causes mount up in time to a ground of coolness or irritation – and at last they break out into open violence as the only amends we can make ourselves for suppressing them so long, or the readiest means of banishing recollections of former kindness, so little compatible with our present feelings. We may try to tamper with the wounds or patch up the carcase of departed friendship, but the one will hardly bear the handling, and the other is not worth the trouble of embalming! The only way to be reconciled to old friends is to part with them for good: at a distance we may chance to be thrown back (in a waking dream) upon old times and old feelings: or at any rate, we should not think of renewing our intimacy, till we have fairly *spit our spite*, or said, thought, and felt all the ill we can of each other. Or if we can pick a quarrel with some one else, and make him the scape-goat, this is an excellent contrivance to heal a broken bone. I think I must be friends with Lamb again, since he has written that magnanimous *Letter to Southey*, and told him a piece of his mind! – I don't know what it is that attaches me to H——[16] so much, except that he and I, whenever we meet, sit in judgment on another set of old friends, and 'carve them as a dish fit for the Gods'.[17] There was L—— H——,[18] John Scott, Mrs ——,[19] whose dark raven locks make a picturesque background to our discourse, B——,[20] who is grown fat, and is, they say, married, R——;[21] these had all separated long ago, and their foibles are the common link that holds us together. We do not affect to condole or whine over their follies; we enjoy, we laugh at them till we are ready to burst our sides, '*sans* intermission, for hours by the dial'.[22] We serve up a course of anecdotes, *traits*, master-strokes of character, and cut and hack at them till we are weary. Perhaps some of them are even with us. For my own part, as I once said, I like a friend the better for having faults that one can talk about. 'Then,' said Mrs —, 'you will never cease to be a philanthropist!' Those in question were some of the choice-spirits of the age, not 'fellows of no mark or likelihood';[23] and we so far did them justice: but it is well they did not hear what we sometimes said of them. I care little what any one says of me, particularly behind my back, and in the way of critical and analytical discussion — it is looks of dislike and scorn, that I answer with the worst venom of my pen. The expression of the face wounds me more than the expressions of the tongue. If I have in one instance mistaken this expression, or resorted to this remedy where I ought not, I am sorry for it. But the face was too fine over which it mantled, and I am too old to have misunderstood it! ... I sometimes go up to —'s;[24] and as often as I do, resolve never to go again. I do not find the old homely welcome. The ghost of friendship meets me at the door, and sits with me all dinner-time. They have got a set of fine notions and new acquaintance. Allusions to past occurrences are thought trivial, nor is it always safe to touch upon more general subjects. M.[25] does not begin as he formerly did every five minutes, 'Fawcett used to say', &c. That topic is something worn. The girls are grown up, and have a thousand accomplishments. I perceive there is a jealousy on both sides. They think I give myself airs, and I fancy the same of them. Every time I am asked, 'If I do not think Mr Washington Irving a very fine writer?' I shall not go again till I receive an invitation for Christmas-day in company with Mr Liston. The only intimacy I never found to flinch or fade was a purely intellectual one. There was none of the cant of candour in it, none of the whine of mawkish sensibility. Our mutual acquaintance were considered merely as subjects of conversation and knowledge, not at all of affection. We regarded them no more in our experiments than 'mice in an air-pump':[26] or like malefactors, they were regularly cut down and given over to the dissecting-knife. We spared neither friend nor foe. We sacrificed human infirmities at the shrine of truth. The skeletons of character might be seen, after the juice was extracted, dangling in the air like flies in cobwebs: or they were kept for future inspection in some refined acid. The demonstration was as beautiful as it was new. There is no surfeiting on gall: nothing keeps so well as a decoction of spleen. We grow tired of every thing but turning others into ridicule, and congratulating ourselves on their defects.

We take a dislike to our favourite books, after a time, for the same reason. We cannot read the same works for ever. Our honey-moon, even though we wed the Muse, must come to an end; and is followed by indifference, if not by disgust. There are some works, those indeed that produce the most striking effect at first by novelty and boldness of outline, that will not bear reading twice: others of a less extravagant character, and that excite and repay attention by a greater nicety of details, have hardly interest enough to keep alive our continued enthusiasm. The popularity of the most successful writers operates to wean us from them, by the cant and fuss that is made about them, by hearing their names everlastingly repeated, and by the number of ignorant and indiscriminate admirers they draw after them: – we as little like to have to drag others from their unmerited obscurity, lest we should be exposed to the charge of affectation and singularity of taste. There is nothing to be said respecting an author that all the world have made up their minds about: it is a thankless as well as hopeless task to recommend one that nobody has ever heard of. To cry up Shakespeare as the God of our idolatry,[27] seems like a vulgar, national prejudice: to take down a volume of Chaucer, or Spenser, or Beaumont and Fletcher, or Ford, or Marlowe, has very much the look of pedantry and egotism. I confess it makes me hate the very name of Fame and Genius when works like these are 'gone into the wastes of time',[28] while each successive generation of fools is busily employed in reading the trash of the day, and women of fashion gravely join with their waiting-maids in discussing the preference between *Paradise Lost* and Mr Moore's *Loves of the Angels*. I was pleased the other day on going into a shop to ask, 'If they had any of the *Scotch Novels*'? to be told – 'That they had just sent out the last, *Sir Andrew Wylie*!'[29] – Mr Galt will also be pleased with this answer! The reputation of some books is raw and *unaired*: that of others is worm-eaten and mouldy. Why fix our affections on that which we cannot bring ourselves to have faith in, or which others have long ceased to trouble themselves about? I am half afraid to look into *Tom Jones*, lest it should not answer my expectations at this time of day; and if it did not, I should certainly be disposed to fling it into the fire, and never look into another novel while I lived. But surely, it may be said, there are some works, that, like nature, can never grow old; and that must always touch the imagination and passions alike! Or there are passages that seem as if we might brood over them all our lives, and not exhaust the sentiments of love and admiration they excite: they become favourites, and we are fond of them to a sort of dotage. Here is one:

> '—Sitting in my window
> Printing my thoughts in lawn, I saw a God,
> I thought (but it was you), enter our gates;
> My blood flew out and back again, as fast
> As I had puffed it forth and sucked it in
> Like breath; then was I called away in haste
> To entertain you: never was a man
> Thrust from a sheepcote to a sceptre, raised
> So high in thoughts as I; you left a kiss
> Upon these lips then, which I mean to keep
> From you for ever. I did hear you talk
> Far above singing!'[30]

A passage like this indeed leaves a taste on the palate like nectar, and we seem in reading it to sit with the Gods at their golden tables: but if we repeat it often in ordinary moods, it loses its flavour, becomes vapid, 'the wine of *poetry* is drank, and but the lees remain'.[31] Or, on the other hand, if we call in the aid of extraordinary circumstances to set it off to advantage, as the reciting it to a friend, or after having our feelings excited by a long walk in some romantic situation, or while we

> '—play with Amaryllis in the shade,
> Or with the tangles of Neæra's hair'[32] —

we afterwards miss the accompanying circumstances, and instead of transferring the recollection of them to the favourable side, regret what we have lost, and strive in vain to bring back 'the irrevocable hour'[33] — wondering in some instances how we survive it, and at the melancholy blank that is left behind! The pleasure rises to its height in some moment of calm solitude or intoxicating sympathy, declines ever after, and from the comparison and a conscious falling-off, leaves rather a sense of satiety and irksomeness behind it . . . 'Is it the same in pictures?' I confess it is, with all but those from Titian's hand. I don't know why, but an air breathes from his landscapes, pure, refreshing as if it came from other years; there is a look in his faces that never passes away. I saw one the other day. Amidst the heartless desolation and glittering finery of Fonthill,[34] there is a portfolio of the Dresden Gallery. It opens, and a young female head looks from it; a child, yet woman grown; with an air of rustic innocence and the graces of a princess, her eyes like those of doves, the lips about to open, a smile of pleasure dimpling the whole face, the jewels sparkling in her crisped hair, her youthful shape compressed in a rich antique dress, as the bursting leaves contain the April buds! Why do I not call up this image of gentle sweetness, and place it as a perpetual barrier between mischance and me? — It is because pleasure asks a greater effort of the mind to support it than pain; and we turn, after a little idle dalliance, from what we love to what we hate!

As to my old opinions, I am heartily sick of them. I have reason, for they have deceived me sadly. I was taught to think, and I was willing to believe, that genius was not a bawd — that virtue was not a mask — that liberty was not a name — that love had its seat in the human heart. Now I would care little if these words were struck out of the dictionary, or if I had never heard them. They are become to my ears a mockery and a dream. Instead of patriots and friends of freedom, I see nothing but the tyrant and the slave, the people linked with kings to rivet on the chains of despotism and superstition. I see folly join with knavery, and together make up public spirit and public opinions. I see the insolent Tory, the blind Reformer, the coward Whig! If mankind had wished for what is right, they might have had it long ago. The theory is plain enough; but they are prone to mischief, 'to every good work reprobate'.[35] I have seen all that had been done by the mighty yearnings of the spirit and intellect of men, 'of whom the world was not worthy',[36] and that promised a proud

opening to truth and good through the vista of future years, undone
by one man, with just glimmering of understanding enough to feel
that he was a king, but not to comprehend how he could be king of
a free people! I have seen this triumph celebrated by poets, the friends
of my youth and the friends of man, but who were carried away by
the infuriate tide that, setting in from a throne, bore down every
distinction of right reason before it; and I have seen all those who
did not join in applauding this insult and outrage on humanity
proscribed, hunted down (they and their friends made a bye-word
of), so that it has become an understood thing that no one can live
by his talents or knowledge who is not ready to prostitute those
talents and that knowledge to betray his species, and prey upon his
fellow-man. 'This was some time a mystery: but the time gives
evidence of it.'[37] The echoes of liberty had awakened once more in
Spain, and the morning of human hope dawned again: but that dawn
has been overcast by the foul breath of bigotry, and those reviving
sounds stifled by fresh cries from the time-rent towers of the Inquisition – man yielding (as it is fit he should) first to brute force, but
more to the innate perversity and dastard spirit of his own nature,
which leaves no room for farther hope or disappointment. And
England, that arch-reformer, that heroic deliverer, that mouther
about liberty and tool of power, stands gaping by, not feeling the
blight and mildew coming over it, nor its very bones crack and turn
to a paste under the grasp and circling folds of this new monster,
Legitimacy! In private life do we not see hypocrisy, servility, selfishness, folly, and impudence succeed, while modesty shrinks from the
encounter, and merit is trodden under foot? How often is 'the rose
plucked from the forehead of a virtuous love to plant a blister there'![38]
What chance is there of the success of real passion? What certainty
of its continuance? Seeing all this as I do, and unravelling the web
of human life into its various threads of meanness, spite, cowardice,
want of feeling, and want of understanding, of indifference towards
others and ignorance of ourselves – seeing custom prevail over all
excellence, itself giving way to infamy – mistaken as I have been in
my public and private hopes, calculating others from myself, and
calculating wrong; always disappointed where I placed most reliance;
the dupe of friendship, and the fool of love; have I not reason to hate

and to despise myself? Indeed I do; and chiefly for not having hated
and despised the world enough.*

* The only exception to the general drift of this Essay (and that is an exception in theory
— I know of none in practice) is, that in reading we always take the right side, and make
the case properly our own. Our imaginations are sufficiently excited, we have nothing to
do with the matter but as a pure creation of the mind, and we therefore yield to the
natural, unwarped impression of good and evil. Our own passions, interests, and prejudices
out of the question, or in an abstracted point of view, we judge fairly and conscientiously;
for conscience is nothing but the abstract idea of right and wrong. But no sooner have we
to act or suffer, than the spirit of contradiction or some other demon comes into play, and
there is an end of common sense and reason. Even the very strength of the speculative
faculty, or the desire to square things with an *ideal* standard of perfection (whether we
can or no) leads perhaps to half the absurdities and miseries of mankind. We are hunting
after what we cannot find, and quarrelling with the good within our reach. Among the
thousands that have read *The Heart of Mid Lothian*[59] there assuredly never was a single
person who did not wish Jeanie Deans success. Even Gentle George was sorry for what he
had done, when it was over, though he would have played the same prank the next day:
and the *unknown* author, in his immediate character of contributor to *Blackwood* and the
Sentinel, is about as respectable a personage as Daddy Ratton himself. On the stage, every
one takes part with Othello against Iago. Do boys at school, in reading Homer, generally
side with the Greeks or Trojans?

Hot and Cold

— 'Hot, cold, moist, and dry, four champions fierce,
Strive here for mastery.' — MILTON[1]

'The Protestants are much cleaner than the Catholics,' said a shop-keeper of Vevey to me. 'They are so,' I replied, 'but why should they?' A prejudice appeared to him a matter-of-fact, and he did not think it necessary to assign reasons for a matter-of-fact. That is not my way. He had not bottomed his proposition on proofs, nor rightly defined it.

Nearly the same remark, as to the extreme cleanliness of the people in this part of the country, had occurred to me as soon as I got to Brigg, where however the inhabitants are Catholics. So the original statement requires some qualification as to the mode of enunciation. I had no sooner arrived in this village, which is situated just under the Simplon, and where you are surrounded with *glaciers* and *goitres*, than the genius of the place struck me on looking out at the pump under my window the next morning, where the 'neat-handed Phyllises'[2] were washing their greens in the water, that not a caterpillar could crawl on them, and scouring their pails and tubs that not a stain should be left in them. The raw, clammy feeling of the air was in unison with the scene. I had not seen such a thing in Italy. They have there no delight in splashing and dabbling in fresh streams and fountains — they have a dread of ablutions and abstersions, almost amounting to *hydrophobia*. Heat has an antipathy in nature to cold. The sanguine Italian is chilled and shudders at the touch of cold water, while the Helvetian boor, whose humours creep through his veins like the dank mists along the sides of his frozen mountains, is 'native and endued unto that element'.[3] Here every thing is purified and filtered: there it is baked and burnt up, and sticks together in a most amicable union of filth and laziness. There is a little mystery and a little contradiction in the case – let us try if we cannot get rid of both by means of caution and daring together. It is not that the difference of latitude between one side of the Alps and the other can signify much: but the phlegmatic blood of their German ancestors is poured down the valleys of the Swiss like water, and *iced* in its progress; whereas that of the Italians, besides its vigorous origin, is enriched and ripened by basking in more genial plains. A single Milanese market-girl (to go no farther south) appeared to me to have more blood in her body, more fire in her eye (as if the sun had made a burning *lens* of it), more spirit and probably more mischief about her than all the nice, *tidy*, good-looking, hard-working girls I have seen in Switzerland. To turn this physiognomical observation to a metaphysical account, I should say then that Northern people are clean and Southern people dirty as a general rule, because where the principle of life is more cold, weak, and impoverished, there is a greater shyness and aversion to come in contact with external matter (with which it does not so easily amalgamate), a greater fastidiousness and delicacy in choosing its sensations, a greater desire to know surrounding objects and to keep them clear of each other, than where this principle being more warm and active, it may be supposed to absorb outward impressions in itself, to melt them into its own essence, to impart its own vital impulses to them, and in fine, instead of shrinking from every thing, to be shocked at nothing. The Southern temperament is (so to speak) more sociable with matter, more gross, impure, indifferent, from relying on its own strength; while that opposed to it, from being less able to react on external applications, is obliged to be more cautious and particular as to the kind of excitement to which it renders itself liable. Hence the timidity, reserve, and occasional hypocrisy of Northern manners; the boldness, freedom, levity, and frequent licentiousness of Southern ones. It would be too much to say, that if there is any thing of which a genuine Italian has a horror, it is of cleanliness; or that if there is any thing which seems ridiculous to a thorough-bred Italian woman, it is modesty: but certainly the degree to which nicety is carried by some

people is a *bore* to an Italian imagination, as the excess of delicacy
which is pretended or practised by some women is quite incomprehen-
sible to the females of the South. It is wrong, however, to make the
greater confidence or forwardness of manners an absolute test of
morals: the love of virtue is a different thing from the fear or even
hatred of vice. The squeamishness and prudery in the one case have
a more plausible appearance; but it does not follow that there may
not be more native goodness and even habitual refinement in the
other, though accompanied with stronger nerves and a less morbid
imagination. But to return to the first question.* – I can readily
understand how a Swiss peasant should stand a whole morning at a
pump, washing cabbages, cauliflowers, salads, and getting rid half a
dozen times over of the sand, dirt, and insects they contain, because
I myself should not only be *gravelled* by meeting with the one at
table, but should be in horrors at the other. A Frenchman or an Italian
would be thrown into convulsions of laughter at this superfluous
delicacy, and would think his repast enriched or none the worse for
such additions. The reluctance to prey on life, or on what once had
it, seems to arise from a sense of incongruity, from the repugnance
between life and death – from the cold, clammy feeling which belongs
to the one, and which is enhanced by the contrast to its former warm,
lively state, and by the circumstance of its being taken into the mouth,
and devoured as food. Hence the desire to get rid of the idea of the
living animal even in ordinary cases by all the disguises of cookery,
of boiled and roast, and by the artifice of changing the name of
the animal into something different when it becomes food.† Hence
sportsmen are not devourers of game, and hence the aversion to kill

* Women abroad (generally speaking) are more like men in the tone of their conversation
and habits of thinking, so that from the same premises you cannot draw the same conclusions
as in England.

† This circumstance is noticed in *Ivanhoe*,⁴ though a different turn is given to it by the
philosopher of Rotherwood.

'Nay, I can tell you more,' said Wamba in the same tone, 'there is old Alderman Ox
continues to hold his Saxon epithet, while he is under the charge of serfs and bondsmen
such as thou; but becomes Beef, a fiery French gallant, when he arrives before the worshipful
jaws that are destined to consume him. Mynheer Calf too becomes Monsieur de Veau in
like manner: he is Saxon when he requires tendance, and takes a Norman name when he
becomes matter of enjoyment.' – Vol. I, Chap. 1.

the animals we eat.* There is a contradiction between the animate
and the inanimate, which is felt as matter of peculiar annoyance by
the more cold and congealed temperament which cannot so well pass
from one to the other; but this objection is easily swallowed by the
inhabitant of gayer and more luxurious regions, who is so full of life
himself that he can at once impart it to all that comes in his way, or
never troubles himself about the difference. So the Neapolitan bandit
takes the life of his victim with little remorse, because he has enough
and to spare in himself: his pulse still beats warm and vigorous, while
the blood of a more humane native of the frozen North would run
cold with horror at the sight of the stiffened corse, and this makes
him pause before he stops in another the gushing source, of which
he has such feeble supplies in himself. The wild Arab of the Desert
can hardly entertain the idea of death, neither dreading it for himself
nor regretting it for others. The Italians, Spaniards, and people of
the South swarm alive without being sick or sorry at the circumstance:
they hunt the accustomed prey in each other's tangled locks openly
in the streets and on the highways, without manifesting shame or
repugnance: combs are an invention of our Northern climes. Now I
can comprehend this, when I look at the dirty, dingy, greasy, sun-burnt
complexion of an Italian peasant or beggar, whose body seems alive
all over with a sort of tingling, oily sensation, so that from any given
particle of his shining skin to the beast 'whose name signifies love'[5]
the transition is but small. This populousness is not unaccountable
where all teems with life, where all is glowing and in motion, and
every pore thrills with an exuberance of feeling. Not so in the dearth
of life and spirit, in the drossy, dry, material texture, the clear
complexions and fair hair of the Saxon races, where the puncture of
an insect's sting is a solution of their personal identity, and the idea
of life attached to and courting an intimacy with them in spite of
themselves, naturally produces all the revulsions of the most violent
antipathy and nearly drives them out of their wits. How well the
smooth ivory comb and auburn hair agree – while the Greek *dandy*,

* Hence the peculiar horror of cannibalism from the stronger sympathy with our own
sensations, and the greater violence that is done to it by the sacrilegious use of what once
possessed human life and feeling.

on entering a room, applies his hand to brush a cloud of busy stragglers from his hair like powder, and gives himself no more concern about them than about the motes dancing in the sun-beams! The dirt of the Italians is as it were baked into them, and so ingrained as to become a part of themselves, and occasion no discontinuity of their being.

I can forgive the dirt and sweat of a gipsy under a hedge, when I consider that the earth is his mother, the sun is his father. He hunts vermin for food: he is himself hunted like vermin for prey. His existence is not one of choice, but of necessity. The hungry Arab devours the raw shoulder of a horse. This again I can conceive. His feverish blood seethes it, and the virulence of his own breath carries off the disagreeableness of the smell. I do not see that the horse should be reckoned among unclean animals, according to any notions I have of the matter. The dividing of the hoof or the contrary, I should think, has not any thing to do with the question. I can understand the distinction between beasts of prey and the herbivorous and domestic animals, but the horse is tame. The natural distinction between clean and unclean animals (which has been sometimes made into a religious one) I take to depend on two circumstances, *viz.* the claws and bristly hide, which generally, though not always, go together. One would not wish to be torn in pieces instead of making a comfortable meal, 'to be supped upon'[6] where we thought of supping. With respect to the wolf, the tiger, and other animals of the same species, it seems a question which of us should devour the other: this baulks our appetite by distracting our attention, and we have so little relish for being eaten ourselves, or for the fangs and teeth of these shocking animals, that it gives us a distaste for their whole bodies. The horror we conceive at preying upon them arises in part from the fear we had of being preyed upon by them. No such apprehension crosses the mind with respect to the deer, the sheep, the hare — 'here all is conscience and tender heart'.[7] These gentle creatures (whom we compliment as useful) offer no resistance to the knife, and there is therefore nothing shocking or repulsive in the idea of devoting them to it. There is no confusion of ideas, but a beautiful simplicity and uniformity in our relation to each other, we as the slayers, they as the slain. A perfect understanding subsists on the subject. The hair of animals of prey is also strong and bristly, and forms an obstacle to our Epicurean designs. The calf or fawn is sleek and smooth: the bristles on a dog's or a cat's back are like 'the quills upon the fretful porcupine',[8] a very impracticable repast to the imagination, that stick in the throat and turn the stomach. Who has not read and been edified by the account of the supper in *Gil Blas?*[9] Besides, there is also in all probability the practical consideration urged by Voltaire's traveller,[10] who being asked 'which he preferred – black mutton or white?' replied, 'Either, provided it was tender.' The greater rankness in the flesh is however accompanied by a corresponding irritability of surface, a tenaciousness, a pruriency, a soreness to attack, and not that fine, round, pampered passiveness to impressions which cuts up into handsome joints and entire pieces without any fidgety process, and with an obvious view to solid, wholesome nourishment. Swine's flesh, the abomination of the Jewish law, certainly comes under the objection here stated; and the bear with its shaggy fur is only smuggled into the Christian larder as half-brother to the wild boar, and because from its lazy, lumpish character and appearance, it seems a matter of indifference whether it eats or is eaten. The horse, with sleek round haunches, is fair game, except from custom; and I think I could survive having swallowed part of an ass's foal without being utterly loathsome to myself.* Mites in a rotten cheese are endurable, from being so small and dry that they are scarce distinguishable from the atoms of the cheese itself, 'so drossy and divisible are they': but the Lord deliver me from their more thriving next-door neighbours! Animals that are made use of as food should either be so small as to be imperceptible, or else we should dig into the quarry of life, hew

---

* Thomas Cooper of Manchester, the able logician and political partisan, tried the experiment some years ago, when he invited a number of gentlemen and officers quartered in the town to dine with him on an ass's foal instead of a calf's-head, on the anniversary of the 30th of January. The circumstance got wind, and gave great offence. Mr Cooper had to attend a county-meeting soon after at Boulton-le-Moors, and one of the country magistrates coming to the inn for the same purpose, and when he asked 'If any one was in the room?' receiving for answer – 'No one but Mr Cooper of Manchester' – ordered out his horse and immediately rode home again. Some verses made on the occasion by Mr Scarlett and Mr Shepherd of Gateacre explained the story thus –

> 'The reason how this came to pass is
> The Justice had heard that Cooper ate asses!'

away the masses, and not leave the form standing to reproach us with our gluttony and cruelty. I hate to see a rabbit trussed, or a hare brought to table in the form which it occupied while living: they seem to me apparitions of the burrowers in the earth or the rovers in the wood, sent to scare away appetite. One reason why toads and serpents are disgusting, is from the way in which they run against or suddenly cling to the skin: the encountering them causes a solution of continuity, and we shudder to feel a life which is not ours in contact with us. It is this disjointed or imperfect sympathy which in the recoil produces the greatest antipathy. Sterne asks[11] why a sword, which takes away life, may be named without offence, though other things, which contribute to perpetuate it, cannot? Because the idea in the one case is merely painful, and there is no mixture of the agreeable to lead the imagination on to a point from which it must make a precipitate retreat. The morally indecent arises from the doubtful conflict between temptation and duty: the physically revolting is the product of alternate attraction and repulsion, of partial adhesion, or of something that is foreign to us sticking closer to our persons than we could wish. The nastiest tastes and smells are not the most pungent and painful, but a compound of sweet and bitter, of the agreeable and disagreeable; where the sense, having been relaxed and rendered effeminate as it were by the first, is unable to contend with the last, faints and sinks under it, and has no way of relieving itself but by violently throwing off the load that oppresses it. Hence loathing and sickness. But these hardly ever arise without something contradictory or *impure* in the objects, or unless the mind, having been invited and prepared to be gratified at first, this expectation is turned to disappointment and disgust. Mere pains, mere pleasures do not have this effect, save from an excess of the first causing insensibility and then a faintness ensues, or of the last, causing what is called a surfeit. Sea-sickness has some analogy to this. It comes on with that unsettled motion of the ship, which takes away the ordinary footing or firm hold we have of things, and by relaxing our perceptions, unbraces the whole nervous system. The giddiness and swimming of the head on looking down a precipice, when we are ready with every breath of imagination to topple down into the abyss, has its source in the same uncertain and rapid whirl of the fancy through possible extremes.

Thus we find that for cases of fainting, sea-sickness, &c. a glass of brandy is recommended as 'the sovereign'st thing on earth',[12] because by grappling with the coats of the stomach and bringing our sensations to a *focus*, it does away that nauseous fluctuation and suspense of feeling which is the root of the mischief. I do not know whether I make myself intelligible, for the utmost I can pretend is to suggest some very subtle and remote analogies: but if I have at all succeeded in opening up the train of argument I intend, it will at least be possible to conceive how the sanguine Italian is less nice in his intercourse with material objects, less startled at incongruities, less liable to take offence, than the more literal and conscientious German, because the more headstrong current of his own sensations fills up the gaps and 'makes the odds all even'.[13] He does not care to have his cabbages and salads washed ten times over, or his beds cleared of vermin: he can lend or borrow satisfaction from all objects indifferently. The air over his head is full of life, of the hum of insects; the grass under his feet rings and is loud with the cry of the grasshopper; innumerable green lizards dart from the rocks and sport before him: what signifies it if any living creature approaches nearer his own person, where all is one vital glow? The Indian even twines the forked serpent round his hand unharmed, copper-coloured like it, his veins as heated; and the Brahmin cherishes life and disregards his own person as an act of his religion – the religion of fire and of the sun! Yet how shall we reconcile to this theory the constant ablutions (five times a day) of the Eastern nations, and the squalid customs of some Northern people, the dirtiness of the Russians and of the Scotch? Superstition may perhaps account for the one, and poverty and barbarism for the other.*

Laziness has a great deal to do in the question, and this again is owing to a state of feeling sufficient to itself, and rich in enjoyment without the help of action. Clothilde (the finest and darkest of the Gensano girls) fixes herself at her door about noon (when her day's

---

* What a plague Moses had with his Jews to make them 'reform and live cleanly'![14] To this day (according to a learned traveller) the Jews, wherever scattered, have an aversion to agriculture and almost to its products; and a Jewish girl will refuse to accept a flower – if you offer her a piece of money, of jewellery or embroidery, she knows well enough what to make of the proffered courtesy. See Hacquet's *Travels in Carpathia*, &c.

work is done): her smile reflects back the brightness of the sun, she
darts upon a little girl with a child in her arms, nearly overturns
both, devours it with kisses, and then resumes her position at the
door, with her hands behind her back and her shoes down at heel.
This slatternliness and negligence is the more remarkable in so fine
a girl, and one whose ordinary costume is a gorgeous picture, but it
is a part of the character; her dress would never have been so rich, if
she could take more pains about it – they have no nervous or fidgety
feeling whether a thing is coming off or not: all their sensations, as
it were, sit loose upon them. Their clothes are no part of themselves,
– they even fling their limbs about as if they scarcely belonged to
them; the heat in summer requires the utmost freedom and airiness
(which becomes a habit), and they have nothing tight-bound or
strait-laced about their minds or bodies. The same girl in winter (for
'dull, cold winter *does* inhabit here'[15] also) would have a *scaldaletto*
(an earthen pan with coals in it) dangling at her wrists for four
months together, without any sense of incumbrance or distraction,
or any other feeling but of the heat it communicated to her hands.
She does not mind its chilling the rest of her body or disfiguring her
hands, making her fingers look like 'long purples'[16] – these children
of nature 'take the good the Gods provide them',[17] and trouble
themselves little about consequences or appearances. Their self-will
is much stronger than their vanity – they have as little curiosity
about others as concern for their good opinion. Two Italian peasants
talking by the roadside will not so much as turn their heads to look
at an English carriage that is passing. They have no interest except
in what is personal, sensual. Hence they have as little tenaciousness
on the score of property as in the acquisition of ideas. They want
neither. Their good spirits are food, clothing, and books to them.
They are fond of comfort too, but their notion of it differs from ours
– ours consists in accumulating the means of enjoyment, theirs in
being free to enjoy, in the dear *far niente*.[18] What need have they to
encumber themselves with furniture or wealth or business, when all
they require (for the most part) is air, a bunch of grapes, bread,
and stone-walls? The Italians, generally speaking, have nothing, do
nothing, want nothing, – to the surprise of foreigners, who ask how
they live? The men are too lazy to be thieves, the women to be

something else. The dependence of the Swiss and English on their comforts, that is, on all 'appliances and means to boot',[19] as helps to enjoyment or hindrances to annoyance, makes them not only eager to procure different objects of accommodation and luxury, but makes them take such pains in their preservation and embellishment, and *pet* them so when acquired. 'A man', says Yorick, 'finds an apple, spits upon it, and calls it his.'[20] The more any one finds himself clinging to material objects for existence or gratification, the more he will take a personal interest in them, and the more will he clean, repair, polish, scrub, scour, and tug at them without end, as if it were his own soul that he was keeping clear from spot or blemish. A Swiss dairy-maid scours the very heart out of a wooden pail; a scullion washes the taste as well as the worms out of a dish of broccoli. The wenches are in like manner neat and clean in their own persons, but insipid. The most coarse and ordinary furniture in Switzerland has more pains bestowed upon it to keep it in order, than the finest works of art in Italy. There the pictures are suffered to moulder on the walls; and the Claudes in the Doria Palace at Rome are black with age and dirt. We set more store by them in England, where we have scarce any other sunshine! At the common inns on this side the Simplon, the very sheets have a character for whiteness to lose: the rods and testers of the beds are like a peeled wand. On the opposite side you are thankful when you are not shown into an apartment resembling a three-stalled stable, with horse-cloths for coverlids to hide the dirt, and beds of horse-hair or withered leaves as harbourage for vermin. The more, the merrier; the dirtier, the warmer; live and let live, seem maxims inculcated by the climate. Wherever things are not kept carefully apart from foreign admixtures and contamination, the distinctions of property itself will not, I conceive, be held exceedingly sacred. This feeling is strong as the passions are weak. A people that are remarkable for cleanliness, will be so for industry, for honesty, for avarice, and *vice versa*. The Italians cheat, steal, rob (when they think it worth their while to do so) with licensed impunity: the Swiss, who feel the value of property, and labour incessantly to acquire it, are afraid to lose it. At Brigg I first heard the cry of watchmen at night, which I had not heard for many months. I was reminded of the traveller who after wandering in remote countries saw a gallows near at hand, and knew by this circumstance that he approached the confines of civilization. The police in Italy is both secret and severe, but it is directed chiefly to political and not to civil matters. Patriot sighs are heaved unheard in the dungeons of St Angelo: the Neapolitan bandit breathes the free air of his native mountains!

It may by this time be conjectured why Catholics are less cleanly than Protestants, because in fact they are less scrupulous, and swallow whatever is set before them in matters of faith as well as other things. Protestants, as such, are captious and scrutinizing, try to pick holes and find fault, – have a dry, meagre, penurious imagination. Catholics are buoyed up over doubts and difficulties by a greater redundance of fancy, and make religion subservient to a sense of enjoyment. The one are for detecting and weeding out all corruptions and abuses in doctrine or worship: the others enrich theirs with the dust and cobwebs of antiquity, and think their ritual none the worse for the tarnish of age. Those of the Catholic Communion are willing to take it for granted that every thing is right; the professors of the Reformed religion have a pleasure in believing that every thing is wrong, in order that they may have to set it right. In morals, again, Protestants are more precise than their Catholic brethren. The creed of the latter absolves them of half their duties, of all those that are a clog on their inclinations, atones for all slips, and patches up all deficiencies. But though this may make them less censorious and sour, I am not sure that it renders them less in earnest in the part they do perform. When more is left to freedom of choice, perhaps the service that is voluntary will be purer and more effectual. That which is not so may as well be done by proxy; or if it does not come from the heart, may be suffered to exhale merely from the lips. If less is owing in this case to a dread of vice and fear of shame, more will proceed from a love of virtue, free from the least sinister construction. It is asserted that Italian women are more gross; I can believe it, and that they are at the same time more refined than others. Their religion is in the same manner more sensual: but is it not to the full as visionary and imaginative as any? I have heard Italian women say things that others would not – it does not therefore follow that they would do them: partly because the knowledge of vice that makes it familiar renders it indifferent; and because the same masculine tone of thinking that enables them to confront vice, may raise them above it into a higher sphere of sentiment. If their senses are more inflammable, their passions (and their love of virtue and of religion among the rest) may glow with proportionable ardour. Indeed the truest virtue is that which is least susceptible of contamination from its opposite. I may admire a Raphael, and yet not swoon at sight of a daub. Why should there not be the same taste in morals as in pictures or poems? Granting that vice has more votaries here, at least it has fewer mercenary ones, and this is no trifling advantage. As to manners, the Catholics must be allowed to carry it over all the world. The better sort not only say nothing to give you pain; they say nothing of others that it would give them pain to hear repeated. Scandal and tittle-tattle are long banished from good society. After all, to be wise is to be humane. What would our English *blue-stockings* say to this? The fault and the excellence of Italian society is, that the shocking or disagreeable is not supposed to have an existence in the nature of things.*

* The dirt and comparative want of conveniences among Catholics is often attributed to the number of their Saints' days and festivals, which divert them from labour, and give them an idle and disorderly turn of mind.

On the Difference between Writing and Speaking

'Some minds are proportioned to that which may be dispatched at
once, or within a short return of time: others to that which begins
afar off, and is to be won with length of pursuit.' LORD BACON[1]

It is a common observation, that few persons can be found who speak
and write equally well. Not only is it obvious that the two faculties
do not always go together in the same proportions: but they are not
unusually in direct opposition to each other. We find that the greatest
authors often make the worst company in the world; and again, some
of the liveliest fellows imaginable in conversation, or extempore
speaking, seem to lose all their vivacity and spirit the moment they
set pen to paper. For this a greater degree of quickness or slowness
of parts, education, habit, temper, turn of mind, and a variety of
collateral and predisposing causes are necessary to account. The subject
is at least curious, and worthy of an attempt to explain it. I shall
endeavour to illustrate the difference by familiar examples rather
than by analytical reasonings. The philosopher of old was not unwise,
who defined motion by getting up and walking.

The great leading distinction between writing and speaking is,
that more time is allowed for the one than the other: and hence
different faculties are required for, and different objects attained by,
each. He is properly the best speaker who can collect together the
greatest number of apposite ideas at a moment's warning: he is
properly the best writer who can give utterance to the greatest quantity
of valuable knowledge in the course of his whole life. The chief
requisite for the one, then, appears to be quickness and facility of
perception – for the other, patience of soul, and a power increasing

with the difficulties it has to master. He cannot be denied to be an expert speaker, a lively companion, who is never at a loss for something to say on every occasion or subject that offers: he, by the same rule, will make a respectable writer, who, by dint of study, can find out any thing good to say upon any one point that has not been touched upon before, or who, by asking for time, can give the most complete and comprehensive view of any question. The one must be done off-hand, at a single blow: the other can only be done by a repetition of blows, by having time to think and do better. In speaking, less is required of you, if you only do it at once, with grace and spirit: in writing, you stipulate for all that you are capable of, but you have the choice of your own time and subject. You do not expect from the manufacturer the same dispatch in executing an order that you do from the shopkeeper or warehouseman. The difference of *quicker* and *slower*, however, is not all: that is merely a difference of comparison in doing the same thing. But the writer and speaker have to do things essentially different. Besides habit, and greater or less facility, there is also a certain reach of capacity, a certain depth or shallowness, grossness or refinement of intellect, which marks out the distinction between those whose chief ambition is to shine by producing an immediate effect, or who are thrown back, by a natural bias, on the severe researches of thought and study.

We see persons of that standard or texture of mind that they can do nothing, but on the spur of the occasion: if they have time to deliberate, they are lost. There are others who have no resource, who cannot advance a step by any efforts or assistance, beyond a successful arrangement of common-places: but these they have always at command, at every body's service. There is F—;[2] meet him where you will in the street, he has his topic ready to discharge in the same breath with the customary forms of salutation; he is hand and glove with it; on it goes and off, and he manages it like Wart[3] his caliver.

> 'Hear him but reason in divinity,
> And, all-admiring, with an inward wish
> You would desire that he were made a prelate.
> Let him but talk of any state-affair,
> You'd say it had been all in all his study.

Turn him to any cause of policy,
The Gordian knot of it he will unloose,
Familiar as his garter. When he speaks,
The air, a charter'd libertine, stands still' — [4]

but, ere you have time to answer him, he is off like a shot, to repeat the same rounded, fluent observations to others: — a perfect master of the sentences, a walking polemic wound up for the day, a smartly bound political pocket-book! Set the same person to write a common paragraph, and he cannot get through it for very weariness: ask him a question, ever so little out of the common road, and he stares you in the face. What does all this bustle, animation, plausibility, and command of words amount to? A lively flow of animal spirits, a good deal of confidence, a communicative turn, and a tolerably tenacious memory with respect to floating opinions and current phrases. Beyond the routine of the daily newspapers and coffee-house criticism, such persons do not venture to think at all: or if they did, it would be so much the worse for them, for they would only be perplexed in the attempt, and would perform their part in the mechanism of society with so much the less alacrity and easy volubility.

The most dashing orator[5] I ever heard is the flattest writer I ever read. In speaking, he was like a volcano vomiting out *lava*; in writing, he is like a volcano burnt out. Nothing but the dry cinders, the hard shell remains. The tongues of flame, with which, in haranguing a mixed assembly, he used to illuminate his subject, and almost scorched up the panting air, do not appear painted on the margin of his works. He was the model of a flashy, powerful demagogue — a madman blest with a fit audience. He was possessed, infuriated with the patriotic *mania*; he seemed to rend and tear the rotten carcase of corruption with the remorseless, indecent rage of a wild beast: he mourned over the bleeding body of his country, like another Antony over the dead body of Cæsar, as if he would 'move the very stones of Rome to rise and mutiny':[6] he pointed to the 'Persian abodes, the glittering temples'[7] of oppression and luxury, with prophetic exultation; and, like another Helen, had almost fired another Troy! The lightning of national indignation flashed from his eye; the workings of the popular mind were seen labouring in his bosom: it writhed

461

and swelled with its rank 'fraught of aspics' tongues',[8] and the poison frothed over at his lips. Thus qualified, he 'wielded at will the fierce democracy, and fulmin'd over'[9] an area of souls, of no mean circumference. He who might be said to have 'roared you in the ears of the groundlings an 'twere any lion, aggravates his voice' on paper, 'like any sucking-dove'.[10] It is not merely that the same individual cannot sit down quietly in his closet, and produce the same, or a correspondent effect – that what he delivers over to the compositor is tame, and trite, and tedious – that he cannot by any means, as it were, 'create a soul under the ribs of death'[11] – but sit down yourself, and read one of these very popular and electrical effusions (for they have been published) and you would not believe it to be the same! The thunder-and-lightning mixture of the orator turns out a mere drab-coloured suit in the person of the prose-writer. We wonder at the change, and think there must be some mistake, some leger-de-main trick played off upon us, by which what before appeared so fine now appears to be so worthless. The deception took place *before*; now it is removed. 'Bottom! thou art translated!'[12] might be placed as a motto under most collections of printed speeches that I have had the good fortune to meet with, whether originally addressed to the people, the senate, or the bar. Burke's and Windham's form an exception: Mr Coleridge's *Conciones ad Populum* do not, any more than Mr Thelwall's *Tribune*. What we read is the same: what we hear and see is different – 'the self-same words, but *not* to the self-same tune'.[13] The orator's vehemence of gesture, the loudness of the voice, the speaking eye, the conscious attitude, the inexplicable dumb show and noise, – all 'those brave sublunary things that made his raptures clear',[14] – are no longer there, and without these he is nothing; – his 'fire and air'[15] turn to puddle and ditch-water, and the God of eloquence and of our idolatry sinks into a common mortal, or an image of lead, with a few labels, nicknames, and party watch-words stuck in his mouth. The truth is, that these always made up the stock of his intellectual wealth; but a certain exaggeration and extravagance of *manner* covered the nakedness, and swelled out the emptiness of the *matter*: the sympathy of angry multitudes with an impassioned theatrical declaimer supplied the place of argument or wit; while the physical animation and ardour of the speaker evaporated in 'sound and fury, signifying nothing',[16] and leaving no trace behind it. A popular speaker (such as I have been here describing) is like a vulgar actor off the stage – take away his cue, and he has nothing to say for himself. Or he is so accustomed to the intoxication of popular applause, that without that stimulus he has no motive or power of exertion left – neither imagination, understanding, liveliness, common sense, words or ideas – he is fairly cleared out; and in the intervals of sober reason, is the dullest and most imbecile of all mortals.

An orator can hardly get beyond *common-places*: if he does, he gets beyond his hearers. The most successful speakers, even in the House of Commons, have not been the best scholars or the finest writers – neither those who took the most profound views of their subject, nor who adorned it with the most original fancy, or the richest combinations of language. Those speeches that in general told best at the time, are not now readable. What were the materials of which they were chiefly composed? An imposing detail of passing events, a formal display of official documents, an appeal to established maxims, an echo of popular clamour, some worn-out metaphor newly vamped-up, – some hackneyed argument used for the hundredth, nay thousandth time, to fall in with the interests, the passions, or prejudices of listening and devoted admirers; – some truth or falsehood, repeated as the Shibboleth of party time out of mind, which gathers strength from sympathy as it spreads, because it is understood or assented to by the million, and finds, in the increased action of the minds of numbers, the weight and force of an instinct. A COMMON-PLACE does not leave the mind 'sceptical, puzzled, and undecided in the moment of action': – 'it gives a body to opinion, and a permanence to fugitive belief'.[17] It operates mechanically, and opens an instantaneous and infallible communication between the hearer and speaker. A set of cant-phrases, arranged in sounding sentences, and pronounced 'with good emphasis and discretion',[18] keep the gross and irritable humours of an audience in constant fermentation; and levy no tax on the understanding. To give a reason for any thing is to breed a doubt of it, which doubt you may not remove in the sequel; either because your reason may not be a good one, or because the person to whom it is addressed may not be able to comprehend it, or because *others* may not be able to comprehend it. He who offers to go into the grounds of an acknowledged axiom, risks the unanimity of the company 'by most admired disorder',[19] as he who digs to the foundation of a building to show its solidity, risks its falling. But a common-place is enshrined in its own unquestioned evidence, and constitutes its own immortal basis. Nature, it has been said, abhors a *vacuum*;[20] and the House of Commons, it might be said, hates every thing but a common-place! – Mr Burke did not often shock the prejudices of the House: he endeavoured to *account for them*, to 'lay the flattering unction' of philosophy 'to their souls'.[21] They could not endure him. Yet he did not attempt this by dry argument alone: he called to his aid the flowers of poetical fiction, and strewed the most dazzling colours of language over the Standing Orders of the House. It was a double offence to them – an aggravation of the encroachments of his genius. They would rather 'hear a cat mew or an axle-tree grate',[22] than hear a man talk philosophy by the hour –

> 'Not harsh and crabbed, as dull fools suppose,
> But musical as is Apollo's lute,
> And a perpetual feast of nectar'd sweets,
> Where no crude surfeit reigns.'[23]

He was emphatically called the *Dinner-Bell*. They went out by shoals when he began to speak. They coughed and shuffled him down. While he was uttering some of the finest observations (to speak in compass) that ever were delivered in that House, they walked out, not as the beasts came out of the ark, by twos and by threes, but in droves and companies of tens, of dozens, and scores! Oh! it is 'the heaviest stone which melancholy can throw at a man',[24] when you are in the middle of a delicate speculation to see 'a robusteous, periwig-pated fellow'[25] deliberately take up his hat and walk out. But what effect could Burke's finest observations be expected to have on the House of Commons in their corporate capacity? On the supposition that they were original, refined, comprehensive, his auditors had never heard, and assuredly they had never thought of them before: how then should they know that they were good or bad, till they had time to consider better of it, or till they were told what to think? In the mean time, their effect would be to stop the question: they were blanks in the debate: they could at best only be laid aside and left *ad referendum*.[26] What would it signify if four or five persons, at the utmost, felt their full force and fascinating power the instant they were delivered? They would be utterly unintelligible to nine-tenths of the persons present, and their impression upon any particular individual, more knowing than the rest, would be involuntarily paralysed by the torpedo touch of the elbow of a country-gentleman or city-orator. There is a reaction in insensibility as well as in enthusiasm; and men in society judge not by their own convictions, but by sympathy with others. In reading, we may go over the page again, whenever any thing new or questionable 'gives us pause':[27] besides, we are by ourselves, and it is *a word to the wise*. We are not afraid of understanding too much, and being called upon to unriddle. In hearing we are (saving the mark!) in the company of fools; and time presses. Was the debate to be suspended while Mr Fox or Mr Windham took this or that Honourable Member aside, to explain to them *that fine observation* of Mr Burke's, and to watch over the new birth of their understandings, the dawn of this new light! If we were to wait till Noble Lords and Honourable Gentlemen were inspired with a relish for abstruse thinking, and a taste for the loftier flights of fancy, the business of this great nation would shortly be at a stand. No: it is too much to ask that our good things should be duly appreciated by the first person we meet, or in the next minute after their disclosure; if the world are a little, a very little, the wiser or better for them a century hence, it is full as much as can be modestly expected! – The impression of any thing delivered in a large assembly must be comparatively null and void, unless you not only understand and feel its value yourself, but are conscious that it is felt and understood by the meanest capacity present. Till that is the case, the speaker is in your power, not you in his. The eloquence that is effectual and irresistible must stir the inert mass of prejudice, and pierce the opaquest shadows of ignorance. Corporate bodies move slow in the progress of intellect, for this reason, that they must keep back, like convoys, for the heaviest sailing vessels under their charge. The sinews of the wisest councils are, after all, impudence and interest: the most enlightened bodies are often but slaves of the weakest intellects they reckon among them, and the best-intentioned are but tools of the greatest hypocrites and knaves. – To conclude what I had to say on the character of Mr Burke's parliamentary style, I will just give an instance of what I mean in affirming that it was too recondite for his hearers; and it shall be even in so obvious a thing as a quotation. Speaking of the newfangled French Constitution, and in particular of the King (Louis XVI) as the chief power in form and appearance only, he repeated the famous lines in Milton describing Death, and concluded with peculiar emphasis,

> —'What *seem'd* its head,
> The *likeness* of a kingly crown had on.'[28]

The person who heard him make the speech said, that, if ever a poet's language had been finely applied by an orator to express his thoughts and make out his purpose, it was in this instance. The passage, I believe, is not in his reported speeches; and I should think, in all likelihood, it 'fell still-born'[29] from his lips; while one of Mr Canning's well-thumbed quotations out of Virgil would electrify the Treasury Benches, and be echoed by all the politicians of his own standing, and the tyros of his own school, from Lord Liverpool in the Upper down to Mr William Ward in the Lower House.

Mr Burke was an author before he was a Member of Parliament: he ascended to that practical eminence from 'the platform' of his literary pursuits. He walked out of his study into the House. But he never became a thorough-bred debater. He was not 'native to that element',[30] nor was he ever 'subdued to the quality'[31] of that motley crew of knights, citizens, and burgesses. The late Lord Chatham was made for, and by it. He seemed to vault into his seat there, like Hotspur, with the exclamation in his mouth – 'that Roan shall be my throne'.[32] Or he sprang out of the genius of the House of Commons, like Pallas from the head of Jupiter, completely armed. He assumed an ascendancy there from the very port and stature of his mind – from his aspiring and fiery temperament. He vanquished, because he could not yield. He controlled the purposes of others, because he was strong in his own obdurate self-will. He convinced his followers, by never doubting himself. He did not argue, but assert; he took what he chose for granted, instead of making a question of it. He was not a dealer in *moot-points*. He seized on some stronghold in the argument, and held it fast with a convulsive grasp – or wrested the weapons out of his adversaries' hands by main force. He entered the lists like a gladiator. He made political controversy a combat of personal skill and courage. He was not for wasting time in long-winded discussions with his opponents, but tried to disarm them by a word, by a glance of his eye, so that they should not dare to contradict or confront him again. He did not wheedle, or palliate, or circumvent, or make a studied appeal to the reason or the passions – he *dictated* his opinions to the House of Commons. 'He spoke as one having authority, and not as the Scribes.'[35] – But if he did not produce such an effect either by reason or imagination, how did he produce it? The principle by which he exerted his influence over others (and it is a principle of which some speakers that I might mention seem not to have an idea, even in possibility) was sympathy. He himself evidently had a strong possession of his subject, a thorough conviction, an intense interest; and this communicated itself from his *manner*, from the tones of his voice, from his commanding attitudes, and eager gestures, instinctively and unavoidably to his hearers. His will was surcharged with electrical matter like a Voltaic battery; and all who stood within its reach felt the full force of the shock. Zeal will do more than knowledge. To say the truth, there is little knowledge, – no ingenuity, no parade of individual details, not much attempt at general argument, neither wit nor fancy in his speeches – but there are a few plain truths told home: whatever he says, he does not mince the matter, but clenches it in the most unequivocal manner, and with the fullest sense of its importance, in clear, short, pithy, old English sentences. The most obvious things, as he puts them, read like axioms – so that he appears, as it were, the genius of common sense personified; and in turning to his speeches you fancy that you have met with (at least) one honest statesman! – Lord Chatham commenced his career in the intrigues of a camp and the bustle of a mess-room; where he probably learnt that the way to govern others, is to make your will your warrant, and your word a law. If he had spent the early part of his life, like Mr Burke, in writing a treatise on the *Sublime and Beautiful*, and in dreaming over the abstract nature and causes of things, he would never have taken the lead he did in the British Senate.

Both Mr Fox and Mr Pitt (though as opposite to each other as possible) were essentially speakers, not authors, in their mode of oratory. Beyond the moment, beyond the occasion, beyond the immediate power shewn, astonishing as that was, there was little remarkable or worth preserving in their speeches. There is no thought in them that implies a habit of deep and refined reflection (more than we are accustomed ordinarily to find in people of education); there is no knowledge that does not lie within the reach of obvious and mechanical search; and as to the powers of language, the chief miracle is, that a source of words so apt, forcible, and well-arranged, so copious and unfailing, should have been found constantly open to express their ideas without any previous preparation. Considered as written style, they are not far out of the common course of things; and perhaps it is assuming too much, and making the wonder greater than it is, with a very natural love of indulging our admiration of extraordinary persons, when we conceive that parliamentary speeches are in general delivered without any previous preparation. They do not, it is true, allow of preparation at the moment, but they have the preparation of the preceding night, and of the night before that, and of nights, weeks, months, and years of the same endless drudgery and routine, in going over the same subjects, argued (with some paltry difference) on the same grounds. *Practice makes perfect.* He who has got a speech by heart on any particular occasion, cannot be much gravelled for lack of matter on any similar occasion in future. Not only are the topics the same; the very same phrases – whole batches of them, – are served up as the Order of the Day; the same parliamentary bead-roll of grave impertinence is twanged off, in full cadence, by the Honourable Member or his Learned and Honourable Friend; and the well-known, voluminous, calculable periods roll over the drowsy ears of the auditors, almost before they are delivered from the vapid tongue that utters them! It may appear, at first sight, that here are a number of persons got together, picked out from the whole nation, who can speak at all times upon all subjects in the most exemplary manner; but the fact is, they only repeat the same things over and over on the same subjects, – and they obtain credit for general capacity and ready wit, like Chaucer's Monk, who, by having three words of Latin always in his mouth, passed for a great scholar.

'A few termes coude he, two or three,
That he had learned out of some decree;
No wonder is, he herd it all the day.'[54]

Try them on any other subject *out of doors*, and see how soon the extempore wit and wisdom 'will halt for it'.[55] See how few of those who have distinguished themselves *in* the House of Commons have done any thing *out of it*; how few that have, shine *there*! Read over the collections of old Debates, twenty, forty, eighty, a hundred years ago; they are the same *mutatis mutandis*, as those of yesterday. You wonder to see how little has been added; you grieve that so little has been lost. Even in their own favourite topics, how much are they to seek! They still talk gravely of the Sinking Fund in St Stephen's Chapel, which has been for some time exploded as a juggle by Mr Place of Charing-Cross; and a few of the principles of Adam Smith, which every one else had been acquainted with long since, are just now beginning to dawn on the collective understanding of the two Houses of Parliament. Instead of an exuberance of sumptuous matter, you have the same meagre standing dishes for every day in the year. You must serve an apprenticeship to a want of originality, to a suspension of thought and feeling. You are in a go-cart of prejudices, in a regularly constructed machine of pretexts and precedents; you are not only to wear the livery of other men's thoughts, but there is a House-of-Commons jargon which must be used for every thing. A man of simplicity and independence of mind cannot easily reconcile himself to all this formality and mummery; yet woe to him that shall attempt to discard it! You can no more move against the stream of custom, than you can make head against a crowd of people; the mob of lords and gentlemen will not let you speak or think but as they do. You are hemmed in, stifled, pinioned, pressed to death, – and if you make one false step, are 'trampled under the hoofs of a swinish multitude'![56] Talk of mobs! Is there any body of people that has this character in a more consummate degree than the House of Commons? Is there any set of men that determines more by acclamation, and less by deliberation and individual conviction? That is moved more *en masse*, in its aggregate capacity, as brute force and physical number? That judges with more Midas ears, blind and sordid, without discrimination of right and wrong? The greatest test of courage I can conceive, is to speak truth in the House of Commons. I have heard Sir Francis Burdett say things there which I could not enough admire; and which he could not have ventured upon saying, if, besides his honesty, he had not been a man of fortune, of family, of character, – aye, and a very good-looking man into the bargain! Dr Johnson had a wish[37] to try his hand in the House of Commons. An elephant might as well have been introduced there, in all the forms: Sir William Curtis makes a better figure. Either he or the Speaker (Onslow) must have resigned. The orbit of his intellect was not the one in which the intellect of the House moved by ancient privilege. *His* common-places were not *their* common-places. – Even Horne Tooke failed, with all his *tact*, his self-possession, his ready talent, and his long practice at the hustings. He had weapons of his own, with which he wished to make play, and did not lay his hand upon the established levers for wielding the House of Commons. A succession of dry, sharp-pointed sayings, which come in excellently well in the pauses or quick turns of conversation, do not make a speech. A series of drops is not a stream. Besides, he had been in the practice of rallying his guests and tampering with his subject; and this ironical tone did not suit his new situation. He had been used to 'give his own little Senate laws',[38] and when he found the resistance of the great one more than he could manage, he shrunk back from the attempt, disheartened and powerless. It is nothing that a man can talk (the better, the worse it is for him) unless he can talk in trammels; he must be drilled into the regiment; he must not run out of the course! The worst thing a man can do is to set up for a wit there – or rather (I should say) for a humourist – to say odd out-of-the-way things, to ape a character, to play the clown or the wag in the House. This is the very forlorn hope of a parliamentary ambition. They may tolerate it till they know what you are at, but no longer. It may succeed once or twice, but the third time you will be sure to break your neck. They know nothing of you, or your whims, nor have they time to look at a puppet-show. 'They look only at the stop-watch, my Lord!'[39] We have seen a very lively sally of this sort which failed lately. The House of Commons is the last place where a man will draw admiration by making a jest of his own character. But if he has a mind to make a jest of humanity, of liberty, and of common sense and decency, he will succeed well enough!

The only person who ever 'hit the House between wind and water'[40] in this way, – who made sport for the Members, and kept his own dignity (in our time at least), was Mr Windham. He carried on the traffic in parliamentary conundrums and enigmas with great *éclat* for more than one season. He mixed up a vein of characteristic eccentricity with a succession of far-fetched and curious speculations, very pleasantly. Extremes meet; and Mr Windham overcame the obstinate attachment of his hearers to fixed opinions by the force of paradoxes. He startled his bed-rid audience effectually. A paradox was a treat to them, on the score of novelty at least; 'the sight of one', according to the Scotch proverb, 'was good for sore eyes'. So Mr Windham humoured them in the thing for once. He took all sorts of commonly received doctrines and notions (with an understood reserve) – reversed them, and set up a fanciful theory of his own, instead. The changes were like those in a pantomime. Ask the first old woman you met her opinion on any subject, and you could get at the statesman's; for his would be just the contrary. He would be wiser than the old woman at any rate. If a thing had been thought cruel, he would prove that it was humane; if barbarous, manly; if wise, foolish; if sense, nonsense. His creed was the antithesis of common sense, loyalty excepted. Economy he could turn into ridicule, 'as a saving of cheese-parings and candle-ends',[41] – and total failure was with him 'negative success'.[42] He had no occasion, in thus setting up for original thinking, to inquire into the truth or falsehood of any proposition, but to ascertain whether it was currently believed in, and then to contradict it point-blank. He made the vulgar prejudices of others 'servile ministers'[43] to his own solecisms. It was not easy always to say whether he was in jest or earnest – but he contrived to hitch his extravagances into the midst of some grave debate; the House had their laugh for nothing; the question got into shape again, and Mr Windham was allowed to have been more *brilliant* than ever.*

Mr Windham was, I have heard, a silent man in company. Indeed

* It must be granted, however, that there was something *piquant* and provoking in his manner of 'making the worse appear the better reason'.[44] In keeping off the ill odour of a bad cause, he applied hartshorn and burnt feathers to the offended sense; and did not, like Mr Canning, treat us with the faded flowers of his oratory, like the faint smell of a perfumer's shop, or try to make Government 'love-locks'[45] of dead men's hair!

his whole style was an artificial and studied imitation, or capricious caricature of Burke's bold, natural, discursive manner. This did not imply much spontaneous power or fertility of invention; he was an intellectual posture-master, rather than a man of real elasticity and vigour of mind. Mr Pitt was also, I believe, somewhat taciturn and reserved. There was nothing clearly in the subject-matter of his speeches to connect with the ordinary topics of discourse, or with any given aspect of human life. One would expect him to be quite as much in the clouds as the automaton chess-player, or the last new Opera-singer. Mr Fox said little in private, and complained that in writing he had no style. So (to compare great things with small) Jack Davies, the unrivalled racket-player, never said any thing at all in company, and was what is understood by a modest man. When the racket was out of his hand, his occupation, his delight, his glory, (that which he excelled all mankind in) was gone! So when Mr Fox had no longer to keep up the ball of debate, with the floor of St Stephen's for a stage, and the world for spectators of the game, it is hardly to be wondered at that he felt a little at a loss – without his usual train of subjects, the same crowd of associations, the same spirit of competition, or stimulus to extraordinary exertion. The excitement of leading in the House of Commons (which, in addition to the immediate attention and applause that follows, is a sort of whispering gallery to all Europe) must act upon the brain like brandy or laudanum upon the stomach; and must, in most cases, produce the same debilitating effects afterwards. A man's faculties must be quite exhausted, his virtue gone out of him. That any one accustomed all his life to the tributary roar of applause from the great council of the nation, should think of dieting himself with the prospect of posthumous fame as an author, is like offering a confirmed dram-drinker a glass of fair water for his morning's draught. Charles Fox is not to be blamed for having written an indifferent history of James II but for having written a history at all. It was not his business to write a history – his business was *not to have made any more Coalitions*! But he found writing so dull, he thought it better to be a colleague of Lord Grenville! He did not want style (to say so is nonsense, because the style of his speeches was just and fine) – he wanted a sounding-board in the ear of posterity to try his periods upon. If he had gone to the House of Commons in the morning, and tried to make a speech fasting, when there was nobody to hear him, he might have been equally disconcerted at his want of style. The habit of speaking is the habit of being heard, and of wanting to be heard; the habit of writing is the habit of thinking aloud, but without the help of an echo. The orator sees his subject in the eager looks of his auditors; and feels doubly conscious, doubly impressed with it in the glow of their sympathy; the author can only look for encouragement in a blank piece of paper. The orator feels the impulse of popular enthusiasm,

– like proud seas under him:[46]

the only Pegasus the writer has to boast, is the hobby-horse of his own thoughts and fancies. How is he to get on then? From the lash of necessity. We accordingly see persons of rank and fortune continually volunteer into the service of oratory – and the State; but we have few authors who are not paid by the sheet! – I myself have heard Charles Fox engaged in familiar conversation. It was in the Louvre. He was describing the pictures to two persons that were with him. He spoke rapidly, but very unaffectedly. I remember his saying – 'All those blues and greens and reds are the Guercinos; you may know them by the colours.' He set Opie right as to Domenichino's *St Jerome*. 'You will find,' he said, 'though you may not be struck with it at first, that there is a great deal of truth and good sense in that picture.' There was a person at one time a good deal with Mr Fox, who, when the opinion of the latter was asked on any subject, very frequently interposed to give the answer. This sort of tantalizing interruption was ingeniously enough compared by some one, to walking up Ludgate-hill, and having the spire of St Martin's constantly getting in your way, when you wish to see the dome of St Paul's! – Burke, it is said, conversed as he spoke in public, and as he wrote. He was communicative, diffuse, magnificent. 'What is the use', said Mr Fox to a friend, 'of Sheridan's trying to swell himself out in this manner, like the frog in the fable?'[47] – alluding to his speech on Warren Hastings's trial. 'It is very well for Burke to express himself in that figurative way. It is natural to him; he talks so to his wife, to his servants, to his children; but as for Sheridan, he either never opens his mouth at all, or if he does, it is to utter some joke. It is out of the question for him to affect these *Orientalisms*.' Burke once came into Sir Joshua Reynolds's painting-room,[48] when one of his pupils was sitting for one of the sons of Count Ugolino;[49] this gentleman was personally introduced to him; – 'Ah! then,' said Burke, 'I find that Mr N— has not only a head that would do for Titian to paint, but is himself a painter.' At another time, he came in when Goldsmith was there, and poured forth such a torrent of violent personal abuse against the King, that they got to high words, and Goldsmith threatened to leave the room if he did not desist. Goldsmith bore testimony to his powers of conversation. Speaking of Johnson, he said, 'Does he wind into a subject like a serpent, as Burke does?'[50] With respect to his facility in composition, there are contradictory accounts. It has been stated by some, that he wrote out a plain sketch first, like a sort of dead colouring, and added the ornaments and tropes afterwards. I have been assured by a person who had the best means of knowing, that the *Letter to a Noble Lord* (the most rapid, impetuous, glancing, and sportive of all his works) was printed off, and the proof sent to him: and that it was returned to the printing-office with so many alterations and passages interlined, that the compositors refused to correct it as it was – took the whole matter in pieces, and re-set the copy. This looks like elaboration and afterthought. It was also one of Burke's latest compositions.* A regularly bred speaker would have made up his mind beforehand; but Burke's mind being, as originally constituted and by its first bias, that of an author, never became set. It was in further search and progress. It had an internal spring left. It was not tied down to the printer's form. It could still project itself into new beauties, and explore strange regions from the unwearied impulse of its own delight or curiosity. Perhaps among the passages interlined, in this case, were the description of the Duke of Bedford, as 'the Leviathan among all the creatures of the crown',[51] – the *catalogue raisonnée* of the Abbé Sieyès's pigeon-holes,[52] – or the comparison of the English Monarch to 'the proud keep of Windsor, with its double belt of kindred and coeval towers'.[53] Were these to

---

* Tom Paine, while he was busy about any of his works, used to walk out, compose a sentence or paragraph in his head, come home and write it down, and never altered it afterwards. He then added another, and so on, till the whole was completed.

be given up? If he had had to make his defence of his pension in the House of Lords, they would not have been ready in time, it appears; and, besides, would have been too difficult of execution on the spot: a speaker must not set his heart on such forbidden fruit. But Mr Burke was an author, and the press did not 'shut the gates of *genius* on mankind'.[54] A set of oratorical flourishes, indeed, is soon exhausted, and is generally all that the extempore speaker can safely aspire to. Not so with the resources of art or nature, which are inexhaustible, and which the writer has time to seek out, to embody, and to fit into shape and use, if he has the strength, the courage, and patience to do so.

There is then a certain range of thought and expression beyond the regular rhetorical routine, on which the author, to vindicate his title, must trench somewhat freely. The proof that this is understood to be so, is, that what is called an oratorical style is exploded from all good writing; that we immediately lay down an article, even in a common newspaper, in which such phrases occur as 'the Angel of Reform', 'the drooping Genius of Albion'; and that a very brilliant speech at a loyal dinner-party makes a very flimsy, insipid pamphlet. The orator has to get up for a certain occasion a striking compilation of partial topics, which, 'to leave no rubs or botches in the work',[55] must be pretty familiar, as well as palatable to his hearers; and in doing this, he may avail himself of all the resources of an artificial memory. The writer must be original, or he is nothing. He is not to take up with ready-made goods; for he has time allowed him to create his own materials, to make novel combinations of thought and fancy, to contend with unforeseen difficulties of style and execution, while we look on, and admire the growing work in secret and at leisure. There is a degree of finishing as well as of solid strength in writing, which is not to be got at every day, and we can wait for perfection. The author owes a debt to truth and nature which he cannot satisfy at sight, but he has pawned his head on redeeming it. It is not a string of clap-traps to answer a temporary or party-purpose, – violent, vulgar, and illiberal, – but general and lasting truth that we require at his hands. We go to him as pupils, not as partisans. We have a right to expect from him profounder views of things; finer observations; more ingenious illustrations; happier and bolder expressions.

He is to give the choice and picked results of a whole life of study; what he has struck out in his most felicitous moods, has treasured up with most pride, has laboured to bring to light with most anxiety and confidence of success. He may turn a period in his head fifty different ways, so that it comes out smooth and round at last. He may have caught a glimpse of a simile, and it may have vanished again: let him be on the watch for it, as the idle boy watches for the lurking-place of the adder. We can wait. He is not satisfied with a reason he has offered for something; let him wait till he finds a better reason. There is some word, some phrase, some idiom that expresses a particular idea better than any other, but he cannot for the life of him recollect it: let him wait till he does. Is it strange that among twenty thousand words in the English language, the one of all others that he most needs should have escaped him? There are more things in nature than there are words in the English language, and he must not expect to lay rash hands on them all at once.

> 'Learn to *write* slow: all other graces
> Will follow in their proper places.'[56]

You allow a writer a year to think of a subject; he should not put you off with a truism at last. You allow him a year more to find out words for his thoughts; he should not give us an echo of all the fine things that have been said a hundred times.* All authors, however, are not so squeamish; but take up with words and ideas as they find them delivered down to them. Happy are they who write Latin verses! Who copy the style of Dr Johnson! Who hold up the phrase of ancient Pistol![57] They do not trouble themselves with those hair-breadth distinctions of thought or meaning that puzzle nicer heads – let us leave them to their repose! A person in habits of composition often hesitates in conversation for a particular word: it is because he is in search of the best word, and *that* he cannot hit upon. In writing he would stop till it came.† It is not true, however, that the scholar could

---

* Just as a poet ought not to cheat us with lame metre and defective rhymes, which might be excusable in an improvisatori versifier.

† That is essentially a bad style which seems as if the person writing it never stopped for breath, nor gave himself a moment's pause, but strove to make up by redundancy and fluency for want of choice and correctness of expression.

avail himself of a more ordinary word if he chose, or readily acquire a command of ordinary language; for his associations are habitually intense, not vague and shallow; and words occur to him only as *tallies* to certain modifications of feeling. They are links in the chain of thought. His imagination is fastidious, and rejects all those that are 'of no mark or likelihood'.[58] Certain words are in his mind indissolubly wedded to certain things; and none are admitted at the *levee* of his thoughts, but those of which the banns have been solemnized with scrupulous propriety. Again, the student finds a stimulus to literary exertion, not in the immediate *éclat* of his undertaking, but in the difficulty of his subject, and the progressive nature of his task. He is not wound up to a sudden and extraordinary effort of presence of mind; but is for ever awake to the silent influxes of things, and his life is one long labour. Are there no sweeteners of his toil? No reflections, in the absence of popular applause or social indulgence, to cheer him on his way? Let the reader judge. *His* pleasure is the counterpart of, and borrowed from the same source as the writer's. A man does not read out of vanity, nor in company, but to amuse his own thoughts. If the reader, from disinterested and merely intellectual motives, relishes an author's 'fancies and good nights',[59] the last may be supposed to have relished them no less. If he laughs at a joke, the inventor chuckled over it to the full as much. If he is delighted with a phrase, he may be sure the writer jumped at it; if he is pleased to cull a straggling flower from the page, he may believe that it was plucked with no less fondness from the face of nature. Does he fasten, with gathering brow and looks intent, on some difficult speculation? He may be convinced that the writer thought it a fine thing to split his brain in solving so curious a problem, and to publish his discovery to the world. There is some satisfaction in the contemplation of power; there is also a little pride in the conscious possession of it. With what pleasure do we read books! If authors could but feel this, or remember what they themselves once felt, they would need no other temptation to persevere.

To conclude this account with what perhaps I ought to have set out with, a definition of the character of an author. There are persons who in society, in public intercourse, feel no excitement,

'Dull as the lake that slumbers in the storm,'[60]

but who, when left alone, can lash themselves into a foam. They are never less alone than when alone. Mount them on a dinner-table, and they have nothing to say; shut them up in a room by themselves, and they are inspired. They are 'made fierce with dark keeping'.[61] In revenge for being tongue-tied, a torrent of words flows from their pens, and the storm which was so long collecting comes down apace. It never rains but it pours. Is not this strange, unaccountable? Not at all so. They have a real interest, a real knowledge of the subject, and they cannot summon up all that interest, or bring all that knowledge to bear, while they have any thing else to attend to. Till they can do justice to the feeling they have, they can do nothing. For this they look into their own minds, not in the faces of a gaping multitude. What they would say (if they could) does not lie at the orifices of the mouth ready for delivery, but is wrapped in the folds of the heart and registered in the chambers of the brain. In the sacred cause of truth that stirs them, they would put their whole strength, their whole being into requisition; and as it implies a greater effort to drag their words and ideas from their lurking-places, so there is no end when they are once set in motion. The whole of a man's thoughts and feelings cannot lie on the surface, made up for use; but the whole must be a greater quantity, a mightier power, if they could be got at, layer under layer, and brought into play by the levers of imagination and reflection. Such a person then sees farther and feels deeper than most others. He plucks up an argument by the roots, he tears out the very heart of his subject. He has more pride in conquering the difficulties of a question, than vanity in courting the favour of an audience. He wishes to satisfy himself before he pretends to enlighten the public. He takes an interest in things in the abstract more than by common consent. Nature is his mistress, truth his idol. The contemplation of a pure idea is the ruling passion of his breast. The intervention of other people's notions, the being the immediate object of their censure or their praise, puts him out. What will tell, what will produce an effect, he cares little about; and therefore he produces the greatest. The *personal* is to him an impertinence; so he conceals himself and writes. Solitude 'becomes his glittering bride, and airy

thoughts his children'.[62] Such a one is a true author; and not a member
of any Debating Club, or Dilettanti Society whatever!*

---

* I have omitted to dwell on some other differences of body and mind that often prevent
the same person from shining in both capacities of speaker and writer. There are natural
impediments to public speaking, such as the want of a strong voice and steady nerves. A
high authority of the present day (Mr Canning) has thought this a matter of so much
importance, that he goes so far as even to let it affect the constitution of Parliament, and
conceives that gentlemen who have not bold foreheads and brazen lungs, but modest
pretensions and patriotic views, should be allowed to creep into the great assembly of the
nation through the avenue of close boroughs, and not be called upon 'to face the storms
of the hustings'.[63] In this point of view, Stentor[64] was a man of genius, and a noisy
jack-pudding may cut a considerable figure in the 'Political House that Jack built'.[65] I
fancy Mr C. Wynn is the only person in the kingdom who has fully made up his mind
that a total defect of voice is the most necessary qualification for a Speaker of the House
of Commons!

Madame Pasta and Mademoiselle Mars

I liked Mademoiselle Mars exceedingly well, till I saw Madame Pasta whom I liked so much better. The reason is, the one is the perfection of French, the other of natural acting. Madame Pasta is Italian, and she might be English – Mademoiselle Mars belongs emphatically to her country; the scene of her triumphs is Paris. She plays naturally too, but it is French nature. Let me explain. She has, it is true, none of the vices of the French theatre, its extravagance, its flutter, its grimace, and affectation, but her merit in these respects is as it were negative, and she seems to put an artificial restraint upon herself. There is still a pettiness, an attention to *minutiæ*, an etiquette, a mannerism about her acting: she does not give an entire loose to her feelings, or trust to the unpremeditated and habitual impulse of her situation. She has greater elegance, perhaps, and precision of style than Madame Pasta, but not half her boldness or grace. In short, every thing she does is voluntary, instead of being spontaneous. It seems as if she might be acting from marginal directions to her part. When not speaking, she stands in general quite still. When she speaks, she extends first one hand and then the other, in a way that you can foresee every time she does so, or in which a machine might be elaborately constructed to develop different successive movements. When she enters, she advances in a straight line from the other end to the middle of the stage with the slight unvarying trip of her country-women, and then stops short, as if under the drill of a *fugal-man*.[1] When she speaks, she articulates with perfect clearness and propriety, but it is the facility of a singer executing a difficult passage. The case is that of habit, not of nature. Whatever she does, is right in the intention, and she takes care not to carry it too far; but

she appears to say beforehand, '*This* I will do, I must not do *that*.'
Her acting is an inimitable study or consummate rehearsal of the
part as a preparatory performance: she hardly yet appears to have
assumed the character; something more is wanting, and that something you find in Madame Pasta. If Mademoiselle Mars has to smile,
a slight and evanescent expression of pleasure passes across the surface
of her face; twinkles in her eyelids, dimples her chin, compresses her
lips, and plays on each feature: when Madame Pasta smiles, a beam
of joy seems to have struck upon her heart, and to irradiate her
countenance. Her whole face is bathed and melted in expression,
instead of its glancing from particular points. When she speaks, it is
in music. When she moves, it is without thinking whether she is
graceful or not. When she weeps, it is a fountain of tears, not a few
trickling drops, that glitter and vanish the instant after. The French
themselves admire Madame Pasta's acting, (who indeed can help it?)
but they go away thinking how much one of her simple movements
would be improved by their extravagant gesticulations, and that her
noble, natural expression would be the better for having twenty airs
of mincing affectation added to it. In her Nina[2] there is a listless
vacancy, an awkward grace, a want of *bienséance*,[3] that is like a child
or a changeling, and that no French actress would venture upon for
a moment, lest she should be suspected of a want of *esprit* or of *bon
mien*. A French actress always plays before the court; she is always
in the presence of an audience, with whom she first settles her personal
pretensions by a significant hint or side-glance, and then as much
nature and simplicity as you please. Poor Madame Pasta thinks no
more of the audience than Nina herself would, if she could be observed
by stealth, or than the fawn that wounded comes to drink, or the
flower that droops in the sun or wags its sweet head in the gale. She
gives herself entirely up to the impression of the part, loses her power
over herself, is led away by her feelings either to an expression of
stupor or of artless joy, borrows beauty from deformity, charms
unconsciously, and is transformed into the very being she represents.
She does not act the character – she *is* it, looks it, breathes it. She
does not study for an effect, but strives to possess herself of the feeling
which should dictate what she is to do, and which gives birth to the
proper degree of grace, dignity, ease, or force. She makes no point all

the way through, but her whole style and manner is in perfect keeping, as if she were really a love-sick, care-crazed maiden, occupied with one deep sorrow, and who had no other idea or interest in the world. This alone is true nature and true art. The rest is sophistical; and French art is not free from the imputation; it never places an implicit faith in nature but always mixes up a certain portion of art, that is, of consciousness and affectation with it. I shall illustrate this subject from a passage in Shakespeare.

'POLIXENES. – Shepherdess,
(A fair one are you) well you fit our ages
With flow'rs of winter.

PERDITA. – Sir, the year growing ancient,
Not yet on summer's death, nor on the birth
Of trembling winter, the fairest flowers o' th' season
Are our carnations and streak'd gilliflowers,
Which some call nature's bastards; of that kind
Our rustic garden's barren, and I care not
To get slips of them.

POLIX. – Wherefore, gentle maiden,
Do you neglect them?

PERDITA. – For I have heard it said,
There is an art which in their piedness shares
With great creating nature.

POLIX. – Say, there be,
Yet nature is made better by no mean,
But nature makes that mean; so o'er that art,
Which you say adds to nature, is an art,
That nature makes; you see, sweet maid, we marry
A gentle scyon to the wildest stock,
And make conceive a bark of baser kind
By bud of nobler race. This is an art,
Which does mend nature, change it rather; but
The art itself is nature.

PERDITA. – So it is.

POLIX. – Then make your garden rich in gilliflowers,
And do not call them bastards.

PERDITA. — I'll not put
A dibble in earth, to set one slip of them;
No more than, were I painted, I should wish
This youth to say, 'twere well; and only therefore
Desire to breed by me.' — *Winter's Tale, Act IV.*

Madame Pasta appears to be of Perdita's mind in respect to her acting, and I applaud her resolution heartily. We English are charged unjustly with wishing to disparage the French: we cannot help it; there is a natural antipathy between the two nations. Thus unable to deny their theatrical merit, we are said insidiously to have invented the appellation, *French nature*, to explain away or throw a stigma on their most successful exertions:

— 'Though that their art be nature,
We throw such changes of vexation on it,
As it may lose some colour.'[4]

The English are a heavy people, and the most like a stone of all others. The French are a lively people, and more like a feather. They are easily moved and by slight causes, and each part of the impression has its separate effect: the English, if they are moved at all (which is a work of time and difficulty), are moved altogether, or in mass, and the impression, if it takes root, strikes deep and spreads wide, involving a number of other impressions in it. If a fragment of a rock wrenched from its place rolls slowly at first, gathers strength and fury as it proceeds, tears up every thing in its way, and thunders to the plain below, there is something noble and imposing in the sight, for it is an image of our own headlong passions and the increasing vehemence of our desires. But we hate to see a feather launched into the air and driven back on the hand that throws it, shifting its course with every puff of wind, and carried no farther by the strongest than by the slightest impulse. It is provoking (is it not?) to see the strength of the blow always defeated by the very insignificance and want of resistance in the object, and the impulse received never answering to the impulse given. It is the very same fluttering, fidgeting, tantalizing, inconsequential, ridiculous process that annoys us in the French character. There seems no *natural* correspondence between objects and feelings, between things and words. By yielding to every impulse at once, nothing produces a powerful or permanent impression; nothing produces an aggregate impression, for every part tells separately. Every idea turns off to something else, or back upon itself; there is no progress made, no blind impulse, no accumulation of imagination with circumstances, no absorption of all other feelings in one overwhelming one, that is, no keeping, no *momentum*, no integrity, no totality, no inflexible sincerity of purpose, and it is this resolution of the sentiments into their detached points and first impressions, so that they do not take an entire and involuntary hold of them, but either they can throw them off from their lightness, or escape from them by reason of their minuteness, that we English complain of as French nature or a want of nature, for by nature is only meant that the mind identifies itself with something so as to be no longer master of itself, and the French mind never identifies itself with any thing, but always has its own consciousness, its own affectation, its own gratification, its own slippery inconstancy or impertinent prolixity interposed between the object and the impression. It is this theatrical or artificial nature with which we cannot and will not sympathize, because it circumscribes the truth of things and the capacities of the human mind within the petty round of vanity, indifference, and physical sensations, stunts the growth of imagination, effaces the broad light of nature, and requires us to look at all things through the prism of their petulance and self-conceit. The French in a word leave *sincerity* out of their nature (not moral but imaginative sincerity), cut down the varieties of feeling to their own narrow and superficial standard, and having clipped and adulterated the current coin of expression, would pass it off as sterling gold. We cannot make an exchange with them. They are affected by things in a different manner from us, not in a different degree; and a mutual understanding is hopeless. We have no dislike to foreigners as such: on the contrary, a rage for foreign artists and works of art is one of our foibles. But if we give up our national pride, it must be to our taste and understandings. Nay, we adopt the manners and the fashions of the French, their dancing and their cooking, – not their music, not their painting, not their poetry, not their metaphysics, not their style of acting. If we are sensible of our own stupidity, we cannot admire *their* vivacity;

if we are sick of our own awkwardness, we like it better than their grace; we cannot part with our grossness for their refinement; if we would be glad to have our lumpish clay animated, it must be with true Promethean heat, not with painted phosphorus: they are not the Frankensteins that must perform this feat. Who among us in reading Schiller's *Robbers* for the first time ever asked if it was German or not? Who in reading Klopstock's *Messiah* did not object that it was German, not because it was German, but because it was heavy; that is, because the imagination and the heart do not act like a machine, so as to be wound up or let down by the pulleys of the will? Do not the French complain (and complain justly), that a picture is English, when it is coarse and unfinished, and leaves out the details which are one part of nature? Do not the English remonstrate against this defect too, and endeavour to cure it? But it may be said we relish Schiller, because he is barbarous, violent, and like Shakespeare. We have the Cartoons of Raphael then, and the Elgin Marbles; and we profess to admire and understand these too, and I think without any affectation. The reason is that there is no affectation in them. We like those noble outlines[5] of the human face at Hampton Court; the sustained dignity of the expression; the broad, ample folds of the drapery; the bold, massive limbs; there is breath and motion in them, and we would willingly be so transformed and spiritualized: but we do not want to have our heavy, stupid faces flittered away into a number of glittering points or transfixed into a smooth petrifaction on French canvas. Our faces, if wanting in expression, have a settled purpose in them; are as solid as they are stupid; and we are at least flesh and blood. We also like the sway of the limbs and negligent grandeur of the Elgin Marbles; in spite of their huge weight and manly strength, they have the buoyancy of a wave of the sea, with all the ease and softness of flesh: they fall into attitudes of themselves: but if they were put into attitudes by the genius of Opera-dancing, we should feel no disposition to imitate or envy them, any more than we do the Zephyr and Flora graces of French statuary. We prefer a single head of Chantrey's to a quarry of French sculpture. The English are a modest people, except in comparing themselves with their next neighbours, and nothing provokes their pride in this case, so much as the self-sufficiency of the latter. When Madame Pasta walks in upon the stage, and looks about her with the same unconsciousness or timid wonder as the young stag in the forest; when she moves her limbs as carelessly as a tree its branches; when she unfolds one of her divine expressions of countenance, which reflect the inmost feelings of the soul, as the calm, deep lake reflects the face of heaven; do we not sufficiently admire her, do we not wish her ours, and feel, with the same cast of thought and character, a want of glow, of grace, and ease in the expression of what we feel? We bow, like Guiderius and Arviragus[6] in the cave when they saw Imogen, as to a thing superior. On the other hand, when Mademoiselle Mars comes on the stage, something in the manner of a fantoccini figure[7] slid along on a wooden frame, and making directly for the point at which her official operations commence — when her face is puckered into a hundred little expressions like the wrinkles on the skin of a bowl of cream, set in a window to cool, her eyes peering out with an ironical meaning, her nose pointing it, and her lips confirming it with a dry pressure — we admire indeed, we are delighted, we may envy, but we do not sympathize or very well know what to make of it. We are not electrified, as in the former instance, but *animal-magnetized*.*[8] We can manage pretty well with any one feeling or expression (like a clown that must be taught his letters one at a time) if it keeps on in the same even course, that expands and deepens by degrees, but we are distracted and puzzled, or at best only amused with that sort of expression which is hardly itself for two moments together, that shifts from point to point, that seems to have no place to rest on, no impulse to urge it forward, and might as well be twenty other things at the same time — where tears come so easily they can hardly be real, where smiles are so playful they appear put on, where you cannot tell what you are to believe, for the parties themselves do not know whether they are in jest or earnest, where the whole tone is ironical, conventional, and where the difference between nature and art is

---

* Even her *j'existe* [9] in Valeria (when she first acquires the use of sight) is pointed like an epigram, and *put in italics*, like a technical or metaphysical distinction, instead of being a pure effusion of joy. Accordingly a French pit-critic took up the phrase, insisting that *to exist* was common to all things, and asked what the expression was in the original German. This treatment of passion is *topical* and extraneous, and seldom strikes at the seat of the disorder, the heart.

nearly imperceptible. This is what we mean by French nature, *viz.* that the feelings and ideas are so slight and discontinuous that they can be changed for others like a dress or visor; or else, to make up for want of truth and breadth, are caricatured into a mask. This is the defect of their tragedy, and the defect and excellence of their comedy; the one is a pompous abortion, the other a *facsimile* of life, almost too close to be agreeable. A French comic actor might be supposed to have left his shop for half an hour to show himself upon a stage – there is no difference, worth speaking of, between the man and the actor – whether on the stage or at home, he is equally full of gesticulation, equally voluble, and without meaning – as their tragic actors are solemn puppets, moved by rules, pulled by wires, and with their mouths stuffed with rant and bombast. This is the harm that can be said of them: they themselves are doubtless best acquainted with the good, and are not too diffident to tell it. Though other people abuse them, they can still praise themselves! I once knew a French lady who said all manner of good things and forgot them the next moment; who maintained an argument with great wit and eloquence, and presently after changed sides, without knowing that she had done so; who invented a story and believed it on the spot; who wept herself and made you weep with the force of her descriptions, and suddenly drying her eyes, laughed at you for looking grave. Is not this like acting? Yet it was not affected in her, but natural, involuntary, incorrigible. The hurry and excitement of her natural spirits was like a species of intoxication, or she resembled a child in thoughtlessness and incoherence. She was a Frenchwoman. It was nature, but nature that had nothing to do with truth or consistency.

In one of the Paris Journals lately, there was a criticism on two pictures by Girodet of Bonchamps and Cathelineau, Vendean chiefs. The paper is well written, and points out the defects of the portraits very fairly and judiciously. These persons are there called 'Illustrious Vendeans'. The dead dogs of 1812 are the illustrious Vendeans of 1824. Monsieur Chateaubriand will have it so, and the French are too polite a nation to contradict him. They split on this rock of complaisance, surrendering every principle to the fear of giving offence, as we do on the opposite one of party-spirit and rancorous hostility, sacrificing the best of causes, and our best friends to the desire of giving offence, to the indulgence of our spleen, and of an ill-tongue. We apply a degrading appellation, or bring an opprobrious charge against an individual; and such is our tenaciousness of the painful and disagreeable, so fond are we of brooding over grievances, so incapable are our imaginations of raising themselves above the lowest scurrility or the dirtiest abuse, that should the person attacked come out an angel from the contest, the prejudice against him remains nearly the same as if the charge had been fully proved. An unpleasant association has been created, and this is too delightful an exercise of the understanding with the English public easily to be parted with. John Bull would as soon give up an estate as a bugbear. Having been once gulled, they are not soon *ungulled.* They are too knowing for that. Nay, they resent the attempt to undeceive them as an injury. The French apply a brilliant epithet to the most vulnerable characters; and thus gloss over a life of treachery or infamy. With them the immediate or last impression is every thing: with us, the first, if it is sufficiently strong and gloomy, never wears out! The French critic observes that M. Girodet has given General Bonchamps, though in a situation of great difficulty and danger, a calm and even smiling air, and that the portrait of Cathelineau, instead of a hero, looks only like an angry peasant. In fact, the lips in the first portrait are made of marmalade, the complexion is cosmetic, and the smile ineffably engaging; while the eye of the peasant Cathelineau darts a beam of light, such as no eye, however illustrious, was ever illumined with. But so it is, the Senses, like a favourite lap-dog, are pampered and indulged at any expense: the Imagination, like a gaunt hound, is starved and driven away. Danger and death, and ferocious courage and stern fortitude, however the subject may exact them, are uncourtly topics and kept out of sight: but smiling lips and glistening eyes are pleasing objects, and there you find them. *The style of portrait requires it.* It is of this varnish and glitter of sentiment that we complain (perhaps it is no business of ours) as what must forever intercept the true feeling and genuine rendering of nature in French art, as what makes it spurious and counterfeit, and strips it of simplicity, force and grandeur. Whatever pleases, whatever strikes, holds out a temptation to the French artist too strong to be resisted, and there is too great a sympathy in the public mind with this view of the subject, to quarrel with or severely criticize what is so congenial with its own feelings. A premature and superficial sensibility is the grave of French genius and of French taste. Beyond the momentary impulse of a lively organization, all the rest is mechanical and pedantic; they give you rules and theories for truth and nature, the Unities for poetry, and the dead body for the living soul of art. They colour a Greek statue ill and call it a picture: they paraphrase a Greek tragedy, and overload it with long-winded speeches, and think they have a national drama of their own. Any other people would be ashamed of such preposterous pretensions. In invention, they do not get beyond models; in imitation, beyond details. Their microscopic vision hinders them from seeing nature. I observed two young students the other day near the top of Montmartre, making oil sketches of a ruinous hovel in one corner of the road. Paris lay below, glittering grey and gold (like a spider's web) in the setting sun, which shot its slant rays upon their shining canvas, and they were busy in giving the finishing touches. The little outhouse was in itself picturesque enough: it was covered with moss, which hung down in a sort of drooping form as the rain had streamed down it, and the walls were loose and crumbling in pieces. Our artists had repaired every thing: not a stone was out of its place: no traces were left of the winter's flaw in the pendent moss. One would think the bricklayer and gardener had been regularly set to work to do away every thing like sentiment or keeping in the object before them. Oh, Paris! it was indeed on this thy weak side (thy inability to connect any two ideas into one) that thy barbarous and ruthless foes entered in! –

The French have a great dislike to any thing obscure. They cannot bear to suppose for a moment there should be any thing they do not understand: they are shockingly afraid of being *mystified*. Hence they have no idea either of mental or aerial perspective. Every thing must be distinctly made out and in the foreground; for if it is not so clear that they can take it up bit by bit, it is wholly lost upon them, and they turn away as from an unmeaning blank. This is the cause of the stiff, unnatural look of their portraits. No allowance is made for the veil that shade as well as an oblique position casts over the different parts of the face; every feature, and every part of every feature is given with the same flat effect, and it is owing to this perverse fidelity of detail, that that which is literally true, is naturally false. The side of a face seen in perspective does not present so many markings as the one that meets your eye full: but if it is put into the *vice* of French portrait, wrenched round by incorrigible affectation and conceit (that insist upon knowing all that is there, and set it down formally, though it is not to be seen), what can be the result, but that the portrait will look like a head stuck in a vice, will be flat, hard, and finished, will have the appearance of reality and at the same time look like paint; in short, will be a French portrait? That is, the artist, from a pettiness of view and want of more enlarged and liberal notions of art, comes forward not to represent nature, but like an impertinent commentator to explain what she has left in doubt, to insist on that which she passes over or touches only slightly, to throw a critical light on what she casts into shade, and to pick out the details of what she blends into masses. I wonder they allow the existence of the term *clair-obscur*[10] at all, but it is a word; and a word is a thing they can repeat and remember. A French gentleman formerly asked me what I thought of a landscape in their Exhibition. I said I thought it too clear. He made answer that he should have conceived that to be impossible. I replied, that what I meant was, that the parts of the several objects were made out with too nearly equal distinctness all over the picture; that the leaves of the trees in shadow were as distinct as those in light, the branches of the trees at a distance as plain as of those near. The perspective arose only from the diminution of objects, and there was no interposition of air. I said, one could not see the leaves of a tree a mile off, but this, I added, appertained to a question in metaphysics. He shook his head, thinking that a young Englishman could know as little of abstruse philosophy as of fine art, and no more was said. I owe to this gentleman (whose name was Mérimée, and who I understand is still living), a grateful sense of many friendly attentions and many useful suggestions, and I take this opportunity of acknowledging my obligations.

Some one was observing of Madame Pasta's acting, that its chief merit consisted in its being natural. To which it was replied, 'Not so, for that there was an ugly and a handsome nature.' There is an old proverb, that 'Home is home, be it never so homely': and so it may be said of nature; that whether ugly or handsome, it is nature still. Besides beauty, there is truth, which is always one principal thing. It doubles the effect of beauty, which is mere affectation without it, and even reconciles us to deformity. Nature, the truth of nature in imitation, denotes a given object, a 'foregone conclusion'[11] in reality, to which the artist is to conform in his copy. In nature real objects exist, real causes act, which are only supposed to act in art; and it is in the subordination of the uncertain and superficial combinations of fancy to the more stable and powerful law of reality that the perfection of art consists. A painter may arrange fine colours on his palette; but if he merely does this, he does nothing. It is accidental or arbitrary. The difficulty and the charm of the combination begins with the truth of imitation, that is, with the resemblance to a given object in nature, or in other words, with the strength, coherence, and justness of our impressions, which must be verified by a reference to a known and determinate class of objects as the test. Art is so far the development or the communication of knowledge, but there can be no knowledge unless it be of some given or standard object which exists independently of the representation and bends the will to an obedience to it. The strokes of the pencil are what the artist pleases, are mere idleness and caprice without meaning, unless they point to nature. Then they are right or wrong, true or false, as they follow in her steps and copy her style. Art must anchor in nature, or it is the sport of every breath of folly. Natural objects convey given or intelligible ideas which art embodies and represents, or it represents nothing, is a mere chimera or bubble; and, farther, natural objects or events cause certain feelings, in expressing which art manifests its power, and genius its prerogative. The capacity of expressing these movements of passion is in proportion to the power with which they are felt; and this is the same as sympathy with the human mind placed in actual situations, and influenced by the real causes that are supposed to act. Genius is the power which equalizes or identifies the imagination with the reality or with nature. Certain events happening to us naturally produce joy, others sorrow, and these feelings, if excessive, lead to other consequences, such as stupor or ecstasy, and express themselves by certain signs in the countenance or voice or gestures; and we admire and applaud an actress accordingly, who gives these tones and gestures as they would follow in the order of things, because we then know that her mind has been affected in like manner, that she enters deeply into the resources of nature, and understands the riches of the human heart. For nothing else can impel and stir her up to the imitation of the truth. The way in which real causes act upon the feelings is not arbitrary, is not fanciful; it is as true as it is powerful and unforeseen; the effects can only be similar when the exciting causes have a correspondence with each other, and there is nothing like feeling *but* feeling. The sense of joy can alone produce the smile of joy; and in proportion to the sweetness, the unconsciousness, and the expansion of the last, we may be sure is the fulness and sincerity of the heart from which it proceeds. The elements of joy at least are there, in their integrity and perfection. The death or absence of a beloved object is nothing as a word, as a mere passing thought, till it comes to be dwelt upon, and we begin to feel the revulsion, the long dreary separation, the stunning sense of the blow to our happiness, as we should in reality. The power of giving this sad and bewildering effect of sorrow on the stage is derived from the force of sympathy with what we should feel in reality. That is, a great histrionic genius is one that approximates the effects of words, or of supposed situations on the mind, most nearly to the deep and vivid effect of real and inevitable ones. Joy produces tears: the violence of passion turns to childish weakness; but this could not be foreseen by study, nor taught by rules, nor mimicked by observation. Natural acting is therefore fine, because it implies and calls forth the most varied and strongest feelings that the supposed characters and circumstances can possibly give birth to: it reaches the height of the subject. The conceiving or entering into a part in this sense is every thing: the acting follows easily and of course. But art without nature is a nickname, a word without meaning, a conclusion without any premises to go upon. The beauty of Madame Pasta's acting in Nina proceeds upon this principle. It is not what she does at any particular juncture, but she seems to be the character, and to be incapable of divesting herself of it. This is true acting: any thing else is playing tricks, may be clever and ingenious, is French Opera-dancing, recitation, heroics or hysterics — but it is not true nature or true art.

On a Portrait of an English Lady, by Vandyke

The portrait I speak of is in the Louvre, where it is numbered 416, and the only account of it in the *Catalogue* is that of a *Lady and her daughter*. It is companion to another whole-length by the same artist, No. 417, of a *Gentleman and a little girl*. Both are evidently English.

The face of the lady has nothing very remarkable in it, but that it may be said to be the very perfection of the English female face. It is not particularly beautiful, but there is a sweetness in it, and a goodness conjoined, which is inexpressibly delightful. The smooth ivory forehead is a little ruffled, as if some slight cause of uneasiness, like a cloud, had just passed over it. The eyes are raised with a look of timid attention; the mouth is compressed with modest sensibility; the complexion is delicate and clear; and over the whole figure (which is seated) there reign the utmost propriety and decorum. The habitual gentleness of the character seems to have been dashed with some anxious thought or momentary disquiet, and, like the shrinking flower, in whose leaves the lucid drop yet trembles, looks out and smiles at the storm that is overblown. A mother's tenderness, a mother's fear, appears to flutter on the surface, and on the extreme verge of the expression, and not to have quite subsided into thoughtless indifference or mild composure. There is a reflection of the same expression in the little child at her knee, who turns her head round with a certain appearance of constraint and innocent wonder; and perhaps it is the difficulty of getting her to sit (or to sit still) that has caused the transient contraction of her mother's brow, — that lovely, unstained mirror of pure affection, too fair, too delicate, too soft and feminine for the breath of serious misfortune ever to come near, or not to crush it. It is a face, in short, of the greatest purity and sensibility, sweetness and simplicity, or such as Chaucer might have described

'Where all is conscience and tender heart'.[1]

I have said that it is an English face; and I may add (without being invidious) that it is not a French one. I will not say that they have no face to equal this; of that I am not a judge; but I am sure they have no face equal to this, in the qualities by which it is distinguished. They may have faces as amiable, but then the possessors of them will be conscious of it. There may be equal elegance, but not the same ease; there may be even greater intelligence, but without the innocence; more vivacity, but then it will run into petulance or coquetry; in short, there may be every other good quality but a total absence of all pretension to or wish to make a display of it, but the same unaffected modesty and simplicity. In French faces (and I have seen some that were charming both for the features and expression) there is a varnish of insincerity, a something theatrical or meretricious; but here, every particle is pure to the 'last recesses of the mind'.[2] The face (such as it is, and it has a considerable share both of beauty and meaning) is without the smallest alloy of affectation. There is no false glitter in the eyes to make them look brighter; no little wrinkles about the corners of the eye-lids, the effect of self-conceit; no pursing up of the mouth, no significant leer, no primness, no extravagance, no assumed levity or gravity. You have the genuine text of nature without gloss or comment. There is no heightening of conscious charms to produce greater effect, no studying of airs and graces in the glass of vanity. You have not the remotest hint of the milliner, the dancing-master, the dealer in paints and patches. You have before you a real English lady of the seventeenth century, who looks like one, because she cannot look otherwise; whose expression of sweetness, intelligence, or concern is just what is natural to her, and what the occasion requires; whose entire demeanour is the emanation of her habitual sentiments and disposition, and who is as free from guile or affectation as the little child by her side. I repeat that this is not the distinguishing character of the French physiognomy, which, at its best, is often spoiled by a consciousness of what it is, and a restless desire to be something more.

Goodness of disposition, with a clear complexion and handsome features, is the chief ingredient in English beauty. There is a great difference in this respect between Vandyke's portraits of women and Titian's, of which we may find examples in the Louvre. The picture, which goes by the name of his *Mistress*, is one of the most celebrated of the latter. The neck of this picture is like a broad crystal mirror; and the hair which she holds so carelessly in her hand is like meshes of beaten gold. The eyes which roll in their ample sockets, like two shining orbs, and which are turned away from the spectator, only dart their glances the more powerfully into the soul; and the whole picture is a paragon of frank cordial grace, and transparent brilliancy of colouring. Her tight bodice compresses her full but finely proportioned waist; while the tucker in part conceals and almost clasps the snowy bosom. But you never think of any thing beyond the personal attractions, and a certain sparkling intelligence. She is not marble, but a fine piece of animated clay. There is none of that retired and shrinking character, that modesty of demeanour, that sensitive delicacy, that starts even at the shadow of evil – that are so evidently to be traced in the portrait by Vandyke. Still there is no positive vice, no meanness, no hypocrisy, but an unconstrained elastic spirit of self-enjoyment, more bent on the end than scrupulous about the means; with firmly braced nerves, and a tincture of vulgarity. She is not like an English lady, nor like a lady at all; but she is a very fine servant-girl, conscious of her advantages, and willing to make the most of them. In fact, Titian's *Mistress* answers exactly, I conceive, to the idea conveyed by the English word, *sweetheart.* – The Marchioness of Guasto is a fairer comparison. She is by the supposition a lady, but still an Italian one. There is a honeyed richness about the texture of the skin, and her air is languid from a sense of pleasure. Her dress, though modest, has the marks of studied coquetry about it; it touches the very limits which it dares not pass; and her eyes which are bashful and downcast, do not seem to droop under the fear of observation, but to retire from the gaze of kindled admiration,

> —'As if they thrill'd
> Frail hearts, yet quenched not!'[3]

One might say, with Othello, of the hand with which she holds the globe that is offered to her acceptance —

> —'This hand of yours requires
> A sequester from liberty, fasting and pray'r,
> Much castigation, exercise devout;
> For here's a young and *melting* devil here,
> That commonly rebels.'[4]

The hands of Vandyke's portrait have the purity and coldness of marble. The colour of the face is such as might be breathed upon it by the refreshing breeze; that of the Marchioness of Guasto's is like the glow it might imbibe from a golden sunset. The expression in the English lady springs from her duties and her affections; that of the Italian Countess inclines more to her ease and pleasures. The Marchioness of Guasto was one of three sisters, to whom, it is said, the inhabitants of Pisa proposed to pay divine honours, in the manner that beauty was worshipped by the fabulous enthusiasts of old. Her husband seems to have participated in the common infatuation, from the fanciful homage that is paid to her in this allegorical composition; and if she was at all intoxicated by the incense offered to her vanity, the painter must be allowed to have 'qualified' the expression of it 'very craftily'.[5]

I pass on to another female face and figure, that of the Virgin, in the beautiful picture of the *Presentation in the Temple*, by Guido. The expression here is *ideal*, and has a reference to visionary objects and feelings. It is marked by an abstraction from outward impressions, a downcast look, an elevated brow, an absorption of purpose, a stillness and resignation, that become the person and the scene in which she is engaged. The colour is pale or gone; so that purified from every grossness, dead to worldly passions, she almost seems like a statue kneeling. With knees bent, and hands uplifted, her motionless figure appears supported by a soul within, all whose thoughts, from the low ground of humility, tend heavenward. We find none of the triumphant buoyancy of health and spirit as in the Titian's *Mistress*, nor the luxurious softness of the portrait of the Marchioness of Guasto, nor the flexible, tremulous sensibility, nor the anxious attention to passing circumstances, nor the familiar look of the lady by Vandyke; on the contrary, there is a complete unity and concentration of expression, the whole is wrought up and moulded into one intense feeling, but that feeling fixed on objects remote, refined, and ethereal as the form of the fair supplicant. A still greater contrast to this internal, or as it were, *introverted* expression, is to be found in the group of female heads by the same artist, Guido, in his picture of the *Flight of Paris and Helen.* They are the three last heads on the left-hand side of the picture. They are thrown into every variety of attitude, as if to take the heart by surprise at every avenue. A tender warmth is suffused over their faces; their head-dresses are airy and fanciful, their complexion sparkling and glossy; their features seem to catch pleasure from every surrounding object, and to reflect it back again. Vanity, beauty, gaiety glance from their conscious looks and wreathed smiles, like the changing colours from the ring-dove's neck. To sharpen the effect and point the moral, they are accompanied by a little negro-boy, who holds up the train of elegance, fashion, and voluptuous grace!

Guido was the 'genteelest' of painters; he was a poetical Vandyke. The latter could give, with inimitable and perfect skill, the airs and graces of people of fashion under their daily and habitual aspects, or as he might see them in a looking-glass. The former saw them in his 'mind's eye',[6] and could transform them into supposed characters and imaginary situations. Still the elements were the same. Vandyke gave them with the *mannerism* of habit and the individual details; Guido, as they were rounded into grace and smoothness by the breath of fancy, and borne along by the tide of sentiment. Guido did not want the *ideal* faculty, though he wanted strength and variety. There is an effeminacy about his pictures, for he gave only the different modifications of beauty. It was the Goddess that inspired him, the Siren that seduced him; and whether as saint or sinner, was equally welcome to him. His creations are as frail as they are fair. They all turn on a passion for beauty, and without this support, are nothing. He could paint beauty combined with pleasure or sweetness, or grief, or devotion; but unless it were the ground-work and the primary condition of his performance, he became insipid, ridiculous, and extravagant. There is one thing to be said in his favour; he knew his own powers or followed his own inclinations; and the delicacy of his *tact* in general prevented him from attempting subjects uncongenial with it. He 'trod the primrose path of dalliance',[7] with equal prudence and modesty. That he is a little monotonous and tame, is all that can be said against him; and he seldom went out of his way to expose his deficiencies in a glaring point of view. He came round to subjects of beauty at last, or gave them that turn. A story is told of his having painted a very lovely head of a girl, and being asked from whom he had taken it, he replied, 'From his old man!' This is not unlikely. He is the only great painter (except Correggio) who appears constantly to have subjected what he saw to an imaginary standard. His Magdalens are more beautiful than sorrowful; in his Madonnas there is more of sweetness and modesty than of elevation. He makes but little difference between his heroes and his heroines; his angels are women, and his women angels! If it be said that he repeated himself too often, and has painted too many Magdalens and Madonnas, I can only say in answer, 'Would he had painted twice as many!' If Guido wanted compass and variety in his art, it signifies little, since what he wanted is abundantly supplied by others. He had softness, delicacy and *ideal* grace in a supreme degree, and his fame rests on these as the cloud on the rock. It is to the highest point of excellence in any art or department that we look back with gratitude and admiration, as it is the highest mountain-peak that we catch in the distance, and lose sight of only when it turns to air.

I know of no other difference between Raphael and Guido, than that the one was twice the man the other was. Raphael was a bolder genius, and invented according to nature: Guido only made draughts after his own disposition and character. There is a common cant of criticism which makes Titian merely a colourist. What he really wanted was invention: he had expression in the highest degree. I declare I have seen heads of his with more meaning in them than any of Raphael's. But he fell short of Raphael in this, that (except in one or two instances) he could not heighten and adapt the expression that he saw to different and more striking circumstances. He gave more of what he saw than any other painter that ever lived, and in the imitative part of his art had a more universal genius than Raphael had in composition and invention. Beyond the actual and habitual look of nature, however, 'the demon that he served'[8] deserted him, or became a very tame one. Vandyke gave more of the general air and manners of fashionable life than of individual character; and the subjects that he treated are neither remarkable for intellect nor passion. They are people of polished manners, and placid constitutions; and many of the very best of them are 'stupidly good'.[9] Titian's portraits, on the other hand, frequently present a much more formidable than inviting appearance. You would hardly trust yourself in a room with them. You do not bestow a cold, leisurely approbation on them, but look to see what they may be thinking of you, not without some apprehension for the result. They have not the clear smooth skins or the even pulse that Vandyke's seem to possess. They are, for the most part, fierce, wary, voluptuous, subtle, haughty. Raphael painted Italian faces as well as Titian. But he threw into them a character of intellect rather than of temperament. In Titian the irritability takes the lead, sharpens and gives direction to the understanding. There seems to be a personal controversy between the spectator and the individual whose portrait he contemplates, which shall be master of the other. I may refer to two portraits in the Louvre, the one by Raphael, the other by Titian, (Nos. 1153 and 1210), in illustration of these remarks. I do not know two finer or more characteristic specimens of these masters, each in its way. The one is of a student dressed in black, absorbed in thought, intent on some problem, with the hands crossed and leaning on a table for support, as it were to give freer scope to the labour of the brain, and though the eyes are directed towards you, it is with evident absence of mind. Not so the other portrait, No. 1210. All its faculties are collected to see what it can make of you, as if you had intruded upon it with some hostile design, it takes a defensive attitude, and shows as much vigilance as dignity. It draws itself up, as if to say, 'Well, what do you think of me?' and exercises a discretionary power over you. It has 'an eye to threaten and command',[10] not to be lost in idle thought, or in ruminating over some abstruse, speculative proposition. It is this intense personal character which, I think, gives the superiority to Titian's portraits over all others, and stamps them with a living and permanent interest. Of other pictures you tire, if you have them constantly before you; of his, never. For other pictures have either an abstracted look and you dismiss them, when you have made up your mind on the subject as a matter of criticism; or an heroic look, and you cannot be always straining your enthusiasm; or an insipid look, and you sicken of it. But whenever you turn to look at Titian's portraits, they appear to be looking at you; there seems to be some question pending between you, as though an intimate friend or inveterate foe were in the room with you; they exert a kind of fascinating power; and there is that exact resemblance of individual nature which is always new and always interesting, because you cannot carry away a mental abstraction of it, and you must recur to the object to revive it in its full force and integrity. I would as soon have Raphael's or most other pictures hanging up in a Collection, that I might pay an occasional visit to them: Titian's are the only ones that I should wish to have hanging in the same room with me for company.

Titian in his portraits appears to have understood the principle of historical design better than any body. Every part tells, and has a bearing on the whole. There is no one who has such simplicity and repose — no violence, no affectation, no attempt at forcing an effect; insomuch that by the uninitiated he is often condemned as unmeaning and insipid. A turn of the eye, a compression of the lip decides the point. He just draws the face out of its most ordinary state, and gives it the direction he would have it take; but then every part takes the same direction, and the effect of this united impression (which is absolutely momentary and all but habitual) is wonderful. It is that which makes his portraits the most natural and the most striking in the world. It may be compared to the effect of a number of small loadstones, that by acting together lift the greatest weights. Titian seized upon the lines of character in the most original and connected point of view. Thus in his celebrated portrait of Hippolito de Medici, there is a keen, sharpened expression that strikes you, like a blow from the spear that he holds in his hand. The look goes through you; yet it has no frown, no startling gesticulation, no affected penetration. It is quiet, simple, but it almost withers you. The whole face and each separate feature is cast in the same acute or wedge-like form. The forehead is high and narrow, the eye-brows raised and coming to a point in the middle, the nose straight and peaked, the mouth contracted and drawn up at the corners, the chin acute, and the two sides of the face slanting to a point. The number of acute angles which the lines of the face form, are, in fact, a net entangling the attention and subduing the will. The effect is felt at once, though it asks time and consideration to understand the cause. It is a face which you would beware of rousing into anger or hostility, as you would beware of setting in motion some complicated and dangerous machinery. The possessor of it, you may be sure, is no trifler. Such, indeed, was the character of the man. This is to paint true portrait and true history. So if our artist painted a mild and thoughtful expression, all the lines of the countenance were softened and relaxed. If the mouth was going to speak, the whole face was going to speak. It was the same in colour. The gradations are infinite, and yet so blended as to be imperceptible. No two tints are the same, though they produce the greatest harmony and simplicity of tone, like flesh itself. 'If', said a person, pointing to the shaded side of a portrait of Titian, 'you could turn this round to the light, you would find it would be of the same colour as the other side!' In short, there is manifest in his portraits a greater tenaciousness and identity of impression than in those of any other painter. Form, colour, feeling, character, seemed to adhere to his eye, and to become part of himself; and his pictures, on this account, 'leave stings'[11] in the minds of the spectators! There is, I grant, the same personal appeal, the same point-blank look in some of Raphael's portraits (see those of a Princess of Aragon and of Count Castiglione, Nos. 1150 and 1151) as in Titian: but they want the texture of the skin and the minute individual details to stamp them with the same reality. And again, as to the uniformity of outline in the features, this principle has been acted upon and carried to excess by Kneller and other artists. The eyes, the eye-brows, the nose, the mouth, the chin, are rounded off as if they were turned in a *lathe*, or as a peruke-maker arranges the curls of a wig. In them it is vile and mechanical, without any reference to truth of character or nature; and instead of being pregnant with meaning and originality of expression, produces only insipidity and monotony.

Perhaps what is offered above as a key to the peculiar expression of Titian's heads may also serve to explain the difference between painting or copying a portrait. As the perfection of his faces consists in the entire unity and coincidence of all the parts, so the difficulty of ordinary portrait-painting is to bring them to bear at all, or to piece one feature, or one day's labour on to another. In copying, this difficulty does not occur at all. The human face is not one thing, as the vulgar suppose, nor does it remain always the same. It has infinite varieties, which the artist is obliged to notice and to reconcile, or he will make strange work. Not only the light and shade upon it do not continue for two minutes the same: the position of the head constantly varies (or if you are strict with a sitter, he grows sullen and stupid), each feature is in motion every moment, even while the artist is working at it, and in the course of a day the whole expression of the countenance undergoes a change, so that the expression which you gave to the forehead or eyes yesterday is totally incompatible with that which you have to give to the mouth to-day. You can only bring it back again to the same point or give it a consistent construction by an effort of imagination, or a strong feeling of character; and you must connect the features together less by the eye than by the mind. The mere setting down what you see in this medley of successive, teasing, contradictory impressions, would never do; either you must continually efface what you have done the instant before, or if you retain it, you will produce a piece of patchwork, worse than any caricature. There must be a comprehension of the whole, and in truth a *moral sense* (as well as a literal one) to unravel the confusion, and guide you through the labyrinth of shifting muscles and features. You must feel what *this* means, and dive into the hidden soul, in order to know whether *that* is as it ought to be; for you cannot be sure that it remains as it was. Portrait-painting is, then, painting from recollection and from a conception of character, with the object before us to assist the memory and understanding. In copying, on the contrary, one part does not run away and leave you in the lurch, while you are intent upon another. You have only to attend to what is before you, and finish it carefully a bit at a time, and you are sure that the whole will come right. One might parcel it out into squares, as in engraving, and copy one at a time, without seeing or thinking of the rest. I do not say that a conception of the whole, and a feeling of the art will not abridge the labour of copying, or produce a truer likeness; but it is the changeableness or identity of the object that chiefly constitutes the difficulty or facility of imitating it, and, in the latter case, reduces it nearly to a mechanical operation. It is the same in the imitation of *still-life*, where real objects have not a principle of motion in them. It is as easy to produce a *facsimile* of a table or a chair as to copy a picture, because these things do not stir from their places any more than the features of a portrait stir from theirs. You may therefore bestow any given degree of minute and continued attention on finishing any given part without being afraid that when finished it will not correspond with the rest. Nay, it requires more talent to copy a fine portrait than to paint an original picture of a table or a chair, for the picture has a soul in it, and the table has not. — It has been made an objection (and I think a just one) against the extreme high-finishing of the drapery and backgrounds in portraits (to which some schools, particularly the French, are addicted), that it gives an unfinished look to the face, the most important part of the picture. A lady or a gentleman cannot sit quite so long or so still as a lay-figure, and if you finish up each part according to the length of time it will remain in one position, the face will seem to have been painted for the sake of the drapery, not the drapery to set off the face. There is an obvious limit to every thing, if we attend to common sense and feeling. If a carpet or a curtain will admit of being finished more than the living face, we finish them less because they excite less interest, and we are less willing to throw away our time and pains upon them. This is the unavoidable result in a natural and well-regulated style of art; but what is to be said of a school where no interest is felt in any thing, where nothing is known of any object but that it is there, and where superficial and petty details which the eye can explore, and the hand execute, with persevering and systematic indifference, constitute the soul of art?

The expression is the great difficulty in history or portrait-painting, and yet it is the great clue to both. It renders forms doubly impressive from the interest and signification attached to them, and at the same time renders the imitation of them critically nice, by making any departure from the line of truth doubly sensible. Mr Coleridge used to say, that what gave the romantic and mysterious interest to Salvator's landscapes was their containing some implicit analogy to human or other living forms. His rocks had a latent resemblance to the outline of a human face; his trees had the distorted jagged shape of a satyr's horns and grotesque features. I do not think this is the case; but it may serve to supply us with an illustration of the present question. Suppose a given outline to represent a human face, but to be so disguised by circumstances and little interruptions as to be mistaken for a projecting fragment of a rock in a natural scenery. As long as we conceive of this outline merely as a representation of a rock or other inanimate substance, any copy of it, however rude, will seem the same and as good as the original. Now let the disguise be removed and the general resemblance to a human face pointed out, and what before seemed perfect, will be found to be deficient in the most essential features. Let it be further understood to be a profile of a particular face that we know, and all likeness will vanish from the want of the individual expression, which can only be given by being felt. That is, the imitation of external and visible form is only correct or nearly perfect, when the information of the eye and the direction of the hand are aided and confirmed by the previous knowledge and actual feeling of character in the object represented. The more there is of character and feeling in any object, and the greater sympathy there is with it in the mind of the artist, the closer will be the affinity between the imitation and the thing imitated; as the more there is of character and expression in the object without a proportionable sympathy with it in the imitator, the more obvious will this defect and the imperfection of the copy become. That is, expression is the great test and measure of a genius for painting, and the fine arts. The mere imitation of *still-life*, however perfect, can never furnish proofs of the highest skill or talent; for there is an inner sense, a deeper intuition into nature that is never unfolded by merely mechanical objects, and which, if it were called out by a new soul being suddenly infused into an inanimate substance, would make the former unconscious representation appear crude and vapid. The eye is sharpened and the hand made more delicate in its tact,

> 'While by the power
> Of harmony, and the deep power of joy,
> We see into the life of things'.[12]

We not only *see*, but *feel* expression, by the help of the finest of all our senses, the sense of pleasure and pain. He then is the greatest painter who can put the greatest quantity of expression into his works, for this is the nicest and most subtle object of imitation; it is that in which any defect is soonest visible, which must be able to stand the severest scrutiny, and where the power of avoiding errors, extravagance, or tameness can only be supplied by the fund of moral feeling, the strength or delicacy of the artist's sympathy with the ideal object of his imitation. To see or imitate any given sensible object is one thing, the effect of attention and practice; but to give expression to a face is to collect its meaning from a thousand other sources, is to bring into play the observation and feeling of one's whole life, or an infinity of knowledge bearing upon a single object in different degrees and manners, and implying a loftiness and refinement of character proportioned to the loftiness and refinement of expression delineated. Expression is of all things the least to be mistaken, and the most evanescent in its manifestations. Pope's lines on the character of women may be addressed to the painter who undertakes to embody it.

> 'Come then, the colours and the ground prepare,
> Dip in the rainbow, trick it off in air;
> Chuse a firm cloud, before it falls, and in it
> Catch, ere it change, the Cynthia of the minute.'[13]

It is a maxim among painters that no one can paint more than his own character, or more than he himself understands or can enter into. Nay, even in copying a head, we have some difficulty in making the features unlike our own. A person with a low forehead or a short chin puts a constraint on himself in painting a high forehead or a long chin. So much has sympathy to do with what is supposed to be a mere act of servile imitation! – To pursue this argument one step farther. People sometimes wonder what difficulty there can be in painting, and ask what you have to do but to set down what you see? This is true, but the difficulty is to see what is before you. This is at least as difficult as to learn any trade or language. We imagine that we see the whole of nature, because we are aware of no more than we see of it. We also suppose that any given object, a head, a hand, is one thing, because we see it at once, and call it by one name. But how little we see or know, even of the most familiar face, beyond a vague abstraction, will be evident to every one who tries to recollect distinctly all its component parts, or to draw the most rude outline of it for the first time; or who considers the variety of surface, the numberless lights and shades, the tints of the skin, every particle and pore of which varies, the forms and markings of the features, the combined expression, and all these caught (as far as common use is concerned) by a random glance, and communicated by a passing word. A student, when he first copies a head, soon comes to a stand, or is at a loss to proceed from seeing nothing more in the face than there is in his copy. After a year or two's practice he never knows when to have done, and the longer he has been occupied in copying a face or any particular feature, sees more and more in it, that he has left undone and can never hope to do. There have been only four or five painters who could ever produce a copy of the human countenance really fit to be seen; and even of these few none was ever perfect, except in giving some single quality or partial aspect of nature, which happened to fall in with his own particular studies and the bias of his genius, as Raphael the drawing, Rembrandt the light and shade, Vandyke ease and delicacy of appearance, &c. Titian gave more than any one else, and yet he had his defects. After this, shall we say that any, the commonest and most uninstructed spectator sees the whole of nature at a single glance, and would be able to stamp a perfect representation of it on the canvas, if he could embody the image in his mind's eye?

I have in this Essay mentioned one or two of the portraits in the Louvre that I like best. The two landscapes which I should most covet, are the one with a Rainbow by Rubens, and the *Adam and Eve in Paradise* by Poussin. In the first, shepherds are reposing with their flocks under the shelter of a breezy grove, the distances are of air, and the whole landscape seems just washed with the shower that has passed off. The Adam and Eve by Poussin is the full growth and luxuriant expansion of the principle of vegetation. It is the first lovely dawn of creation, when nature played her virgin fancies wild; when all was sweetness and freshness, and the heavens dropped fatness. It is the very *ideal* of landscape-painting, and of the scene it is intended to represent. It throws us back to the first ages of the world, and to the only period of perfect human bliss, which is, however, on the point of being soon disturbed.* I should be contented with these four or five pictures, the *Lady* by Vandyke, the Titian, the *Presentation in the Temple*, the Rubens, and the Poussin, or even with faithful copies of them, added to the two which I have of a young Neapolitan Nobleman and of the Hippolito de Medici; and which, when I look at them, recall other times and the feelings with which they were done. It is now twenty years since I made those copies, and I hope to keep them while I live. It seems to me no longer ago than yesterday. Should the next twenty years pass as swiftly, forty years will have glided by me like a dream. By this kind of speculation I can look down as from a slippery height on the beginning, and the end of life beneath my feet, and the thought makes me dizzy!

My taste in pictures is, I believe, very different from that of rich and princely collectors. I would not give two-pence for the whole Gallery at Fonthill. I should like to have a few pictures hung round the room, that speak to me with well-known looks, that touch some string of memory — not a number of varnished, smooth, glittering gewgaws. The taste of the Great in pictures is singular, but not unaccountable. The King is said to prefer the Dutch to the Italian school of painting; and if you hint your surprise at this, you are looked upon as a very Gothic and *outré*[15] sort of person. You are told, however, by way of consolation, — 'To be sure, there is Lord Carlisle likes an Italian picture — Mr Holwell Carr likes an Italian picture —

---

* I may be allowed to mention here (not for the sake of invidious comparison, but to explain my meaning,) Mr Martin's picture of Adam and Eve asleep in Paradise. It has this capital defect, that there is no *repose* in it. You see two insignificant naked figures, and a preposterous architectural landscape, like a range of buildings over-looking them. They might as well have been represented on the top of the pinnacle of the Temple, with the world and all the glories thereof spread out before them. They ought to have been painted imparadised in one another's arms, shut up in measureless content, with Eden's choicest bowers closing round them, and Nature stooping to clothe them with vernal flowers. Nothing could be too retired, too voluptuous, too sacred from 'day's garish eye';[14] on the contrary, you have a gaudy panoramic view, a glittering barren waste, a triple row of clouds, of rocks, and mountains, piled one upon the other, as if the imagination already bent its idle gaze over that wide world which was so soon to be our place of exile, and the aching, restless spirit of the artist was occupied in building a stately prison for our first parents, instead of decking their bridal bed, and wrapping them in a short-lived dream of bliss.

the Marquis of Stafford is fond of an Italian picture – Sir George Beaumont likes an Italian picture!' These, notwithstanding, are regarded as quaint and daring exceptions to the established rule; and their preference is a species of *lèse majesté* in the Fine Arts, as great an eccentricity and want of fashionable etiquette, as if any gentleman or nobleman still preferred old claret to new, when the King is known to have changed his mind on this subject; or was guilty of the offence of dipping his fore-finger and thumb in the middle of a snuff-box, instead of gradually approximating the contents to the edge of the box, according to the most approved models. One would imagine that the great and exalted in station would like lofty subjects in works of art, whereas they seem to have an almost exclusive predilection for the mean and mechanical. One would think those whose word was law, would be pleased with the great and striking effects of the pencil;* on the contrary, they admire nothing but the little and elaborate. They have a fondness for cabinet and *furniture* pictures, and a proportionable antipathy to works of genius. Even art with them must be servile, to be tolerated. Perhaps the seeming contradiction may be explained thus. Such persons are raised so high above the rest of the species, that the more violent and agitating pursuits of mankind appear to them like the turmoil of ants on a mole-hill. Nothing interests them but their own pride and self-importance. Our passions are to them an impertinence; an expression of high sentiment they rather shrink from as a ludicrous and upstart assumption of equality. They therefore like what glitters to the eye, what is smooth to the touch; but they shun, by an instinct of sovereign taste, whatever has a soul in it, or implies a reciprocity of feeling. The Gods of the earth can have no interest in any thing human; they are cut off from all sympathy with the 'bosoms and businesses of men'.[17] Instead of requiring to be wound up beyond their habitual feeling of stately dignity, they wish to have the springs of over-strained pretension let down, to be relaxed with 'trifles light as air',[18] to be amused with the

---

* The Duke of Wellington, it is said, cannot enter into the merits of Raphael; but he admires 'the spirit and fire'[16] of Tintoret. I do not wonder at this bias. A sentiment probably never dawned upon his Grace's mind; but he may be supposed to relish the dashing execution and *hit or miss* manner of the Venetian artist. Oh, Raphael! well is it that it was one who did not understand thee, that blundered upon the destruction of humanity!

familiar and frivolous, and to have the world appear a scene of *still-life*, except as they disturb it! The little in thought and internal sentiment is a natural relief and set off to the oppressive sense of external magnificence. Hence kings babble and repeat they know not what. A childish dotage often accompanies the consciousness of absolute power. Repose is somewhere necessary, and the soul sleeps while the senses gloat around! Besides, the mechanical and high-finished style of art may be considered as something *done to order*. It is a task to be executed more or less perfectly, according to the price given, and the industry of the artist. We stand by, as it were, to see the work done, insist upon a greater degree of neatness and accuracy, and exercise a sort of petty, jealous jurisdiction over each particular. We are judges of the minuteness of the details, and though ever so nicely executed, as they give us no ideas beyond what we had before, we do not feel humbled in the comparison. The artisan scarcely rises into the artist; and the name of genius is degraded rather than exalted in his person. The performance is so far ours that we have paid for it, and the highest price is all that is necessary to produce the highest finishing. But it is not so in works of genius and imagination. Their price is above rubies. The inspiration of the Muse comes not with the *fiat* of a monarch, with the donation of a patron; and, therefore, the Great turn with disgust or effeminate indifference from the mighty masters of the Italian school, because such works baffle and confound their self-love, and make them feel that there is something in the mind of man which they can neither give nor take away.

'Quam nihil ad tuum, Papiniane, ingenium!'[19]

Definition of Wit

Wit is the putting together in jest, i.e. in fancy, or in bare supposition, ideas between which there is a serious, i.e. a customary incompatibility, and by this pretended union, or juxtaposition, to point out more strongly some lurking incongruity. Or, wit is the dividing a sentence or an object into a number of constituent parts, as suddenly and with the same vivacity of apprehension to compound them again with other objects, 'wherein the most distant resemblance or the most partial coincidence may be found'.[1] It is the *polypus*[2] power of the mind, by which a distinct life and meaning is imparted to the different parts of a sentence or object after they are severed from each other; or it is the prism dividing the simplicity and candour of our ideas into a parcel of motley and variegated hues; or it is the mirror broken into pieces, each fragment of which reflects a new light from surrounding objects; or it is the untwisting the chain of our ideas, whereby each link is made to hook on more readily to others than when they were all bound up together by habit, and with a view to a *set* purpose. Ideas exist as a sort of *fixtures* in the understanding; they are like *moveables* (that will also unscrew and take to pieces) in the wit or fancy. If our grave notions were always well founded; if there were no aggregates of power, of prejudice, and absurdity; if the value and importance of an object went on increasing with the opinion entertained of it, and with the surrender of our faith, freedom, and every thing else to aggrandize it, then 'the squandering glances' of the wit, 'whereby the wise man's folly is anatomized',[3] would be as impertinent as they would be useless. But while gravity and imposture not only exist, but reign triumphant; while the proud, obstinate, sacred tumours rear their heads on high, and are trying to get a new lease of for ever and a day; then oh! for the Frenchman's art ('Voltaire's? – the same'[4]) to break the torpid spell, and reduce the bloated mass to its native insignificance! When a Ferdinand still rules,*[5] seated on his throne of darkness and blood, by English bayonets and by English gold (that have no mind to remove him thence) who is not glad that an Englishman has the wit and spirit[6] to translate the title of *King Ferdinand* into *Thing Ferdinand*; and does not regret that, instead of pointing the public scorn and exciting an indignant smile, the stroke of wit has not the power to shatter, to wither, and annihilate in its lightning blaze the monstrous assumption, with all its open or covert abettors? This would be a *set-off*, indeed, to the joint efforts of pride, ignorance, and hypocrisy: as it is, wit plays its part, and does not play it ill, though it is too apt to cut both ways. It may be said that what I have just quoted is not an instance of the decomposition of an idea or word into its elements, and finding a solid sense hid in the unnoticed particles of wit, but is the addition of another element or letter. But it was the same lively perception of individual and salient points, that saw the word KING stuck up in capital letters, as it were, and like a transparency in the *Illuminated Missal* of the Fancy, that enabled the satirist to conjure up the letter T before it, and made the transition (urged by contempt) easy. For myself, with all my blind, rooted prejudices against the name, it would be long enough before I should hit upon so happy a mode of expressing them. My mind is not sufficiently alert and disengaged. I cannot run along the letters composing it like the spider along its web, to see what they are or how to combine them anew; I am crushed like the worm, and writhing beneath the load. I can give no reasons for the faith that is in me, unless I read a novel of Sir Walter's,[7] but there I find plenty of examples to justify my hatred of kings in former times, and to prevent my wishing to 'revive the ancient spirit of loyalty' in this! Wit, then, according to this account of it, depends on the rapid analysis or solution of continuity in our ideas, which, by detaching, puts them into a condition to coalesce more readily with others, and form new and unexpected combinations: but does all analysis imply wit, or where is the difference? Does the examining the flowers and leaves

* This was written in 1829.

in the cover of a chair-bottom, or the several squares in a marble pavement, constitute wit? Does looking through a microscope amount to it? The painter analyses the face into features – nose, eyes, and mouth – the features into their component parts: but this process of observation and attention to details only leads him to discriminate more nicely, and not to confound objects. The mathematician *abstracts* in his reasonings, and considers the same line, now as forming the side of a triangle, now of a square figure; but does he laugh at the discovery, or tell it to any one else as a monstrous good jest? These questions require an answer; and an evasive one will not do. With respect to the wit of words, the explanation is not difficult; and if all wit were verbal, my task would be soon ended. For language, being in its own nature arbitrary and ambiguous; or consisting of 'sounds significant',[8] which are now applied to one thing, now to something wholly different and unconnected, the most opposite and jarring mixtures may be introduced into our ideas by making use of this medium which looks two ways at once, either by applying the same word to two different meanings, or by dividing it into several parts, each probably the sign of a different thing, and which may serve as the starting-post of a different set of associations. The very circumstance which at first one might suppose would convert all the world into punsters and word-catchers, and make a Babel and chaos of language, *viz.* the arbitrary and capricious nature of the symbols it uses, is that which prevents them from becoming so; for words not being substantive things in themselves, and utterly valueless and unimportant except as the index of thought, the mind takes no notice of or lays no kind of stress upon them, passes on to what is to follow, uses them mechanically and almost unconsciously; and thus the syllables of which a word may be composed, are lost in its known import, and the word itself in the general context. We may be said neither to hear nor see the words themselves; we attend only to the inference, the intention they are meant to communicate. This merging of the sound in the sense, of the means in the end, both common sense, the business of life, and the limitation of the human faculties dictate. But men of wit and leisure are not contented with this; in the discursiveness of their imaginations and with their mercurial spirits, they find it an amusement to attend not only to the conclusion or the meaning of words, but to criticize and have an eye to the words themselves. Dull, plodding people go no farther than the literal, or more properly, the practical sense; the parts of a word or phrase are *massed together* in their habitual conceptions; their rigid understandings are confined to the one meaning of any word predetermined by its place in the sentence, and they are propelled forward to the end without looking to the right or the left. The others, who are less the creatures of habit and have a greater quantity of disposable activity, take the same words out of harness, as it were, lend them wings, and flutter round them in all sorts of fantastic combinations, and in every direction that they choose to take. For instance: the word *elder* signifies in the dictionary either *age* or a certain sort of *tree* or *berry*; but if you mention *elder wine* all the other senses sink into the dictionary as superfluous and nonsensical, and you think only of the wine which happens to bear this name. It required, therefore, a man of Mr Lamb's wit and disdain of the ordinary trammels of thought, to cut short a family dispute over some very excellent wine of this description, by saying, 'I wonder what it is that makes *elder wine* so very pleasant, when *elder brothers* are so extremely disagreeable?' *Compagnons du lys*, may mean either the *companions of the order of the flower-de-luce*, or the *companions of Ulysses* – who were transformed into swine – according as you lay the emphasis. The French wits, at the restoration of Louis XVIII, with admirable point and truth, applied it in this latter sense. Two things may thus meet, in the casual construction and artful encounters of language, wide as the poles asunder and yet perfectly alike; and this is the perfection of wit, when the physical sound is the same, the physical sense totally unlike, and the moral sense absolutely identical. What is it that in things supplies the want of the *double-entendre* of language? – ABSURDITY. And this is the very signification of the term. For it is only when the two contradictory natures are found in the same object that the verbal wit holds good, and the real wit or *jeu d'esprit* exists and may be brought out wherever this contradiction is obvious with or without the *jeu-de-mots* to assist it. We can comprehend how the evolving or disentangling an unexpected coincidence, hid under the same name, is full of ambiguity and surprise; but an absurdity may be written on the face of a thing without the help of language; and it is in detecting and embodying this that the finest wit lies. Language is merely one instrument or handle that forwards the operation: Fancy is the midwife of wit. But how? – If we look narrowly and attentively, we shall find that there is a language of things as well as words, and the same variety of meaning, a hidden and an obvious, a partial and a general one, in both the one and the other. For things, any more than words, are not detached, independent existences, but are connected and cohere together by habit and circumstances in certain sets of association, and consist of an alphabet, which is thus formed into words and regular propositions, which being once done and established as the understood order of the world, the particular ideas are either not noticed, or *determined* to a set purpose and 'foregone conclusion',[9] just as the letters of a word are sunk in the word, or the different possible meanings of a word adjusted by the context. One part of an object being habitually associated with others, or one object with a set of other objects, we *lump* the whole together, take the general rule for granted, and merge the details in a blind and confused idea of the aggregate result. This, then, is the province of wit; to penetrate through the disguise or crust with which indolence and custom 'skin and slur over' our ideas, to move this slough of prejudice, and to resolve these aggregates or bundles of things into their component parts by a more lively and unshackled conception of their distinctions, and the possible combinations of these, so as to throw a glancing and fortuitous light upon the whole. There is then, it is obvious, a *double meaning* in things or ideas as well as in words (each being ordinarily regarded by the mind merely as the mechanical signs or links to hold together other ideas connected with them) – and it is in detecting this *double meaning* that wit in either case is shown. Having no books at hand to refer to for examples, and in the dearth of imagination which I naturally labour under, I must look round the room in search of illustrations. I see a number of stars or diamond figures in the carpet, with the violent contrast of red and yellow and fantastic wreaths of flowers twined round them, without being able to extract either edification or a particle of amusement from them: a joint-stool and a fire-screen in a corner are equally silent on the subject – the first hint I receive (or glimmering of light) is from a pair of tongs which, placed formally astride on the fender, bear a sort of resemblance to the human figure called *long legs and no body*. The absurdity is not in the tongs (for that is their usual shape) but in the human figure which has borrowed a likeness foreign to itself. With this *contre-sens*, and the uneasiness and confusion in our habitual ideas which it excites, and the effort to clear up this by throwing it from us into a totally distinct class of objects, where by being made plain and palpable, it is proved to have nothing to do with that into which it has obtruded itself, and to which it makes pretensions, commences the operation of wit and the satisfaction it yields to the mind. This I think is the cause of the delightful nature of wit, and of its relieving, instead of aggravating, the pains of defect or deformity, by pointing it out in the most glaring colours, inasmuch as by so doing, we, as it were, completely detach the peccant part and restore the sense of propriety which, in its undetected and unprobed state, it was beginning to disturb. It is like taking a grain of sand out of the eye, a thorn out of the foot. We have discharged our mental reckoning, and had our revenge. Thus, when we say of a *snub-nose*, that it is like an ace of clubs, it is less out of spite to the individual than to vindicate and place beyond a doubt the propriety of our notions of form in general. Butler compares the knight's red, formal-set beard to a tile: —

> 'In cut and die so like a tile,
> A sudden view it would beguile';[10]

— we laugh in reading this, but the triumph is less over the wretched precisian than it is the triumph of common sense. So Swift exclaims:

> 'The house of brother Van I spy,
> In shape resembling a goose-pie.'[11]

Here, if the satire was just, the characteristics of want of solidity, of incongruity, and fantastical arrangement were inherent in the building, and written on its front to the discerning eye, and only required to be brought out by the simile of the goose-pie, which is an immediate test and illustration (being an extreme case) of those qualities. The absurdity, which before was either admired, or only suspected, now stands revealed, and is turned into a laughing-stock, by the new version of the building into a goose-pie (as much as if the metamorphosis had been effected by a play of words, combining the most opposite things), for the mind in this case having narrowly escaped being imposed upon by taking a trumpery edifice for a stately pile, and perceiving the cheat, naturally wishes to cut short the dispute by finding out the most discordant object possible, and nicknames the building after it. There can be no farther question whether a goose-pie is a fine building. Butler compares the sun rising after the dark night to a lobster boiled, and 'turned from black to red'.[12] This is equally mock-wit and mock-poetry, as the sun can neither be exalted nor degraded by the comparison. It is a play upon the ideas, like what we see in a play upon words, without meaning. In a pantomime at Sadler's Wells, some years ago, they improved upon this hint, and threw a young chimney-sweeper into a cauldron of boiling water, who came out a smart, dapper volunteer. This was *practical wit*; so that wit may exist not only without the play upon words, but even without the use of them. Hogarth may be cited as an instance, who abounds in wit almost as much as he does in humour, considering the inaptitude of the language he used, or in those double allusions which throw a reflected light upon the same object, according to Collins's description of wit,

'Like jewels in his crisped hair'.[13]

Mark Supple's[14] calling out from the Gallery of the House of Commons – 'A song from Mr Speaker!' when Addington was in the chair and there was a pause in the debate, was undoubtedly wit, though the relation of any such absurd circumstance actually taking place, would only have been humour. A gallant calling on a courtesan (for it is fair to illustrate these intricacies how we can) observed, 'he should only make her a present every other time'. She answered, 'Then come only every other time.' This appears to me to offer a sort of touchstone to the question. The sense here is, 'Don't come unless you pay.' There is no wit in this: the wit then consists in the mode of conveying the hint: let us see into what this resolves itself. The object is to point out as strongly as can be, the absurdity of not paying; and in order to do this, an impossibility is assumed by running a parallel on the phrases, 'paying every other time', and 'coming every other time', as if the coming went for nothing without paying, and thus, by the very contrast and contradiction in the terms, showing the most perfect contempt for the literal coming, of which the essence, *viz.* paying, was left out. It is, in short, throwing the most killing scorn upon, and fairly annihilating the coming without paying, as if it were possible to come and not to come at the same time, by virtue of an identical proposition or form of speech applied to contrary things. The wit so far, then, consists in suggesting, or insinuating indirectly, an apparent coincidence between two things, to make the real incongruity, by the recoil of the imagination, more palpable than it could have been without this feigned and artificial approximation to an union between them. This makes the difference between jest and earnest, which is essential to all wit. It is only *make-believe*. It is a false pretence set up, or the making one thing pass in supposition for another, as a foil to the truth when the mask is removed. There need not be laughter, but there must be deception and surprise: otherwise, there can be no wit. When Archer, in order to bind the robbers, suddenly makes an excuse to call out to Dorinda, 'Pray lend me your garter, Madam',[15] this is both witty and laughable. Had there been any propriety in the proposal or chance of compliance with it, it would no longer have been a joke: had the question been quite absurd and uncalled-for, it would have been mere impudence and folly; but it is the mixture of sense and nonsense, that is, the pretext for the request in the fitness of a garter to answer the purpose in question, and the totally opposite train of associations between a lady's garter (particularly in the circumstances which had just happened in the play) and tying a rascally robber's hands behind his back, that produces the delightful *équivoque* and unction of the passage in Farquhar. It is laughable, because the train of inquiry it sets in motion is at once on pleasant and on forbidden ground. We did not laugh in the former case — 'Then only come every other time' — because it was a mere ill-natured exposure of an absurdity, and there was an end of it: but here, the imagination courses up and down along a train of ideas, by which it is alternately repelled and attracted, and this produces the natural drollery or inherent ludicrousness. It is the difference between the wit of humour and the wit of sense. Once more, suppose you take a stupid, unmeaning likeness of a face, and throwing a wig over it, stick it on a peg, to make it look like a barber's block — this is wit without words. You give that which is stupid in itself the additional accompaniments of what is still more stupid, to enhance and verify the idea by a falsehood. We know the head so placed is not a barber's block; but it might, we see, very well pass for one. This is caricature or the *grotesque*. The face itself might be made infinitely laughable, and great humour be shown in the delineation of character: it is in combining this with other artificial and aggravating circumstances, or in the setting of this piece of lead that the wit appears.* RECAPITU-LATION. It is time to stop short in this list of digressions, and try to join the scattered threads together. We are too apt, both from the nature of language and the turn of modern philosophy, which reduces every thing to simple sensations, to consider whatever bears one name as one thing in itself, which prevents our ever properly understanding those *mixed modes* and various clusters of ideas, to which almost all language has a reference. Thus if we regard *wit* as something resembling a drop of quicksilver, or a spangle from off a cloak, a little nimble substance, that is pointed and glitters (we do not know how) we shall make no progress in analysing its varieties or its essence; it is a mere word or an atom: but if we suppose it to consist in, or be the result of, several sets and sorts of ideas combined together or acting upon each other (like the tunes and machinery of a barrel-organ) we may stand some chance of explaining and getting an insight into the process. Wit is not, then, a single idea or object, but it is one mode of viewing and representing nature, or the differences and similitudes, harmonies and discords in the links and chains of our ideas of things at large. If all our ideas were literal, physical, confined to a single impression of the object, there could be no faculty for, or possibility of, the existence of wit, for its first principle is *mocking* or making a jest of any thing, and its first condition or postulate, therefore, is the distinction between jest and earnest. First of all, wit implies a jest, that is, the bringing forward a pretended or counterfeit illustration of a thing; which, being presently withdrawn, makes the naked truth more apparent by contrast. It is lessening and undermining our faith in any thing (in which the serious consists) by heightening

---

* The common trick of making an imitation of the human countenance with a napkin or the ends of the knuckles comes under the head of wit, not humour.

or exaggerating the vividness of our idea of it, so as by carrying it to extremes to show the error in the first concoction, and from a received practical truth and object of grave assent, to turn it into a laughing-stock to the fancy. This will apply to Archer and the lady's garter, which is ironical: but how does it connect with the comparison of Hudibras's beard to a tile, which is only an exaggeration; or the *Compagnons d'Ulysse*, which is meant for a literal and severe truth, as well as a play upon words? More generally then, wit is the conjuring up in the fancy any illustration of an idea by likeness, combination of other images, or by a form of words, that being intended to point out the *eccentricity* or departure of the original idea from the class to which it belongs does so by referring it contingently and obliquely to a totally opposite class, where the surprise and mere possibility of finding it, proves the inherent want of congruity. Hudibras's beard is transformed (by wit) into a tile: a strong man is transformed (by imagination) into a tower. The objects, you will say, are unlike in both cases; yet the comparison in one case is meant seriously, in the other it is merely to tantalize. The imagination is serious, even to passion, and exceeds truth by laying a greater stress on the object; wit has no feeling but contempt, and exceeds truth to make light of it. In a poetical comparison there cannot be a sense of incongruity or surprise; in a witty one there must. The reason is this: It is granted stone is not flesh, a tile is not hair, but the associated feelings are alike, and naturally coalesce in one instance, and are discordant and only forced together by a trick of style in the other. But how can that be, if the objects occasioning these feelings are equally dissimilar? — Because the qualities of stiffness or squareness and colour, objected to in Hudibras's beard, are themselves peculiarities and oddities in a beard, or contrary to the nature or to our habitual notion of that class of objects; and consequently (not being natural or rightful properties of a beard) must be found in the highest degree in, and admit of, a grotesque and irregular comparison with a class of objects, of which squareness and redness* are the essential characteristics (as of a tile), and which can have, accordingly, no common point of union in general qualities or feeling with the first class, but where the ridicule

---

* A red beard is not uncommon, but it is odious.

must be just and pointed from this very circumstance, that is, from the coincidence in that one particular only, which is the flaw and singularity of the first object. On the other hand, size and strength, which are the qualities on which the comparison of a man to a tower hinges, are not repugnant to the general constitution of man, but familiarly associated with our ideas of him: so that there is here no sense of impropriety in the object, nor of incongruity or surprise in the comparison: all is grave and decorous, and instead of burlesque, bears the aspect of a loftier truth. But if strength and magnitude fall within our ordinary contemplations of man as things not out of the course of nature, whereby he is enabled, with the help of imagination, to rival a tower of brass or stone, are not littleness and weakness the counterpart of these, and subject to the same rule? What shall we say, then, to the comparison of a dwarf to a pigmy, or to Falstaff's comparison of *Silence* to 'a forked radish, or a man made after supper of a cheese-paring'?[16] Once more then, strength and magnitude are qualities which impress the imagination in a powerful and substantive manner; if they are an excess above the ordinary or average standard, it is an excess to which we lend a ready and admiring belief, that is, we *will* them to be if they are not, because they *ought to be* – whereas, in the other case of peculiarity and defect, the mind is constantly at war with the impression before it; our affections do not tend that way; we will it *not* to be; reject, detach, and discard it from the object as much and as far as possible; and therefore it is, that there being no voluntary coherence but a constant repugnance between the peculiarity (as of *squareness*) and the object (as a *beard*), the idea of a beard as being both naturally and properly of a certain form and texture remains as remote as ever from that of a tile; and hence the double problem is solved, why the mind is at once surprised and not shocked by the allusion; for first, the mind being made to see a beard so unlike a beard, is glad to have the discordance increased and put beyond controversy, by comparing it to something still more unlike one, *viz.* a tile; and secondly, *squareness* never having been admitted as a desirable and accredited property of a beard as it is of a tile, by which the two classes of ideas might have been reconciled and compromised (like those of a man and a tower) through a feeling or quality common (in will) to both, the transition from one to the other continues as new and startling, that is, as witty as ever; — *which was to be demonstrated.* I think I see my way clearly so far. Wit consists in two things, the perceiving the incongruity between an object and the class to which it generally belongs, and secondly, the pointing out or making this incongruity more manifest, by transposing it to a totally different class of objects in which it is prescriptively found in perfection. The medium or link of connexion between the opposite classes of ideas is in the unlikeness of one of the things in question *to itself, i.e.* the class it belongs to: this peculiarity is the narrow bridge or line along which the fancy runs to link it to a set of objects in all other respects different from the first, and having no sort of communication, either in fact or inclination, with it, and in which the pointedness and brilliancy, or the *surprise* and *contrast* of wit consists. The faculty by which this is done is the rapid, careless decomposition and recomposition of our ideas, by means of which we easily and clearly detach certain links in the chain of our associations from the place where they stand, and where they have an infirm footing, and join them on to others, to show how little intimacy they had with the former set.

The motto of wit seems to be, *Light come, light go.* A touch is sufficient to dissever what already hangs so loose as folly, like froth on the surface of the wave; and an hyperbole, an impossibility, a pun or a nickname will push an absurdity, which is close upon the verge of it, over the precipice. It is astonishing how much wit or laughter there is in the world — it is one of the staple commodities of daily life — and yet, being excited by what is *out of the way* and singular, it ought to be rare, and gravity should be the order of the day. Its constant recurrence from the most trifling and trivial causes, shows that the contradiction is less to what we find things than to what we wish them to be. A circle of milliner's-girls laugh all day long at nothing, or day after day at the same things — the same cant phrase supplies the wags of the town with wit for a month — the same set of nicknames has served the *John Bull* and *Blackwood's Magazine* ever since they started. It would appear by this that its essence consisted in monotony, rather than variety. Some kind of incongruity however seems inseparable from it, either in the object or language. For instance, admiration and flattery become wit by being expressed in a quaint and abrupt way. Thus, when the dustman complimented the Duchess of Devonshire by saying, as she passed, 'I wish that lady would let me light my pipe at her eyes', nothing was meant less than to ridicule or throw contempt, yet the speech was wit and not serious flattery. The putting a wig on a stupid face and setting it on a barber's pole is wit or humour: − the fixing a pair of wings on a beautiful figure to make it look more like an angel is poetry; so that the *grotesque* is either serious or ludicrous, as it professes to exalt or degrade. Whenever any thing is proposed to be *done* in the way of wit, it must be in mockery or jest; since if it were a probable or becoming action, there would be no drollery in suggesting it; but this does not apply to illustrations by comparison, there is here no line drawn between what is to take place and what is not to take place − they must only be extreme and unexpected. Mere nonsense, however, is not wit. For however slight the connexion, it will never do to have none at all; and the more fine and fragile it is in some respects, the more close and deceitful it should be in the particular one insisted on. Farther, mere sense is not wit. Logical subtlety or ingenuity does not amount to wit (although it may mimic it) without an immediate play of fancy, which is a totally different thing. The comparing the phrenologist's division of the same portion of the brain into the organs of form and colour to the cutting a Yorkshire pudding into two parts, and calling the one *custard* and the other *plum-cake* may pass for wit with some, but not with me. I protest (if required) against having a grain of wit.*

---

* Some one compared B—, a tall, awkward country lout to Adam, who came into the world full grown, but without having ever made any use of his limbs. This was wit, though true; where then is the ingredient of incongruity? In altering the idea of Adam at pleasure, or from a mere possibility to make it answer a ludicrous purpose. Adam is generally supposed an active, graceful person: a lad grown up with large bones and muscles, with no more use of them than an infant, is a laughable subject, because it deranges or unhinges our customary associations. The threads of our ideas (so to speak) are strong and tightened by habit and will, just as we tighten the strings of a fiddle with pegs and screws; and when any of these are relaxed, snapped asunder, or unstrung by accident or folly, it is in taking up the odds and ends (like stitches let down) as they hang light and loose, and twisting them into some motley, ill-assorted pattern, so as to present a fantastic and glaring contrast to custom (which is plain sense) or the *ideal*, which strengthens and harmonizes (and which is poetry) − that the web of wit and humour consists. The *serious* is that which is closely cemented together by experience and prejudice, or by common sense: the ludicrous

is the incoherent, or that which wants the cement of habit and purpose; and wit is employed in finding out new and opposite combinations of these detached and broken fragments (or exceptions to established rules) so as to set off the distinction between absurdity and propriety in the most lively and marked manner possible. Proof is not wanted here; illustration is enough, and the more extravagant the better; for the cause being previously condemned in our prosing judgments, we do not stand upon punctilio, but only wait for a smart, sly excuse to get rid of it; and hence *tricking is fair in wit*, as well as in war: where the justice of the cause is not the question, you have only to fight it out or make the best of the case you can.

On Genius and Common Sense

We hear it maintained by people of more gravity than understanding, that genius and taste are strictly reducible to rules, and that there is a rule for every thing. So far is it from being true that the finest breath of fancy is a definable thing, that the plainest common sense is only what Mr Locke would have called a *mixed mode*,[1] subject to a particular sort of acquired and undefinable tact. It is asked, 'If you do not know the rule by which a thing is done, how can you be sure of doing it a second time?' And the answer is, 'If you do not know the muscles by the help of which you walk, how is it you do not fall down at every step you take?' In art, in taste, in life, in speech, you decide from feeling, and not from reason; that is, from the impression of a number of things on the mind, which impression is true and well-founded, though you may not be able to analyse or account for it in the several particulars. In a gesture you use, in a look you see, in a tone you hear, you judge of the expression, propriety, and meaning from habit, not from reason or rules; that is to say, from innumerable instances of like gestures, looks, and tones, in innumerable other circumstances, variously modified, which are too many and too refined to be all distinctly recollected, but which do not therefore operate the less powerfully upon the mind and eye of taste. Shall we say that these impressions (the immediate stamp of nature) do not operate in a given manner till they are classified and reduced to rules, or is not the rule itself grounded upon the truth and certainty of that natural operation? How then can the distinction of the understanding as to the manner in which they operate be necessary to their producing their due and uniform effect upon the mind? If certain effects did not regularly arise out of certain causes in mind as well as matter, there could be no rule given for them: nature does not follow the rule, but suggests it. Reason is the interpreter and critic of nature and genius, not their lawgiver and judge. He must be a poor creature indeed whose practical convictions do not in almost all cases outrun his deliberate understanding, or who does not feel and know much more than he can give a reason for. – Hence the distinction between eloquence and wisdom, between ingenuity and common sense. A man may be dextrous and able in explaining the grounds of his opinions, and yet may be a mere sophist, because he only sees one half of a subject. Another may feel the whole weight of a question, nothing relating to it may be lost upon him, and yet he may be able to give no account of the manner in which it affects him, or to drag his reasons from their silent lurking-places. This last will be a wise man, though neither a logician nor rhetorician. Goldsmith was a fool to Dr Johnson in argument; that is, in assigning the specific grounds of his opinions: Dr Johnson was a fool to Goldsmith in the fine tact, the airy, intuitive faculty with which he skimmed the surfaces of things, and unconsciously formed his opinions. Common sense is the just result of the sum-total of such unconscious impressions in the ordinary occurrences of life, as they are treasured up in the memory, and called out by the occasion. Genius and taste depend much upon the same principle exercised on loftier ground and in more unusual combinations.

I am glad to shelter myself from the charge of affectation or singularity in this view of an often debated but ill-understood point, by quoting a passage from Sir Joshua Reynolds's *Discourses*, which is full, and, I think, conclusive to the purpose. He says,

'I observe, as a fundamental ground common to all the Arts with which we have any concern in this Discourse, that they address themselves only to two faculties of the mind, its imagination and its sensibility.

'All theories which attempt to direct or to control the Art, upon any principles falsely called rational, which we form to ourselves upon a supposition of what ought in reason to be the end or means of Art, independent of the known first effect produced by objects on the imagination, must be false and delusive. For though it may appear bold to say it, the imagination is here the residence of truth. If the imagination be affected, the conclusion is fairly drawn; if it be not affected, the reasoning is erroneous, because the end is not obtained; the effect itself being the test, and the only test, of the truth and efficacy of the means.

'There is in the commerce of life, as in Art, a sagacity which is far from being contradictory to right reason, and is superior to any occasional exercise of that faculty; which supersedes it; and does not wait for the slow progress of deduction, but goes at once, by what appears a kind of intuition, to the conclusion. A man endowed with this faculty feels and acknowledges the truth, though it is not always in his power, perhaps, to give a reason for it; because he cannot recollect and bring before him all the materials that gave birth to his opinion; for very many and very intricate considerations may unite to form the principle, even of small and minute parts, involved in, or dependent on, a great system of things: – though these in process of time are forgotten, the right impression still remains fixed in his mind.

'This impression is the result of the accumulated experience of our whole life, and has been collected, we do not always know how, or when. But this mass of collective observation, however acquired, ought to prevail over that reason, which however powerfully exerted on any particular occasion, will probably comprehend but a partial view of the subject; and our conduct in life, as well as in the arts, is or ought to be generally governed by this habitual reason: it is our happiness that we are enabled to draw on such funds. If we were obliged to enter into a theoretical deliberation on every occasion before we act, life would be at a stand, and Art would be impracticable.

'It appears to me therefore' (continues Sir Joshua) 'that our first thoughts, that is, the effect which any thing produces on our minds, on its first appearance, is never to be forgotten; and it demands for that reason, because it is the first, to be laid up with care. If this be not done, the artist may happen to impose on himself by partial reasoning; by a cold consideration of those animated thoughts which proceed, not perhaps from caprice or rashness (as he may afterwards conceit), but from the fullness of his mind, enriched with the copious stores of all the various inventions which he had ever seen, or had ever passed in his mind. These ideas are infused into his design, without any conscious effort; but if he be not on his guard, he may reconsider and correct them, till the whole matter is reduced to a common-place invention.

'This is sometimes the effect of what I mean to caution you against; that is to say, an unfounded distrust of the imagination and feeling, in favour of narrow, partial, confined, argumentative theories, and of principles that seem to apply to the design in hand; without considering those general impressions on the fancy in which real principles of *sound reason*, and of much more weight and importance, are involved, and, as it were, lie hid under the appearance of a sort of vulgar sentiment. Reason, without doubt, must ultimately determine every thing; at this minute it is required to inform us when that very reason is to give way to feeling.' – *Discourse XIII*. vol. ii. p. 113–17.

Mr Burke, by whom the foregoing train of thinking was probably suggested, has insisted on the same thing, and made rather a perverse use of it in several parts of his *Reflections on the French Revolution*; and Windham in one of his Speeches has clenched it into an aphorism – 'There is nothing so true as habit.'[2] Once more I would say, common sense is tacit reason. Conscience is the same tacit sense of right and wrong, or the impression of our moral experience and moral apprehensions on the mind, which, because it works unseen, yet certainly, we suppose to be an instinct, implanted in the mind; as we sometimes attribute the violent operations of our passions, of which we can neither trace the source nor assign the reason, to the instigation of the Devil!

I shall here try to go more at large into this subject, and to give such instances and illustrations of it as occur to me.

One of the persons[3] who had rendered themselves obnoxious to Government and been included in a charge for high treason in the year 1794, had retired soon after into Wales to write an epic poem and enjoy the luxuries of a rural life. In his peregrinations through that beautiful scenery, he had arrived one fine morning at the inn at Llangollen, in the romantic valley of that name. He had ordered his breakfast, and was sitting at the window in all the dalliance of expectation when a face passed of which he took no notice at the instant – but when his breakfast was brought in presently after, he found his appetite for it gone, the day had lost its freshness in his eye, he was uneasy and spiritless; and without any cause that he could discover, a total change had taken place in his feelings. While he was trying to account for this odd circumstance, the same face passed again – it was the face of Taylor the spy; and he was no longer at a loss to explain the difficulty. He had before caught only a transient glimpse, a passing side-view of the face; but though this was not sufficient to awaken a distinct idea in his memory, his feelings, quicker and surer, had taken the alarm; a string had been touched that gave a jar to his whole frame, and would not let him rest though he could not at all tell what was the matter with him. To the flitting, shadowy, half-distinguished profile that had glided by his window was linked unconsciously and mysteriously, but inseparably, the impression of the trains that had been laid for him by this person; – in this brief moment, in this dim, illegible short-hand of the mind he had just escaped the speeches of the Attorney and Solicitor-General over again; the gaunt figure of Mr Pitt glared by him; the walls of a prison enclosed him; and he felt the hands of the executioner near him, without knowing it till the tremor and disorder of his nerves gave information to his reasoning faculties that all was not well within. That is, the same state of mind was recalled by one circumstance in the series of association that had been produced by the whole set of circumstances at the time, though the manner in which this was done was not immediately perceptible. In other words, the feeling of pleasure or pain, of good or evil, is revived and acts instantaneously upon the mind, before we have time to recollect the precise objects which have originally given birth to it.* The incident here mentioned was merely, then, one case of what the learned understand by the *association of ideas*: but all that is meant by feeling or common sense

---

* Sentiment has the same source as that here pointed out. Thus the *Ranz des Vaches*, [4] which has such an effect on the minds of the Swiss peasantry, when its well-known sound is heard, does not merely recall to them the idea of their country, but has associated with it a thousand nameless ideas, numberless touches of private affection, of early hope, romantic adventure, and national pride, all which rush in (with mingled currents) to swell the tide of fond remembrance, and make them languish or die for home. What a fine instrument the human heart is! Who shall touch it? Who shall fathom it? Who shall 'sound it from its lowest note to the top of its compass'? [5] Who shall put his hand among the strings, and explain their wayward music? The heart alone, when touched by sympathy, trembles and responds to their hidden meaning!

is nothing but the different cases of the association of ideas, more or less true to the impression of the original circumstances, as reason begins with the more formal development of those circumstances, or pretends to account for the different cases of the association of ideas. But it does not follow that the dumb and silent pleading of the former (though sometimes, nay often mistaken) is less true than that of its babbling interpreter, or that we are never to trust its dictates without consulting the express authority of reason. Both are imperfect, both are useful in their way, and therefore both are best together, to correct or to confirm one another. It does not appear that in the singular instance above mentioned, the sudden impression on the mind was superstition or fancy, though it might have been thought so, had it not been proved by the event to have a real physical and moral cause. Had not the same face returned again, the doubt would never have been properly cleared up, but would have remained a puzzle ever after, or perhaps to have been soon forgot. – By the law of association as laid down by physiologists, any impression in a series can recall any other impression in that series without going through the whole in order: so that the mind drops the intermediate links, and passes on rapidly and by stealth to the more striking effects of pleasure or pain which have naturally taken the strongest hold of it. By doing this habitually and skilfully with respect to the various impressions and circumstances with which our experience makes us acquainted, it forms a series of unpremeditated conclusions on almost all subjects that can be brought before it, as just as they are of ready application to human life; and common sense is the name of this body of unassuming but practical wisdom. Common sense, however, is an impartial, instinctive result of truth and nature, and will therefore bear the rest and abide the scrutiny of the most severe and patient reasoning. It is indeed incomplete without it. By ingrafting reason on feeling, we 'make assurance double sure'.[6]

> ''Tis the last key-stone that makes up the arch . . .
> Then stands it a triumphal mark! Then men
> Observe the strength, the height, the why and when
> It was erected; and still walking under,
> Meet some new matter to look up, and wonder.'[7]

But reason, not employed to interpret nature, and to improve and perfect common sense and experience, is, for the most part, a building without a foundation. – The criticism exercised by reason then on common sense may be as severe as it pleases, but it must be as patient as it is severe. Hasty, dogmatical, self-satisfied reason is worse than idle fancy, or bigoted prejudice. It is systematic, ostentatious in error, closes up the avenues of knowledge, and 'shuts the gates of wisdom on mankind'.[8] It is not enough to show that there is no reason for a thing, that we do not see the reason of it: if the common feeling, if the involuntary prejudice sets in strong in favour of it, if in spite of all we can do, there is a lurking suspicion on the side of our first impressions, we must try again, and believe that truth is mightier than we. So, in offering a definition of any subject, if we feel a misgiving that there is any fact or circumstance omitted, but of which we have only a vague apprehension, like a name we cannot recollect, we must ask for more time, and not cut the matter short by an arrogant assumption of the point in dispute. Common sense thus acts as a check-weight on sophistry, and suspends our rash and superficial judgments. On the other hand, if not only no reason can be given for a thing, but every reason is clear against it, and we can account from ignorance, from authority, from interest, from different causes, for the prevalence of an opinion or sentiment, then we have a right to conclude that we have mistaken a prejudice for an instinct, or have confounded a false and partial impression with the fair and unavoidable inference from general observation. Mr Burke said[9] that we ought not to reject every prejudice, but should separate the husk of prejudice from the truth it encloses, and so try to get at the kernel within; and thus far he was right. But he was wrong in insisting that we are to cherish our prejudices, 'because they are prejudices': for if they are all well-founded, there is no occasion to inquire into their origin or use; and he who sets out to philosophize upon them, or make the separation Mr Burke talks of in this spirit and with this previous determination, will be very likely to mistake a maggot or a rotten canker for the precious kernel of truth, as was indeed the case with our political sophist.

There is nothing more distinct than common sense and vulgar opinion. Common sense is only a judge of things that fall under common observation, or immediately come home to the business[10] and bosoms of men. This is of the very essence of its principle, the basis of its pretensions. It rests upon the simple process of feeling, it anchors in experience. It is not, nor it cannot be, the test of abstract, speculative opinions. But half the opinions and prejudices of mankind, those which they hold in the most unqualified approbation and which have been instilled into them under the strongest sanctions, are of this latter kind, that is, opinions, not which they have ever thought, known, or felt one tittle about, but which they have taken up on trust from others, which have been palmed on their understandings by fraud or force, and which they continue to hold at the peril of life, limb, property, and character, with as little warrant from common sense in the first instance as appeal to reason in the last. The *ultima ratio regum* [11] proceeds upon a very different plea. Common sense is neither priestcraft nor state-policy. Yet 'there's the rub that makes absurdity of so long life';[12] and, at the same time, gives the sceptical philosophers the advantage over us. Till nature has fair play allowed it, and is not adulterated by political and polemical quacks, (as it so often has been) it is impossible to appeal to it as a defence against the errors and extravagances of mere reason. If we talk of common sense, we are twitted with vulgar prejudice, and asked how we distinguish the one from the other: but common and received opinion is indeed 'a compost heap'[13] of crude notions, got together by the pride and passions of individuals, and reason is itself the thrall or manumitted slave of the same lordly and besotted masters, dragging its servile chain, or committing all sorts of Saturnalian licences, the moment it feels itself freed from it. – If ten millions of Englishmen are furious in thinking themselves right in making war upon thirty millions of Frenchmen, and if the last are equally bent upon thinking the others always in the wrong, though it is a common and national prejudice, both opinions cannot be the dictate of good sense: but it may be the infatuated policy of one or both governments to keep their subjects always at variance. If a few centuries ago all Europe believed in the infallibility of the Pope, this was not an opinion derived from the proper exercise or erroneous direction of the common sense of the people: common sense had nothing to do with it – they believed whatever their priests told them. England at present is divided into Whigs and Tories, Churchmen and Dissenters: both parties have numbers on their side; but common sense and party-spirit are two different things. Sects and heresies are upheld partly by sympathy, and partly by the love of contradiction; if there was nobody of a different way of thinking, they would fall to pieces of themselves. If a whole court say the same thing, this is no proof that they think it, but that the individual at the head of the court has said it: if a mob agree for a while in shouting the same watch-word, this is not to me an example of the *sensus communis*,[14] they only repeat what they have heard repeated by others. If indeed a large proportion of the people are in want of food, of clothing, of shelter, if they are sick, miserable, scorned, oppressed, and if each feeling it in himself, they all say so with one voice and one heart, and lift up their hands to second their appeal, this I should say was but the dictate of common sense, the cry of nature. But to waive this part of the argument, which it is needless to push farther. — I believe that the best way to instruct mankind is not by pointing out to them their mutual errors, but by teaching them to think rightly on indifferent matters, where they will listen with patience in order to be amused, and where they do not consider a definition or a syllogism as the greatest injury you can offer them.

There is no rule for expression. It is got at solely by *feeling*, that is, on the principle of the association of ideas, and by transferring what has been found to hold good in one case (with the necessary modifications) to others. A certain look has been remarked strongly indicative of a certain passion or trait of character, and we attach the same meaning to it or are affected in the same pleasurable or painful manner by it, where it exists in a less degree, though we can define neither the look itself nor the modification of it. Having got the general clue, the exact result may be left to the imagination to vary, to extenuate, or aggravate it according to circumstances. In the admirable profile of Oliver Cromwell after —,[15] the drooping eye-lids, as if drawing a veil over the fixed, penetrating glance, the nostrils somewhat distended, and lips compressed so as hardly to let the breath escape him, denote the character of the man for high-reaching policy and deep designs as plainly as they can be written. How is it that we decypher this expression in the face? First, by feeling it: and how is it that we feel it? Not by pre-established rules, but by the instinct of analogy, by the principle of association, which is subtle and sure in proportion as it is variable and indefinite. A circumstance, apparently of no value, shall alter the whole interpretation to be put upon an expression or action; and it shall alter it thus powerfully because in proportion to its very insignificance it shows a strong general principle at work that extends in its ramifications to the smallest things. This in fact will make all the difference between minuteness and subtlety or refinement; for a small or trivial effect may in given circumstances imply the operation of a great power. Stillness may be the result of a blow too powerful to be resisted; silence may be imposed by feelings too agonizing for utterance. The minute, the trifling and insipid is that which is little in itself, in its causes and its consequences: the subtle and refined is that which is slight and evanescent at first sight, but which mounts up to a mighty sum in the end, which is an essential part of an important whole, which has consequences greater than itself, and where more is meant than meets the eye or ear. We complain sometimes of littleness in a Dutch picture, where there are a vast number of distinct parts and objects, each small in itself, and leading to nothing else. A sky of Claude's cannot fall under this censure, where one imperceptible gradation is as it were the scale to another, where the broad arch of heaven is piled up of endlessly intermediate gold and azure tints, and where an infinite number of minute, scarce noticed particulars blend and melt into universal harmony. The subtlety in Shakespeare, of which there is an immense deal every where scattered up and down, is always the instrument of passion, the vehicle of character. The action of a man pulling his hat over his forehead is indifferent enough in itself, and generally speaking, may mean any thing or nothing: but in the circumstances in which Macduff is placed, it is neither insignificant nor equivocal.

'What! man, ne'er pull your hat upon your brows', &c.

It admits but of one interpretation or inference, that which follows it: —

'Give sorrow words: the grief that does not speak,
Whispers the o'er-fraught heart, and bids it break.'[16]

The passage in the same play,[17] in which Duncan and his attendants are introduced commenting on the beauty and situation of Macbeth's castle, though familiar in itself, has been often praised for the striking contrast it presents to the scenes which follow. – The same look in different circumstances may convey a totally different expression. Thus the eye turned round to look at you without turning the head indicates generally slyness or suspicion: but if this is combined with large expanded eye-lids or fixed eye-brows, as we see it in Titian's pictures, it will denote calm contemplation or piercing sagacity, without any thing of meanness or fear of being observed. In other cases, it may imply merely indolent enticing voluptuousness, as in Lely's portraits of women. The languor and weakness of the eye-lids gives the amorous turn to the expression. How should there be a rule for all this beforehand, seeing it depends on circumstances ever varying, and scarce discernible but by their effect on the mind? Rules are applicable to abstractions, but expression is concrete and individual. We know the meaning of certain looks, and we feel how they modify one another in conjunction. But we cannot have a separate rule to judge of all their combinations in different degrees and circumstances, without foreseeing all those combinations, which is impossible; or if we did foresee them, we should only be where we are, that is, we could only make the rule as we now judge without it, from imagination and the feeling of the moment. The absurdity of reducing expression to a preconcerted system was perhaps never more evidently shown than in a picture of the Judgment of Solomon by so great a man as N. Poussin, which I once heard admired for the skill and discrimination of the artist in making all the women, who are ranged on one side, in the greatest alarm at the sentence of the judge, while all the men on the opposite side see through the design of it. Nature does not go to work or cast things in a regular mould in this sort of way. I once heard a person remark of another – 'He has an eye like a vicious horse.' This was a fair analogy. We all, I believe, have noticed the look of a horse's eye, just before he is going to bite or kick. But will any one, therefore, describe to me exactly what that look is? It was the same acute observer that said of a self-sufficient prating music-master – 'He talks on all subjects *at sight*' – which expressed the man at once by an allusion to his profession. The coincidence was indeed perfect. Nothing else could compare to the easy assurance with which this gentleman would volunteer an explanation of things of which he was most ignorant but the *nonchalance* with which a musician sits down to a harpsichord to play a piece he has never seen before. My physiognomical friend would not have hit on this mode of illustration without knowing the profession of the subject of his criticism; but having this hint given him, it instantly suggested itself to his 'sure trailing'.[18] The manner of the speaker was evident; and the association of the music-master sitting down to play at sight, lurking in his mind, was immediately called out by the strength of his impression of the character. The feeling of character and the felicity of invention in explaining it were nearly allied to each other. The first was so wrought up and running over that the transition to the last was easy and unavoidable. When Mr Kean was so much praised for the action of Richard in his last struggle with his triumphant antagonist, where he stands, after his sword is wrested from him, with his hands stretched out, 'as if his will could not be disarmed, and the very phantoms of his despair had a withering power',[19] he said that he borrowed it from seeing the last efforts of Painter in his fight with Oliver. This assuredly did not lessen the merit of it. Thus it ever is with the man of real genius. He has the feeling of truth already shrined in his own breast, and his eye is still bent on nature to see how she expresses herself. When we thoroughly understand the subject, it is easy to translate from one language into another. Raphael, in muffling up the figure of Elymas the Sorcerer in his garments,[20] appears to have extended the idea of blindness even to his clothes. Was this design? Probably not; but merely the feeling of analogy thoughtlessly suggesting this device, which being so suggested was retained and carried on, because it flattered or fell in with the original feeling. The tide of passion, when strong, overflows and gradually insinuates itself into all nooks and corners of the mind. Invention (of the best kind) I therefore do not think so distinct a thing from feeling, as some are apt to imagine. The springs of pure feeling will rise and fill the moulds of fancy that are fit to receive it. There are some striking coincidences of colour in well-composed pictures, as in a straggling weed in the foreground streaked with blue or red to answer to a blue or red drapery, to the tone of the flesh or an opening in the sky: – not that this was intended, or done by rule (for then it would presently become affected and ridiculous) but the eye being imbued with a certain colour, repeats and varies it from a natural sense of harmony, a secret craving and appetite for beauty, which in the same manner soothes and gratifies the eye of taste, though the cause is not understood. *Tact, finesse*, is nothing but the being completely aware of the feeling belonging to certain situations, passions, &c. and the being consequently sensible to their slightest indications or movements in others. One of the most remarkable instances of this sort of faculty is the following story, told of Lord Shaftesbury, the grandfather of the author of the *Characteristics*. He had been to dine with Lady Clarendon and her daughter, who was at that time privately married to the Duke of York (afterwards James II) and as he returned home with another nobleman who had accompanied him, he suddenly turned to him, and said, 'Depend upon it, the Duke has married Hyde's daughter.' His companion could not comprehend what he meant; but on explaining himself, he said, 'Her mother behaved to her with an attention and a marked respect that it is impossible to account for in any other way; and I am sure of it.' His conjecture shortly afterwards proved to be the truth. This was carrying the prophetic spirit of common sense as far as it could go. –

A Farewell to Essay-Writing*

'This life is best, if quiet life is best.'[1]

Food, warmth, sleep, and a book; these are all I at present ask — the
ultima thule[2] of my wandering desires. Do you not then wish for

> 'A friend in your retreat,
> Whom you may whisper, solitude is sweet'?[3]

Expected, well enough: — gone, still better. Such attractions are
strengthened by distance. Nor a mistress? 'Beautiful mask! I know
thee!'[4] When I can judge of the heart from the face, of the thoughts
from the lips, I may again trust myself. Instead of these, give me the
robin red-breast, pecking the crumbs at the door, or warbling on the
leafless spray, the same glancing form that has followed me wherever
I have been, and 'done its spiriting gently';[5] or the rich notes of the
thrush that startle the ear of winter, and seem to have drunk up the
full draught of joy from the very sense of contrast. To these I adhere
and am faithful, for they are true to me; and, dear in themselves, are
dearer for the sake of what is departed, leading me back (by the
hand) to that dreaming world, in the innocence of which they sat
and made sweet music, waking the promise of future years, and
answered by the eager throbbings of my own breast. But now 'the
credulous hope of mutual minds is o'er',[6] and I turn back from the
world that has deceived me, to nature that lent it a false beauty, and
that keeps up the illusion of the past. As I quaff my libations of tea

---

* Written at Winterslow Hut, February 20, 1828.

in a morning, I love to watch the clouds sailing from the west, and fancy that 'the spring comes slowly up this way'.[7] In this hope, while 'fields are dank and ways are mire',[8] I follow the same direction to a neighbouring wood, where, having gained the dry, level greensward, I can see my way for a mile before me, closed in on each side by copse-wood, and ending in a point of light more or less brilliant, as the day is bright or cloudy. What a walk is this to me! I have no need of book or companion – the days, the hours, the thoughts of my youth are at my side, and blend with the air that fans my cheek. Here I can saunter for hours, bending my eye forward, stopping and turning to look back, thinking to strike off into some less trodden path, yet hesitating to quit the one I am in, afraid to snap the brittle threads of memory. I remark the shining trunks and slender branches of the birch trees, waving in the idle breeze; or a pheasant springs up on whirring wing; or I recall the spot where I once found a wood-pigeon at the foot of a tree, weltering in its gore, and think how many seasons have flown since 'it left its little life in air'.[9] Dates, names, faces come back – to what purpose? Or why think of them now? Or rather, why not think of them oftener? We walk through life, as through a narrow path, with a thin curtain drawn around it; behind are ranged rich portraits, airy harps are strung – yet we will not stretch forth our hands and lift aside the veil, to catch glimpses of the one, or sweep the chords of the other. As in a theatre, when the old-fashioned green curtain drew up, groups of figures, fantastic dresses, laughing faces, rich banquets, stately columns, gleaming vistas appeared beyond; so we have only at any time to 'peep through the blanket of the past',[10] to possess ourselves at once of all that has regaled our senses, that is stored up in our memory, that has struck our fancy, that has pierced our hearts: – yet to all this we are indifferent, insensible, and seem intent only on the present vexation, the future disappointment. If there is a Titian hanging up in the room with me, I scarcely regard it: how then should I be expected to strain the mental eye so far, or to throw down, by the magic spells of the will, the stone-walls that enclose it in the Louvre? There is one head there of which I have often thought, when looking at it, that nothing should ever disturb me again, and I would become the character it represents – such perfect calmness and self-possession reigns in it! Why do I not hang an image of this in some dusky corner of my brain, and turn an eye upon it ever and anon, as I have need of some such talisman to calm my troubled thoughts? The attempt is fruitless, if not natural; or, like that of the French, to hang garlands on the grave, and to conjure back the dead by miniature pictures of them while living! It is only some actual coincidence, or local association that tends, without violence, to 'open all the cells where memory slept'.[11] I can easily, by stooping over the long-sprent grass and clay-cold clod, recall the tufts of primroses, or purple hyacinths, that formerly grew on the same spot, and cover the bushes with leaves and singing-birds, as they were eighteen summers ago; or prolonging my walk and hearing the sighing gale rustle through a tall, straight wood at the end of it, can fancy that I distinguish the cry of hounds, and the fatal group issuing from it, as in the tale of Theodore and Honoria.[12] A moaning gust of wind aids the belief; I look once more to see whether the trees before me answer to the idea of the horror-stricken grove, and an air-built city towers over their grey tops.

> 'Of all the cities in Romanian lands,
> The chief and most renown'd Ravenna stands.'[13]

I return home resolved to read the entire poem through, and, after dinner, drawing my chair to the fire, and holding a small print close to my eyes, launch into the full tide of Dryden's couplets (a stream of sound), comparing his didactic and descriptive pomp with the simple pathos and picturesque truth of Boccaccio's story, and tasting with a pleasure, which none but an habitual reader can feel, some quaint examples of pronunciation in this accomplished versifier.

> 'Which when Honoria view'd,
> The fresh *impulse* her former fright renew'd.' —[14]
>> *Theodore and Honoria.*

> 'And made th' *insult*, which in his grief appears,
> The means to mourn thee with my pious tears.'[15]
>> *Sigismonda and Guiscardo.*

These trifling instances of the wavering and unsettled state of the language give double effect to the firm and stately march of the verse, and make me dwell with a sort of tender interest on the difficulties and doubts of an earlier period of literature. They pronounced words then in a manner which we should laugh at now; and they wrote verse in a manner which we can do any thing but laugh at. The pride of a new acquisition seems to give fresh confidence to it; to impel the rolling syllables through the moulds provided for them, and to overflow the envious bounds of rhyme into time-honoured triplets. I am much pleased with Leigh Hunt's mention[16] of Moore's involuntary admiration of Dryden's free, unshackled verse, and of his repeating *con amore*, and with an Irish spirit and accent, the fine lines –

> 'Let honour and preferment go for gold,
> But glorious beauty isn't to be sold.'[17]

What sometimes surprises me in looking back to the past, is, with the exception already stated, to find myself so little changed in the time. The same images and trains of thought stick by me: I have the same tastes, likings, sentiments, and wishes that I had then. One great ground of confidence and support has, indeed, been struck from under my feet; but I have made it up to myself by proportionable pertinacity of opinion. The success of the great cause, to which I had vowed myself, was to me more than all the world: I had a strength in its strength, a resource which I knew not of, till it failed me for the second time.

> 'Fall'n was Glenartny's stately tree!
> Oh! ne'er to see Lord Ronald more!'[18]

It was not till I saw the axe laid to the root, that I found the full extent of what I had to lose and suffer. But my conviction of the right was only established by the triumph of the wrong; and my earliest hopes will be my last regrets. One source of this unbendingness, (which some may call obstinacy), is that, though living much alone, I have never worshipped the Echo. I see plainly enough that black is not white, that the grass is green, that kings are not their subjects; and, in such self-evident cases, do not think it necessary to collate my opinions with the received prejudices. In subtler questions, and matters that admit of doubt, as I do not impose my opinion on others without a reason, so I will not give up mine to them without a better reason; and a person calling me names, or giving himself airs of authority, does not convince me of his having taken more pains to find out the truth than I have, but the contrary. Mr Gifford once said,[19] that 'while I was sitting over my gin and tobacco-pipes, I fancied myself a Leibniz'. He did not so much as know that I had ever read a metaphysical book: – was I therefore, out of complaisance or deference to him, to forget whether I had or not? I am rather disappointed, both on my own account and his, that Mr Hunt has missed the opportunity[20] of explaining the character of a friend, as clearly as he might have done. He is puzzled to reconcile the shyness of my pretensions with the inveteracy and sturdiness of my principles. I should have thought they were nearly the same thing. Both from disposition and habit, I can *assume* nothing in word, look, or manner. I cannot steal a march upon public opinion in any way. My standing upright, speaking loud, entering a room gracefully, proves nothing; therefore I neglect these ordinary means of recommending myself to the good graces and admiration of strangers, (and, as it appears, even of philosophers and friends). Why? Because I have other resources, or, at least, am absorbed in other studies and pursuits. Suppose this absorption to be extreme, and even morbid, that I have brooded over an idea till it has become a kind of substance in my brain, that I have reasons for a thing which I have found out with much labour and pains, and to which I can scarcely do justice without the utmost violence of exertion (and that only to a few persons), – is this a reason for my playing off my out-of-the-way notions in all companies, wearing a prim and self-complacent air, as if I were 'the admired of all observers'?[21] or is it not rather an argument, (together with a want of animal spirits), why I should retire into myself, and perhaps acquire a nervous and uneasy look, from a consciousness of the disproportion between the interest and conviction I feel on certain subjects, and my ability to communicate what weighs upon my own mind to others? If my ideas, which I do not avouch, but suppose, lie below the surface, why am I to be always attempting to dazzle superficial people with them, or smiling, delighted, at my own want of success?

What I have here stated is only the excess of the common and well-known English and scholastic character. I am neither a buffoon, a fop, nor a Frenchman, which Mr Hunt would have me to be. He finds it odd that I am a close reasoner and a loose dresser. I have been (among other follies) a hard liver as well as a hard thinker; and the consequences of that will not allow me to dress as I please. People in real life are not like players on a stage, who put on a certain look or *costume*, merely for effect. I am aware, indeed, that the gay and airy pen of the author does not seriously probe the errors or misfortunes of his friends – he only glances at their seeming peculiarities, so as to make them odd and ridiculous; for which forbearance few of them will thank him. Why does he assert that I was vain of my hair when it was black, and am equally vain of it now it is grey, when this is true in neither case? This transposition of motives makes me almost doubt whether Lord Byron was thinking so much of the rings on his fingers as his biographer was. These sort of criticisms should be left to women. I am made to wear a little hat, stuck on the top of my head the wrong way. Nay, I commonly wear a large slouching hat over my eyebrows; and if ever I had another, I must have twisted it about in any shape to get rid of the annoyance. This probably tickled Mr Hunt's fancy, and retains possession of it, to the exclusion of the obvious truism, that I naturally wear 'a melancholy hat'.

I am charged with using strange gestures and contortions of features in argument, in order to 'look energetic'. One would rather suppose that the heat of the argument produced the extravagance of the gestures, as I am said to be calm at other times. It is like saying that a man in a passion clenches his teeth, not because he is, but in order to seem, angry. Why should everything be construed into air and affectation? With Hamlet, I may say, 'I know not *seems*.'[22]

Again, my old friend and pleasant 'Companion' remarks it, as an anomaly in my character, that I crawl about the Fives-Court like a cripple till I get the racket in my hand, when I start up as if I was possessed with a devil. I have then a motive for exertion; I lie by for difficulties and extreme cases. *Aut Cæsar aut nullus*.[23] I have no notion of doing nothing with an air of importance, nor should I ever take a liking to the game of battledore and shuttlecock. I have only seen by accident a page of the unpublished Manuscript relating to the present subject, which I dare say is, on the whole, friendly and just, and which has been suppressed as being too favourable, considering certain prejudices against me.

In matters of taste and feeling, one proof that my conclusions have not been quite shallow or hasty, is the circumstance of their having been lasting. I have the same favourite books, pictures, passages that I ever had: I may therefore presume that they will last me my life – nay, I may indulge a hope that my thoughts will survive me. This continuity of impression is the only thing on which I pride myself. Even L——,[24] whose relish of certain things is as keen and earnest as possible, takes a surfeit of admiration, and I should be afraid to ask about his select authors or particular friends, after a lapse of ten years. As to myself, any one knows where to have me. What I have once made up my mind to, I abide by to the end of the chapter. One cause of my independence of opinion is, I believe, the liberty I give to others, or the very diffidence and distrust of making converts. I should be an excellent man on a jury: I might say little, but should starve 'the other eleven obstinate fellows'[25] out. I remember Mr Godwin writing to Mr Wordsworth, that 'his tragedy of Antonio could not fail of success'. It was damned past all redemption. I said to Mr Wordsworth that I thought this a natural consequence; for how could any one have a dramatic turn of mind who judged entirely of others from himself? Mr Godwin might be convinced of the excellence of his work; but how could he know that others would be convinced of it, unless by supposing that they were as wise as himself, and as infallible critics of dramatic poetry – so many Aristotles sitting in judgment on Euripides! This shows why pride is connected with shyness and reserve; for the really proud have not so high an opinion of the generality as to suppose that they can understand them, or that there is any common measure between them. So Dryden exclaims of his opponents with bitter disdain –

'Nor can I think what thoughts they can conceive.'[26]

I have not sought to make partisans, still less did I dream of making enemies; and have therefore kept my opinions to myself, whether they were currently adopted or not. To get others to come into our ways of thinking, we must go over to theirs; and it is necessary to follow, in order to lead. At the time I lived here formerly, I had no suspicion that I should ever become a voluminous writer; yet I had just the same confidence in my feelings before I had ventured to air them in public as I have now. Neither the outcry *for* or *against* moves me a jot: I do not say that the one is not more agreeable than the other.

Not far from the spot where I write, I first read Chaucer's *Flower and Leaf*,[27] and was charmed with that young beauty, shrouded in her bower, and listening with ever-fresh delight to the repeated song of the nightingale close by her – the impression of the scene, the vernal landscape, the cool of the morning, the gushing notes of the songstress,

> 'And ayen, methought she sung close by mine ear',[28]

is as vivid as if it had been of yesterday; and nothing can persuade me that that is not a fine poem. I do not find this impression conveyed in Dryden's version, and therefore nothing can persuade me that that is as fine. I used to walk out at this time with Mr and Miss L——[29] of an evening, to look at the Claude Lorraine skies over our heads, melting from azure into purple and gold, and to gather mushrooms, that sprung up at our feet, to throw into our hashed mutton at supper. I was at that time an enthusiastic admirer of Claude, and could dwell for ever on one or two of the finest prints from him hung round my little room; the fleecy flocks, the bending trees, the winding streams, the groves, the nodding temples, the air-wove hills, and distant sunny vales; and tried to translate them into their lovely living hues. People then told me that Wilson was much superior to Claude. I did not believe them. Their pictures have since been seen together at the British Institution, and all the world have come into my opinion. I have not, on that account, given it up. I will not compare our hashed mutton with Amelia's;[30] but it put us in mind of it, and led to a discussion, sharply seasoned and well sustained, till midnight, the result of which appeared some years after in the *Edinburgh Review*.[31] Have I a better opinion of those criticisms on that account, or should I therefore maintain them with greater vehemence and tenaciousness? Oh no! Both rather with less, now that they are before the public, and it is for them to make their election.

It is in looking back to such scenes that I draw my best consolation for the future. Later impressions come and go, and serve to fill up the intervals; but these are my standing resource, my true classics. If I have had few real pleasures or advantages, my ideas, from their sinewy texture, have been to me in the nature of realities; and if I should not be able to add to the stock, I can live by husbanding the interest. As to my speculations, there is little to admire in them but my admiration of others; and whether they have an echo in time to come or not, I have learned to set a grateful value on the past, and am content to wind up the account of what is personal only to myself and the immediate circle of objects in which I have moved, with an act of easy oblivion,

'And curtain close such scene from every future view.'[32]

The Letter-Bell

Complaints are frequently made of the vanity and shortness of human life, when, if we examine its smallest details, they present a world by themselves. The most trifling objects, retraced with the eye of memory, assume the vividness, the delicacy, and importance of insects seen through a magnifying glass. There is no end of the brilliancy or the variety. The habitual feeling of the love of life may be compared to 'one entire and perfect chrysolite',[1] which, if analysed, breaks into a thousand shining fragments. Ask the sum-total of the value of human life, and we are puzzled with the length of the account, and the multiplicity of items in it: take any one of them apart, and it is wonderful what matter for reflection will be found in it! As I write this, the *Letter-Bell* passes: it has a lively, pleasant sound with it, and not only fills the street with its importunate clamour, but rings clear through the length of many half-forgotten years. It strikes upon the ear, it vibrates to the brain, it wakes me from the dream of time, it flings me back upon my first entrance into life, the period of my first coming up to town, when all around was strange, uncertain, adverse – a hubbub of confused noises, a chaos of shifting objects – and when this sound alone, startling me with the recollection of a letter I had to send to the friends I had lately left, brought me as it were to myself, made me feel that I had links still connecting me with the universe, and gave me hope and patience to persevere. At that loud-tinkling, interrupted sound (now and then), the long line of blue hills near the place where I was brought up waves in the horizon, a golden sunset hovers over them, the dwarf-oaks rustle their red leaves in the evening-breeze, and the road from — to —,[2] by which I first set out on my journey through life, stares me in the face as plain, but from time and change not less visionary and mysterious, than the pictures in the *Pilgrim's Progress*. I should notice, that at this time the light of the French Revolution circled my head like a glory,[3] though dabbled with drops of crimson gore: I walked confident and cheerful by its side –

> 'And by the vision splendid
> Was on my way attended.'[4]

It rose then in the east: it has again risen in the west.[5] Two suns in one day, two triumphs of liberty in one age, is a miracle which I hope the Laureate will hail in appropriate verse. Or may not Mr Wordsworth give a different turn to the fine passage, beginning –

> 'What, though the radiance which was once so bright,
> Be now for ever vanished from my sight;
> Though nothing can bring back the hour
> Of glory in the grass, of splendour in the flower?'[6]

For is it not brought back, 'like morn risen on mid-*night*';[7] and may he not yet greet the yellow light shining on the evening bank with eyes of youth, of genius, and freedom, as of yore? No, never! But what would not these persons give for the unbroken integrity of their early opinions – for one unshackled, uncontaminated strain – one *Io pæan*[8] to Liberty – one burst of indignation against tyrants and sycophants, who subject other countries to slavery by force, and prepare their own for it by servile sophistry, as we see the huge serpent lick over its trembling, helpless victim with its slime and poison, before it devours it! On every stanza so penned would be written the word RECREANT! Every taunt, every reproach, every note of exultation at restored light and freedom, would recall to them how their hearts failed them in the Valley of the Shadow of Death.[9] And what shall we say to *him* – the sleep-walker,[10] the dreamer, the sophist, the word-hunter, the craver after sympathy, but still vulnerable to truth, accessible to opinion, because not sordid or mechanical? The Bourbons being no longer tied about his neck, he may perhaps recover his original liberty of speculating; so that we may apply to him the lines about his own *Ancient Mariner* –

'And from his neck so free
The Albatross fell off, and sank
Like lead into the sea.'[11]

This is the reason I can write an article on the *Letter-Bell*, and other such subjects; I have never given the lie to my own soul. If I have felt any impression once, I feel it more strongly a second time; and I have no wish to revile and discard my best thoughts. There is at least a thorough *keeping* in what I write – not a line that betrays a principle or disguises a feeling. If my wealth is small, it all goes to enrich the same heap; and trifles in this way accumulate to a tolerable sum. – Or if the Letter-Bell does not lead me a dance into the country, it fixes me in the thick of my town recollections, I know not how long ago. It was a kind of alarm to break off from my work when there happened to be company to dinner or when I was going to the play. *That* was going to the play, indeed, when I went twice a year, and had not been more than half a dozen times in my life. Even the idea that any one else in the house was going, was a sort of reflected enjoyment, and conjured up a lively anticipation of the scene. I remember a Miss D—, a maiden lady from Wales (who in her youth was to have been married to an earl), tantalized me greatly in this way, by talking all day of going to see Mrs Siddons' 'airs and graces'[12] at night in some favourite part; and when the Letter-Bell announced that the time was approaching, and its last receding sound lingered on the ear, or was lost in silence, how anxious and uneasy I became, lest she and her companion should not be in time to get good places – lest the curtain should draw up before they arrived – and lest I should lose one line or look in the intelligent report which I should hear the next morning! The punctuating of time at that early period – every thing that gives it an articulate voice – seems of the utmost consequence; for we do not know what scenes in the *ideal* world may run out of them: a world of interest may hang upon every instant, and we can hardly sustain the weight of future years which are contained in embryo in the most minute and inconsiderable passing events. How often have I put off writing a letter till it was too late! How often had to run after the postman with it – now missing, now recovering, the sound of his bell – breathless, angry with myself –

then hearing the welcome sound come full round a corner – and seeing the scarlet costume which set all my fears and self-reproaches at rest! I do not recollect having ever repented giving a letter to the postman, or wishing to retrieve it after he had once deposited it in his bag. What I have once set my hand to, I take the consequences of, and have been always pretty much of the same humour in this respect. I am not like the person who, having sent off a letter to his mistress, who resided a hundred and twenty miles in the country, and disapproving, on second thoughts, of some expressions contained in it, took a post-chaise and four to follow and intercept it the next morning. At other times, I have sat and watched the decaying embers in a little *back* painting-room (just as the wintry day declined), and brooded over the half-finished copy of a Rembrandt, or a landscape by Van Goyen, placing it where it might catch a dim gleam of light from the fire, while the Letter-Bell was the only sound that drew my thoughts to the world without, and reminded me that I had a task to perform in it. As to that landscape, methinks I see it now –

> 'The slow canal, the yellow-blossomed vale,
> The willow-tufted bank, the gliding sail'.[13]

There was a windmill, too, with a poor low clay-built cottage beside it: – how delighted I was when I had made the tremulous, undulating reflection in the water, and saw the dull canvas become a lucid mirror of the commonest features of nature! Certainly, painting gives one a strong interest in nature and humanity (it is not the *dandy-school* of morals or sentiment) –

> 'While with an eye made quiet by the power
> Of harmony and the deep power of joy,
> We see into the life of things'.[14]

Perhaps there is no part of a painter's life (if we must tell 'the secrets of the prison-house'[15]) in which he has more enjoyment of himself and his art, than that in which after his work is over, and with furtive sidelong glances at what he has done, he is employed in washing his brushes and cleaning his palette for the day. Afterwards, when he gets a servant in livery to do this for him, he may have other and more ostensible sources of satisfaction – greater splendour, wealth, or fame; but he will not be so wholly in his art, nor will his art have such a hold on him as when he was too poor to transfer its meanest drudgery to others – too humble to despise aught that had to do with the object of his glory and his pride, with that on which all his projects of ambition or pleasure were founded. 'Entire affection scorneth nicer hands.'[16] When the professor is above this mechanical part of his business, it may have become a *stalking-horse* to other worldly schemes, but is no longer his *hobby-horse* and the delight of his inmost thoughts –

'His shame in crowds, his solitary pride!'[17]

I used sometimes to hurry through this part of my occupation, while the Letter-Bell (which was my dinner-bell) summoned me to the fraternal board, where youth and hope

'Made good digestion wait on appetite
And health on both' –[18]

or oftener I put it off till after dinner, that I might loiter longer and with more luxurious indolence over it, and connect it with the thoughts of my next day's labours.

The dustman's-bell, with its heavy, monotonous noise, and the brisk, lively tinkle of the muffin-bell, have something in them, but not much. They will bear dilating upon with the utmost licence of inventive prose. All things are not alike *conductors* to the imagination. A learned Scotch professor found fault with an ingenious friend[19] and arch-critic for cultivating a rookery on his grounds: the professor declared 'he would as soon think of encouraging a *froggery*'. This was barbarous as it was senseless. Strange, that a country that has produced the Scotch Novels[20] and *Gertrude of Wyoming*[21] should want sentiment!

The postman's double-knock at the door the next morning is 'more germain to the matter'.[22] How that knock often goes to the heart! We distinguish to a nicety the arrival of the Two-penny or the General Post. The summons of the latter is louder and heavier, as bringing news from a greater distance, and as, the longer it has been delayed, fraught with a deeper interest. We catch the sound of what is to be paid – eight-pence, nine-pence, a shilling – and our hopes generally rise with the postage. How we are provoked at the delay in getting change – at the servant who does not hear the door! Then if the postman passes, and we do not hear the expected knock, what a pang is there! It is like the silence of death – of hope! We think he does it on purpose, and enjoys all the misery of our suspense. I have sometimes walked out to see the Mail-Coach pass, by which I had sent a letter, or to meet it when I expected one. I never see a Mail-Coach, for this reason, but I look at it as the bearer of glad tidings – the messenger of fate. I have reason to say so. – The finest sight in the metropolis is that of the Mail-Coaches setting off from Piccadilly. The horses paw the ground, and are impatient to be gone, as if conscious of the precious burden they convey. There is a peculiar secrecy and despatch, significant and full of meaning, in all the proceedings concerning them. Even the outside passengers have an erect and supercilious air, as if proof against the accidents of the journey. In fact, it seems indifferent whether they are to encounter the summer's heat or winter's cold, since they are borne through the air in a winged chariot. The Mail-Carts drive up; the transfer of packages is made; and, at a signal given, they start off, bearing the irrevocable scrolls that give wings to thought, and that bind or sever hearts for ever. How we hate the Putney and Brentford stages that draw up in a line after they are gone! Some persons think the sublimest object in nature is a ship launched on the bosom of the ocean: but give me, for my private satisfaction, the Mail-Coaches that pour down Piccadilly of an evening, tear up the pavement, and devour the way before them to the Land's-End!

In Cowper's time, Mail-Coaches were hardly set up; but he has beautifully described the coming in of the Post-Boy: –

> 'Hark! 'tis the twanging horn o'er yonder bridge,
> That with its wearisome but needful length
> Bestrides the wintry flood, in which the moon
> Sees her unwrinkled face reflected bright: –
> He comes, the herald of a noisy world,
> With spattered boots, strapped waist, and frozen locks;
> News from all nations lumbering at his back.
> True to his charge, the close-packed load behind,

Yet careless what he brings, his one concern
Is to conduct it to the destined inn;
And having dropped the expected bag, pass on.
He whistles as he goes, light-hearted wretch!
Cold and yet cheerful; messenger of grief
Perhaps to thousands, and of joy to some;
To him indifferent whether grief or joy.
Houses in ashes and the fall of stocks,
Births, deaths, and marriages, epistles wet
With tears that trickled down the writer's cheeks
Fast as the periods from his fluent quill,
Or charged with amorous sighs of absent swains
Or nymphs responsive, equally affect
His horse and him, unconscious of them all.'[23]

And yet, notwithstanding this, and so many other passages that seem like the very marrow of our being, Lord Byron denies[24] that Cowper was a poet! – The Mail-Coach is an improvement on the Post-Boy; but I fear it will hardly bear so poetical a description. The picturesque and dramatic do not keep pace with the useful and mechanical. The telegraphs that lately communicated the intelligence of the new revolution to all France within a few hours, are a wonderful contrivance; but they are less striking and appalling than the beacon-fires (mentioned by Æschylus[25]), which, lighted from hill-top to hill-top, announced the taking of Troy and the return of Agamemnon.

NOTES

Hazlitt is not an easy writer to annotate. He quoted compulsively, often freely adapting the material he was quoting; even when he is not quoting his writing is often densely allusive. His essays are full of references to people and events that most readers today will know little about; moreover many of them contain topical and personal allusions – some obscure, and intended only for the inner circle of his readers. Finally, Hazlitt had regular recourse to Latin and French quotations, proverbs, and tags. The problem for the annotator is knowing when to stop.

This edition is edited with a view to its usefulness to the general and student reader. Basic bibliographical details are supplied. Wherever possible quotations are identified and referenced (this does not apply on the rare occasions where Hazlitt provides an adequate reference himself). Quotations within quotations are only identified in exceptional cases. Allusions are pointed out selectively, on the basis of their contextual significance. Very basic classical ('Pandora's box') and biblical (Noah's ark) allusions are not remarked. Topical, 'background', and 'source' details are generally included only when they are essential to a basic understanding of Hazlitt's text. There is, however, a separate Biographical Index of all the important people mentioned by Hazlitt, except major figures of English literature, biblical characters, modern European monarchs, and those who entered his text simply by owning or being the subject of a painting. All Latin quotations and tags, and such French ones as are likely to offer difficulty, are translated or otherwise explained. For fuller bibliographical, biographical, and background annotation see P. P. Howe's *Collected Works of William Hazlitt* (21 vols, London: J. M. Dent & Sons Ltd, 1930–4) or Duncan Wu's *Selected Works of William Hazlitt* (9 vols, London: Pickering and Chatto, 1998).

Quotations from poems are referenced with a line number, and, where applicable, a book number in small roman numerals (i.e. *Paradise Lost*, vii,

213). Poems divided into both parts (or books) and books (or cantos) are distinguished in the primary instance by a large roman character, and in the secondary instance by a small one (i.e. Samuel Butler, *Hudibras*, I, ii, 36). Quotations from *The Faerie Queene* are further distinguished with a stanza *and* line number (i.e. *Faerie Queene*, II, iv, 17:4). Quotations from Byron's *Don Juan* are given a canto and line reference, but also, for the benefit of readers with older editions, a stanza reference in brackets (i.e. *Don Juan*, II, 1647–8 (ccvi)). In all cases, modern scholarly editions have been used where possible, but line references will sometimes vary slightly from edition to edition. Quotations from plays are, where possible, identified with an act number in large roman numerals, a scene number in small roman numerals, and a line number (i.e. *Hamlet*, I, v, 23). This has generally depended on a modern, scholarly edition being available; where this was not the case, there will often be no line reference. The plays of Shakespeare, from which Hazlitt drew the largest group of his quotations, are referenced to the second Arden edition (in the case of *The Two Noble Kinsmen* to the third Arden edition); line references will vary slightly in other editions. Quotations from prose works, where appropriate, are identified with a chapter number in small roman numerals, while 'Book' or 'Part' numbers are given in large roman numerals (i.e. *Tom Jones*, V, ii). Again, there will be slight variations between editions. The works of Edmund Burke, whom Hazlitt quotes more often than any other non-fiction writer, are an exceptional case and references are keyed, wherever possible, to the standard *Writings and Speeches of Edmund Burke* (Oxford: Clarendon Press, 1981–), still emerging under the general editorship of Paul Langford. James Boswell's *Life of Johnson* is quoted in the edition of George Birkbeck Hill (6 vols, Oxford: Clarendon Press, 1934–50). Biblical references are given in the conventional form (i.e. Mark 10:15).

Shakespeare's plays, the major poems of Milton, *The Canterbury Tales* and *The Faerie Queene* are referenced by title only. Works by major figures of English or European literature are identified by title and the author's last name. The works of lesser writers, or writers of non-literary works, are cited with the author's full name as it is usually known. When Hazlitt is quoting accurately, or nearly so, a simple reference is given. On the many occasions when he misremembers or deliberately adapts a quotation the reference is distinguished by a 'Cf'. Because of limitations of space it is only in exceptional cases that the original is supplied.

It is regretted that limited space has also meant, in most cases, that no account of the whereabouts, modern title, and present attribution of the paintings Hazlitt refers to is included. The reader should be warned, however, that many have been reattributed since the early nineteenth century and will not be found in standard catalogues.

In preparing these notes I have drawn extensively on the edition of P. P. Howe, mentioned above, and, in the final stages, on that of Duncan Wu. I have also made use of George Sampson's thoroughly annotated *Hazlitt: Selected Essays* (Cambridge: Cambridge University Press, 1917) and Jon Cook's *William Hazlitt: Selected Writings* (Oxford: Oxford University Press, 1991). I have rechecked every reference, however, and in some cases have revised these scholars' accounts of Hazlitt's sources. A number of friends have offered valued assistance with particular notes: I must, in particular, mention Maria Serafica and Michael Sharp.

David Chandler

'THE CUSTOMS AND THE GRANDE CHARTREUSE'

An extract from Chapter 14 of *Notes of a Journey through France and Italy* (1826), previously published in the *Morning Chronicle* for 6 April 1825. Hazlitt had made the tour described in the *Notes* between September 1824 and September 1825, with his second wife, Isabella.

1 '*Here was sympathy*': Cf. *Merry Wives of Windsor*, II, i, 7–8 and a passage in Joseph Cottle's *Messiah* (1815) where the fallen Satan says 'here, with spirits lost, is sympathy' (ii, 111).

2 *Douane*: The customs house.

3 *which Bonaparte said . . .* : Hazlitt refers to Napoleon's attack on 'ideology' in his 'Response to the State Consul' of 20 December 1812 (published in the *Moniteur* the following day).

4 '*Sayings and Doings*': Nine novels by Theodore Hook, published 1824–8.

5 '*Irving's Orations*': Edward Irving's *For the Oracles of God* (1823).

6 '*Table-Talk*': By Hazlitt himself (1825).

7 *Lives of the Popes*: A famous book by Bartolomeo Sacchi de Platina (1421–81).

8 '*Like that ensanguined . . .*': 'Lycidas', 106.

9 *sçavoir vivre*: 'Knowledge of living'.

10 *agrémens*: Pleasures.

11 *the winter's flaw*: Hamlet, V, i, 209.

12 *Falstaff took to himself . . .*: See *1 Henry IV*, V, iv, 110–28.

13 *douceur*: A tip.

14 *the Magdalen Muse of Mr Moore* . . .: Hazlitt makes this gibe elsewhere (see, for example, 'Jack Tars'). In Oxford and Cambridge 'Magdalen' is pronounced 'maudlin' (a word derived, in any case, from the name Mary Magdalene, who was depicted as a weeping penitent). Because Mary Magdalene was a prostitute Hazlitt also gestures at the sensuousness and easy appeal of Thomas Moore's poetry.

15 *to unsing!*: 'Extract VIII' of Moore's *Rhymes on the Road* is entitled 'Les Charmettes'.

16 *'where Alps o'er Alps arise'*: Cf. Pope, *Essay on Criticism*, 232.

17 *'this fortress built* . . .': *Richard II*, II, i, 43.

18 *'nodded to him* . . .': Cf. *Midsummer Night's Dream*, III, i, 167.

19 *'c'est un trône'*: 'It's a throne, and the cloud is its glory!' 'Glory' here essentially means 'halo': see Sir Thomas Browne, *Pseudodoxia Epidemica* (1646), V, ix: 'radiant Halo's . . . after the French expression are usually termed, the Glory'. Hazlitt himself liked to use the 'French expression', as in his essay 'The Letter-Bell'.

20 *berceau*: Cradle.

21 *traiteur*: Caterer.

22 *'with cautious* . . .': Cf. 'L'Allegro', 141.

ON THE PLEASURE OF PAINTING

An essay from the first volume of *Table-Talk* (1821). It had previously appeared in the *London Magazine* for December 1820. Hazlitt was invited to write a formal obituary of his father, who died on 16 June 1820, but wrote this essay instead.

1 *'There is a pleasure* . . .': Cf. William Cowper, *The Task*, ii, 285–6.

2 *'no juggling here'*: Kane O'Hara, *April-Day* (1777), II. The context is worth citing: 'This is past coz'nage, no juggling here. / Astrology was ever held a science / Inscrutable, infallible, incredible. / Such hold it I, and therefore hold firm faith in't' (1777 ed. p. 25).

3 *'study with joy* . . .': Cf. Cowper, *The Task*, iii, 227–8.

4 *spolia opima*: 'Rich spoils', specifically those offered to the gods by a Roman general who had killed an enemy leader in single combat.

5 *a passage in Werther* . . .: Goethe's *Die Leiden des jungen Werthers* ('The Sorrows of Young Werther') (1774), Letter viii. Hazlitt quotes the first English translation (1779; many subsequent editions).

6 *'more tedious than* . . .': Cf. *King John*, III, iv, 108.

7 '*My mind to me . . .*': The first line of a well-known poem once attributed to Edward Dyer (1543–1607), but no longer believed to be by him.

8 '*to set a throne . . .*': Cf. Francis Bacon, *Advancement of Learning*, I, viii.

9 '*Pure in the last . . .*': Dryden, *Satires of Aulus Persius Flaccus*, ii, 133.

10 '*palpable to feeling . . .*': Cf. *Macbeth*, II, i, 36–7.

11 '*fleecy fools*': Untraced; possibly a recollection of *As You Like It*, II, i, 22, where deer are described as 'dappled fools'.

12 '*light thickened*': Cf. *Macbeth*, III, ii, 50.

13 *Wilson said . . .*: Hazlitt's source for these stories about Richard Wilson was probably James Northcote's conversation (Hazlitt later assumed the role of Boswell to Northcote's Johnson and published a volume of *Conversations of James Northcote, Esq, RA* in 1830).

14 *The first head . . . an old woman . . .*: The picture is now in the Maidstone Museum.

15 *to see good in every thing*: Cf. *As You Like It*, II, i, 17.

16 *If art was long . . .*: An allusion to the Latin proverb *ars longa, vita brevis* ('art is long, life is short'), adapted from Seneca, *Dialogi*, X, i.

17 *I did not then . . . believe, with Sir Joshua . . .*: The superiority of 'general ideas of nature' is a recurrent theme in Reynolds's writings, and is particularly strongly urged in an essay he contributed to Johnson's *Idler* (No. lxxxii). Hazlitt elsewhere attacks this essay.

18 '*as in a glass darkly . . .*': Cf. 1 Corinthians 13:12.

19 '*sees into the life . . .*': Wordsworth, 'Tintern Abbey', 50.

20 '*mist, the common . . .*': *Paradise Lost*, v, 435–6.

21 *Richardson . . . tells a story . . .*: From a reference he gives in the following essay, it is clear that Hazlitt owned the 1792 complete edition of the *Works of Jonathan Richardson*, in which the Michelangelo story is at p. 209.

22 *The famous Schiller used to say . . .*: Schiller's supposed remark is untraced.

23 '*That you might almost say . . .*': Cf. Donne, 'The second Anniversary', 245–6.

24 *impasting*: Laying on of the paint thickly.

25 *It is related of Sir Joshua Reynolds . . .*: As with the stories about Wilson, the probable source is James Northcote's conversation.

26 '*the source . . . of thirty years*' . . .': A paraphrase of James Northcote, *Memoirs of Sir Joshua Reynolds* (1813), 370.

27 *a picture of my father*: Also in the Maidstone Museum.

28 '*riches fineless*': *Othello*, III, iii, 177.

29 '*ever in the haunch . . .*': *2 Henry IV*, IV, iv, 92.

30 '*I also am a painter!*': An anecdote recorded in Giorgio Vasari's *Lives*.

31 *It was an idle . . .*: Wu points out that Hazlitt quotes A. F. Tytler's 1792

translation of Schiller's *Die Räuber*, III, ii: "Twas an idle thought, a boy's conceit!'

32 *the battle of Austerlitz*: 2 December 1805; Napoleon's victory over the Austrians and Russians was naturally greeted with enthusiasm by Hazlitt, an ardent Napoleonist.

33 *the great Platonic year*: A mythical period in which the heavenly bodies will have returned to the same relative positions they held at the beginning of time; the past will then be repeated. It is explained in Plato's *Timæus*, xxxviii.

34 *full of years* . . .: Hazlitt's father died aged eighty-four.

THE SAME SUBJECT CONTINUED

A sequel to the previous essay, similarly included in the first volume of *Table-Talk* (1821). First published in the *London Magazine* for December 1820 as part of the previous essay.

1 *'Whate'er Lorraine* . . .': James Thomson, *The Castle of Indolence*, i, 341–2.

2 *Lord Radnor's park* . . .: Longford Castle, Wiltshire.

3 *'bosomed high* . . .': 'L'Allegro', 78.

4 *the Orleans Gallery*: Part of a legendary collection of old masters, assembled by Philippe, Duke of Orleans (1674–1723), exhibited for sale in London between December 1798 and July 1799.

5 *'hands that the rod* . . .': Cf. Thomas Gray, 'Elegy Written in a Country Churchyard', 47.

6 *'a forked mountain* . . .': *Antony and Cleopatra*, IV, xiv, 5–7.

7 *'signifying nothing'*: *Macbeth*, V, v, 28.

8 *the Provoked Husband*: A comedy by John Vanbrugh and Colley Cibber (1728).

9 *I went to the Louvre*: In October 1802.

10 *un beau jour*: An allusion to Jean Sylvain Bailly's famous description of a key event in the French Revolution when, on 6 October 1789, Louis XVI was forcibly brought from Versailles to Paris. Burke had ironically referred to this description in his *Reflections on the Revolution in France* (*Works*, viii, 120).

11 *'if thou hast not* . . .': Cf. *As You Like It*, III, ii, 31–42.

12 *experimentum crucis*: 'Decisive experiment'.

13 *'number numberless'*: *Paradise Regained*, iii, 310.

14 *'casual fruition* . . .': *Paradise Lost*, iv, 766–7.

15 *W—*: Both Richard Wilson and David Wilkie have been suggested as possibilities.

16 *a friend of mine . . .*: Benjamin Robert Haydon, whose *Christ's Entry into Jerusalem* was exhibited in March 1820. It was Hazlitt who had praised the work in the *Edinburgh Review*.

17 *Richardson . . . exclaims . . .*: From the reference it is clear that Hazlitt is quoting from the 1792 *Works of Jonathan Richardson*, 249–51.

18 *'swallowing the tailor's . . .'*: *King John*, IV, ii, 195.

19 *'bastards of his genius . . .'*: Howe and Wu both suggest a derivation from *Comus*, 727: 'And live like Nature's bastards, not her sons'. However, Sampson's suggestion that it comes from Shakespeare, *A Lover's Complaint*, 174–5, where one is described who 'Thought characters and words merely but art, / And bastards of his foul adulterate heart' seems more plausible – especially as Hazlitt elsewhere has 'Bastards of his art', which is almost certainly derived from *A Lover's Complaint*.

ON A LANDSCAPE OF NICOLAS POUSSIN

An essay from the second volume of *Table-Talk* (1822). Previously published in the *London Magazine* for August 1821.

1 *'And blind Orion . . .'*: Keats, *Endymion*, ii, 198.

2 *this landscape . . .*: *Paysage avec Orion aveugle*. It was exhibited in London between June and July 1821.

3 *'a hunter of shadows . . .'*: Not an exact quotation, but a reference to *Odyssey*, xi, 703–4, where Odysseus describes how he saw Orion in the underworld, driving a ghostly herd of the beasts he had slain while alive.

4 *'grey dawn . . .'*: *Paradise Lost*, vii, 373–4.

5 *'a forerunner . . .'*: Cf. James Montgomery, 'Departed Days: A Rhapsody', 87; Montgomery has 'day' instead of 'dawn'.

6 *'shadowy sets off'*: *Paradise Lost*, v, 43.

7 *Sir Joshua has . . .*: In *Discourse*, v.

8 *'denote a foregone . . .'*: *Othello*, III, iii, 434.

9 *'take up the isles . . .'*: Isaiah 40:15, combined with 40:12.

10 *high and palmy state*: *Hamlet*, I, i, 116.

11 *'so potent art'*: *Tempest*, V, i, 50.

12 *'more than natural'*: *Hamlet*, II, ii, 363–4.

13 *'gives to airy . . .'*: *Midsummer Night's Dream*, V, i, 16–17.

14 *'I have often admired', says Vignuel de Marville . . .*: Hazlitt quotes Maria

Graham, *Memoirs of the Life of Nicolas Poussin* (1820), Vol. 1, pp. 35–6.

15 *'o'er-informed'*: Dryden, *Absalom and Achitophel*, 158.

16 *'the very stones...'*: Cf. *Macbeth*, II, i, 58.

17 *'Leaping like wanton...'*: *Faerie Queene*, I, vi, 14:4.

18 *ET EGO* ...: 'And I too have dwelt in Arcadia'.

19 *'the valleys low...'*: Cf. 'Lycidas', 136.

20 *'within the book...'*: Cf. *Hamlet*, I, v, 103–4.

21 *'the sober certainty...'*: *Comus*, 262.

22 *'he who knows...'*: Cf. Milton, 'Sonnet 17', 13–14.

23 *'Old GENIUS the porter...'*: *Faerie Queene*, III, vi, 31:8, 32:1.

24 *'there were propagation too!'*: Wu points out that this is a recollection of Bell's 1774 acting edition of *Macbeth*, II, iv: 'Dread horrors still abound/And ev'ry place surround, As if in death were found/Propagation too.'

25 *he, who collected it...*: Napoleon, who had died on 5 May 1821.

MR KEAN'S SHYLOCK

A selection from *A View of the English Stage* (1818). Previously published in the *Morning Chronicle* for 27 January and 2 February 1814, this was a review of Edmund Kean's London début.

1 *'far-darting eye'*: Cf. William Cowper, *The Task*, iii, 602.

2 *in Norval and Richard*: Norval in John Home's tragedy *Douglas* (1756); Richard in *Richard III*.

MR MACREADY'S OTHELLO

Another selection from *A View of the English Stage* (1818). Previously published in the *Examiner* for 13 October 1816.

1 *a majestic serpent wounded...*: Perhaps Hazlitt was thinking of the fight with the Snake God in Robert Southey's *Madoc* (1805), II, vii.

2 *'Let Afric...'*: Cf. Edward Young, *The Revenge*, V, i, 385.

3 *'I do agnise...'*: Cf. *Othello*, I, iii, 231–3.

4 *'No, not much moved'*: Ibid., III, iii, 228.

5 *'Othello's occupation's...'*: Ibid., III, iii, 363.

6 *'Yet, oh the pity...'*: Cf. Ibid., IV, i, 191–2.

7 *'Swell, bosom...'* Ibid., III, iii, 456–7.

8 *'Like to the Pontic...'*: Cf. Ibid., III, iii, 460–2.
9 *'Horror on horror's...'*: Cf. Ibid., III, iii, 376.
10 *'pride, pomp...'*: Ibid., III, iii, 360.
11 *'we never saw a gentleman...'*: Untraced.

MRS SIDDONS

Another selection from *A View of the English Stage* (1818). Previously published in the *Examiner* for 16 June 1816.

1 *'the baby of a girl'*: Macbeth, III, iv, 105.
2 *'Rather than so ... and champion...'*: Ibid., III, i, 70–1.
3 *Genius of Gil Blas...*: *Gil Blas* (1715–35) was a picaresque novel by Alain René Le Sage; the incident referred to occurs in VII, iv.
4 *'Leave me to my repose'*: Cf. Thomas Gray, 'The Descent of Odin. An Ode', 50, 58, 72.
5 *'The line too labours...'*: Pope, *Essay on Criticism*, 371.
6 *'I tell you he cannot...'*: Cf. *Macbeth*, V, i, 60–1.
7 *'Go, go'*: Cf. Ibid., III, iv, 18.
8 *another farewell address...*: Horace Twiss, a nephew of Mrs Siddons, wrote the address which she read on taking her farewell of the stage on 29 June 1812.
9 *'himself again'*: An interpolation by Colley Cibber into *Richard III*, V.
10 *'To-morrow and to-morrow'*: Macbeth, V, v, 19.
11 *printed by a steam-engine*: *The Times* was first printed by a steam-powered printing press in November 1814.

CORIOLANUS

A chapter from *Characters of Shakespeare's Plays* (1817). A part had been previously published in the *Examiner* for 15 December 1815, and this was reprinted in *A View of the English Stage* (1818).

1 *'no jutting frieze ... to make its pendent...'*: Cf. *Macbeth*, I, vi, 6–8.
2 *'it carries noise...'*: Cf. *Coriolanus*, II, i, 157–8.
3 *'Carnage is...'*: Cf. Wordsworth, 'Ode. The Morning of the Day Appointed for a General Thanksgiving. January 18, 1816', 279–82.
4 *'poor rats'*: Cf. *Coriolanus*, I, i, 248.

5 '*as if he were a God...*': Cf. ibid., III, i, 80–1.

6 '*Mark you his absolute...*': Ibid., III, i, 88–9.

7 '*cares*' ... '*fears*': Ibid., III, i, 136.

8 '*Now the red pestilence...*': Ibid., IV, i, 13–14.

9 *those who have little...*: An ironic parody of many of Christ's sayings; see for example Luke 6:20–6.

10 *poetical justice...*: An ironic parody of the title of William Godwin's *Political Justice* (1793).

11 '*Methinks I hither...*': *Coriolanus*, I, iii, 29–30, 32–43.

12 '*These are the ushers...*': Ibid., II, i, 157–60.

13 '*Pray now, no more...*': Ibid., I, ix, 13–15.

'INTRODUCTION TO ELIZABETHAN LITERATURE'

The 'Introductory' 'Lecture I' in *Lectures on the Dramatic Literature of the Age of Elizabeth* (1820). Hazlitt had delivered the lecture on 5 November 1819.

1 '*mere oblivion*': *As You Like It*, II, vii, 165.

2 '*poor, poor dumb...*': Cf. *Julius Caesar*, III, ii, 227.

3 '*How lov'd...*': Cf. Pope, 'Elegy to the Memory of an Unfortunate Lady', 71.

4 '*draw the curtain...*': Cf. *Twelfth Night*, I, v, 236–7.

5 '*of poring pedantry*': Cf. Thomas Warton, 'Sonnet written in a Blank Leaf of Dugdale's Monasticon', 3.

6 '*the sacred influence...*': *Paradise Lost*, ii, 1034–5.

7 '*pomp of elder...*': Thomas Warton, 'Sonnet written in a Blank Leaf of Dugdale's Monasticon', 11.

8 '*nor can we think...*': Cf. Dryden, *The Hind and the Panther*, i, 315.

9 '*there's livers out...*': *Cymbeline*, III, iv, 140–1.

10 *long before it was known...*: An exaggeration: William Harvey's account of his discovery of the circulation of the blood was published in 1628; Claude Lorraine died in 1682.

11 '*by nature's own sweet...*': *Twelfth Night*, I, v, 243.

12 '*where Pan, knit...*': Cf. *Paradise Lost*, iv, 266–8.

13 '*there are more things...*': Cf. *Hamlet*, I, v, 174–5.

14 '*matchless, divine...*': Cf. Pope on Shakespeare, 'The First Epistle of the Second Book of Horace', 70.

15 *Dr Johnson said...*: In his *Preface to Shakespeare* (1765).

16 '*less than smallest dwarfs...*': *Paradise Lost*, i, 779.

17 *'desiring this man's . . .'*: Shakespeare, 'Sonnet 29', 7.

18 *'in shape and gesture . . .'*: *Paradise Lost*, i, 590.

19 *'his soul was . . .'*: Cf. Wordsworth, 'London, 1802', 9.

20 *'drew after him a third . . .'*: Cf. *Paradise Lost*, ii, 692.

21 *Jonson's learned sock*: A quotation from 'L'Allegro', 132.

22 *to know the truth . . .*: An allusion to John 8:32.

23 *'to run and read'*: Cf. Habakkuk 2:2.

24 *'penetrable stuff'*: *Hamlet*, III, iv, 36.

25 *'My peace I give unto you . . .'*: John 14:27.

26 *'they should love . . .'*: Cf. Ibid., 15:12.

27 *'Woman, behold . . .'*: Ibid., 19:26.

28 *'Behold thy mother'*: Ibid., 19:27.

29 *their hearts burned . . .*: See Luke 24:32.

30 *'when the meek Saviour . . .'*: John 19:30.

31 *'who is our neighbour?'*: Cf. Luke 10:29; Christ answers with the Parable of the Good Samaritan.

32 *'to the Jews a stumbling . . .'*: Cf. 1 Corinthians 1:23.

33 *'we perceive a softness . . .'*: Untraced.

34 *'soft as sinews . . .'*: *Hamlet*, III, iii, 71.

35 *principalities and powers*: Ephesians 6:12.

36 *'The best of men . . .'*: Thomas Middleton and Thomas Dekker, *The Honest Whore*, Part One, V, ii, 491–4.

37 *virtù*: 'A love of, or taste for, works of art or curios' (*OED*).

38 *'Fortunate fields . . .'*: *Paradise Lost*, iii, 569–70.

39 *'like those Hesperian . . .'*: Ibid., iii, 568.

40 *'Right well I wote . . .'*: *Faerie Queene*, II, Proem.

41 *'those bodiless creations . . .'*: Cf. *Hamlet*, III, iv, 140–1.

42 *'Your face, my Thane . . .'*: *Macbeth*, I, v, 61–2.

43 *'thick and slab'*: Ibid., IV, i, 32.

44 *hair-breadth accidents . . .*: Cf. *Othello*, I, iii, 135–6.

45 *'snatched a wild . . .'*: Cf. Thomas Gray, 'Ode on a Distant Prospect of Eton College', 40.

46 *'The course of true . . .'*: Cf. *Midsummer Night's Dream*, I, i, 134.

47 *'The age of chivalry . . .'*: Cf. Burke, *Reflections on the Revolution in France* (*Writings*, viii, 127).

48 *'Who prized black eyes . . .'*: John Suckling, 'A Session of the Poets', 78–9.

49 *'Like strength reposing . . .'*: Cf. Keats, 'Sleep and Poetry', 237.

50 *'they heard the tumult . . .'*: Cf. William Cowper, *The Task*, iv, 99–100.

51 *an ingenious and agreeable writer . . .*: Probably Nathan Drake (1766–1836), author of *Shakespeare and his Times* (1817).

52 *'It snowed of meat . . .'*: Cf. *The Canterbury Tales,* 'General Prologue', 345.

53 *as Mr Lamb observes*: In a note to *Specimens of English Dramatic Poets, Who Lived About the Time of Shakspeare* (1808), 84.

54 *'in act and complement . . .'*: Cf. *Othello,* I, i, 62–3.

55 *Dekker has given . . .*: Thomas Middleton and Thomas Dekker, *The Honest Whore,* Part One, V, ii.

56 *'A Mad World, my Masters'*: A play by Thomas Middleton (1608).

57 *'like birdlime . . .'*: Cf. *Othello,* II, i, 126–7.

58 *Materiam superabat . . .*: 'The workmanship was more beautiful than the material.' Ovid, *Metamorphoses,* ii, 5.

59 *'but Pan is a God . . .'*: John Lyly, *Midas,* IV, i, 9.

ON GUSTO

An essay from *The Round Table* (1817). Previously published in the *Examiner* for 26 May 1816.

1 *morbidezza*: Softness.

2 *the Orleans Gallery*: See above, 'The Same Subject Continued', note 4.

3 *'Or where Chineses . . .'*: *Paradise Lost,* iii, 438–9.

4 *'Wild above . . .'*: Ibid., v, 297.

ON SHAKESPEARE AND MILTON

The third lecture in *Lectures on the English Poets* (1818). The opening reproduces part of 'Why the Arts are not Progressive?' in *The Round Table* (1817).

1 *'the human face . . .'*: *Paradise Lost,* iii, 44.

2 *'Circled Una's . . .'*: Cf. *Faerie Queene,* I, iii, 4:6–8.

3 *'fault has been more . . .'*: Cf. *Julius Caesar,* I, ii, 138–9.

4 *excluded from Dr Johnson's Lives . . .*: This was not, however, Johnson's choice; the *Lives of the English Poets* was commissioned by a group of booksellers.

5 *It has been said by some critic . . .*: William Gifford, in the Introduction to his *Plays of Philip Massinger* (1805).

6 *'a mind reflecting . . .'*: From the opening line of a laudatory poem on Shakespeare by 'I.M.S.' prefixed to the Second Folio (1632).

7 'All corners of the earth...': Cymbeline, III, iv, 37–8.

8 'nodded to him...': Cf. Midsummer Night's Dream, III, i, 167.

9 bestrode the blast...: Cf. Macbeth, I, vii, 22.

10 'his so potent art': Cf. Tempest, V, i, 50.

11 'subject to the same...': Cf. Measure for Measure, III, i, 9.

12 'his frequent haunts...': Cf. Comus, 313.

13 'coheres semblably...': Cf. 2 Henry IV, V, i, 62.

14 it has been ingeniously remarked...: By Coleridge, in his lecture 'On Shakespeare and Milton' of 16 December 1811.

15 'Me and thy crying...': Tempest, I, ii, 132.

16 'What! man, ne'er pull...': Macbeth, IV, iii, 208.

17 'Man delights not me...': Hamlet, II, ii, 309–10.

18 'a combination and a form...': Ibid., III, iv, 60.

19 'There is a willow...': Cf. Ibid., IV, vii, 165–6.

20 'He's speaking now...': Antony and Cleopatra, I, v, 24–5.

21 'It is my birth-day...': Ibid., III, xiii, 185–7.

22 'nigh sphered...': William Collins, 'Ode on the Poetical Character', 66.

23 'playing with wisdom': Cf. Paradise Lost, vii, 9–10.

24 'to make society...': Macbeth, III, i, 42.

25 'which, with a little act...': Cf. Othello, III, iii, 333–8.

26 'while rage...': Cf. Troilus and Cressida, I, iii, 52.

27 'in their untroubled...': Cf. Wordsworth, The Excursion, vi, 787–90.

28 Satan's address...: Paradise Lost, iv, 32ff.

29 'Oh, that I were a mockery-king...': Cf. Richard II, IV, i, 260–2.

30 'His form had not yet...': Paradise Lost, i, 591–4.

31 mere effusion...: Probably a dig at Coleridge, who had entitled a number of poems in his 1796 Poems on Various Subjects: 'Effusions', and defended the name in his Preface.

32 Moods of their own Minds: A thrust at Wordsworth, who had titled a section of his 1807 Poems 'Moods of My Own Mind'.

33 'With what measure...': Cf. Mark 4:24 and Luke 6:38.

34 'It glances from heaven...': Cf. Midsummer Night's Dream, V, i, 13.

35 'puts a girdle...': Ibid., II, i, 175–6.

36 'I ask that I may...': Cf. Troilus and Cressida, I, iii, 226–9.

37 'No man is the lord...': Ibid., III, iii, 115–23.

38 'Rouse yourself...': Ibid., III, iii, 221–4.

39 any other word but the true one...: Coleridge makes a very similar point in Biographia Literaria (1817), i.

40 'Light thickens...': Macbeth, III, ii, 50–1.

41 'his whole course...': Cf. Othello, I, iii, 91.

42 *'the business of the state . . .'*: Ibid., IV, ii, 168.

43 *'Of ditties highly . . .'*: *1 Henry IV*, III, i, 202–4.

44 *'And so by many . . .'*: *Two Gentleman of Verona*, II, vii, 31–2.

45 *'great vulgar . . .'*: Abraham Cowley, 'Horace, L. 3. Ode 1', 2.

46 *Voltaire's criticisms . . .*: Voltaire's most important criticism of Shakespeare is found in his *Discours sur la tragédie à Milord Bolingbroke* (1730), *Lettres philosophiques* (1734), and *Du Théâtre anglais* (1761); his main complaint was that Shakespeare did not follow the classical 'rules' of composition.

47 *'his delights did shew . . .'*: Cf. *Antony and Cleopatra*, V, ii, 88–9.

48 *the touch of the ark . . .*: Hazlitt liked this image, which is somewhat ambiguous: when Uzzah touched the ark, 'God smote him there for *his* error; and there he died by the ark of God' (2 Samuel 6:7).

49 *'Blind Thamyris . . .'*: *Paradise Lost*, iii, 35–6.

50 *'With darkness and with . . .'*: *Paradise Lost*, vii, 27.

51 *'piling up every . . .'*: Ibid., xi, 324–5.

52 *'For after . . . I had . . . delightful studies'*: *The Reason of Church Government*, II, Preface.

53 *'The noble heart . . .'*: *Faerie Queene*, I, v, 1:1–4.

54 *'makes Ossa . . .'*: *Hamlet*, V, i, 278.

55 *'Him followed Rimmon . . .'*: *Paradise Lost*, i, 467–9.

56 *'As when a vulture . . .'*: Ibid., iii, 431–9.

57 *'the great vision . . .'*: 'Lycidas', 161.

58 *'the pilot of some . . .'*: *Paradise Lost*, i, 204.

59 *'the wandering moon . . .'*: 'Il Penseroso', 67–70.

60 *'like a steam . . .'*: *Comus*, 555.

61 *'He soon / Saw . . .'*: *Paradise Lost*, iii, 621–44.

62 *'With Atlantean shoulders . . .'*: Ibid., ii, 306–7.

63 *'Leviathan, which God . . .'*: Ibid. i, 200–2.

64 *Dr Johnson . . . condemns . . .*: In his *Life* of Milton (*Lives of the English Poets*).

65 *'His hand was known . . .'*: *Paradise Lost*, i, 732–3, 738–47.

66 *'But chief the spacious . . .'*: Ibid., i, 762, 767–88.

67 *'Round he surveys . . .'*: Ibid., iii, 555–67.

68 *'Such as the meeting . . .'*: 'L'Allegro', 138–40.

69 *'the hidden soul . . .'*: 'L'Allegro', 144.

70 *'God the Father . . .'*: Pope, 'The First Epistle of the Second Book of Horace Imitated', 102.

71 *'As when Heaven's . . .'*: *Paradise Lost*, i, 612–13.

72 *'All is not lost . . .'*: Ibid., i, 106–9.

73 *like a hell within...*: An allusion to *Paradise Lost*, iv, 175, where Satan says 'my self am Hell'.

74 *'that intellectual being...'*: Ibid., ii, 147–8.

75 *'being swallowed...'*: Ibid., ii, 149–50.

76 *'Fallen cherub...'*: Ibid., i, 157–8.

77 *'rising aloft...'*: Ibid., i, 225–6.

78 *'Is this the region...'*: *Paradise Lost*, i, 242–63.

79 *philippics against Salmasius...*: In *Pro Populo Anglicano Defensio* (1651) Milton had replied to Salmasius's *Defensio Regia pro Carolo I* (1649).

80 *'with hideous ruin...'*: *Paradise Lost*, i, 46.

81 *'retreated in a silent...'*: Ibid., ii, 547–50.

82 *a noted political writer...*: John Stoddart; Hazlitt refers to Stoddart's attacks on Napoleon in *The Times*.

83 *Longinus preferred...*: *De Sublimitate*, ix.

84 *'no kind of traffic...'*: Cf. *Tempest*, II, i, 144–57.

85 *'The generations were...'*: Wordsworth, *The Excursion*, vi, 569–72.

86 *our future woe...*: An allusion to *Paradise Lost*, i, 3–4.

87 *'the unapparent deep'*: Ibid., vii, 103.

88 *'know to know...'*: Cf. William Cowper, 'Truth', 327.

89 *'They toiled not...'*: Cf. Matthew 6:28–9.

90 *'In them the burthen...'*: Cf. Wordsworth, 'Tintern Abbey', 39–42.

91 *'such as angels weep'*: *Paradise Lost*, i, 620.

92 *'In either hand...'*: Ibid., xii, 637–47.

'THE MANAGER'

An extract from 'The Drama: No. III' in the *London Magazine* for March 1820. Not republished by Hazlitt.

1 *W—m in S—shire*: Wem in Shropshire, where Hazlitt's family had moved in 1787.

2 *W—ch*: Whitchurch, nine miles from Wem.

3 *J—s*: Jenkins, a friend of Hazlitt's father.

4 *the West-Indian*: A comedy by Richard Cumberland.

5 *No Song No Supper*: By Prince Hoare (1790).

6 *like Nebuchadnezzar's image...*: See Daniel 2:31–3.

7 *'of imagination...'*: *Midsummer Night's Dream*, V, i, 8.

8 *What is it to them...*: An allusion to Matthew 6:25

9 *'Their mind to them...'*: See 'On the Pleasure of Painting', note 7.

10 *'of all earth's bliss...'*: Charles Lamb, 'Ballad from the German' (1802 text), 9–10.

11 *Fortunatus's Wishing Cap...*: A reference to an old European folk story in which the beggar Fortunatus obtains a hat that can transplant the wearer wherever he or she wishes to go.

12 *the philosopher's stone...*: A substance that turned base metals into gold.

13 *aurum potabile*: 'Drinkable gold'.

14 *'by his so potent...'*: Cf. *Tempest*, V, i, 50.

15 *'happy alchemy...'*: Matthew Green, 'The Spleen', 610.

16 *'Severn's sedgy...'*: Cf. *1 Henry IV*, I, iii, 97.

17. *'Alas! how changed...'*: Pope, 'Epistle to Bathurst', 305–6.

THE INDIAN JUGGLERS

An essay from the first volume of *Table-Talk* (1821). The concluding section on John Cavanagh had previously appeared in the *Examiner* for 7 February 1819.

1 *thy ways past finding out!*: Romans 11:33.

2 *rolling a stone up a hill...*: An allusion to the story of Sisyphus in Homer, *Odyssey*, xi, 593–600.

3 *The celebrated Peter Pindar...*: As with most of his anecdotes about artists, Hazlitt probably heard this one from James Northcote.

4 *'In argument they own'd...'*: Cf. Oliver Goldsmith, 'The Deserted Village', 211–12.

5 *Jaggernaut*: A Hindu god whose image was paraded once a year.

6 *'to allow for the wind'*: Scott, *Ivanhoe*, xiii.

7 *'human face...'*: *Paradise Lost*, iii, 44.

8 *H—s and H—s*: Wu records that the manuscript reads 'H—s and Hiltons' (referring to William Hilton, 1786–1839). Howe suggests that Hayman, Highmore and Hudson are all evoked. Sampson adds John Hoppner and (unconvincingly) Benjamin Robert Haydon.

9 *'in tones...'*: Cf. *Paradise Regained*, iv, 255.

10 *To snatch this grace...*: Pope, *Essay on Criticism*, 155.

11 *'commercing with...'*: 'Il Penseroso', 39.

12 *the winter's flaw*: *Hamlet*, V, i, 209.

13 *'And visions, as poetic...'*: Cf. a verse fragment of Thomas Gray, printed by Roger Lonsdale in his *Poems of Gray, Collins, and Goldsmith* (1969) as 'Lines on Beech Trees'.

14 *'Thrills in each...'*: Cf. Pope, *Essay on Man*, i, 209–10.

15 *'half flying...'*: Cf. *Paradise Lost*, ii, 941–2.

16 *I know an individual...*: Leigh Hunt.

17 *nugæ canoræ*: 'Trifling songs'. Cf. Horace, *Ars Poetica*, 322.

18 *Themistocles said...*: The anecdote comes from Plutarch's *Life* of Themistocles, but Hazlitt probably knew it from Francis Bacon, *Advancement of Learning*, I, iii.

19 *Napier's bones will live*: 'Napier's bones' was a calculating device, but Hazlitt also alludes to Ezekiel 37:3.

20 *'he dies and leaves...'*: Cf. *Twelfth Night*, I, v, 245–6.

21 *'great scholar's...'*: Cf. *Hamlet*, III, ii, 129–30.

22 *fives*: 'A game in which a ball is struck by the hand against the front wall of a three-sided court' *(OED)*.

CHARACTER OF COBBETT

Another essay from the first volume of *Table-Talk* (1821). Hazlitt later incorporated it into *The Spirit of the Age* (1825).

1 *'fillips the ear...'*: Cf. *2 Henry IV*, I, ii, 229.

2 *'lays waste'*: Cf. Dryden, *The Hind and the Panther*, i, 158.

3 *fourth estate*: The French Revolution had highlighted the political importance of the 'Third Estate' of the people, in addition to the nobility and clergy. Hazlitt places Cobbett outside all three 'Estates'.

4 *'damnable iteration...'*: Cf. *1 Henry IV*, I, ii, 88.

5 *'to clear it from all...'*: Cf. *Measure for Measure*, IV, ii, 141–2.

6 *nunquam sufflaminandus...*: 'There was no stopping him.' The phrase comes from Ben Jonson's description of Shakespeare in *Timber: or, Discoveries* (1640).

7 *'full of matter'*: *As You Like It*, II, i, 68.

8 *'weary, stale...'*: Cf. *Hamlet*, I, ii, 133.

9 *We sit down at a table...*: The metaphor was common, as in Fielding's *Tom Jones*, X, i.

10 *Barmecide in the Arabian Nights...*: In 'The Story of the Barber's sixth Brother'.

11 *graphical descriptions...*: A reference to Cobbett's *Year's Residence in the United States of America* (1818).

12 *'live in his description'*: Cf. Pope, *Windsor Forest*, 8.

13 *'look green'*: Ibid.

14 *What havoc he makes . . .*: Samuel Parr ('the Whig Dr Johnson') was famous for his large powdered wig. Cobbett seems to have had an affectionate regard for Parr (see *The Works of Samuel Parr* (1828), viii, 21), and is unlikely to have ridiculed him in other than mild terms. But Hazlitt appears to be alluding to a well-publicized incident of 1820. Cobbett published (anonymously) a 'Letter from the Queen to the King' in several newspapers, which, widely believed to be by Parr, inspired some of the most hostile criticism the latter ever received – the unfortunate wig being variously referred to (see *Selections of Cobbett's Political Works* (1835), vi, 33). One must suppose that Cobbett had anticipated this outcome.

15 *Mr* —: [Henry] Brougham.

16 *His Grammar*: Cobbett's *Grammar of the English language, in a Series of Letters* (1818).

17 *the Yanguesian carriers . . .*: See Cervantes, *Don Quixote*, I, xv.

18 *'He has the back-trick . . .'*: Cf. *Twelfth Night*, I, iii, 120–1.

19 *'arrowy sleet'*: Cf. *Paradise Regained*, iii, 323–5.

20 *an Ishmaelite*: See the description of Ishmael at Genesis 16:12.

21 *Boroughmongers*: Traders in parliamentary seats.

22 *'deliberately or for money'*: Cf. John Gay, *Beggar's Opera*, I, viii, 63.

23 *a bill passed the House . . .*: Cobbett's *Political Register* evaded stamp duty until 1819, when a change in the law made it liable.

24 *'the gentleman and scholar'*: Burns, 'The Twa Dogs', 14.

25 *Paine said . . .*: The statement is untraced.

26 *'ample scope and verge . . .'*: Cf. Thomas Gray, 'The Bard', 51.

27 *'He pours out all . . .'*: Pope, 'The First Satire of the Second Book of Horace Imitated', 51–2.

28 *Antipholis of Ephesus cuts . . .*: See *Comedy of Errors*, V, i, 296ff.

29 *bringing over the relics . . .*: Cobbett brought Paine's bones to Liverpool in 1819.

30 *'his canonized . . .'*: Cf. *Hamlet*, I, iv, 47.

31 *Big Ben*: Benjamin Brian, or Bryan (1753–94), a celebrated boxer; he was champion of England 1791–4.

32 *The Edinburgh Review made . . .*: Francis Jeffrey's review of the *Political Register* appeared in the *Edinburgh Review* for July 1807, published 24 August. Cobbett's response appeared in the *Political Register* for 29 August 1807.

THE FIGHT

Published in the *New Monthly Magazine* for February 1822. Not republished by Hazlitt. The fight described took place on 11 December 1821 at Hungerford, Berkshire. For a full account see Henry Downes Miles's *Pugilistica: The History of British Boxing* (1906), vol. ii, 109–14. Miles's work also includes extended profiles of most of the boxers mentioned by Hazlitt. In this essay Hazlitt refers to two of his friends by aliases: 'Joe Toms' is Joseph Parkes (1796–1865) and 'Jack Pigott' is Peter George Patmore (1786–1855).

1 *'The fight, the fight . . .'*: Cf. *Hamlet*, II, ii, 600–1.

2 *'the proverb' nothing . . .*: Cf. Ibid., III, ii, 334–5.

3 *as the author of Waverley would express it . . .*: The 'author of *Waverley*' was Scott. Sampson comments: '"To ask at" is a Scotticism, that is, an expression that might be used by any Scot . . . but I cannot recall an instance of [Scott's] actually using it in any of the novels.'

4 *blue ruin*: Low quality gin.

5 *alter idem*: '[Each] another self'.

6 *'So carelessly did . . .'*: Cf. *As You Like It*, I, i, 118.

7 *'What more felicity . . .'*: Spenser, 'Muiopotmos', 209–10.

8 *'Well, we meet . . .'*: Cf. *Julius Caesar*, IV, iii, 285.

9 *my Rubicon*: In 53 BC Julius Caesar and his army crossed the Rubicon, the boundary between Cisalpine Gaul and Italia proper, and thereby provoked a civil war. To 'cross the Rubicon' therefore came to mean taking a decisive, irrevocable step.

10 *'I follow Fate . . .'*: Dryden, *The Indian Emperor*, IV, iii, 5.

11 *Jehu*: Slang for a driver, from the reference to Jehu's driving at 2 Kings 9:12.

12 *'quite chap-fallen'*: *Hamlet*, V, i, 186.

13 *a word to throw . . .*: Cf. *As You Like It*, I, iii, 2–3.

14 *'where good digestion . . .'*: Cf. *Macbeth*, III, iv, 37–8.

15 *'Follows so the ever-running . . .'*: Cf. *Henry V*, IV, i, 282–3.

16 *Is not this life . . .*: Cf. *As You Like It*, II, i, 2.

17 *'more figures . . .'*: Cf. *Julius Caesar*, II, i, 231.

18 *'denoted a foregone . . .'*: *Othello*, III, iii, 434.

19 *'seriously inclined'*: Cf. Ibid., I, iii, 146.

20 *envious showers . . .*: Cf. *Taming of the Shrew*, Induction, ii, 66.

21 *Gilpin*: The eponymous hero of William Cowper's 'Diverting History of John Gilpin'. The reference is to 165–76.

22 '*A lusty man . . .*': Cf. *The Canterbury Tales*, 'General Prologue', 167.

23 '*standing like greyhounds . . .*': Cf. *Henry V*, III, i, 31.

24 '*he moralized into . . .*': Cf. *As You Like It*, II, i, 44–5.

25 *like Bardolph's*: See *1 Henry IV*, III, iii, 23–47.

26 '*there are three things . . .*': A reference to Georges Jacques Danton's famous statement of 1792: 'De l'audace, encore de l'audace, toujours de l'audace, et la France est sauvée'.

27 '*Alas! the Bristol . . .*': Cf. William Cowper, *The Task*, ii, 322.

28 '*That man was made . . .*': 'Man Was Made to Mourn' is the title of a poem by Burns.

29 '*Between the acting . . .*': *Julius Caesar*, II, i, 63–5.

30 *swells*: Fashionably dressed people.

31 *Ajax*: A Greek warrior in Homer, famous for his size and courage.

32 '*with Atlantean shoulders . . .*': *Paradise Lost*, ii, 306.

33 *Diomed*: A Greek warrior in Homer.

34 *scratch*: A line drawn across the ring, where the boxers would start each round.

35 '*grinned horrible . . .*': *Paradise Lost*, ii, 846.

36 '*like two clouds . . .*': Cf. Ibid., ii, 714–16.

37 '*In doleful dumps . . .*': Quoted from a modernized version of 'The Ancient Ballad of Chevy-Chase', 119–22.

38 *Sir Fopling Flutter*: A character in George Etherege's play *The Man of Mode* (1676). The quotation is from III, ii, 305.

39 *O procul este . . .*: 'You who are profane, stand at a distance', Virgil, *Aeneid*, vi, 258.

40 *a cross*: Slang for 'the fight was fixed'.

41 *sans intermission . . .*: Cf. *As You Like It*, II, vii, 32–3.

42 *New Eloise*: Rousseau's cult novel, *La Nouvelle Héloïse* (1761).

'JACK TARS'

An extract from Chapter 20 of *Notes of a Journey through France and Italy* (1826). Previously published in the *Examiner* for 1 May 1825 under the title 'English and Foreign Manners'.

1 *Jack Tars*: Sailors.

2 *History of a Foundling*: I.e. *Tom Jones*.

3 *mucilage*: A substance that acts as a laxative.

4 *kill him with kindness*: An allusion to the title of Thomas Heywood's play, *A Woman Killed with Kindness*.

5 *John Bull*: A character invented by John Arbuthnot as a representative of England.

6 *according to a happy allusion* . . .: A reference to Robert Southey, 'The March to Moscow' (1813), 25–54. Southey presented the British pacifists as advising John Bull to 'Ask the Emperor Nap[oleon] if he will please / To grant you peace upon your knees' (28–9).

7 *the Bourbons*: The French Royal family.

8 *tub to a whale*: An allusion to George Canning's recognition of the independence of the Spanish American colonies in 1823; a 'tub to a whale' is proverbial for a timely diversion.

9 *fœnum in cornu*: 'The hay is on the horn' (dangerous cattle were thus distinguished). Horace, *Satires*, I, iv, 34.

10 '*Stout Gentleman*': Possibly George IV.

11 *baisés-mains*: 'Hand-kissing'.

12 '*lily-livered*': *Macbeth*, V, iii, 15 and *King Lear*, II, ii, 15.

13 '*perceive a fury* . . .': Cf. *Othello*, II, iii, 281.

14 *riante*: Happy.

15 '*But that two-handed* . . .': 'Lycidas', 130.

16 *the Magdalen Muse* . . .: See 'The Customs and the Grande Chartreuse', note 14

ON HOGARTH'S *MARRIAGE À-LA-MODE*

An essay from *The Round Table* (1817). Previously published in the *Examiner* for 5 June 1814, and subsequently included in *Sketches of the Principal Picture Galleries in England* (1824).

1 '*Of amber-lidded* . . .': Cf. Pope, *The Rape of the Lock*, iv, 123–4.

2 *just at the moment* . . .: Hazlitt was actually thinking of ibid., ii, 9–18.

3 '*a person, and a smooth* . . .': Cf. *Othello*, I, iii, 395–6.

4 '*vice loses half* . . .': Cf. Burke, *Reflections on the Revolution in France* (*Writings*, viii, 127).

5 *cheveux-de-fris*: 'Curly hair'.

THE SUBJECT CONTINUED

A sequel to the previous essay, also from *The Round Table* (1817). Previously published in the *Examiner* for 19 June 1814, and subsequently included in *Sketches of the Principal Picture Galleries in England* (1824).

1 *what Fielding says . . .*: *Tom Jones*, IV, i.
2 *'all the mutually . . .'*: Cf. Burke, *Reflections on the Revolution in France* (*Writings*, viii, 84).
3 *'frequent and full'*: *Paradise Lost*, i, 797.
4 *'In loud recess . . .'*: Cf. Ibid., i, 795.

CHARACTER OF MR BURKE, 1807

An essay from *Political Essays, With Sketches of Public Characters* (1819). Previously published in *The Eloquence of the British Senate* (1807).

1 *The following speech . . .*: 'On Economical Reform', 11 February 1780 (*Writings*, iii, 438–51).
2 *Proteus*: A minor sea-god who knows all things and can assume any shape at will.
3 *'The elephant to make . . .'*: Cf. *Paradise Lost*, iv, 345–7.
4 *'native and endued . . .'*: *Hamlet*, IV, vii, 178–9.
5 *'he was the most . . .'*: Untraced.
6 *'a new creation . . .'*: Oliver Goldsmith, *The Traveller*, 296.
7 *Seneca . . . says . . .*: Wu notes 'Brendan McLaughlin suggests to me that Hazlitt has in mind Seneca's remarks on *subtilis* in *De Beneficiis*.'
8 *'Alas! Leviathan . . .'*: William Cowper, *The Task*, ii, 322.
9 *The corner stone . . .*: An allusion to Psalms 118:22.
10 *to the Jews . . .*: Cf. 1 Corinthians 1:23.
11 *He strove to establish . . .*: In this and the following paragraph Hazlitt summarizes Burke's *Reflections on the Revolution in France* (1790).
12 *'How charming . . .'*: *Comus*, 475–7.
13 *His comparison between our connexion with France . . .*: *First Letter on a Regicide Peace* (*Writings*, ix, 257–9).
14 *his account of the conduct of the war . . .*: *Second Letter on a Regicide Peace* (*Writings*, ix, 273–5).

15 *as Dr Johnson observed . . .*: In his *Life* of Pope (*Lives of the English Poets*).
16 *'proud keep . . .'*: *Letter to a Noble Lord* (*Writings*, ix, 172).

CHARACTER OF MR BURKE [1817]

Another essay from *Political Essays, With Sketches of Public Characters* (1819), obviously intended to be read in conjunction with the earlier 'Character' of Burke. Previously published as part of the article 'Coleridge's Literary Life' in the *Edinburgh Review* for August 1817 and (without the final paragraph) in the *Champion* for 5 October 1817.

1 *his speech on the Begum's affairs . . .*: Of 4 April 1786 (*Writings*, vi, 91–113).
2 *he represented the French priests . . .*: In *Reflections on the Revolution in France* (*Writings*, viii, 183–96).
3 *an interpretation on the word abdication . . .*: Ibid. (*Writings*, viii, 77–8).
4 *His lamentations . . .*: Ibid. (*Writings*, viii, 126–9).
5 *Mr Coleridge thinks . . .*: In *Biographia Literaria* (1817), x, Coleridge had stated approvingly that 'the essays and leading paragraphs of our journals are so many remembrances of EDMUND BURKE'.
6 *'Never so sure . . .'*: Cf. Pope, 'Epistle to a Lady', 51–2.

CHARACTER OF MR FOX, 1807

An essay from *Political Essays, With Sketches of Public Characters* (1819). Previously published in *The Eloquence of the British Senate* (1807).

1 *at present . . .*: The note was added in 1819.
2 *'craftily qualified'*: *Othello*, II, iii, 36.
3 *'what I have written . . .'*: Pilate's words at John 19:22.
4 *'have bared . . .'*: Cf. Oliver Goldsmith, *The Traveller*, 390.
5 *'whose sound reverbed . . .'*: Cf. *King Lear*, I, i, 155.
6 *a celebrated and admirable writer . . .*: William Godwin, whose 'Character of Fox' appeared in the *Morning Chronicle*, 22 November 1806.
7 *in the preface to Spenser . . .*: John Upton's edition of *The Faerie Queene* (1758).
8 *'deaf and dumb things'*: Cf. *Julius Caesar*, I, i, 35: 'You blocks, you stones,

you worse than senseless things!' and (in context) Habakkuk 2: 19: 'Woe
unto to him that saith to the wood, Awake; to the dumb stone, Arise, it shall
teach! . . . *there is* no breath at all in the midst of it.'
9 '*jutting frieze* . . .': Cf. *Macbeth*, I, vi, 6–7.
10 '*with mighty wings* . . .': *Paradise Lost*, i, 20–2.
11 '*the dazzling fence* . . .': Cf. *Comus*, 790–1.
12 '*an honest man's* . . .': Pope, *Essay on Man*, iv, 248.
13 '*To his great* . . .': Burke, speech of 9 February 1790.

WHY THE ARTS ARE NOT PROGRESSIVE? – A FRAGMENT

An essay from *The Round Table* (1817). The first four paragraphs had been
published previously in the *Morning Chronicle* for 11 and 15 January 1814;
the last two paragraphs in the *Champion* for 11 September 1814.

1 '*the human face* . . .': *Paradise Lost*, iii, 44.
2 '*circled Una's* . . .': Cf. *Faerie Queene*, I, iii, 4:6–8.
3 *Prince of Painters*: Raphael.
4 *sorrow of Griselda*: In *The Clerk's Tale*.
5 *the Flower and the Leaf*: A fifteenth-century allegorical poem, no longer
attributed to Chaucer.
6 *story of the Hawk*: *Decameron*, Fifth Day, Novel V.
7 *So Isabella* . . .: Ibid, Fourth Day, Novel V.
8 *So Lear* . . .: *King Lear*, II, iv, 187–90.

POETRY

Published in *The Atlas* for 8 March 1829. Not republished by Hazlitt.

1 '*Daffodils / That come* . . .': *Winter's Tale*, IV, iv, 118–25.
2 *John Bull*: A character invented by John Arbuthnot as a representative of
England.
3 '*that fine madness* . . .': Michael Drayton, 'To My Most Dearely-Loved
Friend Henery Reynolds, Esq.', 107, 109.
4 *one hypercritic*: Hazlitt was probably thinking of Johnson, who had annotated this passage: 'Sweeter than an "eye-lid" is an odd image: but perhaps
he [Shakespeare] uses "sweet" in the general sense, for "delightful".'
5 '*cowslips wan* . . .': 'Lycidas', 147.

6 *'lowly children...'*: Cf. James Thomson, *The Seasons*, 'Spring', 450.

7 *'they came before...'*: Cf. *Winter's Tale*, IV, iv, 119.

8 *vox et preterea...*: 'A voice and nothing more'; a proverb meaning 'empty words'.

9 *'winged words'*: Dryden, *Virgil's Aeneis*, iv, 388.

10 *'ball of dazzling fire'*: Cf. Byron, *Manfred*, II, ii, 14: 'dazzling eyes of glory' and II, ii, 71: 'dazzling lightnings'.

11 *'to elevate...'*: George Villiers, Duke of Buckingham, *The Rehearsal*, I, i.

12 *that it was black*: An idea perhaps inspired by Shelley's *Cenci*, III, i, 14: 'The sunshine on the floor is black!'.

ON THE ELGIN MARBLES: THE ILISSUS

Published in the *London Magazine* for February 1822. Not republished by Hazlitt.

1 *'Who to the life...'*: Abraham Cowley, 'To the Royal Society', 79–88.

2 *'To learn...'*: Cf. William Cowper, *The Task*, iii, 227–8.

3 *'alternate action...'*: Hazlitt quotes from Thomas Lawrence's testimony to the Select Committee of the House of Commons on the Elgin Marbles, 5 March 1816.

4 *Mr Chantrey once...*: Hazlitt had probably heard the story from James Northcote.

5 *'image and superscription'*: Matthew 22:20.

ON THE ELGIN MARBLES

Published in the *London Magazine* for May 1822 as the promised sequel to the previous article. Not republished by Hazlitt.

1 *in rerum...*: 'In the nature of things'.

2 *'So from the ground...'*: Cf. *Paradise Lost*, v, 479–81.

3 *'laborious foolery'*: Cf. *King Lear*, III, i, 16–17.

4 *'fair varieties'*: Cf. Mark Akenside, *The Pleasures of Imagination* (1744), i, 78.

5 *Sir Joshua debated...*: Reynolds's *Journey to Flanders and Holland* concludes with a 'Character of Rubens'.

6 *'gay creatures...'*: Cf. *Comus*, 298–300.

7 *in his mind's eye*: Cf. *Hamlet*, I, ii, 185.

8 *seven-league boots*: Proverbial; 'from the boots in the fairy story of Hop o' my Thumb, which enabled the wearer to cover seven leagues at each step' (*OED*).

9 *H—yd—n's*: [Benjamin] Haydon's.

10 *Sedet, in . . .*: 'Unlucky Theseus sits, and will sit for eternity'. Virgil, *Aeneid*, vi, 617–18.

11 *Honi soit qui . . .*: 'Evil be to him who evil thinks' – the motto of the Order of the Garter.

12 *cum grano . . .*: 'With a pinch of salt'.

13 *it has been remarked*: Coleridge's remark was made in conversation.

14 *Sir Joshua tells us . . .*: In *The Idler*, lxxxii.

15 *'villainous low'*: *Tempest*, IV, i, 249.

16 *'to o'erstep . . .'*: Cf. *Hamlet*, III, ii, 19.

17 *'all we hate'*: Pope, 'Epistle to a Lady', 52.

18 *'Thrills in each . . .'*: Cf. Pope, *Essay on Man*, i, 218.

19 *Sir Joshua lays it down . . .*: A reiterated theme in Reynolds's theoretical writing; the previously cited *Idler* essay is exemplary.

20 *gratis dicta*: 'Things spoken for nothing'.

'PROSE-STYLE AND THE ELGIN MARBLES'

A footnote at the end of Chapter 11 of *Notes of a Journey Through France and Italy* (1826), previously published in the *Morning Chronicle* for 2 November 1824.

FROM A *LETTER TO WILLIAM GIFFORD, ESQ.*

A pamphlet, published at Hazlitt's own expense in 1819. The *Quarterly Review*, of which Gifford was editor, had published three hostile reviews of Hazlitt's works: of *The Round Table*, of *Characters of Shakespear's Plays*, and of *Lectures on the English Poets* . Although these were not, in fact, all authored by Gifford, Hazlitt addresses him as though they were.

1 *'on this bank . . .'*: *Macbeth*, I, vii, 6.

2 *the imagination brooding . . .*: Cf. *Paradise Lost*, i, 19–22.

3 *a broad and beaten way . . .*: Cf. Ibid., ii, 1026–7.

MY FIRST ACQUAINTANCE WITH POETS

Published in the *Liberal* for April 1823. Not republished by Hazlitt. Part of the essay, describing Coleridge's sermon, had been previously published in the *Examiner* for 12 January 1817 and in *Political Essays, With Sketches of Public Characters* (1819).

1 *W–m*: Wem, where Hazlitt's family moved in 1787.

2 *'dreaded name . . .'*: *Paradise Lost*, ii, 964–15.

3 *'fluttering the proud . . .'*: Cf. *Coriolanus*, V, vi, 114–15.

4 *'High-born Hoel's . . .'*: Thomas Gray, 'The Bard', 28.

5 *'bound them/With Styx . . .'*: Cf. Pope, 'Ode for Musick. On St Cecilia's Day', 90–1.

6 *like the fires . . .*: Aeschylus, *Agamemnon*, 281–386.

7 *Il y a des impressions . . .*: 'There are some impressions that neither time nor circumstances can obliterate. Were I to live whole centuries, the sweet days of my youth could never return and never fade from my recollection' (Sampson's translation). Despite other scholars' attempts to be more specific, Sampson's gloss remains the best: 'The passage resembles several sentences in Rousseau's *Confessions* and *La Nouvelle Héloïse*.' Hazlitt moved into French to evoke Rousseau's idiom.

8 *'And he went up . . .'*: Combines Matthew 14:23 and John 6:15.

9 *'rose like a steam . . .'*: *Comus*, 556.

10 *'of one crying . . .'*: Cf. Matthew 3:3–4.

11 *crimped*: Forced into the army.

12 *cue*: Pigtail.

13 *'Such were the notes . . .'*: Cf. Pope, 'Epistle to Robert, Earl of Oxford', 1.

14 *JUS DIVINUM*: 'Divine Right [of Kings]'. By 1816 Hazlitt regarded Coleridge as an apostate willing to uphold the theory of 'Jus Divinum'. As Sampson comments, 'The whole description of the sermon at Wem is plainly written with the intention of emphasizing Coleridge's change of political faith.'

15 *'Like to that sanguine . . .'*: 'Lycidas', 106.

16 *'As are the children . . .'*: Cf. James Thomson, *The Castle of Indolence*, ii, 295.

17 *'A certain tender . . .'*: Cf. Ibid., i, 507.

18 *'somewhat fat . . .'*: Hazlitt confuses *Hamlet*, V, ii, 290 with III, iv, 155.

19 *'no figures nor . . .'*: *Julius Caesar*, II, i, 231.

20 *the age of Methuselah*: Quoted as 969 at Genesis 5:27, making him the oldest of the patriarchs.

21 *attempting to establish...*: In *Political Justice* (1793) Godwin, an atheist, had presented the 'conjecture' that man might one day become immortal simply through 'mind ... becom[ing] omnipotent over matter' (VIII, vii).

22 *Deva's winding...*: Cf. 'Lycidas', 55.

23 *the shores of old romance*: Wordsworth, 'A narrow girdle of rough stones and crags', 40.

24 *the Delectable Mountains*: Part of the allegorical landscape in Bunyan's *Pilgrim's Progress*.

25 *this simile... Cassandra*: Gauthier de Costes de la Calprenède, *Cassandra* (1642), II, v.

26 *'Sounding on...'*: A confused recollection of *The Canterbury Tales*, 'General Prologue', 307. As Sampson pointed out, Hazlitt was confusing this with Wordsworth, *The Excursion*, iii, 701.

27 *Credat Judæus...*: 'Let the Jew Apella believe it!' (Horace, *Satires*, I, v, 100). The name Apella stands for any Jew; the Jews were regarded as particularly credulous by the Romans.

28 *choke-pears*: Sampson notes 'Literally a fruit difficult to swallow because of its rough, astringent nature, and so, metaphorically, anything hard to understand.'

29 *'Thus I confute...'*: Cf. Boswell, *Life of Johnson*, i, 471.

30 *'Kind and affable...'*: Cf. *Paradise Lost*, viii, 648.

31 *has somewhere told himself...*: *Biographia Literaria*, x. Coleridge's version of the story is rather different.

32 *that other Vision*: Byron's. Southey's *Vision* (1821), written in his capacity as Poet-laureate, described George III's entry into heaven; Byron's mocked it by describing Southey's own (unsuccessful) efforts to enter heaven, as well as attacking George III.

33 *the Bridge-street Junto*: 'The Constitutional Association', whose office was in Bridge Street. It was mainly concerned with suppressing seditious publications, and Hazlitt's gibe draws attention to the irony that John Murray was a member despite being the publisher of Byron's seditious *Vision of Judgment*.

34 *Tom Jones and the...*: See Fielding's *Tom Jones* (1749), X, v.

35 *Paul and Virginia*: A translation of Bernardin de St Pierre's enormously popular *Paul et Virginie* (1787).

36 *Camilla*: Frances Burney's novel (1796).

37 *nothing was given...*: Perhaps an allusion to *King Lear*, I, iv, 130: 'Nothing can be made out of nothing'.

38 *a softness might . . .*: This statement and the succeeding quotation had been placed in quotation marks in Hazlitt's 'Introduction to *The Dramatic Literature of the Age of Elizabeth*'.

39 *form of Sybilline Leaves*: Literally 'in loose sheets', but *Sybilline Leaves* was also the title of Coleridge's collected poems (1817).

40 *'hear the loud . . .'*: Ben Jonson, 'To Sir Robert Wroth', 22.

41 *ballad of Betty Foy*: Wordsworth's 'The Idiot Boy'.

42 *'In spite of pride . . .'*: Pope, *Essay on Man*, i, 293.

43 *'While yet the trembling . . .'*: James Thomson, *The Seasons*, 'Spring', 18.

44 *'Of Providence, foreknowledge . . .'*: *Paradise Lost*, ii, 559–60. In *Biographia Literaria*, x, Coleridge quotes this same passage as descriptive of his 'favourite subjects' as a schoolboy.

45 *his own Peter Bell*: The eponymous hero of Wordsworth's *Peter Bell* (1819; written 1798) who is described as having 'a dark and sidelong walk' and a 'long and slouching . . . gait' (316–17).

46 *ad captandum*: Proverbial; in full 'ad captandum vulgus', 'to win over the masses'.

47 *'his face was . . .'*: Cf. *Macbeth*, I, v, 62–3.

48 *flip*: A drink made of sugar and hot cider, wine, spirits or beer.

49 *'followed in the chace . . .'*: Cf. *Othello*, II, iii, 354–5.

50 *the Death of Abel*: Solomon Gessner's enormously successful *Der Tod Abels* (1758). The 'prose-tale' Coleridge referred to was the incomplete *Wanderings of Cain*, published in 1828.

51 *Caleb Williams*: William Godwin's novel (1794).

52 *'ribbed sea-sands'*: 'The Ancient Mariner', 227.

53 *'Oh memory! shield . . .'*: Untraced; used by Hazlitt elsewhere.

54 *'But there is matter . . .'*: Cf. Wordsworth, 'Hart-Leap Well', 95–6.

JEREMY BENTHAM

A portrait from *The Spirit of the Age* (1825). Previously published in the *New Monthly Magazine* for January 1824.

1 *'A prophet has . . .'*: Cf. Matthew 13:57.

2 *'I know thee . . .'*: Cf. *Tempest*, II, ii, 141–2.

3 *'That waft a thought . . .'*: Cf. Pope, *Eloisa and Abelard*, 58.

4 *'lone island . . .'*: Cf. Pope, *Essay on Man*, i, 106.

5 *Chreistomathic School*: Bentham's *Chrestomathia* (1818) advocated the application of Joseph Lancaster's principles to education at secondary schools.

6 *'foregone conclusion'*: *Othello*, III, iii, 434.

7 *'He has not allowed . . .'*: Cf. Scott, *Ivanhoe*, xiii.

8 *petrific, leaden mace*: Cf. *Paradise Lost*, x, 294.

9 *bound volatile . . .'*: Cf. Ibid., iii, 602–3.

10 *caput mortuum*: 'Worthless residue'.

11 *ultima ratio . . .*: 'Ultimate reasoning of philosophers'. A parody of Cardinal Richelieu's maxim, which Hazlitt quotes in 'On Genius and Common Sense'.

12 *'all appliances . . .'*: *2 Henry IV*, III, i, 29.

13 *Posthæc meminisse . . .*: 'Afterwards we will take delight in remembering'. Cf. Virgil, *Aeneid*, i, 203.

14 *Ordinary of Newgate*: The chaplain of Newgate prison, who prepared condemned prisoners for death.

15 *No more than Montaigne . . .*: A reference to Montaigne's 'Apologie de Raimond Sébond'.

16 *Hulks*: Boats serving as prisons.

17 *'All men act . . .'*: Cf. Bentham, *An Introduction to the Principles of Morals and Legislation* (1789), xiv.

18 *Bedlam or St Luke's*: Mental institutions.

19 *the New Drop*: A mechanical device to facilitate executions, introduced in 1783.

20 *Panopticon*: Advocated by Bentham in his *Panopticon, or The Inspection-House* (1791).

21 *'Dip it in . . .'*: Cf. Sterne, *A Sentimental Journey*, 'The Wig'.

22 *Address to the higher . . .*: A dig at Coleridge, the second of whose *Lay Sermons* (1817) was so addressed.

23 *Mr Owen and his parallelograms . . .*: A reference to Robert Owen's *Report to the Committee for the Relief of the Manufacturing Poor* (1817) which outlined new housing ideas.

24 *On Usury*: Bentham's *Defence of Usury* (1816) had been written in 1787.

25 *'in nook monastic'*: Cf. *As You Like It*, III, ii, 408–9.

26 *'men of Ind'*: *Tempest*, II, ii, 59.

27 *Proh pudor!*: 'For shame!'

28 *'to be honest . . .'*: *Hamlet*, II, ii, 178–9.

29 *'looked enough . . .'*: Francis Bacon, *Advancement of Learning*, I, iii.

WILLIAM GODWIN

Another portrait from *The Spirit of the Age* (1825).

1 *as Goldsmith used to say* . . .: Cf. Boswell, *Life of Johnson*, iii, 252.

2 *'Sedet, in* . . .': 'Unlucky Theseus sits, and will sit for eternity.' Virgil, *Aeneid*, vi, 617–18.

3 *like the false Duessa*: See *The Faerie Queene*, I, iv.

4 *'its hinder parts* . . .': Ibid., I, iv, 5:8–9.

5 *'The pillar'd firmament* . . .': *Comus*, 598–9.

6 *'What then, went* . . .': Cf. Matthew 11:7.

7 *the new Gamaliel*: See Acts 22:3.

8 *Mr Southey's Inscriptions*: Radical poems included in *Poems* (1797).

9 *'like Cato* . . .': Pope, 'Epistle to Dr Arbuthnot', 209.

10 *Oh! and is all forgot?*: Cf. *Midsummer Night's Dream*, III, ii, 201.

11 *'by that sin* . . .': *Henry VIII*, III, ii, 441.

12 *'the law of laws* . . .': A significant parody of Revelation 17:14.

13 *'Who is thy neighbour?'*: The question put to Christ at Luke 10:29; Christ then tells the parable of the Good Samaritan.

14 *'Thou shalt love* . . .': Luke 10:27 (in this context).

15 *'There was the rub* . . .': Cf. *Hamlet*, III, i, 65, 68–9.

16 *'trenchant blade'*: Samuel Butler, *Hudibras* I, i, 357.

17 *'all is conscience* . . .': Cf. *The Canterbury Tales*, 'General Prologue', 150.

18 *'so ran the tenour* . . .': Cf. *Merchant of Venice*, IV, i, 231.

19 *'It was well said* . . .': Cf. *Henry VIII*, III, ii, 152–3.

20 *'fallen first* . . .': A parody of *Hamlet*, II, ii, 147–51.

21 *'lost the immortal* . . .': Cf. *Othello*, II, iii, 255–6.

22 *'the guide, the stay* . . .': Cf. Wordsworth, 'Tintern Abbey', 110–12.

23 *'when in Auvergne* . . .': Cf. Scott, *Quentin Durward*, i.

24 *'Reason is the queen* . . .': Hazlitt quotes his own 'Illustrations of Vetus'.

25 *'the unreasonableness* . . .': Cf. Cervantes, *Don Quixote*, I, i.

26 *experimentum crucis*: 'Decisive experiment'.

27 *'flying an eagle* . . .': Cf. *Timon of Athens*, I, i, 49.

28 *'Thus far shalt* . . .': Cf. Job 38:11.

29 *'championing it to the Outrance'*: Cf. *Macbeth*, III, i, 71.

30 *'bastards of his art'*: Cf. Shakespeare, 'A Lover's Complaint', 174–5.

31 *There is no look of patch-work* . . .: The implied comparison is with Scott's novels.

32 *Allen-a-Dale*: A northern minstrel who appears in Scott's *Ivanhoe*.

33 *speech on General Warrants*: As Howe notes, there is a mistake here, for the speech in question, of 7 March 1763, was actually on the Cyder Tax. However, the mistake is Godwin's, not Hazlitt's (see next note).

34 *the printed volume . . .*: Godwin's *History of the Life of William Pitt, Earl of Chatham* (1783); the quoted passage is at v.

35 *Esto perpetua*: 'Let it endure for ever.'

MR COLERIDGE

Another portrait from *The Spirit of the Age* (1825).

1 *'and thank the bounteous . . .'*: Cf. *Comus*, 175–6.

2 *'a mind reflecting . . .'*: From the opening line of a laudatory poem on Shakespeare by 'I.M.S.' prefixed to the Second Folio (1632).

3 *'dark rearward . . .'*: Cf. *Tempest*, I, ii, 50.

4 *'That which was now . . .'*: *Antony and Cleopatra*, IV, xiv, 9–11.

5 *'quick, forgetive . . .'*: Cf. *2 Henry IV*, IV, iii, 97–8.

6 *his Daphne . . .*: An allusion to Ovid, *Metamorphoses*, i, 525–52.

7 *'what in him . . .'*: Cf. *Paradise Lost*, i, 22–3.

8 *'And by the force . . .'*: Cf. *Macbeth*, III, v, 28–9.

9 *'rich strond'*: *Faerie Queene*, III, iv, 34:2.

10 *'goes sounding . . .'*: Cf. Wordsworth, *The Excursion*, iii, 710, significantly quoted by Coleridge, *Biographia Literaria*, v.

11 *'his own nothings . . .'*: Cf. *Coriolanus*, II, ii, 77.

12 *'letting contemplation . . .'*: John Dyer, *Grongar Hill*, 26.

13 *'Sailing with supreme . . .'*: Thomas Gray, 'The Progress of Poesy', 116–17.

14 *'He lisped . . .'*: Cf. Pope, 'Epistle to Dr Arbuthnot', 128.

15 *'whose hearts . . . burnt . . .'*: An allusion to Luke 24:32.

16 *ELIA*: Charles Lamb; the reference is to Lamb's essay 'Christ's Hospital Five and Thirty Years Ago'.

17 *'Struggling in vain . . .'*: Wordsworth, *The Excursion*, vi, 557.

18 *'ethereal braid . . .'*: Cf. William Collins, 'Ode to Evening', 7.

19 *like Ariel . . .*: See *Tempest*, I, ii, 274–81.

20 *'And so by many . . .'*: *Two Gentlemen of Verona*, II, vii, 31–2.

21 *he fell . . . ten thousand fathoms . . .*: Cf. *Paradise Lost*, ii, 933–4.

22 *hortus siccus*: 'Dry garden'. Quoting Burke, *Reflections on the Revolution in France* (*Writings*, viii, 63).

23 *'When he saw . . .'*: Coleridge, *Remorse*, IV, ii, 100–2.

24 *the Sorrows of Werter*: Goethe's popular novel (1774).

25 *'laughed with Rabelais...'*: Cf. Pope, *Dunciad*, i, 22.

26 *the Triumph of Death*: A fresco in the Campo Santo at Pisa, now attributed to Francesco Traini. Coleridge spoke of it as Giotto's in at least two of his lectures.

27 *would have floated his bark...*: A reference to the 'Pantisocracy' project of 1794–5: Coleridge and Robert Southey had planned to found a commune in America.

28 *'In Philarmonia's...'*: Cf. Coleridge, 'Monody on the Death of Chatterton', 151.

29 *'Frailty, thy name...'*: Cf. *Hamlet*, I, ii, 146.

30 *doses of oblivion*: A reference to Coleridge's opium addiction.

31 *a Poet-laureate or stamp-distributor*: References to Southey and Wordsworth.

32 *'bourne from whence...'*: Cf. *Hamlet*, III, i, 79–80.

33 *as if life's business...*: Cf. Wordsworth, 'Resolution and Independence', 37.

34 *'He cannot...'*: Cf. *The Canterbury Tales*, 'The Franklin's Tale', 36.

35 *morning calls from idle visitors...*: An ironic reference to a passage in 'Essay III' of Coleridge's *Friend*.

36 *He has the happiness...*: An allusion to Fielding, *Joseph Andrews*, III, v.

37 *Pas de trois*: A dance for three people.

38 *Pingo in...*: 'I paint for eternity'. Quoted from Joshua Reynolds's third *Discourse*.

39 *'taught with the...'*: Pope, *Essay on Man*, iii, 177.

40 *'Youth at its...'*: Cf. Thomas Gray, 'The Bard', 74.

MR WORDSWORTH

Another portrait from *The Spirit of the Age* (1825).

1 *'lowliness is young...'*: *Julius Caesar*, II, i, 22.

2 *'no figures nor...'*: Cf. Ibid., II, i, 231–2.

3 *'skyey influences'*: *Measure for Measure*, III, i, 9.

4 *'Nihil humani...'*: 'I think nothing pertaining to humanity foreign to me.' Cf. Terence, *Heautontimorumenos*, I, i, 77.

5 *He takes a subject...*: Wordsworth himself had famously stated in the 1800 Preface to *Lyrical Ballads* that the 'feeling' in the poems 'gives importance to the action and situation, and not the action and situation to the feeling'.

6 *'the cloud-capt towers...'*: Cf. *Tempest*, IV, i, 151–6.

7 *de novo*: 'Anew'.

8 *tabula rasa*: 'Clean slate'.

9 *'the judge's robe . . .'*: Cf. *Measure for Measure*, II, ii, 59–61.

10 *jewels in the crisped . . .*: Cf. William Collins, 'The Manners. An Ode', 55.

11 *He gathers manna . . .*: This sentence presents Wordsworth as a Moses figure: see Exodus 16:11–15 and 17:3–6.

12 *'a sense of joy/To the . . .'*: Wordsworth, 'Lines written at a Small Distance from my House', 6–8.

13 *vicissitude of fate*: Edward Young, *Night Thoughts*, vi, 108.

14 *'Beneath the hills . . .'*: Wordsworth, *The Excursion*, vi, 568–72.

15 *the round earth its footstool*: Cf. Isaiah 66:1.

16 *the vain pomp . . .*: *Henry VIII*, III, ii, 365.

17 *'To him the meanest . . .'*: Cf. Wordsworth, 'Intimations Ode', 205–6.

18 *The daisy looks up . . .*: Hazlitt refers to Wordsworth's poem 'To the Daisy'; there follow a series of increasingly imprecise references to other Wordsworth poems: 'To the Cuckoo', 'The Sparrow's Nest' (which Hazlitt confuses with another poem, 'The Green Linnet'), 'The Thorn', and possibly 'Alice Fell'.

19 *Cole-Orton*: Sir George Beaumont's country house, where the Wordsworths frequently stayed.

20 *'Calm contemplation . . .'*: Cf. Wordsworth, 'Laodamia', 72.

21 *'Fall blunted . . .'*: Cf. Oliver Goldsmith, *The Traveller*, 232.

22 *'and fit audience . . .'*: *Paradise Lost*, vii, 31.

23 *still-born from the press*: Cf. Pope, 'Epilogue to the Satires', ii, 226.

24 *toujours perdrix*: 'Always partridge': a comment originally made by the confessor to Henry VI of France when the latter ordered partridge for every course at dinner.

25 *'man of no mark . . .'*: Cf. *1 Henry IV*, III, ii, 45.

26 *'Flushed with a purple . . .'*: Dryden, *Alexander's Feast*, 51–2.

27 *'He hates those . . .'*: Apparently a (misremembered?) quotation from Wordsworth's conversation, which Hazlitt uses elsewhere; there are no such 'interlocutions', however.

28 *'Action is momentary . . .'*: *The Borderers*, III, v, 60–5.

29 *Drawcansir*: A character in George Villiers, Duke of Buckingham, *The Rehearsal* (1671), who enters a battle and kills the combatants on both sides.

30 *'he hates conchology . . .'*: Hazlitt quotes himself, from his *Lectures on the English Poets* (1818).

31 *'Where one for sense . . .'*: Cf. Samuel Butler, *Hudibras*, II, i, 29–30.

32 *'take the good . . .'*: Cf. Dryden, *Alexander's Feast*, 106.

33 '*the spoiled child*...': Hazlitt quotes his account of Byron in *The Spirit of the Age*.

34 *genial current of the soul*: Thomas Gray, 'Elegy written in a Country Churchyard', 52.

35 *the God of his own idolatry*: In David Garrick's celebrated *Ode Upon Dedicating a Building, and Erecting a Statue, to Shakespeare, at Stratford Upon Avon* (1769) it was Shakespeare who was 'The god of our idolatry!' (14).

'VENICE'

An extract from Chapter 22 of *Notes of a Journey through France and Italy* (1826). Previously published in the *Morning Chronicle* for 13 September 1825.

1 *Lord Byron and Lady Morgan*... *quarrelling*...: See the 'Appendix' to Byron's *The Two Foscari*.

2 '*And Ocean smil'd*...': Perhaps a freely adapted quotation. Howe annotates with Coleridge, 'Ode to the Departing Year', 129–30; closer is William Lisle Bowles, *The Missionary*, viii, 195–6: 'ocean smiled / As to the sire I bore his lisping child'.

3 '*And now from out*...': Barry Cornwall, 'A Vision', 59–75.

ON THE PRESENT STATE OF PARLIAMENTARY ELOQUENCE

Published in the *London Magazine* for October 1820. Not republished by Hazlitt.

1 '*Such a one*... *aims*...': Cf. Pliny, *Epistularum*, I, xx.

2 '*domestic treason*...': Cf. *Macbeth*, III, ii, 25.

3 '*make a wanton*': *Hamlet*, V, ii, 25.

4 *de omnibus*...: 'About all things and certain others'.

5 '*plays round*...': Cf. Pope, *Essay on Man*, iv, 254.

6 *sea of speculation*... *curious pebbles*...: The image is Sir Isaac Newton's: see Joseph Spence, *Anecdotes, Observations, and Characters, of Books and Men* (1820), 54.

7 '*roll all his*...': Cf. Andrew Marvell, 'To His Coy Mistress', 41–2.

8 *'kindle them...'*: *Comus*, 793–4.

9 *good hater*: Johnson's description of Richard Bathurst as recorded in Hesther Lynch Piozzi, *Anecdotes of the late Samuel Johnson*.

10 *bellum internecinum*: 'Internecine war'.

11 *'ample scope...'*: Cf. Thomas Gray, 'The Bard', 51.

12 *'would lengthen...'*: Cf. *Macbeth*, IV, i, 117.

13 *a Member of Congress*: Probably Daniel Webster (1782–1852).

14 *It is a custom...*: *Hamlet*, I, iv, 15–16.

15 *'Grove nods to grove...'*: Pope, 'Epistle to Burlington', 117–18.

16 *'Like Juno's Swans...'*: Cf. *As You Like It*, I, iii, 71–2.

17 *Roubiliac ... said ... 'what he...'*: The anecdote is recorded in James Northcote, *Memoirs of Sir Joshua Reynolds* (1813), 44.

18 *'Without o'erflowing...'*: John Denham, *Cooper's Hill*, 192.

19 *'Come then...'*: James Thomson, *The Seasons*, 'A Hymn', 118.

20 *'that speech was given...'*: Hazlitt elsewhere attributes this 'observation' to Talleyrand, but it had been made by Voltaire in the 1760s – and there are several earlier versions. See Burton Stevenson, *Stevenson's Book of Quotations* (1934), pp. 1901–2.

21 *which Isabey has given...*: A reference to Jean-Baptiste Isabey's painting *The Congress of Vienna*.

22 *'In many a winding...'*: Cf. 'L'Allegro', 139–40.

23 *hawk and buzzard*: 'Between hawk and buzzard' was a proverbial phrase for 'in a state of perplexity or indecision'.

24 *'But 'tis the fall...'*: Pope, 'Epilogue to the Satires', i, 143–4.

25 *'Out upon...'*: *1 Henry IV*, I, iii, 206.

26 *Summum jus...*: 'More law, less justice'. Cicero, *De Officiis*, I, x.

27 *'as notorious...'*: Cf. *Tristram Shandy*, I, x: "twas plain as the sun at noon-day'.

28 *toto cælo*: '[In respect of] the whole of heaven'.

29 *'the punto, the stoccado...'*: Cf. *Merry Wives of Windsor*, II, iii, 24.

30 *'no further seek...'*: Cf. Thomas Gray, 'Elegy Written in a Country Churchyard', 125–6.

31 *malice prepense*: 'Premeditated malice'.

32 *'hear him's...'*: Cf. Burke, 'Speech on American Taxation', 19 April 1774 (*Writings*, ii, 455).

33 *'swinging slow...'*: 'Il Penseroso', 76.

34 *'mother-wit and arts...'*: Cf. Dryden, *Alexander's Feast*, 166.

35 *Sidrophel and Whackum*: See Samuel Butler, *Hudibras*, II, ii.

36 *'sole sovereign sway...'*: Cf. *Macbeth*, I, v, 70.

37 *'What's serious...'*: Cf. Matthew Prior, 'The Ladle', 139.

38 *he speaks, and writes . . .*: Hazlitt himself parodies Acts 17:28: 'in him [the Lord] we live, and move, and have our being'.

39 '*a windy fan . . .*': Cf. *Faerie Queene*, III, xii, 8:2, 8.

40 '*As those same plumes . . .*': Ibid., III, xii, 8:5.

41 '*Trifles light . . . confirmations . . .*': *Othello*, III, iii, 327–9.

42 '*to make the worse . . .*': *Paradise Lost*, ii, 113–14.

43 '*takes the rose . . .*': Cf. *Hamlet*, III, iv, 42–4.

44 *Pierre curses the Senate*: Thomas Otway, *Venice Preserv'd*, IV, i, 262–6.

45 *vis inertiæ*: 'Force of inertia'.

46 '*in the extremity . . .*': Apparently a composite quote from Shakespeare: cf. *Richard II*, IV, i, 235 and *As You Like It*, IV, iii, 23.

47 '*his face 'twixt . . .*': Cf. Tobias Smollett, *Sir Launcelot Greaves*, xxi.

ON THE SPIRIT OF MONARCHY

Published in the *Liberal* for January 1823. Not republished by Hazlitt.

1 '*THING Ferdinand . . .*': Leigh Hunt's remark, explained in Hazlitt's 'Definition of Wit'.

2 '*And by the vision . . .*': Cf. Wordsworth, 'Intimations Ode', 73–4.

3 *The Madman in Hogarth*: *The Rake's Progress*, Plate VIII.

4 *A celebrated . . . historian . . .*: William Roscoe (1753–1831).

5 '*A good king . . .*': Untraced; the sentiment is expressed several times in Swift's writings.

6 '*that within which . . .*': *Hamlet*, I, ii, 85.

7 '*to fear, not . . .*': Cf. *Othello*, I, ii, 71.

8 *Voltaic Battery*: The first electric battery, invented by Alessandro Volta (1745–1826) in the 1790s.

9 *Metallic Tractors*: Metallic rods drawn over the skin, believed to relieve rheumatic and other pains.

10 '*peep through . . .*': *Macbeth*, I, v, 53–4.

11 *Great is Diana . . .*: Acts 19:28.

12 '*Your Gods . . .*': Cf. Matthew 13:13, but the larger allusion is to the story of Elijah and the prophets of Baal: see especially 1 Kings 18:27.

13 '*Of whatsoe'er descent . . .*': Dryden, *Absalom and Achitophel*, 100–3.

14 '*Gods partial . . .*': Pope, *Essay on Man*, iii, 257–8.

15 '*any mark, any likelihood . . .*': Cf. *1 Henry IV*, III, ii, 45.

16 '*In fact, the argument . . .*': Hazlitt quotes his own 'What is the People?'

17 '*From the crown . . .*': Cf. Isaiah 1:6.

18 *Virtue, says Montesquieu...*: In *Esprit de Lois*, III, vi.

19 '*honour dishonourable...*': *Paradise Lost*, iv, 314–15.

20 '*Of outward shew...*': Ibid., viii, 538–9.

21 '*to tread the...*': Cf. *Hamlet*, I, iii, 50.

22 '*to scale the...*': Cf. Ibid., I, iii, 48.

23 '*nice customs...*': *Henry V*, V, ii, 284.

24 '*in form...*' Cf. *Hamlet*, II, ii, 304–7.

25 '*Vice is undone...*': Pope, 'Epilogue to the Satires', i, 142–9.

26 '*the same luck...*': Cf. Byron, *Don Juan*, II, 1647–8 (ccvi).

27 '*A present deity...*': Dryden, *Alexander's Feast*, 35–6.

28 '*Worth makes...*': Pope, *Essay on Man*, iv, 203–4.

29 '*The only amaranthine...*': William Cowper, *The Task*, iii, 268–9.

30 '*A man may read...*': Jeremy Taylor, *Holy Dying*, I, i.

ON THE CONNEXION BETWEEN
TOAD-EATERS AND TYRANTS

An essay from *Political Essays, With Sketches of Public Characters* (1819).
Previously published in the *Examiner* for 12 January 1817.

1 '*Doubtless, the pleasure...*': Samuel Butler, *Hudibras*, II, iii, 1–2.

2 *what we said about Coriolanus*: See Hazlitt's essay, *Coriolanus*.

3 '*bore through...*': Cf. *Richard II*, III, ii, 170.

4 '*Oh, name him not...*': *Julius Caesar*, II, i, 150–2.

5 *according to Mr Coleridge's... testimony...*: In *The Statesman's Manual*, 'Appendix C'.

6 '*empty praise...*': Pope, *Dunciad*, i, 54.

7 *Compagnons du Lys*: Hazlitt liked the pun here, which he explains in his 'Definition of Wit'.

8 '*unslacked of motion*': *Julius Caesar*, III, i, 70.

9 *the Jaggernaut*: A Hindu god whose image was paraded once a year.

10 '*of the last successful...*': Wu notes, '[John] Stoddart never uses these exact words, but frequently refers to the French Revolution as a "rebellion".'

11 *Mr Owen... dedicated...*: Robert Owen dedicated his *Address to the Inhabitants of New Lanark* (1816) to 'those ... who are honestly in search of Truth, for the purpose of ameliorating the Condition of Society'.

12 *of the two elder Blifils...*: Fielding, *Tom Jones*, I, x–xiii.

13 '*on some high holiday...*': Cf. Oliver Goldsmith, *The Traveller*, 224.

14 *'I've heard of hearts . . .'*: Wordsworth, 'Simon Lee', 101–4.

15 *'It is no tale . . .'*: Ibid., 79–80.

16 *'of other times'*: James Macpherson, *Temora*, vi, and cf. Scott, *Waverley*, i.

17 *hits . . . between wind and water*: Burke, 'Speech on American Taxation', 19 April 1774 (*Writings*, ii, 452).

18 *'Of whatsoever race . . .'*: Dryden, *Absalom and Achitophel*, 100–3.

19 *omne tulit . . .*: 'It has gained every point'. Horace, *Ars Poetica*, 343.

20 *just failed*: John Stoddart was dismissed as editor of *The Times* at the end of 1816.

21 *'who had seen . . .'*: *Morning Chronicle*, 27 January 1814.

22 *'the true Jacobin . . .'*: *The Times*, 29 January 1814.

23 *'in contempt . . .'*: Cf. Burke, *Reflections on the Revolution in France* (*Writings*, viii, 65).

24 *a good hater*: See 'On the Present State of Parliamentary Eloquence', note 9.

25 *Odia in longum . . .*: 'Casting the seeds of hatred deep within [the Emperor] for him to nurture and produce with increase'. Tacitus, *Annals*, I, lxix.

26 *three poets . . .*: Wordsworth, Southey and Coleridge.

WHAT IS THE PEOPLE?

Another essay from *Political Essays, With Sketches of Public Characters* (1819). This and the following essay were originally published in three parts, in the *Champion* for 12, 19 and 26 October 1817. The final two-part form was reached when they were republished in the *Yellow Dwarf* for 7 and 14 March 1818.

1 *'a vile jelly'*: *King Lear*, III, vii, 81.

2 *'the unbought grace . . .'*: Burke, *Reflections on the Revolution in France* (*Writings*, viii, 127).

3 *'resemble the flies . . .'*: Ibid (*Writings*, viii, 145).

4 *'Fine word . . .'*: *King Lear*, I, ii, 18.

5 *Latter Lammas*: A day that will never come.

6 *'Miraturque novas . . .'*: 'And [it] marvels at its new leaves and fruits not its own'. Virgil, *Georgics*, ii, 82.

7 *a certain author . . .*: John Stoddart, a leader writer and editor of *The Times*.

8 *'the professional gentleman'*: Stoddart's description of himself, apparently.

9 *'Gods to punish ... men ...'*: Cf. *Coriolanus*, III, i, 80–1.

10 *compagnons du lys*: Hazlitt liked the pun here, which he explains in his 'Definition of Wit'.

11 *'Why, what a fool ...'*: Cf. *Tempest*, V, i, 295–6.

12 *'Because men ...'*: William Cowper, *The Task*, v, 192.

13 *'cribbed, confined ...'*: Cf. *Macbeth*, III, iv, 23.

14 *'the right divine ...'*: Pope, *Dunciad*, iv, 188.

15 *'broad and casing'*: Cf. *Macbeth*, III, iv, 21–2.

16 *'Like the rainbow's ...'*: Burns, 'Tam o' Shanter', 61–2, 63–4, 65–6.

17 *'enthroned in the hearts ...'*: *Merchant of Venice*, IV, i, 190.

18 *'and levy cruel ...'*: *Paradise Lost*, ii, 501–2.

19 *'steeped in poverty ...'*: Cf. *Othello*, IV, ii, 51.

20 *'to betray the cause ...'*: Untraced.

21 *'large heart ... confined ...'*: One of Hazlitt's cleverest uses of quotation: he ironically adapts *Paradise Lost*, vii, 484–8 – 'First crept/The Parsimonious Emmet, provident/Of future, in small room large heart enclos'd,/Pattern of just equalitie perhaps/Hereafter' – then increases the irony by substituting 'narrow', 'narrow room' being a common metaphor for the grave.

22 *un peuple serf ...*: 'A servile people, liable to forced labour and exploitation, at the mercy of others' (Cook's translation).

23 *'King's castle'*: Burke, *Reflections on the Revolution in France* (*Writings*, viii, 259).

24 *lettres de cachet*: Documents permitting members of the French nobility or ministry to imprison or deport a person without trial.

25 *corvées*: Rents paid in labour.

26 *menus plaisirs*: 'Small pleasures'.

27 *Count Fathom or Jonathan Wild*: The villainous anti-heroes of Tobias Smollett's *Adventures of Ferdinand Count Fathom* (1753) and Fielding's *Jonathan Wild* (1743).

28 *'O silly sheep ...'*: Cf. *Measure for Measure*, V, i, 295–6.

29 *'any faction ...'*: Cf. Burke, *Appeal from the Old to the New Whigs* (1791), 56–7.

30 *Vox populi*: 'The voice of the people is the voice of God' (proverbial).

31 *Hobbes' Leviathan*: In the introduction to *Leviathan* (1651), Thomas Hobbes explains 'by Art [shaping Nature] is created that great LEVIATHAN called a COMMON-WEALTH'.

WHAT IS THE PEOPLE? (CONCLUDED)

A sequel to the previous essay, again from *Political Essays, With Sketches of Public Characters* (1819). For details of earlier publication see bibliographic note to the previous essay.

1 *'fine word...'*: *King Lear*, I, ii, 18.
2 *'tried wisdom'*: From the Prince Regent's reply to the 'Address of the Corporation of London', December 1816; it was reported in the *Examiner* on 15 December.
3 *'If they had not...'*: Cf. Judges 14:18.
4 *'left his wife...'*: Cf. *The Beauties of the Anti-Jacobin* (1799), 306.
5 *'the universal Spanish...'*: Cf. Canning's speech in the House of Commons, 24 February 1809.
6 *ode, elegy, or sonnet*: Cf. Johnson, 'Lines Written in Ridicule of Thomas Warton's Poems', 8.
7 *'make him a willow...'*: Cf. *Twelfth Night*, I, v, 272–5.
8 *He indeed assures us...*: Hazlitt refers to, and quotes from, Robert Southey's article in the *Quarterly Review*, xvi, 225–78.
9 *'whether the voice...'*: Cf. Ibid., 276.
10 *'persecuted, insulted...'*: Cf. Ibid., 228.
11 *Mr Locke has observed...*: In *An Essay Concerning Human Understanding*, IV, xx.
12 *'stying us'*: Cf. *As You Like It*, I, i, 8. Hazlitt implicitly accepts William Warburton's emendation of 'stays' to 'sties'.
13 *'When the sky...'*: Cf. Matthew 16:1–3. After quoting two 'sky' proverbs, Christ significantly adds: 'O *ye* hypocrites, ye can discern the face of the sky; but can ye not *discern* the signs of the times?'
14 *the proverb is somewhat musty*: Cf. *Hamlet*, III, ii, 334–5.
15 *'hold a barren... wrenched...'*: Cf. *Macbeth*, III, i, 61–2.
16 *'for the Son...'*: Cf. Robert Southey, *Carmen Nuptiale*, 'The Dream', 307–8.
17 *the two Ferdinands*: Ferdinand I of the Two Sicilies and Ferdinand VII of Spain.
18 *a swinish multitude*: A much-quoted phrase from Burke's *Reflections on the Revolution in France* (*Writings*, viii, 130).
19 *'that complex constable'*: Cf. Thomas Heywood, *The second part of King Edward the fourth* and its many references to 'the Constable' – 'the great Constable', 'that trechrous Constable', 'our cunning Constable', etc.
20 *'Liceat, quæso...'*: 'A people that has felt the yoke of slavery heavy on

its neck may well be allowed to be wise and learned and noble enough to know what should be done to its oppressor, though it send not to ask either foreigners or grammarians.' *Pro Populo Anglicano Defensio*, I, i.

21 *'forsooth'*: Hazlitt quotes John Stoddart's account of the Evans story in *The Day* and *New Times*.

22 *Lisbon Job*: In 1814 George Canning had been sent to Lisbon as an 'ambassador extraordinary' to receive the King of Portugal on his return from Brazil. The appointment carried a salary of £14,000, and when the King did not return after all the appointment was represented by the Opposition as a 'job'.

23 *'duller than the fat...'*: Cf. *Hamlet*, I, v, 32–3.

24 *'the dim suffusion'*: *Paradise Lost*, iii, 26.

25 *'the drop serene'*: Ibid., iii, 25.

26 *'they may roll...'*: Ibid., iii, 23–4.

27 *'making Ossa...'*: *Hamlet*, V, i, 278.

28 *'as gross as...'*: *Othello*, III, iii, 410–11.

29 *Wat Tyler... so naturally dramatized...*: The Poet-laureate was Robert Southey, whose radical play *Wat Tyler* was written, but not published, in 1794. In 1817 it had been piratically published to embarrass Southey.

30 *'a necessity that...'*: Burke, *Reflections on the Revolution in France* (*Writings*, viii, 147).

31 *'too foolish fond...'*: Cf. *King Lear*, IV, vii, 60.

32 *written in very choice...*: Cf. *Hamlet*, III, ii, 256–7.

33 *'did never wrong...'*: Cf. *Julius Caesar*, III, i, 47.

34 *Mr Burke, in regretting...*: A general reference to the *Reflections on the Revolution in France*.

35 *Exit by Mistake*: By Robert Francis Jameson (1816); not published.

'PORTRAIT OF CROKER'

Published (anonymously) in the *Examiner* for 1 August 1824. Not republished by Hazlitt. This 'Half-length' of John Wilson Croker was first attributed to Hazlitt by Stanley Jones in 'Three Additions to the Canon of Hazlitt's Political Writings', *Review of English Studies*, xxxviii (1987), 355–63. Duncan Wu has included it in his selection from *The Plain Speaker* as 'a kind of postscript' to *The Spirit of the Age* (1825).

1 *'A dog, in forehead...'*: Cf. Pope, *Homer's Iliad*, i, 297.

2 *— House*: Carlton House, residence of George IV.

3 *Thersites*: Described by Homer as the ugliest man at Troy.

4 *Duke Humphrey*: The Duke of Wellington; the allusion is probably to *2 Henry VI*, I, i, 75–103.

5 *keeps a fellow*: Theodore Hook.

6 *Great Fûm*: George IV; see Byron, *Don Juan*, xi, 620 (lxxviii).

ON THE PROSE-STYLE OF POETS

An essay from *The Plain Speaker* (1826).

1 *'feathered, two-legged . . .'*: Cf. Dryden, *Absalom and Achitophel*, 170.

2 *Author of Waverley*: Scott.

3 *'unpleasing flats . . .'*: Cf. *Romeo and Juliet*, III, v, 28.

4 *'foregone conclusion'*: *Othello*, III, iii, 434.

5 *'He murmurs by . . .'*: Wordsworth, 'A Poet's Epitaph', 39–40.

6 *'to come trippingly . . .'*: Cf. *Hamlet*, III, ii, 2.

7 *invita Minerva*: 'With Minerva [goddess of the arts] unwilling', i.e. 'uninspired'. Cf. Horace, *Ars Poetica*, 385.

8 *ad libitum*: 'Extemporaneously'.

9 *like Goldsmith . . .*: The 'Noble Lord' was the Earl of Northumberland. The story enjoyed wide currency but is probably untrue: see James Prior, *The Life of Oliver Goldsmith* (1836), ii, 66–8.

10 *'treads the primrose . . .'*: Cf. *Hamlet*, I, iii, 50.

11 *'the highest heaven . . .'*: Cf. *Henry V*, 'Prologue', 2.

12 *He is nothing . . .*: Cf. *Othello*, II, i, 119.

13 *Bristol-stones*: Quartz crystals found near Bristol.

14 *'on the unstedfast . . .'*: *1 Henry IV*, I, iii, 191.

15 *browses on the roughest bark*: Cf. *Antony and Cleopatra*, I, iv, 66.

16 *'To make us heirs . . .'*: Cf. Wordsworth, 'I am not One who much or oft delight', 53–4.

17 *'Like beauty making . . .'*: Shakespeare, 'Sonnet 106', 3.

18 *'the proud Keep . . .'*: Burke, *Letter to a Noble Lord* (*Writings*, ix, 172).

19 *'Such are their ideas . . .'*: Ibid., (*Writings*, ix, 172–3).

20 *'Dum domus . . .'*: 'So long as the house of Aeneas shall dwell on the Capitol's unshaken rock, and the Father of Rome hold sovereign sway'. Virgil, *Aeneid*, ix, 448–9.

21 *'buttress, frieze . . . make its pendant . . .'*: Cf. *Macbeth*, I, vi, 6–9.

22 *'at one fell . . .'*: Ibid., IV, iii, 129.

23 *'sharp and sweet'*: Cf. *All's Well that Ends Well*, IV, iv, 33.

24 'durante bene . . .': 'As long as [he] pleased'.

25 'From Windsor's . . .': Thomas Gray, 'Ode on a Distant Prospect of Eton College', 6–7.

26 'now hung like . . .': Cf. Burke, 'Speech on the Nabob of Arcot's Debts', 28 February 1785 (Writings, v, 519).

27 'pigeon-holes': Burke, Letter to a Noble Lord (Writings, ix, 177).

28 'the Leviathan . . .': Ibid. (Writings, ix, 164).

29 'Created hugest . . .': Paradise Lost, i, 202.

30 'put his hook . . .': Cf. Job 41: 1–2.

31 travelling out of the record: Cf. The Preface to The Letters of Junius.

32 'elevate and surprise': George Villiers, Duke of Buckingham, The Rehearsal, I, i.

33 I am indebted to Mr Coleridge . . .: Howe suggests this refers to Coleridge's conversation, though it is possible Hazlitt was (inaccurately) recollecting Coleridge's remarks on prose style in 'Essay III' of The Friend.

34 'forlorn way . . .': Cf. Arthur Golding, Ovid's Metamorphoses, iv, 536: 'irksome way obscure'.

35 'extravagant and erring . . .': Hamlet, I, i, 159.

36 'stoops to earth': Cf. Pope, 'Epistle to Dr Arbuthnot', 341.

37 'The words of Mercury . . .': Love's Labour's Lost, V, ii, 920–1.

38 the Author of Rimini: Leigh Hunt.

ON REASON AND IMAGINATION

Another essay from The Plain Speaker (1826).

1 'this breathing world': Richard III, I, i, 21.

2 'In the world's volume . . .': Cymbeline, III, iv, 138–40.

3 'there are more things . . .': Cf. Hamlet, I, v, 174–5.

4 'as mice . . .': Burke, Letter to a Noble Lord (Writings, ix, 177).

5 'all the mighty . . .': Wordsworth, 'Tintern Abbey', 106–7.

6 in vacuo: 'In a vacuum'.

7 'in a short account . . .': Circumstantial Details of the Long Illness and Last Moments of the Rt. Hon. Charles James Fox [etc.] (1806). Hazlitt draws on pp. 23–4.

8 'words that glow . . . thoughts . . .': Cf. Thomas Gray, 'The Progress of Poesy', 110.

9 spirited remark . . . in Paley . . .: William Paley, The Principles of Moral and Political Philosophy, III, Pt. 2, i: 'There is little besides the consideration

of duty, or an habitual humanity, which comes into the place of consideration, to produce a proper conduct towards those who are beneath us.'

10 *De non apparentibus* . . .: 'That which is not seen must be treated as if it did not exist.' A legal maxim found in Sir Edward Coke's *Reports* (1658), v, 343.

11 *'the tyrant's plea'*: *Paradise Lost*, iv, 393.

12 *'casts its shadow* . . .': Thomas Campbell, 'Lochiel's Warning', 57.

13 *one of this school* . . .: James Mill (1773–1836) whose *History of British India* was published 1817–18.

14 *Ex uno omnes*: 'All from one'. Cf. Virgil, *Aeneid*, ii, 65–6.

15 *'What can we reason* . . .': Pope, *Essay on Man*, i, 18.

16 *'A breath can* . . .': Cf. Oliver Goldsmith, 'The Deserted Village', 54.

17 *'give the mind* . . .': Cf. *Hamlet*, III, i, 68.

18 *'One touch* . . .': *Troilus and Cressida*, III, iii, 175.

19 *'Thou hast no* . . .': Cf. *Macbeth*, III, iv, 93–5.

20 *'both at the first* . . .': Cf. *Hamlet*, III, ii, 21–2.

21 *'To feel what* . . .': Cf. Thomas Gray, 'Ode to Adversity', 48.

WHETHER GENIUS IS CONSCIOUS OF ITS POWERS?

Another essay from *The Plain Speaker* (1826).

1 *'sees not itself* . . .': Cf. *Julius Caesar*, I, ii, 66–8.

2 *'What a pity',* said some one . . .: Probably Charles Lamb.

3 *'a phœnix gazed* . . .': *Paradise Lost*, v, 272.

4 *Materiam superabat* . . .: 'The workmanship was more beautiful than the material', Ovid, *Metamorphoses*, ii, 5.

5 *'Our poesy* . . .' *Timon of Athens*, I, i, 21–5.

6 *He . . . boasted that* . . .: See *The Genuine Works of William Hogarth* (1808–17), ii, 237.

7 *invitâ Minerva*: 'With Minerva [goddess of the arts] unwilling'; i.e. 'uninspired'. Cf. Horace, *Ars Poetica*, 385.

8 *Jacob's Ladder*: *Jacob's Dream*, Dulwich Picture Gallery.

9 *'the glory, the intuition* . . .': Cf. Mary Lamb, 'Lines on the Celebrated Picture by Leonardo da Vinci, called "The Virgin of the Rocks"', 15–16.

10 *Sancho . . . jests . . . fell from him* . . .: See Cervantes, *Don Quixote*, II, xliii and lxvii. It is actually proverbs rather than 'jests' as such that Sancho constantly utters.

11 *'through happiness* . . .': Pope, 'Epistle to Jervas', 68.

12 *I heard a person . . . remark, 'Oh!* . . .': Probably Wordsworth.

13 *'And visions, as poetic...'*: Cf. a verse fragment of Thomas Gray, printed by Roger Lonsdale in his *Poems of Gray, Collins, and Goldsmith* (1969) as 'Lines on Beech Trees'.

14 *'My mind to me...'*: The first line of a well-known poem once attributed to Edward Dyer (1543–1607), but no longer believed to be by him.

15 *character of Millamant*: In Hazlitt's *Lectures on the English Comic Writers* (1819). Millamant is a character in William Congreve's *The Way of the World*.

16 *Orlando Friscobaldo*: A character in Thomas Middleton and Thomas Dekker, *The Honest Whore*.

17 *G*ff***d*: [William] Gifford.

18 *founded as the rock*: *Macbeth*, III, iv, 21.

19 *head and front...*: *Othello*, I, iii, 80.

20 *Leigh Hunt ... flowers*: In his editorials in the *Examiner* Hunt had applauded Napoleon's defeat.

21 *I sat by the waters...*: Cf. Psalms 137:1–2.

22 *the Mighty*: Napoleon.

23 *the BEAST*: Revelation 13:15.

24 *image and superscription*: Matthew 22:20.

25 *'cried out upon...'*: Combines *Hamlet*, II, ii, 338 and III, ii, 357–8.

26 *Mr Jerdan recommends...*: William Jerdan had attacked Hazlitt in the pages of the *Literary Gazette* for years. However, unaware of the authorship of Hazlitt's anonymously published *Characteristics: In the Manner of Rochefoucault's Maxims* (1823), he praised it (*Literary Gazette*, 12 July 1823).

27 *The lively ... Editor*: Leigh Hunt.

28 *'that the most accomplished...'*: Cf. Leigh Hunt's attack on the Prince Regent in the *Examiner* for 22 March 1812, for which he was imprisoned.

29 *Return, Alpheus...*: 'Lycidas', 132–3.

30 *'look abroad...'*: Francis Bacon, *Advancement of Learning*, I, iii.

31 *'they take in vain'*: Cf. Exodus 20:7.

32 *'It is all one...'*: Cf. *All's Well That Ends Well*, I, i, 83–5.

33 *'fast-anchored in the deep...'*: Cf. William Cowper, 'Retirement', 84.

34 *Cassiopeia's chair...*: An allusion to Thomas Randolph's *Poems* (1640), p. 14: 'Ariadne's crowne and Cassiopeia's chayre'.

35 *Berenice's locks*: Pope, *Rape of the Lock*, v, 129.

36 *'The face of heaven...'*: Cf. *Romeo and Juliet*, II, ii, 21–2.

37 *'The high endeavour...'*: Cf. William Cowper, *The Task*, v, 901.

38 *bis repetita...*: 'Twice repeated cabbage', proverbial for 'stale repetition'. Cf. Juvenal, *Satires*, vii, 154.

39 *'Titianus faciebat'*: 'Titian painted this.'

ON THE PLEASURE OF HATING

Another essay from *The Plain Speaker* (1826).

1 *Lines to a Spider*: Leigh Hunt's 'To a Spider Running Across a Room'.

2 *'the milk of human...'*: *Macbeth*, I, v, 17.

3 *Mr Burke observes...*: In *A Philosophical Enquiry into the Origins of our Ideas of the Sublime and Beautiful* (*Writings*, i, 223).

4 *abhor a vacuum*: Cf. 'Nature abhors a vacuum' from François Rabelais, *Gargantua*, I, v.

5 *the Scotch Novels*: Scott's novels.

6 *'Off, you lendings!'*: *King Lear*, III, iv, 106–7.

7 *Panopticons*: See 'Jeremy Bentham', note 20.

8 *Parallelograms*: See 'Jeremy Bentham', note 23.

9 *'Tis pretty...*: *All's Well that Ends Well*, I, i, 90.

10 *snap-dragon*: A game in which raisins are snatched out of a bowl of burning brandy.

11 *'upon this bank...'*: *Macbeth*, I, vii, 6.

12 *'outdo termagant'*: Cf. *Hamlet*, III, ii, 13–14.

13 *'That which was luscious...'*: *Othello*, I, iii, 349–50.

14 *'six days...'*: Richardson, *Clarissa*, Letter 529.

15 ELIA: Charles Lamb.

16 *H—*: [Benjamin] Haydon.

17 *'carve them...'*: Cf. *Julius Caesar*, II, i, 173.

18 *L— H—*: Leigh Hunt.

19 *Mrs —*: [Mary Sabilla] Novello.

20 *B—*: [Thomas] Barnes.

21 *R—*: [John] Rickman.

22 *'sans intermission...'*: Cf. *As You Like It*, II, vii, 32–3.

23 *'fellows of no mark...'*: *1 Henry IV*, III, ii, 45.

24 *—'s*: Perhaps [Basil] Montagu's.

25 *M.*: Perhaps [Basil] Montagu.

26 *'mice in an air-pump'*: Burke, *Letter to a Noble Lord* (*Writings*, ix, 177).

27 *the God of our idolatry*: From David Garrick's celebrated *Ode Upon Dedicating a Building, and Erecting a Statue, to Shakespeare, at Stratford Upon Avon* (1769), 14.

28 *'gone into the wastes...'*: Cf. Shakespeare, 'Sonnet 12', 10.

29 *Sir Andrew Wylie*: A novel by John Galt, regarded by Hazlitt as a poor imitator of Scott.

30 *'Sitting in my window...'*: Francis Beaumont and John Fletcher, *Philaster*, V, v, 156–67.

31 *'the wine of poetry...'*: Cf. *Macbeth*, II, iii, 95–6.

32 *'play with Amaryllis...'*: 'Lycidas', 68–9.

33 *'the irrevocable hour'*: Cf. Wordsworth, 'Intimations Ode', 180.

34 *Fonthill*: The home of William Beckford, in Wiltshire.

35 *'to every good...'*: Titus 1:16.

36 *'of whom the world...'*: Hebrews 11:38.

37 *'This was some time...'*: Cf. *Hamlet*, III, i, 114–15.

38 *'the rose plucked...'*: Cf. Ibid., III, iv, 42–4.

39 *The Heart of Mid Lothian*: Scott's novel (1818).

HOT AND COLD

Another essay from *The Plain Speaker* (1826).

1 *'Hot, cold, moist...'*: *Paradise Lost*, ii, 898–9.

2 *'neat-handed Phyllises'*: Cf. 'L'Allegro', 86.

3 *'native and endued...'*: *Hamlet*, IV, vii, 178–9.

4 *Ivanhoe*: Scott's novel (1819).

5 *'whose name signifies...'*: Cf. *Merry Wives of Windsor*, I, i, 20. The 'beast' in question is a louse.

6 *'to be supped...'*: Cf. *Hamlet*, IV, iii, 19.

7 *'here all is conscience...'*: *The Canterbury Tales*, 'General Prologue', 150.

8 *'the quills upon...'*: *Hamlet*, I, v, 20.

9 *the supper in Gil Blas*: Alain René Le Sage, *Gil Blas*, X, xii; the 'supper' is a 'hash of tame cat'.

10 *Voltaire's traveller*: In his *Histoire des Voyages de Scarmentado*.

11 *Sterne asks...*: In *Tristram Shandy*, IX, xxxiii.

12 *'the sovereign'st...'*: *1 Henry IV*, I, iii, 56.

13 *'makes the odds...'*: *Measure for Measure*, III, i, 41.

14 *'reform and live...'*: Cf. *1 Henry IV*, V, iv, 163.

15 *'dull, cold winter...'*: Cf. *The Two Noble Kinsmen*, II, ii, 45.

16 *'long purples'*: *Hamlet*, IV, vii, 168.

17 *'take the good...'*: Cf. Dryden, *Alexander's Feast*, 106.

18 *far niente*: 'Doing nothing'.

19 *'appliances and...'*: *2 Henry IV*, III, i, 29.

20 *'A man... finds...'*: Cf. Sterne, *Tristram Shandy*, III, xxxiv.

ON THE DIFFERENCE BETWEEN WRITING AND SPEAKING

Another essay from *The Plain Speaker* (1826). Previously published in the *London Magazine* for July 1820.

1 *'Some minds are...'*: Francis Bacon, *Advancement of Learning*, II, xxii.
2 *F—*: Possibly [Peter] Finnerty.
3 *like Wart...*: See *2 Henry IV*, III, ii, 265–81.
4 *Hear him but...*: Cf. *Henry V*, I, i, 38–48.
5 *The most dashing orator...*: John Thelwall.
6 *'move the very stones...'*: Cf. *Julius Caesar*, III, ii, 231–2.
7 *'Persian abodes...'*: Cf. Dryden, *Alexander's Feast*, 144–5.
8 *'fraught of aspics'...'*: Cf. *Othello*, III, iii, 456–7.
9 *'wielded at will...'*: Cf. *Paradise Regained*, iv, 269–70.
10 *'roared you...'*: This and the following quotation rather loosely combine *Hamlet*, III, ii, 10–11 and *Midsummer Night's Dream*, I, ii, 76–9.
11 *'create a soul...'*: *Comus*, 560–1.
12 *'Bottom! thou art...'*: Combines *Midsummer Night's Dream*, III, i, 109 and 113–14.
13 *'the self-same words...'*: Cf. *Macbeth*, I, iii, 88.
14 *'those brave sublunary...'*: Cf. Michael Drayton, 'To My Most Dearely-Loved Friend Henery Reynolds, Esq.', 106–8.
15 *'fire and air'*: Ibid., 108.
16 *'sound and fury...'*: *Macbeth*, V, v, 27–8.
17 *'sceptical, puzzled...it gives...'*: Cf. Burke, *Reflections on the Revolution in France* (*Writings*, viii, 138).
18 *'with good emphasis...'*: Cf. *Hamlet*, II, ii, 462–3.
19 *'by most admired...'*: Cf. *Macbeth*, III, iv, 109.
20 *Nature...abhors a vacuum*: François Rabelais, *Gargantua*, I, v.
21 *'lay the flattering...'*: Cf. *Hamlet*, III, iv, 147.
22 *'hear a cat...'*: Cf. *1 Henry IV*, III, i, 123–6.
23 *'Not harsh...'*: *Comus*, 477–80.
24 *'the heaviest stone...'*: Sir Thomas Browne, *Hydriotaphia*, iv.
25 *'a robusteous, periwig...'*: *Hamlet*, III, ii, 9.
26 *ad referendum*: 'For further consideration'.
27 *'gives us pause'*: Cf. *Hamlet*, III, i, 68.
28 *'What seem'd...'*: *Paradise Lost*, ii, 672–3.
29 *'fell still-born'*: Cf. Pope, 'Epilogue to the Satires', ii, 226.
30 *'native to that element'*: Cf. *Hamlet*, IV, vii, 178–9.

31 '*subdued to the quality*': Cf. *Othello*, I, iii, 250–1.

32 '*that Roan shall*...': *1 Henry IV*, II, iii, 72.

33 '*He spoke as one*...': Cf. Matthew 7:29.

34 '*A few termes*...': *The Canterbury Tales*, 'General Prologue', 639–41.

35 '*will halt for it*': *Hamlet* II, ii, 324.

36 '*trampled under*...': Burke, *Reflections on the Revolution in France* (*Writings*, viii, 130).

37 *Dr Johnson had a wish*...: Boswell, *Life of Johnson*, ii, 138–9.

38 '*give his own*...': Cf. Pope, 'Epistle to Dr Arbuthnot', 209.

39 '*They look only*...': Cf. Sterne, *Tristram Shandy*, III, xii.

40 '*hit the House*...': Burke, 'Speech on American Taxation', 19 April 1774 (*Writings*, ii, 452).

41 '*as a saving*...': William Windham, speech of 13 March 1797.

42 '*negative success*': Windham's description of the war with France, speech of 30 December 1794.

43 '*servile ministers*': *King Lear*, III, ii, 21.

44 '*making the worse*...': Cf. *Paradise Lost*, ii, 113–14.

45 '*love-locks*': Not in Johnson's *Dictionary* (1755), but there is a note on the Elizabethan fashion for 'love-locks' in Johnson and Steevens' classic 1778 edition of *The Plays of William Shakspeare*, ii, 379.

46 '*like proud seas*...': Cf. *The Two Noble Kinsmen*, II, ii, 20.

47 '*like the frog*...': Aesop's fable of 'The Lion and the Frog' (?).

48 *Burke once came into*...: Hazlitt had heard this and the following anecdote from James Northcote, who is the 'Mr N—' of the story. He records them in his *Conversations of James Northcote, Esq.* (1830), 'Conversation the Third'.

49 *Count Ugolino*: A subject from Dante.

50 '*Does he wind*...': Boswell, *Life of Johnson*, ii, 260.

51 '*the Leviathan*...': Burke, *Letter to a Noble Lord* (*Writings*, ix, 164).

52 *Abbé Sieyès's pigeon-holes*: Ibid. (*Writings*, ix, 177–8).

53 '*the proud keep*...': Ibid. (*Writings*, ix, 172).

54 '*shut the gates*...': Cf. Thomas Gray, 'Elegy Written in a Country Churchyard', 68.

55 '*to leave no rubs*...': *Macbeth*, III, i, 133.

56 '*Learn to write*...': Howe and Wu cite lines from William Walker, 'The Art of Reading': 'Learn to read slow; all other graces / Will follow in their proper places.' They give no clue as to the provenance of the poem, however.

57 *ancient Pistol*: A character in *2 Henry IV*, *Henry V* and *Merry Wives of Windsor*.

58 '*of no mark*...': *1 Henry IV*, III, ii, 45.

59 '*fancies and good*...': Cf. *2 Henry IV*, III, ii, 312–13.

60 *'Dull as the lake...'*: Cf. Oliver Goldsmith, *The Traveller*, 312.
61 *'made fierce...'*: Francis Bacon, *Advancement of Learning*, I, iv.
62 *'becomes his glittering...'*: Cf. Wordsworth, *The Excursion*, iii, 743–4.
63 *'to face the storms...'*: Wu notes that this appears in none of Canning's published speeches on reform; Hazlitt is probably parodying the common metaphor of 'the storms of life'.
64 *Stentor*: Homeric warrior distinguished by the power of his voice.
65 *'Political House...'*: A squib of William Hone's, published 1819.

MADAME PASTA AND MADEMOISELLE MARS

Another essay from *The Plain Speaker* (1826). Previously published in the *New Monthly Magazine* for January 1825.

1 *a fugal-man*: I.e. a fugleman, a soldier who serves as a guide for his company.
2 *Nina*: The heroine of Nicolas-Marie Dalayrac's *Nina, ou la folle par amour* (1787).
3 *bienséance*: Propriety, decorum.
4 *'Though that their art...'*: A parody of *Othello*, I, i, 71–3.
5 *those noble outlines*: Raphael's cartoons.
6 *like Guiderius and Arviragus...*: See *Cymbeline*, III, vii, 12ff.
7 *a fantoccini figure*: A puppet manipulated by strings.
8 *animal-magnetized*: Mesmerized.
9 *j'existe*: Eugène Scribe, *Valérie*, ix.
10 *clair-obscur*: Chiaroscuro.
11 *'foregone conclusion'*: *Othello*, III, iii, 434.

ON A PORTRAIT OF AN ENGLISH LADY, BY VANDYKE

Another essay from *The Plain Speaker* (1826).

1 *'Where all is conscience...'*: Cf. *The Canterbury Tales*, 'General Prologue', 150.
2 *'last recesses...'*: Dryden, *Satires of Aulus Persius Flaccus*, ii, 133.
3 *'As if they thrill'd...'*: Cf. *Faerie Queene*, II, xii, 78: 7–8.
4 *'This hand of yours...'*: Cf. *Othello*, III, iv, 35–9.
5 *'qualified...very craftily'*: Cf. Ibid., II, iii, 36.

6 '*mind's eye*': *Hamlet*, I, ii, 185.

7 '*trod the primrose* . . .': Cf. Ibid., I, iii, 50.

8 '*the demon that* . . .': Cf. *Macbeth*, V, viii, 14. Perhaps also an allusion to Socrates and his famous *daimonion*, a spiritual monitor that Socrates considered as restricting and limiting his activity (see Plato's *Apologia Socratis*).

9 '*stupidly good*': *Paradise Lost*, ix, 465.

10 '*an eye to threaten* . . .': Cf. *Hamlet*, III, iv, 57.

11 '*leave stings*': Joseph Addison, *Cato*, I, i, 92.

12 '*While by the power* . . .': Cf. Wordsworth, 'Tintern Abbey', 48–50.

13 '*Come then* . . .': Cf. Pope, 'Epistle to a Lady', 17–20.

14 '*day's garish* . . .': 'Il Penseroso', 141.

15 *outré*: Shocking.

16 '*the spirit and fire*': There are a number of sources for this quotation that Hazlitt could have known – for example, Thomas Heywood, *The Fair Maid of the West*, Part Two, IV, i: 'These bold Englishmen, / I think are all composed of spirit and fire.'

17 '*bosoms and businesses*': Semi-proverbial, but from 'The Epistle Dedicatory' to Francis Bacon's *Essayes or Counsels, Civill and Morall* (1625).

18 '*trifles light* . . .': *Othello*, III, iii, 327.

19 *Quam nihil* . . .: 'Absolutely worthless in comparison with your genius, Papinian!' Hazlitt's recollection of 'Quam nihil ad genium, Papiniane, tuum!', the epigraph to Wordsworth and Coleridge's *Lyrical Ballads*. Wordsworth and Coleridge had found the quotation in the preface to Michael Drayton's *Poly-Olbion* (1613).

DEFINITION OF WIT

Not published by Hazlitt. First published by Hazlitt's son, also William Hazlitt, in *Literary Remains* (1836).

1 '*wherein the most* . . .': Cf. John Locke, *An Essay Concerning Human Understanding* (1690), II, xi.

2 *polypus*: Octopus.

3 '*the squandering glances* . . . *whereby the wise* . . .': Cf. *As You Like It*, II, vii, 56–7.

4 '*Voltaire's?* – *the same*': Hazlitt plays with a cliché of eighteenth- and nineteenth-century stage dialogue.

5 *When a Ferdinand still rules* . . .: Ferdinand VII of Spain reigned from March to May 1808 and from 1814 to 1833.

6 *an Englishman has the wit . . .*: Referring to Leigh Hunt.

7 *Sir Walter's*: I.e. Scott's.

8 *'sounds significant'*: Sir John Davies, 'In Macrum', 2.

9 *'foregone conclusion'*: *Othello*, III, iii, 434.

10 *'In cut and die . . .'*: Samuel Butler, *Hudibras*, I, i, 241–2.

11 *'The house of brother . . .'*: Cf. Swift, 'V——'s House', 96, 103–4.

12 *'turned from black . . .'*: Cf. Samuel Butler, *Hudibras*, II, ii, 32.

13 *'Like jewels . . .'*: Cf. William Collins, 'The Manners, An Ode', 55.

14 *'Mark Supple's . . .'*: The incident is detailed in *The Atlas*, 8 March 1829.

15 *'Pray lend me . . .'*: George Farquhar, *The Beaux' Stratagem*, V, iii, 13–14.

16 *'a forked radish . . .'*: Cf. *2 Henry IV*, III, ii, 303–5.

ON GENIUS AND COMMON SENSE

An essay from the first volume of *Table-Talk* (1821).

1 *a mixed mode . . .*: Cf. John Locke, *An Essay Concerning Human Understanding* (1690), II, xii.

2 *'There is nothing . . .'*: William Windham, speech of 14 March 1809.

3 *'One of the persons . . .'*: John Thelwall.

4 *Ranz des Vaches*: The sound of the cowbells.

5 *'sound it from . . .'*: Cf. *Hamlet*, III, ii, 357–8.

6 *'make assurance . . .'*: *Macbeth*, IV, i, 83.

7 *'Tis the last . . .'*: Ben Jonson, 'An Epistle to Sir Edward Sacvile', 136–7, 139–42.

8 *'shuts the gates . . .'*: Cf. Thomas Gray, 'Elegy Written in a Country Church-Yard', 68.

9 *Mr Burke said . . .*: In *Reflections on the Revolution in France* (*Writings*, viii, 138).

10 *home to the business . . .*: Semi-proverbial, but from 'The Epistle Dedicatory' to Francis Bacon's *Essayes or Counsels, Civill and Morall* (1625).

11 *ultima ratio . . .*: 'Ultimate reasoning of kings'. Cardinal Richelieu's motto.

12 *'there's the rub . . .'*: Combines *Hamlet*, III, i, 65 and 68–9.

13 *'a compost heap'*: Cf. Burke, 'On Economical Reform' (*Writings*, iii, 534).

14 *sensus communis*: 'Common feeling'.

15 *Oliver Cromwell after* ——: Probably Samuel Cooper.

16 *'What! man . . . Give sorrow . . .'*: *Macbeth*, IV, iii, 208–10.

17 *The passage in the same play . . .*: Ibid., I, vi, 1–10.

18 *'sure trailing'*: Cf. *Hamlet*, II, ii, 47–8; and the lament for Ringwood in

Fielding, *Joseph Andrews*, III, vi: 'good at trailing, and sure in a highway'.
19 '*as if his will* . . .': Hazlitt quotes his own account of 'Mr Kean's Richard'.
20 *Raphael, in muffling* . . .: A reference to 'Elymas the Sorcerer' in Raphael's
cartoons (Victoria and Albert Museum, London).

A FAREWELL TO ESSAY-WRITING

Published in the *London Weekly Review* for 29 March 1828. Not republished
by Hazlitt.

1 '*This life is best* . . .': *Cymbeline*, III, iii, 29–30.
2 *ultima thule*: 'The end of the world'; proverbial.
3 '*A friend in your* . . .': Cf. William Cowper, 'Retirement', 741–2.
4 '*Beautiful mask* . . .': Cf. Samuel Whyte, 'Epilogue Spoken by Mrs Gardiner,
After the Tragedy of Macbeth', 64: ' "I know you pretty mask." '
5 '*done its spiriting* . . .': Cf. *Tempest*, I, ii, 298.
6 '*the credulous hope* . . .': Byron, *Don Juan*, I, 1725 (ccxvi).
7 '*the spring comes* . . .': Coleridge, 'Christabel', 22.
8 '*fields are dank* . . .': Milton, 'Sonnet XX', 2.
9 '*it left its little* . . .': Cf. Pope, *Windsor Forest*, 134.
10 '*peep through* . . .': Cf. *Macbeth*, I, v, 53.
11 '*open all the cells* . . .': William Cowper, *The Task*, vi, 11–12.
12 *Theodore and Honoria*: Dryden's verse translation of Boccaccio.
13 '*Of all the cities* . . .': Ibid., 1–2.
14 '*Which when Honoria* . . .': Ibid., 342–3.
15 '*And made th' insult* . . .': Dryden, 'Sigismonda and Guiscardo', 668–9.
16 *Leigh Hunt's mention* . . .: In *Lord Byron and Some of His Contemporaries*
(1828).
17 '*Let honour* . . .': Dryden, 'Epilogue to Mithridates King of Pontus', 16–17.
18 '*Fall'n was Glenartny's* . . .': Cf. Scott, 'Glenfinlas', 263–4.
19 *Mr Gifford once said* . . .: Hazlitt elsewhere mentions this as Gifford's
response to his *Letter to William Gifford, Esq.*
20 *Mr Hunt has missed the opportunity* . . .: Hunt had written a chapter on
Hazlitt for his *Lord Byron and Some of His Contemporaries*, but suppressed
it. He showed it to Hazlitt, however, and much of the remainder of this
essay is taken up with Hazlitt's reflections on his friend's account.
21 '*the admired of all* . . .': Cf. *Hamlet*, III, i, 156.
22 '*I know not seems*': *Hamlet*, I, ii, 76.
23 *Aut Cæsar* . . .: 'All or nothing'.

24 *L—*: Perhaps [Walter Savage] Landor, whom the description certainly fits.

25 *'the other eleven...'*: Untraced.

26 *'Nor can I think...'*: Dryden, *The Hind and the Panther*, i, 315.

27 *Chaucer's Flower and Leaf*: A fifteenth-century allegorical poem, no longer attributed to Chaucer.

28 *'And ayen, methought...'*: Cf. Ibid., 105.

29 *Mr and Miss L—*: Charles and Mary Lamb.

30 *with Amelia's*: A reference to Fielding, *Amelia*, X, v. Hazlitt was probably associating this with V, ii, and, more importantly, II, vi, where it is chicken that inspires Amelia to 'softly whisper ... *that she perceived there might be Happiness in a Cottage*'.

31 *in the Edinburgh Review*: Hazlitt refers to his review of Frances Burney's *The Wanderer*, in which he included an extended account of his favourite novels (xxiv, 320–38).

32 *'And curtain close...'*: Cf. William Collins, 'Ode on the Poetical Character', 76.

THE LETTER-BELL

Not published by Hazlitt. First published in the *Monthly Magazine* for March 1831 as 'by the late William Hazlitt'. A reference to the July Revolution of 1830 (see notes below) suggests that this was Hazlitt's final essay. He died on 16 September 1830.

1 *'one entire...'*: Othello, V, ii, 146.

2 *the road from — to —*: Wem to Shrewsbury.

3 *like a glory*: A halo. See also p. 556, note 19.

4 *'And by the vision...'*: Cf. Wordsworth, 'Intimations Ode', 73–4.

5 *it has again risen...*: A reference to the recent July Revolution in France.

6 *'What, though the radiance...'*: Wordsworth, 'Intimations Ode', 178–81.

7 *'like morn...'*: Cf. *Paradise Lost*, v, 310–11.

8 *Io pæan*: 'Hymn of praise'. Given the context, Hazlitt was probably thinking of Burke's use of the phrase in *Reflections on the Revolution in France* (*Writings*, viii, 123).

9 *the Valley of the Shadow...*: Psalms 23:4.

10 *the sleep-walker...*: Coleridge.

11 *'And from his neck...'*: Cf. 'The Ancient Mariner', 289–91.

12 *'airs and graces'*: Proverbial.

13 *'The slow canal...'*: Oliver Goldsmith, *The Traveller*, 293–4.

14 *'While with an eye...'*: Wordsworth, 'Tintern Abbey', 48–50.

15 *'the secrets of the prison...'*: Cf. *Hamlet*, I, v, 14; also, given the context, Wordsworth, 'Intimations Ode', 67–8.

16 *'Entire affection...'*: Cf. *Faerie Queene*, I, viii, 40:3.

17 *'His shame in crowds...'*: Cf. Oliver Goldsmith, *The Deserted Village*, 412.

18 *'Made good digestion...'*: Cf. *Macbeth*, III, iv, 37–8.

19 *an ingenious friend...*: Probably Francis Jeffrey.

20 *Scotch Novels*: Scott's novels.

21 *Gertrude of Wyoming*: A poem by Thomas Campbell (1809).

22 *'more germain...'*: *Hamlet*, V, ii, 155.

23 *'Hark! 'tis the twanging...'*: William Cowper, *The Task*, iv, 1–22.

24 *Lord Byron denies...*: In his *Letter to John Murray Esqre.* (1821) Byron had stated 'Cowper is no poet'.

25 *mentioned by Æschylus...*: In *Agamemnon*, 281–316.

BIOGRAPHICAL INDEX

As noted already, this index lists all important persons mentioned by Hazlitt, except major figures of English literature, biblical characters and modern European monarchs. Persons mentioned by Hazlitt simply as subjects or owners of a painting are not included. Not all the boxers mentioned in 'The Fight' are included: the interested reader is referred to Henry Downes Miles's *Pugilistica: The History of British Boxing* (3 vols, Edinburgh: John Grant, 1906). All dates are AD unless otherwise specified.

Abbott, Charles (1757–1829). MP from 1795 and Speaker of the House of Commons 1802–17; after his father's death his mother married the father of Jeremy Bentham.

Abelard, Peter (1079–1142). Prominent French advocate of rational theological inquiry who taught at Paris and famously fell in love with Héloïse, one of his pupils.

Addison, Joseph (1672–1719). Whig essayist, poet, dramatist and politician. Best known for his contributions to the periodicals the *Tatler* and the *Spectator*.

Aeschylus (525–456 BC). One of the three great Athenian tragic dramatists (with Euripides and Sophocles); best-known for his *Oresteia* trilogy.

Albano (or Albani), Francesco (1578–1660). Italian painter who trained under Ludovico Caracci (see separate entry) and assisted Guido Reni (see separate entry).

Alcaeus (*c*.620–580 BC). Greek lyric poet, famous in antiquity. Very little of his work survived into modern times.

Andrea del Sarto (1486–1531). Major Italian painter renowned for his graceful, informal style.

Angerstein, John Julius (1735–1823). Successful businessman who established the modern Lloyd's and became famous for his philanthropy and taste for fine arts.

Aquinas, Thomas (*c*.1225–74). Italian philosopher, the greatest of the medieval Scholastic theologians. He attempted to reconcile Christian theology with Aristotelian philosophy.

Arbuthnot, John (1667–1735). Physician and man of letters. A friend of Pope and Swift and a founder member of the Scriblerus Club. His best-known work is *The History of John Bull* (1712).

Aretino, Pietro, or the Aretine (1492–1557). Italian dramatist and satirist; his works were famous for their wit and licentiousness.

Ariosto, Ludovico (1474–1533). Major Italian poet; his most celebrated work is the romantic epic, *Orlando Furioso* (1516).

Aristophanes (*c*.448–388 BC). Athenian comic dramatist who became increasingly popular in nineteenth-century England.

Arkwright, Sir Richard (1732–92). Textile industrialist and inventor who developed a spinning machine.

Athenaeus (flourished *c*.200). Greek grammarian and author of *The Gastronomers*, a work in the form of a symposium which discusses food and other matters.

Bacon, Francis (1561–1626). Celebrated lawyer, statesman, philosopher and scientist; Hazlitt revered his *Essays*.

Ball, John (d.1381). An excommunicated priest, one of the leaders, with Wat Tyler, of the Peasants' Revolt of 1381.

Balmerino, Lord, Arthur Elphinstone (1688–1746). Celebrated Jacobite, pardoned for his involvement in the 1715 rebellion but convicted of treason and executed after his participation in the 1745 rebellion.

Banks, Sir Joseph (1743–1820). Eminent explorer and naturalist as well as a member of Dr Johnson's literary Club. President of the Royal Society 1778–1817.

Bathurst, Lord Henry (1762–1834). A prominent Tory politician who was Secretary of War and the Colonies from 1812 to 1827, and was closely involved with the abolition of the slave trade.

Beaumont, Francis (1584–1616). An important dramatist who collaborated with John Fletcher (see separate entry).

Beaumont, Sir George Howland (1753–1827). Minor painter, but an important patron of art and letters. A friend and benefactor of Wordsworth and Coleridge.

Bedford, Duke of, Francis Russell (1765–1802). Whig politician attacked by Burke after he protested at the latter's being giving a pension.

Belcher, Tom (1783–1854). Boxer, who subsequently taught boxing and kept the Castle Tavern in Holborn, London.

Bell, Andrew (1753–1832). Scottish clergyman and educationalist whose educational theories were set out in *An Experiment in Education* (1797) and later adopted by Joseph Lancaster. Bell advocated the use of cleverer pupils to teach the slower ones.

Bentham, Jeremy (1748–1832). Social philosopher whose name is inseparably associated with utilitarianism, the belief that human motivation is based on self-interest and that the greatest happiness of the greatest number should determine moral and social questions.

Berkeley, George (1685–1753). Anglican bishop and Anglo-Irish philosopher and opponent of deism. As a philosopher he argued that material objects exist only insofar as they are perceived by the senses.

Bewick, Thomas (1753–1828). Famous wood-engraver, best known for his *History of British Birds* (1797–1804). Bewick provided illustrations for many literary works, including Scott's.

Blackwood, William (1776–1834). Scottish publisher and founder of *Blackwood's Edinburgh Magazine*.

Boccaccio, Giovanni (1313–75). Major Italian writer, best known for *The Decameron* (1349–58), a collection of exceptionally influential tales.

Bolingbroke, 1st Viscount, Henry St John (1678–1751). Leading Tory politician in the reign of Queen Anne (1702–14). A historian, controversial philosopher, and libertine.

Bowles, William (1762–1850). Churchman and minor poet whose *Fourteen Sonnets* (1789), published anonymously, captured the spirit of the times and influenced the first-generation Romantic poets, particularly Coleridge.

Brook, Lord, Robert Greville (1608–43). Parliamentary general and mystical philosopher who wrote *The Nature of Truth* (1640).

Broughton, Jack (1704–89). Famous boxer, known as the father of English pugilism. Celebrated for his technique, he later taught boxing.

Brougham, Henry Peter, Baron (1778–1868). Lawyer, Whig politician, reformer and orator, and designer of the eponymous carriage.

Buckingham and Normanby, first Duke of, John Sheffield (1648–1721). English statesman, poet and patron of Dryden. His Toryism brought his active political life to an end at the accession of George I.

Buffamalco. Hazlitt's (or the printer's?) mistake for Bonamico Buffalmacco (*fl.* early fourteenth century), a painter, one of the more considerable contemporaries of Giotto (see separate entry). Much of the work previously attributed to him has now been assigned to other artists.

Buonaparte (or Bonaparte), Napoleon (1769–1821). French general, First Consul (1799–1804) and Emperor of France (1804–14/15). A military genius who attempted to build a European empire; he was greatly admired by Hazlitt, who wrote a biography.

Burdett, Sir Francis (1770–1844). A reforming politician who was imprisoned in 1810.

Burke, Edmund (1729–97). Immensely influential Irish statesman and political thinker. A leading Whig, he supported American independence, but later launched a ferocious attack on the French Revolution in *Reflections on the Revolution in France* (1790).

Burnet, Gilbert (1643–1715). Churchman and man of letters, whose best-known work, *The History of My Own Times*, was published posthumously (1724, 1734).

Burton, Robert (1577–1640). Churchman famous for his *Anatomy of Melancholy* (1621), an ostensibly medical work that is really a satire on human learning.

Butler, Joseph (1692–1752). Anglican bishop and moral philosopher.

Butler, Samuel (1613–80). Royalist poet, famous for *Hudibras* (1663–78), a satirical mock-romance in deliberately cumbersome octosyllabics.

Buxton, Jedediah (1707–72). Illiterate farm labourer who was a mathematical genius; he was 'discovered' by the educated world in 1751.

Calamy, Edmund (1671–1732). Grandson of Edmund Calamy (1600–66), the leader of the Presbyterian ascendancy in Parliament between 1643 and 1653; he wrote a biographical history of Nonconformity.

Canning, George (1770–1827). Minister for Foreign Affairs 1807–9. Foreign Secretary 1822–7; Prime Minister briefly before his death in 1827.

Carlisle, Frederick Howard, 5th Earl (1748–1825). Politician who held a number of offices from 1777. He supported the war with France in 1793 and later opposed the Corn Bill. He was also a minor poet.

Carracci, the: an important and influential family of artists: Agostino (1557–1602), Annibale (1560–1609) and Ludovico (1555–1619). Annibale is much the most significant. They founded an Academy in Bologna and promoted an art that mediates between the High Renaissance and the Baroque.

Carr, William Holwell (1758–1830). Art connoisseur and collector as well as a minor artist; he married into the nobility.

Castiglione, Baldassare, Conte di Novilara (1478–1529). Italian humanist mainly remembered for his *Book of the Courtier* (1528), a discussion of the qualifications needed by an ideal courtier.

Castlereagh, Viscount, Robert Stewart (1769–1822). Reactionary Anglo-Irish politician who suppressed the 1798 rebellion in Ireland. British Foreign Secretary 1811–22 and architect of the Grand Alliance against Napoleon.

Cervantes Saavedra, Miguel de (1547–1616). Major Spanish novelist and dramatist, the author of *Don Quixote* (1605, 1615).

Chantrey, Sir Francis Leggatt (1782–1841). Outstandingly successful sculptor responsible for a great deal of public statuary; his work includes statues of George Washington, George III, George IV and William Pitt.

Chapman, George (?1559–1634). Poet, dramatist and translator. Best known for his translations of Homer (1598–1616) and his tragedy *Bussy D'Ambois* (1607).

Charlotte, Princess (1796–1817). The only child of George IV; she married Prince Leopold of Saxe-Coburg (see separate entry) in 1816, but died the following year after giving birth to a stillborn son. She was a popular favourite and her death provoked a national outburst of grief.

Chateaubriand, François-René, Vicomte de (1768–1848). Major figure of the French Romantic movement, who lived in exile in England between 1793 and 1800. A champion of Christianity.

Chatham, William Pitt, 1st Earl of ('the Elder') (1708–88). Whig Prime Minister 1756–61 and 1766–8 who transformed Britain into an imperial power.

Cibber, Colley (1671–1757). Actor and dramatist who became Poet-laureate in 1730. His reputation was permanently damaged when Pope made him the hero of the final version of *The Dunciad*.

Cicero, Marcus Tullius (106–43 BC). Roman statesman, lawyer, scholar and writer who attempted to uphold republican principles. He wrote on many subjects, including rhetoric, philosophy and politics, and was celebrated as the greatest of Roman orators.

Clarendon, Edward Hyde, Earl of (1609–74). Royalist statesman and historian who was exiled to France in 1667.

Clarke, Samuel (1675–1729). Theologian, philosopher, Anglican cleric and exponent of Newtonian physics. Accused of Arianism.

Claude Lorraine (1600–82). Outstanding French landscape painter whose work is distinguished by a serene classicism.

Cobbett, William (1763–1835). English popular journalist who founded the weekly *Political Register* in 1802. He championed rural England against changes brought about by the Industrial Revolution; his *Rural Rides* was published in 1830.

Coke, Thomas William, Earl of Leicester (1752–1842). A zealous Whig who was MP for Norfolk for several decades; more famous now as an agricultural improver.

Collins, William (1721–59). Major eighteenth-century poet whose *Odes on Several Descriptive and Allegoric Subjects* (1746) appealed to a burgeoning Romantic taste and became extremely influential.

Congreve, William (1670–1729). One of the great masters of Restoration comedy, remembered for plays like *The Way of the World* (1700).

Cooper, Thomas (1759–1839). Natural philosopher, lawyer and politician. He was a textile worker in Manchester before emigrating to America to practise law and involve himself in politics.

Correggio, byname of Antonio Allegri (1494–1534). Major Italian painter whose sensuous style made him a major influence on Baroque and Rococo art.

Cowley, Abraham (1618–67). Royalist poet, whose reputation was based largely on his *Pindarique Odes*, influential attempts to establish the irregular ode in English.

Cowper, William (1731–1800). Major eighteenth-century poet, best known for *The Task* (1785). An important influence on Wordsworth and Coleridge.

Crébillon, Prosper Jolyot (1674–1762). French tragic dramatist whose plays were modelled on those of Seneca (see separate entry); his speciality was horror.

Cribb, Tom (1781–1848). Celebrated boxer; Champion of England 1805–20; known for his forbearing temper.

Croker, John Wilson (1780–1857). Irish politician, essayist and reviewer. A staunch Tory, he was appointed Secretary to the Admiralty.

Cromwell, Oliver (1599–1658). Soldier and statesman who became Lord Protector of England (1653–8). He fought on the Parliamentary side in the Civil War, founding the New Model Army in 1644, and subsequently supported the execution of Charles I.

Cudworth, Ralph (1617–88). English theologian and philosopher of ethics whose best-known work, *The True Intellectual System of the Universe* (1678), sought to refute determinism and prove the reality of human freedom.

Cumberland, Richard (1732–1811). Author of several highly successful 'Sentimental Comedies', as well as *Calvary* (1792), an epic poem. Caricatured by Sheridan as Sir Fretful Plagiary in *The Critic*.

Curran, John Philpot (1750–1817). Celebrated Irish politician and judge who championed Catholic emancipation and attacked ministerial corruption. He became famous for speaking on behalf of the accused in many state trials between 1795 and 1803.

Curtis, Sir William (1752–1829). Merchant who was elected MP for the City of London in 1790 and held the seat for the following twenty-eight years. Known as a pitiably bad speaker.

Dante Alighieri (1265–1321). Great Italian poet, the author of *The Divine Comedy*, one of the major works of European literature.

Danton, Georges Jacques (1759–94). French politician; a leader in the early stages of the French Revolution, his moderation later led to his death at the guillotine.

Davila, Arrigo Caterino (1576–1631). Italian historian famous for his immensely successful *History of the Civil Wars in France* (1630).

Davy, Sir Humphrey (1778–1829). Leading chemist who discovered several chemical elements and invented the miner's safety lamp. Also a poet.

De Stutt-Tracey, see under Tracy.

Dekker, Thomas (?1570–1632). Important and prolific dramatist whose work is distinguished by its realistic portrayal of London life.

Demosthenes (c.383–322 BC). Athenian orator, regarded by ancient critics as the greatest prose stylist.

Devonshire, Duchess of, Georgiana Cavendish (1757–1806). Noted society beauty and leader of fashion who liked to mix with literary and political men. She wrote poetry.

Domenichino (1581–1641). Major Italian painter, trained by the Carracci (see separate entry), who became a leading practitioner of Baroque classicism. In the seventeenth and eighteenth centuries his reputation was enormous, and he was widely considered second only to Raphael as a painter.

Dou (or Douw), Gerard (1613–75). Dutch painter who studied with Rembrandt and became famous for portraits and highly finished interior scenes.

Drake, Sir Francis (?1540–96). Celebrated Elizabethan sea-captain who circumnavigated the world and waged war on the Spaniards.

Du Bartas, Guillaume de Salluste (1544–90). Protestant French poet whose religious epics proved more influential in England than in France.

Duns Scotus, John (c.1266–1308). Scottish Franciscan and Scholastic philosopher whose work was influential in separating theology from philosophy.

Eldon, Lord, John Scott (1751–1838). Reactionary lawyer and Lord Chancellor for much of the period between 1801 and 1827.

Elgin, Thomas Bruce, 7th Earl (1766–1841). Diplomat and art collector, famous for his controversial acquisition of the Elgin Marbles.

Ellenborough, Lord, Edward Law (1750–1818). Lord Chief Justice 1802–18 who was reactionary, overbearing and intolerant.

Elliston, Robert William (1774–1831) Successful actor who became manager of Drury Lane Theatre in 1819.

Erskine, Thomas, Baron (1750–1832). Whig lawyer famous for his defence of political reformers. Raised to the peerage in 1806, he later defended Queen Caroline when she was brought to trial by George IV.

Euripides (480–406 BC). One of the three great Athenian tragic dramatists (with Aeschylus and Sophocles); he called into question the morality of Greek legends.

Evans, Thomas (1766–1823). Welsh poet and Dissenting minister; in 1797 he was convicted of having sung a Welsh song 'On Liberty' and ordered to stand in the pillory in addition to being imprisoned for two years.

Fairfax, Edward (d.1635). Yorkshire scholar and gentleman who translated Tasso's *Jerusalem Delivered*.

Fawcett, Joseph (?1758–1804). Unitarian preacher, poet and writer who influenced Wordsworth and Hazlitt.

Fawkes, Guy (1570–1606). Catholic conspirator who unsuccessfully attempted to blow up the Houses of Parliament.

Fichtè, Johann Gottlieb (1762–1814). German philosopher who argued, against Kant, for a pure idealism in which the thinking self is the only reality.

Filmer, Sir Robert (c.1590–1653). Defender of the divine right of kings, ridiculed by Locke.

Fletcher, John (1579–1625). One of the greatest Jacobean dramatists who famously collaborated with Francis Beaumont (see separate entry) in such masterpieces as *Philaster* (1609) and *The Maid's Tragedy* (1610–11).

Ford, John (1586–after 1639). Major seventeenth-century dramatist, best known for *'Tis Pity She's a Whore* (1633).

Foster, James (1697–1753). Prominent Dissenting minister who attacked deism.

Fox, Charles James (1749–1806). Leading Whig politician who opposed George III's policies. As Leader of the Opposition for most of his political career he supported the French Revolution and all liberal causes.

Fuller, Thomas (1608–61). Royalist churchman and man of letters whose works include *The Historie of the Holy Warre* (1639) and *The History of the Worthies of England* (1662).

Fuseli, Henry (1741–1825). Important Swiss painter and critic who spent most of his working life in London. He treated historical subjects in a fantastic, macabre style. One of the outstanding figures of the Romantic movement.

Galt, John (1779–1839). Scottish novelist, best known for *The Provost* (1822). He regarded his best novels, concerned with country life in Scotland, as 'theoretical histories'.

Gandy, William (d. 1729) Minor portrait painter who influenced the young Joshua Reynolds (see separate entry).

Garrick, David (1717–79). Widely regarded as the greatest actor of the eighteenth century; he also wrote various dramatic works and managed Drury Lane Theatre. In 1773 he was elected a member of Johnson's literary Club.

Garrow, Sir William (1760–1840). Distinguished lawyer and judge and an

MP from 1805. He became Baron of the Exchequer in 1817 and held the post for fifteen years.

Ghirlandaio, Domenico (1449–94). Italian fresco painter.

Gifford, John (1758–1818). Miscellaneous writer who supported the government in the 1790s and founded the successful *Anti-Jacobin Review* in 1798. He later wrote a biography of Pitt, the Younger (see separate entry).

Gifford, William (1756–1826). The son of a glazier who was able to go to Oxford through an act of private patronage. Gifford established himself as a satirist in the early 1790s, edited the *Anti-Jacobin* between 1797 and 1798, and the *Quarterly Review* from 1809 to 1824. Conservative in taste as well as politics, he attacked most of the young innovating writers of the period.

Giorgione da (or Giorgio del) Castelfranco (1476/8–1510). Major painter of the Venetian school, famous for dreamy landscapes that were later understood as reducing the importance of the subject. Giorgione influenced the young Titian, and their work is sometimes indistinguishable.

Giotto di Bondone (*c.*1267–1337). Major Italian painter who introduced a new solidity and sense of narrative drama into the Byzantine tradition, thus anticipating the Renaissance.

Girodet-Trioson, Anne-Louis (1767–1824). French painter who was trained by Jacques-Louis David but who later developed a more emotional, Romantic style.

Godwin, William (1756–1836). Social philosopher, novelist and political journalist. His *Enquiry Concerning Political Justice* (1793), which developed a theory of human perfectability through the proper use of reason, was one of the most discussed books of the 1790s and made Godwin a hero in radical circles. Married Mary Wollstonecraft in 1797.

Goldsmith, Oliver (1730–74). Essayist, poet, novelist and dramatist who was a member of the Johnson circle. His best-known work is the play *She Stoops to Conquer* (1773).

Grattan, Henry (1746–1820). Irish MP from 1805 who was an outspoken champion of Irish interests, especially Catholic emancipation; a famous orator.

Grenville, Lord, William Wyndham (1759–1834). Politician who held several offices under Pitt (see separate entry) and was a powerful supporter of the latter's pro-war and repressive policy-making. Abolished the slave trade.

Guercino (Giovanni Francesco Barbieri) (1591–1666). Major Italian painter who played an important role in the development of Baroque art. He was the leading painter in Bologna after the death of Guido Reni.

Guicciardini, Francesco (1483–1540). Florentine historian and statesman, remembered for his *Storia d'Italia*, a history of Italy from 1494 to 1534.

Gully, John (1783–1863). Boxer, famous for his technique, who became Champion of England; he retired from the ring in 1808 and later became an MP.

Harington, Sir John (c.1561–1612). Godson of Queen Elizabeth I, who (allegedly at her command) translated Ariosto's *Orlando Furioso* (1591). Inventor of the water closet.

Hartley, David (1705–57). Philosopher whose influential *Observations on Man* (1749) drew on the philosophy of John Locke (see separate entry) to give a purely physical explanation of mental processes; Hartley believed that his work supported Christianity.

Hastings, Warren (1732–1818). The first governor-general of British India, famously impeached in 1784 for cruelty and corruption and tried between 1788 and 1795. Burke (see separate entry) was among his prosecutors.

Haydon, Benjamin Robert (1786–1846). Historical painter and writer who was friendly with many literary men.

Helvétius, Claude-Adrien (1715–71). French Enlightenment philosopher and educationalist.

Hemskirk, i.e. Heemskerck, Maerten van (1498–1574). Dutch Mannerist painter who worked in an Italian manner.

Hesiod (8th century BC). Influential early Greek poet, famous for his *Theogony* and *Works and Days*.

Heywood, Thomas (?1574–1641). Exceptionally prolific dramatist who may have written as many as 200 plays. Among the best known is *A Woman Killed With Kindness* (acted 1603).

Hickman, Tom (1785–1822). Boxer, known as 'The Gas-Light man' or simply 'The Gas'. Famous for his boasting, Hickman fought professionally 1819–21.

Hobbema, Meindert (1638–1709). Dutch landscape painter who specialized in thickly wooded scenes. Very popular in Britain in the eighteenth and nineteenth centuries.

Hobbes, Thomas (1588–1679). Philosopher and political theorist whose major work is *Leviathan* (1651). He maintained the essential selfishness of human beings.

Hobhouse, John Cam (1786–1869). Politician and close friend of Byron.

Hogarth, William (1697–1764) Major British painter and engraver who attempted to establish a distinct native style. Best-known for his famous series of narrative engravings, *The Harlot's Progress* (1732), *The Rake's Progress* (1733–5) and *Marriage à la Mode* (1743–5), Hogarth was highly regarded in the Romantic period.

Holbein, Hans (1497/8–1543). Major German portrait painter who worked in England from 1526 and became court painter to Henry VIII in 1537. Known for his stunning realism.

Holcroft, Thomas (1745–1809). Radical dramatist, novelist, journalist and actor. His *Anna St Ives* (1792) is remarkable as the first 'Jacobin' novel, anticipating the philosophy of his friend William Godwin (see separate entry). Hazlitt edited his *Memoirs.*

Holinshed, Raphael (d. ?1580). Editor and part-author of the *Chronicles* (1577), the first authoritative vernacular and continuous account of English history, used by Shakespeare for his history plays.

Holland, Henry Richard Vassall Fox, 3rd Baron (1773–1840). Prominent Whig politician, a nephew and disciple of Charles James Fox (see separate entry). He declined the offer of the Opposition leadership in 1812.

Homer (?8th century BC). Supposed author of the *Iliad* and the *Odyssey*, two of the greatest and most influential works of Western literature.

Hook, Theodore Edward (1788–1841). Minor writer of light verse and popular fiction who successfully edited the Tory *John Bull.*

Hooker, Richard (?1554–1600). Churchman and theologian, remembered for his *Of the Laws of Ecclesiastical Politie* (1593–7).

Hume, David (1711–76). Major philosopher, historian, economist and essayist whose reputation was tarnished by his atheism.

Hunt, Leigh (1784–1859). Essayist, journalist, editor, poet and critic. With his brother John he launched the weekly *Examiner* in 1808. He was a friend of Keats, Shelley and Hazlitt.

Hunter, John (1728–93). Important surgeon who founded the study of pathological anatomy in Britain and did much to win respect for surgery as a profession.

Huss (or Hus), Jan (1369–1415). Important Czech religious reformer whose ideas anticipated the Reformation. He was convicted of heresy and burned at the stake.

Inchbald, Mrs Elizabeth (1753–1821). Successful actress, dramatist and novelist; a friend of William Godwin and other radicals in the 1790s.

Irving, Edward (1792–1834). Church of Scotland minister who was called to the Caledonian Church, Hatton Garden, in 1822. An immensely popular preacher, he was excommunicated by the London presbytery in 1830.

Irving, Washington (1783–1859). American writer who made several trips to England, where he became acquainted with some of the leading literary figures. His *Sketch Book* (1819–20) made him a celebrity on both sides of the Atlantic.

Isabey, Jean-Baptiste (1767–1855). Highly successful French miniature painter who was patronized by Napoleon.

Jerdan, William (1782–1869). Successful journalist and editor who wrote for several papers before acquiring the Tory *Sun* in 1813, an event which procured him the acquaintance and support of several leading Tory statesmen. He later became editor of the *Literary Gazette*.

Jerome of Prague (*c.*1365–1416). Czech philosopher and theologian who espoused Reformation doctrines and was burned for heresy.

Joly de Fleury, Jean-François (1718–1802). Director-General of Finance in France after the resignation of Jacques Necker (1781).

Junius, i.e. Sir Philip Francis (1740–1818), the author of a famous series of political letters in the *Public Advertiser* between 1769 and 1772. These became celebrated as one of the classics of Whiggism, but there was much controversy surrounding the identity of 'Junius'.

Kauffman, Angelica (1741–1807). Neoclassical painter who spent many years in England after 1766; best known for decorative wall paintings.

Kean, Edmund (1789–1833). Celebrated tragic actor who developed an innovative, naturalistic acting style.

Kemble, Charles (1775–1854). One of the most celebrated actors of his day. The brother of Sarah ('Mrs') Siddons (see separate entry) and John Philip Kemble (see separate entry).

Kemble, John Philip (1757–1823). Brother of Charles, and a highly successful actor in his own right. Famous for tragic roles.

Ketch, Jack (John) (d.1686). A notorious executioner, known for his cruelly unprofessional technique.

Klopstock, Friedrich Gottlieb (1724–1803). Major German poet who did much to win respect and self-esteem for German literature in the eighteenth century. His major work was the epic hexameter poem *Messiah* (1748–73).

Kneller, Sir Godfrey (?1646–1723). Flemish portrait painter who came to England in 1676 and enjoyed a hugely successful career at the English court. Few of his pictures show him at his best; most have an insipid, studio quality.

La Fontaine, Jean de (1621–95). French poet, famous for his 12 volumes of *Fables* (1668–94), drawn from Eastern, classical and modern sources.

Lamb, Charles (1775–1834). Essayist and critic, pseudonym 'Elia', best known for his *Essays of Elia* (1823, 1833). A friend of Coleridge, Wordsworth, Southey, Hazlitt and many other literary figures.

Lancaster, Joseph (1778–1838). Founder of a system of education based 'on general Christian principles' which attracted much interest and controversy. He had already adopted the theories of Andrew Bell (see separate entry).

Latimer, Hugh (*c.*1485–1555). Protestant churchman burned at Oxford alongside Ridley in 1555 during the reign of Mary I.

Lawrence, Sir Thomas (1769–1830). A highly successful portrait painter whose work is distinguished by panache and elegance.

Leibniz, Gottfried Wilhelm (1646–1716). German philosopher and mathematician who argued for a 'pre-established harmony' between matter and spirit. His defence of divine justice and argument that this is the best of all possible worlds was mercilessly mocked by Voltaire (see separate entry) in his novel *Candide* (1759).

Leland, John (*c.*1506–52). Churchman and first modern English antiquary.

Lely, Sir Peter (1618–80). Flemish painter who imitated Van Dyck and enjoyed an exceptionally successful career as a portraitist in Restoration England.

Leonardo da Vinci (1452–1519). Italian painter, draughtsman, sculptor, architect and engineer; a polymath whose diverse achievements included not only some of the world's most famous paintings, such as *Mona Lisa* (1503–6), but also the invention of the principle of the helicopter. Revered in his own time and ever since.

Leopold, Prince, i.e. Leopold I of Belgium (1790–1865). Fourth son of Francu, Duke of Saxe-Coburg-Saalfeld, who married Princess Charlotte (see separate entry) in 1816. After her death in 1817 he continued to live in England until 1831, when he accepted his election as the first King of the Belgians.

Lessing, Gotthold Ephraim (1729–81). Important German critic and dramatist. He championed Enlightenment principles and argued for the superiority of English literature over French.

Liston, John (1776–1846). Successful comic actor, greatly admired by Charles Lamb (see separate entry).

Liverpool, Robert Banks Jenkinson, 2nd Earl (1770–1828). Tory Prime Minister 1812–27. He suspended the Habeas Corpus Act in Britain in 1817 and imposed other repressive measures in 1819.

Livy (Titus Livius) (59 BC–?AD17). Major Roman historian who related the history of Rome from its beginnings to 0 BC.

Locke, John (1632–1704). Major philosopher whose *Essay Concerning Human Understanding* (1690) proved extremely influential in the eighteenth century. Best known for the idea of the *tabula rasa*, the featureless mind shaped by sensory impressions. A Whig in politics, Locke was suspected of being a Unitarian.

Longinus. Supposed author of a Greek treatise 'On the Sublime' (probably of the first century AD), which importantly influenced eighteenth-century criticism and aesthetics.

Lovat, Simon Fraser, 11th Baron (1667–1747). Famous turncoat Jacobite who changed his allegiance more than once; after supporting the 1745 rebellion he was executed.

Machiavelli, Niccolò (1469–1527). Florentine statesman and political theorist whose controversial book on statecraft, *The Prince* (1532), has made its author's name part of the language (i.e. Machiavellian, Machiavellianism).

Mackintosh, Sir James (1765–1832). Lawyer and politician whose *Vindiciae Gallicae* (1791) was one of the most successful defences of the French Revolution against Burke (see separate entry). In later renouncing the principles of this work he seemed to symbolize the main political movement of the times.

Macready, William Charles (1793–1873). Actor-manager, a leading figure of the nineteenth-century stage.

Madison, James (1751–1836). Fourth president of the United States (1809–17) who had influenced the shape of the US Constitution. He declared war on Britain in 1812.

Malebranche, Nicolas (1638–1715). French philosopher and theologian who developed the philosophy of Descartes. He is best known for his idea of 'Occasionalism' which maintained that what other philosophers had called 'causes' are merely 'occasions' on which God acts to produce effects.

Malthus, Thomas Robert (1766–1834) Economist and demographer whose famous *Essay on the Principle of Population* argued that population naturally increased faster than food production.

Mandeville, Bernard de (1670–1733). Prose-writer and philosopher who settled in England. Best known for *The Fable of the Bees* (1714).

Manners-Sutton, Charles (1780–1845). Tory MP for Scarborough 1806–32. Appointed Judge-Advocate-General in 1809 and Speaker of the House of Commons in 1817, he opposed Catholic emancipation.

Marivaux, Pierre (1688–1763). Successful French dramatist, renowned for his comedies. In 1722 he founded a *Spectateur français* in imitation of Addison's *Spectator*.

Mars, Anne Françoise (1778–1847). Celebrated French actress, known for her impersonation of Molière's heroines.

Marston, John (?1575–1634). Dramatist and poet, best known for *The Malcontent* (1604); one of the major playwrights of Jacobean England.

Martin, John (1789–1854). English Romantic painter who specialized in huge canvases of apocalyptic scenes; greatly admired in his own day.

Masaccio (byname of Tommaso di Giovanni di Simone Guidi) (1401–28). Outstanding Italian painter, the grandeur and naturalism of whose work did much to influence the shape of Renaissance art.

Mérimée, Jean François Léonor (1757–1836). French painter and chemist.

Michelangelo Buonarroti (1475–1564). Florentine painter, sculptor, architect and poet; his claim to being considered one of the greatest artists of all time has never been seriously challenged. If one of his achievements stands out more than another it is doubtless the monumental Sistine Chapel ceiling (1508–12).

Middleton, Thomas (1580–1627). Major Jacobean dramatist, famous for plays such as *The Honest Whore* (1604) and *Women Beware Women* (1620s).

Mignet, François (1796–1884). Influential French historian and journalist; he founded the important newspaper *Le National* in 1830.

Mirabaud, Jean-Baptiste de (1675–1760). French man of letters; d'Holbach's *Système de la nature* (1770) was published under his name.

Molière, pseudonym of Jean-Baptiste Poquelin (1622–73). French comic dramatist and actor. A major figure in European literature.

Montagu, Basil (1770–1851). Legal and miscellaneous writer and philanthropist. A friend of Hazlitt, Wordsworth and Coleridge.

Montaigne, Michel Eyquem de (1533–92). French moralist and essayist, generally regarded as the inventor of the modern 'essay'. The first book of his *Essais* was published in 1572 and the last in 1588.

Montesquieu, Charles-Louis de Secondat (1689–1755). French social and political philosopher. His masterpiece, *De l'esprit des lois* (1748), is the first European work to employ a sociological method.

Montgomery, James (1771–1854). Poet and journalist whose editorship of the radical *Sheffield Iris* in the 1790s twice led to his prosecution and imprisonment. He established his fame as a poet with *The Wanderer of Switzerland* (1806).

Moore, Edward (1712–57). Dramatist and poet remembered for *The Gamester* (1753), a domestic tragedy.

Moore, Thomas (1779–1852). Irish poet and musician, a friend of Byron and Shelley. Extremely successful in his own day, he is now best known for his *Irish Melodies* (1807–34).

Morgan, Lady, née Sydney Owenson (1776–1859). Successful popular novelist who made her name with *The Wild Irish Girl* (1806).

Murillo, Bartolomé Esteban (1618–82). Major Spanish painter, best known for religious subjects treated in a soft and idealized manner.

Murray, John (1778–1843). Publisher and friend of Byron. With Sir Walter Scott he set up the Tory *Quarterly Review* in 1809.

Murray, Lindley (1745–1826). Successful American lawyer, famous for his *English Grammar* (1795).

Neal, Daniel (1678–1743). Dissenting minister who wrote a party *History of the Puritans* (1733–8).

Neat (or Neate), Bill (1791–1858). Celebrated boxer who fought professionally 1818–23 then retired to become a butcher.

Painter, Edward (1784–1852). Celebrated boxer who enjoyed his heyday 1813–20.

Paley, William (1743–1805). Major proponent of theological utilitarianism whose writings offered a rational support for the established church.

Palladio, Andrea (1508–80). Influential Italian architect whose classical style was inspired by a passion for that of Ancient Rome.

Parmigianino (byname of Girolomo Francesco Maria Mazzola) (1503–40). Important Italian artist whose elegant and sophisticated Mannerist style broke with the naturalism of the High Renaissance.

Parr, Samuel (1747–1825). Scholar, pedagogue and conversationalist who was regarded in his own day as 'the Whig Dr Johnson'.

Pascal, Blaise (1623–62). Influential French mathematician, physicist and moralist. His posthumously published *Pensées* (1670; translated 1688) was part of an unfinished defence of the Christian religion.

Pasta, Giuditta (1798–1865). Italian singer and actress; her greatest triumphs came in London and Paris between 1825 and 1833, during which period she was considered the finest soprano in Europe.

Peel, Sir Robert (1788–1850). Important politician who became Tory MP in 1809. In 1822 he entered the Cabinet as Secretary of State, resigning on the issue of Catholic emancipation in 1827. In the following years he emerged as the leader of the Tory opposition, and became Prime Minister 1834–5 and 1841–6.

Phillips, Charles (?1787–1859). Irish lawyer and miscellaneous writer known for his controversial, extravagant style of oratory.

Pindar (c.518–438 BC). The greatest of the Greek choral lyricists, famous for odes celebrating athletic victories.

Pindar, Peter, *see* Wolcot, John.

Pitt, William ('the Younger') (1759–1806). Son of 1st Earl of Chatham (see separate entry). Became Prime Minister in 1783, at the age of twenty-four. Although reform-minded in the mid-1780s, Pitt's policy-making became increasingly reactionary after the French Revolution.

Plato (c.428–c.348 BC). One of the greatest and most influential philosophers in the Western tradition. His philosophy rests on a belief in eternal Ideas, or Forms, that mediate between 'the One' and the material world.

Pliny, the younger (62–c.113). Roman letter-writer, admired as a prose stylist.

Plotinus (205–70). Major philosopher who founded the Neoplatonic school. His philosophy explains how the individual soul seeks union with 'the One'.

Plunkett, William Conyngham (1764–1854). Lawyer who fiercely opposed the plans of William Pitt (see separate entry) to form an Anglo-Irish legislative union. Between 1812 and 1827 he sat in the House of Commons and attempted to introduce bills that would give increased political rights to Catholics.

Plutarch (*c.*50–*c.*120) Greek biographer and moralist whose *Parallel Lives* and *Moral Essays* became extremely influential in the Renaissance.

Ponsonby, George (1755–1817). Irish lawyer and politician who defended the claims of Catholics from the 1790s on. From 1808 he was the Leader of the Opposition in the Commons.

Poole, Thomas (1765–1837). Farmer and tanner, remembered as a friend of Coleridge and Wordsworth.

Poussin, Gaspard (1615–75). Brother-in-law of Nicolas Poussin (see next entry), with whom he studied. He painted landscapes in a grand, classical style.

Poussin, Nicolas (1593/4–1665). Major French painter who spent most of his career working in Italy. Famous for his austere, 'classical' and intellectual manner, often contrasted with the painterly and sensuous manner of Rubens (see separate entry).

Prior, Matthew (1664–1721). Poet known mainly for his humorous occasional verse.

Probert, William (d.1825). A notorious villain of the 1820s, hanged for horse-stealing.

Proclus (*c.*410–85). The last major Greek philosopher, influential in spreading Neoplatonic ideas.

Rabelais, François (*c.*1494–*c.*1553). French physician, humanist and satirist; his masterpieces are the exuberant comic novels *Pantagruel* (1532) and *Gargantua* (1534).

Rae, Alexander (1782–1820). Successful actor who played many leading roles at Drury Lane between 1812 and 1820.

Racine, Jean (1639–99). French tragic dramatist, one of the major European playwrights. The 'classical' quality of his work was often contrasted with Shakespeare's 'romantic' qualities.

Raleigh, Sir Walter (?1554–1618). Explorer, colonizer, poet and prose-writer, remembered for his pursuit of Eldorado. Accused of treason by James I, he was imprisoned and executed; he remains a very enigmatic personality.

Randall, Jack (1794–1828). Celebrated boxer whose legendary technique earned him the title of 'The Nonpareil'. After a short, unbeaten career 1815–19, he retired to run the Hole in the Wall public house in Chancery Lane, London.

Raphael (Raffaello Sanzio) (1483–1520). Major Italian painter and architect, for three centuries after his death widely revered as the greatest of all painters. He introduced a tenderness and luminosity into the grandeur of Florentine art.

Rembrandt Harmenszoon van Rijn (1606–69). Dutch painter; one of the greatest European artists, famous for his very painterly style and dramatic use of light.

Reni, Guido (1575–1642). Major Italian painter whose work combined Baroque exuberance with classical restraint. Tremendously influential, he enjoyed a huge reputation long after his death.

Reynolds, Sir Joshua (1723–92). Portrait painter and aesthetician who dominated English artistic life in the middle and late eighteenth century. He was the first President of the Royal Academy (1786), to which he delivered his celebrated *Discourses*.

Richardson, Jonathan, the elder (1665–1745). Portrait painter, successful in his own day. Later remembered more for his writings on art; his *Theory of Painting* (1715) was the first significant work on aesthetic theory by an English author and a great influence on the young Reynolds.

Richer, John Oliver (*fl.* 1788–1813). Celebrated rope dancer, dancer and acrobat. For many years he performed at Sadler's Wells.

Rob Roy (born Robert Macgregor) (1671–1734). Scottish clan chief who was outlawed in 1712 and began a career of banditry. Sir Walter Scott's Romantic treatment of the story in *Rob Roy* (1817) ensured Rob Roy's place in the popular imagination.

Rochester, John Wilmot, Earl of (1647–80). Restoration poet, one of the 'court wits' surrounding Charles II. He wrote about sex with (in English) unprecedented frankness, a fact that has inevitably had a major bearing on his fluctuating reputation.

Romilly, Sir Samuel (1757–1818). Legal reformer who attempted to lessen the severity of criminal law; the English reaction to the French Revolution hindered his work.

Ronsard, Pierre de (1524–85). French poet; leader of a group of avant-garde poets known as La Pléiade, best known for his love poetry.

Rosa, Salvator (1615–73). Italian painter, poet, satirist and musician mainly remembered for wildly romantic landscapes that enjoyed a huge vogue in the eighteenth century.

Roubiliac, Louis-François (d. 1762). French sculptor who had a successful career in England. Known for his portrait statues and busts in a Baroque style.

Rousseau, Jean-Jacques (1712–78). Swiss-born philosopher, political theorist, educationalist and novelist. One of the most influential writers of the eighteenth century (especially *The Social Contract* of 1762), Rousseau argued that man was essentially good but corrupted by society.

Rowley, William (?1585–1626). English dramatist and actor, best known for his collaborations with Thomas Middleton (see separate entry).

Rubens, Sir Peter Paul (1577–1640). Flemish Baroque painter whose painterly, sensuous style was often contrasted with the classicism of Poussin (see separate entry).

Ruysdael (or Ruisdael), Jacob van (1628/9–82). Major Dutch landscape painter who developed a dramatic and Romantic style.

Sallust (Gaius Sallustius Crispus) (86–35 BC). Roman historian; one of Julius Caesar's henchmen, he manipulated the truth in favour of the Caesarean party.

Schelling, Friedrich Wilhelm Joseph von (1775–1854). Major German philosopher, the central theme of whose work is the 'Absolute', the unity of the subjective with the objective. He was an important influence on Coleridge.

Schiller, Johann Christoph Friedrich von (1759–1805). Major German dramatist, poet and literary theorist. The constant theme of his work was freedom, whether conceived of politically and physically, or spiritually.

Scott, John (1783–1821). First editor of the *London Magazine* in which De Quincey, Hazlitt, Lamb, Keats and Clare were published. His attacks on *Blackwood's Magazine* culminated in a duel with J. H. Christie in which Scott was killed.

Screib, i.e. Scribe, Augustin-Eugène (1791–1861). Prolific and successful French dramatist who became famous with *Une Nuit de la garde nationale* (1815). Renowned for his versatility and mastery of dramatic construction.

Scroggins, Jack (real name John Palmer) (1787–1836). Ex-Navy boxer who fought professionally with great success 1814–18; he continued to fight, but with little success, until 1822.

Seneca, Lucius Annaeus (c.55BC–40 AD). Roman Stoic philosopher and tragic dramatist who acted as tutor to the young Nero. His plays are marked by a relish for the bloodthirsty and the supernatural.

Shaftesbury, Anthony Ashley Cooper, 3rd Earl (1671–1713). Moral and aesthetic philosopher who opposed Hobbes's (see separate entry) selfish theory of human conduct, arguing that human beings were capable of holding disinterested views and ideas. His works also championed deism.

Sharp, Granville (1735–1813). Noted scholar, who published several books of biblical criticism, but was more famous as a leading campaigner against slavery.

Shenstone, William (1714–63). Poet, essayist and landscape gardener.

Sheridan, Richard Brinsley (1751–1816). Actor-manager, major dramatist and leading Whig politician. A friend of Fox (see separate entry) and Burke (see separate entry), he played a central role in the impeachment of Warren Hastings (see separate entry). *The School for Scandal* and *The Rivals* are his best-known plays.

Sheridan, Thomas (1735–1813). Actor, theatrical manager, educationalist and elocutionist; the father of Richard Brinsley Sheridan (see above entry).

Siddons, Sarah (1755–1831). Outstandingly successful tragic actress, the sister of Charles Kemble (see separate entry) and John Philip Kemble (see separate entry), with whom she often played. She retired in 1812.

Sieyès, Emmanuel-Joseph, Comte de (1748–1836). French churchman and constitutional theorist; an important influence on public affairs in the early stages of the French Revolution, Sieyès later played a major role in organizing the *coup d'état* that brought Napoleon to power.

Skeffington, Sir Lumley St George (1771–1850). Fop and minor playwright whose most successful plays were produced in the years 1802–5.

Smith, Adam (1723–90). Social philosopher and political economist remembered for *The Wealth of Nations* (1776), which established the foundations of 'free-market' economic theory.

Smith, Sarah (1783–1850). Actress who made her first appearance at Covent Garden in 1805, but whose London career was unable to develop until Mrs Siddons (see separate entry) retired in 1812.

Socinus (Lelio Sozini) (1525–62). Italian theologian, founder of the Socinian heresy which holds that Jesus was not God but a divine prophet of God's word.

Sophocles (496–406 BC). One of the three great Athenian tragic dramatists (with Euripides and Aeschylus); *Oedipus Rex* is considered his masterpiece.

South, Robert (1634–1716). Court preacher favoured by Charles II. Known for his wit and dislike of Dissenters.

Southcott, Joanna (1750–1814). Farmer's daughter and religious fanatic whose 'prophecies' acquired her a large following.

Southey, Robert (1774–1843). Poet, historian and political writer associated with Wordsworth and Coleridge. A youthful supporter of the French Revolution, and writer of several radical works, he later became an influential Tory writer and was attacked by Hazlitt and Byron.

Spinoza, Baruch (1632–77). Jewish philosopher who rejected the Cartesian dualism of spirit and matter. His belief in 'one infinite substance' was interpreted variously as pantheist and atheist.

Stafford, Marquis of, Granville Leveson-Gower (1721–83). Influential Whig politician who held various offices and was offered (but refused) the post of Prime Minister in 1783.

in 1798. After the death of George Ponsonby (see separate entry) he became the acknowledged leader of the opposition.

Tillotson, John (1630–94). Latitudinarian divine who became Archbishop of Canterbury; admired as a prose stylist.

Tintoretto (byname of Jacopo Robusti) (1518–94). Major Italian painter who developed exceptionally dramatic ways of handling light and space; to later neoclassical taste his work appeared excessive.

Titian (c.1487/90–1576). Outstanding Italian painter; one of the most influential figures in European art. Titian was understood as championing an art based on colour against one based on form.

Tooke, John Horne (1736–1812). Radical politician and philologist whose *Diversions of Purley* attacked Johnson's views on the English language. He was one of the defendants in the 1794 Treason Trials.

Torrigiano, Pietro (1472–1528). Italian sculptor notorious for having broken Michelangelo's nose. He worked in England c.1511–20.

Toulmin, Joshua (1740–1815). Dissenting clergyman who held Unitarian views and published many historical and biographical works.

Tracy, Antoine Louis Claude Destutt (1754–1836). French philosopher and politician. As a philosopher he stood in the line of Locke and Condillac, arguing that conscious life is wholly shaped by sensory impressions.

Tucker, Abraham (1705–74). One of the earliest utilitarian philosophers; his major work, *The Light of Nature Pursued* (1768–78), argued that the criterion of moral conduct was general happiness.

Twiss, Horace (1787–1849). Lawyer and politician, the nephew of Sarah Siddons (see separate entry); known as a parodist and writer of occasional verse.

Tyler, Wat (d.1381). The leader of the Peasants' Revolt of 1381.

Upton, John (1707–60). Churchman and editor who published a landmark annotated edition of *The Faerie Queene* in 1758.

Vanbrugh, Sir John (1664–1726). Baroque architect whose best-known work is Blenheim Palace (1705–16). He also enjoyed fame as a dramatist with such plays as *The Provok'd Wife* (1697).

Van Dyck, Sir Anthony (1599–1641). Major Flemish painter who came to England in 1632 and became court painter to Charles I. The stylistic verve and elegance of his portraits meant that he was revered by later English portraitists, particularly Gainsborough.

Van Goyen, Jan (1596–1656). One of the greatest Dutch landscape painters, known for his tonal landscapes and subtle atmospheric effects.

Vansittart, Nicholas (1766–1851). Lawyer and politician who supported Pitt's policies in the 1790s. He held various government offices, won a reputation as a financier, and became Chancellor of the Exchequer in 1812.

Vasari, Giorgio (1511–74). Minor Italian painter and architect famous for his *Lives of the most excellent Italian Architects, Painters and Sculptors* (1550 and 1568), one of the most influential art historical works ever written.

Vega Carpio, Lope Félix de (1562–1635). Major Spanish poet and playwright, regarded as the founder of Spanish drama. Several hundred of his plays survive.

Velázquez, Diego (1599–1660). Outstanding Spanish painter, often considered the greatest of all European painters. He became court painter to Philip IV of Spain in 1623; thereafter most of his works were portraits.

Virgil (Publius Vergilius Maro) (70–19 BC). The greatest Roman poet, whose *Eclogues*, *Georgics* and *Aeneid* have been among the most influential works of European literature.

Voltaire, pseudonym of François Marie Arouet (1694–1778). French satirist, novelist, historian, poet, dramatist, polemicist, moralist, critic and correspondent – the universal genius of the Enlightenment, with which his name is inseparably connected, thereby leading to wildly varying valuations of his work.

Waithman, Robert (1764–1833). Political reformer elected MP for the City of London in 1818.

Walton, Izaak (1593–1683). Tradesman who became friendly with several leading literary and religious men, of whom he wrote several biographies. Best known for *The Compleat Angler* (1653), a literary miscellany that idealizes life in the countryside.

Ward, William (1787–1849). Financier who was elected a director of the Bank of England in 1817 and later entered Parliament in the Tory interest.

Waterloo, Antoine (1618–62). Minor Dutch painter and engraver.

Webster, John (*c*.1580–*c*.1634). Major dramatist, best known for *The White Devil* (*c*.1612) and *The Duchess of Malfi* (*c*.1613). His work is marked by a love of horror.

Wedgwood, Thomas (1771–1805). Inventor of the concept of photography who befriended literary men and gave Coleridge an annuity in 1798. Also interested in educational schemes.

Wellesley, Richard Colley, 1st Marquess (1760–1842). Elder brother of the Duke of Wellington (see separate entry) who served as Governor of Madras and Governor-General of Bengal between 1797 and 1805, greatly enlarging the British Empire in India. He later served as Lord Lieutenant of Ireland (1821–8, 1833–4), attempting to reconcile Protestants and Catholics.

Wellington, Arthur Wellesley, Duke of (1769–1852). Brilliant soldier who established his reputation in the Peninsular War (1808–14) and defeated Napoleon at Waterloo (1815). He later moved into politics, becoming a member of Tory anti-reform Cabinets 1818–27 and Prime Minister in 1828. He supported Catholic emancipation and opposed parliamentary reform.

West, Benjamin (1738–1820). American-born history and portrait painter who succeeded Sir Joshua Reynolds as President of the Royal Academy in 1792. Despite its mannered quality, his work proved influential.

Westall, Richard (1765–1836). Minor artist known for his genre subjects; he also produced vignette illustrations to contemporary poetry.

Whitbread, Samuel (1758–1815). Whig politician who entered the Commons in 1790 and steadily opposed Pitt's policies; he continued to be a leading figure in the opposition until his death.

Wilberforce, William (1759–1833). Politician and philanthropist, prominent from 1788 in the struggle to abolish the slave trade.

Wilkie, Sir David (1785–1845). Genre and portrait painter, known for his anecdotal style.

Wilson, Richard (1714–82). Major landscape painter whose earlier Claudian compositions gradually gave way to more powerful and realistic depictions of British scenes.

Windham, William (1750–1810). MP for Norwich from 1784. Originally a Whig and friend of Fox (see separate entry), Windham followed Burke (see separate entry) in condemning the French Revolution and thereafter became a prominent opponent of political reform. He was a member of Pitt's Cabinet.

Wither, George (1588–1667). Versatile poet and pamphleteer whose work was rediscovered in the Romantic period.

Wolcot, John (1738–1819). The best-known satirical poet of the late eighteenth century, who wrote under the pseudonym of 'Peter Pindar'. Also remembered for his 'discovery' of the painter John Opie (see separate entry).

Wollstonecraft, Mary (1759–97). Famous feminist writer, remembered for *A Vindication of the Rights of Woman* (1792). She married William Godwin (see separate entry). Their daughter was Mary Shelley.

Wolsey, Thomas (c.1475–1530). Churchman who became cardinal and Lord Chancellor of England in 1515, pursuing an aggressive foreign policy under Henry VIII. His brilliant career ended abruptly when he failed to support Henry's divorce from Catherine of Aragon.

Wood, Sir Matthew (1768–1843). Lord Mayor of London 1815–17 and MP for the City of London from 1817 until his death. A staunch Whig.

Wynn, Charles Watkin Williams (1775–1850). MP for Montgomeryshire 1799–1850, who held various government offices. He attempted to form a third party in the Commons in 1818–19.

Yorke, Charles Philip (1764–1834). MP for the county of Cambridgeshire 1790–1810, who held various government offices.

Young, Charles Mayne (1777–1856). Important actor who made his first London appearance in 1807, and became one of the leading tragedians of the day.

Young, Edward (1683–1765). Poet, dramatist and churchman whose *Night Thoughts* (1742–5), a long religious meditation, became one of the classic poems of the eighteenth century, enjoying European celebrity.

Ziska, i.e. Žižka, Jan (c.1370–1424). Military commander and national hero of Bohemia who revolutionized warfare by the use of mobile artillery. He was a follower of the religious reformer Jan Huss (see separate entry).